One Billion Rising

Law, Governance, and Development

The Leiden University Press series on Law, Governance, and Development brings together an interdisciplinary body of work about the formation and functioning of legal systems in developing countries, and about interventions to strengthen them. The series aims to engage academics, policy makers and practitioners at the national and international level, thus attempting to stimulate legal reform for good governance and development.

General Editors:
Jan Michiel Otto (Leiden University) and Benjamin van Rooij (Leiden University)

Editorial Board:
Abdullahi Ahmed An-Naím (Emory University)
Keebet von Benda Beckman (Max Planck Institute for Social Anthropology)
John Bruce (Land and Development Solutions International)
Jianfu Chen (La Trobe University)
Sally Engle Merry (New York University)
Julio Faundez (University of Warwick)
Linn Hammergren (World Bank)
Andrew Harding (University of Victoria)
Fu Hualing (Hong Kong University)
Goran Hyden (University of Florida)
Martin Lau (SOAS, University of London)
Christian Lund (Roskilde University)
Barbara Oomen (Amsterdam University and Roosevelt Academy)
Veronica Taylor (University of Washington)
David Trubek (University of Wisconsin)

One Billion Rising

Law, Land and the Alleviation of Global Poverty

Edited by

Roy L. Prosterman
Robert Mitchell
and Tim Hanstad

with a Preface by Joseph E. Stiglitz

Leiden University Press

Cover photo: © 2007 Josh Fredman Photo
Cover design: Studio Jan de Boer, Amsterdam
Layout: The DocWorkers, Almere

ISBN   978 90 8728 064 2
e-ISBN   978 90 4850 833 4
NUR   820

Contents

Acknowledgments

The authors would like to acknowledge the generous support of the Bill & Melinda Gates Foundation, without which this book would not have been possible.

The authors also gratefully acknowledge the support and contributions of Leonard J. Rolfes, Jr. and David Bledsoe, both former Senior Attorneys of the Rural Development Institute, who helped shape the book and contributed to much of the learning represented here. We are grateful to Professor Jan Michiel Otto, Director of the Van Vollenhoven Institute for Law, Governance and Development at the University of Leiden School of Law, for suggesting that we write this book, and to the students and faculty of the institute for reviewing an early draft of the book and providing helpful recommendations. We also wish to thank the many staff members of RDI who helped in assembling and proofreading the book. We especially acknowledge the help given by Gina Zanolli, Leah Shepard, Neal Kingsley, Katharine Bond and Courtney Hudak.

Preface

Joseph E. Stiglitz, Columbia University

It is a great pleasure for me to write this preface for Roy Prosterman's landmark book on land tenure reform. – Roy and his colleagues at the Rural Development Institute have been tilling this soil for four decades – long before the issue became fashionable.[1] They have blended first-rate scholarship with advocacy: an early, and often lonely, voice recognizing the importance that access to land and security of land tenure has in uplifting the lives of the poor in agrarian economies. They have not only detailed these effects but also identified the mechanisms through which these benefits are realized. In most developing countries, most people depend for their livelihood on agriculture. Land is thus an essential part of the means of production, but those at the bottom typically have no land. Giving even small plots of land can make enormous differences to their lives and the lives of their families. Prosterman and his colleagues not only talk about the importance of land, they provide hard evidence.

But Roy and his colleagues are not Panglossian idealists. Their hard-headed research will be a challenge for many a warm-hearted reformer: land reform is not easy. They carefully document the successes and the failures, paying close attention to the differences in circumstances of the different countries. Their conclusions are at the same time sobering and heartening. The numerous failures are often cited by critics of land reform. Prosterman and his colleagues conclude that governments should purchase land, without compulsion, paying market prices; and given the tight budget constraints facing many developing countries, this limits the scope. At the same time, they argue that micro-plots can have very high productivity and make a great deal of difference. That means the government may not have to purchase huge amounts of land to make a big difference to large numbers of the poor in these countries.

I have long been an advocate of land reform, and in the following paragraphs, I want to explain why, provide some suggestions of how governments can lower the costs of market-based land reform, and show what can be done to increase the prospects of successful land reform. Finally, Prosterman and his colleagues argue for the importance of enhanced security of tenure. There are good reasons for this. But in many countries, there is resistance. I want to explain at least part of the cause of that resistance, making some suggestions of how we can square this circle.

The rationale for land reform

One of my earliest papers was on land tenancy.[2] I attempted to explain the widespread practice of sharecropping. To most economists, this institution seemed strange – for sharecropping greatly attenuates incentives. There are widespread complaints in developed countries about tax rates that approach 50%, yet most workers in developing countries have to turn over to their landlord 50% – in some cases 2/3 – of their crop. I explained sharecropping in terms of balancing out concerns over risk (landlords are better able to bear risks) and incentives (workers need some incentives to motivate them, in a context where it is costly for landlords to monitor workers). If workers were risk neutral (and had access to capital), workers would rent land and would have good incentives. If monitoring were costless, landlords would hire workers and pay them a fixed wage, absorbing the risks of fluctuations of output and price. Sharecropping represents a compromise. But while it may be a good compromise, incentives are nonetheless attenuated: workers do in general work less than they would if they owned their own land. Redistributing land to workers should, in this theory, result not only in more equity, but in greater output and efficiency.

These economic theories, based on the New Paradigm of Information Economics,[3] represented a marked break from conventional neoclassical economics, which argued that one could separate issues of distribution from efficiency. The divergence between the distribution of the ownership of land and the ownership of "labor" creates what are called agency problems, which can have a large economic toll.

Perhaps this accounts for why many of the most successful development stories began with land reform: Taiwan, Korea, Japan, and China. In the case of other successes, like America, land was in ample supply. Jefferson thought that the backbone of America was the small farmer *who owned his own plot of land.*[4]

The first problem encountered in land to the tiller programs is that, in most countries, the land has to be taken away from others. Those from whom the land is being taken away don't like it. This gives rise to political problems, and without wholesale revolution (as in China), these cannot be easily ignored. The standard mantra is that expropriation of land undermines security of property rights, which are viewed as sacrosanct. The violation of property rights itself has strong, adverse incentive effects.

But this argument against land expropriation is not always totally persuasive. Property rights are always circumscribed. Someone who buys stolen property will lose that property if the rightful owner makes a claim, even if the new "owner" paid good money for it. But questions may be raised about the legitimacy of many land claims. In South American countries, land was taken from the indigenous inhabitants. Do they not have some legitimacy in reclaiming the land that was theirs? So too in other countries where land is given away by colonial masters. In many countries, there is a rethinking of the rights to land of the aboriginal or indigenous inhabitants. In recent years, similar questions of legitimacy are being raised about property rights acquired in the process of transition from communism to a market economy: many of the old party bosses seemed to have simply grabbed state assets.

Nonetheless, there are many who, while recognizing these problems with the legitimacy of land rights, believe that upsetting security of property rights raises more problems that it resolves. That is perhaps part of the reason that this book (and the World Bank) have in recent years emphasized market-based land reform.

Market-based land reform, in which government purchases land at market prices, faces a problem of finance. Poor countries are poor; money spent to purchase land is money that could be spent on education, rural roads, health, or other development projects. Where, in the list of alternative ways of spending money to promote growth and alleviate poverty, should market-based land reform lie?

In principle, limitations of revenue with which to purchase land should not be as great a problem as it seems to have been. For if the land redistribution increases efficiency (consistent with the fact that productivity on small plots can be high), then the government can lend the money to the poor to buy the land. Large efficiency gains will accrue to the new owners; if the purchase price from the old landowners is based on the older, lower productivity, old landowners are just as well off as they would otherwise have been. But the new formerly-landless are far better off. Everyone is a winner, and none of this costs government anything. The government is just an intermediary, facilitating the efficient reallocation of land.

One problem with this "solution" is that poor tillers lack access to capital and technology; without those, their plots will not be productive. *Thus, an essential aspect of a successful land reform must be the provision of complementary inputs.*

The IMF and its (distorted) accounting practices imposed a second problem. If the government borrows to buy the land from the landlord, and then lends on to the small farmer, its sole role is as an intermediary. It has both an asset (the mortgage) and a liability (the debt). But IMF accounting only recognizes the liability, not the asset, and the

IMF puts developing countries under enormous pressure not to increase their indebtedness. Given the IMF's continued focus on incentives and the enervating effects of taxation, they should be enthusiastic about land reforms that reduce the scope for sharecropping. But their opposition may reflect not so much the economics of land reform but the views of landholding elites, which have resisted such reforms.

Given budget limitations – and the need to finance complementary inputs – it is important for government to reduce the price that it has to pay for the land it acquires. There are three ways that it can do so. First, it can impose a tax on unproductive land. (This can be assessed either in terms of employment or value-added on the land. The latter may be particularly effective if the country imposes a value-added or income tax, because the result of the attempt to avoid the "underutilized land" tax will be increased value-added tax revenue.) This will encourage those who are not using their land to sell it – or alternatively provide the government with more money with which to buy the land from those who are willing to sell it. Second, it can impose a progressive land tax, a tax that increases with the size of landholdings (though there are often problems in implementation, as large landholdings are put into the names of different family members). Third, it can impose a general land tax with a small-holder exemption, allowing landowners to declare the value of their land, with the proviso that the government would have the right to purchase the land at, say, 10% more than the declared price. Again, this proposal has the advantage that if landowners declare a high price – which would forestall purchase – there will be increased tax revenues with which to purchase land from those who have declared a low price. This proposal can be accompanied by a tax on land improvements (e.g., structures), with large penalties for those who do not declare such improvements. In the past, it might have been difficult to implement such a tax in countries with large landholdings, but with satellite imaging, governments can now get an accurate assessment. These measures may be used in combination to lower the costs of acquisition and to generate revenues to facilitate land acquisition in order to provide the complementary inputs necessary for successful land reform.[5]

Security of land tenure

Economists have long argued for the importance of secure property rights; without such security, there will not be the investments required to increase productivity. Secure and transferable property rights facilitate the creation of credit markets, opening up access to the finance required to purchase better seeds, fertilizer, and other improvements.

That is the theory. In practice, there are two problems. The first is that even with secure collateral, credit markets typically do not work well in developing countries, partly because land markets are not sufficiently developed for land to be a good source of collateral, and partly because in some countries, courts may be reluctant to enforce debt contracts (forcing a poor farmer to turn over his land to a rich bank).

The second is that when land markets are working and courts are willing to enforce debt contracts, a new set of problems arise: given the high volatility of output and prices, and given the other vicissitudes facing the lives of the poor (an illness in the family forcing them to borrow to buy medicines) and the absence of insurance, there is a high risk of the poor who borrow on the basis of land as collateral becoming landless. Ironically, secure and transferable property rights can lead to more landless peasants.

We began our discussion pointing out the high social and economic costs of landlessness. But in many developing countries, if individuals can borrow using their land as collateral, there is a significant risk that they will borrow so much that there is a serious probability that they will lose their land. In such societies, individuals face all sorts of large risks – and have little means of insuring themselves against these risks. There is, of course, variability in agricultural output and prices. Matters have become worse: some of the miracle seeds are more sensitive to weather variability. In India, international seed companies have lobbied for weakening of germination standards. The more productive hybrids and genetically modified varieties require the farmer to buy seeds every year.

There is often little public availability of health services. The advances of modern medicine then present a two-edged sword: if a parent gets sick, the child feels a natural obligation to buy the miracle medicines that may prolong their life or alleviate their pain. The parent's life may be prolonged, but the child may become landless. Individuals borrow, moreover, for weddings, funerals, and other social obligations. When two or more of these "risks" occur at once – a parent gets sick and the weather turns bad – the individual is especially likely to lose his land. (In India, matters often turn worse: there has been a rash of suicides, in the thousands, as many think death is the only way of escaping the burden of debt.)

Just as land reform without complementary inputs may be counterproductive, resulting in lower productivity, secure property rights without protective insurance may increase landlessness.[6] By contrast, recent research has called into question the virtues of *full* security of land rights. For instance, China's increase in agrarian productivity occurred well before there was any security of property rights; and even today, there are leaseholds, not freeholds. In countries with limited land turnover, land markets will be thin, and land will still not serve as a good source of collateral. Moreover, as we have noted, courts may be reluctant to enforce credit contracts when it entails dispossessing local inhabitants, and especially so if the inability to repay is a result of, say, bad weather or a family tragedy. The approaches of the Grameen Bank, BRAC, and other micro-credit schemes, which are not based on collateral but on the creation of social capital, seem far more promising in extending access to credit.[7]

Concerns about the creation of new landless peasants as a result of transferable land rights has led some governments to devise still other ways of facilitating credit, e.g., some fraction of the *output* can be used as collateral. Thus, over the long run, in the absence of good insurance markets (and there are never good insurance markets in developing countries), *partial* or *limited* security of property rights (that is, for instance, limitations in the transferability of ownership) may be preferable to fully secure and transferable property rights. This serves as a reminder: in the world of second best, simplistic solutions, based on market fundamentalism, may not serve a country's interest as well as more nuanced "compromises."

Concluding remarks

As we have noted, land reform has been part of the early economic strategies of several of the most successful developing countries. There is a compelling case – made in this book and elsewhere – that providing more land to the tiller would reduce poverty and increase growth. Yet in some places land ownership is becoming more concentrated, as the ruling elites use their political power to garner for themselves one of the country's most important natural resources. Cambodia stands out as an example. And while the international community often talks about the concentration of income and wealth, they seldom discuss the inequality of land ownership – and land may be much more unequally distributed than either income or wealth. A Gini coefficient of income inequality in excess of 0.4 is a sign of a highly unequal society – yet Paraguay's Gini coefficient for land inequality is, according to some sources, in excess of 0.9!

In a world in which we are constantly confronted with equity and efficiency trade-offs, land reform is one of those rare instances of a policy which simultaneously promotes both. Yet the issue has for too long been neglected – perhaps because the elites in many of the developing countries have done well by the status quo. It is a shame that the international institutions have not pushed this agenda more. This book puts the issue back onto the agenda, and Roy Prosterman should be congratulated, not only for his tireless energy as an advocate, but also for his deep work, presented here, providing nuanced arguments and detailed evidence.

Notes

1   See, e.g., H. de Soto, THE MYSTERY OF CAPITAL: WHY CAPITALISM TRIUMPHS IN THE WEST AND FAILS EVERYWHERE ELSE (Basic Books 2000).

2   J.E. Stiglitz, *Incentives and Risk Sharing in Sharecropping*, 41(2) REVIEW OF ECONOMIC STUDIES 219-255 (1974).

3   See J.E. Stiglitz, *Information and the Change in the Paradigm in Economics*, abbreviated version of Nobel lecture, 92(3) AMERICAN ECONOMIC REVIEW 460-502 (2002).

4   I think, however, that there may be more to it than just a matter of incentives, but these are deeper questions which will have to be left to another occasion.

5   There are further advantages of shifting the burden of taxation to land: long ago, Henry George argued for the use of a land tax. See PROGRESS AND POVERTY (Cosimo 2005) (originally published in 1879). For more recent discussions of land taxes, see Karla Hoff, *Land Taxes, Output Taxes, and Sharecropping: Was Henry George Right?*, in K. Hoff, A. Braverman & J.E. Stiglitz, eds., THE ECONOMICS OF RURAL ORGANIZATION: THEORY, PRACTICE, AND POLICY (Oxford University Press 1993).

6   See, e.g., A. Braverman & J.E. Stigltiz, *Credit Rationing, Tenancy, Productivity and the Dynamics of Inequality*, in P. Bardhan, ed., THE ECONOMIC THEORY OF AGRARIAN INSTI-TUTIONS 185-201 (Oxford: Clarendon Press 1989).

7   See, e.g., A. Haldar & J.E. Stiglitz, *The Dialectics of Law and Development: Analyzing Formality and Informality*, paper prepared for the Initiative for Policy Dialogue's China Task Force (2008).

1   Poverty, law and land tenure reform

Tim Hanstad, Roy L. Prosterman and Robert Mitchell

I.   Background

Global poverty is not just another problem. It is the most important problem facing the world today. Despite the substantial economic and social improvements made over the past several decades, the most recent estimates (as calculated for 2005) are that 1.4 billion humans remain in extreme poverty, using the latest research and based on those living on less than US$1.25 a day. This is up from previous estimates of less than 1 billion people living in extreme poverty. According to these new estimates, a total of 2.6 billion people were surviving on less than US$2 per day.[1] These poverty estimates were also made before the recent sharp increases in food and energy prices.

Poverty is devastating wherever it exists. It robs people of life and hope. It is the chief cause of world hunger – as of 2006, the FAO estimated that 854 million people around the world lived in near-constant hunger and malnourishment, an estimate again made before the very large increases in basic food prices since that time.[2] And hunger kills, not usually through starvation, but through chronic malnutrition, which is the most important contributing factor in child mortality.[3]

Globally, poverty remains largely a rural phenomenon. Of the 1.4 billion people in our world living on less than US$1.25 a day, about three-quarters reside in rural areas.[4] Especially in rural areas, and particularly for poor families, land plays a dominant economic, social and political role. For these hundreds of millions of poor people, land is a main vehicle for gaining social status and a political voice within their communities, for providing nutrition and income for their families, for establishing some measure of economic independence, for investing, and for accumulating wealth and transferring it between generations. The manner by which land rights are held, land conflicts are addressed, and land use is regulated affects:

- the ability of families to produce for their subsistence and generate marketable surpluses;
- the social and economic status of families, including their group identity;

- incentives for families to exert their own efforts to improve and invest in the land, and to sustain the natural resource base;
- opportunities for families to access financial services;
- the ability of families to build and improve housing;
- opportunities for families to access government programs and participate in the political process; and
- the capacity of families to build reserves to protect their assets during periods of economic, climatic, health-related or other stress.

In sum, for the vast majority of people in developing countries, the nature of their rights to land largely defines their access to opportunity, income, housing, economic and nutritional security, political power, and social status within their community.[5]

Worldwide, in a macro-scale comparison, systems in which small owner-operated farms dominate tend to achieve the highest yields per hectare.[6] A more specific set of illustrations of productivity comparisons from post-tenure-reform settings is given in Box 1.1.

Box 1.1. Land rights and farm productivity

Various aspects of these linkages are discussed in specific country settings throughout the book. For example:

- Chinese farmers, beneficiaries of an initial reform that turned tenant farmers into individual owners in the years immediately after the Communists came to power (and before the disastrous collectivization), increased grain production by 70% and farm incomes by 85% in the seven years from 1949 to 1956 (Chapter 7).
- Taiwanese farmers, beneficiaries of a parallel reform in 1953 that provided ownership to tenants, increased grain production by 60% and farm income by 150% in the following 10 years (Chapter 2).
- South Vietnamese tenant farmers living in villages that implemented similar reforms during 1970-1973 increased rice production by 30% in that time period, in the midst of a war (Chapter 2).
- In the Mexican state of Laguna, in the wake of the Mexican land reform, small, individually cultivated *ejidal* farms created by the land reform had a total factor productivity – calculated exclusive of the farmer's labor – that was 50% greater than for the collectively farmed *ejidos* and 33% greater than for the pre-existing large farms (Chapter 3).
- When the Chinese collective farms were later broken up, the resulting individual farms initially increased grain production by 8.6% per year during 1980-1984, roughly 10 times the average rate of increase prevailing under collectivitization (Chapter 7).

Household access to land and secure rights to land have impacts beyond the level of individuals and families. Research has documented a positive relationship between equitably distributed land and both economic growth[7] and poverty alleviation at the country level. A study by two leading World Bank economists of 66 countries over the period 1960-2000 found that countries with a more broad-based distribution of land were characterized by higher levels of economic growth.[8] Another study on the relationship between land access and poverty in 21 developing countries found that land concentration and a corresponding lack of land access explained 69% of the variation in poverty levels.[9]

While broader agricultural growth does lead to rural poverty alleviation at the country level, it is not nearly as effective as broadening land access. Analysis of the same 21 countries shows that a decrease in land concentration by one-third leads to a one-half reduction of the poverty level within 12 to 14 years. By contrast, agricultural growth of 3% per year without a reduction in land concentration would take 60 years to produce the same level of poverty reduction.[10]

Broad-based land distributions are also associated with greater social peace and cohesion. History provides many examples where high rates of landlessness, an inequitable distribution of land, or other land rights deprivations have led to large-scale conflicts with devastating consequences.[11] In the 20th century, this included, for example, the great civil conflicts in Mexico, Russia, Spain, China and Vietnam.[12]

For these reasons, many policy makers, development practitioners and researchers have recognized – though with significant fluctuations in the attention paid to the land issue over time – that providing impoverished rural people with access and secure rights to land is central to reducing poverty, empowering poor people and communities, and promoting both broader economic growth and social harmony.

This book explores the intersection of poverty, land and law in an effort to advance our understanding and insight as to how governments might provide the poor with access and secure rights to land. Much of what appears in individual chapters is informed by and documents the experience of a group of lawyers who have had significant experience in working with governments, international development agencies and civil society groups to provide poor people with access and secure rights to land. The approach to this work has been characterized by several important shared values and biases, including a pro-poor bias, a bias for approaches likely to have a large-scale impact, and a belief that the law, in this as in many other aspects of international development, has an important role to play. Over the past four decades, the combined experience of the authors spans more than 40 countries and totals more than 150 person-years. The authors, including the three who act as overall editors of this volume, have accumulated this experience through their joint and collaborative work at the Seattle-based Rural Development Institute, which is affiliated with the University of Washington School of Law.

Improving and securing the relationship of poor families to land persists as a crucial issue in much of the world. This is the central question of "pro-poor land tenure reform" and the defining topic of this book. We use the term "land tenure reform" rather than "land reform" because the latter has often been understood to refer only to redistributing rights to land. We define "*pro-poor* land tenure reform" broadly to include reforms that increase the ability of the rural poor and other socially marginalized groups to gain or protect access and secure rights to land (see Box 1.2). We stress that not all land tenure reforms are pro-poor (Zimbabwe's disastrous "land reform" is a recent and obvious example), but we sometimes use the terms interchangeably.

We write this book as lawyers with multi-disciplinary perspectives who are collaboratively engaged in international development work. This work has included desk and field research, technical assistance, policy advocacy, developing legislation, training, and the design, implementation and assessment of land tenure reform programs. Our perspective as lawyers is likely to differ from that of members of other disciplines – for example, economics, political science, agronomy, sociology and anthropology – although we work with and draw heavily upon insights from other disciplines in formulating our conclusions. And our perspective as persons actively engaged not only in on-the-ground research but in the formulation and implementation of policies, laws and programs affecting land tenure is also likely to be different from the perspective of those who are engaged in either desk or field research that is not similarly action-linked. We hope, however, that we can make the "legal element" of the discussion throughout this book (and the linkages to recommendations for action) sufficiently straightforward and understandable so as to engage and inform those who approach these land tenure issues from other disciplines and perspectives. Indeed, communication about these issues across disciplines and backgrounds is one of our central goals in writing this book.

Box 1.2. Defining terms

"Land tenure," simply put, is the relationship between people and land. That relationship is typically defined in terms of various "land rights" such as rights relating to possession, exclusion, use, transfer and enjoyment.

"Land tenure reforms" are structural and large-scale changes to the relationship between people and land.

"Pro-poor land tenure reforms" are reforms that increase the ability of the poor and other marginalized groups to gain or protect access and secure rights to land. Pro-poor land tenure reforms are typically designed to advance one or more of three objectives, often in concert:

1. Broaden access to land by the poor and other marginalized groups;
2. Improve "land tenure security" (see below) for the poor and other marginalized groups concerning land rights they presently possess;
3. Improve, in terms of both substantive rules and process, the capacity of public sector land-related institutions to serve the public generally and protect the interests of the poor in particular.

"Land tenure security" exists when an individual or group can confidently enjoy rights to a specific piece of land on a long-term basis, protected from dispossession by outside sources, and with the ability to reap the benefits of investments in the land, at least through use and, probably desirably in most settings, also through transfer of the land rights to others.

II.   Characteristics of land tenure systems

Land tenure can generally be defined as the set of rules and relationships among people concerning the use, development, transfer and succession of rights to land. Land tenure rules define the rights held and duties owed concerning land by private and public actors, by individuals and by groups.

Four characteristics of land tenure systems are fundamental for understanding land tenure reforms. First, land tenure systems evolve, and understanding the general patterns of that evolution is crucial in designing reform interventions. Second, land tenure systems are complex, pluralistic and overlapping. Third, land tenure systems vary widely from place to place depending on historic, cultural, social, political and economic factors. Fourth, and finally, the law is an important factor in shaping the structure of a land tenure system. We examine each of the first three characteristics below; since the fourth characteristic is closely connected to the book's central theme, we consider it at greater length and in a separate section.

Evolving nature of land tenure systems

In any given setting, the land tenure system has evolved in response to changing economic, social and political factors and will continue to evolve in response to those factors. Economists have long used the concept of induced innovation to explain how, with increased population density, more intensive economic activity, and advancing technology, societies develop a more precise definition of property rights to provide an improved incentive framework for investment and efficient economic activity.[13] In general, societies tend to adopt more defined and individualized land tenure rights as the population density increases, as land-related investments become more necessary and profitable, and as other factors increase the value of land.[14] This evolutionary pattern is sometimes steady and gradual, but more often long periods of relative stability are punctuated by periods of rapid change brought about by significant economic, political or social events. Understanding the "hows," "whys" and "whens" of land tenure system evolution is crucial for considering whether and how to reform a given system to provide opportunity to the poor and marginalized.

A common theme in the development literature concerning the evolving nature of property rights and land tenure systems is an *efficiency thesis:* that all systems evolve efficiently in a cost-minimizing direction in response to a changing technological and economic environment. According to this thesis, social groups adopt particular property rights regimes and change their land tenure system because the benefits from doing so exceed the costs, implying that society will always gain.[15] A common inference of the thesis is that social groups should be left to themselves to adopt and adapt land tenure systems and the state should generally assume a "hands off" approach other than formalizing what the social groups have developed.

While this efficiency thesis has some explanatory value, it is often faulty, particularly when different social groups interact, a state makes laws, or a strong group overpowers others. Historical examples such as the institution of slavery, the dispossession of indigenous peoples in many regions, and Stalin's treatment of the Ukrainian *kulaks* pose problems for the efficiency thesis.[16]

In this book, we align with the revised version of the efficiency thesis offered by Robert Ellickson who asserts that the thesis applies only to land rules within a closely knit group.[17] However, land rules created in other settings – including rules created by states, which almost always apply to a society larger than the closely knit group – do not necessarily proceed efficiently in a manner that produces overall societal benefits. We take Ellickson's proposition a step further and assert that land tenure rules created by states are likely to generate negative impacts on marginalized groups within the broader society unless the state takes pro-active and informed steps to protect and benefit such groups, including through the design and implementation of land tenure rules. This issue will arise with special acuteness in Chapter 8, which discusses formalization of rural land rights.

Complexity of land tenure systems

One can analyze the complexity and multi-dimensionality of land tenure systems in a number of ways. Our own framework of analysis recognizes four generalizations: (1) there is no single best model for defining land rights or land tenure systems; (2) land tenure systems cannot be considered solely with regard to their material effects; (3) land tenure systems are often pluralistic within a given setting; and (4) such systems vary substantially from country to country.

First, there is no single best model for defining land rights, and wide variation exists even among highly developed land rights systems. Although land rights are often, for purposes of general typology, categorized using terms such as ownership or lease or usufruct, such concepts are deceptively simplistic.

Summary presentations in Western legal theory may focus on two or three aspects of land rights as central. One recent formulation, for example, emphasizes transferability and freedom of use: "Holding a fee simple [*i.e.*, an ownership right] allows owners to convey and devise it to whomever they please. It allows them to use it in ways their own self-interest dictates, free from the claims of their children or their ancestors."[18] Others have emphasized the aspect of exclusivity: "[T]he essence of private property is always the right to exclude others."[19] Each aspect, however, can involve multiple and complex rights.

Especially in Anglo-American legal theory, land property rights are also often analogized as a "bundle of sticks," with significant emphasis given to various legal interests (sticks) into which "complete property" (the bundle) may be divided.[20] European civil law theory takes a more or less similar approach, viewing land tenure rights (and property rights generally) as including six kinds of legally protected "expectations": (i) a right of possession; (ii) a right of exclusion; (iii) a right of disposition; (iv) a right of use; (v) a right to enjoy profits; and (vi) a right of destruction.[21] While none of these theories of land property rights is entirely satisfactory, each illustrates that land rights are complex. Moreover, the limits of the individual incidents vary among Western market economies.[22]

Second, land tenure systems involve much more than economics and cannot be treated in policy terms that consider only material dimensions. Land tenure systems also have anthropological, political and social dimensions that influence the non-material aspects of life in important ways. Land tenure rules set the platform for social and political institutions.[23] Land tenure reform that focuses on only one dimension to the exclusion of others is almost certain to fail to achieve its goals. The importance of the often-ignored social status dimension is discussed in Chapter 4. Broadly speaking, traditional societies based on customary laws tend to emphasize the social dimension of land tenure systems, while modern, market-oriented societies tend to emphasize the economic dimension.[24]

Third, land tenure systems are often pluralistic in developing country settings; that is, in a given setting, one is likely to find a combination of different land tenure systems. Consider the following example. A developing country that was previously colonized by a European power has adopted a land tenure system resembling the system operating in the former colonial power. In a highly commercialized city of the developing country land parcels have been carefully surveyed, are individually owned, and are frequently sold, leased and mortgaged according to the national law. Meanwhile, in a forested, sparsely populated area several hours from that city, a closely knit society of forest dwellers operates under a customary land tenure system that predates the colonial occupation and which evolved separately and slowly over the past 500 years. The forest dwellers do not consider land to be a commodity. They coordinate land use and possession through a complex balancing of community and household rights and duties. Although the country's rulers hold that the statutory land law followed in the city also governs the forest dwellers, the latter are not aware of that law, nor has it much impacted their lives (although that may soon change). Meanwhile, an agricultural area closer to the city involves elements of both land tenure systems. While some residents continue to consider ancestral land as integral to their identity and follow customary land tenure rules, others sell their land to outsiders. Some sell land based on a handshake, without registering the transaction, while others sell using formal written contracts and register the land sales according to the statutory law.

This hypothetical example serves to illustrate how pluralistic land tenure systems can overlap, influence each other, and occupy the same space. Patrick McAuslan uses the notion of three "circuits" of land relations present in many developing countries. The first and lowest circuit is customary land and its regulation via traditional processes. It exists principally, but not exclusively, in certain rural settings. The second circuit is an unofficial or informal market in land regulated by custom and practice, which exists principally in urban and peri-urban areas, but is growing in rural society. The third and upper circuit is the modern official land market regulated by statutory law codes interpreted and applied by professionals and state officials. It exists in both urban and rural settings.[25]

Finally, because land tenure systems evolve and are multi-layered, they vary substantially from country to country. Differing historic, cultural, social, political and economic factors compound the difference. The situational specificity of land tenure systems means that it is usually not possible to take a system that seems to function well in one country and transplant that system into another country. This, too often, was a path followed by colonial powers and is one sometimes followed by international development agencies and development practitioners today.

These issues are touched upon in Chapter 8, which considers problems of possible elimination of some layers of existing rights where formalization attempts to simplify or consolidate multiple customary rights in a single holder; and Chapter 5, which discusses the frequent problem of allocation of rights to the male "head of household," excluding women from the titling or rights certification process.

III.   The role of law in influencing land tenure systems

Development experts and policy makers commonly either over-estimate or under-estimate the role that law plays in influencing land tenure systems. When considering land tenure reform, it is useful to keep in mind several points. First, formal law and customary law often co-exist in a single setting. Second, although law is but one factor influencing people's behavior, it can be a crucial tool for good or ill in reforming land tenure. Finally, the role of formal law in influencing land tenure systems depends on the extent to which the rule of law exists.

Sources of law: formal and customary

Let us start by defining what we mean by the various types of "law" that shape land tenure systems. Many conventional concepts of land tenure focus exclusively on land tenure rules defined in state legislation. In practice, however, many land tenure systems are more properly understood as being comprised of an amalgamation of interacting multiple legal orders – national government, sub-national government,

local, customary and religious – each of which might separately provide
a basis for claiming particular land rights. In approaching land tenure
reform, one must recognize and understand the implications of legal
pluralism where it exists. (One must also recognize that there are developing societies where such pluralism may not be a significant phenomenon, or where it exists primarily with respect to areas inhabited
by small minorities of the population, such as forest dwellers or pastoralists.)

For purposes of this book, we define "law" as a rule of conduct or
procedure established by custom, agreement or authority. Legal orders
can be broadly categorized into either formal law or customary law.
Formal law is written and issued (and expected to be enforced) by a
state authority. It includes constitutional provisions, national statutes,
provincial and local government laws and regulations, judicial case law,
and government program and project rules. Customary law typically is
unwritten, applies within a self-identified group and grows out of that
group's traditions and experience.

Because customary law is typically unwritten, it can be "invisible" to
outsiders. Many traditional societies or subgroups have a deeply embedded preference for customary law approaches regarding questions
of land access, use, inheritance or market transfers. These customary
laws can be fundamental expressions of culture and tradition, derived
in turn from a combination of spiritual beliefs, history, geography, economics and other factors. Although customary law is a prominent legal
regime governing land tenure in many rural areas of developing countries – including large portions of Africa, Southeast Asia and the South
Pacific – customary land tenure law is rarely recognized in formal legal
systems.

Land tenure systems governed by customary law are very often described as "communal tenure" systems. The term "communal" can be
misleading in this context because it can be misunderstood to imply
common ownership of all resources or collective production, each of
which is relatively rare.[26] Customary law systems of land tenure are
generally "communal" only in the sense that the community exercises
a degree of control over who is allowed into the group, and the fact that
group members qualify for an allocation of land for residence and
cropping, as well as rights of access to the group's common property
resources.[27] Such systems are better understood as mixed tenure systems comprised of bundles of individual, family, sub-group and larger
group rights and duties concerning a variety of natural resources. The
community usually allocates residential and arable land to individuals
or families, who most often hold them with strong and secure rights
and cultivate them separately. Families and larger clusters of house-

holds sometimes also have preferential rights to common pool resources such as water sources or desirable grazing areas.

Two important general differences should be noted between formal land tenure law and customary land tenure law. The first is the issue of land alienability (i.e., transferability). Most formal (at least Western) land tenure law systems allow for relatively unrestricted alienation of land rights, or at least do not normally distinguish between alienability within or outside a given social group. Customary land tenure law systems often prohibit alienation of land rights to outsiders, but allow alienation within the group.

The second difference is the degree to which the land possessor may exclude others. Formal systems typically emphasize the right of right-holders to exclude others, whereas customary law more typically emphasizes inclusivity and the right not to be excluded.[28] Depending on the potential uses of the land, this may give rise to multiple or layered rights in which a household that plants and harvests a particu-

Figure 1.1.   *Typology of property rights in land*

		Socially perceived to be legitimate?	
		Yes	No
Strictly legal?	Yes	**Ownership rights**, acquired through inheritance or sale/purchase market (although tenure security for those with little power/voice may be vulnerable, particularly where rights unrecorded in land records) **Customary use rights over village commons** (may not effectively be exercised in practice if land heavily degraded or encroached upon) **Legally protected tenancies under liberalized land-lease market** (social legitimacy may be ambiguous)	**Women's right to own land independently** (usually does not translate into effective control over land, given high opportunity cost to an individual woman in pressing her legal claim) **Legally protected tenancies?** (may not locally be perceived as legitimate if markets for credit and labor highly interlinked with those for land to rent)
	No	**Concealed tenancies** under oral contracts in which rent exceeds legal maximum, and where length of actual occupancy entitles tenant to acquire legal occupancy rights (most likely to prevail where factor markets highly interlinked) **"Illegalize" customary use rights** (e.g., cultivation rights of tribal communities on forest land, forbidden under 1980 Forest Conservation Act)	**Encroachment on commons** (whether or not this translates into effective control over land depends on relative bargaining power/voice: e.g., more powerful groups may gain effective control over land through "illegal" acquisition of occupancy rights, while already landless may lose effective control in spite of legal entitlement) **Alienation of tribal land** (loss of effective control over land owing to indebtedness/land mortgage)

Source: R. Mearns, *Access to Land in Rural India: Policy Issues and Options* 6, Table 1 (World Bank Policy Working Paper May 1999).

lar crop may be different from (or merely included within) other or larger groups that can graze animals, gather branches or mushrooms, selectively harvest trees, etc.

Those considering land tenure reform must understand the extent and nature of customary law regimes that may presently govern portions of national territories and populations that are to be included within the purview of the formal land tenure law. People functioning under such regimes are much more likely to accept the formal law (and the state will consequently find it much easier to implement the formal law) if that law utilizes concepts already present in the customary law.[29] Robin Mearns has distinguished between the legal legitimacy and the social legitimacy of land tenure rights in India and has developed a useful typology of common land tenure rights according to these parameters (see Figure 1.1).

Problems occur when socially legitimate customary land rights are made illegal by formal law (lower left quadrant of Figure 1.1), or when the formal law legalizes land rights that are either not recognized by or prohibited by customary law (upper right quadrant). Where both formal and customary law operate in the same space (as in McAuslan's "second circuit" described earlier) and there is wide and consistent divergence between the formal and customary law, some breakdown in the rule of law typically results – either in the rule of formal law, in the rule of customary law, or both.

Law as one of many factors influencing behavior

Common sense dictates that the behavior of people and government agencies is influenced by much more than just law. Professors Ann and Robert Seidman use models for legal system functioning that portray whether and how laws impact behavior.[30] Efforts to use law as a tool for social and economic transformation – such as land tenure reform – can benefit from these models.[31]

Laws can only facilitate social and economic transformation by changing the repetitive behaviors of both law-implementing institutions and the citizens who are to be governed, benefited or regulated by the law. Formal laws can be thought of as instructions to both audiences: law-implementing institutions and citizens. However, the behavior of both groups is influenced by much more than just the law. Law-implementing institutions and ordinary people decide how to behave by choosing among constraints and resources characteristic of their specific environments – including the law.[32] Non-legal constraints and resources include the objective conditions in which people live (economic, social, geographic, cultural, political, etc.), their subjective interests, values and ideologies, and their expectations as to how the law-implementing institutions will behave. All of this occurs in the context of country-specific circumstances and with dynamic feedback loops among the actors.

It is clear from this model, which accords with our experience in practice, that pro-poor land tenure law reform must be accomplished with an understanding of the "ground realities" – for both the people subject to the law and the institutions tasked with implementing the law. Understanding these ground realities requires research. And the research must go beyond observing behavior and actions to examine the factors that influence such behavior and actions. Law reform not informed by such research will succeed only through serendipity. What kind of research is needed, and how should it be directed?

We identify several categories of legal and non-legal factors that in-fluence the behavior of people and implementing authorities in the face of laws.[33] All should be carefully considered and studied in the early stages of land tenure reform. The following categories of factors can provide a general map to guide research into existing incentives or behaviors embedded in the particular country-specific circumstances that affect reform of land tenure law and institutions:

1. *Rules.* Which existing laws, both formal and customary, apply to the actions of people and implementing authorities, here with respect to the subject of land tenure?
2. *Awareness of rules.* To what extent do people and implementing authorities know of and understand existing rules?
3. *Opportunity and capacity to obey the rules.* Do people and implement-ing authorities have the opportunity and capacity to follow the rules?
4. *Decision to follow the rules.* To what extent are people and imple-menting authorities interested in following the rules, and what fac-tors influence such interest?[34]

Only with research in hand that encompasses these factors will law-makers and their advisors be able to assess the needs and possibilities for fashioning new or additional rules affecting land tenure in a parti-cular setting.

Rule of law

While law does play an important role in shaping land tenure systems, the capacity of the law and legal institutions to help drive land tenure reform depends, in part, on the relative existence of the rule of law or, in other words, the overall effectiveness of the entire legal system.[35] Effective legal systems share certain general characteristics fundamen-tal to facilitating efficient and equitable economic and social development. These include predictability, fairness, rapid adjudication, and the degree to which the legal system is consistent with customs, norms and levels of administrative resources.

Predictability. Predictability of the legal system is important for inducing economic growth. If the legal system allows economic actors to predict the legal consequences of their activities and the state apparatus can be mobilized to enforce those consequences, this is likely to encourage such actors to pursue economic opportunities that they might otherwise consider too risky. A legal system that lacks the element of predictability (e.g., the rule of "readjustment" of land rights in China, discussed in Chapter 7) will not encourage economic initiative. If a legal system is to afford sufficient predictability, it must include substantive and procedural rules that are written, published and widely known – hence not just published, but publicized. The legal system should spell out very clearly the procedures necessary to enforce legally protected rights and interests. The procedural and substantive rules should also be simple, precise and unambiguous.

Fairness. Effective legal systems also place a heavy emphasis on the relative "fairness" of the law. Laws should apply equally to all regardless of public connections or private power. Moreover, both substantive and procedural laws should provide for "due process" – open and unrestricted access to public courts and administrative bodies for airing legal grievances and enforcing legal rights.[36] A legal system that tolerates the unequal application of legal standards or permits the arbitrary exercise of power without legal recourse tends to induce passivity and resentment by citizens, neither of which is conducive to encouraging widespread participation in economic activity. (See, for example, the discussion in Chapter 7 relating to opaque and unequal application of land expropriation rules and the resulting problems in China.)

Rapid adjudication of disputes. Rapid adjudication of disputes facilitates economic initiative and activity. Too many legal systems have an unfortunate propensity for long delays before disputes are finally resolved. Such delays can be addressed by increasing the number of judges or courts to handle anticipated litigation, keeping formalized procedural rules to a minimum, establishing administrative procedures to solve some problems without recourse to courts, and encouraging private dispute resolution through mediation or arbitration. The appropriate balance between rapid adjudication and standards of fairness is likely to include publicized and enforced rules specifically defining and limiting administrative authority and discretion.[37] (Aspects of this are discussed in Chapters 6 and 8.)

Consistency between legal rules and the society's customs, norms and administrative resources. To remain effective, no legal system can depart far from the traditions of the people it serves. Unless the people

consider the laws and law-enforcing mechanisms to be fair and legitimate, the costs of law adjudication and enforcement will be prohibitive.
Law should remain as consistent as possible with a country's economic, social and political fabric even as it attempts to reform that fabric.
The design of the legal system must also reflect the country's administrative resources and capabilities. Law reformers should take into account such resources and capabilities when drafting substantive and
procedural rules to ensure that the administrative structure can actually
implement the rules. These resources and capabilities differ significantly among developing countries.

IV.   Pro-poor land tenure reforms

Pro-poor land tenure reforms increase the ability of the rural poor and
other marginalized groups to gain access to land and also to secure
rights to land already possessed. Pro-poor land tenure reforms can be
designed to advance one or more of three objectives: (1) broadening
land access for the poor and other marginalized groups; (2) improving
land tenure security for the poor and other marginalized groups to
land rights they possess; and (3) improving the capacity of public sector
land institutions to serve the public generally and protect the interests
of the poor in particular (see Box 1.2).

Broadening access to land

Our analysis of land tenure reform objectives distinguishes between access to land and tenure security. The primary distinction between efforts to broaden land access and those that improve land tenure security relates to the fact of land *possession*. Simply put, broadening land
access involves providing possession, at a minimum, to those who lack
possession of land, whereas improving land tenure security involves securing and broadening the rights of those who already possess land.
Land tenure reforms can involve efforts to improve tenure security
without efforts to broaden access to land. But most efforts to broaden
access will also include measures to provide greater tenure security to
those who receive access.

The distinction and interaction between land access and secure
tenure are portrayed in Figure 1.2. A person may have both access and
secure tenure to land, which is represented by the upper left quadrant
of the figure. In general, land tenure reforms should aim to move larger numbers of people into this upper left quadrant. The upper right
quadrant represents those who have access to land, but not secure
rights. Examples include informal, at-will tenants (such a tenancy is ter-

minable at the "will" of either party), most of those women whose husbands have independent legal rights to the "family's" landholding, and "squatters" or informal possessors on land claimed by the government.

When people lack access to land, they almost always lack secure rights. That is, the vast majority of people who exist in the lower half of the matrix exist in the lower right quadrant. Among the rare instances where a person lacks possession, but has a secure right, are cases where the landowner does not have the right of possession. (Note that the figure does not readily accommodate workers or "members" on collective farms, who might be thought of as akin to agricultural laborers on a plantation but, unlike those laborers, usually having secure job rights.)

Figure 1.2.   *Land access and secure tenure*

		Tenure Security	
		Yes	No
Land Access	Yes	Typical owner-operator with title	Tenant at will or for a short term Many women Squatter on government land
	No	(Unusual, but includes:) Landowner with *bargadar* in West Bengal Long-term lessor in Czech Republic	Typical landless laborer

A considerable literature documents the social and economic importance of land access, and especially secure and long-term land access, for individuals and families,[38] as well as the importance of broad access to land at the macro-level for a country's development prospects.[39] Yet large numbers of rural families in many developing countries are completely landless, in the sense that they lack secure and meaningful possession of any land.[40]

Most efforts to carry out large-scale land rights reforms have involved moving poor agricultural families from either the upper-right or lower-right quadrant in Figure 1.2 to the upper-left quadrant: that is, providing for either insecure tenant farmers (and nearly all tenant families who are among the poor have insecure rights) or landless agricultural laborers to become owner-operators.[41]

Reforms aimed at enabling tenants to become owners have typically involved state expropriation – with varying degrees of compensation – of some or all of the land held by landlords that is rented out to tenants. Chapter 2 examines the very successful post-World War II "land-to-the-tiller" programs in Japan, Taiwan and South Korea (and similar successful programs in South Vietnam and El Salvador, with which RDI lawyers were involved), as well as a number of failed programs.

One of the more striking evolutions in our own views on land tenure reform since 1987, when author Prosterman wrote, with Jeffrey Riedinger, "Land Reform and Democratic Development,"[42] is our conclusion that there are very few settings in which state-mandated land-to-the-tiller programs giving ownership to tenant farmers are likely to be feasible today. And, while we continue to hold to the conclusion in the earlier book that legal regimes to regulate the continuing landlord-tenant relationship are unlikely to work in developing countries, we now conclude that lawful and unregulated landlord-tenant arrangements, still vastly inferior to land ownership, nonetheless represent a large step up the ladder out of poverty for agricultural laborers. Hence, in many settings, it may be worth the effort to dismantle restrictions and regulations of the agricultural landlord-tenant relationship that have clearly failed, giving greater scope for legal landlord-tenant arrangements.

Reforms aimed at helping agricultural laborers to become owner-operators have typically involved attempts by the state to expropriate larger landholdings above a certain size or "ceiling," or sometimes expropriation of entire plantations. There have been few successes here, although RDI lawyers have been close observers of one such program, in El Salvador, that was moderately successful, and two programs that failed, in Nicaragua and in the Philippines. Chapter 3 examines these efforts.

Broadening land access through large-scale expropriation of land is a politically charged approach. Success requires strong political resolve and widespread support in society. Both because of the political challenges and the relatively frequent failure of expropriatory reforms, foreign assistance donors, most notably the World Bank, have increasingly promoted voluntary efforts to broaden land access through market mechanisms. As discussed in Chapter 3 (and briefly in Chapter 6), although market-oriented approaches have shown some potential in certain settings, they have also aroused considerable opposition and controversy.

Here we conclude that in the future there may actually be more scope for well-conceived programs to distribute land to agricultural laborers than for land-to-the-tiller programs, whether based on expropriating private land with market-price compensation, on voluntary market-based purchases of private land, or on the distribution of appropriate and existing public land. Such programs to benefit agricultural laborers would likely focus on public land or on low-value unused (or underutilized) large private landholdings.

However, traditional programs to provide land access both for tenants and agricultural laborers have almost always focused on the provision of a "family farm" (or equivalent aliquot share on a larger farming unit) sufficient to provide the beneficiary family's entire livelihood. Providing such farms, usually close to the median size of existing farms in the country, typically requires a set of legal measures that would acquire and distribute anywhere from 10% to 40% of arable land, depending on the proportion of tenants and agricultural laborers in the rural population. The resulting political and financial hurdles are often insuperable, and setting the financial land-valuation hurdle lower inevitably means setting the political feasibility hurdle much higher. Thus, it is of growing interest that programs are now emerging to provide ownership of a micro-plot, often of a house-and-garden plot (or homegarden) of a fraction of an acre, as a supplement to the existing livelihood of a tenant or laborer family that presently lacks any access to land of their own. Such programs may require 1% or less of the country's arable land, be affordable even when paying full market price on a willing seller-willing buyer basis, and hence face far fewer political obstacles. This approach is discussed in Chapter 4, as well as in Chapter 6.

Improving land tenure security

Secure land tenure rights are clearly an important component of economic development generally, and rural development specifically. Such rights are exercised not only by individual possessors, but often by larger social groups.

Land tenure security has been defined and measured in a variety of ways. Although differing notions of land tenure rights make it difficult to develop a simple objective definition of land tenure security, the following definition identifies several key concepts.

Land tenure security exists when an individual or group is confident that they have rights to a piece of land on a long-term basis, protected from dispossession by outside sources, and with the ability to reap the benefits of labor and capital invested in the land, whether through direct use or upon transfer to another holder.[43]

The authors of this definition then go on to suggest, in an analysis that we find highly useful, that regardless of the land tenure system, land tenure security can then be assessed using three important measures: breadth, duration and assurance.[44] Breadth refers to the quantity and quality of the land rights held (the sticks in the bundle),[45] which may include rights to possess land to the exclusion of others, to grow or harvest crops, to pass rights on to heirs, to sell land or to lease it to others, to pledge land rights as security for credit, and to build structures.[46]

One important aspect of breadth involves transferability of rights. The right to transfer one's land rights can encompass market transfers (e.g., sale or rental) as well as non-market transfers (e.g., inheritance). If land possessors can transfer their land rights through sale and rental markets, this can encourage them to invest in their land to increase its productivity and long-term value. The ability to transfer land rights also gives the possessors greater options to diversify their livelihoods and react effectively to changing economic and non-economic forces. The right to mortgage one's land rights can also be a source of finance for major land improvement and acquisition of additional land (through so-called "purchase money mortgages").

In theory, land sale rights are the most effective way of combining efficient transfers of rights without sacrificing long-term tenure security for possessors. However, in environments characterized by market imperfections, especially in credit and insurance markets, land rental transfers may produce greater efficiency and equity than land sales.[47] In any case, land rental markets are likely to develop earlier than land sales markets and are likely to be a more practicable means for the poor to access land. International experience indicates that efforts aimed at encouraging land rental markets that are combined with measures to reduce credit and insurance market imperfections are likely to have much greater benefits than an exclusive concentration on land sales markets.[48]

The second measure of tenure security is duration, which refers to the length of time for which tenure rights are valid. Typically, the same duration applies to every stick in the bundle of rights, but this is not necessarily so. Longer durations imply greater tenure security. Ownership or equivalent rights are perpetual, but other long-term rights may provide similar incentives to land possessors and give rise to similar behavior. Chapter 7 discusses the impact of the 30-year land rights being given in rural China.

Assurance, the third measure, refers to the certainty of the breadth and duration of the land rights. If an individual is said to possess land rights of a specific breadth and duration but has difficulty exerting or enforcing those rights, the assurance of the rights is compromised. A land "right" that cannot be exerted or enforced is not a meaningful right, and the more costly it is to enforce the right (in money, time or effort), the less valuable it is.

In sum, adequate tenure security exists when an individual or group with rights to land possesses key rights for a duration sufficiently long to recoup the value of investments made on the land, and with enough assurance to prevent outside interference. Conversely, tenure insecurity exists where an individual or group possesses an inadequate breadth of meaningful rights, the duration of those rights is insufficient to recoup investments made, or the ability to enforce rights is lacking.[49]

Compared to weak or insecure rights, secure land rights can facilitate economic development in a variety of ways, including:

1. raising productivity through increased agricultural investment;[50]
2. increasing land transactions and facilitating transfer of land from less efficient to more efficient uses (and more efficient users) by increasing the certainty of contracts and lowering enforcement costs;
3. reducing the incidence of land disputes through clearer definition and enforcement of rights;
4. increasing access to and use of credit by improving ability of borrowers to use land as collateral;
5. increasing investments in housing or other structures on the land;
6. increasing the underlying value of the land;[51]
7. reducing the amount of resources individual owners must spend on defending their interests, which allows them to participate more fully in productive work not tied to the land;[52]
8. reducing soil erosion and other environmental degradation to land as the result of incentives to improve stewardship of land;[53]
9. creating political stability by providing farmers a more significant stake in society;[54] and
10. reducing pressure   for farmers to migrate prematurely to urban areas.[55]

These points are further discussed in Chapter 8.

Although tenure security is often promoted for economic objectives, improving tenure security also typically results in less stress, improved peace of mind and a greater hope for the future for those individuals, families or groups who receive it.[56] More broadly, secure land tenure widely held by the rural population may play an important role in political empowerment, democratization and the institutions of civil society.[57] These benefits may be difficult to quantify, but they are just as real – and perhaps even more important – than the quantifiable economic benefits.

Most land tenure reforms include efforts to improve land tenure security for individuals or groups that possess land but have insecure tenure. These efforts include both giving greater rights (sometimes "ownership") to agricultural tenants (the topic of Chapter 2), issuing titles to certify land ownership or other secure rights to land (the topic of Chapter 8), and other measures to increase tenure security for non-tenant possessors (such as those in China which are the topic of Chapter 7).

Titling, customary tenure systems and common property resources

Land tenure reforms often include measures to increase tenure security for land possessors whose possession is not based upon tenancy or license from a landowner. The most common method is generally described as "titling" – issuing titles or functionally equivalent documentation to land possessors to certify that the state acknowledges their right to possess the land. These efforts and variations upon them, their impacts, risks and limitations are discussed in Chapter 8 and are also referenced in Chapters 6 and 7.

Even though formal title can increase tenure security in many situations, experience indicates it is not always necessary for optimal tenure security.[58] Moreover, even when formal title is a necessary condition for tenure security, it is often not a sufficient condition. A variety of methods are available for providing tenure security that can be administered in a cost-effective way through institutions that combine legality with social legitimacy.

Where customary law systems are strong, state recognition of existing customary rights and institutions can be more effective than attempts to provide individual titles based on Western concepts. Legally recognizing customary land rights can improve tenure security for both the customary group as a whole and for its individual members. In particular, demarcating the external boundaries of the group's land can decrease the threat of encroachment by outsiders.[59]

Common property resources (CPR) are often discussed interchangeably with customary land tenure systems, but should be analyzed separately. They may include many areas of forest, dryland pasture, wetlands and surface waters. Most customary tenure systems include some CPRs and some individually held resources, and land tenure systems governed by formal law may also include CPRs. CPRs are resources that are shared by different users, who often hold varying rights. The physical nature or non-continuous and non-intensive use of the resource typically makes it difficult for the primary users to exclude other users, yet the use of the resource by one user necessarily reduces the supply available to others. Many CPRs are common to members of a defined group, and the group actively excludes non-members from use. The group may develop use customs that have the effect of limiting the extent of each member's use of the CPR.

CPRs are of particular importance for securing the livelihoods of poor and marginalized groups in society. Improving their tenure security in CPRs is crucial not only for sustaining and improving livelihoods but for providing the user groups with the necessary tools and incentives for conserving the resource base on which they depend.[60]

Land rights of women

The rights of women deserve special attention in all land tenure reform efforts, but should play a particularly important role in efforts to improve land tenure security. Past land tenure reforms typically ignored women's rights, focusing only on the household as a unit – a unit virtually always taken to be represented by a male (when an adult male is present). Women's land rights almost always require strengthening, under both formal and customary law. On this topic – in which "land law" may overlap and interact with "family law" – the limitations of formal law are particularly evident. While legislative reform has an important role to play in creating "space" for progressive change, it is clearly not sufficient. Cultural action, advocacy and education including legal literacy play crucial roles. Chapters 5 and 8 address this important topic in more detail.

Land rights of indigenous peoples

Indigenous peoples are another marginalized group that require special attention in efforts to strengthen tenure security. Those efforts have the potential both to harm and to benefit indigenous peoples. Past titling efforts in many parts of the world have provided governments with the political cover to dispossess indigenous peoples of land they have traditionally possessed and used.[61]

Three characteristics of indigenous land rights merit emphasis. First, indigenous land rights are a specific concern of international law, including being the subject of the International Labor Organization's Indigenous and Tribal Peoples Convention, now in effect in a number of countries.[62] Second, indigenous lands often constitute quite extensive areas, some of which are endowed with substantial oil and gas, mining, timber and other natural resources. This often results in tensions between the indigenous people and governments and business interests.[63] Third, because indigenous lands are typically under communal tenure systems, efforts to promote tenure security focused only on individual private property are likely to be wholly inadequate. These issues are discussed further in Chapter 8.

Reform of public sector land institutions

Capable land institutions are essential for broadening land access, improving tenure security, defining and protecting public and other group interests in land and, overall, for overseeing land tenure systems that operate equitably and effectively. Thus, land tenure reforms often include some program to reform and build capacity within public sector land institutions. In developing countries, such capacity is often weak, as revealed by inadequate and outdated land records, substantial numbers of land disputes that cannot be addressed expeditiously, high transaction costs and long delays for land transactions, and the government's inability to regulate or tax land effectively.

Efforts to reform public sector land institutions are sometimes combined with land titling efforts. Where capacity is very weak, especially following periods of armed conflict, institutional reform must be approached as a long-term process. The reform of public sector institutions is not a central focus of this book, although Chapter 8 does address the need for competent and committed land registration institutions, where registration of land rights is undertaken.[64]

V.   Guiding principles in approaching land tenure reform

The material in each of this book's chapters is rooted in the work, research and experience of RDI lawyers. The book thus necessarily reflects some principles, biases and values that guide RDI professionals in approaching land tenure reform work in developing countries. Although the principles are general, none is appropriate to every situation. Rather, these are broad themes and touchstones that must be tailored to particular circumstances.

Targeting the poor

Give preference to land tenure reform interventions that directly benefit the poorest and marginalized. The objective of economic development initiatives must be to improve the lives of the least well-off, especially the majority of the poor who live in rural areas. Interventions that purport to reach the poor indirectly, through a "trickle-down" of benefits, should be treated with suspicion. Interventions that provide benefits to both the non-poor and the poor should be analyzed to determine if a portion of intervention resources can be used to target the poor more effectively. A result that is otherwise "efficient" in terms of increasing national production or productivity may sometimes benefit better off segments of society while actually reducing the welfare of the poor.

Given the counter-intuitive reality that small farms are typically more productive than large farms in developing country settings, interventions that create smaller farms can boost efficiency as well as equity (see discussion on this inverse relationship between farm size and productivity in Chapter 3).

Protecting the rights of women should be a paramount consideration in analyzing every land tenure reform intervention. It is important to focus not only on the welfare of poor families, but also the welfare of women within poor families to ensure that they share in the benefits that flow from holding and exercising land rights. Planners should consider not only changes in law and public education to strengthen the rights of women, but should also look for opportunities to design programs that promote the development of assets over which women already exercise a high degree of authority (e.g., homegardens in many settings).

Anticipate and design against program sabotage and elite capture of benefits. It is always important to ensure that reforms carefully target intended beneficiaries. The primary objects of land tenure interventions should be the poor and marginalized, including women. A natural tendency exists for program or intervention benefits to be intercepted and captured by the non-poor ("elite capture"). In addition, local officials may impose barriers to program implementation through aggressive rent seeking behavior. Programs should be designed to minimize opportunities for rent seeking and to prevent capture of benefits by elites. One effective tool for ensuring that benefits reach the poor is to incorporate monitoring processes into program implementation that will ensure the production of quantitative and verifiable assessments of the level of benefits obtained by the target groups.

Assessing land tenure reform needs

Assess the relative importance of land among the other development issues in a given setting. Each developing country setting is unique, and each country may contain a number of unique settings within its territory. And the relative importance of land as a development or poverty issue varies in each setting depending on numerous factors. These factors must be assessed before determining whether, how and how deeply to intervene on land tenure issues. Land is likely to be a particularly important factor in the lives of the rural poor. In some settings it may be that "the horse is already out of the barn" because land tenure reform that might have deserved to be a high priority in past years is no longer likely to be an effective way to benefit the majority of the country's poor.

Recognize that land tenure reform is frequently necessary but is not sufficient for full poverty-fighting impact. Where a family is already on land

and receives new, long-term rights to that land, the immediate benefits (such as status, a sense of security, assured return on investments in the land) will almost certainly be enhanced and complemented by various related measures. Farm credit and micro-credit, access to improved seed and fertilizer, extension advice, appropriate research, marketing information are likely to achieve their optimum response when they reach beneficiaries who can now apply such aid and support to their own land, keep all the resulting profits, and make welcome land improvements. The point can be made in more acute form where a reform gives access to land to a family (for example, agricultural laborers) who had no access before. Such a family has lacked any piece of land to which any such support could even be applied.

Understand ground realities before proposing land tenure reform interventions. This is perhaps best articulated through the Seidmans' approach, which shares many of the biases of RDI's approach. This principle has several corollaries: (1) field research is critical to understanding the ground realities (researchers should go directly to the field and meet with project beneficiaries and prospective beneficiaries rather than only relying on the reports of others); (2) researchers should interview beneficiaries and other actors outside the presence of local officials, plantation owners and others who may have inconsistent interests;[65] (3) field research should include both qualitative and quantitative measures of conditions; (4) choosing among research approaches involves analysis of the costs and benefits of various approaches; and (5) the "80/20 rule" typically applies to the quest for full information (as a very rough approximation, 80% of full information can be attained with the first 20% of resources and time, and the remaining 20% requires four times as much effort and time).

Scope of land tenure reform intervention

In the inevitable trade-off between quantity of beneficiaries and quality of benefits, planners should favor the former. It is better to allocate available benefits (or resources or land) widely among the target group than to give only some members of the target group an ideal portion. We have referred to the latter approach as the "purse of gold" phenomenon.[66]

Pick low-hanging fruit. The "low-hanging fruit" is that which is most easily taken from the tree. Planners should do first that which is most easily accomplished and which provides immediate benefits. A simple cost-benefit analysis approach in analyzing land tenure reform interventions (particularly legal framework interventions) typically reveals some interventions that offer a high likelihood of success and few substantial challenges or obstacles. Reform interventions should be designed to initially achieve what is politically possible and financially affordable in the short to medium term rather than insisting immediately upon tackling larger and more complicated problems that will be resolved, if ever, only in the long term. On the other hand, it is important to make sure that low-hanging fruit is not "sour" in the sense that the intervention will cause harm or will defer energy from more important interventions (e.g., titling and registration programs that are not controversial, but which are not targeted to the needs of the poor).

Do not let the "best" become the enemy of the "good." Seeking an ideal solution that is improbable or impossible can preclude a "second-best" solution that is both extremely beneficial *and* feasible. Effective reform almost always (perhaps always) involves compromise among divergent interests. This maxim is related to but distinct from the low-hanging fruit maxim. Both involve cost-benefit analytic approaches. Examples of "good enough" solutions include long-term use rights (in place of ownership, where the latter would meet strong ideological resistance) and micro-plots (in place of full-size farms, where the latter would be clearly unaffordable). These specific examples are central to our discussion in Chapters 4, 6 and 7.

Choose interventions that are replicable. Gold-plated projects not only waste resources, but undermine future efforts to design and implement affordable solutions that can confer benefits to a larger population. Projects should be measured according to the cost of benefits per family in light of resources available and the number of families needing benefits. Ideally, projects should be affordable by host countries, without outside assistance. This is related to the "purse of gold" phenomenon, selection of low-hanging fruit, and the best being the enemy of the good.

Look for ways to make interventions affordable. When pricing project costs, do not rely solely on competition to produce reasonable prices. A simple competitive bidding regime for awarding contracts will not produce reasonable prices in environments where service suppliers are likely to collude. Other methods can be used to minimize the incidence of collusive pricing. This is a subset of the replicability issue.

Choose interventions that are sustainable. Programs are worthwhile only if results can be sustained over long periods. Interventions whose achievements do not last can undermine the credibility of development efforts and can cause fatigue among implementers. Interventions should not overestimate the capacity of existing administrative structures. While interventions should take advantage of new technologies, technology should be appropriate to host country conditions, including the existing capacity of local clerks. For example, do not install computers where electric service is unreliable, or design programs that require computer literacy even though clerks have never used computers. This is also related to the issue of replicability, since administrative capacity that is sufficient to implement a pilot project may not be able to sustain a larger program.

Timing of land tenure reform interventions

Acting to intervene on land issues involves risks and costs; and not acting also involves risks and costs. Planners often decline to take specific intervening actions on issues of land policy and law because of perceived risks and costs. However, although too rarely done, it is also important for planners to recognize and count the costs of inaction if they are to perform an appropriate cost-benefit analysis.

Recognize and take advantage of political and financial windows of opportunity. Successful interventions to improve land relations often depend upon the alignment of favorable political, financial and other factors. Timing is important, and over-planning can squander opportunities. This is related to the principle of not letting the best be the enemy of the good. It is difficult to plan for specific windows of opportunity, and one cannot be certain how long the window will remain open. Most significant and successful past land tenure reforms occurred because of sudden, well-directed interventions during a temporally limited, political window of opportunity. There is also an associated but perhaps larger point here relating to broader developmental or historical windows as distinct from narrower political windows, which is that rural land tenure reforms, to be most effective, should occur at a stage of development when a large portion of the population depend on rural land for their livelihood. A widespread redistributive land reform would not have the same beneficial impact in Brazil today as it would have had 40 years ago. It should also be recognized that there may be alternatives in program design – homestead plots in lieu of full-size farms is a notable one – that can enlarge, even greatly enlarge, the available windows of opportunity.

Role of law

Embody land rights in law whenever possible. Policy or custom is never as good or as "permanent" as law, and well-formulated law can be fully advertent to existing policy and custom.

Laws are only one of many factors affecting the behavior of the various actors. Many non-legal forces (economic, cultural, sociological, etc.) impact people's behavior. The more aligned the law is with those other factors, the greater the chance that the law can actually be implemented. For example, customary laws typically represent highly evolved (and evolving) and innovative responses to a unique and complex set of economic, sociological and cultural factors (although this does not always mean they represent the best practicable approach, or one geared to recognize women and the marginalized, or one reflecting awareness of other possibilities). Planners must first understand ground realities such as customary law before designing, adopting and implementing land law reforms.

Be alert for perverse, unintended consequences. It is important to learn from past mistakes to avoid doing harm. There are many examples of well-intended laws and programs that have led to results that undermine the objectives they sought (both of the major British efforts to buy white-owned land in Africa for redistribution to poor black farmers – in Kenya in the 1960s and Zimbabwe in the 1980s – went forward with severe design flaws whose adverse consequences are being felt today). Planners must not only understand the ground realities in order to craft effective land tenure reform law and policy; they must also put themselves in the position of the powerful vested interests to determine how such interests are likely to react to changes in policy or law. This also involves determining the "implementability" of a law or policy given the realities of administrative capacity and vested interests. While harmful consequences may be accidental from the standpoint of planners, the results may be intentional from the standpoint of the non-poor (including bureaucrats) who seek to capture benefits or thwart changes in the status quo.

Role of implementation

Achieving policy or legislative reform is at best half the battle. Changes in policy and law are typically necessary but never sufficient. Implementation is key. A policy or law that has not been implemented is worth little or nothing. Moreover, we often hear but rarely believe that "the law is good, but the problem is lack of implementation." Failures in implementation can often be traced to faulty law design. For example, the law drafters may not have taken into account the lack of capacity within the implementing agency or non-legal factors influencing people's behavior that would make the law difficult or impossible to implement.

Test the hypotheses. Do not assume that hypotheses are correct. Revisit hypotheses to test them and seek ways to refine and improve their predictive value. For example, many observers assume that small land plots substantially constrain productivity and design costly and potentially disruptive land consolidation programs based on that assumption without ever empirically testing it.

Set intermediate implementation goals and measure results. Land tenure reforms are often long-term reforms. Such reforms should then be implemented in stages with intermediate benchmarks and incentives for implementers to produce results. The level of future or ongoing funding should depend upon success in achieving intermediate results. Numerous land tenure reform objectives are quantifiable such that "progress payments" can be linked to the level of ongoing achievements. Think of construction mortgages where the bank releases funds as the building goes up.

Local actors

Bureaucrats play key roles. It is critical to understand the interests and motivations of bureaucrats who will implement programs and policies. Bureaucrats are often accustomed to exercising power over land. Programs designed to reward bureaucrats for meeting targets that advance development objectives may prove to be particularly effective.

Make beneficiaries part of the land tenure reform process. Planners should look for ways to help beneficiaries claim and defend their interests, marshalling their energy to press officials to comply with law. Legal aid is an example of a program that makes use of the fact that the motivation of beneficiaries to defend their interests, though often inchoate, generally exceeds the motivation of bureaucrats to ignore or violate those interests. Chapter 9 discusses the topic of land-related legal aid, which is a type of intervention that can give beneficiaries an effective voice and complement almost any type of land tenure reform.

Use public education to create legitimate expectations among the public and among the land tenure reform beneficiaries. Law must be actively publicized. When publicized, law creates expectations among the public and even more pointedly among the beneficiaries, which can be useful in motivating officials to fulfill expectations. Even where the law cannot be implemented fully or immediately throughout the country, the publicization of the law and explanation of its benefits can motivate the public and beneficiaries to demand its implementation.

Civil society organizations play important roles in land tenure reform processes. Civil society organizations are prominent in many, although not all, settings where land tenure reform is needed. They can perform important roles in providing planners with information about the plight of the poor and marginalized, articulating the demands of those groups, reaching consensus among targeted beneficiaries on policy options, "selling" feasible policy choices to their constituencies, and helping in the implementation of reforms.

Weigh the power imbalances. More broadly, weigh and consider the power imbalances that operate against (or sometimes for) the interests of program beneficiaries, and how these imbalances may be altered. Nearly all successful land reforms involved broader arrays of factors that favored the beneficiaries, and most unsuccessful land reforms included the reverse (although a badly designed program can forestall success even with what may seem a winning constellation of forces be-hind the reform). Some of the factors that can redress what appears to be an adverse balance are discussed immediately above, such as legal aid, public education, and the mobilization of civil society actors. De-sign variables can also be crucial: a program that would contemplate mandatory taking of landlords' land for far less than market value will encounter a gauntlet of fierce resistance from the landowners and their allies; a program based upon land being voluntarily sold at market prices (perhaps because the program needs only enough land to distri-bute micro-plots) will encounter virtually no such resistance.

In general, planners should trust land rightholders to exercise transfer rights wisely. We generally presume that land holders should be free to lease out, sell, mortgage and bequeath their land. Restrictions on these freedoms can be warranted in certain settings (typical examples include not allowing men to disinherit their wives, a temporary moratorium on sale by land reform grantees, and prohibiting foreigners from holding agricultural land), but restrictions should be justified by important soci-etal objectives and should be narrowly designed to meet those objec-tives.

VI. Conclusions

The wise application of the law to the reform of land tenure rules and systems remains among the most widely relevant and highly leveraged means of improving the lives of the world's rural poor. This book at-tempts to summarize and synthesize much of the post-World War II experience, both successful and unsuccessful, in applying the law to these issues.

Centrally, we hope that the cumulative experience reflected in this book – that of RDI and that of others – will provide help and guidance in identifying what is needed, and what can be done, to improve the land access and security of the rural poor in a wide variety of national and sub-national settings over the coming years. Ultimately, it is our goal both to show the continuing importance of "the land question," and to demonstrate that there are practical, legal-system answers, sometimes rather new and different answers, to most of the variant renderings of that question. This includes the important goals of public and academic education on land issues, as well as communication to policy makers, program funders, the media and others with special in-terest in land issues.

The discussion unfolds in sequence, intended to form a single, uni-fied volume that reflects the collaborative experience, research and conclusions of the authors and editors, rather than comprising a series of independent chapters or contributions.

Chapters 2, 3 and 4 look, respectively, at two traditional and one promising alternative approach to answering the land question. Chapter 2 discusses one of the two principle arenas in which land tenure reforms have unfolded in the past, that of landlord-tenant systems. There have been a number of successful land-to-the-tiller programs giving ownership to tenants of the land they farm, as well as a number of failures. The design features needed in a successful land-to-the-tiller program can be identified with considerable confidence, but it has been a quarter-century since the last substantially successful program unfolded, and there are generalized factors that make it less likely such reforms will be seriously attempted in the future (e.g., there are fewer land-based communist insurgencies, fewer governments likely to have the necessary political will, and much higher values for agricultural land in many of the potential settings).

One alternative followed in several countries involves an attempt to impose substantial external regulations on tenure security and rent levels in the ongoing landlord-tenant relationship (as distinct from ending that relationship). This alternative has only one sustained success (in the Indian state of West Bengal), but also many failures which have often left tenants in a worse position. A better approach in most settings today is to adopt a more "market friendly" approach to farmland rental markets. Doing so may provide an opportunity for the poorest to move "up the ladder" from agricultural laborer to tenant farmer.

Chapter 3 discusses the other principal arena in which land tenure reforms have unfolded in the past, that of large estates worked by agricultural laborers. There have been fewer successes in such settings, and numerous failures. Again, the design features needed in a successful program can be identified with considerable confidence. Somewhat paradoxically, there may be greater opportunities for successful new programs here, and some serious efforts at such programs continue. The prospects for success appear much greater for underutilized estates or underutilized portions of estates than for intensively used and heavily capitalized lands.

Chapter 4 examines an important alternative or supplemental approach that is gaining favor in some developing-country settings, that of small micro-plots for the rural poor. The chapter reviews scattered experiences from a variety of settings that lead to the recognition that micro-ownership of plots as small as one-twenty-fifth hectare – one-tenth of an acre – or even less can provide vital supplementation to the livelihoods of the rural poor. Compared to the reforms discussed in Chapters 2 and 3, these require far less land and far fewer financial resources. Planning for and design of programs to distribute such plots (using land purchases on the market or existing public land), including important complementary measures, are discussed in Chapter 4.

Chapter 5 analyzes the important ways in which improving women's access to land and strengthening the security of women's rights to land provide both economic access to markets and social access to non-market institutions. The chapter explores how land tenure policy can be shaped to provide benefits to women, as well as the need for planners to take care that policies do not inadvertently reduce women's land rights.

Chapters 6 and 7 focus on the two largest – and very different – contemporary country settings for land tenure reforms, India and China, respectively. Looking first at a developing country whose agriculture was never collectivized, Chapter 6 reviews India's specific experience since Independence in 1947 with the approaches to land tenure reform outlined in the previous chapters, concluding that the greatest hope lies in a combination of micro-plot distribution (now going forward in several Indian states, with market-based acquisition of the needed land) and (with an important exception) credible restoration and deregulation of tenancy.

Chapter 7 looks principally at the processes of transformation of collectivized farming and tenure, reviewing China's specific experience with land tenure reform since the Communist accession to power in 1949. The present efforts to give farmers 30-year land rights, often against the resistance of local cadres and officials, represent the playing out of a dynamic which has parallels in landlord resistance to land-to-the-tiller programs, except for the important fact that the land is already publicly (collectively) owned. It represents a setting in which broader issues as to implementation and achievement of the rule of law are unfolding and being tested in the specific arena of land tenure security, with implications far beyond the Chinese countryside. Full physical reorganization of collective farms into family farms was completed a quarter-century ago in China. This invites comparison with the very different experience seen in the countries that formerly comprised the Soviet Union.

Chapters 8 and 9 deal with two important cross-cutting issues on which the law has a heavy bearing, relating to the access of the rural poor and marginalized to rights in land: the issues of formalization of land rights, and legal aid. Formalization may confer benefits on the poor in some settings, but each circumstance must be evaluated separately to determine whether the poor are likely to benefit, and formalization programs must be designed to ensure that, at the very least, the programs do not adversely affect the poor and marginalized. Land rights legal aid holds great potential for benefitting the poor, whether in concert or independent of land tenure reform programs targeting the poor. Chapter 10 embodies our concluding reflections as to what important changes have occurred with respect to the perception, prospects and practice of land tenure reform since we began our work on those issues some 40 years ago.

Notes

1 See S. Chen & M. Ravallion, Development Research Group, World Bank, *The Developing World Is Poorer Than We Thought, But No Less Successful In the Fight Against Poverty*, Policy Research Working Paper No. 4703, at 3-4, 10-11, 30-31 (Aug. 2008). The "$1.25 a day" international poverty line (based on the poverty lines commonly found in low-income countries) and the "$2 a day" international poverty line (based on the poverty lines more typical of middle-income countries) are calculated using estimated "purchasing power parity," that is, the number of units of a country's currency required to buy the same amounts of goods and services in the domestic market as a U.S. dollar would buy in the United States. Despite the higher-than-previous estimate of the extremely poor, the study still concludes, in revising the whole time series, that their numbers have declined, from 1.9 billion in 1981 (however, if China is excluded, the number has somewhat increased). Id. at 30. See also *An Even Poorer World*, NEW YORK TIMES (editorial), Sept. 2, 2008.
Another well-publicized consequence of the same research was the downward revision of the PPP-based estimates of total GDP for a number of developing countries, including approximately 40% reductions in previous measures of total GDP for China and India. See, e.g., *Chinese, Indian economies "smaller than thought,"* FINANCIAL TIMES, Dec. 18, 2007; World Bank Press Release 2005 *International Comparison Program Preliminary Global Report Compares Size of Economies*, Dec. 17, 2007.
2 Food and Agriculture Organization of the United Nations, *The State of Food Insecurity in the World 2006*, at 10 (FAO 2006).
3 It is estimated that, worldwide, 53% of the approximately 10 million child deaths every year can be attributed to being underweight. R. Black, S. Morris & J. Bryce, *Where and Why are 10 Million Children Dying Every Year?*, 361 THE LANCET 2226-2234 (Elsevier 2003).
4 C. Csaki & C. De Haan, REACHING THE RURAL POOR: A RENEWED STRATEGY FOR RURAL DEVELOPMENT 6 (World Bank 2003).
5 See generally K. Deininger, LAND POLICIES FOR GROWTH AND POVERTY REDUCTION (World Bank Policy Research Report 2003); M.R. El-Ghonemy, *Agrarian Reform Policy Issues Never Die* (speech presented at The American University in Cairo, Mar. 4, 2002), available at http://64.233.179.104/scholar?hl=en&lr=&q=cache:eYw2cIv5 VOEJ:www.aucegypt.edu/src/conf_site/papers/Ghoneim_speech.pdf+el-ghonemy +text+of +speech; R. Prosterman & T. Hanstad, *Land Reform in the Twenty-First Century: New Challenges, New Responses*, 4(2) SEATTLE JOURNAL FOR SOCIAL JUSTICE 763 (2006).
6 On a macro-comparison, 1981-1983 grain productivity per hectare was clearly highest in systems dominated by small owner-operated farms, and the results have not changed dramatically since that time. R. Prosterman & J. Riedinger, LAND REFORM AND DEMOCRATIC DEVELOPMENT ch. 2 (Johns Hopkins 1987); United Nations Food & Agriculture Organization, FAO PRODUCTION YEARBOOK 2003, at 71-73 (UNFAO 2003). One

exception to the general observation was the seemingly highest-producing collective agriculture, North Korea, but it has since been shown to have been "cooking the books" with drastically overstated figures. Using later, corrected production figures, the small, owner-operated farms of the South (arising out of the 1950s land-to-the-tiller program) get grain yields over 90% greater, per hectare, than the collective farms of the North. Id.

7   K. Deininger & L. Squire, *New Ways of Looking at Old Issues: Inequality and Growth*, 57(2) JOURNAL OF DEVELOPMENT ECONOMICS 259-287 (1998).

8   See Deininger, supra note 5, at 18-19.

9   M.R. El Ghonemy, G. Tyler & Y. Couvreur, *Alleviating rural poverty through agricultural growth*, 29 JOURNAL OF DEVELOPMENT STUDIES 358-364 (1993).

10   Id.

11   See Prosterman & Riedinger, supra note 6, ch. 1; see also Deininger, supra note 5, at 157. Prosterman first formulated an "Index of Rural Instability," based on the portion of a country's population that consisted of agricultural families who lacked ownership or owner-like tenure to the land they worked, in the early 1970s. R. Prosterman, *Land Reform as Foreign Aid*, 6 FOREIGN POLICY 130 (1972). This represented a revision and refinement of a relationship between landlessness and instability earlier identified by Bruce Russet in B. Russet, *Inequality and Instability, the Relation of Land Tenure to Politics*, 16(3) WORLD POLITICS 442 (1964).

12   Cycles of land tenure reforms have been carried out in many parts of the world during the distant past. In varying forms and scale, land tenure reform was carried out during ancient times, including by the Greeks and Romans. A periodic land redistribution is contemplated in the Old Testament, but it is uncertain whether it was actually carried out. Much later, a major land tenure reform was implemented in France around the beginning of the French Revolution in 1798, after which the reasonably satisfied French peasantry largely sat out the (mostly urban) violence and upheaval. At about the same time, a democratic and non-violent land tenure reform began in Denmark.

In the 19th century, several land tenure reforms were undertaken in Europe. Notable among them was the emancipation of the Russian serfs by Tsar Alexander II in 1861, accompanied by a major distribution of land. While Abraham Lincoln emancipated the slaves in the United States in 1863 in the midst of the American Civil War, this was unfortunately not followed by redistribution of plantation land to the freed slaves. Separately, President Lincoln's Homestead Act of 1862 granted more than 14 million homesteaders title to government land, largely in the western parts of the country, by 1900.

The 20th century saw a large number of land tenure reforms in a variety of settings, many of which are discussed in the current volume. See generally R. Prosterman & J. Riedinger, supra, note 6, chs. 1 and 2; S.M. Borras, Jr., C. Kay, A. Haron & A. Lodhi, *Agrarian Reform and Rural Development: Historical Overview and Current Issues*, ISS/UNDP Land, Poverty and Public Action Policy Paper No. 1 (ISS/UNDP 2007), available at http://www.iss.nl/land; F. Douring, LAND AND LABOR IN EUROPE IN THE TWENTIETH CENTURY (Martinus Nighoff 1965); G. Myrdal, ASIAN DRAMA: AN INQUIRY INTO THE POVERTY OF NATIONS (Twentieth Century Fund 1968); E. Tuma, TWENTY-SIX CENTURIES OF AGRARIAN REFORM (University of California 1965).

13   H. Demsetz, *Toward a Theory of Property Rights*, 57(2) AMERICAN ECONOMIC REVIEW 347 (1967); see generally Y. Hayami & V.W. Ruttan, AGRICULTURAL DEVELOPMENT: AN INTERNATIONAL PERSPECTIVE (Johns Hopkins University Press 1985).

14   See Deininger, supra note 5, at 9-10. Many experts explain the transformation of land tenure systems within general models in which the historical evolution of tenure follows changes in the economy and society. See, e.g., H. Binswanger, K. Deininger &

G. Feder, *Agricultural Land Relations in the Developing World*, 75(5) AMERICAN JOURNAL
OF AGRICULTURAL ECONOMICS 1242-1248 (1993); Demsetz, supra note 13, at 347-359;
R. Ellickson, *Property in Land* 102(6) YALE LAW JOURNAL 1315 (1993). In this model, a
hunter-gatherer society will be associated with open access to common property resources. The concept of territory develops with the emergence of a communal group
identity. Communal control over land is strengthened as agricultural cultivation expands. As agriculture becomes more sedentary and intensive, individual or household rights to specific plots emerge. The transformation of territory into states results
in government acquiring special powers over land and access to resources. Manorial
systems develop and can lead to either greater rights to cultivators (family farms) or
greater rights to overlords (landlord estates or haciendas). Economic and political
ideologies also play a role. Capitalism tends to push for land to be more easily alienated and the removal of communal or other restrictions on use and transfer. Communism has typically resulted in state ownership of land. Where communism has
collapsed or been modified, there is typically a return to private ownership. While
these simple historical models do help to demonstrate ways in which land tenure systems may mirror wider changes in society, they necessarily fail to take into account
all the unique and diverse factors that influence land tenure systems within a given
setting and the complexity of changes that they undergo. See, e.g., M. Cleary & P. Ea-
ton, TRADITION AND REFORM: LAND TENURE AND RURAL DEVELOPMENT IN SOUTH EAST
ASIA 1-12 (Oxford University Press 1996).
15 See Demsetz, supra note 13, at 347.
16 See Ellickson, supra note 14, at 1321. Observers from a range of perspectives have
also asserted theories that would conflict with the proposition that land tenure systems always evolve efficiently. Institutional economists Douglass North and Robert
Thomas find that while governments are better able than private groups to enforce
property rights, they are also more prone to capture by rent seekers. D.P. North & R.
P. Thomas, THE RISE OF THE WESTERN WORLD: A NEW ECONOMIC HISTORY (Cambridge
University Press 1973). Karl Marx both observed and predicted that capitalists will
use force and fraud to obtain land from customary groups. K. Marx, CAPITAL, pt. 8
(1867). Klaus Deininger, an economist and land expert of the World Bank, notes that
"there are many examples throughout history where failure to establish the necessary
property rights institutions has led to conflict and resource dissipation rather than investments that would enhance resource values and productivity," which shows the
limits of a property rights evolution theory that predicts a virtuous cycle. See Deininger, supra note 5, at 10.
17 See Ellickson, supra note 14, at 1320-1321.
18 B. Burke, A.M. Burke & R.H. Helmholz, FUNDAMENTALS OF PROPERTY LAW 221 (Lexis
Law Publishing 1999).
19 See, e.g., M.R. Cohen, *Property and Sovereignty*, 13(1) CORNELL LAW QUARTERLY 8, 12
(1927).
20 R. Cunningham, W. Stoebuck & D. Whitman, THE LAW OF PROPERTY 7 (West Publishing 1993). A.M. Honore proposed a list of eleven "standard incidents" that he claims
make up private property, including the crucial rights to exclusive possession, personal use, and alienation. Honore's full list of incidents is: (1) right to exclusive possession; (2) right to personal use and enjoyment; (3) right to the capital value, including
alienation, consumption, waste or destruction; (4) right to transmit by gift, devise or
descent; (5) right to manage use by others; (6) right to the income from use by
others; (7) right to tenure security (that is, immunity from confiscatory expropriation); (8) lack of any term on these rights; (9) residual rights on the reversion of
lapsed ownership rights held by others; (10) duty to refrain from using the object in
ways that harm others; and (11) liability to execution for repayment of debts. A.M.

Honore, *Ownership*, in A.G. Guest, ed., OXFORD ESSAYS IN JURISPRUDENCE 107, 112-28 (University of Toronto Press 1961). Honore's list is now commonly accepted by property theorists as a starting point for describing the core bundle of private property rights in Western market economies, although many theorists challenge the inclusion of one incident or another. M. Heller, *The Tragedy of the Anticommons: Property in the Transition from Marx to Markets*, 111(3) HARVARD LAW REVIEW 621, 623, nn. 187-89 and accompanying text (1998).

21   See Cunningham, et al., supra note 20, at 7, citing R. Pound, *The Law of Property and Recent Juristic Thought*, 25(12) AMERICAN BAR ASSOCIATION JOURNAL 993 (1939).

22   There are, for example, considerable differences in the purposes for which, and the compensation to be paid when, the state takes private land for some other use – "expropriation" in some definitions of the term – an issue discussed in Chapter 7.

23   See Ellickson, supra note 14, at 1344-1362.

24   Moreover, a traditional society based on customary law tends not to differentiate between economic and social relations in society: economic relations are merely a part of social relations, and social relations are all important. Modern societies, in contrast, which tend to be dominated by the market, are inclined to keep market and social relations compartmentalized and to view land primarily as a commodity and factor of production. P. McAuslan, BRINGING THE LAW BACK IN: ESSAYS IN LAND, LAW AND DEVELOPMENT 5 (Ashgate 2003).

25   See id. at 6-8. McAuslan notes that the three sets of relations or circuits overlap in two senses. People move between the circuits both in terms of their actual relationship to the land and the transactions in which they engage. Moreover, it can be difficult to determine whether a particular piece of land is within a particular circuit; and it may be within more than one circuit, giving rise to a unique combination of rights and duties. See id. at 8.

26   J.W. Bruce & S.E. Migot-Adholla, INTRODUCTION TO SEARCHING FOR LAND TENURE SECURITY IN AFRICA 4-5 (Kendall-Hunt 1994).

27   B. Cousins & A. Claassens, *Communal Tenure "From Above" and "From Below": Land Rights, Authority and Livelihoods in Rural South Africa*, in S. Evers, M. Spierenburg & H. West, eds., COMPETING JURISDICTIONS: SETTLING LAND CLAIMS IN AFRICA 22 (Brill 2005).

28   P. Peters, *The Erosion of Commons and the Emergence of Property: Problems for Social Analysis*, in R.C. Hunt & A. Gilman, eds., PROPERTY IN ECONOMIC CONTEXT 356-361 (University Press of America 1998).

29   El-Ghonemy cautions that those who rush to privatize customary land tenure in tropical Africa should note that it took Great Britain six centuries between the Norman Conquest in 1066 and the Act of Settlement in 1700 to transform a tribal subsistence society into a market-centered society and to establish private, individual property in land without monopoly and governed by formal law; a principle that became the foundation of the Anglo-Saxon political economy. El-Ghonemy, supra note 5. This did not, however, forestall the abuses of enclosure, in which the aristocracy or other well-off farmers often gained rights over former "common" land at the expense of ordinary villagers.

30   See generally A. Seidman, R. Seidman & N. Abeyesekere, LEGISLATIVE DRAFTING FOR DEMOCRATIC SOCIAL CHANGE: A MANUAL FOR DRAFTERS (Kluwer Law International 2001).

31   The law's potential as a tool for social and economic transformation is a matter of dispute. Marxist theory holds that the mode of production determines the law. Others view law as only reflecting the sum of existing socio-economic-political vectors in a given setting, which, like the Marxist approach, denies its potential for social and economic transformation. The British analytical positivist school holds that law's central

POVERTY, LAW AND LAND TENURE REFORM

function is to guide courts in the resolution of disputes by declaring rights and duties. All these approaches deny or at least limit the law's role as a tool for social and
economic change. Based on our experience, we follow a different school and believe
law does have a central role in effectuating social and economic change, although
realizing some important limitations. Laws are the building blocks of society. How
else but through law and state power can governments restructure institutions to
benefit the mass of their populations? Alternatives would seem to be either adoption
of non-law-based authoritarian engineering (e.g., the Cultural Revolution in China,
personality cult in North Korea, or Cambodia's Khmer Rouge) or doing nothing and
waiting for other evolutionary socio-economic-political factors to make changes on
the ground that the law then tries to reflect. Both options are problematic. Social and
economic transformation through law *can* prove highly authoritarian and manipula-
tive or can be participatory and democratic. RDI promotes the latter. Those who reject using law as a tool for social and economic change because of its authoritarian
potential (e.g., Peter Fitzpatrick, Brian Tamanaha) are, in our view, throwing the baby
out with the bathwater.

32 See Seidman, et al., supra note 30, at 16.

33 This list of categories is adapted from a list developed by Ann and Robert Seidman.

34 For actors that are complex organizations, it is also important to consider the process
by which actors decide whether or not to follow the rules. For all actors, interests will
be influenced by their values, attitudes and assumptions. Referred to as "domain assumptions," these are the typically unexamined collection of myths, assumptions and
valuations through which most people assess reality. See generally A.W. Gouldner,
THE COMING CRISIS OF WESTERN SOCIOLOGY (Basic Books 1970).

35 The World Justice Project has developed a working definition for the rule of law that
comprises four universal principles: (1) the government and its officials and agents
are accountable under the law; (2) the laws are clear, publicized, stable and fair, and
protect fundamental rights, including the security of persons and property; (3) the
process by which the laws are enacted, administered and enforced is accessible, fair
and efficient; and (4) the laws are upheld, and access to justice is provided by competent, independent, and ethical law enforcement officials, attorneys or representatives,
and judges, who are of sufficient number, have adequate resources, and reflect the
makeup of the communities they serve. See World Justice Project, *About the World
Justice Project, Universal Principles of the Rule of Law* (visited July 22, 2008) http://
www.abanet.org/wjp/about.html.

36 W.L. Church, *Legal Systems,* in M.G. Blasé, ed., INSTITUTIONS IN AGRICULTURAL DEVEL-
OPMENT 223-24 (Iowa State University Press 1971).

37 Adjudicative processes must also be designed to follow the "fairness" principle such
that they can fairly govern disputes between parties who have different socio-economic positions. This is particularly important in many land tenure reform settings
where disputes may be between a wealthy and powerful landowner and a relatively
weak and land-poor person or involve a woman asserting her rights against men or
her in-laws.

38 See generally Deininger, supra note 5; Prosterman & Hanstad, supra note 5.

39 See generally Deininger & Squire, supra note 7; and El-Ghonemy, supra note 9.

40 See Prosterman & Riedinger, supra note 6, at Chapter 2.

41 If the agricultural laborers work in the plantation sector rather than for various
small-or medium landholders, there may also be an effort to keep them working "at
scale" on some variant of a collective or cooperative farm. Also, an exception to the
general insecurity of tenant farmers is sometimes found in cases of "reverse
tenancy", where the landowner is small and the tenant is large and resourceful, perhaps bargaining for long-term lease rights from many small lessors, as is often the

case for the large lessees who are successor enterprises of the former collectives in the Czech Republic (the small lessors thus, paradoxically, have the security of being owners, but have given up access for an extended time, and are therefore shown in the lower-left quadrant, as being without access).

42   See generally Prosterman & Riedinger, supra note 6. Riedinger, also a lawyer, is now Professor of Political Science and Dean of International Programs at Michigan State University. See generally J. Riedinger, AGRARIAN REFORM IN THE PHILIPPINES: DEMO-CRATIC TRANSITIONS AND REDISTRIBUTIVE REFORMS (Stanford University Press 1995).

43   Based on a definition in F. Place, et al., *Land Tenure Security and Agricultural Performance in Africa: Overview of Research Methodology*, in J.W. Bruce & S.E. Migot-Adholla, eds., SEARCHING FOR LAND TENURE SECURITY IN AFRICA 15, 19 (Kendall-Hunt 1994).

44   See id. at 20.

45   See earlier discussion at notes 20 through 22 and accompanying text.

46   J.L. Knetsch, *Land Use: Values, Controls, and Compensation*, in E. Quah & W. Neilson, eds., LAW AND ECONOMIC DEVELOPMENT: CASES AND MATERIALS FROM SOUTHEAST ASIA 302 (Longman 1993).

47   See Deininger, supra note 5, at 80.

48   See Deininger, supra note 5, at 86-93.

49   See Place, supra note 43, at 20-21.

50   Deininger, supra note 5, at 42-48.

51   G. Feder, *The Intricacies of Land Markets: Why the World Bank Succeeds in Economic Reform through Land Registration and Tenure Security* (paper presented at the Conference of the International Federation of Surveyors, April 19-26 2002, Washington D.C.); Prosterman & Riedinger, supra note 6, ch. 1.

52   Deininger, supra note 5, at 40.

53   R. Mitchell, *Property Rights and Environmentally Sound Management of Farmland and Forests*, in J.W. Bruce, et al., eds., LAND LAW REFORM: ACHIEVING DEVELOPMENT POLICY OBJECTIVES 191 (World Bank 2006).

54   See G. Feder, et al., LAND POLICIES AND AGRICULTURAL PRODUCTIVITY IN THAILAND (World Bank 1988), cited in Bruce & Migot-Adholla, supra note 43, at 15.

55   See M. Fay & C. Opal, *Urbanizations without Growth, A Not-So-Uncommon Phenomenon*, World Bank Policy Research Working Paper 2412, at 6 (World Bank 2000); D.F. Byceson & V. Jamal, FAREWELL TO FARMS: DE-AGRARIANISATION AND EMPLOYMENT IN AFRICA (Ashgate 1997).

56   R. DiTella, S. Galiani & E. Schargrodsky, *The Formation of Beliefs: Evidence From the Allocation of Land Titles to Squatters*, 122 (1) QUARTERLY JOURNAL OF ECONOMICS 209-241 (Feb. 2007).

57   See generally F. Zakaria, THE FUTURE OF FREEDOM: ILLIBERAL DEMOCRACY AT HOME AND ABROAD 77-78 (Norton & Company 2007). To like effect, on the key, and neglected, issues of failure to empower the freed slaves of the post-Civil War South in the U.S. by giving them land of their own, see E. Foner & J. Brown, FOREVER FREE XXV-XXVI, at 141-142, 164-165, 202 (Knopf 2005) ("The Radicals' failure to achieve land reform had ensured that most black southerners would be tied to agricultural labor on white-owned land, or menial jobs in southern cities"). See also H.L. Gates, Jr., *Forty Acres and a Gap in Wealth*, NEW YORK TIMES, Nov. 18, 2007 ("we can only imagine how different black-white relations would be" if land distribution had then been official government policy).

58   For discussion of the current debate over Hernando de Soto's emphasis on of the importance of formal individual titling in his widely read book, THE MYSTERY OF CAPITAL: WHY CAPITALISM TRIUMPHS IN THE WEST FAILS EVERYWHERE ELSE ch. 6 (Basic Books 2000), see R. Home & H. Lim, eds., DEMYSTIFYING THE MYSTERY OF CAPITAL

(Routledge Cavendish 2004); B. Cousins & D. Homby, *De Soto Solution not for South Africa*, BUSINESS DAY, Jan 13, 2007; and http://www.landrightswatch.net.

59 D. Fitzpatrick, *Best Practice for the Legal Recognition of Customary Tenure*, 36(3) DEVELOPMENT & CHANGE 449, 465 (2005).

60 See generally, e.g., D.W. Bromley, ed., MAKING THE COMMONS WORK – THEORY, PRACTICE, AND POLICY (ICS Press 1992). For specifics on consequences of a well-known reversal of a CPR regime, the Enclosure Movement in England, see, for example, J.L. Hammond & B. Hammond, THE VILLAGE LABOURER (Longman 1966, originally published 1911); J.A. Yelling, COMMON FIELD AND ENCLOSURE IN ENGLAND 1450-1850 (MacMillan Press 1977).

61 See, e.g., C.D. Brockett, LAND, POWER, AND POVERTY: AGRARIAN TRANSFORMATION AND POLITICAL CONFLICT IN CENTRAL AMERICA 23-26 (Unwin Hyman 1990).

62 L. Cotula, C. Toulmin & J. Quan, *Policies and Practices for Securing and Improving Access to Land*, International Conference on Agrarian Reform and Rural Development Issue Paper No. 1, at 20 (presented at Porto Alegre, Brazil, Mar. 2006), available at www.icarrd.org. ILO Convention 169, which was adopted in 1989, but has not yet received sufficient ratifications to come into formal effect, recognizes the "rights of ownership and possession" of indigenous peoples, and requires states to consult indigenous peoples on the allocation of licenses to exploit natural resources in or on indigenous lands.

63 See, e.g., J. Perlez, *The Papuans Say, This Land and Its Ores Are Ours*, NEW YORK TIMES, Apr. 5, 2006, at A4; J. Perlez, *Forests in Southeast Asia Fall to Prosperity's Ax*, NEW YORK TIMES, Apr. 29, 2006, at A1 (dilemmas posed for the environment where indigenous people perceive economic advantage in rapid exploitation of timber resources).

64 For a comprehensive and comparative overview of reforming non-judicial public sector land institutions, see T. Burns, C. Grant, A.M. Brits & K. Nettle, COMPARATIVE STUDY OF LAND ADMINISTRATION SYSTEMS: CRITICAL ISSUES AND FUTURE CHALLENGES (World Bank 2003). For a comparative discussion of land-related judicial institutions, see B. Schwarzwalder, *Land-Related Judicial Institutions*, in R. Prosterman & T. Hanstad, eds., LEGAL IMPEDIMENTS TO EFFECTIVE LAND RELATIONS IN EASTERN EUROPE AND CENTRAL ASIA: A COMPARATIVE PERSPECTIVE (World Bank 1999).

65 The views and perspectives of local officials, large landowners, and others whose interests may be inconsistent with the targeted beneficiaries should also be sought and considered in crafting reforms.

66 The phrase is taken from a children's story in which a king, traveling among his thronging and poor subjects, tells his groom to throw a purse of gold to one of them who has caught the king's attention. Naturally, the subject lives "happily ever after," although the persisting poverty of the others is not addressed.

2 Tenancy reform

Roy L. Prosterman and Jennifer Brown

I. Introduction

This chapter covers one of the principal potential beneficiary groups of land reform programs: those whose chief source of livelihood comes from cultivating, as tenant farmers, land owned by others. The chapter will focus on the experience with redistribution of land to tenant farmers, as well as alternatives to distribution such as regulation of landlord-tenant relationships, and will offer recommendations as to what should be done, or sometimes undone, in programmatic terms with respect to landlord-tenant relationships. In the category of "tenant farmers" we include not only those who pay a fixed amount of rent, but also sharecroppers, who are simply tenants whose rent is set as a percentage of the actual crop harvested.[1]

Both theory and policy as to agricultural land tenancy have evolved considerably over the course of the last half-century. The initial stance of many policy makers and advisors, implemented most notably in the years following World War II, was that tenancy was a negative and exploitative practice where landlords held all the power, with tenants holding little tenure security and largely being at their landlord's mercy with regard to the terms of the tenancy arrangement. Especially in that period of intensely impoverished and highly agrarian societies, there was considerable empirical support for this view, extending to a range of countries, especially in Asia.[2]

As one prominent outcome, this vision strongly supported ownership as a better alternative for existing tenants, leading to the successful postwar land-to-the-tiller programs of East Asia in which governments took ownership from landlords and transferred it to tenants. Later successful, or largely successful, land-to-the-tiller programs can also be found, extending into the 1980s, but there were also a number of unsuccessful programs during this period. An alternative, or sometimes supplementary, outcome of the widely negative view of tenancy was the widespread adoption of laws heavily regulating tenancy. Still other legislative reforms – generally in the context of efforts to give ownership to the existing tenants – attempted to ban all tenancy from that time onward.

The common stance among many policy makers and advisors that has evolved over the course of the past two decades views tenancy much more positively and optimistically as an effective mechanism (or at least a more realistic mechanism than sales markets or administratively imposed land tenure reform) for increasing access to land for land-poor but labor-rich producers and for ensuring that land and labor are both being fully and efficiently used. Government program planning has begun to follow suit, and some governments that previously sought to stamp out or carefully regulate tenancy have lifted restrictions (Mexico)[3] or are urging the rolling back of tenancy restrictions (India).[4]

Rural relationships have evolved over the past half-century in a number of societies, from virtually feudal arrangements based on highly imbalanced power relationships, to arrangements in which landlords and tenants may have more equitable bargaining positions and where both increasingly have alternative sources of income outside of agriculture. Land tenure reforms, including land-to-the-tiller programs, are at least partially responsible for this shift in rural power relationships. Landlord-tenant relationships are certainly not universally equitable now; however, in many settings tenants today are in a much improved bargaining position relative to that which existed when World War II was ending.[5]

Another part of the shift in perspective lies in the realization that many countries that might consider widespread reforms aimed at benefiting tenant farmers – such as land-to-the-tiller, or extensive regulation of the tenancy relationship – do not presently have the resources or political will to implement such reforms. Indeed, many impractical or poorly thought-through programs of the last 50 years remained unimplemented or only partially implemented, sometimes having led to much worse consequences – such as massive evictions of existing tenants – than if the government had not attempted them.

The economic, demographic and political landscapes have changed in many ways over the past half-century, but the issues revolving around agricultural tenancy and what, if anything, to do about it are still prominent today in much of South and Southeast Asia, and are also found, though to a lesser degree, in parts of Latin America and Africa.

The Rural Development Institute has worked extensively in a number of the settings where tenancy questions have been important, among them India, the Philippines, Vietnam, El Salvador and Egypt. In addition, RDI has done past fieldwork that encompassed the tenancy issue in Pakistan, Bangladesh and Brazil. As in later chapters, we shall draw significantly here on RDI's own practical experience in the field.

We divide the further discussion in this chapter into four sections. Section II will focus on land-to-the-tiller programs, Section III will focus on programs emphasizing substantial regulation of tenancy relationships, and Section IV will consider "freed" tenancy markets. Finally, Section V will summarize the practical conclusions as to policy and design for possible future programs.

All three policy approaches to tenancy – conferral of ownership, substantial regulation or letting the market prevail – may produce negative as well as positive impacts. For example, land-to-the-tiller approaches can greatly undermine the tenure security of landowners, making them unwilling to rent out land for fear such a reform is coming, and even leading them to evict current tenants. The positive impacts are more obvious, and include a long time horizon for land investments by tenants who have become owners, with concomitant increases in production and crop diversification; wealth creation (assuming the land rights are made transferable); and escape of the tenant from the "power domain" of the landlord, thus enhancing the tenant's status.[6] The key questions concern the extent to which the positive impacts can be achieved without the negative ones, and the degree to which various factors, including the specific features of program design, are likely to determine whether the result is positive or negative.

The alternative approach of heavily regulating the tenancy relationship may produce some of the same negative impacts and is likely to produce far fewer positive impacts. The administrative difficulty of enforcing these rules on an ongoing basis (however well-designed) greatly limits the positive potential of this approach. Whereas land-to-the-tiller is a one-time reform, regulation of tenancy relationships is ongoing.

The third approach, in which the state either does not regulate tenancy, or regulates it in a very limited way, assumes that tenancy can be an effective mechanism for increasing land access if largely left to market forces. Many commentators have come to the conclusion that tenancy today could be an important means of increasing access to land for land-poor rural families and have recommended that presently existing but poorly implemented tenancy regulations should be repealed. Little grounded data exist on whether the hoped-for outcomes from rolling back tenancy restrictions would be seen in practice, but we close the chapter by providing recommendations on how to end such regulation in ways most likely to achieve improved land access for the land-poor.

II.   Land-to-the-tiller

There are three fairly well-known and notably successful post-war land-to-the-tiller programs, each of which made a substantial majority of tenant farmers – who at that time constituted a large part of the rural population and were the dominant group among those who were landless – into owners of the same land which they had farmed as tenants. We examine briefly in turn the cases of Japan, South Korea and Taiwan. RDI has also done village fieldwork in each of these three settings, two decades or more after the reform was carried out, to talk with farmer beneficiaries – and also with former landlords – about the effects of the reforms on their lives and livelihoods.

In Japan, the land tenure reform was carried out soon after World War II under the American military occupation, and to a large degree at the insistence of General Douglas MacArthur.[7] To summarize its characteristics briefly[8]: The two main sources of land for distribution to tenants were the land of absentee landlords, *all* of which was to be taken, and the land of village landlords, who were permitted to keep up to 1 hectare of tenanted land in their village of residence. Thus, there was what may be referred to as a "zero ceiling" permitted for absentee-owned land, and a "1-hectare ceiling" for resident-landlord land with tenants on it. In each case, the tenant received in ownership exactly the same land he or she farmed as a tenant. (The parcels of tenanted land that were to be retained by resident landlords, with the tenants remaining upon the land, were determined by the Village Land Committee.[9])

The land price to be paid to the landlords by the Japanese government, and repaid to the government by the ex-tenants, was very low as a result of the extreme post-war inflation. It was calculated in 1945 prices, and to be paid mostly in bonds redeemable after 30 years, bearing 3.6% annual interest. Indeed, from a landlord standpoint, the practical result was virtually equivalent to confiscation of the land, and from a tenant standpoint virtually equivalent to free distribution.[10]

The land reform transferred nearly 80% of the previously tenanted area and affected about 37% of all agricultural land.[11] The small number of tenants who continued renting (on the retained land of resident small landlords) received strict legislative protection as to both tenure security and rent levels they could be charged. The tenants who became owners could sell the land they received, though only with administrative permission, and only to someone who would cultivate it and who remained below a 3-hectare maximum for owner-operated land.[12] The distributed land could also be mortgaged, including for purchase money mortgage.[13]

By 1970, both the ceilings on landholdings and the regulation of tenancy had been eliminated, and absentees could now own land and make their own market arrangements with their tenants. Of course, by then the Japanese economy was transformed.[14]

Administration of the Japanese land reform program at the grass-roots village level was carried out in a highly public and transparent manner, by a Village Land Committee on which tenants and small owner-operators held most seats.[15] Implementation by these village level groups was instrumental to the success of the reform, because local groups understood local tenure arrangements and were able to implement the reforms swiftly.

Another large land reform occurred in South Korea, beginning in 1950 shortly before the Korean War, and continuing during the war. The reform was carried out under the authoritarian government of Syngman Rhee and, as in Japan, was implemented with substantial American support.

The South Korean land reform law terminated ownership of all tenanted land, whether the owner was an absentee or a resident landlord, with minor exemptions.[16] In addition, there was a 3-hectare maximum for owner-operated land but very few holdings reached this size. As in the Japanese reform, tenants received ownership of the same land they presently farmed. Land compensation was, unlike that in Japan, at least meaningful, though far from generous. For annual cropland the government paid the landlord 1.5 times the gross value of one year's annual production,[17] dividing the payment into equal installments over a five-year period. Thus, during each of the five years the landlord received 30% of the value of the initial or baseline annual gross crop as his entire compensation, as compared to a previous expectation of rents that had ranged from a 30% to 80% share of the gross crop in an ongoing (theoretically perpetual) stream, with a 50% landlord share (and the tenant bearing all expenses) being a common rate.[18] The customary valuation formula for farmland in Korea had been 10 times the annual rent,[19] which would have yielded a total price of 3 to 8 times gross crop value, and typically 5 times that value. Clearly, most of the value of the land was being commandeered by the government while landowners received only a fraction of the actual value.

The beneficiaries repaid the government the same 30% per year for five years, thus receiving an immediate increment in income (compared with the rents they had paid) that was typically 20% of their previous gross crop level plus 100% of whatever additional crops they were now producing above the previous gross crop level. After completing payment, the new owners could sell or mortgage their land, but not rent it out, since all tenancy was prohibited. The South Korean land reform reached about 69% of the intended land and affected about 30% of all arable land.[20]

A third post-war land reform occurred on Taiwan. Shortly after fleeing to Taiwan from the mainland with the remnants of his army and administration in 1949, Chiang Kai-shek carried out a major land-to-the-tiller program that was completed in 1953.[21] This was likely done, in large part, in recognition that the failure to address the land-based grievances of mainland China's tenant farmers had been a decisive factor in the victory of the Communists over Chiang's Nationalists in the civil war.[22] For the Taiwanese program, too, there was substantial American support.

The Taiwanese reform began in 1949 with a rigorous reduction of tenant rents from an average of 50-60% of the gross crop value to a maximum of 37.5%.[23] The reform continued with distribution of tenanted public lands, then went on, in 1953, to take most private landlord-owned lands for redistribution to their tenants. Taiwan allowed both absentee and resident landlords to retain a portion of their tenanted land, taking all tenanted land above approximately 3 hectares for average paddy land and 6 hectares for average dry land.[24] The government paid landlords an amount equal to 2.5 times the gross value of the main annual crop, with 70% of that paid in bonds linked to the price of rice (for paddy land) or sweet potato (for dry land), payable with 4% interest in equal installments over 10 years. The remaining 30% was paid with shares of stock in major industrial or utility enterprises that the government was privatizing. It appears that 2.5 times gross crop value was not greatly out of line with the market value of land, which had apparently been worth roughly 4 times gross crop value before the 1949 rent reduction.[25]

The ex-tenants repaid the government the same total amount, spread over 10 years. This amortization meant a yearly payment equal to about 30% of their initial gross crop value, versus the existing rent of 37.5%, and versus a prior rent level around 50% to 60%. In addition, the new owner gained the full income from any increased value of production. The law allowed sale and mortgage, but not lease, after the beneficiary had made full payment.

The Taiwanese reform distributed about 71% of tenanted croplands into ownership[26] – mostly through taking it from private landlords, but also including distribution of tenanted public lands and negotiated tenant purchases from landlords that had been largely due to the rent reduction and the prospect of further land reform. The distribution covered about 30% of Taiwan's cultivated land.[27] Nearly all remaining tenanted lands came under protected-tenancy restrictions, which were not substantially lifted until 2000.[28]

A number of commentators have concluded that the major land ten-ure reforms in Japan, South Korea and Taiwan were key to the rapid post-war growth of these economies.[29] In Taiwan, for example, where very extensive data collection took place, annual rice yields per hectare increased 60% on average in the decade following the land-to-the-tiller program of 1949-1953, and the average income of farm households rose by 150%.[30] Much of the dramatic increase in farm incomes was due to diversification into higher value production: between 1952 and 1979, rice (despite a large increase in its total production) declined as a relative proportion of the value of all agricultural production from 50% to 27%, while fruits, vegetables and livestock grew from 21.5% of such value to 60.5%.[31] Higher farm incomes quickly translated into substan-tial improvements in living conditions: "This can be seen from pay-ments for food, clothing, dwellings, travel, education and entertain-ment, and from the number of children attending school." There were also large increases in farmers' community participation and holding of public office at the village, county and province level.[32]

Over the longer term, Taiwan's small owner-operator farmers trans-formed themselves into entrepreneurs and modern consumers. Field-work conducted by RDI in 2000 (the third round of such fieldwork in Taiwan since the 1970s) found that the great majority of farmers inter-viewed not only owned cars, computers and cell phones, but had also bought stocks and traveled overseas.

In addition to the programs in Japan, South Korea and Taiwan, four lesser known land-to-the-tiller programs were carried out in the time span between 1949 and 1984 which accomplished much the same dis-tributional results. These occurred in mainland China, South Vietnam, Kerala State in India, and El Salvador. All four programs – like that in South Korea – terminated ownership of all tenanted land, whether the owner was an absentee or a resident landlord. And all but the China re-form hold important lessons for program design.

After the Communists came to power in 1949, China carried out a massive program giving full private ownership to the former tenant farmers (who had provided the core support for Mao's revolution). The program was superseded by the mandatory collectivization of China's farming after 1956, and thus has been largely forgotten, although its production and farm-income results were highly impressive, and these may provide useful lessons for the current Chinese tenure reforms. Over the period 1949 to 1956, grain production increased by 70% and total farm income rose 85%.[33] However, its lessons for program design are likely to have very limited application for other countries. It is briefly discussed in Chapter 7.

South Vietnam carried out a large-scale program in 1969-1973, giv-ing ownership of some 44% of total farm area to approximately three-

quarters of all tenant families. The reform produced a number of positive results both economic and political, but came too late to affect the
outcome of the conflict. The positive results included a roughly 30%
increase in rice production in the villages – comprising the majority of
all villages – where land reform was implemented,[34] and an overall decline of approximately four-fifths in indigenous recruitment within the
South by the communist Vietcong.[35]

In addition, a 1972 sample survey of nearly a thousand respondents
found that farmers in villages that had high implementation (with ex-
tenants receiving written titles confirming their ownership) were twice
as likely to keep chickens or ducks or have fish ponds and four times
as likely to keep pigs than were farmers living in villages that had not
yet distributed titles.[36] Over 70% of those who had received their titles
made comments to the effect that the program was bringing about
"the beginning of the good life," more than twice the proportion of
those who had not yet received titles. And the interviewers concluded
that "ex-tenants who have become farm owners want to produce more,
venture into other crops, risk cash outlays to improve or increase their
yields, and work harder and longer. Many say this."[37]

Although largely lost to view after the Communists took power in the
South in 1975, the land-to-the-tiller program remained in substantial
part viable and helped lay the groundwork for the individual family
farming that eventually came to be practiced countrywide in the 1990s
after break-up of the collective farms, although under 20-year use rights
rather than private ownership for the resulting family farmers.[38] Box
2.1 describes aspects of RDI's experience with the 1969-1973 program.

Kerala State in India carried out a near-universal program giving
ownership to almost all tenant farmers in the state beginning in
1970.[39] The 1.3 million tenant family beneficiaries comprised 43% of
all agricultural households and received, in place, about the same percentage of all land planted in annual crops. For a number of reasons,
this substantially successful program deserves more attention than it
has received, not least because it was carried out by a democratic, non-
authoritarian government and in the absence of war or major civil conflict (although there were grassroots demonstrations by supporters and
– mostly nonviolent – political turmoil at the outset). It has lacked high
visibility, both because of the generally low-key and undramatic setting,
and because it affected only a single, relatively small Indian state.

Box 2.1. Land-to-the-Tiller in South Vietnam

The Land-to-the-Tiller law, based on a 1967 prototype drafted by one of the present authors, was adopted in nearly its original form on March 26, 1970.

The intent was to "eliminate tenancy," affecting all tenanted crop-land except for the small amounts under industrial crops and orchards.

Primary administration was through a Village Land Distribution Committee, comprised of elected officials and skewed towards tenants and small owner-operators. In a highly public application process, the committee assisted the former tenants in preparing applications and briefly inspected each claimed piece of land (normally with an accompanying crowd of villagers) and marked that applicant's land with an identification number on an aerial photograph of the village, placing the same number on the application form. Unless there were conflicting claims to a particular piece of land that could not be resolved on the spot, the committee approved the applicants' claims and forwarded them to Saigon, where a USAID-supplied computer printed out final titles. These were then sent back down to the village and distributed. This was sometimes referred to as a "once up – once down" administrative process, with only two contacts required in the case of the great bulk of beneficiaries – one contact to receive the application and gather all essential information and a second contact to deliver the final title. Copies of all titles were placed in the land registry.

At its inception, *The New York Times* (editorial April 9, 1970) called it "probably the most ambitious and progressive non-Communist land reform of the twentieth century." Ultimately, nearly a million final titles were distributed, reaching approximately 75% of all wholly or partly tenant families in the South.

For a detailed account of the South Vietnamese reform, see R. Prosterman & J. Riedinger, *Land Reform and Democratic Development*, Chapter 5 (John Hopkins 1987).

El Salvador carried out a program giving ownership to approximately 30% of its tenant farmers and, as in Vietnam, implemented it in the midst of a civil conflict.[40] In El Salvador, however, the program (paralleled by a program to give estate lands to agricultural laborers, discussed in Chapter 3) was timely enough to play a likely role in tipping the result against the Communist insurgency.[41] This program, under which land distribution began in 1980 and substantially ended in 1984, is the most recent on the planet to have made a significant effort to make tenants owners of the land they till. While this program was also broadly successful in both political and economic terms,[42] it did not benefit as high a proportion of tenant families as the Asian programs discussed above. Some reasons for this are described later in this chapter and in Box 2.2.

We will describe selectively further elements of each of these programs in what follows. We will also refer to elements of the generally (or even wholly) unsuccessful land-to-the-tiller programs in Pakistan, Bangladesh, most Indian states other than Kerala, the Philippines, and the earlier South Vietnamese land reform program of the 1950s.[43] Both the successes and the failures of the various programs may offer lessons as to the extent to which it is still feasible, in the early twenty-first century, to design and undertake programs that will successfully confer upon tenants ownership of the land they till.

Lessons to be learned

Examination of the existing body of experience with land-to-the-tiller programs indicates that a complex of mutually interacting variables – beginning with geopolitical and financing issues – are likely to bear on the feasibility and success of such a program in any given country setting. In effect, for each setting one must attempt to predict how likely there is to be a positive alignment of these variables, and whether any of these variables might be influenced in a direction more likely to support the reform. In most cases today the answer is very likely to be that it is probably not possible to successfully launch and carry out a reform in which tenant farmers receive ownership, or equivalent rights, to land they farm as tenants. Many of the lessons, however, remain highly relevant today in the design of other kinds of land tenure reform programs.

The geopolitical "macro" environment

Of course, a threshold condition for a land-to-the-tiller program is the presence of a large population of tenant farmers mired in poverty and insecurity. Beyond this, we note that six of the seven successful land-to-the-tiller reforms involved "macro" factors that are generally unlikely to be duplicated – and, perhaps more to the point, that one would not wish to duplicate deliberately. At least four (Japan, South Korea, Taiwan and China) involved highly authoritarian forms of government in power at the time of the reform; two others (South Vietnam and El Salvador) were carried out under weakened, but certainly not democratic, governments fighting for their existence against strong Communist forces attempting to overthrow them. All of the programs except that in Kerala State reflected situations of chaos and disruption either immediately post-conflict or with violent conflicts actually ongoing. Also, except for Kerala (and of course, China), all featured a degree of official U.S. advocacy and support for the land reform that went well beyond mere technical assistance or "foreign aid" and seems unlikely to be duplicated (the least U.S. pressure or insistence having been needed in Taiwan, whose leadership had just been traumatized by the loss of the mainland, the most pressure having been applied in Japan). Kerala, as already noted, was exceptional: land tenure reform went forward under Communist or left-front governments, but ones that were elected and could be replaced through the ballot; conditions were peaceful, with the reform neither preceded nor accompanied by major conflict; and there was certainly no U.S. pressure to carry out the reform – indeed, there was barely any awareness outside India of its existence. In Kerala, it was extensive grass-roots political organizing, building on a history of radicalism that had grown out of landlord abuses, coupled with a simple land reform program design (universal transfer to tenant farmers, no land retention by landlords – to be discussed below) that made land reform possible.[44]

Thus, today, apart from possible exceptional situations of violent Maoist movements rooted to a significant degree in the land-based grievances of tenant farmers (it is unclear, as this is being written, whether Nepal's new government, largely traceable to such an insurgency, will provide a contemporary example), one might wish to consider the extent to which the very different factors present in Kerala might now exist or be created. And one must also consider the extent to which entirely distinct, but still democratic and non-violent, models might be developed.

Landlord compensation

Since the earliest days of our involvement with the land reform issue, we have urged adequate compensation to land-losing owners.[45] Such compensation need not necessarily be full "market value" in all circumstances. And planners may recognize the general impracticality of paying the entire sum – or even most of it – in cash in the case of a large-scale land redistribution. Indeed, such large payments in unrestricted cash would be likely to fuel inflation, which might eat away at the value of such cash even as it was received. But adequate compensation should be that which, at least, creates a fund likely to be sufficient to replace, in perpetuity, the net income that the land had produced for the landowner. In cases of tenanted land, this amount would equal the annual rent received. And former owners should be able to use such compensation very quickly for making investments, for example by using bonds paid as compensation as collateral for loans to make such investments.[46] Of the seven successful post-war land-to-the-tiller programs, Taiwan probably came closest to providing adequate compensation, but none of the programs paid, or purported to pay, full market value.[47]

What should not be attempted, however, is a taking of private land rights for little or no compensation. This happened in China, in an ideologically motivated and deliberate way as part of the communist revolution there, and also happened in the Japanese reform, nominally blamable on the great post-war inflation, but readily avoidable had the law been written differently, and to that extent also deliberate.[48]

Intermediate approaches are found in the other successful programs, including in El Salvador, where payment was based on the landlord's own earlier declarations of land value for property tax purposes,[49] which of course erred on the low side, but allowed the argument by the takers, "what's sauce for the goose, is sauce for the gander." An interesting variation was also used in Kerala State, where the payment for tenanted paddy land was inversely progressive, ranging, very roughly, from 4 times gross crop value for the smallest landlords down to 2 times gross crop value for the largest, according to a statutory formula.[50]

An important related variable, even if the compensation formula appears reasonably adequate, is whether the government's promises to pay in a deferred form such as bonds will be viewed as credible by landowners. For example, the largely unsuccessful 1972 Philippine program to give land to tenant farmers provided that most of the payment would be in government bonds. But the bonds did not carry the "full faith and credit" of the Philippine government; that is, they were not backed by the full revenues and taxing power of the government like other government bonds. Rather, they were to be vaguely financed and guaranteed (apart from collection of repayment from the beneficiaries) by shares in government-owned enterprises.[51]

And even where cash payment is to form a significant portion of compensation – as in El Salvador, for example, where landlords who owned less than 100 hectares were to receive 50% of their compensation in cash[52] – the government must still be willing to appropriate the necessary funds in a timely way. Failure to do this during the early period of implementation of the Salvadoran land-to-the-tiller program contributed to landlord opposition.[53]

A number of mutually reinforcing reasons support payment of adequate compensation:

(1) To the extent that any future land-to-the-tiller programs are unlikely to rely on authoritarian government, and are instead more likely to resemble the "Kerala approach,"[54] something close to adequate com-

pensation will probably be a pre-condition for success. Especially if the government is neither authoritarian nor one with a strong electoral mandate, this is likely to be a threshold practical consideration: in a democracy, even in cases where there may not be sympathy or focused political opposition on behalf of what is likely to be a relatively well-off and well-educated group (the affected landlords), inadequate compensation for land takings will still be unsettling for many other voters who are property owners and so will be opposed on those grounds.

(2) To the degree that landowners consider the offered compensation to be unreasonably low, the result may go well beyond voting for the opposition, and entail social instability or violent protest, perhaps even the overthrow of a democratic but weak government. Although involving chiefly plantation land and not tenanted land, this was a factor in the initiation of the Spanish Civil War in the 1930s, was clearly a precipitating factor in the U.S.-sponsored overthrow of the Guatemalan government in the 1950s, and may have been a factor in the military coup in Brazil in the 1960s.[55]

(3) Even if it does not lead to overt violence, poor compensation is likely to give rise to strenuous landowner efforts to undermine and sabotage the program by various means discussed later in this section. Such pressure makes it much more difficult to design a workable program.

(4) Closely related to the foregoing point, severely inadequate compensation makes it more difficult to threaten credible penalties for landowners who obstruct the program. Assuming that landlords who evade the land reform law through non-violent means will not believe that courts will apply criminal penalties to them, the most effective civil penalty for program obstruction (e.g., the landlord's failure to declare all the land he owns) may be the loss of the land without compensation. However, precisely to the degree that the proffered compensation is quite low or merely nominal, landowners may feel they have nothing to lose from attempting to keep land outside the reach of the program.

(5) In some settings, providing low compensation for the land to be taken may represent a generalized attempt to punish all landlords or plantation owners as a class or group through the political system. Such generalized condemnations have always been extremely difficult to justify, and they have become even more so as rural societies lose feudal characteristics. The public, even if desiring more equitable land-ownership patterns as a social goal, is increasingly less likely to support "punishing" landlords as a means of achieving this goal.

(6) If low compensation or no compensation for land is sought to be justified as being more in the nature of an adjudicated fine for specific past landlord behavior, then due process, which is increasingly ac-

cepted as an international norm, demands that distinctions be made based on the actual facts with respect to each owner. Even in a situation as extreme as that of deprivation of black farmers' lands solely because of race, done in South Africa for decades after 1913, that country's 1994 restitution law requires specific factual findings as to how the present white holder of the land obtained it before a decision can be made as to whether and how much the government will pay to the present holder.[56] These provisions are discussed in Chapter 3. The present point together with point (5) support the case that the determination of land compensation should not rest on generalized ideological grounds.

We thus conclude that, in any projected universal or near-universal distribution of land to tenant farmers, it will be desirable to determine: (a) how many hectares are to be redistributed;[57] (b) the market value of the land;[58] (c) the level of reasonably adequate compensation for the land, taking account of market value, rent levels, deferred payment and other factors; (d) a realistic schedule of payment to landlords, including any deferral; (e) a realistic schedule of beneficiary repayment – contemplating that they should receive immediate economic benefits, and thus pay substantially less than their previous rents; (f) based on all of the foregoing, how much government financing is likely to be needed;[59] and (g) whether and how the government can credibly mobilize the resources that would thus be necessary. If the clear answer to the final question is, "It cannot!," then reformers will need to identify some alternative to a traditional land-to-the-tiller program.

Market-assisted land reform

One variant approach attempted in recent years is "market-assisted land reform." Under this approach, the land market itself is used to acquire land on the basis of a willing buyer and willing seller. The government (or other funder) provides credit to the intended beneficiary to purchase land on the open market. Alternatively, the government may buy the land and then transfer it to the ownership of the intended beneficiary. This approach has been championed by the World Bank, and the longest experience with it has been in non-tenant, large-estate settings such as Brazil and South Africa. Hence our discussion of its strengths and weaknesses appears in Chapter 3. There is, however, no inherent reason why this approach cannot be used – to the extent it shows itself to be practical – in a sector of small and medium-sized landholdings as well, including tenant-occupied holdings. Indeed, it is presently being implemented in the three Indian states of Andhra Pradesh, Karnataka and West Bengal, in programs that have focused on allowing landless agricultural laborers to acquire ownership of very small plots. Chapter 6 discusses this experience. Tenant farm families who own no agricultural land can also qualify as beneficiaries though the land they receive is not normally part of the land on which they are tenants.

Beneficiary selection

Most land-to-the-tiller programs have involved in-place distribution to existing tenants, which means that beneficiary designation should be fairly straightforward. Some potential issues can arise, however, including in relation to possible landlord attempts to undermine land-to-the-tiller legislation.

A frequent and highly important issue that has arisen as to beneficiary designation is that of an artificially narrow definition of "tenant." This term should include all those who possess an agricultural holding continuously over the course of one crop season or longer while recognizing the superior rights of another (usually denominated the "landlord") and paying to the latter a rent for the possession and use of the land. It should make no difference whether the rent is calculated as a fixed amount set in advance (a "fixed-rent" tenancy) or as a specified share of the crop actually produced (a "sharecropping" tenancy). Nor should it matter whether the rent is paid in kind or in cash, or whether cash rent is paid before or after the harvest.

Of the foregoing possibilities for fastening on a "distinction without a difference," a common mistake in unsuccessful land-to-the-tiller programs has been to deny tenant status to sharecroppers. This unwarranted limitation is found in several state-level land reform laws in India, and is discussed in Chapter 6. The fact that such a limitation has been inserted in the law at all is, in itself, generally sufficient to cast grave doubt on the political will of the legislating government to carry out a meaningful land tenure reform.

A related problem is that of sub-lease, in which the original tenant leases the land to a third person who becomes the actual cultivator and pays rent (which may be different from the original tenant's rent) to the original tenant. Some land-to-the-tiller laws deem the original tenant, sometimes referred to as the sub-lessor, to hold a superior right vis-à-vis the cultivating sub-lessee. Such sub-tenancy is likely to be present with respect to only a very small fraction of tenanted land, largely because owner-landlords much prefer to choose their own actual cultivator. For this small fraction of cases in which sub-leases exist, the best general practice for land-to-the-tiller programs is to entitle the actual cultivator – whether tenant or sub-tenant – to claim rights and benefits under the program.[60]

A further issue is whether the law will impose a ceiling on the amount of land that tenant farmers can receive. Many laws that abolish landlord ownership of tenanted land have also applied ceilings (sometimes the same, sometimes lower) on what the ex-tenant may own following the reform. The concern here is over the "reverse" of what is often thought of as typical tenancy: instead of small tenants renting in land from large owners, in some settings large tenants are increasingly renting in land from small owners. Even where the overall land tenure reform has been successfully implemented, one may find that this additional provision is being ignored, as not worth the administrative effort and political fallout of implementation. The most criticized example of an in-place distribution to tenants without a sufficient limit on land to be received has been Kerala State, where tenants using more than 2 hectares, a relatively large holding by local standards, received 64% of the land redistributed.[61] One strong policy consideration for including a lower maximum provision in Kerala (the actual ceiling was 4.85 to 6.1 hectares) would have been that it would have allowed the government to acquire excess lands, at the expense of larger tenants, to provide to the many non-tenant agricultural laborer families.[62]

A somewhat different setting of large holdings held by tenant entities that lease in land from small owners is found in parts of the former USSR and is discussed in the final section of Chapter 7.

It should be noted that without an enforced ceiling on what tenant beneficiaries receive, an in-place land-to-the-tiller program yields no land for distribution to non-tenants. Notably, it provides none for agricultural laborers, especially that category of laborers who work peripatetically for various cultivators (including both tenants and owner-operators). Another potential source of land for such families is a ceiling on self-cultivated land, as discussed in Chapter 3, but one must raise the policy question of whether it is possible to argue persuasively for a ceiling that would only apply to pre-existing owner-cultivators, or whether the same ceiling must also apply to new owner-cultivators (land-to-the-tiller beneficiaries) who were formerly tenants.

Another consideration involves the potentially competing interests of tenants who cultivate the land of the same landlord. If the law allows the landlord to retain some tenanted land, which tenants of a particular landlord will become owners – to some degree – and which tenants will not? Will this still be an in-place distribution and depend wholly on which land gets taken and which land the landlord retains? This would seem to be the simplest solution, but may often not prove the fairest. This issue is related to the question of who ultimately chooses the retained portion of the land – the landlord or the administering agency. If the landlord is permitted to choose the retained land, does the law impose restrictions, such as a requirement that the landlord se-

lect "average" land, or select a single contiguous part of the total holding? And if the administering agency chooses the land to be taken,
should it do so with an eye to spreading "in place" benefits to as many
of the landlord's tenants as possible?[63]

A final issue as to beneficiary identification is one that has almost
never been addressed, even in land-to-the-tiller programs that are
counted among the most successful.[64] This is the question not of
which tenant families should benefit or to what extent, but of who
within those tenant families should be recognized as a beneficiary. In
particular, should the law recognize a wife as receiving the same benefits as the husband, and equal status as a beneficiary? Because wives
the world over jointly cultivate land with their husbands as farmers
and depend on family land for their livelihoods, they also deserve the
security of receiving land tenure reform benefits. This raises program
design questions as to how to ensure that all documentation issued will
include the name of the wife as well as that of the husband, and what
provisions in the law can help safeguard the wife's interest in case of
inheritance, divorce, separation or abandonment. These issues are discussed principally in Chapter 5 on gender.

Ensuring presumptive beneficiaries are not evicted

A serious issue in achieving land distribution goals under land-to-the-
tiller programs has been anticipatory eviction of tenant farmers before
the law is formally adopted, or between the time it is adopted and the
time it is actually implemented. This was, for example, a huge problem
in most of India's state-level land reform programs undertaken in the
1950s and 1960s, as discussed in Chapter 6. Several variables can
make this a greater problem. A long period of public debate, during
which landlords come to understand that a law redistributing some or
all tenanted land is very likely to be adopted, increases opportunities
for evasion, although at the same time, public debate on legislation is
necessary and desired in a democratic society. This problem could be
partially surmounted by retroactively applying the legislation from a
point in time prior to the start of debate. But this will not be possible if
there are constitutional or other legal constraints that prevent the law
from having retrospective application, and it will still leave the potentially daunting administrative task of going back in time to trace and
undo past evictions. Some countries have overcome these problems by
legislating an enforced "freeze" on tenant evictions while the land reform law is being developed. Kerala is one such example, where legislation to halt evictions was passed to protect tenants during the period
while the legislation was drafted but before its implementation.[65] Finally, evictions are more likely if the government fails to ensure admin-

istrative capacity to uncover violations or apply credible penalties against violators.

In Taiwan, the combination of legal protection for tenants' existing possession and administrative follow-up to reinstate illegally evicted tenants kept problems to a minimum. These measures responded to a significant wave of illegal anticipatory tenant evictions or coerced tenant "surrenders" of their land rights that occurred after adoption of the 37.5% limitation on rents but before adoption of the land-to-the-tiller program. Out of 393,000 lease contracts entered into by June 1949, over 35,000 (around 9%) had purportedly been terminated before the land-to-the-tiller program got underway.[66] The government responded by introducing a comprehensive system employing 62 inspectors to provide information, conduct inspections and settle disputes. By June 1952, fewer than one-half of 1% of protected tenants had lost their lands.[67]

A number of factors can help restrain anticipatory evictions of tenant farmers. First, tenants' rights under any program, including restraints on their eviction by landlords, should be persistently publicized, through publicity channels most likely to reach them.[68]

Second, a program that does not allow landlords to retain ownership of any tenanted land – a so-called "zero ceiling" approach, as in South Korea, South Vietnam, Kerala State or El Salvador – may provide tenants with the confidence to resist eviction. This signals to tenants that each of them – not just some presently unknown portion – will become owners, and free of the landlord's influence in the future. This probably gives all tenants a greater sense of their capacity to resist landlord demands that they surrender their leases in return for some small payment. Thus, if all landlords will soon be out of the picture, their tenants need not stay in the landlord's "good graces" (hoping, for example, to be leased another piece of land later, or at least hired as an agricultural laborer). Moreover, only regimes with a strong political commitment to carrying out land reform have ever adopted a zero ceiling on landlord retention of tenanted land.[69]

Third, evictions may be restrained by strong administrative capacity combined with political will and a firm central authority, as in Taiwan or Japan. As in those cases, this combination may restrain evictions even where landlords are allowed to retain some tenanted land, and there is therefore the prospect that some tenants (even if under "regulated" tenancy) will remain tenants after the land reform.

Also related to outright eviction of tenants is the problem of allowing landlords to evict tenants "legally" by reclaiming the land for personal cultivation. Many Indian states with less successful land-to-the-tiller programs permitted landowners to evict tenants if the landlord planned to cultivate the land personally, and such "personal cultivation" was often defined to include the use of hired wage laborers under the landowner's supposed supervision. Allowing landlords to resume cultivation, especially when implemented in a way so as to allow the use of hired laborers, defeats the main purpose of the reform – moving land ownership into the hands of tenants who are the actual cultivators. It also harms the tenants' interests by incentivizing their eviction. This issue is discussed further in Chapter 6.

In terms of program design, as distinct from exogenous political or other factors,[70] it is clear that the principal step that program drafters can take to help forestall anticipatory evictions is by designing a program that prohibits landlords from retaining any tenanted land or resuming personal cultivation on formerly tenanted land. These rules must, in turn, be effectively publicized as a basic step in their enforcement.

Anticipatory transfers

Where governments have attempted reform programs that allow landlords to retain some portion of their tenanted land, the largest single problem of evasion and program sabotage has usually arisen from the landlords' anticipatory transfer of above-ceiling land to relatives, friends or strawmen.[71] Thus there is created at least the appearance (and perhaps the reality) that such landlords hold no tenanted land in excess of the ceiling as of the effective date of the land reform law.[72] This is an "appearance" if the transferees are simply nominal holders of title to the formerly above-ceiling land, with the landlord still collecting the rents and exercising ultimate control over such land, but is a "reality" if it is a *bona fide* transfer of all rights to the land, as, for example, a transfer made during the landlord's life to adult children or others who might have been presumptive heirs upon the owner's death. In some cases, the transfer is not even actually made before the land-to-the-tiller law becomes effective, but is fraudulently pre-dated, sometimes with the collusion of a corrupt local notary.

This method of evasion through anticipatory transfer of above-ceiling land is easier for many landlords than tenant eviction, since it both avoids possible physical confrontation and removes the need to find some other way of cultivating the land, especially if the landlord does not wish to self-cultivate directly.

The measures that may deter such anticipatory (or pre-dated) transfers include most of those discussed above in relation to anticipatory eviction of tenants in cases where landlords retain tenanted land. These include retroactive application of the law, a preliminary freeze on transfers prior to full adoption of the land reform, publicizing the rights of tenants, and a grass-roots administrative effort. If a program is adopted that does allow landlords to retain some tenanted land, the following additional design elements may also play a useful role.

First, the legislation should be drafted to disregard any transfers made after the law's adoption by the landlord to members of the landlord's immediate family. Certainly this should include the wife and minor children, as well as adult children or parents living under the same roof and should preferably extend to adult children living apart. In this way landlords would not be allowed to transfer to those they might most easily use as nominal transferees, while retaining actual benefit from the land for themselves (what some legal systems might denominate "beneficial enjoyment").

Second, the law should forbid bogus transfers by explicitly providing that post-law transfers will be recognized as valid only if the landlord has parted with all rights and benefits. This, in turn, opens up at least the theoretical possibility that program administrators could question tenants as to whether their obligations as tenant had now shifted to the supposed new owner, and in particular whether they still pay rent to the old owner.

Third, the law could require that any claimed transfer of above-ceiling land not only be evidenced by a deed dated before the effective date of the law, but by a registry record of the transfer that pre-dated the law. Fraudulent pre-dating of entries in the land register is possible – and indeed RDI has been told that this was sometimes done in the Philippines, under non-zero-ceiling laws there – but tampering with the land register is at least more difficult than getting a pre-dated notarization on a non-registered deed, and may require the knowledge and collusion of more than one registry official.[73]

Fourth, other design measures may deter anticipatory transfers. In particular, provided that village-level bodies are not dominated by landlords, the law could make them responsible for fact finding and administration at the village level. Such bodies functioned in the Japanese reform, where resident landlords were allowed to retain one hectare of tenanted land. And in Taiwan an administrative presence extending to the grass-roots level may have served a similar function, again in the context of a program that allowed landlords to retain some tenanted land.[74]

Finally, the combination of a reasonable level of compensation and the threat that it will be withheld if the landlord makes false statements or obstructs the program may serve as a deterrent. Both the promise and the threat, however, must be perceived as reasonably credible. This being said, we are not aware of any program in which sanctions were actually applied. In Taiwan, where landlords were allowed to retain some tenanted land and where compensation was not insignificant, local administrators seem to have relied far more on persuasion and "jaw-boning" than on the use of formal penalties.[75] Of course, this was in the context of a strong government with strong political will and (being under the control of the Nationalists, who had fled from the mainland in 1949) with few connections to indigenous Taiwanese landlords.

Beneficiary rights

When former tenants do receive land as a result of the reform program, further questions concern how "owner-like" will be the bundle of rights they receive.[76] (A set of parallel issues is discussed in Chapter 7.)

Where the reform provides that the government shall acquire existing landlord rights of ownership, governments have provided, correspondingly, perpetual rights to tenant beneficiaries. The principal issue that arises in such cases is the breadth of the rights beneficiaries will receive; that is, how "owner-like" are such rights? For example, some reforms have limited the rights of beneficiaries to transfer the rights they have received. Transfer restrictions are often adopted either because policy makers regard transfers by beneficiaries as inconsistent with basic concepts embedded in the land reform program, as for example, where the land-to-the-tiller law forbids landlords from retaining tenanted land and also ban the creation of any future tenancies. Such a ban would logically include any attempted leasing by the beneficiaries. Or policy makers may wish to limit transfer (or mortgage) of the land by the new owners because they believe that the new owners must be protected against their own unwise or imprudent actions. On the other hand, consistent with the concept of the perpetual duration of the rights being given to former tenants, land-to-the-tiller programs always allow rights to be passed on to succeeding generations, although there may sometimes be restrictions as to beneficiary-directed dispositions by will as distinct from predetermined dispositions to presumptive or statutory heirs.

Restrictions on transfers, where they exist, may be unlimited in time or may take the form of a time-bound moratorium (e.g., no sales for the first 10 years) or a contingent limitation (e.g., no sales until the beneficiary has paid the government for the land). Even where restrictions are initially without time limit, lawmakers may subsequently decide to abolish the restrictions, thus bringing the beneficiaries' rights in line with those held by other landowners in the society.

To obtain the fullest benefits of the land distribution in both enhancing political stability and beneficiary motivation, unlimited restrictions on either transfer or mortgage appear to be generally undesirable and unadministratable. If there is to be restriction, at most a moratorium or contingent limitation should be used, after which the new owners should be treated like any other owner. As to regulation or prohibition of leasing, see the discussion in section III below, as well as Chapter 6.

Another type of limitation on transfer sometimes found is one that allows transfer only to transferees with certain characteristics. For example, the law might provide that the total area of land the transferee proposes to acquire plus the land already held will not exceed some statutory ceiling on owner-cultivated land. Or the law might provide that a transferee must indeed be an agriculturalist who will self-cultivate (rather than an investor or "speculator"), or is not a foreigner, or is a natural person and not a corporation. Sometimes there is provision for local administrators to approve transactions to verify that they meet these or other criteria. Again, in terms of program design, it is desirable that any such restrictions, at least after some initial time period, not be any more limiting for new owners than for agricultural landowners generally.[77]

Aside from duration and breadth, the further dimension of assurance in the "bundle" of land rights is usually provided principally through some type of formal documentation given to the beneficiaries.[78] A persistent problem in some land-to-the-tiller efforts has been that the documents endorsing beneficiary rights have simply not been issued, or issuance has been subject to long delays. This may, in turn, reflect a range of circumstances, from those in which the government has paid the old landlord but has failed to prepare and physically hand over the title documents to the tenant, to those in which the landlord is contesting the propriety of the taking, perhaps frivolously, and the dispute remains tied up in a laborious court system, possibly for years.

Several program design steps can help ensure documentation of beneficiary rights, thereby greatly improving the assurance with which those rights are held. These measures are discussed in Chapter 8, which deals with titling and registration issues generally. There is a growing body of evidence (also discussed in that chapter, and in Chapter 7) that, in many country settings, issuance of formal documentation is important in generating behavior that land tenure reform programs seek to bring about, such as beneficiary investment in land improvements.

Time-bound implementation

The available experience suggests it is unwise to set deadlines for key aspects of program implementation. Of the seven land-to-the-tiller programs that we consider largely successful, only El Salvador used an implementation deadline. And that program was the least far-reaching of the seven, with about 30% of tenant farmers benefiting versus large majorities in the other six. The more modest success in El Salvador can be traced at least in part to the vulnerabilities created by a deadline, under which the program initially provided that beneficiaries had to submit their applications for ownership within one year of the adoption of implementing regulations.[79] This provision in itself might not have definitively limited the program, but for two additional factors.

First, the implementation process was not localized and contained unnecessary complications. For example, beneficiaries generally had to submit applications at the county seat rather than in the village; the law required issuance of a "provisional title" as a separate step, rather than simply letting the applicant retain a verified copy of the application; and the procedure called for time-consuming on-the-ground land surveying rather than relying largely or entirely on aerial surveying, a technology that had been successfully used in South Vietnam a decade earlier. These features slowed down the implementation process. But a second and unpredicted factor, political changes in El Salvador that brought to power both an administration and a legislature that were less supportive, or were even hostile, to the reform process proved even deadlier in conjunction with the deadlines, through the machinations described in Box 2.2.

Nor did the absence of a deadline in other land-to-the-tiller settings lead to drawn-out implementation. Of the other six land-to-the-tiller reforms we characterize here as successes – indeed, all of them greater programmatic successes than the Salvadoran reform in terms of the proportion of tenants who became owners – none had a deadline, yet none took more than five years to implement.

Presumed tenancy

As noted above, local village bodies that are not dominated by landlords are probably in the best position to adjudicate the reforms and determine who has a rightful claim as a tenant. Without such local knowledge it may be easy for politically connected landlords to succeed in disputing the existence of a tenancy relationship in the first place, or to coerce tenants into not claiming their rights. Kerala State's reform included another interesting variation: it created a series of presumptions as to the existence of the landlord-tenant relationship, placing the burden of proof on the landlord to show that there was not a tenancy relationship, rather than on the tenant to show that there was a tenancy relationship.[80] The existence of landlord-tenant relationships is so well and widely known at the village level that the issue has hardly arisen where the law provided for a public, local, non-landlord-dominated fact-finding process.

Box 2.2. Time-bound implementation in El Salvador

Advising the Salvadoran government, RDI argued against any deadline provision for beneficiary applications, but ultimately had to withdraw that opposition to get the land-to-the-tiller decree approved at all.

We anticipated that the Salvadoran government, with urging from the U.S., would extend the deadline, and initially they did. But the new and much-less-favorably disposed legislature ultimately took advantage of the deadline provision through a rather sophisticated pair of legal maneuvers:

(1) They adopted a law requiring that any land not applied for by the deadline would return to the ownership of the former landlord. This effectively negated a provision of the original law that had taken all tenanted land out of the landlord's ownership and conferred it on the tenants "by operation of law" as of the law's effective date, April 28, 1980. That provision had made the original application process merely a confirmatory one, rather than the source of the tenant's title.

(2) Under intense pressure from supporters of the reform in the U.S. Congress, the legislature had previously extended the application process for further one-year periods, but now having made timely applications necessary for the tenant's title, they balked at further extensions, and the time for beneficiary applications was allowed to expire on June 30, 1984.

Thus, the provision of a deadline in El Salvador proved to be decisively negative in its ultimate consequences, allowing not only a cutoff of further applications but allowing former landlords to reclaim ownership of all land not yet applied for.

For a detailed account of the Salvadoran reform, see R. Prosterman & J. Riedinger, *Land Reform and Democratic Development*, Chapter 6 (John Hopkins 1987).

Outside support

Leaving China aside, as a post-revolutionary reform in which no outside support would be expected or needed, five of the land-to-the-tiller reforms we discuss received varying outside support from the U.S. (those of Japan, Taiwan, South Korea, South Vietnam and El Salvador). Kerala carried out a successful program without any foreign support, having been implemented by a fully committed state government with extensive grass-roots outreach and support, and in a peaceful countryside.

Looking to settings where one or more of these factors – government commitment, grass-roots outreach and peace – is either missing or variable over the period of implementation, the contrast between U.S. support in South Vietnam and that in El Salvador is instructive. In both cases, RDI provided the principal technical assistance for the initial formulation of the land-to-the-tiller program.[81] In South Vietnam, the Nixon administration fully and consistently supported the land tenure reform, and had put 30 of USAID's own direct-hire staff on the ground within weeks after the adoption of the land-to-the-tiller law to assist in the implementation and monitoring of the program. There was also continuous random-sample surveying to verify progress and results. In El Salvador, the Carter administration was supportive, but was greatly distracted by the 1980 U.S. election campaign; it was succeeded by the Reagan administration, which might be characterized as a "net supporter" on the whole, but which went through various stages and was pulled in various directions (e.g., a supportive USAID administrator, but an initially hostile U.S. ambassador, only later succeeded by a supportive ambassador, Thomas Pickering; and with a powerful conservative senator, the late Jesse Helms, persistently in opposition).

The ultimate result in El Salvador was that the USAID mission in that country failed to include *any* full-time direct-hire professional staff support for the Salvadoran land-to-the-tiller program until a single position was created towards the end of 1982, more than two years after the land tenure reform was adopted. Only in 1984 was this commitment gradually increased to seven full- and part-time staff devoted to the program, but with time running out. USAID also engaged a number of outside contract technicians, but they had little apparent influence or power with respect to either Salvadoran or U.S. land tenure reform policies. Based upon RDI's own experience with the Salvadoran reform, we can say that this paucity of assistance contributed to the Salvadoran government's persistence in an implementation process that was too centralized and unnecessarily complex.

If a land-to-the-tiller program were to be adopted anywhere today, past experience strongly suggests that external support from bilateral or multilateral public agencies – if desired by the implementing country and judged to be worth providing at all by the outside actors – must be fully sufficient, highly timely and non-grudging. However, no widespread, mandated land-to-the-tiller reform to confer ownership upon tenant farmers has been initiated since that of El Salvador commenced in 1980. The closest to an exception is the Philippines, where a program initiated under martial law by President Ferdinand Marcos in 1972 had largely languished, but was partially revived after 1986 under the post-Marcos Aquino and Ramos presidencies.[82]

Even where all of the foregoing "design" lessons can be absorbed and applied, we believe that the combination of political and financial constraints – especially of generally less-authoritarian governments and fewer threatening, land-based rural rebellions in potential candidate countries, together with generally much-higher rural land prices – will make the incidence of such land-to-the-tiller reforms in the future rare.[83]

III.   Regulating tenancy

As an alternative to land-to-the-tiller reforms, many governments have sought to provide benefits to tenants through substantial regulation of the ongoing landlord-tenant relationship. One seeming attraction to this approach is that it does not require the government to purchase land for redistribution to the tenants. From an administrative perspective, regulation has the appearance of being easier because policy makers can simply legislate a ceiling to rents and a minimum period of tenure (perhaps even making tenants' rights perpetual and inheritable) that they hope will transform the tenant's economic situation. The central problem, however, is that this type of reform is not possible by the stroke of a pen, and considerable and ongoing oversight is required for it to have any chance of working. For example, the law would at a minimum need to require a new, written lease between each tenant and his or her landlord embodying the new, mandatory terms of the tenancy. And the process of entering into, verifying and enforcing such new leases would presumably require a continuing active government role.

Indeed, in virtually all less-developed country settings in which they have been tried on any scale, such programs to regulate the tenancy relationship in substantial ways have proven unworkable.[84] They do not, therefore, represent a practicable solution to the problems of tenure insecurity, concomitant inability to make long-term investments, high rent levels, or poverty that typically affect small tenant farmers in less-developed countries.

In contrast to the land-to-the-tiller discussion, where we were able to cite and describe seven generally successful programs, we can cite only one success in broad regulation of the landlord-tenant relationship in a less-developed-country setting – that of the state of West Bengal in India – and even this success must be weighed against a lengthy list of failures. Moreover, in some of the failures many or even most existing tenant farmers not only gained no protection from the purported regulatory improvements, but actually ended up substantially worse off than they were before the attempted reform, sometimes subject to widespread evictions. Apart from the one success in West Bengal, failures have included most other Indian states, Pakistan, Bangladesh, the Philippines, South Vietnam in the 1950s and up to the land-to-the-tiller program, and the Chinese mainland under the Nationalists, before the Communists took power in 1949.[85] There is also evidence in parts of Africa and in India that regulation resulted in widespread evictions of existing tenants.[86]

The central problem with landlord-tenant regulation is that virtually none of the less-developed countries where such regulation has been tried, or where it might be attempted now, has the administrative capacity to constrain and regulate successfully – in the tenant's favor – the ongoing landlord-tenant relationship. We identify at least three key reasons that tenancy regulations have not been successfully implemented in these settings.

First, unlike the land-to-the-tiller programs, which are characterized by a complete severing of the landlord-tenant relationship, all landlord-tenant regulation efforts, by their very definition, must deal with a continuing relationship, one which is intended to go on year after year and must keep that relationship always within the prescribed bounds. Successful implementation, correspondingly, will require an ongoing allocation of financial resources and personnel by the government.

Second, the landlord's motivation to cheat is likely to be strong precisely to the extent that the new regulation attempts to make significant – and from the landlord's standpoint, economically adverse – changes to the previously existing market-driven terms of the tenancy. Thus, a problem arises which is the direct counterpart of the adequate-compensation point that figured prominently in our discussion of land-to-the-tiller programs, but a problem which here has no even theoretically possible solution, because here there is no attempt to provide "compensation" to the landlord for whatever economic loss the landlord experiences as a result of the regulation, nor any thought of compensation.

Third, and greatly compounding the difficulties raised by the first two points, much of the regulatory effort must deal with matters that are non-transparent and easily hidden, especially in so far as the power relationship of the parties tends strongly to favor the landlord and thus keeps the tenant from coming forward to government administrators with complaints about landlord cheating.[87]

The central conclusion here is that in virtually any developing country setting, there are probably *no* design features that will make landlord-tenant regulation predictably or probably feasible over its necessarily extended and indefinite time-span. At most, it may be said that the least-hurtful programs have been those that tolerate, in practice, landlords who demand rents in excess of the amount permitted by law, while the existing tenant is at least allowed to remain on the land. Such has largely been the case with landlord-tenant regulation in the Philippines, and was the case in South Vietnam in the late 1950s and until the successful land-to-the-tiller program. In both cases landlords charged tenants an agreed-on rent much higher than the statutory level, and there was virtually no state enforcement activity.[88] However, even in settings where effective administration of regulatory measures seems unlikely, landlords may engage in precautionary evictions. This has occurred, for example, in some African settings.[89] Some of the worst results have been experienced in India.

We save a more detailed discussion of attempted regulation of the landlord-tenant relationship for Chapter 6, which is focused on India, where individual states have demonstrated most of the variations on failure. Here we briefly describe what began as an exceptionally effective tenancy regulation program but ended as an abject failure – the attempt in Egypt – and point out the lessons that this failure may hold for the single current success story in a developing-country setting: landlord-tenant regulation in West Bengal. Egypt's regulation of the landlord-tenant relationship spanned 40 years (45 if we include the years during which it was fully phased out). This was among the most extreme of such initiatives with respect to the extent to which it sought to divorce both duration of tenure and rent levels from market conditions. The Agrarian Reform Law establishing the regulation of tenancy was adopted just six weeks after the July 1952 Revolution that overthrew the monarchy and brought to power the socialist-military regime associated from 1954 until 1970 with Gamel Abdul Nasser.[90] As long as they paid their rent, the law guaranteed tenants perpetual tenure, required written tenancy contracts which they could continually renew, and allowed tenants to pass their tenancy rights to their heirs. Rent was fixed at seven times the land tax, which, even after some increase in that tax after Anwar Sadat succeeded Nasser in 1970, typically translated (as our own village interviewing in the late 1970s and into the 1980s indicated) into a very low rent level of 15-20% of the gross value of the crops produced. In addition, the tenant was entitled to receive one-half the sale price if the landlord sold the land for non-agricultural purposes. The effects of the law were widely felt, since tenants farmed as much as 60% of Egypt's cropland at the time the law was introduced.[91] The rights of such a tenant, under a regime of full enforcement, could be characterized as "owner-like" for the 40 years the law was enforced.[92]

That the Egyptian legal regime with respect to landlord-tenant relations was successfully enforced may have resulted from a combination of factors not commonly found in other developing-country settings where such regulation has been attempted. These included a considerable tradition of respect for the law, a grassroots bureaucratic and administrative presence (facilitated by a cultivated area that was limited to about 2.5 million hectares, concentrated in the Nile Valley and Nile Delta) and, perhaps most important, the fact that the program was initiated by a government that came to power as a revolutionary regime, and one whose socialist ideology made the threat of punishing non-complying landlords a credible one.

After Nasser's death in 1970, and with a gradual softening of the regime's ideology, there were muted calls for a rollback of the reform by landlords and their supporters, but there was also a clear opportunity, at least until the beginning of the 1990s, for a more progressive course. If there had been even modest political will at the top, the reform could have been "perfected" in favor of the tenants, by buying out the relatively small residual rights of the landlords that had been left with them after the 1952 reform, and giving the tenants full ownership.

We urged such a course on the Egyptian government in the 1980s,[93] pointing out that the old landlords by then mostly lived in the cities, had diversified to other sources of income, and had had over three decades to reconcile themselves to a situation that most recognized as a *fait accompli*. Thus, we argued, it was highly desirable to obtain an "insurance policy," at modest cost,[94] by buying out the remaining rights of the nominal landlords and completing the transfer of rights to the tenants. Otherwise, we pointed out that from a pro-reform point of view (which was still the government's position) there remained a continuing risk of the landlords gaining the ability to overturn the law at some future time.

However, the government rejected this course and subsequently fulfilled these warnings by annulling the long-standing protection of tenants with dazzling speed as the 1990s began. A good deal of the blame for catalyzing and encouraging the reversal lies with the World Bank and the International Monetary Fund, which, in the early euphoria over the rollback of communist economies in Europe, decided to insist on the rollback of Nasserite "socialism" in Egypt, a longstanding symbol of which was the regulation of agricultural tenancy (never mind that Egypt had made no attempt at collectivization of agriculture, or that a number of non-socialist societies had tried landlord-tenant regulation). The law reversing tenant protection was adopted pursuant to the World Bank–IMF "structural adjustment" program in the early 1990s.[95]

In the end, Egypt's parliament, in which the landlords held the upper hand (there were no tenant members), and without hindrance or objection from the Mubarak government, lifted the tenancy protections.[96] This occurred in 1992 and was accompanied by an immediate tripling of the rent level, from seven times the land tax to 22 times the land tax. In 1997, after a five-year transitional period, landowners were allowed to evict any tenant family, many of whom had held secure cultivation rights since 1952. After 1997 they could also charge rents not subject to any legal limit.[97] These huge changes in the law impacted an estimated 1 million tenant families (6 million individuals, or 1/10th of the population) who at the time cultivated one-quarter of Egypt's farmland.[98]

Research by Bush found that this policy reversal caused widespread dispossessions of former tenants, increased rural poverty and indebtedness, and spurred an increase in urban migration by the young.[99] Another study found that rents increased by 300% and that small farmers and rural tenants were not able to compete with wealthier interests to rent or purchase Egypt's scarce arable land.[100]

The ultimate psychological and political impact of the Egyptian rollback of their successful landlord-tenant regulation may take many years to make itself felt and, of course, relates not only to the current economic situation of the tenants or ex-tenants viewed in isolation, but also to the enormous worsening of that situation relative to what it had been – essentially as a fixed expectation – for decades prior to 1992. Psychologists in such circumstances may refer to potential aggression arising out of the frustration of an ongoing activity (here, secure possession of land which is the source of livelihood, at a low rent).[101] Such aggression may take a variety of forms: one might wonder, for example, what has been the subsequent life-experience of the young men who were driven to migrate to the cities by the reversal of their family's economic fortunes at the hands of the landowners, the lawmakers and the government.[102]

The tenancy reforms in the Indian state of West Bengal are now the last remaining tenancy reforms with broad application that are still effective in a less-developed country setting. The Egyptian experience may suggest that West Bengal should seek to achieve what Egypt failed to do while it is still politically feasible: as much full ownership for the protected tenants as possible, as soon as possible. These possibilities are discussed in Chapter 6.

A final issue concerns what may be regarded as the most extreme form of tenancy "regulation": a total ban on tenancy or the creation of new tenancies.[103] Such bans were implicitly or explicitly based on the then-prevalent view that agricultural tenancy is inherently exploitative and undesirable. These attempted bans have usually been enacted as part of a land-to-the-tiller program in which those tenants or other non-owners who would be affected are first entitled to receive ownership or owner-like rights to their existing land, and thereafter forbidden to become landlords themselves. This was done, with narrowly defined exceptions, in South Korea, for example, although RDI interviewing of

older and retired Korean farmers indicated that friendly tenancy arrangements subsequently developed, and the ban did not remain
broadly enforced.[104] The generally negative impact of the tenancy prohibitions found in several Indian states is discussed in Chapter 6.

Notably, the most recent enactment of legislation providing for the
widespread conferral of ownership upon existing tenants was more
than a quarter-century ago, in El Salvador in 1980. To the extent that
governments are unlikely to enact such legislation in most contemporary tenancy settings, and to the extent that existing legislation prohibits
or otherwise reduces landowner willingness either to maintain or create tenancy relationships, large numbers of the rural poor can be severely disadvantaged. Having thus been denied the ability to lease in
land, they are thereby pressed towards earning their livelihood as temporary agricultural laborers. Such work is much less desirable than the
option of working land as tenant farmers who possess land for at least
one crop season at a time – and usually for at least one year – and who
typically have some scope for deciding how to operate that land. In
most agricultural settings, tenancy is likely to represent a step up the
ladder out of poverty compared with the status of temporary laborers.
One recent World Bank analysis for India, for example, suggests substantially higher remuneration per day worked for tenant farmers than
for wage laborers.[105]

IV.   Freeing tenancy markets

Having examined the many problems that can plague government attempts to regulate landlord-tenant relations, in this section we argue
that governments should consider formally restoring and deregulating
the tenancy option in settings where it is currently the subject of such
unsuccessful restriction or regulation.

As a threshold matter, we should be clear about one point: market-
based (unregulated) tenancy is a severely inferior second-best in comparison to poor family becoming owner-operators of that same land.
Such a family is left in the "power domain" of the landowner, even if
some of the most feudal practices have receded over the past half-century in many settings. Tenants are likely to have far less status in the
community than they would as owners of the same land. In terms of
production, they are highly unlikely to have the security of tenure that
allows mid- to long-term investments in the land, thus constraining
many of the potential increases or diversifications of production on the
land they farm.[106] And they will have no realizable wealth based on
that land.[107]

Yet we have seen in Section II above that legislative provision of ownership under land-to-the-tiller reform is not likely to be a realistic option today in most settings where widespread tenancy persists; nor, as seen in Section III, is it realistic to expect successful regulation of the landlord-tenant relationship that gives more "ownerlike" rights and mitigates or partially reverses some of the problems (such as uncertain length of tenure and perceived high or at least rising rents) that inhere in most market-based tenancy relationships.

Thus, to insist upon ownership via land-to-the-tiller or nothing, is to permit the (unattainable) "best" to be the enemy of the "good," or at least the enemy of the "adequate." In this context the "adequate" outcome would be a lawful tenancy relationship, which is preferable to the generally much less favorable outcome of being only a casual agricultural laborer. And to insist upon substantial pro-tenant regulation or nothing, is to let that (also unattainable) "good" be the enemy of the same, at-least "adequate" achievement of market-based tenancy.

The first consequence of this reasoning would seem to be that minimally regulated free-market tenancy, in the great majority of those settings where it currently exists, should be left alone: the downside risks of most attempted regulation are likely to far outweigh the probable upside potential.

But if deregulation is to occur and tenancy markets are to be promoted in settings where the present legal regime does not freely allow such tenancy for agricultural land, advocates must address three important issues, depending upon the specifics of the setting.

First, to the extent that those who are presently cultivating the land have already received long-term tenure security benefits under a regulatory regime, those benefits must be preserved, and, when possible, such tenants should be converted to owners by compensating landlords for the market value of their remaining land rights.

Second, landowners are likely to enter into newly lawful, unregulated tenancy arrangements only if they are persuaded that the rules restricting tenancy have now changed and can be relied upon to remain so.

Third, where possible, reformers should consider whether any aspects of the landlord-tenant relationship can be incrementally improved to reduce the common disadvantages of the tenant, without making landowners substantially more reluctant to enter into formal and legally recognized tenancy agreements. That is, the law should provide some regulation of the landlord-tenant relationship that leads to both predictability and certain basic protections for the tenant and the landlord.[108]

A problem lurks here, however, that did not exist in our analyses above of what makes land-to-the-tiller programs workable or unworkable, or what makes landlord-tenant regulation programs workable or (usually) unworkable. In each of those other instances, we were able to draw upon a substantial body of comparative experience with actual programs, often including RDI's own experience with implementation or in observing attempted implementation. But a program to carry out a general reversal of an unsuccessful tenancy-prohibition or tenancy-regulation program, while it may be strongly supported in theory, is something that has been attempted in only one case, so far as we are aware.[109]

That one possibly instructive case is in Mexico, where until 1992 the law prohibited *ejidatarios*, who received land under the land reform, from renting out their holdings. Despite the change that permitted the leasing of these plots, RDI research found that as of 2001, *ejidatarios* interviewed in Mexico's Oaxaca state were still nervous about openly leasing out their land (although some had been leasing out the land illegally prior to the repeal of the ban, as appears to be have been widely true in Mexico) and were confused about their ability to lease out the land legally.[110] This bears on the second of the three points above, suggesting that tenancy regulations might tend to distort tenancy markets even after policy makers scale back or repeal them. This, in turn, underscores that such scale-back or repeal, if done, should be accompanied by reiterated grass roots publicity and education. Publicity and education are among the seemingly easiest measures for implementing legal rules in general (not only in the land tenure area) but are ones which, in RDI's experience, governments often do not focus on, do not budget for, and tend ultimately to ignore.

However, the Mexican experience offers no guidance on our first point above as to the need to identify and protect existing tenants who may already have received some benefits (a point further discussed in Chapter 6). That concern relates largely to settings in which traditional landlords – who may fear being subjected to future land-to-the-tiller or ceilings legislation – might seize upon tenancy deregulation measures as an occasion to evict an existing minority of tenants who, contrary to the landowner's wishes, had actually received tenure security benefits from the regulations that were being undone.[111]

What the concern expressed in our first point does suggest, in other settings in which at least some tenants are supposed to have received some benefits (even becoming owners under certain circumstances), is that at a minimum, reform proponents must conduct careful field research to determine whether there is a sector of families who have benefited from landlord-tenant regulation (even though most families may not have done so) contrary to the landowner's will, and how they might be adversely affected by the contemplated measures of deregulation.[112]

Nor does the isolated Mexican example offer much guidance on our third point, which relates to redressing the relative power relationship. On that point, it appears in principle that reformers should consider at least four issues when devising rules that may help prospective tenants while not alienating prospective landlords.

Process-facilitating measures. The designers of the rules should consider adopting seemingly "neutral" measures – either as part of deregulation or in settings where tenancy already operates entirely under the free market – that may make the situation more transparent or otherwise facilitate tenancy contracting. These might include, for example, drafting and publicizing non-mandatory model rental contracts. Also, "listing" services – such as a village bulletin board or local radio program or newspaper – to bring together prospective lessors and lessees.[113] Reduced-fee or free-of-charge formalization and public registration of longer-term leases may also encourage parties to conclude formal rental contracts.

The FAO's Good Practice Guidelines for agricultural leasing arrangements offer, among others, these recommendations:[114]
– The preparation of a model lease or lease terms
– An undertaking to refer to a model agreement when lease terms are in dispute (this would not supersede agreements by the parties, but would fill the gap on matters where a clear agreement was lacking)
– Improvements in transparency (either registration of leases, or a senior member of the local community to act as a recorder or repository)
– Access to appropriate information (a simple recording system for rents, fees and input/output shares)

Stable tenancy relations. Some regulatory changes seem overwhelmingly likely to benefit both prospective landlords and prospective tenants. Here, for example, we would include the termination of an existing rule providing that anyone who was allowed to be a tenant on the same parcel for more than one year was entitled to become a permanent tenant or, perhaps, was entitled to claim the right to become owner of that parcel. Where such a provision is law, the general result is likely to be either frequent shuffling of tenants from parcel to parcel or owners not renting out their land at all, seemingly disadvantageous to both landlords and tenants. Still, one would have to investigate whether some existing tenants might already be entitled to benefits – though not yet actually claimed – under the existing rules, and if so whether these benefits could be successfully "grandfathered in" and preserved.

Rules that reinforce access for small tenants. In many settings, especially developing country settings where non-mechanized agriculture is used and labor is readily available, tenancy can more equitably distribute access to land. This is the opposite of the common fear by some policy makers that tenancy will concentrate landholdings, with the powerful renting in plots from smallholders. Evidence that smallholders and the landless most commonly rent in land and that rental markets act to equalize operational holdings has been uncovered by researchers in a number of different country settings.[115] Conversely, reverse tenancy, whereby large holders rent in land from smaller holders, is more common in regions that practice capital-intensive and land-extensive agriculture – less characteristic of most developing country settings where, more typically, plentiful labor and relatively little land or spare capital is available.[116]

This raises the important question of whether anything can be done to enhance this effect of tenancy markets in tending to equalize holdings in developing country settings (benefiting especially those with little land but surplus family labor) by restraining the concentration of landholdings through lease. Some measures would seem self-evident, such as ending any existing subsidies for farm-machinery purchase, which artificially inflate the competitiveness of larger operational units (whether owned or rented in) as against small, labor-intensive units.[117]

But is it possible – and even if possible, would it be desirable – to introduce effective direct limits on the size of rented-in holdings or of total operational holdings, whether rented in or owned? Administratively, as discussed in Chapter 3, it appears more feasible to limit the size of holdings operated as a single unit than to try to place ceilings on "ownership" divorced from usership. But, politically, existing large tenants are likely to oppose the imposition of such ceilings on the amount of land tenants may rent in almost as much as existing owners would oppose ceilings on ownership of unitary operational holdings. Moreover, ceilings on already rented-in lands, if successfully implemented, would seemingly cause the large tenant simply to return the land to a number of small owners from whom the tenant had rented it, many or most of them because it was the best deal those small owners could make. And, as the discussion of Ukraine in Chapter 7 makes clear, there may be settings (especially where land is plentiful but local capital is not) in which many of the rural poor can benefit from renting to large, well-financed tenants.

All of this argues for any new ceiling affecting tenanted land to be applied only prospectively, to land that large holders attempt to rent in after the new rule becomes effective.[118] Even then, where such reverse leasing to large tenants represents the only, or nearly the only, option in a very limited land-rental market, it should be generally presumed that such ceilings are inappropriate. By contrast, where a robust rental market among smallholders or involving the landless exists, it might be a concern that large tenants were exercising their "clout" or winning leases for non-market reasons that might be hard to detect. Hence one might, prospectively, apply ceilings in such cases.

Carrots for landlords who go further. In some settings, it might also be possible to create material inducements for landlords who voluntarily agreed to provide tenants, or some tenants, more protection than they would receive in a free tenancy market. For example, on leases of more than a given length to small cultivators, the state might forgive the collection of any agricultural land taxes. All fees for registration of such transactions – such registration being a protection for both parties – might also be waived.

V. Conclusions

The classic land-to-the-tiller approach of giving ownership of "full-size" farms to tenant farmers – usually of the land the tenants presently cultivate – had a number of successes, as well as many failures, in the period from the end of World War II to the beginning of the 1980s. While one can distill from that body of experience lessons in program design that would likely lead to successful land-to-the-tiller programs in the future if it were merely a matter of such design, it is not simply a design question. Rather, there are threshold issues of political will and financial feasibility that make such programs generally unlikely in the future (and for the past quarter-century no government has seriously attempted to initiate a land-to-the-tiller program on a major scale). However, this chapter's detailed discussion of program design is important for at least three reasons: (i) some of the analysis will prove useful in our discussion of the redistribution of large estates in the next chapter, an arena in which there is somewhat more scope for future action; (ii) some design lessons here may also bear on "market-assisted land reform" programs likely to affect smaller, or much smaller, portions of a country's arable land, whether in the context of the next chapter, or that of Chapter 4 on micro-plots; and (iii) there may still be exceptional situations where compulsory redistribution on a land-to-the-tiller model remains an option, with Nepal a possible example.[119]

Past regulation of the ongoing landlord-tenant relationship, unlike the outright transfer of ownership through land-to-the-tiller, has had an almost uniformly dismal track record. Thus, our central conclusion on that subject is that tenancy regulation cannot be viewed as a feasible or desirable option. The leading exception to such universal failure is West Bengal. One notable lesson – this from past experience in Egypt, where long-standing protections were rolled back, resulting in widespread evictions – would seem to be that the West Bengal state government should move to achieve as much full ownership for the protected *bargadars* as possible, as rapidly as possible. These issues are further discussed in Chapter 6.

Finally, it seems desirable to deregulate the landlord-tenant relationship in many, and perhaps most, settings where regulation of tenancy has failed. However, while some improvements in tenancy markets can probably be identified that are fairly easy and non-controversial, others must be thought through carefully if policy makers are to satisfy the important threshold standard of "do no harm." Moreover, a general caveat attached to the deregulation discussion is that – with the exception of the only tangentially relevant experience in Mexico – deregulation has never been seriously attempted in practice in a setting where past regulation has been unsuccessful. Thus, while deregulation may potentially be the most widely applicable of the approaches canvassed in the present chapter, the discussion of deregulation is less empirically grounded than the discussions of lessons learned with respect to land-to-the-tiller and mandated regulation.

Notes

1   A good basic introduction to the important distinctions between these arrangements is available in UNFAO, *Good Practice Guidelines for Agricultural Leasing Arrangements*, FAO Land Tenure Studies No. 2 (UNFAO May 2001), available at http://www.fao.org/DOCREP/004/Y2560E/Y2560E00.HTM.

2   See, e.g., W. Hinton, FANSHEN: A DOCUMENTARY OF REVOLUTION IN A CHINESE VILLAGE (Vintage 1967); S. Clark, THE SOCIAL ORIGINS OF THE IRISH LAND WAR (Princeton University Press 1979).

3   J. Brown, *Ejidos and Comunidades in Oaxaca, Mexico: Impact of the 1992 Reforms*, Rural Development Institute Reports on Foreign Aid and Development No. 120, at 5 (Rural Development Institute 2004), available at http://www.rdiland.org/PDF/PDF_Reports/RDI_120.pdf.

4   Government of India, *Eleventh Five-Year Plan, 2007-2012*, secs. 1.109-1.113 (Dec. 2007). Several individual Indian states, which make the operative land tenure rules under India's Constitution, have such loosening of tenancy restrictions under active discussion.

5   Significant locales remain, however, in which the situation of tenants remains repugnant, such as Bihar state in India. See K.G. Iyer, *Concealed Tenancy: Dilemmas of Share-Croppers in Bihar,* in B.N. Yugandhar & K.G. Iyer, eds., LAND REFORMS IN INDIA, VOLUME 1: BIHAR—INSTITUTIONAL CONSTRAINTS 247-65 (Sage Publications 1993).

6   See generally K. Deininger, LAND POLICIES FOR GROWTH AND POVERTY REDUCTION (World Bank & Oxford University Press 2003). For the "power domain" concept, see E. Wolf, PEASANT WARS OF THE TWENTIETH CENTURY 290-91 (Harper & Row 1969).

7   This has been contrasted with MacArthur's failure to pursue such reforms during the period after his 1944 return (as liberator from the Japanese occupation) to the Philippines, ascribed largely to a new American staff member who had been a Manila corporation lawyer. But, "Later, in Japan, where Americans owned no stock and the General had time to devise his own civil policies, MacArthur would execute a

spectacular 'about-face.'" See W. Manchester, AMERICAN CAESAR: DOUGLAS MACARTHUR 1880-1964, at 378-379 (Little Brown 1978).

8   For good discussions of the Japanese land reform, see R.P. Dore, LAND REFORM IN JAPAN (Oxford University Press 1959); T. Kawagoe, *Agricultural Land Reform in Post-war Japan; Experience and Issues*, World Bank Policy Research Working Paper 2111 (World Bank 1999); H.E. Voelkner, *Land Reform in Japan*, AID SPRING REVIEW (USAID 1970).

9   See Dore, supra note 8, at 138-139. There was also a limit on owner-operators of agricultural land to a maximum of 3 hectares of land – a limit that also applied to tenants who became owners under the reform – but very few operational holdings were that large.

10   R.P. Dore recounts an estimate by A.J. Grad: "He estimates that the price of a tan [about 1/10 hectare] of good rice land in 1939 would have bought over 3,000 packets of cigarettes or 31 tons of coal. In 1948 it would have bought 13 packets of cigarettes or 0.24 tons of coal." Id. at 139, citing A.J. Grad, LAND AND PEASANT IN JAPAN (1952). This would indicate land-price erosion in inflation-adjusted (purchasing power) terms of over 99%.

11   See id. at 174 & table 8. The tenant-cultivated proportion of riceland had declined from 53.1% in 1941 to 10.9% by the final report of the Land Committee in August 1950, and the tenant-cultivated proportion of upland had declined from 37.2% to 8.5%. A total of about 1,915,000 hectares had been distributed to 4,748,000 tenant families.

12   Theoretically, the beneficiaries could also lease out the land, but few wished to do so, since both new and old lessees were afforded the strict legislative protection of tenancy.

13   In purchase money mortgage, the land being sold is used by the buyer as security for the loan by which he acquires the land. Thus, those who do not have enough cash of their own to pay for land are enabled to be buyers, assuming banks are present that are willing to lend on the security of that land.

14   Dore, as an observer through the post-land reform period, offers an intriguing picture of the transformation of the Japanese rural economy in his preface to the 1985 American edition. See R.P. Dore, LAND REFORM IN JAPAN, Preface to the New Edition (Schocken 1985).

15   See Kawagoe, supra note 8, at 31; Dore, supra note 8, at 149-173.

16   Land Reform Law of South Korea, Law No. 108, art. 5(2)(a), (b); J. Yoong-Deok & Y. Kim, *Land Reform, Income Redistribution, and Agricultural Production in Korea*, 48(2) ECONOMIC DEVELOPMENT AND CULTURAL CHANGE 253 (2000); G. Henderson, KOREA: THE POLITICS OF THE VORTEX (Harvard University Press 1968); R. Morrow & K. Sherper, *Land Reform in South Korea*, AID SPRING REVIEW 26-27 (USAID 1970).

17   See Morrow & Sherper, supra note 16, at 30-31.

18   See id. at 5-6.

19   See id. at 30.

20   See Yoong-Deok & Kim, supra note 16, at 257. "Voluntary land sales by Korean landlords prior to implementation," under pressure from local leftist organizations, account for some of the difference (69% accomplishment) between the formal reach and intended reach of the land reform implementation process. See Morrow & Sherper, supra note 16, at 6, 30. The reform also included ex-Japanese-owned land, which was distributed by the U.S. military authorities beginning in 1948.

21   C. Chen, LAND REFORM IN TAIWAN (China Publishing 1961); S.W.Y. Koo, G. Ranis & J. C.H. Fei, THE TAIWAN SUCCESS STORY: RAPID GROWTH WITH IMPROVED DISTRIBUTION IN THE REPUBLIC OF CHINA, 1952-1979 (Westview 1981); A.Y.C. Koo, *Land Reform in Taiwan*, AID SPRING REVIEW (USAID 1970); C. Liu, *Diversification of the Rural Economy in*

Taiwan, Working Paper 16: The Japan Program Working Paper Series on Priorities and Strategies in Rural Poverty Reduction: Experiences from Latin America and Asia (paper presented at the Japan Program/INDES 2001 Conference, Japan).

22 See Chen, supra note 21, at 113-14.

23 The 37.5% was arrived at by excluding 25% as belonging solely to the tenant, then dividing the remaining 75% between tenant and landlord. A survey done prior to the reform showed average rents were 56.8% of the tenant's harvest in 1948. See id. at 20.

24 The retainable amount was then varied upward for lower-quality land, and downward for higher-quality land, both paddy and dry land being divided into 26 "grades" (for the highest-quality paddy land, for example, grades 1 through 6, only 1.45 tenanted hectares could be retained). The Land-to-the-Tiller Act, art. 10 states landlord retention of paddy field cultivated by tenants was to be 3 chia or 7.1901 acres for average-grade land – 7th to 12th grade – that is, 2,9109 hectares, and dryland retention was set at two times the retention for equivalent grades of paddy field. For the relevant articles, see Chen, supra note 21, at 204-05.

25 Koo provides data indicating that the average value of paddy land in relation to gross crop value had been fairly stable at ratios between 4.0 and 4.3 throughout the prewar period 1926-1940. See Koo, supra note 21, at 12, table II.D. Land values had certainly not surged in in-kind terms: Chen indicates a value (adjusted for hectares versus *chia*) of 23,880 kg of unhulled rice for high-grade paddy field in 1948, compared to Koo's figure of 22,387 for an average paddy field in 1936-1940. Chen, supra note 23, at 45. If one considers rent reduction followed by transfer of ownership as a single integral program, then what was being paid was roughly 62% (a multiplier of 2.5 versus one of 4.0) of the market value of the land before land reform began.

26 See Chen, supra note 21, at 82.

27 See id. at 307 (table 1), 312 (table 10).

28 See C.-Z. Liu, *Diversification of the Rural Economy in Taiwan*, The Japan Program Working Series Paper No. 16, at 12 (presented at the Japan Program/INDES 2001 Conference, Japan).

29 See generally A. Alesina & D. Roderik, *Distribution, Political Conflict, and Economic Growth: A Simple Theory and Some Empirical Evidence*, in A. Cukierman, Z. Hercowitz & L. Leiderman, eds., POLITICAL ECONOMY, GROWTH, AND BUSINESS CYCLES 46 (MIT Press 1992).

30 Chen, supra note 23, at 84, chart 12.

31 S. Kuo, G. Ranis & J. Fei, THE TAIWAN SUCCESS STORY: RAPID GROWTH WITH IMPROVED DISTRIBUTION IN THE REPUBLIC OF CHINA, 1952-1979, at 57, 59 (Westview 1981). See also E. Thorbecke, *Agricultural Development*, in W. Galenson, ed., ECONOMIC GROWTH AND STRUCTURAL CHANGE IN TAIWAN 142-43 (Cornell University Press 1979).

32 Chen, supra note 23, at 87-89.

33 China Institute of Reform & Development, HISTORY OF CHANGES AND INNOVATIONS OF CHINA'S RURAL LAND SYSTEM 32 (1999); G. Zhang, RURAL REFORM IN CHINA 3-4 (Haitian Publishing House 2001).

34 H.C. Bush, G.H. Messegee & R.V. Russell, THE IMPACT OF THE LAND-TO-THE-TILLER PROGRAM IN THE MEKONG DELTA 16 (Control Data Corporation/AID Dec. 1972). See also C.S. Callison, LAND-TO-THE-TILLER IN THE MEKONG DELTA 199 (University Press of America 1983).

35 R. Prosterman & J. Riedinger, LAND REFORM AND DEMOCRATIC DEVELOPMENT 139-41 (Johns Hopkins 1987). See generally id., ch. 5; C.L. Sulzberger, *Vietnamizing the Peace*, NEW YORK TIMES, Feb. 27, 1972. Despite the impact within the South, the reform could not, of course, affect divisions coming across the border from the North,

as the conflict became increasingly "inter-statal" rather than predominantly "civil" in nature.

36 Bush, et al., supra note 34, at 17.

37 Id. at 50. Another researcher, doing an intensive three-village survey, found that the land-to the-tiller program "was clearly stimulating rural investment in both house improvements and consumer durables and thereby increasing market demand for these domestic industries." Callison, supra note 34, at 218.

38 The South Vietnamese experience also holds important lessons with respect to the earlier, failed land-to-the-tiller program attempted after 1956, following the initial peace agreement between the Communists and the French that had divided the country into North and South. That program had involved a high ceiling for landlord retention – 100 hectares – and even that went largely unenforced by a government that had little political commitment to the program. Most of the land that was acquired came from the departing French landlords, and from Vietnamese landlords who feared a Communist takeover of the South, but most of this land was permitted to be rented out by local officials rather than being actually given to tenants. See Prosterman and Riedinger, supra note 35, ch. 5.

39 P. Radhakrishnan, PEASANT STRUGGLES, LAND REFORMS AND SOCIAL CHANGE: MALABAR 1836-1983, at 149-163 (Sage Publications 1989); R.J. Herring, LAND TO THE TILLER: THE POLITICAL ECONOMY OF AGRARIAN REFORM IN SOUTH ASIA 196, 210-12 (Yale University Press 1983).

40 Estimates of beneficiary numbers range from about 43,000 to 52,000 out of El Salvador's roughly 160,000 tenant households (a further element of the reform, taking large estates, benefited about 27,000 additional households, and is discussed in Chapter 3). For the 52,000 estimate, see J. Strasma, *Unfinished Business: Consolidating Land Reform in El Salvador,* in W. Thiesenhusen, ed., SEARCHING FOR AGRARIAN REFORM IN LATIN AMERICA 411 (Unwin Hyman 1989), and for the 43,000 estimate, see R.W. Scofield, *Land Reform in Central America,* in R. Prosterman, M. Temple & T. Hanstad, eds., AGRARIAN REFORM AND GRASSROOTS DEVELOPMENT: TEN CASE STUDIES 144 (L. Rienner 1990). See generally Prosterman & Riedinger, supra note 35, ch. 6.

41 *Land Reform: An Ambassador's Views,* text of remarks delivered by Ambassador Thomas R. Pickering, former U.S. Undersecretary of State for Political Affairs, and former U.S. Ambassador to El Salvador, Seattle, Jan. 12, 2004, on file with Rural Development Institute.

42 See Strasma, supra note 40, at 422. Strasma cites research soon after the reform showing both income increases and substantial land investments by beneficiaries: 21% of former tenants had made soil conservation investments such as terracing; 13% had planted trees; and 6% had improved upon irrigation or drainage. Also, between 1982 and 1984, income from the distributed parcels rose 9% in real (after inflation) terms (note this did not include the new trees, which were not yet mature) and "off-farm income rose even more strongly [apparently by more than one-half in real terms], perhaps because the former tenants now had a secure base. No longer did they have to spend time and energy to please a landlord or to find a parcel to rent the following year." Strasma, supra note 40, at 427 n. 5. Compare the findings on titling of urban squatters in Peru, where research showed that "Individuals in titled households spend fewer hours inside the home guarding property and engaging in home-based entrepreneurial activities, and a greater number of hours in both employment and private leisure activities outside the home. . . . These results provide empirical support for the anecdotal evidence that untitled squatters commonly attain informal rights by taking time off from work to participate in such activities as guarding their property, participating in community groups, and filing administrative claims for formalization." E. Field, *Property Rights, Community Public Goods, and*

Household Time Allocation in Urban Squatter Communities: Evidence from Peru, 45(3) WILLIAM AND MARY LAW REVIEW 837, 867-868 (2004).

43 We categorize the failed Indonesian land reform program of 1960-1965 as one that was never likely to include tenant farmers as the main beneficiary group, and discuss this program briefly in Chapter 3.

44 See, e.g., R.J. Herring, *Explaining the Anomalies in Agrarian Reform: Lessons from South India*, in Prosterman, et al., supra note 40 at 49, 53-65.

45 See R. Prosterman, *Land Reform in Latin America: How to Have a Revolution Without a Revolution*, 42 WASHINGTON LAW REVIEW 189 (1966); R. Prosterman, *Land Reform as Foreign Aid*, 6 FOREIGN POLICY 128-141 (1972); Prosterman & Riedinger, supra note 35, at 194-202; T. Hanstad, *Philippine Land Reform: The Just Compensation Issue*, 63 WASHINGTON LAW REVIEW 417 (1988).

46 A decree was issued governing the bond portion of compensation in the Salvadoran reform (covering both tenanted and plantation lands affected) which authorized such a bond monetization option, but that option never appears to have been implemented. See Decree No. 220 of the Revolutionary Junta of Government, Special Law for the Issuance of the Agrarian Reform Bonds, clauses (h) and (j) (1980). There was also discussion of such a bond-monetization possibility for the Aquino-era stages of the Philippine reform, around 1986. See J. Riedinger, AGRARIAN REFORM IN THE PHILIPPINES: DEMOCRATIC TRANSITIONS AND REDISTRIBUTIVE REFORM 171 (Stanford University Press 1995). Other possible options for converting deferred payments to immediate use, non-inflationary at least to the extent that some spare capacity exists in those sectors of the economy, might be to make them usable to pay for school expenses for the ex-landlord's children, or medical expenses for the ex-landlord's family.

47 There have, however, been other land tenure reform programs that have paid full market value, or even more than full market value. These include the taking of land of large landlords in Japan under the Meiji Restoration in the late 19th century; the buying-out of the large intermediaries (Zamindars) in India in the years immediately following Independence in 1947; the rather small-scale acquisition of large private estates in Venezuela in the 1960s; and some of the more recent, again small-scale, "market-assisted land reform" efforts of the World Bank in Brazil and elsewhere. Some aspects of these are discussed in Chapters 3, 4 and 6.

48 To some degree that may simply have been done to save money by a military administration that had the power to do it; perhaps the landlords were also considered as allies of the political elements that had been responsible for Japan's aggressive war-making, and thus deserving of punishment.

49 See Basic Law of Agrarian Reform (Decree No. 153) of the Revolutionary Junta of Government, art. 13 (1980).

50 See Kerala Land Reforms Act (1963), sec. 72A and table 1 (reflecting a sliding scale based on total amount of the otherwise-calculated compensation from "100%" down to "50%" as a minimum), and secs. 27, 33, 35 (the effect of which is to make the "fair rent," which is to be multiplied by sixteen in order to arrive at the 100% compensation figure generally be 25% of the gross crop, leading to the calculation of 16 x 25%, or 4 times gross crop value for the smallest landlords).

51 Our direct impression from interviewing after the promulgation of the 1972 reform was that landlords were skeptical of the value of such enterprises as a back-up guarantee for the payment. However, by the time of the 1987 Aquino reforms, the possible distribution of stock shares as part of a direct landowner compensation package had become quite attractive, since this now included an array of "sequestered" properties that the new Aquino government had seized from ousted President Ferdinand Marcos and his cronies, as alleged ill-gotten gains of his rule. Riedinger, supra note 46, at 171 & n.83.

52 See Decree No. 207 of the Revolutionary Junta of Government, Law for the Expro-
    priation and Transfer of Land to the Tiller, art. 5 (1980).
53 There were later efforts to remedy this shortcoming, including changes to the U.S.
    Foreign Assistance Act. See Prosterman & Riedinger, supra note 35, at 166, 171-73,
    286-87 nn.84-86.
54 Kerala was, after Taiwan, probably the closest to meeting the adequate compensation
    standard.
55 See further discussion in Chapter 3. Also see, e.g., H. Thomas, THE SPANISH CIVIL
    WAR 81-82 (Harper & Row 1977).
56 Restitution of Land Rights Act, 1994, ch. 3, sec. 33 (South Africa).
57 If this is to be an in-place distribution, the number of hectares to be distributed will
    turn on the size of existing tenanted holdings, subject to possible maximum caps on
    what can be received by larger tenants.
58 There may be wide variations in land values in different settings: from $10,000 or
    more per hectare in densely populated East Java with its rich volcanic soils and ample
    rainfall, to the low hundreds of dollars per hectare in semi-arid areas of the sparsely
    populated Brazilian northeast.
59 Also taking into account contingencies such as drought or crop failure affecting ben-
    eficiary repayment.
60 The program should probably allow for the non-cultivating tenant to retain benefi-
    ciary status where there are special circumstances leading to the creation of the sub-
    tenancy, such as illness, widowhood or temporary status as a student or military con-
    script.
61 R. Herring, LAND TO THE TILLER 212 (Yale University Press 1983). The Kerala land ten-
    ure reform law set a ceiling on self-cultivated land (also applicable to the tenant bene-
    ficiaries who became owners) that was twelve to fifteen acres (4.85 to 6.1 hectares)
    for most families; Kerala Land Reforms Act (1963), secs. 82, 16, 16A, 17. Pushing this
    to a logical extreme, one would conclude that a universal land-to-the-tiller approach,
    which set no limit on land received, would certainly be undesirable in a setting of
    widespread "reverse tenancy" where a substantial proportion of tenanted land was
    held by large tenants who were renting it from small owners.
62 Such a provision was put into law in South Vietnam, but the limitation was deferred
    and never implemented due to the perceived administrative, and possibly political,
    difficulties of implementation. It was adopted in a form (3 hectares maximum in the
    Mekong Delta and 1 hectare maximum in the Central Lowlands) that would have af-
    fected an estimated 10% of land reform beneficiaries, taking back a portion of the
    land they received, but was then indefinitely deferred as to actual application by the
    implementing regulations. See Prosterman & Riedinger, supra note 35, at 136.
63 A potentially horrendous example of (apparently) ignoring the administrative ease
    and fairness of giving "in place" benefits, combined with a poorly thought through
    attempt (apparently) to give idealized benefits was found in Presidential Decree No.
    27 by the President of the Philippines, Decreeing the Emancipation of Tenants from
    the Bondage of the Soil Transferring to Them the Ownership of the Land They Till
    and Providing the Instruments and Mechanism Therefor (1972). This decree seemed
    to contemplate that each tenant to be benefited would receive ownership of 3 hectares
    of the irrigated or 5 hectares of the unirrigated lands that were presently tenanted.
    Since a holding of such size, however, would be approximately three times the aver-
    age size of existing tenant holdings, a literal interpretation might have suggested
    that, on average, two existing tenant families would have to be evicted in order to cre-
    ate an idealized holding of the required size for a fortunate third family of existing
    tenants. When this consequence of a literal interpretation was pointed out, the gov-
    ernment effectively abrogated the "3-hectare" and "5-hectare" provisions and pro-

ceeded to carry the program out (to a limited extent) or an in-place distribution to the existing tenants. Implementation was further limited by the presence of a non-zero, seven-hectare retention area of tenant farmed land for each landlord.

64 This may in large part be due to the fact that most, if not all, of those successful programs were completed before policy makers in most settings had even gained awareness that this was an issue.

65 See Herring, supra note 61, at 186.

66 See Chen, supra note 21, at 27, 32.

67 See id. at 33 (estimating that only 5% of the evictions had not yet been resolved by that date; 5% of 9% evicted equals 0.45% of all tenants). Chen adds: ". . . the remaining five percent [of cases] were being settled one by one." Id.

68 See Chapter 7 on China for a discussion of the impact of publicity on implementation.

69 In the case of El Salvador, successive regimes came in through elections that had varying, sometimes much lesser, degrees of commitment; under some subsequent less-committed administrations, an effort was made to include a seven-hectare retention area for landlords (when supposedly accompanied by one of five criteria, such as the owner being a widow with children), although without any warrant in the governing law. It was clear from the beginning, however, that the *campesinos* themselves, where there was obvious inequity, were highly unlikely to apply for the land: self-administration by them of such tacit limits would have been a far better approach. See Prosterman & Riedinger, supra note 35, at 167-68, 285-86 n.71.

70 The fact that a strong insurgency was underway was almost certainly a further factor in limiting anticipatory evictions in South Vietnam and El Salvador. In some areas of the Vietnamese and Salvadoran countryside, landlords could not even have full access or be able to remain in the village overnight. Moreover, in each case landlords were to receive at least moderate compensation, versus the risk of losing the land without any compensation if the revolutionaries won (as they ultimately did in South Vietnam). Of course, in China, where the revolutionaries had already won, and were carrying out a zero-ceiling program, landlords had become an officially reviled group, and were probably generally more concerned about losing their lives than their land.

71 There may also be cases where the "ceiling" is set at such a high level to begin with that most landlords escape the program even without such evasion: that was the case with the "100-hectare" ceiling of the initial, failed program in 1950s South Vietnam under President Ngo Dinh Diem. Stanford Research Institute, LAND REFORM IN VIETNAM, SUMMARY VOL. 5, at 68-70, 185-188 (Stanford Research Institute 1968). In a number of other settings, the combination of high ceilings on land ownership and poor compensation proffered for land, accompanied by anticipatory and often fraudulent transfers of above-ceiling land by landowners, has rendered land-to-the-tiller programs ineffectual. This was true of successive programs in Pakistan and Bangladesh, in both of which the principal beneficiaries would have been the sharecropping tenant farmers. See R. Herring, LAND TO THE TILLER: THE POLITICAL ECONOMY OF AGRARIAN REFORM IN SOUTH ASIA ch. 4 (Yale University Press 1983); M. Khan, UNDERDEVELOPMENT AND AGRARIAN STRUCTURE IN PAKISTAN chs. 4 & 5 (Westview 1981); F. Jannuzi & J. Peach, THE AGRARIAN STRUCTURE OF BANGLADESH: AN IMPEDIMENT TO DEVELOPMENT chs. 1 & 2 (Westview 1980). Further on the method of calculating the ceilings in Pakistan, see note 75 to Chapter 3. Even with a ceiling as low as seven hectares, a land-to-the-tiller program in the Philippines confronting similar landlord responses had provided ownership of land to only a small minority of tenants 13 years after its inception. See J. Riedinger, AGRARIAN REFORM IN THE PHILIPPINES: DEMOCRATIC TRANSITIONS AND REDISTRIBUTIVE REFORM 91-96 (Stanford University Press 1995) (under Operation Land Transfer, which became a national program in 1972, a

potential beneficiary universe of at least 914,000 tenant families initially identified shrank to an estimate of 587,000 families and then, apparently, to 427,000 because of the seven-hectare retention limit. But by the end of 1985 only 137,000 titles had been printed and about 134,000 beneficiaries had begun their amortization payments to the government).

72 See Chapter 6 regarding India; O.B. Jones, PAKISTAN: EYE OF THE STORM 245-249 (Yale University Press 2002); F.T. Jannuzi & J.T. Peach, THE AGRARIAN STRUCTURE OF BANGLADESH: AN IMPEDIMENT TO DEVELOPMENT 50-53 (Westview 1980); Riedinger, supra note 46, at 160, 218.

73 To forestall and uncover such predating one could theoretically ask tenants when, if ever, they started paying rent to the supposed new "owner."

74 Among the successful programs that forbade landlords from retaining tenanted land, South Vietnam and Kerala State also had variations on local-level administration in which beneficiaries were substantially involved. South Korea was a seeming exception (at least in the formal way contemplated in its land reform law) due to the pendency of the Korean War during much of the time the land reform was being implemented. In El Salvador, the democratic *campesino* organizations played an important local role, but an unofficial one; for various bureaucratic and political reasons, implementation there had no official local involvement, was more complicated and slow, and (for this reason among others, discussed below) reached the smallest fraction of intended tenant beneficiaries (about 30%) among the seven programs we consider largely successful. See generally Prosterman & Riedinger, supra note 35, at ch. 6.

75 See Chen, supra note 21, at 33.

76 See Chapter 1 for a discussion of property rights as a "bundle of sticks."

77 Still another limitation sometimes found is a restriction on divisibility, or on "minimum size" of permitted parcels. Some warrant can be found for such restrictions with respect to subdivision as a consequence of inheritance of agricultural land, especially in the case of statutorily mandated succession not done at the landowner's direction; however, it seems very difficult to justify "minimum size" limitations where there are market transfers being made. There, it seems that private parties are likely to know better what constitutes an efficient size landholding than any general, *a priori* determination that legislators have embodied in the law. This approach also finds support in the general evidence that smaller holdings are more productive and efficient than larger holdings, discussed in Chapter 3. (And Chapter 4, on benefits of micro-holdings.)

78 See Chapter 8 on formalization of land rights.

79 See Prosterman & Riedinger, supra note 35, at 160-161, 163, 165. RDI had argued against this deadline provision in working with the drafters, but the Christian Democrats who were then a key supporting constituency were adamantly opposed to dropping it; ultimately, it came down to having an otherwise well-conceived decree with such a limitation, or having no land tenure reform at all for tenant farmers.

80 See Kerala Land Reforms Act (1963), secs. 4-12.

81 Compare generally chapters 5 (South Vietnam) and 6 (El Salvador) in Prosterman & Riedinger, supra note 35.

82 See generally Riedinger, supra note 46.

83 For a discussion of the factors at a macro level that are likely to be implicated in the creation of much higher market prices for land, see Chapter 1. To complete the logic of this analysis, we also point out that achieving ownership of full-size farms for the majority of tenants in a setting where tenancy is widespread, via financing for voluntary market-price purchases is no more financially feasible than mandatory land-to-the-tiller redistribution at or near market-price levels. Indeed, it is less so, to the extent that lack of the mandatory feature is likely to cause landowners' asking prices –

where one may be talking of the need to acquire 20%, 30% or 40% of total arable land – to rise sharply. The issue of voluntary market-based acquisition for full-size farms or equivalent per-family allocations is further discussed in Chapter 3. The distinct issue of market-based land acquisition for allocation of micro-plots is discussed in Chapter 4.

84 In developed market economies with fully developed legal systems, regulation of the landlord-tenant relationship in the agricultural sector (including perpetual or very long-term tenure and fixed lower-than-free-market rents) has been successfully introduced and maintained, for periods now sometimes very close to a century. That is the case in the Netherlands, Great Britain, Belgium and France. It was also done, starting in the English colonial era, in the territories that became the Republic of Ireland and Northern Ireland, from 1881 until 1923 and 1925, respectively, then to be superseded by full-scale programs giving ownership to the tenants. See J.E.W. Wylie, IRISH LAND LAW 21-52 (2d ed. Butterworths 1986) (noting, at 30, "But the cost and time consumed in the exercise were enormous" for the Irish and British administrators and tribunals implementing the 1881 landlord-tenant regulation law); C. O'Grada, IRELAND BEFORE AND AFTER THE FAMINE: EXPLORATIONS IN ECONOMIC HISTORY 1800-1925, at ch. 4 (2d ed. Manchester University Press 1993). There was also successful regulation for decades-long periods in both Japan and Taiwan, as to the minor sectors of tenanted land that remained after their land-to-the-tiller programs due to the law's allowance of some landlord retention of tenanted lands (about 2.9 hectares of average paddy land in Taiwan, and 1 hectare of resident-owned land in Japan, were permitted to be retained). Japan ended its regulation of remaining landlord-tenant relationships in 1970, and Taiwan largely did so in 2000.

85 See discussion in Chapter 6 (India); N. Islam, *Growth, Poverty, and Human Development: Pakistan*, UNDP Occasional Paper 31, available at http://gd.tuwien.ac.at/soc/ undp/oc31aa.htm (Pakistan); Jannuzi & Peach, supra note 72, at 52-53 (Bangladesh); Riedinger, supra note 46, at 75, 259 n.11 (Philippines); Prosterman & Riedinger, supra note 35, at 122-24 (South Vietnam); Chen, supra note 21, at 18-21 (mainland China).

86 For Africa, see, for example, A.F. Robertson, THE DYNAMICS OF PRODUCTIVE RELATIONSHIPS: AFRICAN SHARE CONTRACTS IN COMPARATIVE PERSPECTIVE 27-30, 275 (Cambridge University Press 1987), who finds that sharecropping levels were reduced by state control over sharecropping conditions. South Africa has experienced extensive evictions of tenants and other occupiers despite post-apartheid legislation intended to secure their possession without transferring ownership. See M. Wegerif, et al., STILL SEARCHING FOR SECURITY: THE REALITY OF FARM DWELLER EVICTIONS IN SOUTH AFRICA (Social Surveys and Nkuzi Development Association, Pretoria 2005). For discussion of the situation in India, see Chapter 6.

87 Two examples, derived from RDI field experience and interviews with supposedly "protected" tenants: (1) On the important matter of rent levels, the tenancy contract may correctly specify a level of "rent" within the limits imposed by the law. But what real option does the tenant have – if he is fearful of his future access to the land, or of impairing his future relationship with this landlord or with the village landlords generally – if the landlord demands that the tenant pay an additional amount "under the table"? How are administrators to learn of such payments, their frequency, or amount? (2) In an alternative cheating scenario the tenant agrees to the landlord's demand that the contract specify an inflated production or land-area figure, so that what appears to be a legal rent level in relation to that figure is a much higher rent in proportion to actual production or land area. This, in turn, can thrive under a process of governmental oversight of such contracts which – whether distant, under-

staffed, uncaring, or corrupt – fails to detect such overestimates of production or land area.

88 For South Vietnamese tenants, see the results of the 1000-household sample survey carried out in 1967-1968, in Stanford Research Institute, LAND REFORM IN VIETNAM: WORKING PAPERS, VOL. 4, at parts 1 and 2 (Menlo Park, Cal. 1968, Mimeo). The primary author of the present chapter, R. Prosterman, acted as land-law consultant to the survey. For the Philippines, see Riedinger, supra note 46, at 96; G.M. Bautista, W.C. Thiesenhusen & D.J. King, *Farm Households on Rice and Sugar Lands: Margen's Village Economy in Transition*, in A.J. Ledesma, P.Q. Makil & V.A. Miralao, eds., SECOND VIEW FROM THE PADDY: MORE EMPIRICAL STUDIES ON PHILIPPINE RICE FARMING AND TENANCY 73-92 (Institute of Philippine Culture, Ateneo de Manila University 1983).

89 See Robertson, supra note 86, at 275.

90 Law No. 178 of 1952 (Egypt). See R. Saad, *Egyptian Politics and the Tenancy Law*, in R. Bush, ed., COUNTER-REVOLUTION IN EGYPT'S COUNTRYSIDE 105 (Zed Books 2002).

91 J.S. Oweis, *The Impact of Land Reform on Egyptian Agriculture: 1952-65*, INTERMOUNTAIN ECONOMIC REVIEW 54 (Spring 1971) (reprint published by the University of Wisconsin Land Tenure Center).

92 RDI fieldwork in Egypt confirmed the law's continuing enforcement during the period from the late 1970s until the law's demise. We were surprised to find widespread enforcement of the law, especially after our earlier fieldwork showing the prevailing non-enforcement of landlord-tenant regulations in many parts of Asia.

93 Letter from R. Prosterman, Professor University of Washington School of Law, and Jeffrey Riedinger (now Professor and Dean of International Studies and Programs, Michigan State University), to Dr. Youssef Wally, Minister of Agriculture Egypt (July 12, 1984) (on file with the Rural Development Institute) [hereinafter the Wally Letter].

94 See id. at 6. "We would ourselves most prefer an alternative that reflects the fact that the 'registered tenants' are much more like *owners* – and have been for 30 years – than the nominal 'owners' who were the previous landlords of the land. Our own preference would thus be to ultimately transfer *full ownership* directly to the present registered tenants. Possibly this could be done through increasing the payment by the registered tenants to the old owners by 50% or thereabouts, to be made during the next 30 years, but treating those payments as full and final payments for **ownership** of the land. Thus, from the year 2015 onward, all such payments would end, and the registered tenant would be the sole owner." (Emphasis in original.)

95 See M. Aal, *Agrarian Reform and Tenancy Problems in Upper Egypt*, Paper presented at South Africa Conference on Land Tenure Issues, Capetown, South Africa, 2001. For a description of landlords' arguments for rollback, see R. Springborg, *State-Society Relations in Egypt: The Debate Over Owner-Tenant Relations*, 45(2) MIDDLE EAST JOURNAL 232, 240 (1991).

96 Law 96 of 1992. See R. Bush, *An Agricultural Strategy Without Farmers: Egypt's Countryside in the New Millennium*, 27(84) REVIEW OF AFRICAN POLITICAL ECONOMY 235 (2000).

97 R. Bush, *Land Reform and Counter-Revolution*, in Bush, supra note 96, at 18.

98 R. Saad, supra note 90, at 106. It is not clear what brought about the apparent decline in percentage of tenanted cropland from 1952 (estimated at 60%). Some of it may have been due to buy-out agreements in which tenants became owners of some, or all, of the land, or landlords became owners (without tenants) of some or all of the land. See the discussion of such processes as seen in India's West Bengal state, in Chapter 6. Some tenant acquisition of land from landlords also occurred in Taiwan

in the period following the initial rent reduction and preceding the program to transfer full ownership. See Chen, supra note 21, at 46-47.

99 Bush, supra note 96, at 238.

100 FIAN International, THE RIGHT TO ADEQUATE FOOD IN EGYPT: FIAN PARALLEL REPORT 11-12 (FIAN 2000).

101 See generally J. Dollard, et al., FRUSTRATION AND AGGRESSION (Yale University Press 1939). The psychological mechanism at work may be regarded as a specific form of "frustration aggression" sometimes referred to as "relative deprivation." See Prosterman & Riedinger, supra note 35, at 7-10, 253-54 nn.1-6; see generally T.R. Gurr, WHY MEN REBEL (Princeton University Press 1970); S. Clark, THE SOCIAL ORIGINS OF THE IRISH LAND WAR (Princeton University Press 1979).

102 One might also wonder about the possible contribution of those tenant or ex-tenant households, or their migrant sons, to the greatly enlarged strength of the Muslim Brotherhood in recent parliamentary elections. See generally I. Johnson, *Islam and Europe: A Volatile Mix Reaching Out to Islam*, WALL STREET JOURNAL EUROPE, Dec. 29, 2005, A-1, European edition. Hopefully, such issues will be the subject of research, perhaps of future doctorial dissertations. Our working hypothesis would be that some fraction of the household members of the one million affected tenant families – to a significantly greater extent than for a "control group" of one million small owner-operator families – have been radicalized, and turned into strong opponents of the Mubarak government, reflected in various kinds of behavior, some though not all of it of a kind open to the inquiry of researchers. See generally Prosterman & Riedinger, supra note 35, at ch. 1.

103 Or there may be lesser bans on tenancy in certain agricultural sectors or on certain kinds of tenancy, such as fixed-rent tenancy.

104 R. Prosterman & P. Li, *South Korea NCM Program: Analysis of Administrative Implementation* (Sept. 19, 2006) (unpublished memorandum on file with the Rural Development Institute). A further variant is seen in Mexico, where non-landholding families received land rights on the *ejidal* enterprises which the great majority of *ejidatarios* chose to farm individually rather than collectively. The resulting individual land rights were perpetual usufruct, unlimited in duration and inheritable by an heir who would directly farm the land. The reform law prohibited the lease (and sale) of such land rights until 1994, although there was widespread evasion. Leasing is now permitted, as are sales under certain conditions. The original Mexican land tenure reform primarily affected large estate lands, rather than existing tenanted lands, and is discussed in Chapter 3.

105 In India, the World Bank calculated the marginal product of labor from agricultural cultivation compared with the wage rate of casual agricultural labor, concluding "that both males and females obtain a value marginal product of about Rs 150 per day engaged in agricultural self-cultivation. . . . Noting that the casual wage rate in agriculture as well as non-agriculture is less than Rs 50 per day, it appears that land rental provides a very attractive opportunity to improve household well-being even after subtracting the rental payment." World Bank, INDIA: LAND POLICIES FOR GROWTH AND POVERTY REDUCTION 75 (Oxford 2007). Indeed, even if we assume and subtract a relatively high 50% share cropping rental, the net remuneration per cultivator-day from tenant farming appears to be more than one-and-a-half times that from casual wage labor in (or out of) agriculture (Rs 75 versus less than Rs 50). This is a huge difference for a poor rural family.

106 On this issue of ability to invest, see also Chapter 7 on China.

107 See generally H. de Soto, THE MYSTERY OF CAPITAL: WHY CAPITALISM TRIUMPHS IN THE WEST AND FAILS EVERYWHERE ELSE (Basic Books 2000). This highly popular book focuses, however, on land that is held, or supposedly held, insecurely by the poor –

without formalization of their rights – but not on cases where such land is already owned by private landlords and such "formalization" would entail redistributive land reform.

108 See generally UNFAO, supra note 1.

109 We exclude the ending of rare successful programs: the deliberate and seemingly disastrous (from the tenants' point of view) dismantling of the rare successful landlord-tenant regulation program in Egypt, discussed above, as well as the eventual ending or reduction of restrictions in the small residual landlord-tenant sectors of Taiwan and Japan after decades of successful implementation, done at a time when those had become fully developed market economies, with much smaller agricultural populations and extensive non-agricultural opportunities.

110 See Brown, supra note 3, at 23.

111 This was not an issue in Mexico, where any existing "tenant" of an *ejidatario* – his tenancy illegal under the old rule but now legal under the new – was there only because the *ejidatario* wanted him there.

112 Such fieldwork should embrace, besides those potentially affected families, others who are stakeholders or knowledgeable: landlords (who may be more candid about their incentives under deregulation than some might expect), the rural poor not presently benefiting from regulation, government and village officials, local NGOs, local academics, etc.

113 Taking care, however, not to introduce too soon any mode of listing likely to be biased in favor of the potential "big" tenant. RDI saw an impressive example of an accessible marketplace for information on urban residential property in Wuhan City, China, in 1998, apparently repeated in many other Chinese cities. See B. Schwarzwalder, *Land Planning Report, Shekou Township, Hubei Province, Xindeng Township, Zhejiang Province* (Jan. 28, 1999) (unpublished memorandum on file with the Rural Development Institute); R. Prosterman, *Small Township Development Project Land Market Assessment Final Report*, Dec. 1998 (unpublished memorandum on file with the Rural Development Institute).

114 FAO, supra note 1, at point 6.

115 See E. Sadoulet, R. Murgai & A. De Janvry, *Access to Land via Land Rental Markets*, in A. De Janvry, et al., eds., ACCESS TO LAND, RURAL POVERTY, AND PUBLIC ACTION 211-212 (Oxford University Press 2001); M. Kevane, *Agrarian Structure and Agricultural Practice: Typology and Application to Western Sudan*, 78(1) AMERICAN JOURNAL OF AGRICULTURAL ECONOMICS 236-45 (1996); C. Pant, *Tenancy and Family Resources: A Model and Some Empirical Analysis*, 12(1-2) JOURNAL OF DEVELOPMENT ECONOMICS 27-39 (1983); E. Skoufias, *Household Resources, Transaction Costs, and Adjustment through Land Tenancy*, 71(1) LAND ECONOMICS 42-56 (1995); G. Parthasarthy, *Lease Market, Poverty Alleviation and Policy Options*, 26(13) ECONOMIC AND POLITICAL WEEKLY A31-A38 (30 Mar. 1991); G.K. Chadha & S.K. Bhaumik, *Changing Tenancy Relations in West Bengal: Popular Notions, Grassroots Realities*, 27(19) ECONOMIC & POLITICAL WEEKLY 1009-1017, 1089-1098 (1992). Of farmers renting in land in Nicaragua, 80% were found to be completely landless. K. Deininger, E. Zegarra & I. Lavandenz, *Determinants and Impacts of Rural Land Market Activity: Evidence from Nicaragua*, 31(8) WORLD DEVELOPMENT 1385, 1393 (2003). In Uganda land rental markets were found to provide access to land for those in need, especially the landless. See generally K. Deininger & P. Mpuga, *Land Markets in Uganda: Incidence, Impact, and Evolution over Time*, World Bank Discussion Paper 347 (World Bank 2003).

116 See Sadoulet, Murgai & De Janvry, supra note 115, at 211. See discussion of reverse tenancy arrangements occurring in the former Soviet Union in Section VII of Chapter 7.

117 See the discussion of the generally greater productivity of small farms in less-developed country settings in Chapter 3.

118 Because of the likely much greater political resistance, we would be inclined not to make such a rule applicable to renewal of existing leases after the law's effective date, but only to such new leases as enlarged the big "tenant" holding to a size exceeding, or further exceeding, the ceiling.

119 Another potential arena, at least over the longer term, may be Pakistan, with large feudal landlords still playing a huge role in the society. S.S. Hasan, *Feudal Shadow Over Pakistan Elections*, 2008, available at http://news.bbc.co.uk/2/hi/south_asia/7239466.stm. Past land-to-the-tiller efforts have been lackadaisical at best, and have withered under the heat of landlord opposition, but the need to do something significant about the land issue is great and seems likely to grow even greater. However, Herring concludes that the 1959 and 1972 reforms together succeeded in resuming and redistributing only a tiny percentage of total farm area (the 1959 reform "resumed" about 3.9% of farmland – but did not distribute all of it – the 1972 reform "redistributed" about 2.5% of farmland; landowners could choose which land they would keep, so that "a great deal of land resumed ... was waste"). Herring, supra note 71, at 98, 112. Khan concludes that the latest, January 1977 reform was a subject of "benign neglect" under the military government that overthrew the Bhutto government in July that same year, giving miniscule actual figures for resumption. M.H. Khan supra note 71, at 183-184, and note 62, at 190.

3 Redistributing land to agricultural laborers

Roy L. Prosterman

This chapter will focus primarily on land redistribution affecting all types of large agricultural estates in which all or the bulk of the land is operated as a single production unit, and on which workers who are not the landowner or members of the landowner's family provide the great majority of the labor.[1] This includes privately owned plantation land, haciendas (a term sometimes used in the Latin American setting to refer to large estates not used intensively or effectively), and other large farms or ranches (the latter being of interest for reform especially where land suitable for crop production is instead being used to graze animals). Also included are public or state lands, and plantations operated by private corporations using state land (as in Indonesia).[2]

This chapter complements Chapter 2. The two chapters together cover the main potential beneficiary groups – respectively, tenant farmers and agricultural laborers – that stand to benefit from land tenure reform programs in settings of traditional, non-collectivized agriculture. These groups have in common the fact that their predominant source of livelihood comes from cultivating land owned by others.[3]

Large estates worked by agricultural laborers are found today in Latin America, and in some portions of Africa that were temperate enough to attract European colonists to farming. They are also found in scattered parts of Asia, especially in the Philippines, but also in a minor agricultural role in places such as Indonesia (state lands privately worked) and India. The Rural Development Institute has worked in a number of countries where these issues have been salient, among them El Salvador, pre-collectivization Nicaragua, Brazil, the Philippines, Indonesia and India. And, while we discuss issues relating to the possible break-up and privatization of collective farms (with a special focus on China) in Chapter 7, it should be borne in mind that there are some interesting parallels there to issues and questions that may arise from the break-up of large estates and the distribution of those estate lands to agricultural workers. These include the impact of eliminating supervision and shedding "free rider" problems, the possibility for increases in motivation and production, issues surrounding marketability of individualized land rights, and prospects for other kinds of empowerment of the beneficiaries.

The discussion in this chapter proceeds in four sections. The first highlights the main features likely to differentiate land tenure reform programs benefiting agricultural laborers from those benefiting tenant farmers. The second section reviews the global evidence as to whether larger operational holdings may be characterized by "economies of scale," an argument sometimes made for exempting such holdings from land tenure reform legislation. The third section discusses major themes and substantive lessons as to what types of land tenure reform provisions have been most likely to provide actual benefit to agricultural laborers. The final section discusses practical lessons gleaned for designing future programs to distribute estate land to agricultural laborers in countries where this issue may arise.

I.   Distinct characteristics of reforms to benefit estate laborers

Identification of land to be taken

The first major difference between reforms to redistribute estate land and reforms to redistribute tenanted land relates to identifying the extent of the landlord's holding. When tenant farmers are the intended beneficiaries, there is almost always a wide discrepancy between the amount of land the landlord owns and the size of each farm operated by the landlord's tenants. However, when laborers on plantations or other large holdings are the intended beneficiaries, the size of the holding owned is the size of the farm operated.[4]

That is, in tenancy settings a single owner holds land rights with respect to numerous separate holdings operated by individual tenants. The visible facts on the ground with respect to each operational holding thus do not normally reveal how much total land any particular landlord owns. Where a land-to-the-tiller law prohibits landlords from retaining ownership of any tenanted land, the extent of the landlord's holdings do not affect the redistribution since as soon as the program administrator finds that a specific piece of land is tenant-cultivated, he knows that such land is to be taken from the landlord and transferred to that tenant farmer. However, in any land reform program that allows the landlord to retain ownership of tenanted land above a specific ceiling, the program administrator is faced with the task of determining the total amount of tenanted land owned by each landlord. As we saw in Chapter 2 (and as also discussed in Chapter 6 in the specific context of India), this is likely to be a highly demanding undertaking, and it is often the case that a significant portion of the anticipated "above ceiling" land eludes successful capture.

By contrast, the taking of land in estates that are above a certain size usually avoids these problems since the size of the holding owned equals the size of the holding as it is actually operated. Once the program administrator views the operational holding on the ground (or looks at a map or an aerial or satellite image of known scale), he can make a well-informed initial judgment as to whether the holding exceeds the ceiling size established by law. If the holding exceeds the ceiling, the law may require the government to acquire all or a portion of the estate.[5] Thus, the application of quantitative ceilings on ownership in order to identify lands subject to the reform is likely to be much simpler and more assured in the taking of large estates.[6]

However, this may not be the end of the land identification story, for many laws intended to take large operational holdings have introduced additional qualitative factors rarely if ever found in laws intended to take tenanted land. These may create problems which can be just as great as the land identification problems present in land-to-the-tiller reforms.

Capital stripping

Large estates often employ machinery, or have herds of animals or other moveable property, that is not under the continuous control of specific workers. Thus, where the estate owner has advance notice of a coming reform that will encompass his lands – and especially to the extent that payment will be below market value or deferred or uncertain – he may engage in "capital stripping," clandestinely removing whatever can be moved to some other location. Tenant farms are less likely to contain such landowner-owned moveable property, and what they do contain is likely to be under the immediate control and watchful eye of the tenant. Capital stripping has occurred in El Salvador, Chile, Portugal and other settings where acquisition of estates was either underway or an immediate prospect.[7]

Identification of those who are to benefit

Most reforms affecting tenanted lands have been land-to-the-tiller reforms, with "tiller" used to mean the existing tenant farmers who cultivate particular parcels of land. Some such reforms establish (but have rarely enforced) limits on how much total land a benefiting tenant farmer can receive, with the excess land supposed to go back into the land tenure reform pot for distribution to another qualifying family. And the law may allow the landlord to keep a part of the tenanted land despite the fact that a specific tenant is cultivating that land. But with those two exceptions, nearly all land-to-the-tiller reforms have been designed to transform the tenant into the owner of exactly the same land that he or she presently farms as a tenant. Thus, there is generally an obvious and automatic match between particular beneficiaries and particular pieces of land.

By contrast, there is often no such obvious match when the government takes an estate for distribution. The most likely beneficiaries are, of course, the permanent workers employed on the estate. But the government may not view them as the exclusive beneficiaries.[8] This may be because the resulting amount of land per household seems excessively large. Or it may be because there are other groups who seem at least as needy and equally deserving of land. Such groups might include temporary laborers who work on the holding at peak times of planting and harvest.

Moreover, if policy makers consider the amount of the land that will be available for distribution per household to be very large in relation to the permanent labor force, and even somewhat large relative to the entire existing labor force (including temporary laborers), they may design the reform program to include still other groups. Such additional beneficiaries might, for example, be members of nearby communities that claimed and used the land prior to the creation of the estate; other agricultural laborer families not associated with the estate (including some working in the medium- or small-holding sector); nearby tenant farm households; nearby owner-operators whose holdings are very small; or landless households who make their present living outside agriculture.

In some cases, groups may invade estate lands to occupy and control them by force in the hope that the government will subsequently confer legal rights upon them. This tactic may bring together a variegated group of would-be beneficiaries, perhaps assembled through common political affiliation. This appears true of the Movement of the Landless (MST) in Brazil, whose land-invading groups may also include households of the urban poor.[9] We are unaware of any case in which the attempted self-selection of beneficiaries and identification of land to be taken, via the phenomenon of land invasions, has been encountered in land tenure reforms involving tenanted land.

In cases where the beneficiary group expands beyond permanent laborers on the estate and those temporary laborers or others who live within easy distance of the estate, further questions arise regarding resettlement needs and costs. If resettlement costs are added as part of the government outlays for the land tenure reform program, average costs incurred per household benefited may increase substantially, and prospects for wider replicability of the reform may become less certain.

Land per family benefited

Whenever there is no automatic or nearly automatic link between beneficiaries and land, the question arises as to how much land should be
allocated per household. This question is presented regardless whether
future utilization of that land will be joint or individual. For example,
by what process will program administrators decide whether the
amount of useable land on the estate would yield an "excessive" figure,
if it were divided only by the number of permanent worker households? Clearly the answers to such questions should also take into account the characteristics of the land being taken. Is it cropland or pastureland, irrigated or unirrigated, single-crop or double-crop? If it is
presently used as pasture, is it nonetheless suitable for crop production? The issue of land productivity is sometimes addressed in the law
through the concept of a "standard" hectare as a land unit, with less-
than-average land requiring more than one physical hectare to com-
prise one "standard" hectare, and better-than-average land requiring
less than one physical hectare.[10] Where the pool of program beneficiaries includes groups besides the permanent workers, and land is to be
individually farmed, program guidelines may provide that they shall receive a smaller allocation per household or per capital.

Individual versus joint cultivation

The question of whether beneficiaries should henceforth cultivate the
land individually or jointly almost never arises under land-to-the-tiller
programs in which tenant farmers become owners of the same parcels
they farmed as tenants.[11] Tenant farmers are accustomed to farming individually, and continue to do so after the reform is implemented, but
now with a greater psychological and economic stake in that particular
land and with the motivation to invest in and improve it for the long
term.

By contrast, when the government takes large estates the existing
workforce has, by definition, been working that land – or the great bulk
of it – as a single production unit. Experience has taught, however, that
given a free choice, even permanent workers often prefer to divide the
estate land and cultivate individual parcels that will be identifiably
"theirs," and on which they can realize directly the benefit of the effort
they expend in cultivation.[12] Other beneficiary groups from outside the
estate may be accustomed to working land either individually or in
common, but have no habits of cultivation on the land of the particular
estate.

Thus, the question of subsequent mode-of-operation – i.e., whether
it is to be individual or joint, or perhaps partly both – often arises in an

acute fashion where the government is taking large estates for redistribution. Beyond the threshold question of whether the law should allow beneficiaries to choose the mode of subsequent operation, planners should consider how the program design can ensure that such a choice is reasonably well-informed and freely made. In settings of "export crops" or capital-intensive plantations, some opinion leaders (government officials, union leaders, academics, journalists, etc.) may call for excluding such choice entirely in drafting the enabling law, arguing that it would be economically damaging to allow beneficiaries to subdivide such estates into individual holdings. This point is closely related to our discussion in Section II below.

Limiting transferability and transactability

To the extent the governing rules will require beneficiaries to continue cultivating the estate land as a unitary operation, such rules must logically constrain any subsequent sale or lease of any part of the land less than the whole, or at least any part of the land whose loss would be inconsistent with unitary operation. Even if the law allows sale or lease of the whole estate, the law must require a decision by the enterprise through which the beneficiaries hold the land – often a cooperative in form – to approve such a transaction. Thus, no individual household could separately decide to transfer any portion of jointly owned land.

One important consequence is that there is likely to be a much more limited wealth-creation effect on a jointly owned and non-subdivisible enterprise: children or other heirs who do not wish to live and work on the enterprise would stand to inherit only a very limited benefit, if any, and the original beneficiary households might find few opportunities to "cash out" their interest in the jointly owned land. There are, of course, some intermediate possibilities, such as allowing production cooperatives formed as a result of a land tenure reform to adopt a governing charter under which members can depart and be "bought out" by the enterprise (in effect, by the remaining members) upon departure. This in turn raises the question of how one can diminish the impact of having such a monopsonistic, one-buyer "market"; for example, through requiring third-party appraisal.

Also, if the law is to allow beneficiaries to choose between individual and joint modes of ownership and operation, will the law require the beneficiaries initially to choose one or another outcome with regard to all land and other assets of the enterprise, or can some beneficiaries choose to withdraw a proportionate amount of the land and other assets to use individually? And must the beneficiaries make such a choice once-and-for-all at the beginning, or may beneficiaries make a subsequent choice to subdivide all or a portion of the land and assets, either to operate an individual farm or to sell the land and assets?

II.   "Economies of scale"

Related to the question of subdividing large estates many people assume that smaller farm sizes are a major constraint upon increasing agricultural productivity. Some would then argue either that large estates should not be taken in a land tenure reform program or, if they ever are to be taken, that the law should prohibit any subdivision of that holding, regardless what the beneficiaries might desire if allowed to choose.

However, "[a] large literature has demonstrated that many agricultural activities do not exhibit true economies of scale in production."[13] This is particularly true when agriculture is unmechanized, which is the case in most developing country settings characterized by an abundance of labor and a lack of capital. Most studies find a negative relationship between farm size and productivity (i.e., a larger farm produces less per unit area),[14] and others are unable to reject the hypothesis of constant returns to scale in agricultural production.[15] In fact, a World Bank study asserts that "the literature contains no single example of economies of scale arising for farm sizes exceeding what one family with a medium tractor could comfortably manage."[16] That is, contrary to the conventional wisdom of casual observers, small family farms are almost always more productive than large farms in developing country settings.[17] The few exceptions include cases of highly specialized machinery, livestock production, and certain plantation crops, discussed below.[18]

The exception of plantation crops exists only for certain crops and is related to scale economies for processing and marketing rather than for crop production itself. Plantation crops, especially, are typically characterized by a dualistic system of production in most countries: large farms employing substantial numbers of hired wage labor and small family farms relying mainly on family labor, which is supplemented by casual labor during harvesting seasons. Each mode of production has its own advantages and disadvantages.

The advantage of small family farms – for all crops, including plantation crops – lies in their predominant reliance on the labor of family members. Family members have a strong incentive to work hard for the family's well-being, unlike hired wage laborers, who tend to require close supervision. Thus, any potential economies of scale are offset by costs resulting from the need to monitor the quality and amount of effort expended by plantation workers (or, in the case of a cooperative, "members"). Such costs are sometimes referred to as "agency costs." The need to supervise labor has profound implications for the organization of industrial production, in particular the optimal size of the firm.[19] These agency costs are particularly important in agricultural production due to the large area over which production occurs and the need for the manager or workers to constantly adjust cultivation practices to micro-variations of the natural environment.[20] An estate of 1000 hectares utilizing primarily hired laborers under supervision can, for example, be thought of as a "factory floor" of 10 square kilometers in size – vast almost beyond imagining for any actual industrial factory – where such operations must be carried out. Analysts have long recognized that family-operated farms tend to be superior to wage-operated large-scale agricultural enterprises in this regard because family farms tend to minimize the agency costs.[21]

Considering the unique advantage of family farms in agricultural production, why did large-farm plantation systems originate? Primarily for two reasons. The first – applicable only to certain crops – is that economies of scale can exist at the level of processing or marketing. Vertical integration of a large plantation with a large-scale central processing unit can make sense when the crop is best processed within a short time after harvest. This is the case for palm oil, sisal and certain types of tea.[22] Large-scale production can also have marketing advantages that, in certain settings, may offset disadvantages relating to agency costs. This is particularly true for overseas markets. Traders dealing with commodities in bulk quantities prefer standardized products that are preferably guaranteed by a brand name, which can give large-scale producers advantages.[23] Even despite the possible processing and marketing advantages for certain crops, many of these crops are often grown by small family farms, which address the scale economies in processing or marketing through the use of nuclear estates[24] or marketing cooperatives.

A second reason for the existence of large-scale plantation systems relates to the establishment costs of plantations in many developing country settings. The establishment of many plantations was driven by the sharply increasing demand for many tropical products in the latter half of the 19th century. At that time, many regions physically suited for growing such products were remote, sparsely populated and uncultivated. Opening these lands for growing new crops involved substantial capital for clearing and developing land and constructing the needed physical infrastructure such as roads, irrigation systems and ports. Large farm sizes were necessary for the investors to internalize gains. However, once the infrastructure was developed, the share of smaller family farms in the area tended to increase, particularly where the specific crops did not present significant scale economies in processing and marketing.[25]

In sum, for most crops in most developing country settings, small family farms are more productive than large farms.

The issue of parcel fragmentation is related to farm size, but differs in several respects. An owner's agricultural landholdings may be fragmented – that is, may be spread among separate plots – and this may be true whether the owner owns much land or very little. It might seem intuitively apparent that a single farmer's cultivation of plots located in different places leads to productivity loss, even in the absence of economies of scale, because of increased transport costs among fields and the apparent loss of arable land to boundaries separating fields. However, empirical evidence for such productivity losses is weak. Binswanger argues that the productivity costs of fragmentation are often overstated or, in some cases, even outweighed by benefits that fragmentation may provide.[26] Moreover, of potentially great importance to the farmers themselves in assuring a minimum adequate livelihood, fragmentation can act as an insurance mechanism similar to growing several different crops.[27] It is noteworthy that in China, where average grain yields per hectare are more than double those in India, average farm size is not only small – around two-thirds of a hectare in China versus around two hectares in India – but the average Chinese farm contains more than six parcels.

The general superiority of small farms in developing country settings does not mean, however, that small farms will always remain small. International experience shows that as a country's economy develops, farm size tends to grow because better paying non-agricultural job opportunities gradually attract labor from agriculture to the non-agricultural sector (while the amount of cultivated land remains relatively constant).[28] Moreover, increasing agricultural wages gives farm owners an incentive to replace labor with farm machinery. Thus, farm size is greatly affected by a country's changing factor endowments,[29] and growing farm sizes are a consequence and not a cause of economic development and growth.

There might, however, be additional considerations if the question were one of transforming an existing large estate – by virtue of its acquisition under a land tenure reform program, coupled with giving recipient families the option to farm individually – into a series of much smaller individual farms on the same land. One consideration would be the extent to which there were "sunk costs" on the existing estate. Thus there may be a distinction between modern, capital-intensive, already heavily improved "plantations," and largely unimproved, low utilization "haciendas" (a terminological distinction sometimes used in the Latin American setting), or nominal "ranches" that are really more suitable for planting crops rather than for grazing cattle.

However, not all "sunk costs" are identical, in the sense that many existing capital improvements are fully capable of being utilized by a series of individual small farmers on the same land, and this is especially so if the beneficiaries agree to maintain the same crop or crops on the bulk of the estate's former land.

Still, even if one could thus make a reasonable theoretical argument for acquiring and redistributing plantation land and assets, even where there were large sunk costs, such heavily improved estates are likely to be very costly for the government to acquire under the principle of adequate compensation, a principle which we have argued in Chapter 2 is strongly supported by a series of mutually reinforcing policy considerations. In most settings we believe this cost argument should be dispositive – although only as to portions of the holding that are actually intensively used and capital intensive.

Unimproved haciendas of low productivity, or large "ranches" actually suitable for planting crops, where the land may have even a full market value that is only in the low hundreds of dollars per hectare may be more suitable candidates for acquisition and – if wished by the beneficiaries – subdivision. The same would hold true for portions of plantations not the subject of large sunk costs that remained unimproved or poorly utilized. In these cases, the subdivided land will almost certainly also be more productive than the same land is in its present use, quite apart from any theoretical debate as to the potential productivity of large estates versus small farms.

A further exception, where compensation for land would not be required at all, arises where such underused estates exist on government-owned land on which no private party has any continuing claim of right.[30] But the cases where such an exception might come into play are limited: one can, for example, identify such government-owned estate lands in Indonesia and the Dominican Republic. The preeminent situations of state or publicly owned land with no need for compensation for the land or improvements are, of course, those encountered in formerly centrally planned economies. See the discussion in Chapter 7.

III. Designing programs to benefit agricultural laborers

Many of the differences identified in Section I above, which distinguish the present reforms from those intended to benefit tenant farmers, also figure among the themes in this section, as we examine how programs might be designed to benefit agricultural laborers, chiefly using land from estates or other large operational holdings. And there may also be relevant lessons on program design and benefits to be gleaned both from the termination of collective-farming systems (discussed in Chapter 7), and from programs to allocate individual rights to micro-plots (discussed in Chapter 4 and also in Chapter 6).

Overall experience with success and failure

As compared to land-to-the-tiller programs, it is more difficult to identify clear successes in programs that have taken large estates for allocation to agricultural laborers.[31] For estate agriculture, probably the most notable experiences – in terms of successfully taking most of the land in a dominant estate sector and transferring that land to agricultural workers – have been those of Mexico and Bolivia.[32]

After its 1910 revolution and violent civil war, Mexico undertook an initially delayed and then very gradual program that unfolded from the 1930s to the 1970s, and Bolivia carried out a much quicker program after its much-less-violent 1952 revolution.[33] In both countries, at the time their land tenure reforms began, there was a dominant sector of very large estates,[34] which could be broadly described as having the following characteristics:

- Low productivity and low capital investment, with large areas of the estates suitable for planted crops often used instead as low-intensity pasture.
- A permanent workforce – denominated peons or *colonos* – that often operated without a cash wage and was often "paid" with use of a small piece of land for their work on the dominant central hacienda.[35]
- A broader system having many characteristics that might be described as feudal: workers were often tied permanently to the estate by debt or custom, owed money to the "company store," were returned by the police if they sought to run away, and were otherwise completely within the power domain of the landowner.[36]

Interestingly, from the beginning the Mexican and Bolivian land reforms clearly allowed beneficiaries on the redistributed estates freely to choose to farm individually. As a result, well over 90% of beneficiaries on Mexico's reform *ejidos* chose individual farming, and the proportion choosing individual farming was similarly high in Bolivia.[37]

The Mexican land tenure reform was unusual, and seemingly unique, in being carried out in "slow motion," over a period of roughly four decades. After its completion, it was estimated by Thiesenhusen that the reform had reached "about half the farmland in Mexico," and that "some 3.1 million peasant families are *ejidatarios*."[38] This would appear to have been very roughly 65% of total agricultural households at that time.[39] To be an individually cultivating *ejidatario*, until the recent changes discussed below, meant having perpetual usufructuary rights to arable land (but not to pasture land or forest, which were held in common under the Mexican *ejido*), which could be passed by inheritance but not sold or leased. See Box 3.1.

The 1952-1956 Bolivian land reform appears to have distributed over three-quarters of all cropland and over half of all pastureland[40] to around a quarter-million peasant families, or around 49% of total agricultural households at the time of the reform.[41] The land was generally granted in ownership to the individual beneficiaries and could be sold, but not leased out or mortgaged. Titling of beneficiaries proceeded very slowly, with only a minority apparently titled even four decades after the reform.[42]

One might speculate that the giving of choice as to mode of farming, and the perceived benefit of individual farming pursuant to that choice, were important in mobilizing grass-roots political and psychological support for carrying through the Mexican reform and maintaining at least the bulk of the Bolivian reform against the opposition of estate owners who were receiving little or no compensation. Certainly, the existence and accommodation of strong beneficiary preferences as to mode of farm organization are significant factors in determining whether the relevant social, political and economic forces will combine to produce a consistently implemented land tenure reform program.

RDI's own research with agricultural laborers in both the Philippines and Nicaragua (the latter conducted on the eve of the Sandinista's initially collectivist reform, which later moved substantially to individual farming) appeared to indicate that the great majority of these workers, given a free choice, would choose individual farming rather than a unitary cooperative or collective organization of production. Indeed, on the initially seized Samoza lands in Nicaragua, a flexible mix of individual holdings, small co-ops, and larger units were allowed.[43]

On the other hand, there have been settings in which intense organizational or ideological considerations seemed to have led beneficiaries to support the idea of unitary operation, at least at the leadership level, and brought initial successes in the taking of estate lands. For example, the militant left in Portugal in 1975-1977 after the overthrow of the long dictatorship, and the *campesino* unions in El Salvador in 1980-1981 in the midst of the civil war, were intent upon creating unitary large enterprises that could maintain a high level of common mobilization for political or even (in El Salvador) mutual-protection purposes. A similar militancy and desire for unitary operation appears characteristic on the estates expropriated in Brazil in recent years after occupation by groups formed by the Movement of the Landless.[44]

Box 3.1 Factor productivity after the Mexican land tenure reform

One study that provides an unusually comprehensive picture of the relative efficiency of large farms, small farms and collective farms was carried out in the Mexican district of Laguna in 1967 by Shlomo Eckstein for the World Bank. It included large private farmers with an average of 93.9 cultivated hectares each; small private farmers with an average of 3.8 cultivated hectares each; *ejidatarios* farming individual plots averaging 2.2 cultivated hectares each that were distributed in the Mexican land reform process; and *ejidatarios* farming collectively on land reform holdings whose per-family aliquot share would average 2.5 cultivated hectares (nationwide, 10% or fewer of *ejidal* families opted to farm collectively). Cotton was the largest single crop in the district, but a number of other crops were grown. What emerged was a sophisticated and persuasive picture of relative agricultural performance, which called forth this judgment as to the small-owner farms and individual *ejidatarios* groups from the World Bank analysts: "Together these two groups, which have small individually operated farms, are clearly above the larger farm operations – private or collective – on all measure of total factor productivity, i.e., in general economic efficiency."

The study looked closely at the gross value of production per hectare, versus the value of all of the inputs that went into such production: land value, capital invested, purchased inputs, cost of hired labor, and imputed value of owner's family labor.

For "total factor productivity," that is, gross value of production divided by value of all inputs, the small farmers showed a ratio of 1.29, the individual *ejidos* 1.24, the large farmers 1.15 and the collective *ejidos* were loss-making at 0.90. Thus, the individual *ejidos* had a total factor productivity that was 38% greater than the collective *ejidos* (1.24/0.90), and 8% greater than the pre-existing large farms (1.24/1.15). At 1.29, the pre-existing small farms did even better.[45]

Source: S. Eckstein, et al., *Land Reform in Latin America: Bolivia, Chile, Mexico, Peru, and Venezuela,* World Bank Staff Working Paper No. 275 (World Bank 1978). See also R. Prosterman & J. Riedinger, LAND REFORM AND DEMOCRATIC DEVELOPMENT 57-60, 261 (Johns Hopkins 1987), from which portions of the above are adapted.

Whether due to their initial cooperativist bent, or for other reasons, and in contrast to the programs in Mexico and Bolivia that gave beneficiaries a choice as to the mode of operation from the beginning, programs intended to take estate land primarily to benefit agricultural laborers have fallen considerably short of meeting goals or perceived needs in Brazil, Peru, Colombia, El Salvador, the Philippines, South Africa, Namibia, and Portugal, among others. Of these, the most success was achieved in Peru and El Salvador. In Peru, the most significant aspect of the reform was that which took the large coastal plantations; after roughly a decade of unitary operation, most of these expropriated estates were broken up by the beneficiaries to farm individually.[46] In El Salvador, the largest size-category of estates, those over 500 hectares, were taken; but political will was insufficient to follow up by implementing the land tenure reform law with respect to the more numerous medium-large size-category of estates down to a ceiling of 100-150 hectares.[47] Apart from programs focused on large estates, other programs have been intended to set ceilings low enough to capture portions of non-tenanted holdings operated by medium- or even smaller-size owners, chiefly to benefit paid agricultural laborers working in that sector. These have almost all been failures, for reasons discussed below. The experience with such programs in India is further explored in Chapter 6.

The current program in Zimbabwe, which has now taken most of the former large-estate land, may be said to be *sui generis* and does not qualify as a "reform" in any normal sense of that word. It was not implemented for the benefit of agricultural workers; most allocations appear to have gone to well-connected cronies of President Mugabe, and recent estimates are that over 80% of the 4,500 former white-owned commercial farms are no longer even in production.[48] Indeed, the normal core group of beneficiaries for such a land distribution – the permanent workers on the estates – seem largely to have been driven off those lands by threats and violence at the hands of thugs organized by Mugabe's ruling party.[49]

While the misallocation was less extreme, there is some analogy to the post-independence Kenyan allocations of rural land, beginning in the 1960s and sporadically continuing for decades. Many of these programs, largely distributing land acquired from large white-owned farms that were established in the colonial era (but later extended and including so-called "public" lands) were carried out in the Rift Valley. In initial planning, "it was intended that settlement areas would be taken up by communities already living in adjacent areas – so allowing local communities to 'take back' lands that they had claimed prior to the advent of European settlement, or to take ownership of lands upon which they may have 'squatted' as tied labourers over many years."[50] But things turned out differently under the successive presidencies of Jomo Kenyatta and Daniel arap Moi, with a combination of ethnic Kikuyu from other geographic areas and persons who were better-connected preempting many of the local poor as recipients, who were ethnic Kalenjin and who often considered the land as originally or historically theirs.

These grievances, stirred up by local and national politicians, gave rise to episodes of substantial violence and displacement in 1992 and 1997, and most recently in January-February 2008 after the disputed national election of December 2007. Many of those displaced appear to be Kikuyu who are perceived as having earlier displaced rightful Kalenjin holders, but the large, new, commercial and politically connected landholders in the Rift Valley seem at least as much precipitators as the Kikuyu settlers.[51]

Focus on the poor

Apart from the crippling impact of inadequate financing and compensation arrangements common to both kinds of programs, programs to redistribute estate lands have given rise to a varied litany of design flaws often different from those found in programs targeting tenanted lands. These are flaws that make it difficult to replicate the estate programs broadly or achieve a comprehensive reform.

One persistent feature of programs to redistribute estate land has been a tendency to include too few beneficiaries relative to the amount of land intended to be taken. Thus, there has been little or no prospect, even if there were full implementation of the program, that most potential beneficiary families would be reached. One such flaw is the establishment of an unreasonably large "minimum" amount of land to be distributed per beneficiary family. Where the minimum distributed holding is unreasonably large, the program exhausts the available land long before reaching most of the potential beneficiary universe.[52] This may be considered an example of what has elsewhere been called the "purse of gold" phenomenon.[53] We have referred in note 49 to the unduly large 60-hectare average distribution made in the earlier phase of Zimbabwe's reform.[54] Brazil now employs a 30-hectare per family target,[55] far too high when considering the number of needy families, likely available land and costs. South Africa is apparently now emphasizing the creation of so-called "commercial" black-owned farms, as distinct from smallholder farms, on acquired land.[56]

Except for the last example – which may also deliberately deemphasize the poorest as beneficiaries – the foregoing country programs appear at least broadly neutral on the question of which categories of beneficiaries would receive the generous per capita benefits being contemplated. In contrast, other country programs (besides South Africa currently) have limited the program's reach and pro-poor impact by targeting a narrow group of households to be benefited. This can be seen in the distribution of large plantations in Peru,[57] of estates exceeding 500 hectares in El Salvador,[58] and the large estates that became *asentamientos* in Chile.[59] Each of these reforms substantially limited the class of beneficiaries to the well-organized permanent laborers on those plantations. Each of these foregoing reforms also contemplated, at least initially, the continuing operation of the holding as a single unit, probably in each case reflecting the proclivities of the union leadership or affiliated political movement that had demanded the reform. RDI saw this directly in its own field research during the land reforms in El Salvador.[60]

In the ongoing (if just barely) allocation of financial grants for land tenure reform beneficiaries in South Africa, under the program of Land Redistribution for Agricultural Development LRAD, at least some provinces appear to interpret the legal rules to limit beneficiaries to permanent laborers on the affected large (white-owned) farms. When thus interpreted, as one analyst notes, "LRAD will do little to redistribute wealth, income, and skills to the poorest people in the Province."[61]

The Indonesian land reform of the early 1960s, which set a low enough ceiling to have affected medium and even smaller non-tenanted holdings (as small as five hectares), was supposed to ensure that at the end of the program the beneficiaries would each own 2 hectares of agricultural land, even though most of the actual farming was on a far smaller scale than that at the time.[62] The first priority group for beneficiaries, under the Indonesian law, moreover, was "cultivators who cultivate the land concerned," followed by "permanent peasant laborers . . . who cultivate the land concerned," with "peasants or other peasant laborers" (the latter a very large group including itinerant or temporary agricultural laborers) listed only in eighth place.[63] Little land acquisition or redistribution, however, actually occurred.

Many of the foregoing examples of high per-household minimums or a stringently narrow beneficiary group can probably be traced at least in part to variations of the persistent and erroneous view that larger farms are better, and that there are economies of scale. Another potent factor, however, is that in many settings the poorest rural families are less likely to be literate, less likely to be connected to various activist groups, and generally less able to give effective voice to their needs.[64]

Another reason programs become restricted in scope and non-replicable is excessive cost per family benefited. Flaws in the procedures for calculating compensation for land to be acquired – discussed below in the sub-section on compensation – may sometimes lead to excessive compensation, thereby raising the cost of the program per beneficiary. This appears to have been a problem in the earlier land reform in Venezuela, in the Brazilian land reform, and perhaps in at least some of the "market-assisted land reform" programs promoted by the World Bank in Brazil, South Africa, and elsewhere.[65]

Resettlement

A sub-case of excessive cost per family benefited also arises where planners define the beneficiary group to encompass families that live sufficiently far from the land being distributed to require program administrators to resettle the families closer to the land. Such cases are, for example, found with respect to land-invading groups in Brazil and Indonesia, to the extent the government then legally acknowledges their claims. (It has also been found in programs to reallocate supposedly vacant and already publicly owned land located at a long distance from beneficiaries, in settings such as Indonesia and the Philippines.[66]) Resettlement programs are costly. Even if resettlement is to be on lands already under cultivation, side-by-side with an existing farm-laborer population – so that the government need not bear costs to open up new lands, support settlers until new crops are planted and harvested for the first time, or establish marketing outlets – other resettlement costs are likely to arise for housing, schools, medical facilities and other basic infrastructure. Even where resettlement costs are incurred in an effort to reach poorer groups in the rural population, such as casual, non-permanent laborers, resettlement often does not represent the best or most cost-effective way of extending land rights to such families.

Criteria for acquiring land

Most land reform laws intended to use compulsion to acquire estate, ranch or similar large-scale unitary operations proceed by establishing a maximum size limit for such holdings. The government then uses the maximum in one of two ways: either (1) it acquires land that exceeds the ceiling, or (2) it acquires all land in the holding. However, many laws aimed at taking land from large-scale holdings set forth additional criteria that must be satisfied for the land to be subject to acquisition. These additional criteria often make the taking process far more complicated and uncertain than it would have been if based solely on the quantity of land in the holding. Some examples of such additional criteria:

– Only lazy, "underutilized," or "uncultivated" land in the holding will be taken, or such land will be taken first, followed only later by other land in the holding.[67]
– "Intensively used" holdings (i.e., holdings that are capital-intensive or have been the subject of significant investment) are not subject to taking.[68]

- A further quantitative standard, often based on land quality or supposed productive capacity, is used in parallel with a purely quantitative area maximum.[69]
- An even more layered and complicated formula is used to determine whether the holding qualifies for taking (in Brazil, one study
  suggested the ceiling law's application in one southern state would
  exempt holdings with at least 30,000 hectares of grazing land or
  21,000 hectares of unused land).[70]

Such criteria may be very difficult to apply consistently, either because
they require complex factual determinations or because they grant too
much discretion to program administrators.

Such problems are greatly compounded when the law also provides
that the landowner's claims that his land is not properly subject to taking under the law must be adjudicated in court before the government
can physically take and distribute the land. A far better approach is one
in which the law authorizes the agency administering the program to
make an initial determination that the land is subject to taking, which
the law then deems a sufficient basis for the agency to take the land
and redistribute it to the beneficiaries. The owner may contest the taking by filing a claim in court, whereupon the agency pays the appropriate compensation into the court, to be held by the court pending final
adjudication of the owner's claim.[71] If the owner wins, he gets his land
back (plus some fair recompense for the interval when he lost possession); if he loses, he receives the money that was paid into court (or
more money, if he successfully persuades the court that the proffered
compensation is insufficient). This approach also motivates the owner
to seek a rapid determination of his claims, in contrast to the no-physi-
cal-taking-until-formal-adjudication approach, in which owners are
usually motivated to seek protracted delay in the adjudication.

Public or state lands

An important use of public lands in some parts of the world takes the
form of a reservation for use by the local rural poor as "common property resources" (CPR).[72] Sometimes, however, these benefits are appro-
priated by local elites, as in densely populated east and central Java,
where such traditional community lands (*tanah bengkok*) are now used
as "village salary lands," in very generous allocations in lieu of cash salaries to the elected village officials.[73] One of the most striking historical
examples of appropriation of such village common lands by elites was
the Enclosure Movement in England, in which the landed gentry, over
the course of more than a century, were able (largely through indivi-

dual acts of Parliament) to separate or "enclose" most CPRs and add them to their private estates.[74]

Where local CPRs still exist, they are sometimes used for the common grazing of animals and sometimes for individual crop-growing under short-term allocations to the needy. The challenge today is often the preservation of the remaining CPRs against individualization and full privatization – for example, by auction to the highest bidder – under the heavy pressures of population growth, urbanization and increased land values.

It sometimes occurs that planners propose using areas of supposedly unused public lands as a source for land to be redistributed to the landless.[75] Sometimes such lands can, indeed, make a significant contribution to meeting the needs of the landless (see the discussion of land allocation programs in India's Andhra Pradesh state, in Chapter 6). But over the years there has been a series of reasons why "solving the land problem through distribution of public lands" proves to be unsatisfactory:

– In the government's records, located perhaps in a far away capital city, the land is shown as "unused." But in fact it is being used, largely by the rural poor, forming part of what they regard as local CPRs, perhaps under long-established customary regimes of use and allocation.

– If the land is not being used but is near to needy populations, this may signal that it is of very poor quality and not suitable for productive agricultural use.

– If the land is not being used but is distant in location, the government will be faced with the manifold problems and high costs (discussed above) of resettling beneficiaries to those distant areas. Only where such resettlement is *sua sponte*, self-initiated, and largely unsubsidized (as under the U.S. Homestead Acts) is there likely to be a prospect for widespread replication.

Land invasion

Land invasions, which almost always relate to land in large estates and almost never to tenanted land, raise difficult issues of policy, law and politics. In considering whether the law should, at least in some circumstances, recognize land invaders as rightholders on the invaded lands, a series of questions should be answered:

First, would the land that has been invaded have been subject to distribution under existing land tenure reform laws and regulations (even if the government has routinely failed to follow the law's procedure for land acquisition)? If the land would not have been subject to distribution even under proper procedures, the case for recognizing invaders must be considered severely weakened.

Second, does a present private rightholder claim existing rights regarding the land invaded? If the land is neither privately claimed nor subject to an ongoing valid lease or concession from the state, the invaders' case is likely to appear more acceptable.

Third, have the invaders excluded the pre-existing labor force on the invaded holding from receiving benefits? Normally that labor force would be a priority group in benefiting from the taking of that land under a land tenure reform law. Inclusion of the existing workers, as in Brazil, rather than exclusion, as in Zimbabwe, builds a far more plausible case for legalizing the invasion (assuming the invaders themselves have some claim to be members of at least some potential beneficiary group under land tenure reform, and even this apparently is often not the case in Zimbabwe).

Fourth, do the invaders act under some historical claim of right, even if any relevant period of limitations for bringing such a claim has expired? Put another way, is this largely a newly forged or *ad hoc* group of claimants, or are they the remnants of, or direct successors to, historical occupants of these same lands? Such a historical factor may help legitimize the invaders' claim to recognition, subject, however, to questions of social and political stability discussed below.

Where the core beneficiary group of permanent laborers have themselves seized estate land, this should perhaps not even be classified as a "land invasion." This becomes still more complicated in a setting like that of the tea plantations of the state of West Bengal in India, where seizures by a plantation's labor force have occurred: (a) on plantations that are excluded from the land reform *ab initio*, by virtue of their crop[76] but (b) on which the labor force has not been paid for an extended period, and thus may have a lien on the enterprise's assets – including its land – for unpaid wages, but again (c) on which there has simply been direct self-help through seizure of the land rather than formal enforcement of the possible wage lien according to procedures prescribed by law.

Beyond specifically legal questions, any land invasion raises broader issues relating to social and political stability. Notably, will recognition of one or a few groups of existing land invaders as rightholders trigger a wave of additional land invasions? Moreover, is there a danger that widespread and formally illegal land invasions might lead to a violent response by large landowners and their allies, perhaps even to a coup d'etat or civil war? This question may also be related to the government's willingness and ability to pay appropriate and credible compensation to landowners who lose their land through invasions: an ability which grows less credible if invasions become widespread and extend to highly valuable capital-intensive holdings. Such a reaction by the landowners and their allies may be a real danger in some settings and historically was probably at least a significant factor in catalyzing Franco's ultimately successful seizure of power in Spain through the civil war of 1936-1939 and the Brazilian generals' coup d'etat and overthrow of a weak democratic regime in 1965.[77]

Outright reversals

The most striking case of reversal of a land tenure reform in which estates were taken occurred in Guatemala, following a 1954 coup against the regime of Jacobo Arbenz. This is now widely recognized as having been collusively organized by the United Fruit Company – which had seen around two-thirds of its vast, but largely unused, banana plantations expropriated for a compensation based on the previously declared tax value of about US$8.20 per hectare[78] – and (via the CIA) the United States, which feared "communist" incursions. For the United States this marked a stunning reversal of its post-war record of support for land tenure reforms in Japan, Taiwan and South Korea (although the U.S. was later to return to support for land tenure reform in South Vietnam and even in Guatemala's Central American neighbor, El Salvador, as well as theoretically but largely ineffectively having supported land tenure reform under Kennedy's "Alliance for Progress"). After the coup, virtually all of the Guatemalan land tenure reform was reversed.[79]

Another example of a partial reversal was the experience in Chile following the military coup against Salvador Allende in 1973 (which was largely motivated by concerns unrelated to the land tenure reform). About half of the land tenure reform beneficiaries[80] were allowed to retain about 57%, by value, of the estate lands previously expropriated. The new military government largely subdivided the land into family holdings, something most beneficiaries had apparently wished to do from early in the reform, but had been forestalled from doing both by an initial legislated moratorium on subdivision and by an ideology that had favored cooperative farms. But the new government sold off the machinery and animals to pay off debts previously amassed by the cooperatives and also cut off credit to the new individual farmers, leading many to sell their land.[81]

The violent reactions to land invasions in 1930s Spain and 1960s Brazil, and the reversals of formal, legislated land acquisitions in 1950s Guatemala (and partial reversal in 1970s Chile) are sobering. They remind the designers of land tenure reforms, and emphatically so in democratic settings, that they must make informed and reasonable efforts to take the interests of existing landowners into account.[82]

A further point of interest is that there have been no outright reversals of land-to-the-tiller reforms that predominantly gave in-place ownership rights to existing tenants in the traditional developing country
settings. This suggests, perhaps, that stronger ties come out of individual ownership rights and are politically harder to undo. The nearest
thing to an exception would be under communism, in China's collectivization of farmland (not a return to the former owners, but a disaster
in its own right) in the mid-1950s, after first purportedly giving it in
ownership to tenant farmers. The Chinese experience is discussed in
Chapter 7.

Compensation issues

Most compensation issues related to takings of estate land are similar
to those discussed for acquisitions of tenanted lands in Chapter 2. But
several matters concerning compensation, while not inherently limited
to land tenure reforms involving large estates, have tended to arise primarily in relation to such lands: (1) arrangements leading to above-market compensation, (2) "market-assisted land reform," (3) restitution, (4)
enforcement of wage liens, and (5) equity in lieu of land.

Arrangements leading to above-market compensation have occasionally
been present in programs to acquire large estates. Examples are found
in the limited land tenure reforms in Venezuela in the 1950s and
1960s and currently in Brazil. The essential problem in the rules governing compensation in these cases has been that the fair market price
of land existing just prior to the program has not served as a limit on
compensation paid. In the Venezuelan case, with respect to the earlier
land tenure reform attempt of the 1950s and 1960s, "this oil-rich country . . . paid handsome compensation to landowners whose estates were
expropriated."[83] The law did not specify that the program itself was not
intended to bid up the land price from what it would have been in the
absence of the program.[84] Consequently, prices asked by landowners
skyrocketed and, as one consequence, the program shifted away from
its original focus on taking and distributing cultivated private lands to
a much more dubious emphasis on largely unused (and perhaps unu-
sable) public lands. In Brazil, the ultimate possibility of expropriation
by the government exists, but only after potentially protracted litigation
in the courts and the satisfying of complex threshold criteria stated in
the law; thus, the government often takes the easier path of agreeing
on a "negotiated price," frequently resulting in payments well above
the previous market price.[85]

Market-assisted land reform is, as the name suggests, an approach by
which the government (or beneficiaries subsidized by government
grants or loans) aims to acquire land through voluntary sales at, or

close to, pre-existing market price, although in theory accompanied by the motivating factor for the landowners that the government might invoke compulsory taking procedures under existing law if too few landowners are willing to negotiate. This approach has been used in recent years in World Bank-supported programs to acquire estate lands in Brazil, South Africa and elsewhere.

Questions have arisen as to possible excessive compensation to landowners under this approach and as to other matters involving program design. In many settings, existing land markets are quite "thin," involving relatively few transactions. If, for example, the setting is one in which only 1% or 2% of estate land would "normally" come onto the market for sale each year, but the population of landless laborers is so sizeable that one might want to acquire 50% of the estate land, then to carry out a full-scale program over a 10-year period would involve an average acquisition of 5% of the estate land per year. But such a large increase in estate land coming onto the market is highly unlikely unless the existing "market" price increases greatly. It would seem likely that a government could acquire such large amounts of land at the pre-existing market price only by invoking eminent domain powers and compulsorily acquiring that land rather than relying upon voluntary negotiation.

Moreover, if there is to be an acquisition on a negotiated basis through the land-acquiring beneficiaries (to whom the government then loans the funds to make the purchase) and the owner who is selling his land, extensive safeguards may be needed to ensure that an adequate amount of land of appropriate quality and location is acquired, within the maximum land costs permitted.

The redistribution aspect of the South African program has proceeded almost entirely on a market-assisted basis without expropriatory takings and has moved slowly relative to the overall goal of transferring 30% of agricultural land (inclusive of pasture land) by 2014. Current estimates are that restitution plus redistribution have together transferred only 4% of agricultural land – of which 90% was white-owned at the end of apartheid – to blacks.[86]

Apart from the question of excessive compensation and willingness of owners to sell, commentators have questioned whether such market-based programs primarily benefit the truly poor. Thus, an argument is made that, at least in settings like Brazil, the "groups" that are formed to avail themselves of the proffered program-supported loans may be constituted by better-informed, better-connected and more entrepreneurial *campesinos*, and consequently tend to exclude the poorest households.[87] In response to these criticisms, several design changes have been introduced in the market-assisted land tenure reform programs in Brazil[88] and South Africa.[89] Under a program recently initiated in the Indian state of Andhra Pradesh, the government acquires land that comes onto the market from landowners who are not below the poverty line and allocates it to benefit landless women from below the poverty line, principally agricultural-laborer households. Design changes for this program, discussed further in Chapter 6, show early promise for resolving problems encountered in the earlier programs of other countries.

Restitution programs that return land to its former small or medium owners may involve special compensation issues. These programs have usually been introduced in settings of previous seizure and forced collectivization of land that had occurred under the prior communist regimes in eastern Europe.[90] But at least one program of restitution, that in South Africa, has involved undoing seizures of black-owned land that were made for private use in a non-communist setting. This is the branch of the three-branch South African land tenure reform program (restitution, redistribution and reform of tenure for existing holders[91]) that attempts to reverse, in part, the seizures of black-owned farmland that occurred over the decades from the Native Lands Act of 1913 until the later stages of white-minority government under apartheid. Some land seizures at issue go back more than 80 years and may involve several generations with differing relationships to the land initially taken from its black owners. For example, the original white beneficiary of land seized from black farmers in the 1920s may have sold the land in the 1940s, and that buyer might have resold it in the 1960s to a farmer whose grandson may now be farming the land, held under inheritance, and with a long series of investments and improvements having been made over the intervening years.

Many potential complexities and variables are reflected in the key language of South Africa's Restitution of Land Rights Act of 1994, setting the criteria and modalities for return of land or cash compensation for its loss. Under the Act as amended in 1997, the Land Claims Court is to consider 10 separately listed factors, including such broad ones as "the requirements of equity and justice," as well as such demandingly specific ones as "the history of the dispossession, the hardship caused, the current use of the land and the history of the acquisition and use of the land." There can also be "an order for equitable redress in the form of financial compensation" rather than return of the land itself.

With nearly all claims supposedly now settled after a slow start, close to 60,000 rural households should now have benefited.[92] Perhaps the two key, interrelated criticisms are that: (1) financial compensation, rather than actual land restoration, had been the remedy in nearly three-fifths of settled claims at least as of 2004, and (2) the total area of actual land transferred to claimants is still only about 2% of South Africa's agricultural land (inclusive of pastures).[93]

Assertion and foreclosure of liens relating to unpaid wages of workers on the estate is another possibility in some circumstances, and one which appears to have been used on some tea plantations in India.[94] These transfers of land use to the workers may not have involved formal foreclosures based on assertion of a worker's lien on the assets of their employer for unpaid wages. But the availability of the legal claim – and the underlying fact of wages owed and unpaid, contemporary in time and upon which no statute of limitations has run – should substantially distinguish this situation from more usual cases of "land invasion," as discussed earlier.[95]

Equity-in-lieu-of-land rights may best be considered as a kind of "negative land reform" scheme because it has arisen in settings in which the government asks potential or actual beneficiaries of land redistribution measures to give up their benefits (or promised benefits) in return for an equity interest – common stock or its equivalent – in an enterprise that will use the land that the same beneficiaries either used (or owned) or had expectation of using (and perhaps owning) under a land tenure reform program.[96]

This issue has arisen with greatest persistence in China, where some schemes have offered farmers "equity" in resulting enterprises in return for giving up their present land rights for use by those enterprises. RDI's field review of the most prominent of the Chinese stock-share programs, that in Nanhai County of Guangdong Province, found numerous problems in actual practice. Among these were the nearly complete lack of meaningful participation or oversight by the farmers who had ceded their land rights; the lack of transparency as to enterprise operations, including such key issues as the calculation of profits or the incurring of expenses, which could lend itself to management manipulation of calculated profits; "dividends" to the farmer-share-holders which appeared to be only about 10% of acknowledged profits; and what appeared to be generous outlays on offices and transport for the local officials who managed the stock-share enterprise.[97] Another country setting where equity or equivalent participation is permitted is South Africa, where a number of examples exist and have been studied.[98] The government wants to assist and empower black farmworkers – and the desire is probably even stronger if it can do so while preserving effective unitary operation on many of the larger, presently white-owned farms. The law does not specify in detail the modalities for such "equity share" arrangements, and much seems to depend on what is worked out between the white owners and the black workers or other residents on a particular holding. NGO or government representatives often assist, and beneficiaries receive government Land Redistribution for Agricultural Development (LRAD) grants of R20,000 (currently equivalent to about US$2,600) per household – and more with sufficient self-contribution – as a contribution they can bring to the transaction.[99] The resulting enterprise – and these are all cases where continuing unitary operation is contemplated – may take any of a number of institutional forms allowed under general South African law.

The arrangements must clearly be negotiated and are consensual, in form at least. Still, a number of problems appear to exist. The choices to be made and their implementation mechanisms are clearly complex, requiring a great deal of outside technical support and leaving considerable doubt about whether many participating families adequately understand their new rights. The genuineness and durability of empowerment for black workers who become equity holders may also be questionable, especially given that they often, perhaps in all cases, hold a minority interest and have only minority representation on the board, and given that the former owner (though this is usually a mutually desired result, to ensure adequate management skills) normally stays on as the manager of the enterprise. These concerns seem to be given further weight by initial research that indicates widely varying results from holding to holding where equity-share schemes have been put in place.[100]

Individual versus joint operation

Section I has already raised the issue of whether the large unitary holding that is being transferred to its workers is to be operated henceforth as a single unit, as a series of individual family farms, or as some combination of these. Do the beneficiaries have a choice in this matter, or has the issue been decided in the governing law and regulations? Is the decision on this issue to be made once-and-for-all at the beginning, or can a majority (or super-majority) of the beneficiaries change their minds later? Can individuals "opt out," either initially or later, with their allocable shares of both land and other assets? And if the beneficiaries are to have any of these choices, how can they meaningfully exercise them?[101]

These questions also suggest the need, implicit in any situation where a group of workers gain control over a unitary estate and must make at least some group decisions – whether only for definitive break-up, or continuing with partial or fully fledged group functioning – to settle on modes of decision making and modes of self-governance (for the longer term).

On these primarily procedural issues there appears to be a long-standing best-practices example found in the Mexican *ejidos*, initially pursuant to the Agrarian Code of 1934, and then amplified under the reform of 1992.[102] These self-government arrangements remain relevant for both the collective and individual *ejidos*, and cover a wide range of the organization's internal affairs. (The Israeli *moshav* is broadly similar to the individual *ejido* in Mexico, though its governance structures exist in what is essentially a developed-country setting.[103])

The key elements of *ejido* governance that appear most empowering for the member households are the following:[104]

(1) The community requests the grant of land (a process ended in 1992), either on the basis of restitution if the community previously held title or non-restitutionary expropriation if there was no previous title.[105]

(2) After government approval and the formal grant of land to the *ejidal* community, the community elects an *ejidal* commissariat to provide daily management and a vigilance council to act as a watchdog.[106]

(3) Ultimate authority is vested in a General Assembly of all members that meets once a month.

(4) Very importantly, voting for the councils is by secret ballot.[107] And if there is a divided vote on the election of the commissariat, the vigilance council must be elected from among members of the losing minority.

(5) All terms of office are for three years, and re-election, which is considered rare,[108] requires a two-thirds vote, not just a simple majority.

(6) Although the president is the leading official, "The intent of the *ejido* system is egalitarianism and the president is meant to be first among equals."[109]

(7) There are also well-developed federal oversight mechanisms in place to ensure *ejidal* democracy, now including an Agrarian Tribunal for dispute resolution established in 1992.

One weakness in the Mexican scheme, however, is that only one person per household is normally a voting member in the General Assembly, and almost invariably that person is the husband and not the wife.[110]

Mexico adopted its constitutional mandate for land reform in 1917 after a polarizing and bloody revolution and adopted more specific governing rules in 1934 in an era when "private property" was ideologically suspect there and in many other country settings. Consequently, Mexican law severely restricted the individual's right to opt out, whether or not the *ejido* had individualized its holdings. Members could not sell or rent their land rights or sell their undivided share, nor even hire labor to help work their land; however, they could pass their rights to a single heir, but only if that person was or became a member of the *ejidal* community and continued to work the land.

As often happens where provisions of law forbid what large numbers of people consider to be appropriate and beneficial activity, these re-

strictions came to be widely ignored, and an informal "shadow market"
in *ejidal* land rights grew up over time.[111] Thus, in 1992, Mexico
amended both its Constitution and the law[112] to allow formal titling of
individualized holdings on the *ejidos* pursuant to a two-thirds vote of
the members. A large majority of *ejidos* have now completed the voluntary no-cost registration process that leads to the distribution of certificates for individual parcels. Today, *ejidatorios* can lease out their land
and can sell it within the *ejidal* community. But only if the land is formally privatized (either in full, with the *ejido* disbanding, or partially,
for members wishing to exercise this option) can the land be sold to an
outsider, and even then the sale remains subject to a right of first refusal by *ejidatorios.*[113]

As a final point under this individual-versus-joint operation heading,
it should be noted that, in a number of reforms where operations began as joint ones, most large holdings were later divided among the
beneficiaries for individual farming.[114]

Nuclear estates

Closely related to the previous point is a model of operation that is
partly unitary and partly individual. As one clearly identified variant,
the so-called "nuclear estate" approach has been used, in such countries as Indonesia, Malaysia and Kenya. In the "nuclear estate" (or "nucleus estate") model, a "nucleus" or core part of the large holding is
used for production of an export crop (such as oil palm) using capital-
intensive methods and a force of permanent workers. This core area of
joint farming is then accompanied by a large number of much smaller
family-size farms, producing the same crop and cultivated mostly by
the families that provide the permanent work force on the core estate.
The management of the core farm provides support to the entire operation, gathers in the entire crop (including purchase of the raw crop
produced on the family plots), processes the crop and markets the final
product.[115] The land used often consists of large tracts of (supposedly)
public land, either allocated to a private investor or to a state-owned
company. Sometimes this has been done in conjunction with resettlement programs, such as the Indonesian transmigration program, discussed in note 66. Similar problems, such as the existence of conflicting customary users, can often arise.[116]

To the extent that a particular land tenure reform program will deal
with existing large holdings in which a substantial portion of the estate
land is presently used for capital-intensive production, the "nuclear estates" model may offer a useful option. Even if one is inclined (as we
recommend) to exclude capital-intensive portions of estates from a redistribution program, this may still leave other, peripheral or non-capi-

tal-intensive portions of such holdings appropriately subject to taking, and in such cases these additional lands might be distributed as family farms. If the family farms produce the same crop as that produced on the portion of the holding that remains undivided, the effect would be to create an overall operation similar to a nuclear estate.

In some Latin American settings, such peripheral lands might already be farmed individually, for subsistence crops, by laborers working on the central estates, under the *colono* system.[117] In the traditional setting, the central estate in such cases would not be capital intensive, and thus would also be subject to taking and redistribution under the assumption (taking of non-capital-intensive lands) made in the previous paragraph. It should also be noted that in some Latin American settings, the beneficiaries who received estate lands have ended up by farming individual parcels, as well as farming together on a central "core" holding. But the individual parcels, like pre-reform *colono* parcels (although they may now be owned by the beneficiaries) are usually farmed with subsistence crops rather than cash crops, and there is probably a tendency to subdivision of the "core" holding by the beneficiaries (now the joint owners), at least in part because of "free rider" and supervision problems.[118] We are not aware of any systematic attempt to compare the "free rider" and supervision problems on different kinds of large holdings, but we would hypothesize that they are likely to be inversely related to the power of supervisors or management to dismiss non-performing workers: hence, a smaller problem on privately owned large plantations, more of a problem on large collective farms, and an even greater problem on large holdings that remain jointly operated by land tenure reform beneficiaries.

Ceilings that capture medium-size and small holdings

In a number of countries, ownership "ceilings" laws have been adopted in the past that would have taken non-tenant-farmed lands operated in holdings much smaller in size than what would usually be thought of as "estates," "plantations," or "ranches." These laws, affecting what most might characterize as "medium-size" – or even "smaller" – holdings, not cultivated by tenants, have been adopted in several Asian settings and have generally failed to achieve any significant degree of land redistribution.

For example, in the 1950s and 1960s, various Indian states adopted ownership ceilings on non-tenanted landholdings typically ranging from 10 to 20 acres (4 to 8 hectares) for irrigated land, and up to 50 acres (20 hectares) or more for lesser-quality land, with the excess to be taken and redistributed.[119] Indonesia sought to take holdings above five hectares in more densely populated parts of the country (with higher ceilings, up to 20 hectares, in more thinly populated areas) and also sought to take the entirety of the holdings of absentee owners.[120] The list might be extended.

Through a combination of usually unchallenged false or anticipatory transfers to relatives or strawmen and simple governmental non-implementation (which may be further abetted by administrative complications the landowners succeed in inserting into the governing law), the great majority of such land has escaped acquisition.[121] Several factors may be at work here to defeat implementation:

First, there is a relatively large political counterweight of owners who would be affected.[122] And, as with almost all of these earlier post-World War II land tenure reforms, the proffered compensation for land was far below market value, exacerbating the owners' reaction.

Second, there is often not a well-identified beneficiary group, in contrast to situations where either large estates or tenanted farms are to be taken and redistributed. In the former case, the permanent workers are generally the presumptive core beneficiary group, and in the latter case, the tenants are almost always the in-place beneficiaries. But with medium and smaller non-tenanted holdings, there are often few or no permanent laborers: beneficiaries are expected to be drawn from the ranks of temporary or itinerant workers, who may consist of different people from season to season and year to year, whose levels of work on the particular land may differ considerably, and who in any event have no links with either particular parcels (as do tenants) or at least specific larger fields (as do permanent laborers). Hence, putative beneficiaries may be less expectant, less organized, and exert less countervailing pressure against that of the existing landowners.

Third, as a further complication, some temporary or itinerant workers may own (or be tenants on) other parcels of land, changing or perhaps eliminating their status as potential beneficiaries. Thus, the completely landless among them – who should be preferred beneficiaries – may lack to an even greater degree the kind of cohesiveness often found among tenant farmers in a small village or permanent workers on a single estate. Yet the law is often written – unwisely, and as one of the administrative complications the landowners may succeed in implanting – to require the would-be beneficiaries to take the initiative in making a claim to particular land.

And, finally, even though legal provisions potentially affecting medium or small holdings did find their way into the statute books in some countries early in the post-war era, they may have lacked much of the broader political and ideological support which underpinned parallel and contemporaneous legal provisions dealing with tenanted lands or large estates.

IV. Possible future approaches to distributing land to benefit agricultural laborers

Drawing together the principal threads of the previous discussion, the following points, both positive and negative, seem vital ones to keep in view when designing and implementing programs to benefit agricultural laborers.[123]

There should be a general presumption against taking capital-intensive estate lands that are privately owned. These lands are likely to involve a relatively high cost per family benefited. It may be necessary to continue operation of these lands in a unitary mode, with beneficiaries of any redistribution limited largely or entirely to the existing permanent labor force. Indeed, an initial litmus test here might be "if the private estate holding is such that the beneficiaries will not be given the option of subdividing it into individual family farms, do not take it." Although this should be a strong presumption, there may be exceptional political circumstances – perhaps in South Africa and Namibia, for example[124] – in which social stability will demand that the government take and redistribute such holdings.

In other country settings one option might be for the government to allow the present owners to retain core estates while taking a portion of the estate using compulsory purchase powers. The government might encourage owners to improve and intensify operations on the retained core estate by using compensation they received for the remaining portions of their land. The government would allocate the taken lands to beneficiaries and allow them to operate such lands in any mode they choose, which in most cases is likely to be on an individual basis. The new small holders might produce largely the same crop as the core estate – in which case the entire operation might approximate the "nuclear estate" model – or might produce other crops chiefly for subsistence and local marketing. It should also be borne in mind that beneficiaries might in many cases operate both field parcels and home-garden plots received under the reform. This option might make sense in Brazil and some other parts of Latin America.

Thus, with rare exceptions, there should be a general presumption against acquiring any portions of private estate lands that are already intensively used. Rather, governments should focus on acquiring underutilized lands, including lands presently used for extensive grazing that are agronomically suitable for cropping (for example, some valley lands such as those RDI has seen in Colombia used for grazing cattle, while small farmers used steep hillsides for crop production, the reverse of ecologically and agriculturally sensible usage patterns). In such cases, except for lands suitable only for extensive pasture,[125] beneficiaries should always be given the choice of farming the land on an individualized basis.

In some settings, the government may acquire underutilized estate land at a per hectare market price in the low hundreds of dollars or even less. This can provide a potentially large "replicability dividend" in reaching larger numbers of beneficiaries. Program designers must be careful not to squander such a prospect of wide replication by then proceeding to allocate excessively large amounts of land per beneficiary family.

In a related vein, there should be a focus on benefiting poorer rural households by ensuring that the beneficiary group prominently includes temporary or casual laborers who are presently landless. But in this case as well there should be a strong presumption against paying any substantial resettlement costs, and against using resources to pay for housing. In general, if the estate lands that are candidates for acquisition are located so far away from most putative beneficiaries that relocation seems impractical – at least without large resettlement subsidies – then one should look carefully at possible candidate lands closer to the beneficiaries, including considering such variables as the distribution of smaller homegarden plots.

Considerations as to whether and to what extent the government might legalize land invasions involve a complex of factors, as discussed above.[126] In general, there should be a presumption against legalizing the results of this kind of self-help. Where the circumstances warrant legalization of the seized land, at a minimum the government should use the invasion to identify land that the government will formally acquire by eminent domain, paying adequate compensation to the owners.

With rare exceptions, beneficiaries of estate land acquisitions should have broad options, both at the start and continuing subsequently, as to their desired mode of cultivating the land. For this and other governance purposes, where at least some group decisions will continue to be made, the procedures used on the Mexican *ejidos* can serve as a useful model. Some potential options for enterprise organization, notably those identified as "stock share" or "equity participation" that do not provide beneficiaries with any substantial voice in enterprise management, are likely to be so inimical to beneficiary interests that they should almost never be included among the governance options.

Where estate lands are not available or otherwise an appropriate source of land for large numbers of non-permanent agricultural laborers or other poor landless families, planners might be inclined to consider using eminent domain power to acquire and distribute medium-sized holdings, using a ceiling low enough to capture a significant amount of non-tenanted, self-cultivated land. This option seems highly problematic because of likely widespread opposition and in light of the lack of success in using such an approach in the past (e.g., Kerala, Indonesia). Indeed, it is likely to invoke all the problems cited against the prospects of contemporary land-to-the-tiller programs in Chapter 2, without even offering the political counterweight of beneficiaries who are already on the land as tenants. But in occasional settings the government can perhaps use negotiated acquisition via "market-assisted land reform" to acquire enough land from medium as well as large holdings to allocate even full-sized plots to significant numbers of the rural poor, as distinct from allocating small homestead plots. As experience with market-assisted land tenure reform accumulates and program methods improve, governments may find they are able to acquire sufficient land to do this, at least in settings where land prices are low.

Notes

1   Large size is not an exclusive touchstone for determining whether non-family labor predominates, as can be seen in some settings where ample capital can be mobilized to substitute for labor. For example, in the United States it is common to find "family farms" of 400 hectares (1000 acres) or more, on which the preponderance of the labor is provided by a single family or siblings, using hundreds of thousands of dollars in farming equipment.

2   This chapter will not discuss collectivized or state-operated lands, or successor operations, in the former Soviet Union, or in Cuba, North Korea, or Nicaragua in the Sandinista era. The present chapter will, however, include situations where the law establishes land ownership "ceilings" that are set low enough that medium-sized and even smaller (non-tenanted) operational holdings may theoretically be impacted.

3   Or, to put it more exactly, their predominant source of income derives from cultivating land to which some other party holds and exercises a superior right, such that they require a payment from the tenant for the privilege of cultivating, or limit the agricultural laborer to a wage or other work-related emolument – in some cases, the temporary use of another, small piece of land – while themselves disposing of what the laborer has produced. Our principal focus in Chapters 2 and 3 thus differs from the principal focus of Peruvian economist Hernando de Soto, author of a popular book on land rights, THE MYSTERY OF CAPITAL: WHY CAPITALISM TRIUMPHS IN THE WEST AND FAILS EVERYWHERE ELSE (Basic Books 2000). Among other differences, whereas we are focused on creating new rights for persons cultivating land to which another party is clearly asserting the dominant right, de Soto's focus is the formalization of land rights that are already being exercised without the presence of any separate private owner or other active paramount right-holder. Chapter 8 and also Chapter 7 bear on these latter issues.

4   Though the discrepancy does not disappear entirely. In the Salvadoran reform, for example, some owners held more than the triggering amount of land only by virtue of lumping together two or three physically distinct holdings. J. Strasma, *Unfinished Business: Consolidating Land Reform in El Salvador*, in W. Thiesenhusen, ed., SEARCHING FOR LAND REFORM IN LATIN AMERICA 408, 425 (Unwin Hyman 1989).

5   The applicable law may, in general, be framed in one of two ways insofar as quantitative ceilings are concerned. Either an estate that is found to exceed the ceiling is then

taken in its entirety, or only that portion of the estate which is in excess of the ceiling is taken. In the latter case, as with tenanted land that has been determined to exceed a non-zero ceiling, there is the further question of who chooses which portion is to be taken and which portion retained by the owner.

6   This may also include the situation on large holdings in Latin American settings in which a single unitary holding is divided into a majority portion managed directly by the owner using agricultural laborers, and a minority portion divided into individual parcels which those laborers are allowed to cultivate (usually used for subsistence crops). In the more traditional version of this *colono* system, the laborers gave their labor on the centrally managed lands as payment for use of their individual parcels, with neither a separate wage paid to them nor a separate rent paid by them. See, e.g., S. Lastarria-Cornhiel, *Agrarian Reforms of the 1960s and 1970s in Peru*, in Thiesenhusen, supra note 4, at 127, 131.

7   W.C. Thiesenhusen, BROKEN PROMISES: AGRARIAN REFORM AND THE LATIN AMERICAN CAMPESINO 106 (Westview 1995); S. Clark & B. O'Neill, *Agrarian Reform in Southern Portugal*, 4 CRITIQUE OF ANTHROPOLOGY 47, 50-51 (1980).

8   Rarely, a government with a particular political agenda may not consider the estate workers to be beneficiaries at all. This appears to be the case in Zimbabwe currently, in a program that must generally be viewed as a travesty of "land reform." For the position of estate workers in Zimbabwe, see International Crisis Group, *Blood and Soil: Land, Politics, and Conflict Prevention in Zimbabwe and South Africa*, ICG Africa Report No. 85, at 92-94 (International Crisis Group Press 2004).

9   W. Wolford, *Producing Community: The MST and Land Reform Settlements in Brazil*, 3 (4) JOURNAL OF AGRARIAN CHANGE 500-501, 505-510, 518 (2003). Such land-invading groups may also accommodate the existing workforce, as they do in Brazil, or may exclude them, as in Zimbabwe.

10 In the Mexican land reform, basic retention was cast in terms of irrigated cropland, one hectare of which was equal to roughly two hectares of rainfed cropland. A far greater amount of pastureland was taken as equivalent. S. Eckstein, G. Donald, D. Horton & T. Carroll, *Land Reform in Latin America: Bolivia, Chile, Mexico, Peru, and Venezuela*, World Bank Staff Working Paper No. 275, at 18 (World Bank 1978). Compare the division of Taiwan's land into 26 grades of paddy land and 26 grades of dryland for purposes of deciding how much a landlord could retain. See Chapter 2, n. 26.

11 Apart, of course, from questions of forced collectivization of such households in two-step processes – land-to-the-tiller followed by collectivization – that occurred under earlier communist regimes, such as those in China and North Vietnam in the 1950s.

12 Factors that have influenced decisions in broadly parallel circumstances – where members of collective farms are given the choice of exiting with an aliquot portion of the enterprise land to farm individually – are discussed in Section VII of Chapter 7.

13 K. Deininger, *Land Policies for Growth and Poverty Reduction*, World Bank Policy Research Report 83 (World Bank & Oxford University Press 2003).

14 See generally R.A. Berry & W.R. Cline, AGRARIAN STRUCTURE AND PRODUCTIVITY IN DEVELOPING COUNTRIES (John Hopkins University Press 1979); R. Burgess, *Land and Welfare: Theory and Evidence from China*, Working Paper (London School of Economics 2001); R.M. Netting, SMALLHOLDERS, HOUSEHOLDERS: FARM FAMILIES AND THE ECOLOGY OF INTENSIVE, SUSTAINABLE AGRICULTURE 146-56 (Stanford University Press 1993); M.R. Carter, *Identification of the Inverse Relationship between Farm Size and Productivity: An Empirical Analysis of Peasant Agricultural Production*, 36(1) OXFORD ECONOMIC PAPERS 131-145 (1984); H.P. Binswanger, K. Deininger & G. Feder, *Power, Distortions, Revolt, and Reform in Agricultural Land Relations*, in J. Behrman & T.N. Srinivasan, eds., HANDBOOK OF DEVELOPMENT ECONOMICS 41-49 (Elsevier Science 1995);

N.L. Johnson & V.W. Ruttan, *Why are Farms so Small?*, 22(5) WORLD DEVELOPMENT 691-709 (1994); G.P. Kutcher & P.L. Scandizzo, THE AGRICULTURAL ECONOMY OF NORTHEAST BRAZIL (World Bank 1981); C. Udry, *Recent Advances in Empirical Microeconomic Research in Poor Countries: An Annotated Bibliography*, 28(1) JOURNAL OF ECONOMIC EDUCATION 58-75 (1997). Some of the observed inverse relationship can be explained by differences in land quality, yet even after controlling for land quality and other differences associated with farm size, empirical studies still indicate a significant inverse correlation. Deininger, supra note 13, at 83.

15   See generally R. Burgess, LAND, WELFARE, AND EFFICIENCY IN RURAL CHINA (London School of Economics 1997); X.L. Dong & L. Putterman, *Preform Industry and State Monopsony in China*, 28(1) JOURNAL OF COMPARATIVE ECONOMICS 32-60 (2000); O.J. Lanjouw, *Information and the Operation of Markets: Tests Based on a General Equilibrium Model of Land Leasing in India*, 60(2) JOURNAL OF DEVELOPMENT ECONOMICS 497-527 (1999); G.H. Wan & E. Cheng, *Effects of Lang Fragmentation and Returns to Scale in the Chinese Farming Sector*, 33(2) APPLIED ECONOMICS 183-194 (2001).

16   H. Binswanger & K. Deininger, *South African Land Policy: The Legacy of History and Current Options*, in J. van Zyl, J. Kirsten & H.P. Binswanger, eds., AGRICULTURAL LAND REFORM IN SOUTH AFRICA: POLICIES, MARKETS AND MECHANISMS 64 (Oxford University Press 1996).

17   One study in India found that for an average farm size of 2.9 acres the income per acre was 737 rupees; for an average farm size of 9.3 acres it was 607 rupees; for 19.5 acres, 482 rupees; and for 42.6 acres, 346 rupees. Netting, supra note 14, at 147-148. A study in Brazil using 1970-1980 data found that net income per hectare consistently decreased as farm size increased. Net income per hectare for farms less than one hectare was almost three times greater than for farms between one and 10 hectares and nearly 30 times greater than for farms between 200 and 2,000 hectares. W.C. Thiesenhusen & J. Melmed-Sanjak, *Brazil's Agrarian Structure: Changes from 1970 through 1980*, 18(3) WORLD DEVELOPMENT 402 (1990). A World Bank study on the higher efficiency of small versus large farms in Kenya found that output per hectare was 19 times higher and employment per hectare was 30 times higher on holdings under 0.5 hectare than on holdings over eight hectares. World Bank, KENYA GROWTH AND STRUCTURAL CHANGE: ISSUES IN KENYAN AGRICULTURAL DEVELOPMENT, VOL. 2, at 372 and table 22, 373 at n.105, 380-382 (World Bank 1983). Author Prosterman and Jeffrey Riedinger, using data from 117 countries, found that 11 of the top 14 countries in terms of grain yields per hectare are countries in which small-scale family farming dominates. R. Prosterman & J. Riedinger, LAND REFORM AND DEMOCRATIC DEVELOPMENT 44 (Johns Hopkins 1987).

18   Deininger, supra note 13, at 83.

19   G.A. Calvo & S. Wellisz, *Supervision, Loss of Control, and the Optimum Size of the Firm*, 86(5) JOURNAL OF POLITICAL ECONOMY 943-952 (1978).

20   Mechanization in industry involves stationary machinery, which implies that the number of workers can be increased substantially without increasing labor supervision costs. In agriculture, labor and machines are both mobile, making supervision expensive and increasing management costs. Agricultural tasks are also sequential in nature due to the annual cycle of production. This limits the opportunities for specialization and division of labor, which creates few advantages to expansion beyond the size of the family farm. J. van Zyl, THE FARM SIZE-EFFICIENCY RELATIONSHIP, in J. van Zyl, J. Kirsten & H.P. Binswanger, eds., AGRICULTURAL LAND REFORM IN SOUTH AFRICA: POLICIES, MARKETS AND MECHANISMS 267 (Oxford University Press 1996).

21   K. Deininger, *Cooperatives and the Break-up of Large Mechanized Farms: Theoretical Perspectives and Empirical Evidence*, World Bank Discussion Paper 218, at 6 (Nov. 1993). See also R.C. Ellickson, *Property Rights in Land*, 102(6) YALE LAW JOURNAL 1327-1332

(1993). On family farms, because family members receive the benefits of all profits, family members: (a) have higher incentives to provide effort than do hired labor, (b) share in the risk, and (c) can be employed more flexibly without incurring hiring or search costs. Thus, important negative economies of scale exist when farming operations are conducted in a manner, or on a territory sufficiently large, as to require a significant proportion of non-family labor. Compare the discussion of the parallel point in Chapter 7, dealing with successive organizations of production in China under individual and collective farming.

22 Y. Hayami & A. Damodaran, *Toward an Alternative Agrarian Reform: Tea Plantations in South India*, 39(36) ECONOMIC & POLITICAL WEEKLY 3993 (2004). The authors compare the manufacturing of black tea and green tea to explain the point. The manufacturing of black tea at standardized quality for export requires processing within a few hours of plucking. Green tea, however, does not. This difference explains the traditional use of the plantation system for black tea and the predominant mode of family farming for green tea.

23 Id. at 3993. On the other hand, in some instances, traders will deliberately favor small producers as in the fair trade movement. For examples of programs that favor small producers, see generally Transfair USA, *Producer Profiles*, http://www.transfair-usa.org/content/certification/profiles.php.

24 Hayami & Damodraran, supra note 22, at 3995.

25 Id. at 3997. See also Y. Hayami, *Family Farms and Plantations in Tropical Development*, 19(2) Asian Development Review 67-89 (2002).

26 H. Binswanger, *Agriculture and Rural Development: Painful Lessons*, paper presented to the 32nd annual meeting of the South African Agricultural Economics Association (Johannesburg, South Africa 1994).

27 See generally R.M. Townsend, *Risk and Insurance in Village India*, 62(3) ECONOMETRICA (1994); D.N. McCloskey, *English Open Fields as Behavior Towards Risk*, in P. Uselding, ed., RESEARCH IN ECONOMIC HISTORY: AN ANNUAL COMPILATION OF RESEARCH VOL. 1, at 125-126, 161-165 (JAI Press 1976).

28 G.M. Meier, LEADING ISSUES IN ECONOMIC DEVELOPMENT, 8TH ED. 381-387 (Oxford University Press 2005).

29 If land and the capital needed for mechanization are both scarce and labor is abundant, then small, labor-intensive family farms make both economic and equitable sense. Where labor is abundant and relatively inexpensive, using capital to mechanize farms carries a high opportunity cost, while the more intensive application of motivated family labor (including "sweat equity" for improvement to the land) carries low opportunity cost. As agricultural labor becomes more scarce and expensive (because of job growth in non-agricultural sectors) and capital becomes more abundant, farm sizes will naturally grow (assuming, that is, the absence of substantial legal or other constraints on the transferability of land rights).

30 Even if no compensation for the land is required, questions as to subdivisibility may still arise in these instances, to the extent the operation has been capital intensive, at least if the capital has been efficiently used.

31 This is in contrast to the clear evidence of post-war successes for land-to-the-tenant programs in at least six settings (not counting pre-collectivization China), detailed in Chapter 2.

32 There have been very recent programs, begun or announced, again in Bolivia, and in Venezuela and Paraguay, all probably too new to incorporate meaningfully in our present analysis. We should note, however, that their prospect or undertaking seems generally supportive of the twin conclusions that substantial land tenure reforms involving large estates may not yet be occurrences virtually all of the past, and therefore that examination of earlier experiences may take on added significance. See, e.g., D.

Hertzler & K. Ledebur, *Bolivia's Land Reform Legislation* (Andean Information Network, Jan. 2007). Some of the limitations that have given rise to a second round of Bolivian reform are outlined in note 42 below; J. Suggett, *Venezuelan Government Takes Over 32 Landholdings for Land Reform*, Venezuelanalysis.com, Apr. 14, 2008; J. Suggett, *Land Reform Conflict in Venezuela's Strategic Water Source*, id., Aug. 11, 2008. Compare the more moderate approach apparently being pursued by the new president of Paraguay as reported in A. Glendenning, *Anti-corruption bishop becomes Paraguay president*, Associated Press dispatch (Aug. 15, 2008); A. Barrionuevo, *Difficult Road Ahead for New Paraguay Leader*, NEW YORK TIMES (Aug. 16, 2008).

33 See Thiesenhusen, supra note 7, at chs. 2 (Mexico) and 3 (Bolivia); Eckstein, et al., supra note 10, at 19-20 (Mexico) and 22 (Bolivia); G. Otero, *Agrarian Reform in Mexico: Capitalism and the State*, in W. Thiesenhusen, ed., SEARCHING FOR AGRARIAN REFORM IN LATIN AMERICA 276 (Unwin Hyman 1989) (Mexico); D.B. Heath, C.J. Erasmus & H.C. Buechler, LAND REFORM AND SOCIAL REVOLUTION IN BOLIVIA (Praeger 1969).

34 In pre-reform Mexico (1923) and pre-reform Bolivia (1950) estates of more than 1,000 hectares were estimated to hold, respectively, 70% and 79% of cropland, and an even higher proportion of total farmland including pasture. Eckstein, et al., supra note 10, at 13.

35 Thiesenhusen states in *Broken Promises* that in Mexico the usual ratio was six days a week worked in the landowner's fields and one day on the individually allocated plot. Thiesenhusen, supra note 7, at 31. And in Bolivia, at least in some cases, workers labored in the landowner's fields five or six days a week during the growing season and every day at harvest time. Sometimes, especially in Bolivia, workers also had to pay a share of the crops from that small parcel in rent to the estate owner. Id. at 54. Where land tenure reforms give ownership of the small *peon-* or *colono*-operated plots to those workers, the result can perhaps to that degree be assimilated to the land-to-the-tiller programs described in Chapter 2 (insecure holder of small plot gains in-place ownership or equivalent rights to that self-same plot), although the context is a reform whose basic design needs follow those of the estate takings discussed in the present chapter.

36 For the "power domain" concept, see E.R. Wolf, PEASANT WARS OF THE TWENTIETH CENTURY 290-91 (Harper & Row 1969).

37 Eckstein finds that in Mexico by 1960 about 95% of all *ejidos* were farmed individually with the remainder being collective or semi-collective. In Bolivia following the Revolution of 1952 and the agrarian reform law of 1953, approximately 25% of all cultivatable land going to beneficiaries was collectively titled, but these production cooperatives did not function for long and by the early 1970s almost all the land had been distributed for individual farming. Eckstein, et al., supra note 10, at 20 (Mexico) and 22 (Bolivia). Thiesenhusen estimates in 1995, after the completion of the long Mexican reform, that "perhaps 3% of the total of 23,000 *ejidos* were organized as collective *ejidos*". Thiesenhusen, supra note 7, at 40.

38 Thiesenhusen, supra note 7, at 40.

39 Thiesenhusen does not give a direct percentage estimate, but the 1995 FAO estimate of 24.2 million in Mexico's agricultural population, using 5 persons per average rural household, would yield a total of roughly 4.8 million agricultural households. UN Food and Agricultural Organization, 2003 PRODUCTION YEARBOOK, Table 3 (UNFAO 2004). The 3.1 million figure in text, divided by the 4.8 million total figure, yields the rough 65% proportion. Given the extended time span, it is not meaningful to pinpoint the percentage benefited at any specific date closer to the beginning of the reform.

40 Eckstein, et al., supra note 10, at 14, Table 4.

41 Thiesenhusen, supra note 7, at 63; Eckstein, et al., supra note 10, at 11 (table 2) and
    16 (table 5).

42 Writing even in 1995, Thiesenhusen notes there had been little improvement in the
    title issuance situation that had existed in 1972, when "titles had reached only 30 per-
    cent of beneficiaries." Thiesenhusen, supra note 7, at 62. While the Bolivian reform
    had considerable initial success in terms of land distributed and poor households af-
    fected, the significance of agriculture grew over succeeding decades in the geographic
    regions that had not been substantially affected – together with in-migration by the
    still-numerous rural poor and the increasing role of very large and not very produc-
    tive "*latifundios*" in those regions. These exacerbations of the land problem were ac-
    companied by the overthrow of the pro-reform government in 1964, to be succeeded
    by hostile and authoritarian military governments from 1964 to 1978, which also in
    some degree connived at the *de facto* reversal of the previous reforms. All this has
    laid the groundwork for the current attempt to expand and strongly renew the re-
    form. See Hertzler and Ledebur, supra note 32. See generally World Bank, *Country
    Social Assessment for Bolivia: Bolivia Towards a New Social Contract – Options for the
    Constituent Assembly* (World Bank 2006).

43 See R. Prosterman & J. Riedinger, *Shore Up Nicaragua's Moderates*, WALL STREET JOUR-
    NAL, Oct. 2, 1979. See also R. Scofield, *Land Reform in Central America*, in R. Proster-
    man, M. Temple & T. Hanstad, eds., AGRARIAN REFORM AND GRASSROOTS DEVELOP-
    MENT 139, 153-161 (Lynne Rienner 1990).

44 The comparisons become even more striking when excluding the farm families' la-
    bor, and thus focusing on the relatively more scarce factors of production – land, ca-
    pital and inputs – where the small farms show a ratio of 1.53, the individual *ejidos*
    1.54, the large farms 1.16, and the collective *ejidos* 1.03. Here the individual *ejidos*
    show a factor productivity 50% greater than the collectives, and 33% greater than the
    large farms (if all labor is excluded, their advantage over the collectives grows to
    62%, while it shrinks slightly to 28% over the large farms).

45 Paradoxically, many of these estates may have been selected for occupation due to
    perceived underutilization of their extensive lands, giving rise to a stronger economic
    case (in comparison with capital-intensive plantations with large "sunk costs" such as
    many of those in Portugal and El Salvador) for immediate break-up and individua-
    lized farming.

46 J.S. Melmed, *Interpreting the Parcellation of Peruvian Agricultural Producer Cooperatives*,
    Land Tenure Center Research Paper No. 96, at 8-9 (Land Tenure Center 1988).

47 See generally Strasma, supra note 4; Thiesenhusen, supra note 7. It should be borne
    in mind, however, that taking account of the reserve-area claims for the first 100-150
    hectares (the exact amount depending on land quality), even full implementation of
    this "Phase II" of the Salvadoran land reform would have likely produced a net area
    for distribution substantially less than that affected in the "Phase I" over-500-hectare
    estates program. Prosterman & Riedinger, supra note 17, at 153 & 282 n. 37. Govern-
    ments also carried out major reforms involving estate lands in Guatemala in the
    early 1950s and Chile up to the early 1970s, both of which were substantially or
    wholly reversed by subsequent anti-reformist regimes.

48 International Crisis Group, supra note 8, at 92-93, 107.

49 Id. at 92-94. Almost forgotten now, an earlier and much more meaningful land ten-
    ure reform was carried out immediately after Mugabe's revolution ousted the break-
    away white government in 1980, with significant financial support from Great Brit-
    ain and other donors for buying underutilized white-owned land on a willing buyer-
    willing seller basis. The program acquired and redistributed 3.3 million hectares be-
    tween 1980 and 1989, amounting to about one-fifth of the white-owned agricultural
    land in Zimbabwe. Unfortunately, although beneficiaries overwhelmingly chose to re-

ceive and use the land for individual farming, the average amount of land distributed per family benefited was around 60 hectares and thus the program reached only 54,000 families. Id. at 32 (for white-owned land) and 39 (for 1980-1989 redistribution); M. Bratton, *Ten Years After: Land Redistribution in Zimbabwe, 1980-1990*, in R. Prosterman, M. Temple & T. Hanstad, eds., AGRARIAN REFORM AND GRASSROOTS DEVELOPMENT 273-290 (Lynne Reinner 1990).

50   D. Anderson & E. Lochery, *Violence and Exodus in Kenya's Rift Valley, 2008: Predictable and Preventable?*, 2(2) JOURNAL OF EASTERN AFRICAN STUDIES 328,335 (July 2008).

51   Id. at 335-339; J. Klopp & P. Kamungi, *Violence and Elections: Will Kenya Collapse?*, Winter 2007/2008 WORLD POLICY JOURNAL 11, 13 (Feb. 16, 2008).

52   There have sometimes been attempts to set minimums in reforms affecting tenanted land, but these efforts have generally been forestalled, perhaps because of the obvious common-sense link between the existing pattern of tenant holdings and the amounts of land to be distributed to each. See the discussions of Marcos' initial "5 hectare" and "3 hectare" goals in the Philippines in Chapter 2. Maximums in land-to-the-tiller programs, on the other hand, may enjoy a fairly strong policy rationale – see Kerala discussion in Chapter 2 – but have rarely, if ever, proven enforceable.

53   Prosterman & Riedinger, supra note 17, at 191 (the reference is to the fairy-tale phenomenon in which the king orders his groom to throw a purse of gold to someone in the crowd who has caught the king's eye, leaving the great majority of his subjects just as impoverished as before).

54   See supra note 49.

55   A.M. Buainain, J.M.F.J. da Silveira & M. Magalhães, *Decentralized Access to Land: Issues for Debate*, Regional Workshop of Land Issues in Latin America and the Caribbean Panel on Redistributive Land Reform 3 (World Bank 2002).

56   Noting that, "the most significant change made to the land reform program by the Mbeki administration has been in land redistribution . . . [which is now] focused on creating 70,000 new black commercial farmers by 2017, with less emphasis on smallholder agriculture and poverty alleviation." International Crisis Group, supra note 8, at 165.

57   Strasma, supra note 5, at 425.

58   Id.

59   Thiesenhusen, supra note 7, at 98-102.

60   In El Salvador the bulk of the permanent workers on the estates identified for redistribution had been organized by the *campesino* union that was supportive of the Christian Democrats and non-violent reform (with both the violent left and the violent right arrayed against them in the setting of Salvador's civil conflict). There was a more fluid situation in the occupation of estates in southern Portugal in the mid-1970s, a setting where RDI also carried out field research. The occupancies were carried out largely through a grassroots imitative, without direction from political parties or unions (although many of the beneficiaries were, or became, members, especially of the Communist Party), and the occupiers were a mix of permanent and temporary workers, sometimes from other estates. As in El Salvador, operation as a single production unit generally continued, perhaps in part because the members of many of the new cooperatives perceived considerable hostility from the outside, especially from those who wished to return the land to the former owners: "Hostility from outside the new production units created a sort of 'siege mentality' within them. The need for 'solidarity' was underscored time and again in conversations and in meetings." N. Berneo, THE REVOLT FROM WITHIN THE REVOLUTION: WORKERS' CONTROL IN RURAL PORTUGAL 116 & ch. 5 (Princeton University Press 1986). Ultimately, the "solidarity" availed little, and much of the land was restored to the old owners.

61 P. Greene, *Design and Implementation of an Equity-Share Scheme on Sherwood Farm in the Midlands of Kwazulu-Natal*, in M. Lyne & M. Roth, eds., ESTABLISHING FARM-BASED EQUITY-SHARE SCHEMES IN KWAZULU NATAL: LESSONS FROM USAID'S BASIS RESEARCH PROGRAMME, PROCEEDINGS OF A MINI-CONFERENCE HELD 26 JULY 2004, at 43 (Nov. 2004).

62 This was soon scaled back to goals of allocating holdings of not more than 0.5 or 1 hectare of land, depending on beneficiary category. The 2 hectares was not mandatory, and families who already owned land could receive enough to bring their holding up to 2 hectares. Indonesia, Government Regulation No. 224 of 1961 Concerning Implementation of Redistribution of Land and Provision of Compensation, art. 10.

63 Id. art. 8.

64 See generally R. Chambers, RURAL DEVELOPMENT: PUTTING THE LAST FIRST 18-20 (Longman 1983).

65 Eckstein, et al., supra note 10, at 24, 88 (Venezuela); K. Mitchell, *Market-Assisted Land Reform in Brazil: A New Approach to Address an Old Problem*, 22(3) NEW YORK LAW SCHOOL JOURNAL OF INTERNATIONAL AND COMPARATIVE LAW 576-583 (2003); J. Frank, *Two Models of Land Reform and Development*, 15(11) Z MAGAZINE (2002) (Brazil); K. Deininger, *Making Negotiated Land Reform Work: Initial Experience from Brazil, Colombia, and South Africa*, World Bank Development Research Working Paper 2040, at 24-27 (World Bank 1999) (South Africa).

66 Indonesia's "transmigration" program of planned and supposedly voluntary resettlement of rural poor people from the crowded island of Java to land on other, less densely populated islands, encountered serious problems as to cost, return on investment, sustainability of land, land-claims of traditional users, and environmental degradation. Even when little or no cost for land (which was regarded as public) was included, the program at its peak – resettling 366,000 families at a total cost of $2.3 billion in 1979-1984 – required $6,300 per family benefited. Adjusting 1979-1984 dollars, the equivalent cost in current dollars would be more than $15,000. The World Bank had supported part of the cost, but eventually became quite critical of the prospects. See World Bank Country Study, *Indonesia – The Transmigration Program in Perspective* xx-xxxix (World Bank 1988).

67 Eckstein, et al., supra note 10, at 12.

68 Id. Broadly to the same effect, but affording less discretion and cause for protracted dispute, are provisions in the land tenure reform law simply excluding holdings that produce specifically named crops, often crops that are thought of as "export" crops. See, e.g., N.C. Behuria, LAND REFORMS LEGISLATION IN INDIA 137 (Vikas Publishing 1997) (exemptions of tea plantations and other plantations from state Ceiling Laws on landholding size).

69 In Pakistan, the successive land tenure reforms of 1959, 1972 and 1977 each established successively lower ceilings for irrigated and unirrigated land, together with a parallel set of Produce Index Units (PIUs), supposedly reflecting the productivity of that land. The owner was then permitted to retain the higher of the two actual amounts of land thus determined, for example under the latest reform (Land Reforms Act II of 1977), 100 irrigated acres or 8,000 PIUs could be retained. But the PIU calculation dated back, unchanged, to 1947, at a time of substantially lower productivity, and one author estimates that the earlier 1972 ceiling, 50% higher at 150 irrigated acres and 12,000 PIUs, would allow actual retention of about 400 irrigated acres in Punjab province and 480 irrigated acres in Sind province (ceilings on unirrigated land were twice those for irrigated land). See M.H. Khan, UNDERDEVELOPMENT AND AGRARIAN STRUCTURE IN PAKISTAN 155 (Westview 1981).

70 Under Brazil's 1964 Land Statute – still in effect – it appears that a first-step consequence of allowing the statutory exemption of 600 "modules" in one Brazilian state

would be to allow a landowner to retain up to 1,800 hectares if used for vegetables, 9,600 hectares if used for grain, 30,000 hectares if used for grazing cattle, and 21,000 hectares even if not used at all. See P. Kluck, *Small Farmers and Agricultural Development Policy: A Look at Brazil's Land Reform Statute*, 38(1) Human Organization 44, 45 (Spring 1979). For a partial English translation of the Land Statute, see Food and Agriculture Organization (FAO), XIV(2)/V 1b *Food and Agriculture Legislation – Brazil* 1-49 (especially arts. 2 & 4).

71 The landowner's claim may also, or alternatively, involve the calculation of compensation to be paid. In this case, the compensation originally offered may, as a provisional matter, be paid into court.

72 See generally D.W. Bromley, ed., MAKING THE COMMONS WORK—THEORY, PRACTICE AND POLICY (ICS Press 1992); N.S. Jodha, *Common Property Resources, A Missing Dimension of Development Strategies*, World Bank Discussion Paper No. 169 (World Bank 1992).

73 See E. Rajagukguk, *Agrarian law, land tenure and subsistence in Java: Case study of the villages of Sukoharjo and Medayu* 128-29, 167-69, 226-27, 262-64, 267-72 (Ph.D. dissertation, University of Washington, available from UMI Dissertation Services, Ann Arbor).

74 See, e.g., J.L. & B. Hammond, THE VILLAGE LABOURER (Longman 1966, originally published in 1911); J.A. Yelling, COMMON FIELD AND ENCLOSURES IN ENGLAND 1450-1850 (MacMillan Press 1977).

75 There are, of course, far fewer unsettled "frontiers" on a planet with 6.7 billion people than on one, say, with 3 billion, the population as recently as 1960. Large-scale settlements on public lands, with accompanying privatization occurred, for example, in the United States throughout the late 19th and early 20th centuries under the Homestead Acts.

76 Department-Related Parliamentary Standing Committee on Commerce of the Parliament of India, *Sixty-Fourth Report on Export of Tea* 14-16 (Aug. 2003). See generally Behuria, supra note 68.

77 H. Thomas, THE SPANISH CIVIL WAR 45-46, 50-57 (Harper & Brothers 1961); see also W. Wolford, *Producing Community: The MST and Land Reform Settlement in Brazil*, 3 (4) JOURNAL OF AGRARIAN CHANGE 503-505 (2003).

78 Thiesenhusen states, "Over 99 percent of the land distributed in the agrarian reform was returned to its owners, including that of the United Fruit Company." Thiesenhusen, supra note 7, at 76 & 79. US$1.2 million was paid to UFC for 146,000 expropriated hectares. The land tenure reform law took all uncultivated land in private farms of more than 270 hectares in size (and down to farms of 90 hectares, where less than two-thirds was under cultivation).

79 Id. at 80.

80 The beneficiary group had consisted largely of the better off, permanent workers.

81 Id. at 99-114.

82 A somewhat different example of government hostility and eventual substantial reversal came in Portugal, after the Socialists came to power two years following the 1974 overthrow of the long Salazar dictatorship. See the background and discussion supra, note 63 and Berneo, there cited. From RDI's fieldwork and discussions with policy makers during the two years just after the restoration of democracy and the formation of the Socialist government, we would suggest that the subsequent pressure to reverse a great part of the 1974-1976 takings of the large southern estates – and meanwhile to give the land takers little credit or support – had its roots in the considerable ill-feeling between the Socialists, committed to democracy, and a Communist Party that was authoritarian in bent and had not wished to see the dictatorship suc-

ceeded by democracy, and for whom the expropriation and collective operation of the plantations was a "signature issue."

83 Eckstein, et al., supra note 10, at 24-25.

84 The general rule, for example in the United States, is that the taking itself should not be allowed to drive up the market price from what it would have been in the absence of the taking. See generally I.W. Bonbright, VALUATION OF PROPERTY: VOLUME I, at 413-431 (Michie 1965).

85 See A. Hall, *Land Tenure and Land Reform in Brazil*, in Prosterman, et al., supra note 43, at 205, 227-228 (as of 1990: "agrarian reform becomes little more than an *ad hoc* process of crisis management in areas of acute land conflict, the benefits of which accrue primarily to landowners in the form of generous compensation.")

86 See generally International Crisis Group, supra note 9, at 135-195. See BBC NEWS, *S. Africa land reform bill shelved*, http://news.bbc.co.uk/go/pr/fr/-/2/hi/africa/ 7583487.stm.

87 In some settings there might be a separate concern over whether the laborers on the estate may be displaced by an externally formed "group" seeking the funding to make the land acquisition, and as to whether there may be additional outlays needed to physically resettle the acquiring group onto the estate – another form of the excessive-costs question.

88 "Market-Assisted Land Reform" through World Bank financing of negotiated purchase in Brazil, with a "focus on poor and underutilized lands" and operating on a small scale (16,439 families) has seen, on the positive side, cost per beneficiary family reduced from $11,600 to around $3,000. More questionably, perhaps, beneficiaries included not only landless rural workers, but also "rural workers owning land sufficient only for subsistence farming," certainly not the poorest rural group. See World Bank *Module 10: Investments in Land Administration, Policy, and Markets*, in AGRICULTURAL INVESTMENT SOURCEBOOK 33-34 (May 2006).

89 The World Bank's "Community Managed Land Reform" program in South Africa encountered initial problems which included "the exclusion of women" as beneficiaries, and limited beneficiary participation in planning, which resulted in "large projects based on collective production, which have not done well." Some changes have since occurred. See World Bank, supra note 88, at 24-26.

90 See generally R. Prosterman & T. Hanstad, eds., *Legal Impediments to Effective Rural Land Relations in Eastern Europe and Central Asia: A Comparative Perspective*, World Bank Technical Paper No. 436, ch. 4 (World Bank 1999).

91 International Crisis Group, supra note 8, at 142.

92 See id. at 177. There had been close to 80,000 claims filed (id. at 163), of which nearly 75,000 had been reportedly settled by March 2008. See Commission on Restitution of Land Rights, ANNUAL REPORT 2007/2008, at 57 (Table of Statistics for Settled Restitution Claims, 1995-31) (Mar. 2008).

93 Projected from current figure of around two million rural hectares restored in kind, based on calculations in International Crisis Group, supra note 8, at 149, 163-64, 166.

94 See Parliament of India (Rajya Sabha), *Department-Related Parliamentary Standing Committee on Commerce, Sixty-Fourth Report on Export of Tea* paras. 7.2-7.7 (Aug. 2003), available at http://rajyasabha.nie.in/book2/reports/commerce/64th report.htm.

95 It is true that some land-invading groups make historical claims to be successors to communities or individuals wrongfully deprived of those lands at an earlier time. But that time is often many years in the past, and countervailing arguments as to repose of claims and the long-since running of any applicable period of limitations may seem persuasive. Compare R. Prosterman, *Land Reform in Latin America: How to Have a Revolution Without a Revolution*, 41 WASHINGTON LAW REVIEW 189-211 (1966),

with K. Karst, *Latin-American Land Reform: The Uses of Confiscation*, 63 MICHIGAN LAW REVIEW 327-72 (1964). Though not in a land invasion setting, and under circumstances where any claim would have been impossible in the intervening years, the complex rules worked out in South Africa and discussed above are instructive. Note that the result there has more often been cash payment than restitution of the land in-kind.

96 A parallel set of issues has arisen in China, with respect to some farmers' rights to the lands distributed after the break-up of the collectives. See Chapter 7.

97 See D. Bledsoe & R. Prosterman, *The Joint Stock Share System in China's Nanhai County*, RDI Reports No. 103 (Feb. 2000). It is, however, possible that at least the legal position of these stockholders has improved recently with general improvements in China's corporate-governance legislation. See China's 2006 Company Law and 2006 Securities Law. The question remains, of course, whether "grassroots" stockholders such as these erstwhile small farmers have received adequate information as to such new rights. See the discussion of implementation of China's laws on land tenure security in Chapter 7.

98 See Lyne & Roth, supra note 61.

99 See Ministry for Agricultural and Land Affairs, *Land Redistribution for Agricultural Development: A Sub-Programme of the Land Redistribution Programme, Final Document*, box 1 at 6 (undated).

100 See generally M. Roth, S. Knight & M. Lyne, *Best Institutional Arrangements for Farmworker Equity-Share Schemes in South Africa* (Land Tenure Center 2003). One companion study of a single farm expresses confidence on training of participants but goes on to say that beneficiary representatives "will require ongoing mentoring and skills transfer." Id. at 44. This may raise questions of replicability, even assuming that a large number of white farm owners would participate in this (presently at least) non-mandatory program.

101 Parallel issues exist for the system of "land shares" for members and pensioners, introduced on the successor enterprises to the old collective farms in most of the former Soviet Union. See Section VII of Chapter 7 for a discussion of the land shares.

102 See C. Thoms, *The Inadequacy of Article 27 Reform in Shaping Sustainable Ejidos* (paper presented at *Constituting the Commons: Crafting Sustainable Commons in the New Millennium*, the Eighth Conference of the International Association for the Study of Common Property, Bloomington, Indiana, May 31-June 4. 2000). As we noted above, upon their formation well over 90% of the *ejidos*, using the free choices permitted under the procedures, chose individual rather than unitary operation for the arable land of the enterprise. See generally supra note 37. Pasture and forest land had to remain under unitary operation. The types of procedures adopted in Mexico would often appear beneficial and empowering for members of unitary operations, as well as for individualized ones with umbrella services. For an English translation of the 1992 Agrarian Law, see translation by FTL, edited by M.M. Quick (on file with the Rural Development Institute).

103 See P. Zusman, INDIVIDUAL BEHAVIOR AND SOCIAL CHOICE IN A COOPERATIVE SETTLEMENT—THE THEORY AND PRACTICE OF THE ISRAELI MOSHAV 39-44, 72-95, 98-112, 219-245 (Magnes Press, Hebrew University 1988) (also noting that over time there came to be more governance difficulties, including "free rider" problems).

104 Adapted from Thoms, supra note 102.

105 The relevant title was generally pre-1857 (when new legal "reforms" had enabled widespread land-grabbing from traditional communities), and because of the difficulties in establishing such titles, non-restitutionary expropriation based on the community's need for land was usually the route successfully followed. Thiesenhusen, supra note 7, at 30, 37-38. This process was terminated in 1992.

106 Thoms, supra note 102, at 8.
107 Id. Government observers can attend General Assembly meetings where elections are held, considered to be meetings that are political in nature. Other meetings are open to non-*ejidatorios*. On the importance of secret-ballot elections for representation votes, see generally the provisions of the National Labor Relations Act in the United States discussing the purpose and importance of secret ballot procedures 29 U.S.C. sec. 481(b) (secret ballot election requirements); sec. 402(k) (defining secret ballots); and see also *Marshall v. United Steelworkers of America Local Union 12447*, 591 F.2d 199, 204-205 (1978).
108 Thoms, supra note 102, at 8.
109 Id. at 9.
110 As to the inadequacy of women's rights under the Mexican land tenure reforms (though improved by 1971 changes), see generally L. Stephen, *Too Little, Too Late? The Impact of Article 27 on Women in Oaxaca*, in L. Randell, ed., REFORMING MEXICO'S AGRARIAN REFORM 289 (M.E. Sharpe 1996).
111 Compare discussion of tenancy delegitimization in various states of India in Chapter 6.
112 Constitution of Mexico Art. 27 (as amended in 1992); Ley Agraria (1992) (translated by Foreign Tax Law, Marsh McFadden Quick, ed., National Law Center for Inter-American Free Trade).
113 See J. Brown, *Ejidos and Communidales in Oaxaca, Mexico: Impact of the 1992 Reforms*, RDI Reports No. 120, at 4-5, 15-17, 20-23 (Rural Development Institute 2004).
114 See, e.g., Melmed, supra note 46, at 33-34. On experience with subdivision of holdings in collective-farming settings, see Chapter 7.
115 M. Colchester, et al., PROMISED LAND: PALM OIL AND LAND ACQUISITION IN INDONESIA—IMPLICATIONS FOR LOCAL COMMUNITIES AND INDIGENOUS PEOPLE 42-46, 97-98, 150-155 (Forest People's Programme, Perkumpulan Sawit Watch, HuMA and the World Agro-Forestry Centre 2006).
116 Id. See also World Bank Country Study, supra, note 66.
117 Lastarria-Cornhiel, supra note 6, at 131 (describing *colonos* in Peru).
118 See the discussion of the Peruvian and Chilean experiences.
119 Behuria, supra note 68, annexure III, at 168-183. See generally our discussion in Chapter 6.
120 Government Regulation in Lieu of Act, No. 56 of 1960, *Concerning Fixation of the Size of Agricultural Land*, art. 1 (ceilings); Government Regulation No. 224 of 1961, *Concerning the Implementation of Redistribution of Land and Provision of Compensation*, art. 3 (absentee-owned land).
121 Or, in the case of "absentee" land in Indonesia, through a combination of ambiguity as to what constituted an "absentee"; and a six-month time period to become a resident owner or transfer (or purport to transfer) the land to a resident owner.
122 Such countervailing impact may be felt, exacerbated by unattractive compensation, even when the reform reaches down only modestly below the largest category of estates. Note that, in El Salvador, the 469 over-500 hectare estates covered by "Phase I" of the law were rapidly taken over, but the approximately 1700 smaller (but by local standards quite large) estates covered by "Phase II" were never touched by implementation. Prosterman & Riedinger, supra note 17, at ch. 6. Efforts to include an additional category of somewhat smaller estates in the takings process in Peru also seem to have faltered. Lastarria-Cornhiel, supra note 6, at 149-150.
123 These points do not include, however, programs to provide small homegarden plots for supplemental income and nutrition to such families, which are discussed in Chapter 4.

124 In any ultimate, post-Mugabe reworking of the land reform process in Zimbabwe, what were formerly (but are no longer) capital-intensive estate lands will hopefully be in part redistributed, perhaps with some core holding returned to original owners who wish to resume, and might then be required to agree to provide assistance to small black holders on the remaining estate lands through technical advice, marketing, and other services. Owners not wishing to resume would receive compensation, with the entire holding then available for the option of subdivision by (genuinely poor and needy) recipients.

125 See T. Hanstad & J. Duncan, *Land Reform in Mongolia: Observations and Recommendations*, RDI Reports No. 109 (Rural Development Institute 2001); B. Schwarzwalder, Zheng Baohua, et al., *Tenure and Management for China's Forestland and Grassland Resources: Fieldwork Findings and Legal and Policy Recommendations*, a joint paper of RDI and the Center for Community Development Studies of Yunnan Province (Nov. 2001).

4 Micro-plots for the rural poor

Robert Mitchell, Tim Hanstad and Robin Nielsen

Most redistributional land reform efforts around the globe have been founded on the assumption that the government should give poor rural households at least one hectare (10,000 square meters) of land and often much more. Distribution of such "full-size" or "typical" individual farms (typical according to local standards) essentially forms the assumption behind attempts to implement land-to-the-tiller programs for tenants and, to a somewhat lesser degree, takings of large estates for reallocation to agricultural laborers. That assumption, however, has stalled many if not most large-scale land redistribution efforts.

In many settings, government attempts at traditional land reform confront inflexible financial and political realities. The sheer numbers of tenants and laborers would require the government to acquire so much of the country's total arable land for such traditional reform methods as to render the program financially unaffordable. If the government attempts to reduce the costs of reform by paying little or nothing for the land acquired for redistribution, the program becomes politically untenable and administratively unfeasible in the face of landowner resistance.

Micro-plot allocation programs offer a viable alternative. Micro-plots are plots of land comprising one acre or less that include or are located near the household's house. When sufficient in size and location to erect basic shelter and engage in vegetable gardening, tree cultivation, small-scale livestock raising, home-based businesses, and other income-generating activities, these small plots immediately diversify livelihood strategies and provide a cushion for the most vulnerable populations against economic and environmental shocks. Developed with what is typically the family's most abundant resource – their own labor – such plots often serve several functions simultaneously, including increasing family income, enhancing family nutrition, providing physical security, serving as a vehicle for generating wealth, and securing the family's status within the community.

Micro-plot allocation programs are distinguished from traditional methods of land tenure reform discussed in Chapters 2 and 3 because they require only a small fraction of the amount of land traditional land reforms require and, in many settings of the greatest need, appear capable of being carried out – at least in significant part – using land purchases from willing sellers to obtain the needed land. Under such circumstances, there is no need for mandatory taking from the haves to benefit the have-nots, no need for exercise of eminent domain powers, and little or no need to focus on local power relations that often undermine efforts to carry out traditional land tenure reforms. In this sense, micro-plot allocation programs using a land purchase approach can be understood as a sub-class of the "market-assisted land reform" programs discussed in Chapter 3. Moreover, market purchasing of land in service of a micro-plot program has special characteristics (notably the much smaller amount of land required) that allow it to avoid some of the problematic issues that have arisen when a market-assisted land reform is attempted in support of a land redistribution program involving greater amounts of land.

Despite the important benefits that can be obtained from small amounts of land, the poorest of the poor often do not have access or clear property rights to micro-plots of adequate size. Where the poorest families have permanent shelter on lands of their own, the plot is often so small that the dwelling occupies almost the entire land plot, allowing essentially no additional use of the land. Alternatively, they may own no land, and rely on a landlord for occupancy of a tiny hut. In many settings, allocating adequately sized micro-plots to landless and land poor families in rural and peri-urban areas is a highly feasible, cost-effective way of improving the livelihoods of the poor. Unfortunately, this simple and implementable approach to poverty alleviation remains largely unrecognized in the arenas of international development planning and foreign economic assistance.

India represents a notable exception. After several years of increasing interest in alternatives to traditional land reforms, India's central government recently embraced the concept of allocating micro-plots to landless laborers. India's recently adopted 11th Five-Year Plan (2007-2012) identifies the enormous need within the population of landless households that micro-plots can address:

> An estimated 13 to 18 million families in rural India today are reported to be landless, of which about 8 million lack homes of their own. They either live in a house constructed on the land of others, or provided by land-owners in return for some forced labour. Some of these persons do not have land to construct a house, while others may have small patches of land but no resources to build a hutment.
>
> The right to a roof over one's head needs to be seen as a basic human right, along with the right to freedom from hunger and

right to education. . . . The Eleventh Five-Year Plan provides the opportunity to realize this vision.[1]

The Plan notes that several state governments have recognized the role that micro-plots can play in improving the livelihoods of previously landless rural households and directs the extension of such programs countrywide:

> Several State Governments have already taken steps to provide each family with a minimum size of land (10-15 cents) [0.10 to 0.15 acres], so that they have enough space to live and, also a little extra space for supplementary livelihood activities, such as growing fodder and keeping livestock, planting fruit trees or vegetables, or undertaking other land-based economic activities (farm or non-farm) to improve their food, nutrition and livelihood security. Kerala has a scheme of providing 10 cents of land to each landless family and this has had a notable impact on poverty reduction in the state. Similarly, in 2005, the Governments of Karnataka and West Bengal initiated schemes to give homestead–cum-garden plots to landless families. These experiments should be generalized across all states.
>
> All landless families with no homestead land as well as those without regularized homesteads should be allotted 10-15 cents of land each. Female headed families should have priority.[2]

RDI has been working with the states of Karnataka, West Bengal, Orissa and Andhra Pradesh,[3] and with a planned micro-plot pilot program in Pakistan's Punjab province. RDI has also done research and advisory work on micro-plots in Indonesia and has advised on the tenure reforms related to similar small plots in the former Soviet Union. The knowledge and experience that RDI gained from this work informs the discussion that follows.

This chapter is divided into four sections. The first examines ways in which micro-plot programs can provide the poor with small amounts of land to use for homegardens and other activities that advance livelihood objectives. The second section discusses factors bearing upon the development of micro-plots on newly allocated land or through intensified use of existing micro-plots. The third section discusses how planners can assess the suitability of micro-plot allocation in a particular setting. The fourth section discusses steps for implementing a micro-plot allocation program, from selecting beneficiaries and acquiring land, to monitoring program outcomes.

An important caveat qualifies the discussion that follows. Although micro-plots may make a substantial difference in the livelihoods of the

poor, planners should not consider allocation of micro-plots as a substitute for more traditional land tenure reform that provides larger plots
in settings, such as those identified in Chapters 2 and 3, where such
reform may be possible. Traditional land tenure reforms that provide
larger field plots are designed to create sustainable livelihoods for farmers, and if such reforms are feasible, they should be pursued. In contrast, micro-plots supplement and diversify existing livelihood strategies, and flexible micro-plot allocation programs can be targeted to
reach different (and broader) rural and peri-urban populations than
those targeted by traditional land tenure reforms.

I.   Characteristics and potential benefits of micro-plots

Intensive gardening and other productive use of micro-plots appear to
have developed independently on the Indian subcontinent, Indonesia
and other parts of Southeast Asia, the tropical Pacific islands, the Caribbean, and various parts of tropical Latin America and Africa. Such diverse and intensive productive use of micro-plots – variously referred
to as homegardens, kitchen gardens, house-and-garden plots and
homestead plots – is found in almost all tropical and subtropical eco-
zones where subsistence land-use systems predominate.[4]

Micro-plots have several identifying characteristics. First, they include the household's residence or are located nearby the residence.
Second, micro-plots usually contain a garden and are used for keeping
poultry, livestock or other animals. The proximity of these to the house
makes it easier and less time-consuming for residents to care for and
protect these assets. Third, the garden contains a high diversity of
plants. Fourth, production on the micro-plot is typically supplemental
to rather than the primary source of family income or consumption.
Fifth, the micro-plot occupies a small area, which makes it easier to
fence the plot, further reducing the risk of crop damage from animals
or loss of assets to theft.[5]

The issue of micro-plot size is of particular interest. Although most
commentators identify homegardens as occupying "small" plots, this
criterion is applied to a wide range of plot sizes, varying from a few
square meters to more than one hectare.[6] Because we are interested in
examining how poor households can obtain and beneficially use micro-
plots, we focus on plots of one acre (0.40 hectare) or less. If limited
public resources are to be used to provide the poor with land for housing and gardening, the size of parcels distributed will determine the
number of households benefited.

A sixth distinguishing characteristic of micro-plots is their support
of activities that the poor can easily enter at some level. For example,

families may begin a vegetable garden or tree cultivation with virtually no economic resources, using locally available planting materials, natural manures, and indigenous methods of pest control.[7] At its most basic level homegardening does not require any members of the household to be "entrepreneurial" in any sense: one need only to be able to plant seeds to raise a few basic crops. Similarly, engaging in composting or vermiculture requires simple skills and little initial outlay of capital, and rearing small livestock requires an initial investment in the animals, but the necessary skills are easily learned.

Depending on how they are used, micro-plots can provide a number of benefits to families, ranging from improving nutrition to improving the status of women within the household, as described below.

Improved nutrition

Homegardens are one strategy for addressing two of the most recalcitrant elements of severe poverty – malnutrition and micronutrient deficiencies – by providing poor families with an immediate source of animal products, vegetables and fruits. A number of studies have reported that homegardens produce a high percentage of the fruits and vegetables consumed by homegardening families.[8] A study of wage-earning families in India's Kerala state who cultivate micro-plots revealed that the value of micro-plot production was the most consistent positive predictor of child nutrition, especially during the slack employment season, as well as in households in which the mother is not employed outside the home.[9]

Families often combine gardening with keeping animals on micro-plots. The household uses the animal manure as fertilizer for the garden and as a fuel source. In Javanese homegardens, animals are not confined and receive only minimal feeding: chickens range freely and eat leftovers from the kitchen, while buffalo, cows, goats and sheep graze on village common lands and are fed additional food at night from grasses cut from dykes of rice fields and other areas.[10]

Homegardens and animal rearing can provide important protections against family food insecurity. On Java, climatic conditions mean that owners of homegardens have plants and animal products available for harvest throughout the year. This year-round production is especially important to the economic stability of poor households, particularly during the period between rice harvests.[11] Homegardens may become the principal source of household food and income during periods of stress, as in Kampala, Uganda, after the civil war, where urban agriculture is reported to have substantially fed the city.[12]

The household garden plots on the former Soviet collectives and the "dacha plots" held by urban residents in the former Soviet Union (discussed in Section VII of Chapter 7), have played a major role in ensuring household food security in both the Soviet and post-Soviet era. Such plots – occupying approximately 5% of the arable land – played a similar role in China during the collective farm era. And in then-impoverished Puerto Rico, a 1941 Land Law that provided for allocation of house-and-garden plots to landless agricultural workers helped to ensure food security for recipient families.[13]

Increased and diversified household income

It is a common misconception that micro-plot production is exclusively oriented towards subsistence; in fact, returns to land and labor are often higher for such small plots than for field agriculture.[14] Micro-plots can contribute to household income in several ways. The household may sell products produced on the plot, including fruits, vegetables, animal products and other valuable materials such as bamboo and wood for construction or fuel. The household may also use the micro-plot to conduct cottage industries to produce crafts or manufactured items for sale to third parties.

In addition to direct earnings from the sale of micro-plot production, production consumed by the household frees up household earnings for other purchases.[15] Alternatively, families may use a portion of the cash income from micro-plot activities to purchase additional food for household consumption. Micro-plots provide households with a number of options for satisfying their livelihood objectives, and each household can determine for itself what combination of consumption, trade and sale of micro-plot production best fits its livelihood strategy.

Enhanced wage security and household status

Ownership of a micro-plot can make important contributions to improved and sustainable livelihoods in ways that are often overlooked, including improved leverage in labor markets, enhanced social status and greater political participation. In the 1940s the Puerto Rican government distributed small micro-plots of between one-quarter acre and one acre to the families of agricultural laborers. The law recognized:

> [a] fundamental human right of all the human beings who live
> exclusively by the tilling of the soil, to be the owners of at least a
> piece of land which they may use to erect thereon . . . their own
> homes, thereby delivering them from coercion and leaving them
> free to sell their labor through fair and equitable bargaining.[16]

Roughly 50,000 families received micro-plots under the law, along with a degree of "peace and spiritual satisfaction."[17] Access to small plots of land also allowed the agricultural laborers to participate in elections without selling their votes to the landlord.[18]

As noted in Box 4.1, for rural households in Karnataka, India, increased status within the village was the most cited benefit of new land ownership, surpassing even income and nutrition benefits.[19] Increases in household status not only provide psychological benefits to household members but are believed to provide better access to trade relations within the village as well as better access to government programs serving village households. Micro-plots can also contribute to a more cohesive social environment.[20]

Box 4.1. Additional benefits of owning a residential micro-plot

For otherwise landless families, ownership of a micro-plot used for construction of a house can provide numerous livelihood benefits beyond those derived directly from the activity itself:

1. *Place for residence.* Although perhaps the most obvious, this benefit should not be overlooked when millions of households lack secure rights to land for a house. Secure legal rights to the plot also provide the family with proper incentives to construct a quality house and make other long-term improvements to the plot.

2. *Status.* Studies in India indicate that formerly landless recipients of government-allocated micro-plots cite their increased status as landowners as the most important benefit derived from the plot (more important even than increased income and food consumption).[21]

3. *Wealth generation.* Micro-plots and occupying structures are typically the most important wealth asset of poor households. As these poor households build and improve their house, build wells and other structures, plant trees, and make other labor-intensive improvements to their plots, they create wealth for themselves.

4. *Bargaining leverage in labor markets.* Agricultural laborers who do not own their own house site frequently rely upon their employers for a place to live. This often creates a dependency relationship that severely limits the laborers' bargaining leverage for wages. RDI researchers interviewed a group of landless women in Madhya Pradesh state in India who had been living on their landlord's land for decades. Although they did not pay rent, the landlord paid them only half of market wage rates, did not allow them to work for other farmers, and at times even prevented them from leaving or entering their homes.

5. *Post-harvest activities and storage.* In many settings, the micro-plot is the site for important post-harvest activities such as drying and threshing. The plots also typically provide space for storing food, tools and other capital assets.
6. *Non-agricultural income generation.* Owning a micro-plot with some extra space can enable poor households to pursue non-agricultural production, service or retailing activities such as handicraft production, bicycle repair, blacksmithing or petty shop.
7. *Access to credit.* In a study of government-allocated house-and-garden plots in Karnataka, India, more than one-third of respondents reported that obtaining the plot had increased their access to credit, and nearly one-quarter reported actually receiving credit as a result of owning the plot.[22]

Benefits to women

Rural women are primarily responsible for raising children and, often, caring for elderly parents and relatives – activities that tie them to the house site for long periods of their lives. During these periods, women may be unable to engage in wage labor, migrate to jobs, or work on family-held agricultural land. Even when women are able to work away from the residence, they usually have primary responsibility for numerous residence-based tasks, such as cooking and cleaning, and caring for livestock and poultry. Women are most likely to be physically close to the home and are thus often in the best position to develop micro-plots to suit the needs of the household.

Significant benefits can accrue to women and their households when women have space under their control that can support various home-based activities. A micro-plot of sufficient size for a range of uses and activities can provide a foundation for a woman to contribute to the family's food and income through cultivating a homegarden, raising livestock and poultry, and engaging in income-generation activities. Program designers should therefore consider the possibility that receipt of a micro-plot may add to the workload of women members of households.[23] However, the micro-plot may also provide women with some control over household assets and valuable experience. Sale of micro-plot production may be one of the only sources of independent income for women and may become an important income source.[24] Where women control micro-plot garden resources, household nutrition – especially nutrition of the children – may improve.[25] A home-based enterprise may be a first step toward the woman's management of larger enterprises, such as agricultural land or a small shop, and can be an important source of status for women.[26]

Environmental benefits

Distribution of micro-plots may have beneficial environmental effects on nearby land. For example, where population pressures and lack of arable land threaten to push families to resettle in forests and wetlands, the distribution of micro-plots to landless and land-poor families can reduce pressures to migrate. This not only helps to reduce conversion of lands better left as forests and wetlands, but also limits the growth of unplanned informal settlements and allows families to remain in areas with established social services and markets in which to sell surpluses produced on the micro-plot.[27]

On the micro-plot itself, cultivation of homegardens, composting and vermiculture may assist in recycling nutrients in the soil. A detailed study of four traditional Thai homegardens found that the household practice of refraining from harvesting everything that could be harvested ensured minimal nutrient export from the system.[28] Another potential impact of homegardening is land conservation: terraced micro-plots have been recommended to preserve soils on sloping areas, and fruit trees, bamboo and other trees can be used to rejuvenate infertile soils.[29]

II. Factors related to developing productive micro-plots for the poor

A number of factors combine to determine whether micro-plots are an appropriate strategy for improving the livelihood of poor families. Among these, perhaps the most fundamental factor is access to suitable land – that is, a land plot that is large enough and otherwise physically suitable for the potential uses of the plot, and to which the family has ownership or ownership-like rights. Where access to suitable land is not a constraint to establishing micro-plots (or once planners have arranged to provide secure access to suitable land), other important factors become relevant. Depending on the potential uses for the micro-plots, such factors may include access to water, access to information, and access to stocks of appropriate plants and animals. Cultural acceptance of homegardening, livestock rearing, vermiculture, and other contemplated home-based activities are equally important, as are access to sufficient capital and labor.

Land

Although some poor populations have adequate access to land for micro-plot activities,[30] inadequate access to land remains a significant problem for poor families worldwide, even in areas that commentators commonly associate with micro-plots, such as Java.[31] Even where a family has nominal access to land, the insecurity of their rights to such land may dissuade the family from making long-term investments to improve the land, such as by planting trees, improving drainage, installing fencing or building a fishpond. Squatters and others with particularly insecure rights may even worry that their improvement of the land may lead to eviction as others seek to reap the benefits of the investment. Thus, not only the quality and size of the land, but the nature of the family's right to control the land are critical.

The optimal size of a of micro-plot depends, to some extent, on the activities that the household will undertake. In the case of vegetable and tree cultivation, the size of micro-plots varies considerably across cultures, and even within the same community. In a study of 62 rural homegardening households in Karnataka, India, RDI researchers found that cultivation of trees increased markedly once plot size reached 1800 square feet (about 170 square meters) (see Figure 4.1),[32] suggesting there is likely to be a critical minimum plot size above

Fig. 4.1 Trees planted by Karnataka homegardening househoulds.

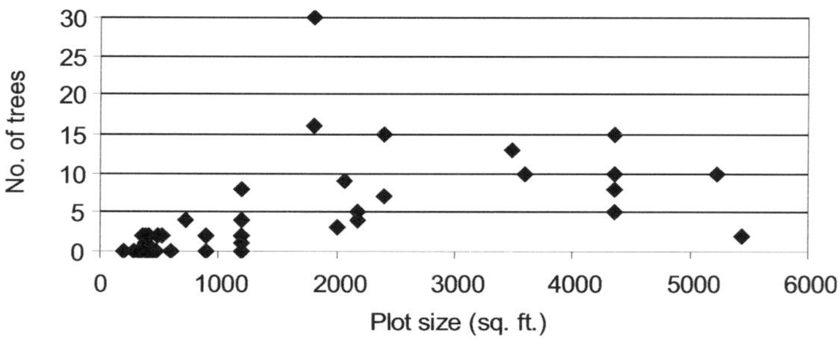

Source: Hanstad & Lokesh 2003 (unpublished data).

which households will begin planting more trees. The footprint of the house itself, which commonly occupies 500 square feet or more, is presumed to reduce greatly the number of trees that can be planted on the smallest parcels.

In a separate study, RDI researchers identified Karnataka households making intensive use of land. Researchers found that families who receive land from the government appear to be as likely to plant trees or raise animals as are families who inherit or purchase the micro-plot,[33] which suggests that for some families in Karnataka, access to land of adequate size is a primary barrier to tree planting and animal raising.[34]

Water

Some micro-plot activities, such as vegetable gardening and livestock raising, require attention to the availability of water. Although gardens on micro-plots are primarily rainfed, homegardeners commonly irrigate during the dry season. Watering depends on the type of crop and can vary from twice daily to twice annually.[35] Several studies have found that drawing and transporting water and hand irrigating the garden are the most onerous and time-consuming gardening tasks.[36] Homegardens that require even a few gallons of water per day may require too much labor to be worthwhile, depending on the location of the water source.

In some areas, lack of water may be the major factor limiting the use of micro-plots for gardens. In Papua New Guinea, potable, piped water for irrigation is the most expensive input for urban homegardeners, and water is especially expensive during the dry season.[37] It can be prohibitively expensive for the household to install a system for bringing water to the house, and there is a large social cost for providing irrigation water to households, especially in urban areas.[38] On the other hand, labor-intensive and appropriate technology improvements such as micro-catchments for holding rainwater or scavenged and plastic containers perforated to function as a no-cost substitute for drip irrigation may allow the maximum use of the available water.

Capital

The need for capital to invest in micro-plot activities varies according to which activities the household selects and the physical attributes of the plot. Where households have access to capital, their micro-plots can be more productive.[39] However, capital is not always necessary for gardening if households use sustainable practices, such as composting, terracing land, and planting leguminous trees to improve soil fertility. These activities may be labor intensive (and require the household to value the benefits of such activities), but do not require large amounts of capital.

Other activities, such as livestock rearing, may require initial investments in stock and construction of fencing and shelters, but thereafter require only limited on-going expenditures. The capital requirements of home-based businesses will necessarily depend on the nature of the business. For example, stocking a small shop or establishing a handicraft business from scratch will require an initial outlay of capital, but expanding an existing enterprise may require far less.

Culture and experience

Cultural norms, traditional practices, personal preferences, and local experience may all influence the activities selected for micro-plot development. Although projects to promote gardening often prefer to work with communal organizations, household-level food production must be a family undertaking since labor, space and time are valuable resources to poor households. Thus, the presence of viable homegardens in the immediate vicinity of the project area is the best predictor of success since such homegardens demonstrate that homegardening is socially and culturally acceptable and is valued by households.[40]

Cultural preferences may inhibit households from taking up gardening. Households may associate homegardening with poverty and therefore decline to establish gardens. Public education may be very useful in promoting gardening, poultry and livestock raising, and other beneficial uses such as vermiculture and composting. And in different settings, different uses may be emphasized: RDI researchers in the south of Pakistan's Punjab province, for example, observed a strong local preference for varied animal husbandry on micro-plots, while in the Indian state of Gujarat, one micro-pilot colony of weavers used their house plots to support their weaving business, including building covered areas for their looms and sheds for storing materials and finished products.

III.   Assessing the suitability of micro-plot programs

In what settings does it make sense to consider using public or private resources to help poor populations gain possession of micro-plots? As an initial matter, policy makers and planners should determine whether traditional land tenure reform measures remain viable, including in circumstances such settings that may emerge unpredictably as, for example, through changes in political leadership. In such settings the allocation of micro-plots should not be considered a substitute for more traditional land tenure reform that would benefit families whose income derives primarily from farming land, but who do not own the land on which they work.

For example, some Indonesian NGOs assert that traditional land tenure reform may be necessary both to correct fundamental inequities in the distribution of farmland and to correct government policies that have deprived farm families of access to land they or their ancestors have farmed historically. As this is written, it remains unclear whether Indonesia may be a setting where traditional land tenure reform, which was neither politically nor financially supported and a failure under President Sukarno's earlier attempt in the 1960s, is presently a serious possibility.

Identifying potential beneficiary populations

In determining whether to adopt micro-plot allocation as a strategy for improving the livelihood of poor families, planners must begin by defining the class of prospective beneficiaries. Definition of the general class of beneficiaries is presumed to depend upon the base poverty line, family ownership of land and various other assets, established residency in the target region, and other measurements already familiar to planners. Using the program's threshold eligibility requirements, planners should gather preliminary information regarding the populations of potential beneficiaries in a given area. Based on the survey findings, planners can determine target areas for assessing the general suitability of the program. Where planners find that potential beneficiaries are located throughout the state or country, more specific inquiries will help identify areas where the program can be initiated to best effect.

Assessing general suitability of micro-plots in target area

A second threshold question is whether allocation of micro-plots, as well as improvement of existing micro-plots, are likely to benefit substantial numbers of the rural poor in the target areas. To answer this question, planners should first ask whether micro-plots presently provide benefits to families in the vicinity of the target areas. The analysis of the extent of beneficial use of micro-plots in a region should encompass all productive uses. Areas in which households have historically been unable to overcome climatic, economic and cultural constraints to homegardening may not be appropriate areas for homegardening interventions. However, the same areas may be conducive to other uses of micro-plots, such as livestock rearing or handicraft production.

If micro-plot gardens do not exist or do not appear to be providing substantial benefits to families within the target area, planners can consider whether micro-plots are providing benefits in settings that planners judge to be analogous to the target setting, including settings in other communities with comparable climates and cultural norms and similar resource constraints. Planners should draw upon the knowledge and experience of NGOs, local leaders, teachers and other individuals with a good knowledge of the target area and potential beneficiaries. In some areas, circumstances may suggest that residents are well equipped to make use of new micro-plots. For example, the target area may include potential beneficiaries with no house plot or permanent shelter who would obtain immediate benefits from receiving micro-plots, or a local NGO may already be working with the poor on projects such as vermiculture, composting or production of handicrafts that families could expand on land received in a micro-plot allocation program.

The preliminary assessment should examine the availability and cost of land and water in the target area, and the cost of other inputs such as capital and plant and animal stocks. Where land is prohibitively expensive to purchase, or where adequate water cannot be brought to the micro-plot site for a reasonable cost, allocation of micro-plots may be impractical. Figure 4.2 presents a decision tree summarizing some of these considerations, which are explored in more detail in the remainder of the chapter.

In assessing whether micro-plots might provide benefits to the target population, planners will likely gain important knowledge from field inquiries, using rapid or participatory appraisal methods[41] to investigate the following issues:

(1) *What are the existing typical uses of micro-plots by the local population, what typical benefits do families derive, and what constraints to plot use do families confront?* Inquiries should focus on a representative sample of the beneficiary population using micro-plots of various sizes.

(2) *What potential uses and benefits do micro-plots offer the beneficiary population?* Inquiries should focus on a purposively selected sample of the local population that have well-developed micro-plots, looking also at why such families are able to use their micro-plots productively.

(3) *What best practices have emerged from NGO or other interventions related to micro-plots in the target area?* In some areas, NGOs or government departments may work with the local population on projects that involve micro-plots, such as vegetable growing, tree cultivation, animal husbandry, and home-based businesses. Project implementers and beneficiaries can reveal what is working (and not working), and such populations may be good candidates for the allocation of new (or larger) micro-plots.

Selection of target area and teaming with local groups

Once planners have evaluated the preliminary information gathered, they can select specific locales for micro-plot projects and assign project staff. Project staff, who will often be local government officials, should ideally have some experience in rural development and working

Figure 4.2. *Analyzing appropriateness of micro-plot allocation*

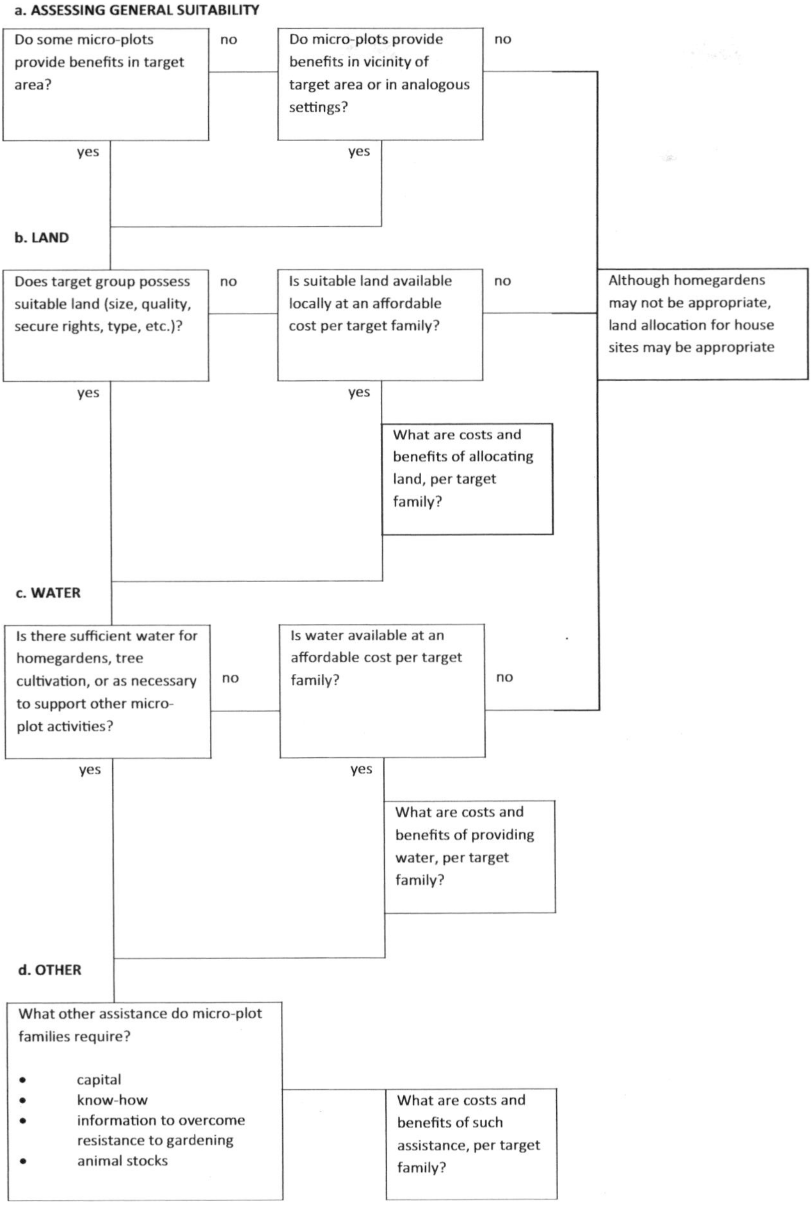

a. ASSESSING GENERAL SUITABILITY

Do some micro-plots provide benefits in target area?	no →	Do micro-plots provide benefits in vicinity of target area or in analogous settings?	no →
yes		yes	

b. LAND

Does target group possess suitable land (size, quality, secure rights, type, etc.)?	no →	Is suitable land available locally at an affordable cost per target family?	no →	Although homegardens may not be appropriate, land allocation for house sites may be appropriate
yes		yes		

What are costs and benefits of allocating land, per target family?

c. WATER

Is there sufficient water for homegardens, tree cultivation, or as necessary to support other micro-plot activities?	no →	Is water available at an affordable cost per target family?	no →
yes		yes	

What are costs and benefits of providing water, per target family?

d. OTHER

What other assistance do micro-plot families require?

- capital
- know-how
- information to overcome resistance to gardening
- animal stocks

What are costs and benefits of such assistance, per target family?

Adapted from R. Mitchell & T. Hanstad, *Small Homegarden Plots and Sustainable Livelihoods for the Poor* 26 (FAO, Rome 2004).

with poor and marginalized groups. Project staff should also consider teaming with local NGOs that have worked with the local community. The process of gathering information and making decisions relating to project implementation will benefit greatly from the expertise available through local NGOs, community workers, and others with local knowledge. Project staff should, however, take care that NGO partners are well established and have solid records of success with local communities, and particularly with the poorest members of the communities. Project staff should be alert to any biases or pre-existing relationships between NGOs and potential beneficiaries of the project.

Review of the legal framework

At the planning stage it is useful to consider legal issues likely to affect the allocation and future use of micro-plots so that these can be addressed at the program level. Planners should be aware of current land uses, classifications and restrictions that might impact the allocation and development of the land. Where politically feasible, government programs should streamline the administrative requirements (such as the need to convert land from agricultural to non-agricultural use) and eliminate or reduce fees to facilitate projects and reduce opportunities for bribes and rent seeking at local levels. However, even if some legal issues can be addressed at a program level, at the local level project staff must also be able to identify legal issues and take appropriate action. For example, project staff must know how they will determine the lawful owner of the land that is to be acquired, sub-divided and allocated as micro-plots, and should be able to determine whether the land is subject to unregistered rights, such as squatter rights.

Finally, prior to finalizing the design of the program, planners should determine what rights can be granted to beneficiaries (e.g., ownership versus restricted rights), what restrictions will accompany the allocation (including whether the beneficiaries will have the right to transfer the land), whether the rights will be registered in the names of both women and men, whether the government will retain rights to the land (such as for community uses), and what additional support beneficiaries can receive. For example, the program may allow beneficiaries to qualify for low-cost financing for investment in the micro-plot, requiring a financing framework and links to a financial institution.

IV.   Implementation of micro-plot programs

Implementation of a micro-plot program requires a great deal of detailed work at the village level, and large-scale projects will require a significant number of local staff. Planners of a large-scale project should give substantial thought to the design of the framework for staff training and project management. In some settings, local government bodies with experience in implementing economic and social programs and land initiatives may have the capacity, experience and human resources to implement a micro-plot project independently. In other settings, the government may need to partner with an NGO or other entity to ensure successful implementation. We divide implementation considerations into eleven steps, discussed in the following pages.

Step 1: Select beneficiary households

Selection of beneficiaries for a micro-plot project begins with creating a list of selection criteria. At the time project staff begin identifying potential beneficiary households, staff may not know how many households will ultimately be included in the project since it may not yet be clear how much suitable land is available.

Adopt site-specific criteria. Programs should focus on households that do not own a suitable micro-plot, and basic threshold selection criteria, such as income and asset levels, should apply to all beneficiaries. In addition, the program should allow project staff to apply additional site-specific criteria tailored to the population in the target area. Project staff should choose the additional criteria to take into account the objectives of the micro-plot project and any special characteristics of the target area. Local NGOs and community workers can often help identify useful criteria. These criteria will provide project staff a basis for prioritizing among poor households and organizing households into residential colonies. Examples of additional criteria include households headed by women, households containing members suffering from HIV/AIDS, and households displaced by regional conflicts.

Define household. In many settings it is common to find that married children occupy the homesite of their parents, such that several generations comprised of several nuclear families occupy the same homesite. Often, the second generation is functionally landless since they own no land of their own, and the homesite is too small to support significant non-housing uses by the occupying nuclear families. Planners may therefore be inclined to adopt a definition of household that refers to nuclear families consisting of parents and unmarried children, such that the family of each married child is considered a separate household. Planners might consider drafting parameters to include in the program any household that does not have access to an adequate amount of land, whether owned by that household or a relative.[42]

Use existing lists of disadvantaged families. When program managers identify certain areas or villages for a micro-plot project, project staff may receive a list of potential beneficiaries from that area – lists prepared earlier by project staff while investigating the target area, prepared in the past by other poverty alleviation programs, or prepared as part of a general census. Such lists form a useful starting point but should be verified in the field to determine the eligibility of each listed household and to make certain that no eligible family has been overlooked. In particular, lists may not include the poorest and most marginalized families since these are often the least visible members of rural society, the least likely to have learned of a census or other survey, and the least able to protect their own interests.[43]

Meet with prospective beneficiaries. In applying the site-specific criteria to make the final selection of beneficiaries, project staff should meet with each prospective beneficiary family. The more project staff can learn about the population, the better able the staff will be to make good decisions about the selection of beneficiaries and tailor the project to their needs.

Box 4.2. Characteristics of successful micro-plot families

Research on new colony developments in India indicates that, in addition to the formal eligibility requirements imposed, beneficiaries with the following characteristics contribute to the success of a micro-plot project:
- A genuine desire to relocate to the new homesite;
- Expressed interest in preparing a plan for using the micro-plot to benefit the household;
- A willingness to contribute their own labor or resources to the micro-plot project – to improve both their individual plots, and roads and other shared land; and
- Confidence that participating in the micro-plot project will ultimately have a positive impact on their lives.

Focus on women beneficiaries. Project staff should pay special attention to women throughout the implementation process. As was noted earlier, women are most likely to spend a significant amount of time on the micro-plot, and to the extent women control the use of the plot and its production, their children and households benefit. Project staff should conduct a separate evaluation of the village population to identify any widows, single women and women heads of household (who otherwise satisfy program criteria) to ensure their inclusion in the program, and should take particular note of women's opinions and interests in the project design and implementation.[44] Because women's voices may be muffled by more powerful voices in the community, project staff should meet separately with women individually and in groups to ensure their voices are heard at every stage of the process.

Composition of micro-plot colonies. In many cases, project staff will be designing a project that involves the creation of new colonies of micro-plots, which may be adjacent to an existing settlement or separately located (see discussion of locating new colonies in step 2). Practical considerations of land availability, numbers of local beneficiaries, economies of scale relating to infrastructure development, project resources, and management and governance of the site will likely result in initial colonies of between ten and 50 households.

Although the homogeneity or heterogeneity of the beneficiary group does not necessarily affect the success of the projects, research conducted in India suggests that beneficiaries are generally most comfortable with an environment that reproduces their current living situation.[45] Thus, where prospective beneficiaries live in ethnically mixed villages, they tend to be comfortable with a mixed group, and where prospective beneficiaries live in a more homogeneous environment, they prefer a community of a single social or economic group.[46]

Step 2: Identify sources of land

Ideally, the beneficiaries should participate in the land selection, and the final land selection should therefore follow beneficiary selection; however, since land is a critical component of the project, project staff should begin considering land selection issues as soon as they select the target area.

Enlarging existing micro-plots. In the course of selecting beneficiaries, project staff will simultaneously determine the need for land. Some potential beneficiary households may own a micro-plot that is too small for anything other than habitation. Others may be nuclear families crowded onto land owned by parents or other relatives, and thus have insufficient land for gardening or income-generating activities. Where households already use very small micro-plots, project staff should investigate whether it is possible to acquire land adjacent to those plots that could be used to enlarge the plots to provide each nuclear family ownership of an adequately sized plot.

Creating new micro-plots. In most cases, land will not be available adjacent to the plot currently occupied by the household. Project staff must therefore identify "new" land that can be acquired and used to create new micro-plots for allocation to beneficiaries. This will require project staff to determine the basic characteristics of land sought and possible sources. At this stage, project staff should identify as many parcels as possible. Project staff can work through this list of possibilities as they visit the parcels and learn more about the needs, interests and capacities of the beneficiary households.[47]

Siting new micro-plots. In some cases, project staff will identify available land – such as degraded communal land or abandoned private land – within existing boundaries of the village where beneficiary households reside. If such land is available, project staff should consult with the owners and users of such land, as well as with prospective beneficiaries of the project, to determine the land's suitability for new micro-plots.

Where sufficient land is not available in the village, project staff must seek land outside the village to create a new residential colony, having in mind the following: (1) proximity to beneficiaries' village; (2) proximity to beneficiaries' employment; (3) availability of water for drinking and for watering livestock and gardens; (4) access to main road, markets and primary schools; and (5) soil quality and slope of the ground. Project staff should also confirm that a colony would not create an environmental problem or place stress on natural resources in a given area.

The proximity of the planned colony to the village and employment is often critical to the success of the project, and project staff should openly discuss the issue with the group of prospective beneficiaries prior to selecting the land. In some cases, prospective beneficiaries will only be interested in a colony that is adjacent to the village, or no further than a certain distance, often measured by the time it takes to walk from the nearest settlement or employment. In other cases, prospective beneficiaries may be willing to move farther, particularly if the new colony will be large and will include significant infrastructure. Culture also plays a role: in some cultures, people take security and pleasure in living in more dense arrangements, while other cultures value open space and independent living.[48]

In addition, because women often have primary responsibility for childrearing, caring for elderly relatives, food preparation and maintaining the house, they are more likely to spend time in and around the micro-plot, and their experiences will inform their opinions regarding land location. Women often have specific concerns about how the organization of plots relates to their physical safety and the safety of their children, and may also be concerned about the distance between the micro-plot and schools and opportunities for day labor.

Land sources. Some programs will limit land sources to publicly owned land, others may require consideration of available public land but allow the project to purchase private land, and other programs may deal exclusively with purchased private land.

Programs allowing land purchase should have clear guidelines for the process of identifying private land for purchase to prevent existing landowners from taking advantage of the program to drive up land prices and dispose of unsuitable land (see Box 4.3). The guidelines should also include safeguards, such as disclosure of the economic position and status of the landholder, to prevent the government from purchasing land from impoverished owners through distress sales. In all cases, the project plan must include procedures whereby project staff verify that landholders have clear ownership rights and the legal authority to sell.

If the project is implemented by the government, as it usually will be when on any large scale, there may be a preference for using public land, where available and suitable, to avoid the need to purchase land. In addition, local officials may be less familiar with sources of private land, and it may take longer for project staff to locate private sellers, inspect the land, confirm the ownership, and negotiate the purchase. However, public land should not be used for micro-plot projects simply because it is available; public land must meet the same criteria demanded for private land to be regarded as suitable for the program.

Plot size. How big should micro-plots be in order for the household to reap the substantial benefits available? In determining optimum plot size, planners should consider that the goal of the allocation is not to provide each household with a plot it will use to earn its primary source of income but to provide a plot that the household can use to meet a portion of its food needs and supplement family income. The plot should be large enough that the majority of the micro-plot can be devoted to activities beyond simply sheltering the household, but small enough that a household can develop it, maintain it, and invest in activities on the plot without crippling the household's resources. In addition, limiting the size of the micro-plot and siting them in colonies comprised of poor households may also reduce the threat that local elites will seek to capture the benefits of the program.

In part, the optimum size of the plot depends on the activities planned for the plot. RDI's research in India leads us to conclude that in many Indian settings a minimum plot size of 1800 square feet (170 square meters) is necessary to allow a household to garden intensively and raise small livestock, and that a plot size of 3000 to 4000 square feet (280 to 370 square meters) is much preferred. Our preliminary research in Java has revealed that households are able to garden intensively on plots in the same size range.[49] The question of what minimum micro-plot size is sufficient to allow a household to garden, raise livestock, and make other economic use of the plot is an empirical one that must be answered with reference to local practices, local economic conditions, and the productive potential of the land itself. However, in the early design of programs, planners can use a plot of 3000 to 4000

square feet (280 to 370 square meters) for planning, and later refine
the range after collecting more information.

Land cost. While the cost of purchasing private land on the market
may be quite affordable, the nature of land – the fact that it is immovable, and the fact that access to land can have important social and political implications – makes its allocation more complicated than allocation of other inputs such as water, know-how, and plant and animal
stocks. For these reasons, it is appropriate for planners to evaluate the
costs of identifying, obtaining and allocating land independent of other
costs.

In Karnataka, India, a November 2001 sample of 400 rural households in four districts estimated the value of unimproved and non-irrigated agricultural land to be between 21,000 and 44,000 rupees per
acre, with an average of 33,250 rupees per acre,[50] which equates to approximately US$694 per acre (US$1714 per hectare) at then current exchange rates. This represents an average cost of approximately US$64
per family if each receives 370 square meters (4000 square feet) of
land.[51] These estimates reflect the likely purchase price of acquiring
agricultural land at market prices, but do not include administrative
costs of acquisition and allocation, or costs of constructing simple
roads, tubewells and electrification. Although such costs are likely to
be low in comparison to land acquisition costs, they are not negligible.

If planners determine that appropriate land is available in the vicinity of the target population, they should then calculate the cost of purchasing such land (if it is private), as well as the administrative costs of
obtaining and allocating the land, calculated in terms of costs per family benefited. Planners must also consider whether and to what extent the beneficiaries should share in the costs of land purchase as well
as other costs. Important factors to consider include: affordability for
what are likely to be among the society's poorest households, administra-
trative costs of collection (relative to benefits of such collection), and
the desirability of cost-sharing by beneficiaries to promote their "ownership" of the program activities.

Step 3: Evaluate possibility of adverse impacts

During selection of land for the micro-plot project, project staff should
be alert for any potential adverse impacts from the project. In most
cases, such impacts can be avoided through adequate planning. This
step occurs during identification of the land.

Common property resources. Project staff should take special care to
verify all the users of the land to be allocated as micro-plots. The government often claims ownership of common property resources such
as community forests or wastelands located near villages and suggests

Box 4.3. Controlling the purchase price for land

Project staff often cite program ceilings on the rate they can pay for land as the most significant factor inhibiting the process of finding land to purchase for projects. Some tactics that program designers and project staff can consider to create more options for land purchases include:

- Advertise the project's ability to pay for the land immediately and in a lump sum. Landowners selling to private parties often receive payment over time and may worry whether they have sufficient security for the unpaid balance. Even if the seller's retention of title until final payment is considered sufficient security, the opportunity to obtain a lump sum payment versus smaller payments spread over years is very attractive to sellers. Landowners may be willing to sell to the government for a lower price – or be willing to sell land they would otherwise not sell – if they receive an immediate, lump sum payment.
- Consider offering a landowner other benefits in addition to cash payment for the land. For example, if the project purchases a portion of the landowner's land and will be making improvements on that section, offer to make similar improvements on land retained by the owner, such as providing a bore well, extending a road, or providing electricity service.
- If large rural development projects are acquiring land, such as for an irrigation project, include some land for micro-plot colonies in the plans for the larger project.
- Possibly use a "Dutch auction," where landowners compete to offer the lowest price for a given size (including quality and location) of land parcel.

that the project use those lands. Project staff should determine who is using such land; the poorest families often depend on access to and use of forests and other public lands to hunt, graze livestock and gather plants for consumption, fodder, medicine and fuel.[52] Even where the staff recognize that such activities occur, they may underestimate the importance of these activities in the household economy of the poorest families. It would be counterproductive to eliminate a common property resource that provides a low level of support to a large number of poor families in order to distribute micro-plots to a smaller number of families, even if the total economic use of the land would be enhanced by such a use conversion.

Arable land. In siting projects, project staff should consider whether the creation of micro-plots will reduce the amount of arable land, possibly causing a fall in overall agricultural production or exacerbating food security concerns. In Indonesia, some government planners have expressed concern that land located near rural villages on Java is prime irrigated rice paddy land, the terracing of which has been undertaken at great social cost. Strict policies are in place to prevent the conversion of such land to other uses, though the conversion of rice paddy land to residential land sometimes continues to occur.

Even if arable land is used to create micro-plots, the new uses are likely to be beneficial for several reasons. First, since only very small plots are needed to provide important benefits to families, the total amount of land needed for a micro-plot colony is modest. Assuming that 5% of the acquired land is used to construct roads, drainage and other infrastructure, a one hectare plot could provide 380 square meter plots (4100 square feet) to 25 households. To place this in perspective, in India, distribution of 380 square meter plots to each of the nation's estimated roughly 15 million completely landless rural families would require only 600,000 hectares of land, which is approximately 4/10 of 1% of the nation's 161.8 million hectares of arable land.[53]

Second, if households develop their plots for homegardens and livestock at a moderate intensity, the plots will likely produce as least as much agricultural value per unit area as had been produced on the arable land. A study of Javanese homegardens found that net income per square meter of homegardens was higher than for rice fields and required much lower costs of production.[54] The latter is particularly important for poor households, who typically have less access to credit and are less able to insure against risk. A study of well-developed homegardens in Karnataka indicates that the income per square meter is several times higher than arable land in the same area used for grain crops.[55]

Finally, even if homegardens on micro-plots did not produce as much per hectare as arable land in some specific setting, any general social loss would be offset to the degree that micro-plots efficiently provide foods to one of the most food-insecure segments of the population. Homegardens are likely to make such foods available to the poor more efficiently than other government food programs since the poor themselves control the choice, use and distribution of homegarden products.

Women's workload. One potential adverse impact of micro-plot allocation programs is an increase in the workload of women beneficiaries. Because women tend to be the primary caretakers of children and the elderly and often have full responsibility for house-related tasks such as cooking and cleaning, they are likely to spend more time near the family residence than men. If the household receives a larger plot, particularly with the expectation that the new micro-plot will support one or more activities, women's workloads will likely increase.

As an initial matter of simple equity, the likely increase in women's workload and responsibilities requires that they receive joint or individual title to the micro-plot. In many cases, women may welcome the opportunities presented in micro-plot programs. Because of their physical connection to the micro-plot, women may have a greater input into decision making regarding micro-plot activities and more significant control over the production from the micro-plot, including the management of any income earned.

In addition, women may have an opportunity to obtain skills and experience in new areas, such as raising livestock and growing vegetables for household consumption and sale in the market. RDI researchers working in the Indian state of Karnataka found that women who received house plots from a government program and technical assistance with income-generation activities from a local NGO used their plots to begin a diverse range of income-producing activities, including egg production, tailoring and milk production. In South Sulawesi, Indonesia, RDI researchers met a self-help group of women who used credit available through a local women's cooperative to begin businesses on their micro-plots selling baked goods and dried seaweed. In both cases, aided by capacity building and NGOs, the women had substantial control over their activities and the earnings from those activities.

These positive impacts and achievements are by no means assured, however. Programs that best serve the interests of women and their families include early and consistent involvement of women in all stages of the program design, focused attention on the issue of titling of the micro-plots, and capacity building for beneficiaries (both individuals and households) on issues of gender equity, and also recognize the value of linking micro-plot programs with local NGOs with experience working with local communities, including specific programs for women.

Step 4: Ensure access to water

Water deserves special consideration during project planning. In many environments, water is likely to be the most important consideration after land. Access to water is necessary for consumption (household and livestock), washing and bathing, and garden irrigation. In some environments, water may be even more scarce than land and more expensive to supply during the dry season. Where water is scarce throughout the year, its absence may preclude establishing new colonies or encouraging homegardening as a viable strategy for the use of micro-plots.

On the other hand, the amount of water needed for homegardening is often not great, and carrying water to the garden may be a reasonable solution. In addition, water availability should be considered when identifying which trees and other plantings to promote in homegardening. Project planners may be able to reduce garden water demand by providing extension advice on water conservation and subsidizing low-cost techniques home gardeners can use to collect, store and use rainwater and household wastewater efficiently.[56]

Step 5: Consider housing options

Housing is a critical element of a micro-plot allocation program, and project staff should determine at the design stage how housing requirements will be addressed and communicate those program terms to prospective beneficiaries to ensure that expectations match the project realities.

Where separate government housing programs exist, project managers can assist beneficiaries in applying for benefits under the appropriate program. Where such programs do not exist, project managers must discuss with prospective micro-plot beneficiaries the options for house construction, including the need for beneficiaries to rely on their own resources. Some households will be prepared to construct a permanent house on the micro-plot, while others may opt to build a temporary shelter with plans to replace it later with a more permanent structure. Others may be unwilling to build a house unless the project finances construction.

In evaluating the social value of distributing micro-plots, it is useful to evaluate the efficacy of alternative programs targeted to assist the same populations. In India, for example, RDI has found that government resources devoted to constructing housing for landless families would reach more beneficiaries if some portion of program resources were diverted from housing construction and instead used to obtain larger house sites that provide space for gardening, livestock rearing, and other activities. Our own field research in India indicates that even the poorest rural households are able to accumulate the resources to construct a house (in stages) if they have secure rights to an adequate house site.[57]

Step 6: Issue ownership titles to land

Programs often contain requirements relating to title to the land and to any house constructed on the land. Requirements may include factors such as whose name must be on the title and restrictions on the use or sale of the land. The following recommendations can maximize benefits to micro-plot beneficiaries (also discussed more broadly in Chapter 8):

First, project guidelines should require the micro-plot (and any new house provided) to be titled jointly in the name of husband and wife, with a clear right of survivorship, or titled individually in the name of the woman beneficiary (whether single, married, widowed or head of household). This provides some additional protection to women in the event of abandonment, divorce or death of the husband. In addition, where women have land rights and control production from the land, they tend to use the assets to care for the welfare of children and the household. In addition, land rights increase the respect women receive within their marriages, households, and communities.[58] These and other benefits of protecting women's land rights are examined in detail in Chapter 5.

Joint titling may also provide another incremental advantage (legally irrelevant, but potentially significant psychologically) by requiring the wife's name to be listed first in the title documents. Listing the woman's name first helps maintain accurate records of ownership since drafters and clerks may be tempted to list only one of multiple right-holders to save time. If women's names are in the primary position, the drafters and clerks are less likely to drop the second name.

Second, project guidelines should include providing beneficiary households with education relating to women's property rights, and the positive impact of such rights on the family.

Third, the guidelines should require registration of the title in accordance with applicable procedures and law.

Fourth, the guidelines should require that project staff provide beneficiaries with a copy of the title document.

Fifth, where land is restricted to agriculture or other non-residential uses, the guidelines should require project staff to work with the local government to amend the classification of the land to allow the construction of houses. Project staff should ensure that such changes occur prior to subdividing and titling the land in the name of beneficiaries. As an alternative to addressing the issue locally, the state or central government may include a general enabling provision as part of a broad micro-plot distribution program.

Finally, if the government places restrictions on future transfers of the property, planners should work with the government to limit the restrictions to a reasonable period (e.g., five or ten years) and also limit the scope of the restrictions (e.g., allowing short-term leases). The limited restrictions will help ensure that the household directly realizes the benefits of the asset, but will also allow the household to sell or lease the land in the future to accommodate the changing needs of the household. RDI's observations in a variety of field settings suggest, however, that even in the complete absence of legal restrictions households are generally not likely to sell such plots in the early years, and micro-plots occupied by a house are almost never leased out.

Step 7: Design and develop residential colony

Project staff should work in partnership with a committee representing the beneficiaries regarding design of the micro-plot residential colony. Issues that the team should decide include how the space will be laid out, and what infrastructure and common areas will be provided within the colony. The team should plan the development and identify the parties responsible for implementing each element of the development. The project staff together with beneficiaries should consider incorporating "covenants" or other requirements concerning the micro-plots.

Typically, colony development will ultimately include: (a) developing water sources; (b) platting plot sites, roads and common spaces; (c) preparing the land through clearing, leveling, draining, etc.; (d) building roads to link the colony to existing roads and provide access to each plot; and (e) installing infrastructure such as electricity and sanitation. Depending on their size and resources, some colonies may wish to include construction of a place of worship, community buildings, and development of green spaces or other common areas. As a practical matter, all desired infrastructure may not be possible in the early stages, and project staff and beneficiaries should prioritize various types of infrastructure in the development plan.

The development plan should also address how the colony will govern itself. An informal committee or governing body can assist a new colony in handling issues that arise in the early days, such as development of infrastructure and use of common facilities. The committee should include at least one member from each represented community or sub-community and should include both women and men. The committee should be responsible for ensuring that the project provides equal treatment to various groups and households. The committee should appoint one or more individuals to be the spokesperson in dealings with local government and project staff.

Step 8: Address cultural barriers

Cultural issues are among the most powerful forces determining the success or failure of poverty alleviation projects, yet among the least recognized. Cultural preferences and attitudes may impact all aspects of a project, such as defining who are appropriate beneficiaries, what kind of land beneficiaries prefer to receive, what groups should be included in a new colony, what activities are appropriate to engage in on the house plot, who in the household should perform the tasks related to the activity, and who should control income generated on the plot. In planning projects, staff should be alert to the impact of cultural preferences and traditions. In some cases, projects may be redesigned to harmonize with cultural preferences, while in other cases, the project may see whether it is possible, through public education, to modify some practice or attitude that threatens to undermine the objectives of the project.

As examples, some cultural practices and beliefs may impact the success of homegardens. In India, many rural Hindu households that have only a small space beyond the footprint of the house will elect to use the space to grow flowers for religious ceremonies and decorations before considering vegetables. In some areas of the world, households may associate homegardening with poverty and therefore decline to establish gardens.[59] In Nepal, dark green leafy vegetables are often considered low-status foods, which might help to explain why researchers found that consumption of vitamin A-rich foods did not increase along with homegarden size in the studied groups.[60]

Public information campaigns can play an important role in addressing some cultural barriers to the effective use of micro-plots. Many families are not aware, for example, that vegetables and fruits are nutritious. In Bangladesh, for example, researchers found that dark green leafy vegetables are widely believed to be bad for young children,[61] while a study of Philippine urban homegardeners found that mothers generally had no knowledge of vitamins and iron in foods until informed by community health workers.[62] The good news is that there is evidence that poor families who receive health information will respond by planting more fruits and vegetables, including dark green leafy vegetables, than families who have not received such information, regardless of socio-economic status, size of the micro-plot, and general knowledge of nutrition.[63]

Step 9: Provide access to capital and inputs

Most beneficiaries of micro-plot allocation programs will, by definition, have little or no capital to invest in the development and operation of any activity on their micro-plot.[64] However, as was noted earlier, one important characteristic of homegardening is that the poor may produce returns without making large investments of capital. For example, in India, a "kitchen garden kit" developed for a pilot activity containing seven varieties of tree seedlings, high-quality vegetable seeds and five hybrid chicks cost 600 Rupees, or about US$16 at current exchange rates. Elsewhere in India, businesses that sell products such as woven cloth or incense hire households to produce the finished product in their homes, supplying the households with the raw materials and deducting the cost of materials from the final price paid for the completed product.

Ultimately, allocation of micro-plots is most likely to be a useful strategy for improving the livelihoods of poor households to the extent that they are willing to invest scarce savings in productive activities. For example, in India, we have met very poor agricultural laborer families who invested scarce family capital to construct housing, plant trees and raise poultry and livestock once they obtained secure ownership of small plots of land. These families received no government assistance in purchasing inputs for homegardening and instead decided to use their own very limited resources to invest in their micro-plot.

As with many development interventions, programs to distribute micro-plots to the poor bring with them the risk that beneficiary families will not value what they receive free of charge. One solution to this problem is for program guidelines to require that micro-plot recipients invest their own time and labor to make improvements to the plot, such as construction of a house. Families are likely to value such assets more if they make active investments of this type. Some programs also provide the land at a non-zero, but subsidized price, payable by the family over a period of years. If the family purchases the land over a period of years, there are nevertheless sound reasons for the family to receive ownership of the land at the time of allocation (and attach a mortgage on the land as security for payment of the debt), rather than delaying transfer of ownership until payments have been completed. The more that can be done to instill a sense of ownership in the land, the more likely the family is to invest its time and scarce capital to improve it.

The introduction of improved inputs can make a significant contribution to micro-plot productivity. One illustrative example is a project undertaken by Helen Keller International to improve animal husbandry in rural Nepal, Cambodia and Bangladesh. In all three countries, within a year the number of eggs consumed in the household rose from a weekly average of 5 to a weekly average of 12, while the number of eggs consumed weekly by household children rose from an average of 2 to an average of 3.[65]

Another important limiting factor in micro-plot cultivation is the use of inputs to improve soil fertility. Where soils contain insufficient nutrients to support gardening, extension advice should include instruction on accelerated composting and the benefits of gardening in containers while establishing better soils.[66] Households might also benefit from instruction on the construction of terraces to improve soils.

Where gardening tools and other inputs are absolutely necessary, the government may find it useful to establish small local stores to sell simple tools and supplies at affordable prices. Where fencing is required to reduce foraging by animals or theft of micro-plot production, live fencing can be used to reduce costs. Plants used in fencing can also provide additional products for household use or sale.

One promising approach related to plant stocks involves the creation of local private nurseries to satisfy the needs of gardeners while earning a profit for the nursery. Sometimes homegardeners and self-help groups can cultivate nursery stocks for certain plants or trees, selling them to other gardeners or to small farmers. Planners should avoid introducing plant species that are locally unknown, no matter how nutritious and economical the plants are.[67]

Step 10: Provide extension services and technical advice

Education on nutrition. Project staff should consider providing all beneficiaries with education on nutrition and the nutritional benefits of plants, fruits and livestock before beneficiaries develop plans for their micro-plots. All community members will likely benefit from the information, and even those planning to use their plots for a small shop or cottage industry may decide to devote space to a garden and area for livestock. The education on nutrition can also assist families purchasing items for their families' consumption.

Extension. An extension service can provide beneficiaries engaging in homegardening and raising livestock with help designing the layout of the plot for the best results, selecting appropriate plants, trees and fertilizers, and addressing animal husbandry issues. Agricultural extension can contribute significantly, and sometimes to an extraordinary degree, to micro-plot production. At the beginning of the Helen Keller International pilot homegardening project in Bangladesh, 50% of households reported having a garden with mean size of 61 square meters and growing an average of 3.1 varieties of vegetables, whereas after two years with the project 100% of households reported having a garden with mean size of 138 square meters and growing an average of 17 varieties.[68]

When designing effective means for communicating an appropriate nutrition strategy, planners must understand the traditional diet and food taboos, seasonal food shortages, food storage practices, food cooking practices, and distribution of food within the household. With this nutritional information, homegardening households can select plant varieties that meet taste preferences and will supply nutrients year-round.[69]

Skills training. In areas where micro-plot beneficiaries contemplate taking up other specialized activities, such as handicrafts or other home-based businesses, project staff should evaluate the needs of the beneficiaries for training in necessary production skills, as well as marketing, recordkeeping and money management.

Labor. Although projects to promote gardening and other activities sometimes prefer to work with communal organizations, household-level food production must be a family undertaking since labor, space and time are valuable resources to poor households and "cannot be risked on the uncertain participation of a number of individuals," even on a small scale.[70]

Homegardens typically are cultivated using "marginal" labor, which is marginal in the sense that it is flexible and its use reflects low opportunities for alternative employment.[71] Although there is not much data on the volume and timing of labor inputs,[72] commentators tend to agree that most traditional gardening practices involve only a few days of preparation and less than an hour per day for maintenance and harvesting.[73]

However, it is important to appreciate that the opportunity cost of spending time on gardening is not zero, and labor-intensive technologies may not be appropriate in many contexts since household members do not have unlimited time available for gardening.[74] Homegardens are more sustainable if labor requirements are low and somewhat flexible.[75] Planners contemplating homegardening projects should consider the availability of marginal labor among households targeted for assistance.

Labor needs will vary by task and household. In India's Gujarat state, RDI researchers met with families who, in addition to maintaining home gardens, produced incense sticks to supplement often erratic wage labor. The families used the space on their plots to store the raw materials, lay out the materials during production, and produce the sticks. The families sold the finished product to a buyer and controlled the volume of sticks produced to suit their needs. The families gave priority to agricultural labor, which paid more per hour, and during the growing season limited their work on the incense sticks to the evenings. When agricultural labor was not available, or when one head of household injured himself and was unable to work in the fields, they increased the time devoted to producing incense sticks.

Conservation. Even where homegardening families have experience in producing various plants and animals, they may not fully understand the long-term consequences of various production techniques. For example, gardeners who do not take proper steps to preserve soil fertility may eventually find that the soil is exhausted. Extension agents can explain the benefits of using animal manures, and composting of kitchen wastes can help restore nutrients to soils. The persistence of homegardens for generations in some societies without the addition of artificial fertilizers suggests that viable low-cost strategies exist for preserving soil fertility. Programs promoting homegardening should include advice that helps families to appreciate the importance of soil fertility and affordable techniques that will preserve soil nutrients.

Ideally, the local community will value homegardening and other micro-plot activities as an appropriate strategy for all families rather than as either a leisure activity of wealthier households or a mark of household poverty. For example, if program managers present home-gardens as a universal strategy for improving household nutrition and household independence (rather than as a "poor man's" strategy of subsistence), any social stigma of gardening as an activity of the poor fades, and the relative status of poor families improves because they share an activity with wealthier families. For these reasons, agricultural extension should ideally include households of all economic brackets.[76]

Step 11: Monitor and evaluate outcomes

Monitoring the project following beneficiary occupancy and development of the micro-plots is an essential part of the program's success. Project staff should review specific project components at regular intervals, and should be in active communication with the beneficiary committee for the six to twelve months following habitation of the micro-plots (which in some cases may be several years after the plots are allocated). If the project has been fortunate enough to partner with an experienced NGO, that organization will also play an important role in ensuring the project provides the anticipated benefits to the households as the months pass.

Many government programs measure success by the numbers: number of households benefited, number of acres distributed, number of houses constructed. The numbers often do not sufficiently reflect whether a project has been successful, especially from the perspective of the intended beneficiaries. As program managers design programs, they should set objectives for the program that include not only the numbers of beneficiaries served but the impact of the project on their lives and livelihoods. Section I discusses a number of potential benefits. Success should also be measured in relation to the achievement of those objectives.

Over a broader project area, baseline and follow-up random sample surveys can provide detailed information on results. In the case of smaller or pilot projects, such results can help inform government decisions to replicate the project widely. Collection of data about results can also be critical for "mid-course corrections" to refine project design and implementation to improve the benefits received.

V.   Conclusion

In the right settings, the allocation of micro-plots is a viable alternative to traditional land reform. In areas where the availability of land, numbers of landless families, program financing, and political realities dictate against traditional reforms, micro-plot programs can substantially improve the lives of the landless rural poor. Micro-plots provide landless households with the means to diversify livelihood strategies by providing secure access to land and water, improved financial security, improved leverage in wage bargaining, improved nutrition, improved social status and political weight, and better access to basic infrastructure.

Where poor families lack secure rights to micro-plots of suitable size and quality, programs to obtain and allocate land to such families will often be a constructive and socially beneficial use of government resources. Where low-income families already have secure rights to micro-plots of suitable size and quality, governments should consider investing in water infrastructure, agricultural extension and nutritional education, as well as programs to ensure that appropriate stocks of plants and animals are available to homegardening families. Although some public funds will doubtless be necessary to establish or strengthen homegardening for landless and land poor families, a successful micro-plot intervention will be one in which the micro-plots become self-sustaining, satisfying the particular livelihood objectives of the recipient family, while reducing the family's continued dependence on public resources.

We would like to see international donors advance the issue of micro-plots as an alternative to traditional land reforms, including the idea of allocating micro-plots to establish homegardens and other livelihood-enhancing activities, in three principal ways: through supporting research, by promoting consensus building among donors, government planners and project implementers, and by directly supporting government or NGO micro-plot projects. Research and implementation projects can both drive the consensus-building process and benefit from the consensus reached at any given stage.

The process of developing and implementing a micro-plot strategy will itself require cultivation and some degree of risk taking. One way to focus the sequencing of decisions is suggested above in Figure 4.2, which includes a strong focus on ensuring access and secure rights to land that will be used for homegardening and house construction. Donors, government planners and project implementers can gain a head start in planning by conducting rapid rural appraisal to assess the opportunities for establishing and promoting homegardens in a particular setting. Donors in particular should look for ways to encourage government planners to assess such opportunities, including by learning from NGOs that have practical experience in implementing micro-plot projects.

Research should generally focus on documenting and studying the costs and benefits of existing micro-plot projects to determine which models hold the most promise. A special subject of research is the ongoing assessment of micro-plot project impacts, particularly from a sustainable livelihoods perspective. Successful projects and resulting best practices should be reported widely in the donor community. At the international level, donors could usefully support research that attempts to establish uniform standards and benchmarks for measuring and analyzing the costs and benefits of micro-plot projects.

But research on existing micro-plots and encouraging consensus-building should not be substitutes for acting to allocate new micro-plots and improve existing micro-plots. Once donors, government planners or NGOs conclude that micro-plots are likely to provide an acceptable threshold of benefits to target beneficiaries in that setting, they should fund, implement and monitor micro-plot programs. In this way, the potential for micro-plots can be explored in the process of providing current benefits to those most in need.

Notes

1   Government of India, 2008. Eleventh Five-Year Plan (2007-2012), sec. 1.105-1.108. The Plan further provides the states with further direction on establishing colonies, linking with existing housing programs, and providing infrastructure.

2   Id. sec 1.108.

3   In Karnataka, the *Namma Bhoomi Namma Thota* ("My Land, My Garden") program provides landless agricultural laborers with small plots of between 2,250 and 4,500 square feet. In West Bengal, the *Chash-O-Basobaser Bhumi-dan Prakalpa* ("Cultivation and Dwelling Plot Allocation") program allots plots of between 1,740 and 7,000 square feet (160 to 650 square meters) to rural households. In Orissa, the *Basundhara* program distributes wasteland and ceiling-surplus land to landless rural families. Most plots have been about 1,740 square feet, but the government recently lifted the size limit to 4,400 square feet.

4   R. Mitchell & T. Hanstad, SMALL HOMEGARDEN PLOTS AND SUSTAINABLE LIVELIHOODS FOR THE POOR (FAO 2004); K. Landauer & M. Brazil, *Introduction,* in K. Landauer & M. Brazil, eds., TROPICAL HOME GARDENS: SELECTED PAPERS FROM AN INTERNATIONAL WORKSHOP HELD AT THE INSTITUTE OF ECOLOGY, PADJADJARAN UNIVERSITY, BANDUNG, INDONESIA, 2-9 DECEMBER 1985, at viii (United Nations University Press 1990); P.K.R. Nair, AN INTRODUCTION TO AGROFORESTRY 86 (Kluwer Academic Publishers 1993).

5   See generally L. Brownrigg, HOME GARDENING IN INTERNATIONAL DEVELOPMENT: WHAT
     THE LITERATURE SHOWS (League for International Food Education 1985). Vasey de-
     scribes experience in Papua New Guinea in which a government program to allocate
     gardening land away from the house failed since it was too difficult for the cultivators
     to guard against theft and vandalism. D. Vasey, *Household gardens and their niche in
     Port Moresby, Papua New Guinea*, 7(3) FOOD & NUTRITION BULLETIN (UNFAO 1985),
     available at http://www.unu.edu/unupress/ food/8F073e/8F073E07.htm.
6   For example, on the Indonesian island of Java, the great majority of micro-plots are
     smaller than 200 square meters, R. Prosterman & R. Mitchell, *Concept for Land Re-
     form on Java* 7 (paper presented at the *Rethinking Land Reform in Indonesia Seminar*,
     Jakarta, Indonesia, May 8, 2002) (on file with the Rural Development Institute). On
     other less densely populated Indonesian islands they average 2,500 square meters
     and can reach sizes of 3 hectares. L. Christanty, HOME GARDENS IN TROPICAL ASIA,
     WITH SPECIAL REFERENCE TO INDONESIA, in Landauer & Brazil, supra note 4, at 10.
7   R. Marsh, *Building on Traditional Gardening to Improve Household Food Security*, Food,
     Nutrition and Agriculture No. 22, at 5-6 (Food and Agriculture Organization 1998),
     available at ftp://ftp.fao.org/docrep/fao/X0051t/X0051t02.pdf.
8   Sri Lankan homegardens have been reported to produce 60% of leaf vegetables and
     20% of all vegetables consumed by the household. I. Hoogerbrugge & L.O. Fresco,
     Homegarden Systems: Agricultural Characteristics and Challenges, International Institute
     for Environment and Development, Gatekeeper Series No. 39, at 11 (1993), citing B.
     Ensing, G. Freeks & S. Sangers, *Homestead Plots and Homegardening in the Matara
     District: The Present Situation and Future Prospects*, Masters of Science thesis, Social
     Science and Economics Department, University of Leiden, Netherlands (1985).
9   S.K. Kumar, *Role of the Household Economy in Child Nutrition at Low Incomes: A Case
     Study in Kerala*, Occasional Paper No. 95, at 60-61 (Department of Agricultural Eco-
     nomics, Cornell University 1978).
10   O. Soemarwoto, I. Soemarwoto, Karyono, et al., *The Javanese Home Garden as an inte-
     grated Agro-Ecosystem*, 7(3) FOOD & NUTRITION BULLETIN (1985), available at http://
     www.unu.edu/unupress/food/8F073e/8F073E08.htm.
11   See Soemarwoto, et al., supra note 10.
12   Marsh, supra note 7, at 6. In the context of a study of land-poor households in Kera-
     la, India, homegardening production has been observed to have a "buffering effect"
     on household consumption when there are shortfalls in wage income. Kumar, supra
     note 9, at 61.
13   The 1941 Land Law (28 L.P.R.A. secs. 241) included this key land tenure reform that
     gave garden plots suitable for raising food crops to landless wage laborers (known as
     agregados). The beneficiaries had to put a simple house on the land, but received as-
     sistance in doing so. The plot size, when adjacent to urban areas, could be as small
     as 1/4-acre or less. See K.S. Rosenn, *Puerto Rican Land Reform: The History of an In-
     structive Experiment*, 73 YALE LAW JOURNAL 334, 343-349 (1963-1964); T.D. Curtis,
     Employment and Land Reform in a Labor-Surplus Economy: A Case Study of Puerto Rico,
     43(4) LAND ECONOMICS 451, 453-455 (1967).
14   See, e.g., M. Andrew & R. Fox, *Undercultivation and Intensification in the Transkei: A
     Case Study of Historical Changes in the Use of Arable Land in Nompa, Shixini*, 21(4)
     DEVELOPMENT IN SOUTHERN AFRICA 700 (2004).
15   In a large-scale Bangladesh homegarden project, the income value of homegarden
     production increased from 14% of average monthly income to 25% after taking into
     account the market price of consumed fruits and vegetables. Marsh, supra note 7, at
     6.
16   Rosenn, supra note 13 at 344, quoting 28 L.P.R.A. (1955).

17 R. Pico, *Problems of Tenure Reform in Latin America*, 6(2) JOURNAL INTER-AMERICAN STUDIES 153 (1964).

18 "The landowners finally realized that laborers had rights that must be respected and the workers realized that selling their votes to the landowners not only was immoral but very bad business. Democracy started to function then and there, a real revolution occurred in the electoral process in Puerto Rico." Pico, supra note 17, at 153. Several states in India have provided ownership of (typically) small house plots to agricultural laborer families in order to remove them from feudal-type dependence on employers on whose land they had been living.

19 T. Hanstad, J. Brown & R. Prosterman, *Larger Homestead Plots as Land Reform?: International Experience and Analysis from Karnataka*, 37(29) ECONOMIC & POLITICAL WEEKLY 3058 (2002). Poorer households cited increased status even more often than other households.

20 In the Saraguro community of Ecuador, micro-plots were observed to "make a contribution far greater than that to diet, ritual life and remedy; the gardens are themselves a manifest representation of the community's most deeply held values: autonomy, status, religious piety, and personal investment in family." R. Finerman & R. Sackett, *Using Home Gardens to Decipher Health and Healing in the Andes*, 17(4) MEDICAL ANTHROPOLOGY QUARTERLY 477 (2003).

21 Hanstad, et al., supra note 19, at 3057.

22 Id. This may perhaps represent any one of three effects, alone or in combination: it gives the family a known address; it provides collateral; and it offers an assured location to conduct many activities that can benefit from credit.

23 This topic is discussed more fully in Section IV below.

24 Marsh, supra note 7, at 11.

25 Kumar, supra note 9, at 61; A. Talukder, L. Kiess, N. Huq, S. de Pee, I. Darnton-Hill & M. Bloem, *Increasing the production and consumption of vitamin A-rich fruits and vegetables: Lessons learned in taking the Bangladesh homestead gardening programme to a national scale*, 21(2) FOOD AND NUTRITION BULLETIN 115, 168 (2000).

26 While visiting villages in Davangere and Gulbarga districts of Karnataka state, RDI witnessed women using their house plots for small restaurants and shops. Their ability to generate income for the activities (versus engaging in activities for household consumption) was restricted, at least in part, by the small size of the plots. Finerman and Sackett report that having an abundant homegarden is an important source of status for Saraguro women in Ecuador, and conclude that homegardens demonstrate the woman's freedom from dependence on vendors and neighbors, her ability to expend resources on developing the garden demonstrate her fiscal standing, her production of flowers to adorn the church demonstrate her piety, and her investment in cultivation demonstrates her devotion to family. Finerman & Sackett, supra note 20, at 477.

27 R. Mitchell, PROPERTY RIGHTS AND ENVIRONMENTALLY SOUND MANAGEMENT OF FARMLAND AND FORESTS in J.W. Bruce, et al., eds., LAND LAW REFORM: ACHIEVING DEVELOPMENT POLICY OBJECTIVES 175, 203 (World Bank 2006). In addition, allocation of micro-plots may reduce the need for land-poor families to gather fodder and fuelwood from marginal lands, contributing to the sustainability of such lands. Id. at 204.

28 J. Gajaseni & N. Gajaseni, *Ecological rationalities of the traditional homegarden system in the Chao Phraya Basin, Thailand*, 46(1) AGROFORESTRY SYSTEMS 3, 20 (1999). Micro-plots may improve or exacerbate public sanitation, depending upon the care with which household wastes are handled. In West Java, it is common for micro-plots to contain fishponds. Fish are fed kitchen waste, and the pond is fertilized by animal and human waste, including waste from toilets built above the fishpond. See generally Soemarwoto, et al., supra note 10.

29 G.J.A. Terra, *Mixed-Garden Horticulture on Java*, 3 THE MALAYAN JOURNAL OF TROPICAL
    GEOGRAPHY 34, 41 (1954).
30 As is the case, for example, with respect to rural families in Russia and most other
    countries that emerged from the Soviet Union. Such land is usually located immedi-
    ately adjacent to a family's house or on sub-divided arable fields near the village. Dur-
    ing the harvest season, owners take turns guarding the plots on the arable fields to
    prevent theft.
31 On crowded Java, a significant proportion of micro-plots (known locally as *pekaran-*
    gan) are smaller than 200 square meters. See Prosterman & Mitchell, supra note 5.
    In a study of a lowland rural village in Central Java, Rajagukguk found that of 1,002
    village families, 44 families (4%) owned no *pekarangan* or micro-plot, 347 families
    (35%) owned 50 square meters or less, 328 families (33%) owned 50-100 square me-
    ters, 259 (26%) owned 100-500 square meters and only 24 families (2%) owned
    more than 500 square meters. E. Rajagukguk, AGRARIAN LAW, LAND TENURE AND SUB-
    SISTENCE IN JAVA: CASE STUDY OF THE VILLAGES OF SUKOHARJO AND MEDAYU, Ph.D. dis-
    sertation, University of Washington (1988). The size of rural *pekarangan* plots is de-
    clining over time, which Arifin attributes in part to the widespread practice of par-
    ents allowing their children to build houses on the pekarangan plots, which are then
    divided among the children upon the death of the parents. H.S. Arifin, *Ecological and*
    Socio-Economic Benefits of Pekarangan Land, Ph.D. dissertation (2002). This appears
    to reflect a situation in which villages are not allowing what is regarded as agricultur-
    al land (rice paddy and dryland) to be used in part for residential purpose – in effect
    prohibiting land from being converted to *pekarangan*.
32 Of 14 households that grew five or more trees, only one had a micro-plot smaller
    than 1800 square feet, while of the 16 households with plots 1800 square feet or lar-
    ger, 13 households (72%) grew five or more trees. T. Hanstad & S.B. Lokesh (2003)
    (unpublished data, on file with the Rural Development Institute).
33 T. Hanstad, S.B. Lokesh & M. Arun, *Reaping the Rewards of Homestead Gardens: Nutri-*
    tional and Income Benefits from Homestead Plots in Karnataka (forthcoming).
34 In a sample survey of 97 land-poor households that had received houseplots under
    government housing schemes in West Bengal, RDI researches found that the produc-
    tive value of plots increased significantly with plot size until plot size reached ap-
    proximately 3000 square feet (280 square meters). T. Hanstad & S.B. Lokesh, *Allocat-*
    ing Homestead Plots as Land Reform: Analysis from West Bengal, RDI Reports on For-
    eign Aid and Development No. 115, at 10-11 (Rural Development Institute 2002).
    More detailed interviews of 45 similarly situated West Bengal households revealed si-
    milar results. In the smaller sample, micro-plots smaller than 1000 square feet (90
    square meters) were found to provide the fewest benefits. Productive value and re-
    ported benefits increased significantly for plots of 1000-2999 square feet (90-280
    square meters), but then plateaued or even decreased for plots above this level. The
    types of and critical "trigger" points for various kinds of homegarden intensification
    appear to vary considerably with the setting.
35 Hoogerbrugge & Fresco, supra note 8, at 10.
36 For example, Russian women expend considerable effort and time carrying water to
    irrigate home production gardens, although Russian gardens are much larger on
    average than tropical homegardens and are thus likely to require much more water.
    H. tho Seeth, S. Chachnov, A. Surinov & J. von Braun *Russian Poverty: Muddling*
    Through Economic Transition with Garden Plots, 26(9) WORLD DEVELOPMENT 1620
    (1998).
37 Vasey, supra note 5.
38 Homegarden irrigation is rarely a consideration in the design of a reticulated water
    system, and it may be too expensive to make the capital improvements to an existing

system necessary to accommodate demand for irrigation water. For urban homegardens in Papua New Guinea, use of unmetered water for irrigation during the dry season exceeded the value of the crops produced, while metered households found it uneconomic to use water for irrigation. Id.

39 One reason that homegardens cultivated by rural households in Russia are more productive than those cultivated by urban households is that the rural households have easier access to inputs and implements that originated from the former collective farms, some of which they may receive as a part of their wage for work on agricultural enterprises that replaced the collective farms, and some of which they may "divert" from such enterprises. tho Seeth, et al., supra note 36, at 1620.

40 Marsh, supra note 7, at 8.

41 R. Chambers, RURAL DEVELOPMENT: PUTTING THE LAST FIRST Chapter 6 (Longman Group Limited 1983).

42 In this way, related households that share a large plot of land would not qualify, while households that share a small plot would qualify for the program.

43 See generally R. Chambers, supra note 41.

44 Project staff might also consider a project or portion of a project – such as an area within a new micro-plot development complex – aimed at providing only for these individuals.

45 R. Nielsen, T. Hanstad & L. Rolfes, *Implementing homestead plot programmes: Experience from India*, LSP Working Paper No. 23, at 57 (FAO 2006).

46 Project staff can anticipate issues that may arise and prepare mitigating measures. For example, in a mixed colony, members of sub-groups may feel isolated unless there are three or four households from the group in the colony, and they can arrange their plots together. Mixed groups may be less able to rely on traditional institutions to organize themselves or resolve disputes, and project planners should consider encouraging the colony to establish a governance structure representative of all groups.

47 We advise against any program to reorganize landholdings within the village such that existing ownership is readjusted to equalize the distribution of micro-plot land among village families. Such a process is not only likely to be very expensive to administer, but would create unnecessary friction among families. Any program to acquire land from one village family and distribute it to another family must be undertaken in a voluntary process in which project implementers purchase the land at a negotiated (i.e., market) price.

48 The issue of how far and where beneficiaries will move may be tied to multiple factors, including the nature of their current house and house plot, locations of present sources of wage labor or other gainful activities, income-generation potential of household members, location of extended family members, ages of children, numbers of residents in the new colony, and composition of the colony.

49 R. Mitchell, R. Prosterman & A. Safik, *Productivity of Intensively Used Homestead Plots in a Central Javan Village*, RDI Reports on Foreign Aid and Development No. 122 (Rural Development Institute 2006).

50 Hanstad, et al., supra note 19, at 3057.

51 This equates to 20 families per hectare. In a December 2000 survey of 500 rural households in West Bengal, respondents estimated the average cost of non-irrigated arable land to be 46,975 Rupees per acre, which is equivalent to approximately US $1006 per acre (US$2487 per hectare) at December 2000 exchange rates. Hanstad & Lokesh, supra note 34, at 25. If one hectare is divided such that 20 families receive 500 square meters of land each, this represents an average acquisition cost of approximately $124 per family benefited.

52 N.S. Jodha, *Rural Common Property Resources: Contributions and Crisis* (May 1990)
     (lecture given at Foundation Day of the Society for Promotion of Wastelands Develop-
     ment) (on file with the Rural Development Insitute); H.W. Blair, *Democracy, Equity
     and Common Property Resource Management in the Indian Subcontinent*, 27(3) DEVELOP-
     MENT & CHANGE 475-499 (1996); R. Meinzen-Dick, A. Knox & M. DiGregorio, eds.,
     PROPERTY RIGHTS AND DEVOLUTION OF NATURAL RESOURCE MANAGEMENT: EXCHANGE
     OF KNOWLEDGE AND IMPLICATIONS FOR POLICY 9 (DSE/ZEL 2001).

53 Mitchell & Hanstad, supra note 4, at 33. The figure for landless families in India re-
     fers to families that own no land as well as those who own less than 20 square me-
     ters (215 square feet) of land. The Eleventh Five-Year Plan states that an estimated 13
     to 18 million families in rural India are landless. Sec. 1.105.

54 Christanty, supra note 6 at 10, citing H. Danoesastro, THE ROLE OF THE HOME GARDEN
     AS A SOURCE OF ADDITIONAL FAMILY INCOME in SEMINAR ON THE ECOLOGY OF HOME-
     STEAD PLOTS iii (Institute of Ecology, Bandung, Indonesia 1980). Marten reports that
     a study of households in West Java revealed that although rice fields controlled by
     the poorest households produced a higher gross value of products per square meter
     as compared to the value produced per square meter on the homegarden, the cost of
     purchased inputs for homegardening was much less; for the better-off households
     (defined as any household earning more than US$100 per year as of 1986) the value
     of homegarden production per square meter equaled the value produced per square
     meter on rice fields. G.G. Marten, *A Nutritional Calculus for Home Garden Design:
     Case-Study from West Java*, in Landauer & Brazil, supra note 4, at 157.

55 Hanstad, et al., supra note 33. Studies in the Nompa area of South Africa found that
     yields per unit area from gardens were much higher than those for fields. Andrew &
     Fox, supra note 14, at 699-700. See also the discussion of the high productivity of
     the small plots in Russia and China in Section VII of Chapter [6].

56 A. Agarwal & S. Narain, *Making Water Management Everybody's Business: Water Har-
     vesting and Rural Development in India*, Gatekeeper Series No. 87, at 3-5 (International
     Institute for Environment and Development 1999). India has developed and success-
     fully marketed several low-technology, low-cost micro-irrigation systems that are ap-
     propriate for micro-plots ranging in size from 20 to 1000 square meters and cost
     from US$5 to US$90. International Development Enterprises, *Micro Irrigation Pro-
     gramme*, available at http://www.ide-india.org/micro_programme.htm. Households
     may also use household wastewater. Marsh, supra note 7, at 10. Water conservation
     strategies can reduce homegarden demand for water. Such strategies include terra-
     cing, trenching, deep mulch and surface mulch (including living mulch and ground
     cover creepers). Plant spacing and mulch may be used to conserve moisture, and
     drought-tolerant plants can reduce the impact of water shortfalls. In areas of high
     rainfall, canopy layers, raised beds and drainage canals may help to prevent flooding,
     Brownrigg, supra note 5. The use of water-loving plants and plastic coverings can
     help to reduce the effects of water abundance. Id.

57 For example, in one study of 45 households who had received house sites from the
     government, 32 had constructed housing without government assistance, indicating
     that these families had the personal incentive, as well as access to sufficient materials
     or sufficient savings or access to credit to construct the house once they received
     land. Hanstad & Lokesh, supra note 34, at 22.

58 B. Agarwal, A FIELD OF ONE'S OWN: GENDER AND LAND RIGHTS IN SOUTH ASIA 37 (Cam-
     bridge University Press 1994); D. Deere & M. Leon, EMPOWERING WOMEN: LAND AND
     PROPERTY RIGHTS IN LATIN AMERICA 16 (University of Pittsburgh Press 2001); K. Dei-
     ninger, LAND POLICIES FOR GROWTH AND POVERTY REDUCTION 61 (World Bank 2003).

59 See, *e.g.*, S. Miura, O. Kunii & S. Wakai, *Home Gardening in Urban Poor Communities of the Philippines*, 54(1) INTERNATIONAL JOURNAL OF FOOD SCIENCES & NUTRITION 77, 86 (2003).

60 A. Shankar, J. Gittelsohn, E.K. Prahdan, et al., *Home Gardening and Access to Animals in Households with Xerophthalmic Children in Rural Nepal*, 19(1) FOOD & NUTRITION BULLETIN 34-41, 39 (1998).

61 N. Cohen, M.A. Jalil, H. Rahman, et al., *Landholding, Wealth and Risk of Blinding Malnutrition in Rural Bangladeshi Households*, 21(11) SOCIAL SCIENCE & MEDICINE 1269-1272 (1985).

62 Miura, et al., supra note 59, at 86. Before they learned about the nutritional value of vegetables, some families mistakenly believed that micronutrient tablets distributed by the government were more desirable than the consumption of vegetables, and that vegetables were the poor man's substitute for tablets. Id. Brun recounts the case of a village studied in west Senegal, where mothers cultivating homegardens did not seem to understand that vegetables were good for their children, and most mothers stopped growing carrots when their children snuck through homegarden fences to eat them raw. T. Brun, J. Reynaud & S. Chevassus-Agnes, *Food and Nutritional Impact of One Home Garden Project in Senegal*, 23 ECOLOGY OF FOOD & NUTRITION 91-108, 106-107 (1989).

63 Miura, et al., supra note 59, at 81.

64 Vasey, supra note 5; V.E. Méndez, R. Lok & E. Somarriba, *Interdisciplinary Analysis of Homestead Plots in Nicaragua: Micro-Zonation, Plant Use and Socioeconomic Importance*, 51(2) AGROFORESTRY SYSTEMS 90 (2001). Where households have access to capital, it is not surprising to find that the households make more productive use of their plots. For example, one reason that homegardens cultivated by rural households in Russia are more productive than those cultivated by urban households is that the rural households have easier access to inputs and implements that originated from the former collective farms, some of which they may receive as a part of their wage for work on agricultural enterprises that replaced the collective farms, and some of which they may "divert" from such enterprises. tho Seeth, et al., supra note 36, at 1620.

65 Helen Keller International, *Integration of Animal Husbandry into Home Gardening Programs to Increase Vitamin A Intake from Foods: Bangladesh, Cambodia and Nepal* 3 (HKI/Asia-Pacific Regional Office 2003). In addition, households in which chicken liver had been consumed within the past week rose from 21% of households to 35% of households. Id.

66 Brownrigg, supra note 5, at 109.

67 In many situations planners may determine that some level of public subsidy of inputs is justified, at least with respect to start-up costs such as the purchase of seedlings and seeds, livestock, or materials for cottage industries. If the project subsidizes these or other inputs, it should consider providing them to beneficiaries at a reduced price for a limited time, rather than making outright gifts of inputs. This approach has been found to legitimize projects as something other than an attempt to "help the poor," which poor families in some settings resent. V. Ninez, *Working at half-potential: Constructive analysis of home garden programmes in the Lima slums with suggestions for an alternative approach*, 7(3) FOOD AND NUTRITION BULLETIN (2005). Planners should avoid any project design that calls for ongoing subsidy of inputs.

68 Marsh, supra note 7, at 7.

69 Id.

70 Ninez, supra note 67.

71 Hoogerbrugge & Fresco, supra note 8, at 4.

72 Id. at 6.

73 During the five-month growing season in one urban setting, it was estimated that homegardens in urban Lima required an average of 50 minutes per day to prepare soil, plant, cultivate, water and harvest. Ninez, supra note 67.
74 Brownrigg, supra note 5, at 13, 15.
75 Marsh, supra note 7, at 10.
76 It may be better to avoid creating "demonstration" homegardens that are separate from those of any particular family, and focus instead on working with a local family which is willing, in the spirit of experimentation and cooperation, to allow their homegarden to be used as a demonstration garden for the village. Brownrigg, supra note 5, at 102.

5   Gender and land tenure reform

Renée Giovarelli

I.   Introduction

In most developing countries, land is a critical asset for women and men, and especially for the urban and rural poor. Property rights in land – whether customary or formal in nature – act as a form of both *economic access* to key markets and *social access* to non-market institutions such as household and community-level governance structures. Because of land's fundamental importance in conferring such access, it is essential that policies seeking in any way to alter the distribution or to formalize property rights in land provide benefits to women and take great care not to disenfranchise the most vulnerable members of the target population, including women.[1]

Women's economic development and their rights to land are intrinsically linked. More than half of all women in the developing world still work in agriculture. Africa's women produce 78% of the continent's food, mainly through subsistence agriculture and small landholding.[2] In India, 86% of rural women workers work in agriculture as compared with 74% of rural male workers. In addition, females head a large percentage of households: 20% in Bangladesh and India and 30% in sub-Saharan Africa.[3] Among the poor, women and women-headed households are the most vulnerable and account for a growing majority of the extreme poor.[4] Land ownership can ensure safety, status, and adequate housing and food security for women and children.[5]

Land rights clearly confer direct economic benefits to women. Land is a key input into agricultural production, it can be a source of income from rental or sale, and can be used as collateral for credit that can be used for either consumption or investment purposes. Moreover, if women are unable to legally own, control and inherit property they have little economic autonomy because they lack access to wealth, and their contribution to the household can remain unremunerated and invisible.[6] Comparative analysis of data from Nicaragua and Honduras, for example, suggests a positive correlation between women's property rights and their overall role in the household economy; women with property rights have greater control over agricultural income, higher shares of business and labor market earnings, and more frequent receipt of credit.[7]

In addition to the short- and medium-term economic gains generated by greater access to product, capital and land markets, women with stronger property rights are also less likely to become economically vulnerable in their old age, or in the event of the death of or divorce from their spouse. In her study of gender and inheritance in rural Honduras, for example, Roquas finds that widows (and women landowners in general) are more likely than men to work their lands indirectly – relying on some combination of hired labor, family labor, and rental to generate income – or to use the land as collateral for loans for non-agricultural undertakings.[8] Moreover, land ownership may be one of the few vehicles through which elderly women can elicit economic support from their children, either in the form of labor contributions to agricultural production or receipt of cash or in-kind transfers for use of the land. In the absence of other forms of social security, the elderly rural population relies heavily on inter-generational transfers for their livelihoods, and children are more likely to contribute to their parents' well-being if the latter retain control over a key productive, and inheritable, resource such as land.[9]

Land is a particularly critical resource for a woman in the event she becomes a *de facto* household head as a result of male migration, abandonment, divorce or death. In both urban and rural settings, independent real property rights under these circumstances can mean the difference between dependence on support from her birth family and the ability to form a viable, self-reliant, female-headed household. Women's land rights within marriage may afford them greater claims on the disposition of assets upon divorce or the death of their husband.[10]

Property rights may also empower women in their household and within the community and society at large. In the event of a disagreement within a household, resolution may depend on the relative bargaining power of each individual within the household, and control over assets is one determinant of bargaining power.[11] Intra-household economic research suggests that the strength of each spouse's "fallback positions," that is, how well they can do in the absence of economic cooperation with their partners, is an important determinant of their ability to shape household preferences and decisions about allocating resources.[12] Data from Central America, for example, indicate that increasing the size of female landholdings is associated with modest increases in food expenditures and child educational attainment.[13] Another study found a positive relationship between the amount of assets (including land) that a woman possesses at the time of marriage and the shares of household expenditures devoted to food, education, health care, and children's clothing during marriage.[14]

5.1. Land rights and vulnerability within the household

Land rights can alleviate some of the collateral effects of women's lower status to men in society, like domestic violence. Women generally have less power and lower status than men, and are very often dependent on men for their well-being. This means that in situations of abuse within the household, which is pervasive worldwide, women may find themselves not only physically and emotionally vulnerable but also without resources, making escape from an abusive situation difficult.

Studies and interviews with women from many parts of the world who have experienced domestic violence attest to the fact that they feel trapped with no place to go because their home and land are owned and controlled by the perpetrator of the violence. One study in India found that women with property who experienced violence from their husbands were far more likely to leave their marital home (71%) than those women who did not own property (19%). Another study of 450 women in West Bengal, India, found that among women without property, 57% said they experience some form of violence, compared with 35% of women with property. A third study in Kerala, India, found that while 49.1% of women without property experienced long-term physical violence in their relationship, only 6.8% of those who owned both land and other property experienced long-term physical violence.

Without direct property rights women are only able to gain access to resources through their partners or fathers, perpetuating dependency. Thus, property rights for women may reduce domestic violence as it can interrupt the dependency on the abuser.

Sources: P. Panda & B. Agarwal, *Marital Violence, Human Development and Women's Property Status in India,* 33(5) WORLD DEVELOPMENT 836 (2005) (women with property more likely to leave home); J. Gupta, *Property Ownership of Women as Protection for Domestic Violence: The West Bengal Experience,* Sept. 2005, ICRW Summary Brief (study from West Bengal), and P. Panda, *Domestic Violence and Women's Property Ownership: Delving deeper into the Linkages in Kerala,* Sept. 2005, ICRW Summary Brief (study from Kerala).

In many countries, both law and practice discriminate against women with regard to land rights. Land rights that are taken for granted by men may not even exist for women.[15] Unlike their male counterparts, women may lose rights to land or not gain rights to land for a number of reasons. First, it may be culturally or legally impossible for women to acquire land rights through markets, inheritance, transfer or gift. Second, marriage, divorce, bride price, dowry or polygamy may create barriers to women's land rights. Third, privatization or individualization of land may result in loss of non-ownership rights that women have to land (e.g., the right to use land). Finally, land titling programs may fail to formalize women's rights.

Entrenched customary laws or practice may limit the type of rights a woman may freely exercise. In many countries, while women have access to land through their husbands or fathers, they do not own land or have ownership-like rights to land. Moreover, cultural prohibitions against women's ownership of land can be more powerful than written laws allowing women's ownership of land and may limit the type of rights to land a woman may freely exercise. For example, in sub-Saharan Africa, women may have a right to cultivate and dispose of a crop, but do not have the right to allocate or alienate land, although their husbands and fathers do have this right.[16]

Women may have inferior rights to land as a result of laws or administrative policies. The laws or policies may be outright discriminatory or simply poorly drafted, failing to state clearly what rights women may exercise. Moreover, legislation is powerful but may not be sufficient alone, since rights to land and other property must be both legally and socially recognized to be usable and enforceable. Thus, overcoming gender biases in property rights systems requires overcoming gender biases within the social and cultural context in which the property right system is created and functions.

In spite of all this, laws can legitimize the possibility of change. While legislation does not itself change custom, it allows those who are brave enough or desperate enough or organized enough to use the law to support change. Additionally, equity is increased when women directly participate in the design of a policy. In many cases, increased gender equality can also lead to increased economic equality.[17]

Land tenure reform policies should address gender biases in access to property rights. This can be done by: (1) identifying the social and cultural factors and limitations that constrain women's property rights; (2) drafting legislation that both takes account of the reality of customary practices, and also ensures that women and men have equal access to property rights; and (3) designing and implementing social and cultural programs that help women overcome cultural obstacles and realize their property rights.

The remainder of this chapter reviews gender issues in the context of land tenure reform. Section II covers gender issues in programs that create new rights to land through privatization of state land. Section III gives an overview of issues that arise when communal land is individualized. Gender concerns that arise in the formation of land rights through titling are covered in Section IV. Section V discusses legal rules related to shared tenure. Section VI reviews women's access and barriers to land markets. Intra-household transactions, including divorce and inheritance, and their impact on women are discussed in Section VII. Section VIII further discusses inheritance issues. Section IX emphasizes the critical role that women's knowledge of land rights plays in the implementation of land legislation. Gender biases within statutory law, customary law and in practice are pertinent to each section and are addressed in each. Section X summarizes recommendations and lessons learned.

II.   Privatization and distribution of state land

Depending on the country, privatization programs usually distribute legal title to the household, the individual, or the head of household. Each of these affects women and their immediate and future rights to land in different ways.

Distribution of land to the household

Government policy makers may choose to distribute and title agricultural land in the name of households when the cultural unit of farm operation is the household or when there is a concern about fragmentation of land. For instance, in China and the Kyrgyz Republic, the cultural unit of farm operation is the household, and the population-to-land ratio is quite high.[18] Distribution of land to individuals would have created very small plots of land and would not have made sense in either country. Thus, land was distributed to families based on family size, with larger families receiving more land. However, in neither case did the legislation define the individual's rights within the family; this was due in part to cultural norms, which do not emphasize individual property rights.

When a household is the legal unit with the right to land, women generally have rights to land through their status as daughters or wives, especially if the custom is for a wife to live with her husband's family. In the land distributions of both China and the Kyrgyz Republic mentioned above, even when women were not disadvantaged in the initial land distribution, problems arose as populations grew, and women left their families to live with their husbands on his family's land. Additionally, custom generally dictates that men make the final decisions regarding what to plant and when to plant it, how to improve the land, or whether or not to sell or lease out the land. Thus, in practice, the male head of household has greater actual rights to the land than his wife or daughter, even though all members of the household are nominally considered rightholders to an equal "share."

In China, land contracts, where they exist, are issued in the name of the head of household. Household member names are usually not listed in the contract, and the contracting party is the household head. Even if family names are listed, no specific land parcel or parcels are attributed to individual members. Contrary to the intent of the 1998 Land Management Law, which provides farmers with a 30-year use right to land, some communities give young men more land on the assumption that they will later marry and bring a woman to their household; other communities do not give unmarried young women land because the community assumes the women will marry and leave the village within the 30 years.[19]

The 2002 Rural Land Contracting Law intends to protect existing contracted land rights from readjustments while also allowing villages to reserve land to designate to new entrants to the village. The law also provides that women have equal rights to land. Under this law, if a woman does not receive a land share in her new village, she retains her land share in her family's village. However, practical issues and cultural norms may obfuscate the efficacy of this law as well. The author interviewed women farmers in China and found that few women would exercise the right to continue farming their portion of the land after they are married. One reason for this is that women who leave their village to marry are not able to travel back and forth to the land. Also, exercising the right to a portion of the family's land is shameful for many women. On the other hand, families that are able to keep their daughter's land are more likely to allow a divorced or abandoned daughter to return home and assert her right to that land.

Similar contradictory results can be found in the Kyrgyz Republic. While land legislation provided for individual rights to land within the family, division of the household parcel during the first nine years of the law's implementation was prohibited. The primary impetus for this rule was a concern about land fragmentation. Nearly 10 years after the land reform began, legislation was enacted that allowed individuals the right to the value of their portion of the land, but not to demarcate or partition the land.[20] In the Kyrgyz Republic, women leave their households to join their husband's families upon marriage. Thus, to receive the value of the land apportioned to a woman when she leaves her family, the remaining co-owners of the land (her family) must purchase her share of the land value. However, very few women request the value of their land when they leave to join their husband's household as the request would be considered shameful for her and her family.[21]

Additionally, three events create land pressures on families in the Kyrgyz Republic: daughters-in-law who join households, children who are born after land distribution, and divorce of daughters. Each of these events requires caring for additional people without the provision of additional land. With no access to credit, a very limited land market, and little rural industry, economic well-being of the family decreases with each new addition to the household. Thus, women who return to their families after divorce (often bringing children with them) can create enormous land pressure on their families.[22]

Distribution of land to individuals

Individual titles to former state land have succeeded in securing women's right to land in societies where women have the cultural and social right to own land, but have not succeeded in societies where women do not. For instance, state land was distributed to individuals and not families in Russia (and most of the European former Soviet Republics), and the distribution was based on the status as a member or former member of a collective or state farm. In Bulgaria land was restituted to those who owned the land before collectivization and to their heirs, regardless of gender or marital status. In both of these cases, women are able to exercise full ownership rights to their land because in addition to the legal right to land, they have a socially accepted right to own land. However, when state land is distributed to individuals in cultures where individual ownership of land is not the custom and is not socially accepted, women do not necessarily gain equal rights to land.

The unequal outcome may be related to cultural practices and biases. Even when land is individually titled to women, it may shift back to male control because women may not be permitted to produce efficiently on their land. Take for example, the land reform in Tigray, Ethiopia. The Tigrean People's Liberation Front (TPLF), during its liberation movement in Ethiopia, carried out land reform between 1975 and 1989 in Tigray, which was a contested area. The TPLF held military control there in early 1980, and they developed a land distribution plan where all land became public property and was equitably distributed among all males above 22 years of age and females above 15 years of age.[23] The TPLF gave all use rights over land to individual members of the household.[24] Children then living had a right to a share of land, but children born after the distribution did not. Such a seemingly equitable distribution did not, however, produce equal success for women and men. Later studies found that oxen ownership (not land ownership) is the best predictor of farming success in Tigray. Thus, although women in Tigray became owners of land, in most study areas land was transferred through tenancy from women-headed households to households capable of farming with traction power, oxen or labor.[25] In the end, primarily female-headed households were limited in their ability to farm because of both cultural taboos and a lack of resources.

Villages in the Indian state of Karnataka offer a unique opportunity to witness an ongoing evolution from the situation in Tigray to that in Bulgaria. Beginning in 2000, a Karnataka housing program required state-allocated houses and house plots to be titled individually in the name of women beneficiaries. Field research confirms almost uniform compliance with the requirement beginning in 2003; however, in areas where no education or instruction accompanied the grant of title, the impact on women is virtually nonexistent. As one woman noted, how could it matter to her what a "small writing on a small paper" said? If her husband told her to leave the house, she would go.[26]

In contrast, other villages that included education of the community, the house plot program met with great success. In successful villages local officials and community workers educated women and men regarding the titling requirement and potential benefits to women, their households and their communities. Also, local NGOs provided training on home-based income-generation schemes and helped establish banking relationships, village committees, and project self-help groups. Far from being dismissive of the power of a piece of paper, the women actively contemplate how their ownership rights can enlarge their livelihood options, including allowing them to establish small home-based businesses, and they openly acknowledge the physical and psychological security they gain from their new rights.[27]

Distribution of land to head of household

In other instances, government schemes have titled land solely in the name of the male head of household. Although Karnataka has been praised among Indian states for the success of its land reform efforts,[28] the earliest programs did not target women as beneficiaries, and the state granted titles to agricultural land almost exclusively in the name of the male head of household.[29]

III.   Individualization of communal land

In many African countries, individualization of customary land tenure is a major objective of land tenure reform programs.[30] The oft-cited reason for this is that market forces should determine the efficient allocation of land. In many cases, individualization comes to mean that the state replaces local customary institutions as both the source and arbiter of rights. However, recently some countries have come to regard communal tenure as a legitimate and legal form of land tenure (e.g., Uganda and Tanzania). Moreover, the underlying notion that individualization of land is necessary for investment in communal land has been challenged by studies that found that customary communal tenure can have a strong positive impact on investment as well as land values.[31] See Chapter 8 for a general discussion of the relationship between tenure security and investment.

Individualization of communal land often results in women losing rather than gaining rights to land. If communal land, which was formally held by the tribe, is titled to the heads of households, wives may lose their property rights, especially if joint ownership is not compulsory under formal law. Moreover, customary rights of women for seasonal or other shared use of land can be eliminated in the process of individualization of ownership rights. Individualization that occurred under British rule, for example, did not take into account that male community members were obliged to provide women with temporary usufruct; consequently, the formal registration of only ownership rights deprived women of this "secondary" right of access.[32] In fact, formal ownership of land and property, in communal land settings, has in general strengthened the control of already powerful groups, has rendered women's rights and access to resources less secure, and has caused women to lose their rights in many cases.[33]

In addition to women's secondary rights on tribal land, women tend to have equal access for gathering or grazing in the commons areas, owned by communities due to custom (not necessarily one tribe). In fact, women tend to rely upon these lands disproportionately to men. If commons land is titled to households, and women's rights to gather or graze are not specifically preserved by registering them, women's rights can be lost.

Under a patrilineal and communal land tenure system, women have always been vulnerable to losing use of communal land in the event of the husband's death, divorce or polygamy. As land becomes more valuable due to cash cropping and increasing population, women stand an even greater risk of losing their rights to land when a family breaks down. For example, in Tanzania, widowed women who had previously been permitted to remain on communal land are now being dispossessed of that land as it increases in value.[34] This practice may cause women to respond by not improving the value of the land for fear of losing it to a husband or male relative. There are cases found in sub-Saharan Africa where women have lost control over land after they introduced irrigation and other improvements.[35]

In some parts of Africa, controversy has surrounded legislation encouraging joint titling of land in the names of husbands and wives to ensure women's rights to land during the individualization process. For example, in Tanzania, the Land Commission promoted a provision requiring joint ownership of land between spouses, but the provision was not included in the final land policy of 1995.[36] Likewise, in Uganda, drafts of the Land Act of 1998 provided for co-ownership of land by married spouses. By all appearances, the Ugandan parliament agreed that customary land on which the family lived or depended for sustenance should be held in co-ownership, but the final enactment of the Land Act contained no such provision.[37]

During the transition process from communal to individual tenure, legislation should make co-ownership the presumption in a marital relationship. However, this is an enormous legal step that will not likely have the acceptance of the community. In that case, donor-funded projects should educate policy makers and local customary leaders on the economic value of women having secure rights to land. Such projects should also provide funding to ensure women have access to some form of dispute resolution to enforce and guard against interference with their tentative rights.

IV.   Formalization of land rights: titling and registration

While in many cases women have *access* to land, they do not have a formal right to land. Rights to land imply security that is tied to an enforceable claim, while access to land is more informal and less enforceable.[38] Because women spend their incomes differently than men and generally have greater responsibility for improving the nutritional well-being of their children, a woman's formal right to and control over land can determine her income generating ability and therefore the well-being of her family.[39] Furthermore, formal title to land may empower women. Focus group interviews in Uganda, the Kyrgyz Republic and India indicate that women regard formal title to land as a means to make them less vulnerable to divorce or abandonment and in some cases less likely to suffer violence from their husbands.[40]

However, the design and implementation of titling programs have not generally made an effort to include women. A review of the "one title holder per household" practice has shown that, typically: (a) titling guidelines do not call for the identification of more than one property rightholder in the household; (b) titling procedures do not allow for enquiry into the number of property rightholders in the household; (c) titling forms do not permit the listing of more than one property rightholder; (d) titling brigades are not trained to look for and identify more than one property rightholder; and (e) titling activities with communities and households (informational meetings, workshops, etc.) focus on male heads of household and do not encourage or facilitate the participation of women and other persons.[41]

In Bolivia, for example, the legal framework is very positive with respect to women's land rights; however, regulations governing land ti-

tling did not provide any guidance in safeguarding those rights. Therefore, during its first three to four years, the title regularization process
was implemented without regard for women's land rights and without
monitoring whether titles were being issued to women either as individuals or as joint owners. The registration forms did not include a place
for more than one name as titleholder. Personnel were not instructed
to identify all landowners within the household. Women were not encouraged to attend public meetings and workshops, nor were they
sought out when the titling brigade visited their land for adjudication
and parcel measurement.

After several years and after critiques by civil society, the implementing agency, INRA, began to design and implement procedures to
increase the participation of women in the process and on the titles.
Gender training workshops were also implemented.[42] In areas where
gender training has taken place with staff, titling brigades and beneficiaries, there appears to be a positive impact on women's knowledge
and assertiveness with regard to their land rights.[43]

Joint titling has been recommended as a means of targeting women
and ensuring that their name is included in the title documents for
lands acquired by the family. However, joint titling often confronts the
same difficulties and constraints in extending property rights to women that are confronted by "traditional" titling programs (in which
state authorities name only one household head in the land title certificate). While specific legislation, regulations, and procedures that focus
on women's rights to land are needed to title women both as individual
owners and as joint owners, cultural constraints to recognising women
as full citizens, with the same and equal set of rights that men enjoy,
may undermine those efforts.

Formalizing land rights raises several issues specific to women. On
one level, women are not often made aware that they have a right to
title their land. On another level, local governments and registration offices may not register land in the names of both spouses if it is customary for only the head of the household to have a formal right to
land ownership. In addition, many rural women do not have formal,
statutorily required, legal documentation for their marriage, especially
if the marriage occurred under customary law or religious law. Some titling rules may exclude titling for couples living in a consensual union
without a legal marriage and this may impact the woman in the union
more severely than the man if it is not customary for a woman to hold
land in her name.[44]

Many Latin American countries took up the issue of how to treat
consensual unions in their titling and registration projects by applying
principles of co-ownership.[45] In many property systems, any two people can be co-owners, while married people can be co-owners or joint

owners. Co-owners can independently use or transfer their share of the property, although the co-owner wishing to use a portion of the property must request a partition of the property first. By contrast, a joint owner cannot transfer his or her share separately and must instead agree with other joint owners regarding any action affecting the property. Joint ownership requires the permission of both owners before a sale or mortgage can occur, while co-ownership does not. Also, joint owners can choose to partition their property and become co-owners. In Peru and in Ecuador, people who live together but who are not married are registered as co-property owners[46] as distinct from joint property owners; thus, their marital status is not important because they both own a separate share of the property rather than owning the property together as a whole, as would be the case if they held the land jointly. This means that both the man and the woman in a consensual union has an equal right to a separate portion of the land, and consent to use that land is not required from the other owner.

Public awareness and training of officials

Education, training and communication are essential for promoting gender equity in land administration projects. Public awareness and training programs serve three main purposes. First, they raise awareness about the rights of men and women with respect to land and property within the country. Second, they provide guidelines for project implementers and improve their awareness of the social and cultural implications of land administration. Finally, they increase the participation of women and men in the land titling process, subsequent registration and other related activities.

Studies have shown how critical public awareness is for the beneficiaries. For example, a study looking at six land titling projects in Latin America found that in Honduras, where joint titling was voluntary, only 16.7% of titles corresponded to women, all other titles were issued to men only. The joint titling program was weak because women were rarely aware of their rights under the program, and the titling of land to women varied across the country according to the willingness of regional functionaries to issue joint titles.[47]

Awareness programs and training can also ensure that program implementers are aware of the social context in which they work. In the Lao People's Democratic Republic, women from most ethnic groups benefit from a tradition of matrilineal inheritance (traced through the maternal side of the family), and the family law states that land purchased during marriage shall be regarded as joint property.[48] Despite this, women's rights to land were not always recognized in practice, and it was found that land titling was only done in the name of males.

The initial reason given for this was that men were the public face of the family, and titling and registration were seen as public activities. However, after a local women's non-governmental organization provided training to community women and the staff of the Department of Land on the topic of women's right to receive land titles, surveys showed an increase in the number of titles in the name of women and an increase in the number of joint titles.[49]

V.   Legal rules regarding shared tenure

Titling and registration serve to formalize land rights, and joint ownership of land is sometimes thought of as the equivalent of jointly titled land. However, most countries have separate family law or land law that provides how land is owned and distributed among married people, regardless whether the right has been formalized.

Shared tenure is the term used to refer to the broad category of rights to land and housing shared by two or more people. Shared tenure can be formal or informal. Formal shared tenure conventionally refers to legal co-ownership or co-lease rights. In most countries, a range of land rights and tenure types exist that form a continuum from informal to formal. For all tenure rights along the continuum, secure tenure for women within the household and within the community remains a crucial issue.[50]

A specific, formal form of shared tenure is *joint tenure*. Joint tenure refers to land or housing held by both spouses – or by both members of a couple living in consensual union – wherein both spouses have equal rights over the marital property.[51] Joint tenure rights may be held whether the tenure has been formally titled and registered or is instead created through operation of law applicable to marital property. While any tenure type can be jointly held, joint tenure usually refers to ownership. According to this concept, more than one person owns the *whole* of the property. Each owner of land held in joint tenure can only deal with the land with the consent of all the owners, as each owner acts on behalf of all owners on the whole of the property. For example, for land to be disposed of, all the joint owners must agree to do so.[52]

Joint titling can satisfy two objectives related to legal rights for women. The fundamental objective is to enhance the status and power of women by improving their access to and control over land. The other objective derives from these property rights: by virtue of having property rights to land and housing, women are able to make decisions on the use of that property, are able to, in conjunction with their husbands, use the property as collateral to secure credit (including credit to finance improvements to the property), and increase their ability to provide for the well-being of themselves and their family.

Joint tenure forms can be universal or presumed, and compulsory or voluntary in law. *Universal* joint tenure means that *all* property brought into or acquired in marriage in any manner is jointly held. *Presumed* joint tenure means that there is a presumption that a married couple holds the property acquired during marriage jointly, but either spouse can prove that certain property is individually held (usually property that is inherited or gifted to one of the spouses only).

Compulsory joint tenure indicates that the law mandates joint tenure in certain circumstances (marriage, for example). A presumption of joint tenure can therefore be compulsory by law and not dependent on whether the property is formalized (titled and registered) in the name of both parties. In much of Eastern Europe, community property for marital couples is compulsory (Russia, Bulgaria, Czech Republic, and Croatia, for example), though the rate of legal marriage appears to be declining in these areas.[53] In unregistered marriages the compulsory joint title provisions will not take effect.

Voluntary tenure means that all parties must choose who will be property owners or occupiers and what form the ownership will take. This can be done in a marriage contract or through the titling and registration process.

Larger groups (such as customary communal tenure, family tenure, community titling, or co-operatives) may hold land and property in either joint tenure or tenure in common, depending upon law and custom.[55] *Tenancy in common* means that each person owns a *portion* of the whole of the not-yet-demarcated property. If the amount each person holds is not specifically stated, the assumption is that the owners own equal parts. Each owner can request demarcation of his or her portion of the land and thereafter deal with that portion independently.

Separate property for married couples or household members is also a possibility under the law in some countries. Countries that have a separate property regime as the default regime have the presumption that both members of a couple (married or not) have a separate right to land or property acquired during a marriage or consensual union.

Table 5.1 illustrates the three tenure arrangements described above and whether they are voluntary or compulsory under civil or family law and then whether they are voluntary or compulsory under land law and what the arrangements mean in terms of inheritance and transfer rights.

Even when the concept of compulsory joint tenure is a part of formal law, there can be many variations in implementation. The specific parameters of the presumption of joint tenure can have a major influ-

Table 5.1. *Forms of property tenure*

	Tenancy in Common: Each party owns a separate share of the whole	Joint Tenure: Parties own the property together as a whole or undivided share (each owns the whole)	Separate Tenure: Each party owns property separately
Compulsory or Voluntary (Civil Law)	Usually voluntary.	Can be compulsory or presumed compulsory (unless contract to the contrary) for married couples, those in consensual unions, or household members of a farm. Can also be voluntary.	Can be the presumption for married couples and those in consensual union.
Compulsory or Voluntary (Land Law)	Can be compulsory when land is privatized or individualized (land is distributed to all, or all adult, household members on a per capita basis).	Can be compulsory when land is privatized or individualized for married couples or families living in one household.	Can be compulsory as part of state distribution of land.
Inheritance	Can bequeath a separate share of the property by will, or share will be distributed according to intestacy rules.	Either the deceased's share of the control of the whole automatically vests in the remaining owners, or the property must be divided and becomes a tenancy in common.	Separate bequests.
Transfer	Can transfer a separate share of the property without permission from other co-owners.	Usually permission of other joint tenants is required for any transfer of any right in the property.[54]	Can transfer without permission.

Source: Adapted from R. Giovarelli & S. Lastarria-Cornhiel, *Shared Tenure Options for Women: A Global Overview*, Table 2.1.1 (UNHABITAT July 2005).

ence on the implementation of this concept. The variations in joint titling regimes are related to the following issues:

1. When does property become the property of the marital community (joint owners)?
2. Which property is jointly owned?
3. Who will manage the joint property?
4. If there is separate property, will the income from that property be owned by the individual or the joint owners?

5. Do consensual unions trigger the joint titling rules and protections?
6. If a presumption of joint tenure is created by civil law, does the land law mandate that all land that is jointly held also be jointly titled and registered?[56]

Both compulsory and non-compulsory joint tenure rights can be adversely affected by legal regulations, customary or religious practices and norms, gaps in legislation, and poorly implemented laws. While civil legislation establishes marital property regimes, the procedures regulating documentation and registration of joint ownership, usually found in land legislation, greatly influence the frequency with which women formalize their rights to land and other property. Procedures can be complicated, time consuming, and expensive. Formalization of ownership may require evidence that women do not have.

VI. Land markets

Apart from privatization of land, women may acquire land rights through purchase, inheritance, labor or other investment in improving the resource, adverse possession, prescription, or leasing.

The customs and attitudes of society toward the purchase and sale of land by women can have a significant effect on women's involvement in the land market. For instance, in some parts of Uganda, village men often oppose women purchasing land during the marriage because it indicates that she intends to divorce. Men will only allow such purchases if they are convinced of the economic benefit of women owning land.[57] To illustrate, in a 100-person household survey in Uganda fewer men and women thought married women should have the right to purchase land than thought widows or single women should have such purchase rights.[58]

In Karnataka State in India, women have the legal right to own land but rarely do so in practice due to traditional gender roles and lack of

Table 5.2.   *Ugandan attitudes to whether women should own land*

Marital Status	Men who condone female ownership (%)	Women who condone female ownership (%)
Widows	68.2	98.2
Single Women	67.4	96.5
Married Women	46.5	69.5

Source: R. Giovarelli & E. Eilor, *Land Sector Analysis: Gender/Family Issues and Land Rights Study* (unpublished report, Government of Uganda 2002), Table 3-1.

independent financial resources. Household land is most commonly titled only in the name of the male head.[59] Likewise, in Chile, because women only participate in the land market when they have resources at their disposal, only 8% of women who owned farms acquired them through purchase as compared to one-quarter of the men.[60]

Another reason why women may not purchase land is because of the perceived collateral effect it may have. Since land ownership is economically empowering for women, women's land ownership can be regarded as threatening to men or to the family as a unit. This perceived threat may underlie legal barriers to women's land rights; for example, under Muslim personal law in the Philippines, a woman must have her husband's consent to acquire any property even if by gift, except from her relatives.[61]

Clearly, land market programs should not focus exclusively on ownership; it may be easier for women to lease land than to purchase it. Leasing land can present less of a threat to men and the social order than purchasing land, and leasing requires less money. Of course, leasing is perceived to be less threatening because it does pose less of a threat – it does *not* create permanent, secure property rights in the lessee. In Burkina Faso, for example, the increased and changing market value of land has had the surprise effect of creating non-traditional avenues for women to lease land long-term on an anonymous basis where they might not have been able to in the past.[62] Male landholders are more willing to lease to women because women cannot claim permanent rights to land. Husbands generally support this borrowing of land by their wives, and women are therefore better able to cultivate land independently, even though they do not own it.[63]

An additional consideration affecting their participation in land markets is women's access to resources. Women who are able to accumulate their own resources are often able to acquire land. Rural women may have limited access to money, credit and information that would allow them to take advantage of land markets both because they are poor and because of their status in the family and society.[64] Women who are able to purchase agricultural land usually live in urban areas and are employed or live in peri-urban areas and grow food for the urban market.[65]

There are ways that poor rural women can work around the restriction of resources. For example, pooled resources can make it easier for women to receive credit using social collateral.[66] Additionally, pooling resources may allow women to purchase land without credit at all.

VII.   Intra-household rights to land

Women's rights to land are almost always related to their relationship to a family. Within a household, there are two separate questions related to women's land rights. First, do women have the right to use, control, own, sell, lease, bequeath or gift land within a marriage, a consensual union, or her birth family? Second, do women who are divorced, widowed, abandoned, or who are second wives have the right to use, control, own, sell, lease, bequeath, or gift land? This section looks at several barriers to women's rights to land in relation to their family relationships. Legal reform efforts to enhance women's land rights seldom focus on the intra-household distribution of land, yet such provisions and practices can have a potentially great impact on women.

Control over land within the marriage

Beyond the legality of the title and the continued use of that property to provide for and shelter their family, do women have effective rights such as the ability to control the use of the property and the right to benefit from the property? One study of agricultural land in Nicaragua found that women who have either individual title or joint title administer over half (52%) of crop income while women who have no land rights only control 14% of crop income.[67] This would seem to suggest, at least in this Nicaraguan case, that extending legal land rights to women, including joint ownership rights, increases their effective rights over land.

However, use rights may be insecure, even within the marriage. Many laws or customs allow husbands to sell land without the permission of their wives. Husbands may also choose what crops to grow, and control any money generated from harvests.

The situation in Uganda provides a particularly pertinent illustration. In Uganda, one family will usually possess several different fields, separated geographically from each other and often separated from the family home. At the time of marriage, the family often gives the woman a specific field to cultivate. In times where the family or the husband needs money, it is the fields designated to the women that are frequently sold by the husband, without her knowledge or consent. The Land Bill of 1998 originally included a provision, referred to as the "consent clause," for which women NGOs fought hard. It was intended to stop the sale of any household land by one spouse unless the other spouse gave written permission. However, the intent of the consent clause was undermined. When it was eventually enacted, section 40 of the Land Act provided:

No one can transfer land without the prior written consent of the spouse if: (1) the spouse ordinarily resides on this land, and (2) the spouse derives sustenance from this land.

Transfer includes: sale, exchange, transfer, pledge, mortgage, lease or *inter vivos* gift – or enter [sic] into a contract for these purposes.[68]

Thus, the consent clause, as enacted, can be read to apply only to land that is *both* residential and used for sustenance, but not to apply to land farther from the house. This interpretation does not in practice provide equal rights for women as promised under the constitution. In a land market survey in Uganda, respondents stated that the formal written consent required under section 40 of the Land Act is rarely obtained. Most respondents were not sure if the consent requirement covered all land plots of a household, just the plot on which the family actually lived, or plots that were used for family sustenance.[69]

By contrast, the legal obligation for consent in other countries is much broader. For instance, in the Philippines, transactions in agricultural land distributed to agrarian reform beneficiaries during marriage or cohabitation require the written consent of both spouses regardless of whether the land is registered in the name of both spouses or just one.[70] Other property of the marriage or cohabitation can be sold only with the consent of both parties.

However, formal rights to land by virtue of marriage may not guarantee that women have input into or control over land production. In Zimbabwe, even with the legal right to land, women report that their husbands control the use of the land; they do not allow women to plant anything but maize, and though the women do all the work, they are not permitted to be involved in any planning related to crop growing.[71]

Even when Pakistani women formally own land, custom may limit their rights to use or dispose of this land. Although women have the legal right to own land independently and jointly with their husbands, according to lending institutions surveyed for a micro-finance study, "women's right to own property does not automatically translate into the right to develop or dispose of it as they see fit."[72] There are no specific legal requirements as to women's rights to control or dispose of land.

Ultimately, it may be that the law can do little to safeguard women's control over land within the family, and laws that do attempt to safeguard women's rights to land, like consent laws, may create other problems. For example, a law that requires written consent for any transfer of household land can make the land market less efficient. Where polygamy exists, and marriages and land are unregistered, keeping track of whose consent is required can be difficult for banks or potential buyers. Bankers in Uganda have complained about the consent requirements imposed by section 40 of the Land Act: they report that it is impossible for them to verify that all the required consents had been obtained prior to granting a loan using land as collateral.[73]

However, there are potential solutions to the issue with consent laws cited above. One possibility is to provide in law that a sale or mortgage is valid even if later contested for lack of consent, provided that the purchaser or mortgagee made a reasonable effort to obtain consent. Reasonable effort could be defined as creating a balance between the needs of the lender or seller for efficiency and clarity and a woman's need to protect her rights to land. If the purchaser or mortgagee cannot prove that such care was taken, he or she could be required to give land or equivalent compensation to the wife who did not provide consent. Of course, while this may be an adequate legal solution, there may be social mores that restrict a women's access to the court system, and the rule may provide more protection to lenders and purchasers than to women.

Divorce

Upon divorce, abandonment or termination of a consensual union, there are three main factors that affect a woman's right to land. First, divorce may carry a stigma that impacts a woman's right to use or own land. In some countries divorce is not allowed, and in others, division of property is based on the guilt of the parties.[74] Second, in many instances women move to their husband's family household upon marriage and are reluctant to claim their land upon divorce because it belongs to the husband's family or it is located in the husband's village. Third, women often lack information about their right to receive land from the marital household upon dissolution of the marriage or union.[75]

Mandatory joint ownership is the legal solution most often promoted to protect women's property rights upon divorce or abandonment. As discussed in various other contexts above, custom and practice play into the effectiveness of a solely legal solution. As noted by gender and land scholars, "where customary or traditional property rights and gender relations are strong, they are likely to dominate the distribution of rights within and around the landscape."[76]

Laws, however, can provide room for change within a culture. A good illustration of this is found in the Ethiopian state of Tigray. During the Tigrean land reform, the law mandated joint registration of property in marriage or in the woman's name alone in the case of non-formalized unions. A woman has the right upon divorce to take the property she brought to the marriage as dowry, as well as her half of the marital land. Other property obtained during the marriage is divided equally. Women state that if they are able to own land and property upon divorce, they cannot be forced to stay with men.[77] In fact, a recent study indicates that this change in the law has caused Tigrean men to become conscious of women's rights to their land, to be more cautious about beating them, and to be more cautious about initiating divorce. However, the rate of divorce has increased in recent years because women are leaving relationships that are violent or in which the husband does not contribute to the family. Women state that the land reform has made them independent.

The absence of laws can negatively impact divorced women's rights to land. In India, although Hindu, Muslim and Christian law all require the husband to provide maintenance to the wife upon divorce, in the Indian state of Karnataka, separated or divorced Hindu women are often socially stigmatized and rarely receive maintenance. Also, women in Karnataka do not have the right to receive any of the husband's ancestral land or separate property. Nor does the civil law provide for co-ownership of marital land.[78] Divorced women in most cases must support themselves, unless they have adult sons who can assist them. Women nearly always lose access to land they previously cultivated and typically do not receive the return of any dowry that was paid on their behalf.

Even where general legislation regarding divorce exists and is positive for women, implementing regulations may thwart women's access to court. For example, in Kyrgyzstan, the person who applies for property division (almost always the woman) must pay the state fee, a percentage of the value of the property.[79] Article 102 of the Civil Code provides that the court can exempt payment, and poor women often do pay less. However, they must pay something, and usually any amount is too much. Moreover, the amount must be paid in advance and provides grounds for commencing the judicial procedure. The full burden for payment falls on the person requesting the property division and is not later reimbursed by the opposing party.[80]

Those working on land law reform in developing countries do not generally analyze rules regarding division of property upon divorce. However, the legal framework surrounding divorce and division of property can have a major impact on women's right to land and on women's status within the family.

Bride price and dowry

The various customs of bride price and dowry, which involve the exchange of wealth upon marriage, are often linked to women's ability to own land.[81] In some countries, like India and the Kyrgyz Republic, dowry is seen as the daughter's pre-mortem inheritance, and she may not have a customary right to inherit land from her birth family. In some cases women may be allowed control over their dowry throughout their married life, and it remains with them upon divorce or death of the husband.[82]

Dowry is not returned upon divorce in the Indian state of Karnataka. Similarly, women in Uganda are left with no marital property or wealth from the bride price after divorce. A Ugandan husband's family pays the wife's family for the bride. When women are asked why women do not or should not own land, they cite bride price as the reason. Payment of bride price simultaneously indicates respect and love for the bride and deems her the property of her husband. Thus, upon divorce, the woman's family is expected to return the bride price and the woman is left with no marital property or wealth. In fact, in interviews, men stated that women cannot own land because "property cannot own property."[83]

Legislating against the practices of dowry and bride price will probably not solve these problems; in fact they may cause them to increase. Although India has outlawed dowry since the 1961 passage of the Dowry Prohibition Act, dowry is still not only practiced, it is more common and more expensive today than in the past. Since dowry and bride price continue to be practiced, legal solutions to the land issues associated with these practices may need to be broader than outright prohibition. For instance, where dowry and bride price are practiced, women's leverage in the household may be improved if countries instituted a universal community property system in which all property brought into and acquired after marriage belongs equally to both spouses. This would be different from the community property laws commonly in place in the West, where property brought to the marriage separately by each spouse is usually excluded from the joint property calculation, but it may be effective in containing some of the negative effects of these practices.

Polygamy

Many societies allow polygamy, and in settings where polygamy is customary or traditional, attempts to prohibit it through legislation are generally ineffective. However, polygamy seriously affects women's rights to property and is the source of much tension over land rights in many countries, especially because it is not often acknowledged by either men or women. Polygamy complicates legislation requiring written consent of spouses for the disposition of property. It also complicates provisions on inheritance and co-ownership of land. While legislating around polygamy is difficult, ignoring it would inadequately protect women's property rights.

Polygamy, along with land shortages and rising populations, are the predominant reasons for intra-familial land disputes in Uganda, according to a 1993 study. Specifically, the problem with polygamy arises because of the allocation of land to multiple children and multiple wives.[84] New wives often receive land at the expense of previous wives, and the children's inheritance may depend on their mother's status at the time of their father's death. Also, because the eldest son of the most senior wife is likely to receive the largest share of the property[85] and is responsible for administration of the estate, children of other wives may not fare well in the allocation.[86]

On August 24, 2004, the President of Benin signed into law the Persons and Family Code, which states that only monogamous marriage will be legally recognized. While polygamy is still allowed under the law, subsequent wives will not have the same legal protections as the first wife or the wife with whom the man is legally registered. Wives subsequent to the first wife in a polygamous marriage, do not have a legal right to land under the Persons and Family Code 2004. It is unclear from the law what will happen to all the polygamous marriages that were in effect at the time of this law in 2004. Do those second and third wives have any legal rights? How might this affect titling now since most of the marriages that exist would have been made under the old law that allowed for polygamy? If women are the second or third wife, they will have no legal rights, making them more vulnerable.

It would be counterproductive for the law to make broad proclamations about the relative worth of marriages (such as a rule that holds that the first is the most important one, or that marriages with children are superior, etc.); however, the law can make determinations about property ownership. One possible rule that could alleviate some of the problems associated with polygamy would be to require that upon taking of a second wife, the husband and first wife must partition all property belonging to the first marriage or consensual union so that the husband has only his half-share to distribute to his new wife and children. Of course, the law is a very cumbersome tool for dealing with complicated family relationships.

VIII.   Inheritance and inter vivos transfers

Inheritance of land by daughters or widows is often the main way that women acquire ownership rights to land. Data from several countries in Latin America indicate that inheritance is the most important medium through which women become independent landowners: 54% of female-owned land in Brazil was inherited, 84% in Chile, 43% in Ecuador, 76% in Mexico, 75% in Peru, 47% in Nicaragua, and 57% in Honduras.[87]

Laws and customs governing inheritance are therefore key to the gender distribution of land. Inheritance law may be ineffective at ensuring land rights for women. For instance, laws often exclude large segments of the female population such as unmarried women, women in cohabitation relationships and women married under customary or religious regimes but not married legally or, as seen above, polygamous wives.[88]

Transfers by inheritance happen either by will or by law. Succession by will must satisfy the legal requirements of a will to be effective. A will specifies how the deceased's property is to be distributed. Usually the testator (the writer of the will) may bequeath all or part of his or her property to any person, but the law may also establish obligatory minimum shares for children or spouses. If a person dies without a will (intestate) or when the will covers only a part of the estate, laws of intestate succession apply. This means the law will govern the division of the estate among classes of heirs.[89]

Written wills are a rarity in rural communities of developing countries, and rules related to intestate succession are therefore important. Intestacy rules usually provide that the spouse and each child receive a certain share of the deceased's property. Many pluralistic legal systems provide that the religion of the spouses will determine which inheritance regime applies. For example, if a person marries as a Muslim in India, the inheritance rules are different than if a person marries as a Hindu.[90]

Many Latin American countries limit how much property an individual can freely will to others and subject the remainder to certain rules regarding the distribution to surviving spouses and children. In Nicaragua and Honduras, for example, property owners may cede up to 75% of their estate – high by Latin American standards – to anyone, and the remaining 25% (porción conyugal) is set aside for widows.[91]

Where a person dies without a will, all Latin American countries designate the legitimate children of the deceased, regardless of sex, as the first beneficiaries of equal shares of the property owned by the individual. However, given widespread land scarcity, it is common for families to consolidate inherited property through sales or informal arrangements that allow one or several (usually male) children to retain control of the land. In most of the region, only if there are no living children do wives become the primary beneficiaries, eligible to share the estate with the parents of the deceased, who are also secondary beneficiaries.[92]

In Latin America, inter-generational inheritance patterns demonstrate greater gender equality over time. In one study, this is attributed to four factors: (1) rising literacy, which raises the awareness of wives and children regarding their rights of inheritance; (2) smaller family size associated with falling fertility, which leads parents to divide property more equally among male and female siblings; (3) higher urban migration rates of young people, further reducing the number of potential heirs interested in remaining in the agricultural sector; and (4) the declining importance of agriculture in the livelihood strategies of rural households, reducing the income value of land and therefore making it less critical to male family members.[93]

Customary law also plays a major role in inheritance practices. Customary rules do not necessarily directly provide for the spouse or for all children, and in some cases customary rules exclude women from inheriting land even as daughters or widows. In other cases, daughters can only inherit land, under certain circumstances, for example, if there are no sons or if they are single, divorced, or widowed and have returned home. In these cases, women may continue to have use rights to land through their sons or brothers, but not ownership of the land. By custom if a woman must move to her husband's village upon marriage, her ability to inherit as a widow may be impeded since the husband's relatives may have no interest in caring for an outsider to the patrilineal line.

In some settings, courts may enforce customary law over civil law, making it difficult for women to inherit land even if the civil law favors such inheritance. In Zimbabwe, the civil legislation provides for equality between men and women; nevertheless, in *Magaya v. Magaya*,[94] the Zimbabwe Supreme Court ruled that under customary law women are juveniles, and therefore a woman could not inherit her father's property even though she was named in his will.

Box 5.2. Crises and coping strategies

People who are forced to depend on their good relationships with others for their most basic rights to shelter and the means to make a living are vulnerable to appalling abuse and exploitation. Once crisis strikes – whether in the form of economic crisis following the HIV/AIDS pandemic, conflict as in Rwanda or Burundi in the 1990s, battles over eroding natural resources, or the undermining of traditional views of rights and obligations that occurs once people's attitudes and beliefs change in response to international media – people must decide where their first loyalties lie. Social obligations to those beyond one's immediate loved ones feel less important, and if they have property which will ensure one's own survival, it is tempting to grab it.

Source: C. Sweetman, How Title Deeds Make Sex Safer: Women's Property Rights in an Era of HIV (Oxfam: July 2006).

Widows

In many countries, a woman's access to her husband's land upon his death is determined by whether there are still living children. If there are no children, a woman who has moved to her husband's village is often expected to return to her father. Even with children, a woman may not inherit land from her husband because the land belongs to her husband's family and not to her. In most countries, ancestral land is treated differently under customary law than purchased land.

In much of rural Africa, access to land is obtained through inheritance of ancestral lands. Patrilineal inheritance patterns of ancestral land (land passing to males) often correspond to patrilocal residence patterns (women moving to their husband's home upon marriage). In many cases, widows do not inherit land from their husbands but may obtain use rights to the land until the children are able to manage the property. Evidence from a number of countries suggests that even if women have a statutory right to land, they may lose their land to male relatives. When women bring their cases to court, courts often favor the rights of men over women, following customary law rather than formal law.

The Succession Act in Uganda treats widows and widowers similarly, although customary law favors widowers. Under the Succession Act, a surviving spouse has the right to occupy, but not own, the house and the land immediately adjoining the house plot, even if the woman farmed land away from the house during the marriage.[95] Moreover, the Succession Act limits what can be done on this land; a widow or widower must farm the land and cannot cut down trees, erect or change buildings, nor use the land for other purposes.[96] They have no right to sell the land. Intestate surviving spouses inherit only a 15% share in other property, including other plots of land, with lineal descendents receiving the majority of the rest of the property. There may be room for improvement to women's land rights via inheritance in Uganda through legislation; however, all the attention has been focused on Uganda's land law, and thus the problematic inheritance rules have remained unchanged.

Another issue related to widow's inheritance is the practice of property grabbing. This is where the in-laws of the deceased take over the home and land of the widow by means of threats, humiliation or physical violence.[97] This is an even greater problem in societies where it is inappropriate for a woman to return to her family upon the death of her spouse. In one study in Uganda, out of 204 widows, 29% said that property was taken from them at the time of the husband's death.[98] The widow's land is divided among her husband's male relatives, many of who may have assisted in gathering the bride price at the time of her marriage.[99] This is a particularly important issue in Uganda where widow-headed households are the most over-represented among the poor, comprising 13% of the poorest quartile of the Ugandan population.[100]

In countries where the impacts of HIV/AIDS on land tenure systems have been studied (e.g., Lesotho, South Africa, Kenya, Tanzania, Malawi) one major impact of the epidemic was identified to be the increase in the vulnerability of women, children and poor households to dispossession by patrilineal kin on the death of male household heads. HIV/AIDS widows may suffer total or partial loss of assets to relatives of their deceased spouses. Furthermore, women who do not have their own rights to land will not have land to pass to their children, making them much more vulnerable. Inheritance rights are especially critical for women in post-conflict situations since many more women are being widowed at a relatively young age, with dependent children to care for and educate. The organization Widows' Rights International conducted a recent survey in Uganda and found that almost 30% of widows were under 40.[101]

Further potentially impoverishing effects of HIV/AIDS may come from the stigma associated with the disease itself. What little research has been done in this area suggests that there may be a stigma associated with HIV/AIDS that especially impacts women's land rights and results in discriminatory practices that disproportionately affect women. Widowed women may be blamed for their husband's death and thus lose the right to use land, or they may lose jobs, be shunned by customers, or forced to surrender property or assets to relatives.

Daughters

Inheritance of land by daughters in a given country is directly related to marital residence and to the customary means of distributing wealth. A woman who leaves her parental home and joins her husband's family often loses any right to inherit her parents' land.[102] As discussed above, she also does not generally have the right to inherit her husband's land because it belongs to her husband's ancestral family. This in effect creates a double bind and ultimately eliminates inheritance as a means of acquiring land for many women.

Frequently, however, daughters in patrilocal societies are not concerned about inheriting land from their birth family because they no longer live in the family's village. These customary practices manifest themselves in different ways in different places. For example, almost all women interviewed during field research in the Kyrgyz Republic and India stated that they would not request land from their families even if they were legally entitled to family land because they moved away from their birth family.

Also, in traditional African communal tenure systems, daughters did not need to inherit the property of their parents to protect them except when they were unmarried or had divorced and returned home, at which time an arrangement was negotiated with their parents' clan so that they would have access to land.[103] Even though in Uganda, the Succession Act provides that children have the right to share seventy-five percent of their parents' land equally among themselves, few daughters inherit land, and those who do usually only retain the use of the land while they are living with their family and do not have the right to sell the land.[104]

India provides a good example of how law and custom work in the area of women's right to land via inheritance as daughters. In India, the Hindu Succession Act provides that daughters can inherit the property of their parents. Hindu personal law, as followed in most of India other than West Bengal, divides property into two classes: separate property and joint family property. Separate property is usually self-acquired and includes land the deceased purchased or received from the government, devolves in the first instance in equal shares to the deceased's sons, daughters, surviving spouse and, if the deceased is a man, to his mother.[105] Joint family property is ancestral property. Traditionally, only males were eligible to become "co-parceners" and receive a share of the joint family property at birth. But a 2005 amendment to the Hindu Succession Act gives both sons and daughters independent birth rights as co-parceners in joint family property.[106]

Despite the positive change for women brought with the Succession Act, field research in Karnataka State (which had amended the Hindu Succession Act to allow daughters to be co-parceners years before the 2005 amendment to the federal act) revealed that daughters generally do not exercise their right to inherit land from their natal families, nor do they exercise their present ownership right to the joint family land as co-parceners. The only exception to these findings was when a woman did not have brothers. Two common reasons were given for why daughters were not asserting their rights under the Succession Act: (1) their families had paid or would pay very high dowries and other expenses to get them married; or (2) their families had limited land and they felt uncomfortable asking to take a share of that small parcel of land away from their brothers. From the perspective of these women, they received their share of the family property through their dowry and wedding expenses even though dowry was not given to them but rather to the groom and his family.[107]

IX.   Women's knowledge of land rights and ability to enforce these rights

While countries and legislatures should enact or amend legislation – family law, civil law and property registration laws – to provide women with equal access to and security in land, it is equally important to educate women and men about these rights. Women need to know their rights and be able to use their rights once they have them.

Women must be educated about the complexity of land issues, the nature of rights and obligations, the relationship between different laws and practices, the options available for enforcing land rights, and the limitations of the legislation and the implementing bodies. Knowledge of both formal systems and informal systems for exercising land rights is critical in most parts of the world.

To ensure land rights for women, land rights literacy and notions of gender equity must be mainstreamed into society. Women and men, male local leaders, farmers, judges and land professionals must understand the law and its implications. Property law will have greater value if there are many people who understand it and are empowered to use it to protect their rights, and if people respect the decisions that may be obtained from a formal process.

Major legal changes will not be effective without a sustained effort to implement them and to gain broad public support for them. While national workshops, training material and mass media campaigns are able to alert the public to new laws, they do little toward effecting a change in attitude or action unless they are augmented by efforts of local people who both understand and support the changes. Combining a mass media effort with a sustained presence of knowledgeable people at the village level will have a much more lasting effect.

For real change to occur there must be several different levels of legal literacy and education regarding women's economic and legal rights:

- Educating policy makers and local customary leaders on the economic value of women having secure rights to land;
- Educating husbands regarding the economic benefits available when their wives purchase land or have rights to land;
- Educating women regarding dispute resolution if rights to land are impeded;
- Educating everyone on new laws and programs; and
- Educating women regarding their right to land from the marital household.

Women's NGOs and other groups can be especially helpful in educating and including women. One example is the role of the Laos

Women's Union (LWU) in educating women regarding their land rights in relation to the Lao PDR titling and registration project, financed with funds loaned by the World Bank. LWU is the official state organization that advocates for gender equity and has been very active and effective in working with legislators and state programs to extend legal rights to women. LWU has also been a very active and integrated member of the registration project's systematic adjudication teams since 1998, when it was perceived that women were being excluded from the land adjudication process. This was an innovative action as most land titling projects in any region have not attempted to work with women's organizations.

One major role of LWU in the land titling process is that of information dissemination, particularly to women, regarding the process itself. LWU produces and distributes communication materials such as calendars, posters, TV and radio spots, and song tapes in villages. It is also involved in educating citizens who receive land titles with regard to the risks and benefits of such titles. LWU produced a booklet in 2002 on the legal situation of women in Lao PDR, extracting sections and articles from several laws relating to land and women. This booklet was being updated in late 2004 with recent legislation such as the new law, Development and Protection of Women, recently approved by the National Assembly.

At the first village meeting with the titling project's systematic adjudication team, mostly village men are present. Several days or a week later, LWU organizes a meeting with village women. The gender issue is treated in depth at this meeting, particularly women's property rights. LWU staff interviewed in Vientiane feel that it is for this reason that the number of titles issued to women and joint titles has increased.[108]

X.   Recommendations and lessons learned

Anyone concerned with promoting the capacity of the poor to improve their well-being must also be concerned with the capacity of women to improve their well-being and the well-being of their children. In most of the developing world, women's sphere of operation is the household, and land programs must reach inside the household to be effective.

While women produce a large percentage of the world's food, they continue to be disadvantaged in terms of their ability to purchase land, to receive land through inheritance or government programs, to have secure rights to land and to dispose of land. Changing these facts will require not only legal change but also societal change. It is critical, therefore, that male and female leaders both within the country and within donor organizations make a commitment to change that includes speaking out publicly against gender bias and making the elimination of gender bias a priority issue.

Policy and legal change

Even though policy and legal change alone will not be sufficient to effectuate gender equity in land rights, many legal steps can be taken to move toward this outcome. Donor projects and government efforts will not only need to address property law and contract law, but also family law. At a minimum, a review of the family code, the inheritance rules and civil legislation related to co-ownership will be necessary to understand fully women's rights to land within the specific legal system. Legal interventions should be reviewed periodically to gauge whether they are having their desired effect and whether they are known and being used by women.

The key issues for a woman's rights to land all revolve around her status in a family – whether she is a wife, mother or daughter, and whether she is unmarried, married, divorced or widowed, and this status may change over time. Each role entails different rights related to property within the tribal, community or family system. Legislation and regulations that affect women's status in the family also affect her ability and right to land.

The legal requirement that land that is acquired during a marriage or consensual union belongs to both partners will probably have the biggest impact on a woman's rights to land because it will affect her ability to keep land in case the marriage dissolves through death, divorce, separation, or abandonment. Where dowry is given, one way to eliminate the situation where men receive money or property when marrying but women receive nothing would be to mandate universal co-ownership by law; that is, provide in legislation that all property that is accrued after or on behalf of the marriage be deemed to be jointly owned by the married couple, with no exceptions for gifts or inheritance. A different rule would be necessary for bride price, which is traditionally given to the bride's family and not the bride. Depending on the country context, the law might require that the bride price be held by the bride's family in trust for her or that she be given a portion of the bride price at the time of marriage. The difficulty with dowry and bride price is that legislation without community acceptance is ineffective. It may be an effective use of donor funds to help broker these types of community agreements and could potentially have an impact on the economic and physical security of women and children.

An additional safeguard for women would be to ensure that registration legislation and regulations specifically require that registration officials register land and other immovable property in the names of women and men who are married or living in consensual unions. Even without co-ownership, however, the law should require both husband and wife to consent in writing to a transaction to dispose of land acquired during the marriage or cohabitation, regardless in whose name the land is registered. A further safeguard would be to require that a wife appear before the notary to consent to the transaction. The right to consent to disposal of land is certainly less than the right to co-ownership, but it is critical for women's use rights to land within their unions. This is especially true in customary land systems in Africa.

For countries where polygamy is practiced, with or without protection under the law, legislation is needed that would essentially protect the first wife's share of the marital property from the other wives. This could be achieved if upon taking of a second wife, all property belonging to the first marriage or consensual union would be partitioned and divided. In this case the husband would only have his share to distribute to his new wife and children. Then subsequent wives should have the same legal protection as first wives (co-ownership) in relation to the remaining property.

The privatization and land tenure reform processes offer an especially promising opportunity for ensuring women's rights to land because the State has complete power to determine who will own the land. State land that is privatized (or private land that is transferred to the landless) should be titled at least in the name of husband and wife, either through joint titling or distribution of individual titles to women as well as men.

Finally, women must have effective mechanisms to enforce their land rights. The closer the dispute resolution body is to the home, the more likely women will be able to make use of it. A legislative review of dispute resolution mechanisms should look at where disputes are adjudicated, what is required for a dispute to be heard, and how the issues of money, time and literacy influence the dispute resolution process. In areas where customary or religious law is strong, involvement of the recognized community elders or religious authorities can facilitate dispute resolution, but they may or may not be inclined to recognize women's land rights. Qualitative field research can evaluate which are the best types of dispute resolution bodies for women.

Customary law

Although formal legal change is important, to reach women effectively requires understanding customary law and traditions, and also understanding what is possible and what is not, what women do and do not want to change. Field information must be gathered separately for men and women, and data must be disaggregated by gender. Rural women understand where to focus change and what is possible within their communities. In Uganda, for example, rural women are not calling for co-ownership of land. They call instead for rights for widows, an achievable goal within the social context, and one supported by both men and women. In Kyrgyzstan, rural women did not want an inheritance law that divided property equally between the spouse and all children. Rather, they felt protected by their customary law, which provides that the house and land go to the youngest son who is responsible for the well-being of his parents until they die. Customary laws vary greatly, even within one country, and it is critical to understand the rules as they relate to families, family wealth and property ownership. In many settings, customary law is much more powerful than statutory law, especially in rural communities and with respect to family matters. Where there is a difference between the two in such a setting, customary law and not statutory law will generally be followed.

Information and education

Educating women about their rights to land is key to any improvement in gender equity. Project designers and implementers should have a plan for communicating the importance of gender issues from the early project design phase. They must also educate project managers and implementers and include women in all aspects of project design. Where possible, local experts (e.g., local NGOs, other ministries, universities) with local level resources and understanding of local cultures and traditions should be used in project communication and community training.

Information campaigns and education must include men as well as women and must focus on issues that specifically affect women. In many cases, separate informational meetings for women and men are necessary as their schedules and customs are different. A variety of media and messages may be necessary to ensure that all potential beneficiaries are included, especially considering the constraints of literacy, language and mass media access. It should be kept in mind that in many rural settings women, especially poor women, are not literate.

XI. Conclusion

Women's rights to ownership, use and control over land are generally affected by their family status as daughter, wife, widow or mother. Property should be viewed in the context of the whole family and the distribution of wealth within the family. However, as land becomes more valuable relative to moveable property, a system that once may have been equitable and functional under customary law may no longer be equitable. Property systems must be reviewed in the present context for their impact on women and adjusted as necessary through formal law, case law, education and training. It is too easy to dismiss equality for men and women in a property rights system as either impossible to achieve or as a second, less important step. In fact, if gender bias is to be overcome, it must be a priority from the beginning and throughout the life of any project or reform.

Notes

1   1 World Bank Agriculture & Rural Development Department, *Gender Issues and Best Practices in Land Administration Projects: A Synthesis Report*, Report No. 32571-GLB (World Bank 2005) [hereinafter *Gender Issues and Best Practices*].

2   Center on Housing Rights and Evictions, *Bringing Equality Home: Promoting and Protecting the Inheritance Rights of Women: A Survey of Law and Practice in Sub-Saharan Africa* 26 (Geneva 2004) [hereinafter COHRE].

3   United Nations Department of Economic & Social Affairs, *1999 World Survey on the Role of Women in Development: Globalization, Gender and Work* 85 (United Nations 1999) [hereinafter *1999 World Survey*].

4   International Land Coalition, *Towards a Common Platform on Access to Land: The Catalyst to Reduce Rural Poverty and the Incentive for Sustainable Natural Resource Management*, report prepared for the World Bank Regional Workshop on Land Issues in Asia, Phnom Penh, Cambodia, June 3–6, 2002, at 4 (ILC 2003), available at: http://www.landcoalition.org/pdf/CPe.pdf.

5   COHRE, supra note 2, at 30. It should also be noted that women's empowerment in the household creates the likelihood that her children will be better educated and nourished because women tend to prioritize family welfare higher than their male counterparts. See United Nations Children Fund (UNICEF), THE STATE OF THE WORLD'S CHILDREN 2007: WOMEN AND CHILDREN: THE DOUBLE DIVIDEND OF GENDER EQUALITY 16 (UNICEF 2006).

6   COHRE, supra note 2, at 30.

7   E. Katz & J.S. Chamorro, *Gender, Land Rights and the Household Economy in Rural Nicaragua and Honduras*, paper prepared for the Regional Workshop on Land Issues in Latin America and the Caribbean (USAID 2002).

8   E. Roquas, *Gender, Agrarian Property and the Politics of Inheritance in Honduras* (paper presented at the *Agrarian Questions: The Politics of Farming anno 1995* conference, Wageningen, Netherlands, May 22-24) (Agrarian Questions Organizing Committee 1995).

9   See id.

10 Fafchamps and Quisumbing found this to be the case in rural Ethiopia. See generally M. Fafchamps & A.R. Quisumbing, *Control and ownership of assets within rural Ethiopian households*, 38(6) JOURNAL OF DEVELOPMENT STUDIES (2002).

11 A.R. Quisumbing & B. McClafferty, USING GENDER IN RESEARCH DEVELOPMENT 8 (International Food and Policy Research Institute 2003).

12 E. Katz, *The Intra-Household Economics of Voice and Exit*, 3(3) FEMINIST ECONOMICS 25-46 (1997).

13 See generally Katz & Chamorro, supra note 7.

14 A.R. Quisumbing & J.A. Maluccio, *Resources at Marriage and Intrahousehold Alloca-*
    tion: Evidence from Bangladesh, Ethiopia, Indonesia, and South Africa, 65(3) OXFORD
    BULLETIN OF ECONOMICS & STATISTICS 283-327 (2003).

15 In the Near East, for example, women rarely own arable land, although civil and reli-
    gious law permits ownership as well as the buying and selling of land by women.
    For example, in Jordan, women own 28.6% of the land; in the United Arab Emirates,
    women own 4.9% of land; and in Oman, women own 0.4% of land. In selected re-
    gions of Egypt, 24% of landowners are women; in Morocco, 14.3% of landowners are
    women; and in Lebanon, 1% of landowners are women. Cyprus is an exception, with
    51.4% of the land owned by women. Female holdings are generally smaller than male
    holdings. See generally UN Food & Agriculture Organization, *Women, Agriculture,*
    and Rural Development: A Synthesis Report of the Near East Region (FAO 1995), avail-
    able at http://www.fao.org/documents/show_cdr.asp?url_file=/docrep/X0176E/
    X0176E00.htm.

16 M. Kevane & L.C. Gray, *A Woman's Field is Made at Night: Gendered Land Rights and*
    Norms in Burkina Faso, 5(3) FEMINIST ECONOMICS 2 (1999).

17 See generally P. Mock, *The Efficiency of Women as Farm Managers: Kenya,* 58(5) AMERI-
    CAN JOURNAL OF AGRICULTURAL ECONOMICS 831-836 (1976); R.S. Meinzen-Dick, L.R.
    Brown, H.S. Feldstein & A.S. Quisumbing, *Gender, Property Rights, and Natural Re-*
    sources, 25(8) WORLD DEVELOPMENT 1303-1315 (1997). Also, for agricultural sector poli-
    cies, women's access to land is a major component of their success, See M. Fong,
    Gender Analysis in Sector Wide Assistance in Agriculture Productivity, in P. Webb & K.
    Weinberger, eds., WOMEN FARMERS: ENHANCING RIGHTS, RECOGNITION AND PRODUCTIV-
    ITY, 23 DEVELOPMENT ECONOMICS AND POLICY 251 (Peter Lang Publishing 2001).

18 In China, the average per capita land allocation was approximately 1.32 mu (approxi-
    mately 0.086 hectares) according to a national survey conducted in 1999. R. Proster-
    man, B. Schwarzwalder & J. Ye, *Implementation of 30-Year Land Use Rights for Farmers*
    Under China's 1998 Land Management Law: An Analysis and Recommendations Based
    on a 17-Province Survey, 9(3) PACIFIC RIM & POLICY JOURNAL 516 (2000). In the Kyrgyz
    Republic, the per capita distribution was approximately 0.75 to 1.5 hectares in north-
    ern provinces and between 0.1 and 0.3 hectares in southern provinces. R. Giovarelli,
    C. Aidarbekova, J. Duncan, K. Rasmussen & A. Tabyshalieva, *Women's Rights to Land*
    in the Kyrgyz Republic 10 (World Bank 2001).

19 Z. Li, *Women's Land Rights in Rural China: A Synthesis,* Ford Foundation Working Pa-
    per No. 6 (Ford Foundation 2002). See also Z. Li & J. Bruce, *Gender, Landlessness and*
    Equity in Rural China, in P. Ho, ed., DEVELOPMENTAL DILEMMAS: LAND REFORM AND
    INSTITUTIONAL CHANGE IN CHINA 315-317 (Routledge 2005).

20 The Law on the Administration of Agricultural Land (2001) (Kyrgyz Republic).

21 See generally Giovarelli, et al., supra note 18.

22 Id. at 11.

23 M. Berhane & M. Haile, *Impacts of the Allocation of Land to Women in Tigray Under*
    the TPLF's Land Reform, unpublished Research Paper, Preface (Institute of Develop-
    ment Research (IDR), Addis Ababa University, Mekelle University College 1999).

24 Id. at 14.

25 Id. at 23.

26 R. Nielsen & T. Hanstad, *In Her Own Name: An Examination of the Legislative and Pol-*
    icy Framework, Implementation, and Impact of Karnataka State's Policy Titling Rural
    Housing Benefits in the Name of Women 66-67 (paper prepared in conjunction with
    the ICRW-RDI study on women's property rights, on file with the Rural Development
    Institute 2006).

27 See id.

28 A. Aziz & S. Krishna, LAND REFORMS IN INDIA: KARNATAKA PROMISES KEPT AND MISSED (Sage Publication 1997).
29 See, e.g., Karnataka Land Reform Rules, 1974, Forms 7, 7A, 11, 12. Some forms routi-nely provide space for "self" and "head of the family," followed by "wife," reflecting an assumption that the household head will be male.
30 See generally K. Izumi, Liberalisation, Gender, and the Land Question in Sub-Saharan Africa, in C. Sweetman, ed., WOMEN, LAND, AND AGRICULTURE VOL. 9, at 9 (Oxfam Pub-lishing 1999). Examples include Tanzania and Zimbabwe.
31 K. Deininger & G. Feder, Land Institutions and Land Markets, World Bank Policy Re-search Working Paper No. 2014, at 9 (World Bank 1998).
32 See generally id.
33 See 1999 World Survey, supra note 3, at 90. See also S. Lastarria-Cornhiel, Impact of Privatization on Gender and Property Rights in Africa, 25(8) WORLD DEVELOPMENT 1317-1333 (1997); J. Dey-Abbas, Gender Asymmetries in Intrahousehold Resource Allocation in Sub-Saharan Africa: Some Policy Implications for Land and Labor Productivity, in L. Ha-daad, J. Hoddinott & H. Alderman, eds., INTRAHOUSEHOLD RESOURCE ALLOCATION IN DEVELOPING COUNTRIES: MODELS, METHODS, AND POLICY 249-262 (Johns Hopkins Uni-versity Press for International Food Policy Research Institute 1992).
34 Izumi, supra note 30, at 13.
35 See 1999 World Survey, supra note 3, at 91-92.
36 Izumi, supra note 30, at 12.
37 See R. Giovarelli & E. Eilor, Land Sector Analysis, Gender/Family Issues and Land Rights Study (Government of Uganda 2002).
38 C.D. Deere & M. León, EMPOWERING WOMEN, LAND AND PROPERTY RIGHTS IN LATIN AMERICA 3 (University of Pittsburgh Press 2001).
39 Id. at 11-12, discussing B. Agarwal, A FIELD OF ONE'S OWN: GENDER AND LAND RIGHTS IN SOUTH ASIA 31 (Cambridge University Press 1994).
40 See generally Giovarelli, et al., supra note 18; Giovarelli & Eilor, supra note 37; J. Brown, et al., Women's Access and Rights to Land in Karnataka, RDI Reports on For-eign Aid and Development No. 114 (Rural Development Institute 2002).
41 Gender Issues and Best Practices, supra note 1, at 27.
42 Id.
43 Id.
44 For example, in the Cajamarca region of Peru over 60% of couples live in a consen-sual union. Deere & León, supra note 38, at 306. Field research in the Kyrgyz Repub-lic found that once the Soviet Union collapsed and legal marriage was no longer re-quired or enforced, a majority of women in rural areas did not register their marriage and were therefore not legally married, although they participated in a religious mar-riage ceremony. See generally Giovarelli, et al., supra note 18, at 20.
45 See generally C.D. Deere & M. León, Who Owns the Land? Gender and Land-Titling Programmes in Latin America, 1(3) JOURNAL OF AGRARIAN CHANGE 440-467 (2001).
46 Under the property law system in the United States, the formal legal term is "tenancy in common."
47 Deere & León, supra note 38, at 295.
48 World Bank, Agricultural Investment Sourcebook 411–412 (World Bank 2004), available at http://www-esd.worldbank.org/ais.
49 Id. at 412. On the island of Java in Indonesia, although formal law and customary law recognize that husband and wife are co-owners of land acquired during marriage, marital property is almost always titled in the name of the husband. Most land-owners are not aware that land can be jointly titled, and application forms do not in-dicate that land can be registered in more than one name. The registration law and accompanying regulations are silent on the issue and some registration officials were

not certain that land could be titled jointly. See also J. Brown, *Rural Women's Land Rights in Java, Indonesia: Strengthened by Family Law, but Weakened by Land Registration*, 1(2) PACIFIC RIM & POLICY JOURNAL 646-647 (May 2003).

50 R. Giovarelli & S. Lastarria-Cornhiel, *Shared Tenure Options for Women: A Global Overview* UN-HABITAT AS/785/05E, at 39 (UN-HABITAT July 2005) [hereinafter *Shared Tenure*].

51 Usually, joint tenure is used when referring to land, but in law joint tenure provisions generally apply to the whole of the household property, including land, other immovable assets (e.g., houses and fixtures), as well as moveable property (e.g., vehicles, animals and cookware).

52 *Shared Tenure*, supra note 50. See also J. Bruce & J.W. Ely, Jr., MODERN PROPERTY LAW, 4TH ED. 277-326 (West Group 1999).

53 Although marriage registration in Eastern Europe and the Soviet Union was mandatory under the old regimes, research indicates that legal marriage rates are decreasing in many of these areas today. In Bulgaria, legal marriage dropped from 9 per one thousand in the 1970s to 4.2 per one thousand in 1997. According to sociological research on tendencies among young people conducted in May 1999, 60% of respondents stated that they did not prefer marriage as a form of cohabitation. R. Giovarelli, *Women's Land Rights in Bulgaria* (unpublished report on file with the Rural Development Institute 2004).

54 Technically, in common-law systems, one of the tenants can transfer his or her share (not demarcated or "undivided") of the property to another, in which case the property is held from then on as a tenancy in common by the tenant that did not transfer his/her interest and the new property rightholder.

55 Upon death, the owner's portion of the whole is part of his or her estate. If a husband and wife hold land as tenants in common and one dies without leaving a will, his or her share will be part of his or her estate and will be distributed to his or her heirs rather than automatically go to the spouse.

56 If not, as is often the case, in a dispute a woman would need to go to a civil court to claim her legal right to the land that is registered only in her husband's name. This can be expensive and difficult for women.

57 Giovarelli & Eilor, supra note 37, at 34.

58 See id. at 26. Not every person answered every question.

59 See Brown, et al., supra note 40, at 15.

60 Deere & León, supra note 38, at 315.

61 M. Judd & J. Dulnuan, *Women's Legal and Customary Access to Land in the Philippines*, World Bank Report 29 (World Bank 2001).

62 See Kevane & Gray, supra note 16, at 14.

63 See id. For an examples of land lease programs that assist women in India, see also R. Nielsen, *If He Asks Me to Leave This Place, I Will Go: The Challenge to Secure Equitable Land Rights for Rural Women*, in H. De Soto & F. Cheneval, eds., REALIZING PROPERTY RIGHTS 216-217 (Rufer & Rub 2006).

64 See *1999 World Survey*, supra note 3, at 92.

65 See id.; Lastarria-Cornhiel, supra note 33, at 1329.

66 Social collateral is generally used in terms of micro-credit lending to members of a group. Generally, the social relationships are the collateral for the loan because if one member does not pay back her share, the other members will suffer.

67 See generally Katz & Chamorro, supra note 7.

68 Land Act of Uganda, sec. 40 (1998).

69 R. Mwebaza & R. Gaynor, *Land Sector Analysis: Land Markets, Land Consolidation, and Land Readjustment Component* 13 (unpublished report, Government of Uganda 2002).

While it is "clear" in the law that the coverage only extends to plots that meet both of these criteria, there was confusion even among policy makers.

70 Judd & Dulnuan, supra note 61, at 13.
71 M. Mushunje, *Women's Land Rights in Zimbabwe*, Report of Land Tenure Center 11 (University of Wisconsin 2001).
72 R. Deshpande & D.M. Burjorjee, INCREASING ACCESS AND BENEFITS FOR WOMEN: PRACTICES AND INNOVATIONS AMONG MICROFINANCE INSTITUTIONS, SURVEY RESULTS (UN Capital Development Fund 2002).
73 Mwebaza & Gaynor, supra note 69, at 13.
74 Judd & Dulnuan, supra note 61, at 11.
75 Berhane & Haile, supra note 23, at 37.
76 Meinzen-Dick, et al., supra note 17, at 1310.
77 See Berhane & Hale, supra note 23, at 38.
78 See Brown, et al., supra note 40, at 8.
79 Law on State Duties (2000), Article 4 (Kyrgyz Republic). Judges in the Kyrgyz Republic pointed out this regulation as a major impediment to women's access to court for property division.
80 Giovarelli, et al., supra note 18, at 21.
81 Dowry is generally money or goods given by the bride's family to the groom or the bride. Bride price is generally money or goods given by the groom's family to the bride's family. Sometimes these words are used interchangeably.
82 Giovarelli, et al., supra note 18, at 23.
83 Giovarelli & Eilor, supra note 37, at 18.
84 J. Kigula, *Land Disputes in Uganda: An Overview of the Types of Land Disputes and Dispute Settlement*, Research and Policy Development Project Paper No. 3 (unpublished paper, Makerere Institute of Social Research, Uganda, and the Land Tenure Center, University of Wisconsin 1993).
85 T. Hilhorst, *Women's Land Rights: Current Developments in Sub-Saharan Africa*, in C. Toulmin & J. Quan, eds., EVOLVING LAND RIGHTS, POLICY AND TENURE IN AFRICA 186 (DFID/IIED/NRI 2000).
86 Hilhorst, supra note 85, at 186.
87 See Deere & León, supra note 38, at 314-318; Katz & Chamorro, supra note 7.
88 COHRE, supra note 2, at 27.
89 See generally G. Nelson, W. Stoebuck & D. Whitman, THE LAW OF PROPERTY (West Group Publishing 2002).
90 See Agarwal, supra note 39, at 198-232.
91 Deere & León, supra note 38, at 60.
92 In Latin America, laws governing inheritance of property do not necessarily apply to land acquired under government-sponsored agrarian reform programs; provisions for the latter are often more geared toward preventing fragmentation of holdings by limiting the number of inheritance beneficiaries to a surviving spouse or single child.
93 See Deere & León, supra note 38, at 264-329.
94 ICHRL 14 (Feb. 16, 1999). The Supreme Court ruled 5–0 that customary law had precedence over the Constitution. Venia Magaya, a 58-year-old, sued her half-brother for ownership of her deceased father's land after her brother evicted her from the home. Under the Zimbabwean Constitution and international human rights treaties, Magaya had a right to the land. The court ruled that women should not be able to inherit land "because of the considerations in African society." The court used Article 23 of the Constitution of Zimbabwe, which prohibits discrimination in the application of African customary law.
95 Succession Act of Uganda, sched. 2, para. 1 (1964, as amended 1972).
96 Id., sched. 2, para. 7.

97   COHRE, supra note 2, at 21.

98   L.Z. Gilborn, R. Nyonyintono, R. Kabumbuli & G. Jagwe-Wadda, *Making a Difference for Children Affected by AIDS: Baseline Findings from Operations Research in Uganda Report* 1 (Population Council 2001), available at http://www.popcouncil.org/pdfs/horizons/orphansbsln.pdf.

99   Giovarelli & Eilor, supra note 37, at 10.

100 S. Appleton, *Women-Headed Households and Household Welfare: An Empirical Deconstruction for Uganda*, 24(12) WORLD DEVELOPMENT 18-19 (1996).

101 K. Young, *Widows Without Rights: Challenging Marginalisation and Dispossession*, 14(2) GENDER AND DEVELOPMENT 199 (2006).

102 On the other hand, women in matrilineal societies are often in a very powerful position in relation to land rights. See generally R. Strickland, *To Have and to Hold: Women's Property and Inheritance Rights in the Context of HIV/AIDS in Sub-Saharan Africa*, ICRW Working Paper (ICRW June 2004).

103 G. Gopal, *Gender-Related Legal Reform and Access to Economic Resources in Eastern Africa*, WORLD BANK DISCUSSION PAPER NO. 405, at 21 (World Bank 1999).

104 Giovarelli & Eilor, supra note 37, at 10.

105 Hindu Succession Act, No. 30 of 1956 (as amended) secs. 8, 15; India Code (2007), accessed Dec. 20, 2007 http://indiacode.nic.in/.

106 Id. sec. 6.

107 S. Arun, *Does Land Ownership Make a Difference? Women's Roles in Agriculture in Kerala, India*, in C. Sweetman, ed., WOMEN, LAND, AND AGRICULTURE VOL. 9, at 19-20 (Oxfam Publishing 1999). See also Brown, et al., supra note 40, at 17-24.

108 *Gender Issues and Best Practices*, supra note 1, at 53-54.

6 Land tenure reform in India

Tim Hanstad and Robin Nielsen

I. Introduction

India's efforts to address the unequal distribution of rural land span almost a century, with their origins rooted in the colonial period and stretching to the present day. Initiatives range from broad legislative mandates imposed by state governments to a single man walking down rural roads seeking donations of farmland for redistribution to the landless poor. India's extensive experience with land tenure reform provides critical insight into many of the concepts that are the focus of the preceding chapters, including tenancy reforms, agricultural land ownership ceilings, and the allocation of micro-plots to landless households.

The results of the decades of reform efforts in India have been predictably varied, often reflecting not only the design and implementation of particular reforms, but also the economic, political, and social environments in which they arose. Through a review of the history of India's land tenure reforms, this chapter provides an opportunity to witness a country's efforts to address the challenge of rural poverty and inequality with specific policies, targeted legislation and directed programs. Examination of India's experience provides a unique opportunity to chronicle the effects of specific policies and legislative language as they play out over time.

Moreover, India's experience with land tenure reform is far from over. Perhaps more than in any other country, policy makers in India have demonstrated a willingness to examine past and existing reforms with a critical eye and to consider new approaches that draw on those experiences, to reflect on the lessons learned, and also to recognize new rural realities. India's highest policy-making body, the National Development Council (consisting of the most senior central and state-level policy makers) recently adopted India's 11th Five-Year Plan.[1] The Plan recognizes the achievements (and failures) of past land tenure reforms and expressly notes the continued relevance of land rights, the significant challenges remaining, and the need to consider new methods to bring the promised benefits of land tenure reform to the rural poor. At the state level, some policy makers have already taken up the challenge. Demonstrating significant initiative, officials in several states have taken bold and creative steps to reconsider land policies. The need for such efforts is acute, and the new policy directives and programs show early promise.

India's business, technology and manufacturing sectors have been major sources of rapid economic growth in recent years. However, much of India's population has not shared in these economic gains. Approximately 70% of India's estimated 1.1 billion people live in rural areas, and 60% of the total workforce works primarily in agriculture.[2] Some 35% of India's population still survives on less than one dollar per day; 70% exists on two dollars a day or less, a higher proportion than in Africa.[3]

India contains the largest concentration of rural poor people and the largest number of landless households on the planet.[4] The grim statistics are connected: while India faces significant and entrenched problems stemming from an inadequate system of education and the persistence of caste distinctions, landlessness is a better predictor of poverty than either illiteracy or membership in the lower castes.[5] In large measure, land access determines a rural family's status, their livelihood options and their prospects for the future.

The link between landlessness and poverty in India has been long recognized. Perhaps no country has matched the volume of land tenure reform legislation produced by India since its independence in 1947, an amount amplified by the rare constitutional requirement that each individual state must enact its own laws on this subject.[6] India's experience demonstrates, however, that adopting well-intended laws does not, by itself, guarantee intended results. From the perspective of most rural poor, most Indian land tenure reform laws have not had the desired effect, and some legislative provisions have had perverse and unintended consequences. As a result, despite decades of well intentioned effort, India's poorest households still struggle for access to rural land and land tenure security.

This chapter describes India's legislatively driven efforts to provide the rural poor with access to agricultural land. Section II describes India's post-Independence legislative initiatives to increase land access. Most prominent among these first-generation initiatives are the abolition of intermediaries, reform of tenancy relations and imposition of ceilings on landholdings. The chapter discusses these and other efforts in some detail because India's experience offers insight into the design, implementation and impact of these more traditional land tenure reforms. India's experience with these initiatives forms the foundation for the country's movement toward a second generation of land reforms.

As described in Section III, India's current efforts to rethink and revise approaches to increasing land access and land tenure security are yielding promising early results – in large measure because policy makers and planners are absorbing some of the lessons of the post-Independence land reforms. This portion of the chapter discusses the lessons of the first generation of land reforms and describes several new approaches designed to increase land access and improve land tenure security for rural poor households. India's recent experiences challenging old assumptions with new initiatives point toward a promising future in which land policies, laws and programs make it possible for secure rights to land to improve the livelihoods of the single largest concentration of the poorest and most disadvantaged people.

II.   India's first-generation land reforms

A.   Abolition of intermediaries

At the time of independence in 1947, Indian agricultural land was administered under three broad types of land tenure systems: the *zamindari* system, the *ryotwari* system, and the *mahalwari* system. The *zamindari* system was the most widespread, covering 57% of cultivated land in British India.[7] Under this system, feudal lords and land tax collectors were proprietors of the land with the authority to collect rent. The tillers of the land became tenants whose fortunes were dependent upon the wishes and whims of the *zamindars*. Over time, the larger *zamindars* freed themselves from the burden of managing their estates and collecting rents from cultivators by contracting out the rent-collecting rights. In some areas, multiple layers of intermediaries separated the *zamindar* from the actual cultivator.[8]

The second type of land tenure system was the *ryotwari* system, which covered about 38% of cultivated land in British India, mostly in southern India.[9] The *ryotwari* system recognized individual cultivators as proprietors of their land with generally recognized rights to transfer their land. The system did not legally recognize any kind of intermediary interest between the cultivator and the state; the proprietors paid land revenue directly to the colonial administration. Nonetheless, informal intermediaries of the *zamindari* type emerged even in areas where the *ryotwari* systems had strongholds, partly as the result of the infiltration of traders and moneylenders into agriculture. Over time, many *ryots* took advantage of their power to transfer by renting out part or all of their land to tenants, mostly sharecroppers.

Only approximately 5% of British India's cultivated land was administered under the third type of land tenure scheme, the *mahalwari* system. Under this system, village units paid land revenue. Peasant farmers contributed shares of the total amount of land revenue owed by the village in proportion to their holdings. The *mahalwari* system existed in most of present-day Punjab and Haryana, as well as parts of Madhya Pradesh, Orissa, and Uttar Pradesh.

The existence of intermediary interests fostered inefficiency and inequity. British authorities had assumed that by giving *zamindars* and other tax-collecting authorities proprietary rights and fixed tax amounts, efficient collaboration between landlords and tenants would follow. The authorities assumed that *zamindars* would provide managerial expertise, technical knowledge and capital, while tenants would supply their labor – a symbiotic relationship that would increase agricultural production and productivity. Such symmetry of contribution was never achieved on a large scale. Many *zamindars* mistreated tenants through practices such as rack-renting and summary evictions.[10]

The abuses of the intermediary systems attracted attention during the struggle to end British rule, and in the period immediately following Independence the country's new leaders paid particular attention to the abolition of intermediary interests in land. The Indian Constitution, which grants the states exclusive authority to enact land tenure legislation, provided a starting point.[11] By the end of the 1950s, almost all states had enacted legislation abolishing intermediary interests upon payment of compensation.

Results were mixed. On one hand, the legislation transformed roughly 25 million "superior" tenants (not necessarily the tillers) into landowners or tenants holding land directly under the government,[12] intermediaries lost status and power, and the legislation reduced incidents of forced labor and other forms of oppression.[13] As *zamindars* were forced to share power with their former "superior" tenants, these beneficiaries of the reforming legislation gained in social status and political power. The abolition of intermediaries also reduced the multiplicity of legal land tenures that previously existed, simplifying and clarifying land tenure law in most Indian states, to the benefit of the poorer members of society. Finally, legislation abolishing intermediaries brought large areas of cultivable wasteland, forests and *abadi* land (house plots and other land in villages) under state ownership. States subsequently distributed a considerable amount of this land to poor beneficiaries (as discussed in Section II D below).

For all the benefits realized, however, laws to abolish intermediary interests still fell well short of their potential. First, the laws created the impetus for *zamindars* to evict substantial numbers of tenants through various methods, including taking advantage of loopholes in the laws;[14] the *zamindars* were particularly successful at evicting "non-superior" tenants (a classification that included the poorest farmers), many of whom had directly farmed the land from which they were evicted for generations.[15]

Second, the combination of these loopholes and other shortcomings in the laws opened the door for intermediaries to gain ownership over much or even all of the land for which they had previously held only an intermediary interest.[16] Meanwhile, the states generally compensated the ex-intermediaries more than adequately for the rights they did lose – as high as 15 to 30 times their annual net income derived from the land.[17] Frustratingly, most did not repay the favor: the ex-intermediaries were generally disinclined to invest their windfalls in industry or other activities beneficial to the economy.[18]

Third, while state laws often granted tenants the right to purchase lands from willing landlords at set rates, the states set high purchase prices, and the rules required tenants to make installment payments within a relatively short period.[19] Few could afford the purchase prices, and an opportunity for tenants to become landowners slipped by.

In sum, the legislation reduced the feudal nature of agrarian relationships in much of India, and despite deficiencies in the legislation, overall the states implemented this phase of India's land reforms more successfully than they implemented the land ceiling and tenancy reforms that followed. However, flawed legal provisions and less-than-effective implementation led to large-scale evictions and missed opportunities to protect and empower many tenants. A stronger focus on providing rights to those who actually tilled the land, as in the contemporaneous land tenure reforms in Japan, South Korea and Taiwan, would almost certainly have achieved better results.[20]

B. Tenancy reforms

The weaknesses in legislation and implementation that limited the effectiveness of the abolition of intermediaries were more pronounced in India's efforts at tenancy reform. In the period immediately after Independence, tenant farmers comprised an estimated 35% of India's rural population.[21] The tenancy system favored powerful landlords at the expense of their tenants. Most tenancies were oral and terminable at will, and most tenants had no other economic opportunities and therefore were severely disadvantaged in their bargaining relationships with their landlords.[22] These exploitive tenancy relationships were ripe for legislative intervention.

In the 1960s and 1970s, every Indian state passed tenancy reform legislation. As with the efforts to abolish intermediaries, equity and efficiency concerns supplied the fuel for the tenancy reform. Unlike legislation to abolish intermediaries, central government policy guidelines directed state tenancy legislation. Unfortunately, central government guidance on matters such as maximum rents and the ability of land-owners to resume tenanted land brought little additional success dur-ing the first-generation land reforms.[23]

In most states, tenants who remained on tenanted land became en-titled to permanent rights, with a significant exception for "resumable" land. While the legislative approaches varied by state, most tenancy laws permitted landowners to resume tenanted land for personal culti-vation, which was often broadly defined to include land farmed by la-borers. Landowners took full advantage of the liberal definition to re-tain ownership of tenanted land.[24]

Half-conceived, often lackluster implementation methods led to even wider gaps between the declared objectives of the tenancy reform policy and law and actual achievements in the field. For example, a village-level examination of the implementation of the tenancy reforms in Ma-harashtra found that local officials were unable to enforce the terms of the legislation: tenants were dispossessed and previously tenanted land vested in landlords because tenant names were removed from revenue records, revenue officials could not establish tenancy relationships be-cause of a lack of documentation, or tenants were coerced to surrender their rights. Researchers concluded that in some villages half of the tenants lost land rights as a result of the reforms.[25]

Perhaps the most controversial aspect of the tenancy laws related to the creation of new tenancies. The laws fall on a continuum. Some states such as Karnataka prohibit tenancy altogether, with a few minor exceptions. Karnataka's tenancy law gives the state the power to seize leased-out land without compensating the landowner and to distribute the land to land-poor families.[26] In contrast, while West Bengal gener-ally does not allow fixed-rent tenancies, the state does permit share-cropping (although, because the law thereby gives permanent rights to such sharecroppers, the law discourages landowners from entering into new sharecropping relationships).[27] At the far end of the spectrum, Maharashtra's laws permit tenancy relationships but grant tenants rights to purchase leased land, creating a disincentive for landowners to enter into leasing relationships.[28]

Impact of tenancy reform

India's tenancy reform legislation largely failed to achieve its goals of protecting tenants and providing land ownership rights to the landless rural poor. In the decades following enactment, the laws provided 12.4 million tenants with rights to 15.6 million acres of land.[29] This com-prises about 8% of rural households and 4% of India's agricultural land.[30] While the achievement cannot be discounted for those who benefited, significant negative impacts experienced by a far larger group offset the positive results. First, tenancy reform caused the large-scale eviction of tenants. One study estimates that the legislation caused landlords to evict tenant families from as much as 33% of India's agricultural land.[31]

Second, the tenancy laws prevented poor farmers from accessing land through tenancy. Rural households often believe that landowners risk losing some rights to their land when they rent it out. As a result some landowners let their land lie fallow rather than assume risks associated with leasing it out, and landowners who rent out land tend to rent only to those whom they trust not to assert rights. For extra protection, the landowner may also rotate tenants to different parcels, often every year.[32]

Third, broad restrictions on tenancy also act to deny women and other marginalized groups a reasonable means of safeguarding land access. In many cases, village elites and male relatives may usurp land owned by women. Where such practices exist, women's land tenure security may be best served through long-term lease arrangements to her male relatives. Restrictions against tenancy frequently prohibit such arrangements, undermining a female landowner's efforts to enter into protective contractual arrangements on favorable market terms. And while groups of women have often found leasing to be a useful tool for accessing land, this approach is constrained because of the legislative restrictions.[33]

Rethinking restrictions on tenancy to help the poor

Throughout much of the 20th century, tenancy in many parts of the developing world – including India – was cast in the role of an exploitative institution and charged with negatively impacting socially optimal equity and productivity outcomes. This perception was understandable in the period before and immediately after Indian independence. In an agrarian setting characterized by strict social and economic hierarchy where overwhelming numbers of rural poor lacked access to land other than as insecure tenants and any other economic opportunity, tenants had little bargaining power, and many landlords exploited their positions of economic and social privilege.

These characterizations are, overall, considerably less accurate today. While still present, economic and social hierarchies have weakened. A growing economy along with targeted social, political and economic interventions have helped to reduce poverty, increase social empowerment, and provide other opportunities to an increasing number of poor rural households. This progress is reflected, in part, by higher (albeit

still low) agricultural labor wages and a shrinking proportion of the
working population in agriculture in many parts of the country.

Moreover, since the enactment of tenancy reform legislation in India
decades ago, a broader consensus in the economic literature has
emerged that concludes land rental markets in general – and sharecropping relationships in particular – can play a substantial role in
increasing land access for the poor. Rental markets can supply a critical
rung on the "agricultural ladder" toward land ownership, particularly
as growing economic opportunity (especially non-agricultural opportunity) and sociopolitical advancements erode feudal-like vestiges and improve the bargaining position of poor tenants.[34] Both land sales and
land rental markets are capable of enhancing transfers of land from
land-rich to land-poor households. Of the two, theory and empirical evidence indicate that the rental market supplies the more commonly
practicable conduit.[35] Land ownership conveys much greater benefits
(particularly concerning credit access, tenure security, social and political empowerment, and wealth), but access to land via land rental is often a more feasible, albeit decidedly second-best alternative to land
ownership. While being a tenant farmer is rarely as beneficial as being
an owner-operator, tenants are generally better off than evicted ex-
tenants working as agricultural laborers.[36]

A systematic economic analysis of tenancy in India provides strong
empirical support that legislatively placed restrictions on tenancy in India result in decreased land access by both the landless and more efficient producers.[37] A 5,000-household survey conducted in India that
collected data over a 17-year period found that tenancy restrictions limit
the supply and demand for agricultural land and prevent access to land
by the landless and most efficient producers.[38] These findings are supported by results of a smaller survey of 400 households that RDI conducted in Karnataka in 2001. That survey interviewed members of
landless households, tenant households that had received occupancy
rights to tenanted land through land reform, households that received
house plots through some type of government program, and those that
received agricultural land through land reform initiatives.[39] This mix-
ture of respondents expressed remarkably similar attitudes toward tenancy restrictions. Of those respondents expressing an opinion, 91% stated that existing tenancy restrictions harm landowners, 94% stated that
existing tenancy restrictions harm the landless, 38% reported that at
least one farmer in their village keeps land fallow rather than renting it
out because renting may lead to the loss of such land, and 45% stated
that tenancy prohibitions should be lifted.[40]

Land tenancy markets can also reduce the vulnerability of poor
households by offering a more stable livelihood source than frequently
volatile labor markets.[41] As opportunities in the non-farm economy in-

crease, tenancy markets can facilitate a broader choice of livelihood opportunities such as migration, specialization and investment. Land rental markets have more potential to provide land access to poor farmers in settings where agriculture is not capital-intensive,[42] which is most of the agriculture in a large majority of the settings that form our focus in this book. In addition, small owner households in positions to pursue non-farm livelihoods will benefit if they are able to rent out some or all of their land for others to cultivate, and devote their personal energies to non-farm activities. Looking to other countries, China's experience – a setting where leasing-out is essentially legal and safe – indicates that in a growing economy, the role of land tenancy can be significant.[43]

In the course of ongoing rapid rural appraisal research in various Indian states, RDI generally finds that: (1) knowledge of the specific tenancy reform provisions in the law is low, but most rural households believe that landowners risk losing some (often substantial) rights to their land when they rent it out; (2) consequently, when land is rented, it is given to people who can be trusted not to assert rights and, for an extra measure of protection, those tenants are typically rotated, often every year; (3) although tenancy reform laws are rarely implemented, they often play a major role in landowner decisions about renting-out land and lead to less active rental markets than would otherwise be expected and to some sub-optimal utilization of land, thus creating a classic lose-lose situation (i.e., the non-implemented law brings few benefits, but its overhang distorts the rental market, with a considerable negative impact); and (4) land-poor households almost always wish that more land was available for rental; they do not fear exploitive landlord practices nearly as much as they fear not being able to access land to improve their livelihoods.[44] The conclusions are supported by the findings of the 5,000-household survey noted above, which suggests that lifting tenancy restrictions would lead to increased land access and income for many poor and landless families and increase agricultural productivity.[45]

India's policy makers echo these conclusions in the 11th Five-Year Plan, issued in December 2007. The Plan notes that although some former tenants benefited from tenancy laws by receiving ownership rights to land, the laws in some areas are now restricting access to land by the landless and marginal farmers wishing to lease in land, reducing productivity of the land and the supply of agricultural land due to landowners' fear of losing land rights under tenancy laws, and creating an unregulated tenancy market that permits exploitative relationships. The Plan recognizes the need to revisit tenancy legislation and revise restrictions in a manner that recognizes the need to balance the interests of landowners, tenants and prospective tenants.[46] Several states are considering such revisions to their tenancy laws (see discussion in Section III E).

C.   Agricultural landownership ceilings

As the third major legislative effort to equalize land ownership in the years following Independence, all Indian states placed ceilings on the amount of agricultural land a person or family can own, with the objective of equalizing landownership. The laws authorized states to take land that exceeded the ceiling from larger landowners and redistribute that land to poor, landless or marginal farmers.

The policy of imposing landownership ceilings evolved slowly after Indian independence and generally enjoyed less consensus than land tenancy reforms. The lengthy, somewhat troubled history of ceiling legislation reflects an inherent dichotomy at the national level and in some states: policy makers are philosophically committed to the imposition of land ceilings, yet at local levels implementation poses an enormous threat to the interests of landowners and leaders alike.

Indian states enacted and enforced ceiling laws in two phases: the period from 1960 to 1972, when no specific policy guidelines yet existed, and the period since 1972, after adoption of national policy guidelines. Laws adopted in the first round were ripe for constitutional challenge and full of loopholes that large landowners used to circumvent the legislative objectives.[47] The laws set high ceilings[48] and did not prohibit anticipatory transfers (which enabled large landowners, in anticipation of the law, to conduct partitions and fictitious transfers). Exemptions were numerous,[49] and ceiling limits were set on the basis of individual holders as the unit and not on a family basis, thus allowing partitions among family members to evade the ceiling legally.[50]

The central government enacted national guidelines to give the effort some teeth, and states responded by lowering ceilings, refining definitions, and limiting some exemptions.[51] The ceilings now range from nine standard acres (3.6 hectares)[52] in parts of Jammu and Kashmir to 54 standard acres (21.8 hectares) for certain circumstances in Gujarat, Haryana, Karnataka, Madhya Pradesh, Punjab, Rajasthan and Tamil Nadu.[53] In nearly every law, however, the compensation paid is negligible when compared with the market value of the land. In all states, the landowner with land in excess of the ceiling may choose which land the government will take.[54]

The national guidelines stipulate that priority in ceiling-surplus land distribution should be given to landless agricultural workers, particularly those belonging to Scheduled Castes and Scheduled Tribes. Most states have generally followed this advice. In some states, first priority is given in the distribution of ceiling land to tenants dispossessed in that area; other states provide no such priority. Some states provide for distributing the ceiling-surplus land free-of-charge to beneficiaries (including West Bengal, Bihar, Orissa and Uttar Pradesh). Other states require beneficiaries to pay a specified amount in suitable installments, which in some cases is equal to the amount paid by the state government to the dispossessed landowner. State laws also vary in the type of rights received by the beneficiaries. Many states permanently prohibit transfers by beneficiaries. Other states, such as Karnataka, prohibit the beneficiaries from transferring their land for a period of years (ranging from 10 to 20 years). Still other states allow such transfers only with the permission of the local land revenue authority.[55]

Overall impact of ceiling laws

By the end of 2005, state governments across India had declared 7.3 million acres of above-ceiling land, which is approximately 1.8% of India's agricultural land. Of that land, the governments had taken possession of 6.5 million acres and had distributed 5.4 million acres to a total of 5.6 million households. The total of ceiling-surplus land distributed amounts to approximately 1% of India's agricultural land and 4% of rural households.[56]

The only states where more than 5% of the cultivated agricultural land area has been redistributed as ceiling-surplus land are West Bengal, Jammu and Kashmir, and (perhaps) Assam.[57] West Bengal leads India, accounting for 40% of the ceiling-surplus land beneficiaries and about 20% of the distributed ceiling-surplus land in India. West Bengal's ceiling legislation set a relatively lower landownership ceiling than the other states and redistributed the surplus land in smaller plots. In addition, the law has fewer loopholes than most other land ceiling provisions, and the state government's emphasis on distributing the benefits widely (but in smaller plots) led to more grassroots support for the process.[58]

The impact of ceiling legislation in West Bengal has been substantial: 34% of all agricultural households have received ceiling-surplus land, in amounts averaging 0.4 acre per household, and studies have documented the importance of the ceiling-surplus distribution in both bettering the livelihoods of beneficiaries and promoting agricultural growth and stability in the countryside.[59]

In other states, the impact of ceiling laws fell short of expectations for several reasons: (1) the state governments paid inadequate compensation for the land taken, which made the programs unpopular with landowners; (2) landowners used gaps and loopholes in the laws to their advantage; (3) states often distributed the relatively small amount of land obtained in relatively large parcels, benefiting only a small percentage of landless families; and (4) outdated and incomplete land records made implementation of the ceiling legislation more difficult.

The disappointing impact of ceiling laws is largely due to persistent deficiencies in the legislation and a similarly persistent lack of political will to implement the legislation effectively. In many cases, ceiling legislation was incomplete and allowed large landowners to avoid the law. Most significantly, however, the laws failed to provide fair compensation to landowners. Even after policy makers revised the laws to provide more favorable payments, government officials lacked the will to make compulsory land purchases from the relatively powerful landowning class. The lack of adequate land records also made redistribution efforts more difficult.[60]

The lack of political will to confront and dismantle existing power structures, to trace land rights through incomplete, outdated (or otherwise poor or nonexistent) record-keeping systems, and to dedicate time and resources to programs unpopular with politically influential landowners has continued to the present day. The 11th Five-Year Plan specifically recognizes the small percentage of land distributed and the extent to which much of the area declared surplus but undistributed is held up in litigation or from which the beneficiaries have been dispossessed. The Plan calls for the speedy disposition of land cases pending in courts, the identification of cases where beneficiaries have been dispossessed and land restored, and joint investigation by Revenue Department officials and Gram Sabha members of fictitious transactions and transfers made to avoid the law.[61]

D.   Allocation of Bhoodan land, government wasteland and house sites

India's land reform efforts are typically described as comprising only the three categories of reforms discussed above: abolition of intermediaries, tenancy reform and ceiling-surplus redistribution. The reforms, however, also included other significant and sometimes overlapping measures. These measures, which are briefly outlined below, include the distribution of *Bhoodan* land, the allocation of government wasteland, and the allocation or regularization of land for house sites (or homesteads).

Distribution of Bhoodan land

Vinob Bhave, a disciple of Mahatma Ghandi, started the *Bhoodan* (land gift) movement in 1951 in the Telengana region of Andhra Pradesh. Bhave took up the cause at a time when armed land grabbing ostensibly to aid the landless poor was gathering momentum. Bhave asked landowners to donate a portion of their land for peaceful distribution to the landless. With a goal to obtain 50 million acres of donated land, Bhave traveled on foot throughout India requesting donations.

Before he ceased his work in 1969, Bhave received 39 million acres of land through the *Bhoodan* movement. However, of the land donated, only 22 million acres has been formally distributed to the poor.[62] The remainder has not been distributed for a variety of reasons. In some cases, the land was unfit for agriculture or had been encroached upon. In other cases, heirs contested the land donation or land documents were missing or contained irregularities. Some researchers also note that the land that has been allocated is of poor quality.[63]

The actual distribution of *Bhoodan* land with legal documents has continued in a sluggish manner through the present day.[64] Dissatisfied with the pace of progress, the Ministry of Rural Development tasked the Committee on State Agrarian Relations and the Unfinished Task of Land Reforms[65] to review the progress of distribution of *Bhoodan* land in all states and suggest measures for distribution of the remaining land to the landless.[66]

Allocation of government wasteland

"Wastelands" are lands that are either entirely barren or are producing significantly below their economic potential.[67] An estimated 150 million acres of India's total land mass of 810 million acres are wastelands. This total acreage includes wastelands under the authority of the Forest Department, controlled by state revenue departments, those used for communal purposes and managed by villages or local governments, and privately owned wastelands.[68]

State laws provide for the allocation of government wasteland to poor rural households under a variety of schemes, and as of 2004, state governments reported allocating 14.7 million acres of government wasteland to such households.[69] Most of the allocation took place in the 1970s and 1980s, and six states have allocated 80% of the wasteland granted, led by Andhra Pradesh (28% of the national total) and Uttar Pradesh (17% of the national total). The national government does not, however, maintain statistics on how many households have actually received such land.[70]

In terms of total acreage, the amount of allocated government wastelands is nearly three times the amount of ceiling-surplus land redistributed. However, in contrast to the studies and literature devoted to ceiling-surplus redistribution, the topic of government wasteland allocation is rarely mentioned, perhaps because the quality of such allocated wastelands is often very poor. Our own fieldwork indicates that such land is not only often (although not always) of poor quality, but would require significant investment to bring it under cultivation – investment that is frequently beyond the means of the beneficiary. In isolated studies, researchers have typically found that a majority of the government wastelands allocated are not utilized.[71]

The possibility of "soft" data may also be partially responsible for the lack of attention to government wasteland allocation figures. In Andhra Pradesh, for example, where more than one-quarter of such allocated land exists, informed observers estimate that the reported grantees are not in legal or physical possession of approximately 30% of the reportedly allocated wastelands. In some cases, lands were distributed "on paper" but not on the ground, or lands were distributed on the ground but without formal legal documentation. In other cases, the grantees were forced off the land by more powerful interests in the village.[72] Section III B of this chapter discusses a project undertaken in Andhra Pradesh to identify and correct irregularities in the distribution of such land.

Allocation or regularization of house sites

Another feature of the first-generation land reform measures in some Indian states is the provision of house sites or homestead plots to landless laborers and other land-poor households. States have provided the land in various ways, including: (1) allocating state government land; (2) allocating vested ceiling-surplus land; (3) allocating land under the control of village *panchayats*; (4) allocating ownership of land held by residential tenants; and (5) regularizing the possession of illegally occupied land. Neither the national government nor most states maintain systematically collected data on the numbers of households that have received ownership of house sites by these various means, but estimates place the number at about four million households nationwide.[73] Nationwide, plots granted typically have ranged in size from 0.015 acre (about 700 square feet) to 0.10 acre (about 4,300 square feet), with most closer to the lower end of the range.

Some states, such as West Bengal and Bihar, have enacted separate laws allocating or regularizing house sites, but most states have incorporated provisions in their land reform laws, land revenue laws, or both. A prominent example is the state of Kerala, which gave landless agricultural laborers known as *kudikidappukaran* the right to obtain permanent, heritable rights to their dwellings and the land surrounding the dwelling.[74] *Kudikidappukaran* could obtain a maximum of 0.10 acre in rural areas and townships, and 0.03 to 0.05 acres in municipalities. The law required *kudikidappukaran* to pay the landowner 25% of the market value, half of which was to be subsidized by the Kudikidappukar's Benefit Fund. The remaining half of the purchase price was payable by the *kudikidappukar* in twelve annual installments.[75]

An estimated 421,000 *kudikidappukaran* received ownership rights
to their dwellings and surrounding land.[76] Most received ownership in
the 1970s and many of the claims were settled outside of the official
channels.[77] Statewide, 21,000 acres were transferred to agricultural laborers as homestead plots, or roughly 0.08 acres per family.[78] The micro-plots gave the laborers security from eviction and, for those who
cultivated their plots, a source of food and additional income.[79]

In the years following Independence, the primary purpose of the
house site allocations was to provide land for a residence and (sometimes) to free agricultural laborers from the power of their employers
who are also their residential landlords. More recently, state programs
allocating micro-plots reflect recognition among policy makers that relatively small amounts of land can provide a household with valuable
non-residential benefits, including increased income, improved nutrition, and greater status in the community, and micro-plot allocation
programs are a practical alternative to traditional land reforms (see discussion in Section III D and Chapter 4).[80]

III.   Toward a second generation of land reform

A.   Lessons learned from first-generation reforms

India's' first generation land reform efforts had some positive results,
particularly in a few states where they were well implemented. As of
2002, state governments had transferred 21 million acres under the
ceiling-surplus and tenancy reform legislation.[81] Moreover, results of a
nationally representative survey of approximately 5,000 rural households interviewed in 1982 and again in 1999 reveal that where states
implemented land reforms, the measures had a positive impact on livelihoods. Households in states that implemented tenancy reforms and
land ceiling legislation experienced higher growth in income, asset ac-
cumulation and childhood education than those in states with lower
levels of land reform efforts.[82]

Overall, however, the first-generation land reforms fell far short of
accomplishing their objectives. Research indicates that the reform programs have not uniformly benefited the poorest and the landless and
the neediest households also lost some of the potentially beneficial impacts because the state failed to provide essential supporting non-land
inputs. In addition, first-generation reforms missed a significant opportunity to provide rural women with rights to land. India's central government directed states allocating government land (e.g., wasteland,
ceiling-surplus land) to title the land jointly in the name of husbands
and wives or individually in the name of the women. However, only a

handful of states even included the directive in state allocation programs, and none were initially successful in implementing their directives.[83] Only recently have the directives begun to take hold, most notably in the state of Karnataka.[84]

The neediest beneficiaries also lost some of the potentially beneficial
impacts of reform because the state failed to provide essential supporting non-land inputs. Finally, the positive impacts of the reforms that
beneficiaries realized have declined as implementation efforts have slowed over time or were temporally limited, and fewer poor households
benefit from reforms. In some settings, the negative impacts of reforms, such as restrictions on tenancy limiting access to land by landless agricultural laborers, may now be outweighing the positive benefits attributable to the reform effort.[85]

The first-generation land reforms offered India's policy makers several general lessons. First, in designing land reforms, governments
should respect the rights of those with existing land interests by providing adequate compensation when extinguishing or restricting their
rights. One reason why the states were able to implement abolition of
intermediary laws more fully than land ceiling laws is that they paid
substantially higher compensation under the former, and the higher levels of compensation tended to result in less resistance from those
whose land rights were to be taken. In designing reforming laws, compensation need not always be full market value, but should be meaningful. At a minimum, it should supply a capital fund adequate to re-
produce, *ad infinitum*, the present net income received from the land
being taken, assuming a conservative constant return.

Second, policy makers and legislative drafters should strive for simple, comprehensible laws and legislative language. Complex legislation
creates a barrier for poor and marginalized people. Those who can afford lawyers can exploit lengthy technical definitions, dense language
and complicated procedures to their advantage and to the disadvantage
of those with fewer resources, less education and less experience with
legal matters.[86]

Third, policy makers should reconsider outdated concepts regarding
appropriate land grants. States wishing to make allocations of land of a
size such that the income from the land is by itself sufficient to provide
the entire livelihood and raise the beneficiary households above the
poverty line have often found themselves paralyzed because sufficient
land of an appropriate quality cannot realistically be acquired to meet
that standard. The experience of the first-generation reforms has
taught that a more relevant standard exists. A sustainable livelihoods
approach recognizes that people draw on a range of capital assets to
further their livelihood objectives and acknowledges that in many cases
a diversity of assets – to which the land distributed will contribute sig-

nificantly – will be an adequate response, including providing the best buffer against the vulnerability factors that threaten the rural poor.[87]

Fourth, reform of land law and land policy can lead to beneficial social change that is at least as important as the direct economic benefits intended for beneficiaries. The equalization of status between the *zamindars* and "superior" tenants increased the tenants' bargaining power and reduced opportunities for oppression. In considering land policy reform alternatives and their possible impacts, policy makers should give consideration to the potential non-material benefits in addition to the material benefits.

Policy makers at the central and state levels have increasingly absorbed the lessons of the first-generation land reforms, as evidenced by the 11th Five-Year Plan and several innovative state programs.[88] Sections III B and C discuss programs that increase land access using land purchase. The 11th Five-Year Plan recognizes that in some areas there may be insufficient amounts of good-quality government land to meet the needs of landless and near-landless households. The Plan identifies land purchase programs as a means by which states can obtain quality land.[89] The state governments in Karnataka, West Bengal, and Andhra Pradesh recently initiated projects to provide micro-plots and field plots of land to landless laborers and other groups through land purchase programs. In these programs, the land is obtained only through voluntary purchase. The voluntary nature of the programs avoids the problems of past land reform approaches that relied on involuntary takings of land. All three programs purchase land in parcels of several acres or more and divide the land among multiple beneficiaries.

Section III D highlights another program in Andhra Pradesh that, with the land purchase program, is housed within the state's Department of Rural Development and Panchayat Raj. This program focuses on providing rural poor households with the intended benefits of prior land reforms by identifying gaps between promised land rights and ground-level realities and using project-trained community surveyors and paralegals to assist the state to provide secure land rights.

The final section discusses three areas of legislative reform: a recent national law granting land rights to forest dwellers and two areas of potential state-level legislative reform: relaxation of tenancy restrictions and legislative support for turning West Bengal's sharecroppers (*bargadars*) into landowners.

B.   Micro-plot land purchase programs

As discussed in detail in Chapter 4, large-scale micro-plot programs offer a practical, cost-effective and politically palatable alternative to traditional land reforms. Micro-plot programs, which allocate plots that include or are located near the household's house, require only a fraction of the amount of land considered necessary in traditional land reforms. Land for micro-plots, which may range in size from a few square meters to roughly one acre, may be acquired through market acquisition as opposed to controversial land takings that can quickly erode political support for a program.

Micro-plot programs recognize that small plots of land of a size sufficient to allow for a house and enough room for vegetable gardening, small animal husbandry, tree cultivation and home-based businesses can diversify livelihood strategies and can provide protection against environmental and economic shocks. If a household is able to make productive use of the micro-plot, the plot can provide shelter for the household, increase the household's income, enhance household nutrition, provide for the household's social status within the community, and serve as a vehicle for improving the household's economic status by providing access to credit.[90]

India's 11th Five-Year Plan recognizes the enormous potential in micro-plot programs to meet the basic needs and provide for the futures of the 13 to 18 million landless households, eight million of which also have no home of their own. The Plan references micro-plot programs in the states of Kerala (described in Section II), Karnataka and West Bengal.[91] The details of the Karnataka and West Bengal programs are described below.

Karnataka's micro-plot program

Based in large measure on RDI's research findings and advocacy efforts, in 2006 Karnataka's Department of Rural Development and Panchayat Raj initiated a five-year program, entitled *Namma Bhoomi – Namma Thota* (Our Land – Our Garden), to provide landless agricultural laborers with micro-plots with the objective of improving their social and economic stability. Beneficiaries of the program come from families that have not owned agricultural land for at least two generations and are dependent on agriculture for their livelihoods. The program anticipates providing 500,000 landless rural households with such plots, using either existing government land or purchasing private land. Individual plots are between 2,250 and 4,500 square feet, depending on whether the land is dry or irrigated and encourages the local government officials implementing the programs to assist beneficiaries by linking them with existing programs for plot development and house construction. The program provides beneficiaries with title to the plots, which must be registered in the name of both the wife and husband.[92]

Karnataka's micro-plot program is administered by the local governing body, the gram panchayat. The gram panchayats identify and pur-

chase eligible land from willing sellers and create a list of eligible beneficiaries to which subdivided plots from the purchased land is assigned.
As of May 2008, approximately 17,000 landless families had received
micro-plots.

West Bengal's field and micro-plot program

In January 2006, the government of West Bengal's Department of
Land and Land Reforms adopted *Chash-O-Basobaser Bhumi-dan Prakalpa* (Cultivation and Dwelling Plot Allocation Scheme) to provide landless and houseless households with micro-plots and field plots for use
as homesteads, for cultivation and to diversify their livelihood options.
The program's objective is to provide (1) each rural family that has no
house with at least a 1,740 square feet (0.04 acre) micro-plot on which
to build a residence; and (2) each landless rural household that relies
on agricultural labor, food gathering from common property resources,
or menial labor for its livelihood and is below the poverty line with a
field plot of at least 7,000 square feet (0.16 acre) of cultivable land.[93]

The state Land and Land Reforms Department is charged with implementing the project, primarily through sub-district level Land Purchase and Land Distribution Committees, which include local officials
and members of India's local democratically elected governing body,
the panchayat. The committees are responsible for obtaining land for
the project through purchase from willing private landowners who
wish to sell suitable land to the state for use in the project. The state officials evaluate each offer of sale from landowners for suitability and
negotiate for the purchase of selected parcels. The program guidelines
initially set ceilings on rates paid for various types of land. After early
experience suggested that the ceilings were too low, the state revised
the guidelines to allow the state to pay the market rate for land and to
exceed that rate with authorization. The program guidelines encourage
officials to purchase land in parcels large enough to create clustered
communities that share infrastructure and extension services.

The program requires the committee to select the poorest households from among landless and houseless agricultural laborer households. Of the benefits, 40% are targeted for members of scheduled
tribes and scheduled castes, 20% for tribals who are not members of
scheduled tribes, and 40% for other landless agricultural households.
Rural artisans are also eligible for homestead plots under the project.

Both the Karnataka and West Bengal programs are in their early
stages, but their designs appear to be well considered. The programs'
strengths include use of a decentralized management structure that devolves authority to local government officials. In addition, both programs require local officials to assist beneficiaries to obtain benefits

from existing programs providing assistance with house construction, micro-irrigation plans, inputs such as seeds, membership in credit organizations and participation in economic development schemes. Embedding these linkages within the program design helps ensure that the beneficiaries are actually able to realize the potential benefits that can flow from the ownership and development of micro-plots.

C.   Land purchase by women's self-help group members

In contrast to the micro-plot programs of West Bengal and Karnataka, Andhra Pradesh's land purchase program aims to provide field plots of up to one acre of irrigated land per beneficiary.[94] While Karnataka's program operates through village governments and West Bengal's through the state government line departments, Andhra Pradesh's program operates primarily through women's self-help groups. The land purchase activity is one component of the state government's Indira Kranthi Patham (IKP) program.[95]

The program uses institution-building and the creation and enhancement of livelihood opportunities to empower rural poor people. At the village level, women are organized into self-help groups of roughly 10-15 women, which begin with capacity building and savings activities before graduating to income generation schemes. The self-help group leaders form village organizations representing the interests of all self-help groups in a village. Village organizations are further federated at the *mandal* (sub-district) level and at the district level.

Targeting the poorest of the poor, the program initially attempted to improve their livelihoods through institution-building and financing for income-generating activities. However, for many within this population, access and rights to land were primary, unaddressed issues; for the landless, financing income generating activities (such as livestock rearing) had proven largely ineffective because they lacked the land base required for most such activities.

RDI worked with the state government and project staff to add a land component that included two sets of activities: (1) land purchase by women members of self-help groups, which is the subject of this part; and (2) activities designed to increase land access and tenure security for the poor such as identifying government land available for assignment to poor households and facilitating resolution of pending land cases, which are known as non-purchase or legal aid activities (discussed in Section III D).

With the support and assistance of their village organizations, women agricultural laborers who are members of self-help groups search for prospective land sellers, evaluate land available for purchase, and negotiate with the sellers to arrive at a purchase price for the land. The Andhra Pradesh program has the following features:[96]

- *Beneficiary-driven process.* The self-help group members initiate the land purchase activity, not government officials or landowners. These self-selected beneficiaries who have shown the capacity for land purchase identify the land, negotiate a price and develop a business plan for farming the land.

- *Purchase plus improvements; business plan requirement.* The program requires the self-help group members to consider what improvements (such as adding a bore well) are necessary and to include such improvements in their business plan. The requirement of a business plan focuses the women on the economic feasibility of their land purchase and requires consideration of options for land development and cultivation.

- *Cost recovery plan.* The program includes a substantial grant component and reasonable repayment terms so the self-help group members do not end up with burdensome debt. The program allows up to 75% of the total cost of the land purchase and any improvements to be paid with grant funds. Each women is responsible for 25% of the total costs, no less than 2/5 of which must be the woman's personal contribution, either in cash or in kind. The women can pay the balance with loans advanced from the self-help group or project. Repayment of any loan can be spread over 15 years and carries a market rate of interest.[97] The debt repayment plan is included in the business plan so beneficiaries can understand their financial obligation and how it affects the overall economics of the land purchase option.

The program's early experience is promising. One preliminary four-district study of 223 households, of which 63 were beneficiary households, found that beneficiary households experienced significantly higher levels of food security, improvements in health and education, and less migration. For example, 76% of beneficiary households reported having two meals per day compared to 50-57% of non-beneficiary households. Beneficiary households also had a far lower rate of seasonal migration (4%) than landless households (45%).[98] However, the possibility of providing a majority of the landless poor with one acre of land through land purchase is questionable, because of the relatively high costs per beneficiary (about US$1200) and the limited supply of appropriate land available for sale. State officials and project staff are evaluating designs that extend the project to include purchases of micro-plots and support for land leasing activities.

D.   Securing land rights through legal aid

In addition to providing rural poor women with access to land through the land purchase activity described above, Andhra Pradesh's World Bank-funded Andhra Pradesh Rural Poverty Alleviation Project has a series of activities designed to improve land access and tenure security for poor households, which it collectively refers to as "legal aid." These legal aid activities are an innovative, collaborative, community-based and highly adaptable approach to providing poor households with the promised benefits of land reforms.[99] In addition, the bottom-up, participatory approach of the legal aid activities empowers the local communities served to develop relationships with local government officials and experience the process of asserting and defending their legal rights to land.

Like most Indian states, Andhra Pradesh enacted post-Independence legislative reforms, and the state reports allocating 5.4 million acres of land to almost three million rural poor households. However, field investigations funded by the state project found that many of the intended beneficiaries had not received the intended benefits of secure land rights. Gaps between the reported numbers and secure land rights occur for a variety of reasons, including: (1) the assignment of land is on paper only, and the physical possession has not been given; (2) beneficiaries have been evicted from their lands; and (3) in numerous cases, especially in areas where large compact blocks have been assigned to the poor (e.g., 150 acres are assigned to 100 poor families), the survey subdivision work has not been done, so the beneficiaries have not received their individual parcels of land. Similar circumstances concerning past government land allocation programs have been reported in other states. In some cases, beneficiaries received land but had no record of their rights. Other groups have been unable to take possession of their land because of a lack of surveys.[100]

Andhra Pradesh's efforts to address the shortcomings in earlier "allocations" of government land provide a model for other states to consider. The model begins with multi-faceted and decentralized efforts to identify "gaps" of the type listed above (see Box 6.1) or other opportunities to allocate unallocated government land. These gaps or opportunities are then classified by project staff, after which they determine the most appropriate approach, select a course of action, and see that action to completion. As these activities have matured over several years, they have become institutionalized within a framework of legal aid activities.

Box 6.1. Addressing "gaps" in past land allocations

Identifying "gaps" in past government land allocations and related opportunities to provide secure land rights to the poor is a threshold activity. The Indian state of Andhra Pradesh has used various methods for identifying and documenting this information:

Working in conjunction with community-based organizations. Relationships with community-based organizations have provided the best source of information regarding opportunities to provide secure rights to poor households. The project's district-level officials keep in touch with organizations familiar with and trusted by local people and provide a conduit through which land information can be passed and acted upon by appropriate officials.

Jamma bhoomi petitions. Jamma bhoomi is a people-centered development process launched in Andhra Pradesh in 1997. The process involves taking the state and district government administration "to the door of the people." Each year, more than 1,000 teams of state and district officials hold local public meetings to listen to people's grievances and accept their written petitions. The project works with local groups to facilitate applications pertaining to land issues in the government's *Jamma bhoomi* program. The information in such petitions provided on land issues is computerized and may be acted upon by various groups.

Survey and inventory of government land. In an effort to identify problems relating to the assignment of government wasteland, the state government initiated in January 2003 a massive, statewide, physical inventory of existing and allocated government wasteland. Although the survey was not completely finished, this information has proven helpful in identifying problems with past allocation of government land and identifying opportunities to address the shortcomings.

Official land records. Project paralegals and law students review land records and cases maintained by the Revenue Department and compare them to the results of field interviews to identify areas where the land records do not reflect the ground-level reality.

In the early days of the project's land-related work, project staff recognized that the land rights of poor households were often the subject of cases pending for years before the Revenue Department, the government division responsible for land matters, in addition to numerous other areas of responsibility. For example, numerous landowners contested the state's acquisition of their land under land ceiling laws and allocation to poor households. Procedural law requires maintenance of the status quo until the claims are decided, preventing allocation of the land to intended beneficiaries. The project engaged a lawyer and in co-operation with Revenue Department officials, project staff reviewed the backlog of cases in selected areas in two districts and identified those involving the project's target population of rural poor. Project staff, law students and the Revenue Department worked together to determine appropriate resolutions.

The initial Revenue Department case work revealed the potential for legal aid to strengthen the land rights of poor households and identified two areas where the project could usefully expand: (1) through use of the community-based organization structure to identify and resolve land issues that never reach the Revenue Court system; and (2) by providing surveying assistance to overburdened government surveyors so that cases requiring surveys can be resolved.

Elements of the land-related legal aid activities

The project developed a framework for legal aid activities based on the following elements: employment and training of local youth as paralegals[101] and community surveyors, management of legal aid staff by the community-based organizations, and establishment of district land centers and community partnerships.

Paralegals. The project hires one educated youth from a disadvantaged family in each sub-district to train as a paralegal.[102] The project trains the paralegals on working with the members of self-help groups and the community-based organization structure, on land laws and records, Revenue Department procedures and village inventories.[103] The paralegal also must complete coursework on land rights and poverty law offered through the national law school.

The paralegals work directly with the self-help groups, building awareness of land issues within self-help groups, identifying land issues impacting the members, and helping the community-based organization to bring issues before the Revenue Department for resolution. Paralegals also support the Revenue Department by providing assistance with fact-finding, obtaining surveys through coordination with the community surveyors, and arranging for legal opinions as necessary.

Community surveyors. Like many states, Andhra Pradesh has a limited number of trained surveyors and a multitude of land issues that require surveying as a precondition to resolution.[104] Because the lack of trained surveyors is delaying the ability of poor households to realize the benefits of secure land rights, the project trains local youth as community surveyors as part of the legal aid activity. The community surveyors work in cooperation with local government surveyors and the paralegals in an effort to increase the state's ability to survey land, especially in cases where the resolution of land cases and receipt of title has been pending because of a lack of surveys.

Community surveyors must successfully complete a surveying course, receive training on land laws and records, village inventories and working with the self-help group members. The community surveyors must complete an apprenticeship with a government surveyor. Once trained, the community surveyors conduct land surveys in coordination with the paralegals and the local government surveyors.

The legal aid activity also includes partnerships with law schools to conduct clinical programs for law students and offer law students opportunities to work on land cases on a volunteer basis and has plans to create district-level panels of lawyers to support legal aid activities. All of the legal aid activities are centered in district-level Land Rights and Legal Assistance Centers, which provide office space for staff, access to land records and research materials, and assist the Revenue Department with court procedures.

Early achievements

At the time of this writing, the legal aid activities are in their early stages in Andhra Pradesh. However, the achievements of the method of improving land rights are substantial. In the year in which the activities expanded statewide, legal aid staff identified land issues impacting roughly 80,000 poor households and had resolved approximately 27% of these problems. The issues addressed include matters relating to issuance of pattadar passbooks (which prove land ownership, use and encumbrances), boundaries and possession of land.

Just as significant are the less tangible benefits of the project. Legal aid staff trained hundreds of self-help group members on land rights and drafted handbooks on land issues for use by community members, paralegals and Revenue Department officials. Legal aid staff helped the Revenue Department identify areas where land may be available for use by the poor and policy decisions that would benefit the poor. Self-help group members report that they consider themselves capable of discussing their legal rights and applying to government officials for enforcement of those rights. Many Revenue Department officials have begun to look to the legal aid staff to assist them in land matters. Finally, training large numbers of local youth as paralegals and community surveyors provides job skills to rural youth and grounds the knowledge regarding land rights in the community.

The legal aid project in Andhra Pradesh has been assisted by several factors, including project staff recruited from the ranks of former rev-

enue department officers, which gives them an advantage in identifying areas with significant land issues adversely affecting the poor and
local officials interested in resolving the issues, and a strong community-based organization structure. However, the framework is highly
adaptable to other institutional and organizational settings. In some
environments, NGOs may undertake village inventories, raise awareness of land rights among poor households, and develop action plans
for resolving land issues. In other areas, local governments may undertake legal aid activities as a means of systematizing their efforts to assist the poorest groups obtain access and secure rights to land.

In all settings, legal aid activities will be most successful where the
disadvantaged groups drive the process by helping to identify and
prioritize land issues and actively participating in the process of resolving those issues. Participation in the process of identifying and asserting legal rights to land not only provides the poor with improved land
rights but empowers them within their households and communities.
The legal aid approach to addressing the gaps between the promised
benefits of land reforms and rural realities not only can provide poor
households with intended land rights, but also the skills and experience that form the basis for social change through legal empowerment.

E.   Increasing land rights with legislative change

In addition to the new programs for micro-plot allocation and legal aid
described in the earlier parts of this chapter, India's policy makers also
have opportunities to improve the land rights of rural poor households
through legislative change. This section discusses the central government's effort to secure land rights for traditional forest dwellers and
two opportunities for future legislative change at the state level: relaxation of legislative restrictions on tenancy and assisting West Bengal's
sharecroppers to become landowners.

Forest rights legislation

After years of debate, in December 2006 India's parliament took a substantial and highly controversial step toward improving the livelihoods
of some of the country's poorest and most vulnerable communities –
tribals living in or near India's forests. A new national law grants forest
dwellers, most of whom are tribals, rights to forest land and forest products. The law, which is entitled the Scheduled Tribes[105] and Other Traditional Forest Dwellers (Recognition of Forest Rights) Act, 2006, is a
legislative effort to acknowledge the historical injustices suffered by the

millions of tribals and other forest dwellers who rely on India's forests and forest products for their livelihoods.

India is home to approximately 68 million tribals, constituting roughly 7% of India's population.[106] Historically, India's tribals have been distinguished from other rural communities in part by their dependence on and communal use of land and its resources.[107] Despite the range of tribal habitations and an increasing volume of tribal migration into towns and cities for employment, the tribal economy of the 21st century remains highly land-based.[108] In particular, tribal livelihoods are closely linked to India's forests, on which tribals rely for shelter, food, fuel wood, spiritual and religious locales, and products for sale or trade.[109]

As India began to formalize land rights in the 19th century, the tribals' occupation and customary use of the forest land and its resources never translated into formal legal rights. From its initial announcement of sovereignty over the forests, the government's grip on forests and forest resources has been almost absolute.[110] Tribal land use resided at the level of a discretionary privilege, which could be withdrawn at any time and without recourse.[111] Tribal rights to the land they occupy and cultivate outside the reach of forest laws have been similarly insecure. State and central governments have usurped large tracts of tribal land for public projects and industrial activities, and the land has in many areas been indiscriminately stripped of minerals and resources.[112] In addition, the precarious economic circumstances of many tribals have resulted in the chronic and continuing alienation of tribal land to non-tribals.[113]

In the last few decades, India's central and state governments have passed significant amounts of legislation specifically aimed at securing tribal land rights. However, even where legislation is designed to protect tribal land interests, such as restricting alienation of tribal land or ensuring tribals receive the benefit of land tenure reforms, the results have been disappointing.[114]

The new Forest Rights Act is a departure from previous legislation intended to protect tribal land rights in at least three important respects. First, the law's primary purpose is to secure existing (albeit informally held) rights. Specifically, the law grants forest-dwelling scheduled tribes and other traditional forest dwellers the right to cultivate forest land to the extent of their occupation, up to four hectares per individual, family or community. The law also grants ownership rights to certain minor forest products, grazing areas and pastoralist corridors that forest dwellers have traditionally used.[115] As such, the law's initial effect is to enhance existing rights rather than constricting them or expanding them, ensuring greater interest among intended beneficiaries and reducing opposition.[116]

Second, the law vests authority for determining forest rights with the local community (gram sabha and community-established committees), trumps any conflicting law, provides enforcement powers, and (in a lesson learned from first-generation land reforms) expressly prohibits eviction of any forest dweller prior to the determination of his or her rights under the law.[117] With this combination of legislative provisions, the law's devolution of authority over forest land matters to local communities may accomplish what prior legislation, the Panchayats (Extension to Scheduled Areas) Act, 1996 (PESA), did not. The PESA provides for tribal self-rule on matters affecting tribal society and economy at the village level and enlarged the authority of local government to include various levels of control over local resources and programs.[118] But implementation of the PESA and realization of its goals have been spotty, in large measure because the PESA granted local communities authority over resources in conflict with existing rights, enforcement powers were not secured,[119] and only a handful of states adopted the PESA – with much diluted terms.[120] The Forest Rights Law's supremacy clause and enforcement provisions give teeth to the formalization of the rights of tribals.

Third, the rules require all three relevant authorities – the tribal welfare office, Revenue Department and Forest Department – to sign off on rights granted under the law. This requirement should help reinforce the extent to which the drafters intended the Forest Rights Law to govern rights previously subject to the Forest and Revenue Departments.

The rules implementing the Forest Rights Law were published on January 1, 2008, and it remains to be seen whether the law will meet expectations. Some success can already be claimed: the enactment of the law reflects the central government's continuing recognition of the importance of land rights in addressing rural poverty; the law formalizes long-standing informal rights of one of the poorest sections of India's society; and the content of the law and the implementing rules reflect the ability of India's policy makers to review the successes and challenges of past efforts and respond with new approaches.

Removing restrictions on tenancy

The 11th Five-Year Plan recognizes that while the tenancy restrictions enacted after Independence fulfilled a purpose and a percentage of the poorer members of rural society benefited, as discussed in Section II of this chapter, the benefits have now been realized, and the restrictions are now causing harm. Specifically, the Plan notes that existing restrictions may restrict the ability of landless poor households to access land through leasing it in, may cause some landowners to fear losing their rights to lessees and thus allow land to lie fallow, and may result in concealed tenancies that exploit tenants.[121] The Plan calls for revisiting the issues of tenancy relationships and, in appropriate areas, revising legislation to relax – if not extinguish – prohibitions against tenancy:

> Tenancy should be legalized in a "limited" manner. It should provide security to the tenant for a contractual period, which could be long enough to encourage long term investment by the tenant. It should also protect the rights to the land of the landowner so that he has an incentive to lease his land rather than keeping it fallow or underutilizing it. Long term tenure arrangements should thus maximize agricultural production and increase the returns to both the famer and landlord and tenant.[122]

The Plan expressly recognizes that conditions vary across the states, and no single manner of addressing tenancy restrictions is advisable. For example, in areas where landowners dominate and feudal relationships prevail, special protections for tenants may need to be imposed.[123] Once research is completed to determine states in which revisions to tenancy laws are appropriate,[124] the process should involve two sequential, or in some settings, simultaneous steps.[125]

As an initial matter, legislation should consolidate the benefits of past tenancy reform by converting "protected," "registered," or "occupancy" tenants into owners.[126] This would require legislative changes that differ from state to state. For example, as discussed in the following section in more detail, in West Bengal, the law could be improved by giving sharecroppers (bargadars) a unilateral right to become owners by "buying out" the landlord for a government-determined sum, by providing for a streamlined voluntary transaction process, or by activating the financing mechanism for sharecropper purchases of barga land that is already contemplated in West Bengal's Land Reform Act.[127]

The second step (either taken simultaneously or following the preservation and enhancement of existing rights of tenants) should focus on liberalizing ongoing tenancy prohibitions and excessive tenant "protections." The specific content of these amendments will differ from state to state and will necessarily be dependent on the nature of the existing legislation. In general, however, policy and legislative changes under consideration include the following provisions. First, where tenancy is now prohibited, allow for tenancy but include provisions that balance the interests of the tenants and landlords. Second, require lease agreements to be in writing, using a standardized form that requires the parties to state the rent amount, the lease length and other important terms of the lease. Third, guarantee the tenant the right of

exclusive possession for the duration of their agreement, but avoid un-
enforceable maximum rent payments or minimum length of terms.
Fourth, expressly provide that neither the law nor any practice will
grant new tenants any long-term rights to land or other rights beyond
what may be mutually agreed to by the parties, as evidenced in a written agreement.

In settings where tenancy might become legally permissible or be
deregulated, our more general discussion in Chapter 2, Section IV,
must also be borne in mind. There we point out the dearth of practical
experience around the globe in designing and implementing measures
permitting or deregulating tenancy in settings where it had been un-
successfully prohibited or regulated, the principal exception being the
case of Mexico.[128] In India, perhaps the prime initial candidates for deregulation would be the four states where government statistics indicate that tenancy reforms did not confer ownership rights on, or protect the rights of, any tenants in the state: Bihar, Madhya Pradesh, Rajasthan and Uttar Pradesh. If these results are verified, these states
have no existing beneficiaries with rights dependent on the maintenance of protective laws nominally on the statute books. In such settings, the states can immediately focus on options for eliminating
tenancy restrictions in a manner that balances the needs and interests
of landowners and prospective tenants.

Turning protected tenants into landowners

West Bengal provides another opportunity for improving land rights
through legislative change. In its initial legislative reforms, West Bengal gave its sharecroppers (known as *bargadars*) substantial rights and
protections. Under the *West Bengal Land Reforms Act*, sharecroppers
are entitled to permanent and non-transferable (except by inheritance)
rights to farm the sharecropped land and to keep a legally determined
share of the production. In addition, sharecroppers have a right of first
refusal to buy the sharecropped land. Thus, if a landowner wants to
sell his land, he must first offer it at the same price for sale to the
sharecropper. A sharecropper keeps his rights even if the owner sells
the land to a third party.[129]

For many years, sharecroppers were unable to enforce these rights.
In an effort to help sharecroppers realize the benefit of the law, in the
late 1970s the West Bengal government initiated *Operation Barga* – a
campaign to register and enforce sharecropper rights. The state has registered more than 1.4 million sharecroppers, and field studies confirm
that their rights under the law are now generally respected and enforced.

However, while West Bengal's sharecroppers have benefited from stronger tenure security and lower crop share payments, virtually all of them would prefer to have ownership of the land. In addition, as non-agricultural opportunities have increased, many landowners would like to sell their land in order to engage in other business activities. The law has not kept pace with these changes. Instead, the law has frozen sharecroppers in their position as tenants and effectively prevents landowners from selling the sharecropped land to third parties.

West Bengal can expand its already significant land reform achievements by allowing its protected sharecroppers to become landowners. However, land sales between the many landowners and sharecroppers who want to do business have often been prevented by legal restrictions on the transferability of sharecropped land and the sharecroppers' lack of purchasing power.

The West Bengal government is now exploring legislative revisions and other steps to support the sharecroppers who wish to become owners (and helping those landlords who want to sell). These include funding a land corporation to help sharecroppers purchase the land they farm, adopting a simpler and less costly process for the sale or exchange of sharecropped land to sharecroppers that includes safeguards to prevent abuse by landowners, and setting a standard or minimum price to be used when a sharecropper wishes to sell or purchase sharecropped land.

At the time this went to press, neither legislative reforms relating to tenancy generally nor to West Bengal's sharecroppers, had been enacted. However, given the admirable willingness of India's policy makers to evaluate past actions and change course as needed to meet the needs of the poorest members of their populations, these legislative revisions seem likely.

IV. Conclusion

The legislative foundations of land tenure reform in India (abolition of intermediaries, tenancy reform and land ceilings) were designed to increase the poor's access to rural land. The effectiveness of the legislation has been mixed, and in some cases decidedly negative. In recent decades, progress under these first-generation efforts has substantially slowed or stalled altogether.

India's policy makers have distinguished themselves by their willingness to review the impact of the first-generation reforms, identify successes and recognize continuing challenges. At the central level, the 11th Five-Year Plan is a distinct departure from past plans, providing unequivocal statements regarding the achievements of past reforms, continuing evidence of the need for further reforms, and specific guidance for policy and legislative change in the areas of tenancy, land ceilings and the allocation of micro-plots. At the state level, some policy makers and program staff have taken bold and creative steps to address rural poverty with innovative land programs. These programs are leading the way toward a second generation of land tenure reforms capable of significantly improving the lives of the country's rural poor. As these efforts are developed and refined, that vast majority of other Indian states that have yet to act must step forward to make land reforms newly relevant to address the issues facing their populations of rural poor. These state policy makers and planners can take advantage of the experience of the handful of pioneering states while creating programs of their own that are tailored to the unique challenges of their locale.

Furthermore, the influence of India's experience with land tenure reform – both in the years following Independence and in its recent new approaches – should not be limited to its borders. India's successes, but equally significantly its recognition of the weaknesses in some of its legislation and implementation efforts, offer valuable lessons to other countries. In particular, countries such as Pakistan and Bangladesh, which have large numbers of tenant farmers without any real prospect of land ownership and access to full-size farms, and those like Indonesia with large numbers of agricultural laborers working on small and medium holdings will benefit from India's experience with land allocations.

Notes

1   National Development Council, Government of India, Eleventh Five-Year Plan, 2007-
2012.
2   Census of India, available at www.censusofindia.net.
3   World Bank, India Country Overview, at www.worldbank.org.in (accessed 2006).
Some sources report higher figures. See, e.g., National Commission for Enterprises,
Report of the National Commission for Enterprises in Unorganized Sector 8 (NCE, Aug.
2007), which reports that three-quarters of the population lives on less than one dollar a day, www.necus.gov.in. The recent large downward revision of purchasing power
parity (PPP) based estimates of average GDP for a number of countries, including India and China, by a consortium paid by the World Bank, would seem to make it
likely that a higher estimate than the Bank's earlier one for the numbers living under
one US dollar a day (estimate that uses PPP figures) will shortly follow. See generally
World Bank, *International Comparison Program Results 2005*, at App. G (World Bank
2007). Under prior estimates, it could be calculated that the absolute number living
under US$1 a day in India exceeded (as of 2004) the total number living under $1 a
day in sub-Saharan Africa by about 18%. A.U. Ahmed, et al., THE WORLD'S MOST DE-
PRIVED: CHARACTERISTICS AND CAUSES OF EXTREME POVERTY AND HUNGER 4 (fig. 2.1) &
33 (table 3.2) (International Food and Policy Research Institute, Oct. 2007).

4   India has approximately 15 million functionally landless households and another 45
     million rural households that own less than one-tenth of an acre. Of the 15 million
     household figure (recently recast in the 11th Five-Year Plan as a 13-18 million house-
     hold range), approximately ten million households own no land, and another five
     million own less than 20 square meters (215 square feet). Government of India, Na-
     tional Sample Survey Organization, Household Ownership Holdings in India, 2003,
     at 10 and table 6R; see Government of India 11th Five-Year Plan, sec. 1.105.
5   World Bank, INDIA: ACHIEVEMENTS AND CHALLENGES IN REDUCING POVERTY, WORLD
     BANK COUNTRY STUDY xiii-xiv (World Bank 1997).
6   Constitution of India, art. 246(3) and Seventh Schedule.
7   The zamandari system prevailed in Bengal, Uttar Pradesh, Bihar, Rajasthan and Oris-
     sa, and was significant but not dominant in parts of Assam, Andhra Pradesh and
     Madhya Pradesh. P.S. Appu, LAND REFORMS IN INDIA 5-19, 48 (New Delhi: Vikas Pub-
     lishing 1996).
8   Id. at 8-9.
9   The ryotwari system prevailed in present-day Maharashtra, Karnataka, Tamil Nadu, as
     well as most of Andhra Pradesh and Madhya Pradesh and parts of Assam, Bihar and
     Rajasthan.
10   Appu, supra note 7, at 48-52.
11   See Constitution of India, art. 246(3) and Seventh Schedule. Despite the states' exclu-
     sive jurisdiction to enact land reform legislation, the central government does play
     and has played an important guiding and consultative role in land policy and legisla-
     tion, enabled in large part by the money it directs to the state for various rural devel-
     opment and poverty alleviation schemes.
12   The net economic benefits realized by these beneficiaries were qualified somewhat
     by obligations to pay for the newly acquired rights and the beneficiaries' prior enjoy-
     ment of a measure of tenure security and rent regulation under pre-Independence
     legislation. Appu, supra note 7, at 71-79.
13   Id.; see also T. Haque & A.S. Sirohi, AGRARIAN REFORM AND INSTITUTIONAL CHANGES
     IN INDIA 38 (New Delhi: Concept Publishing 1986).
14   Substantial loopholes in the laws allowed zamindars to accomplish many of these
     evictions through largely legal means. In every state, legislation permitted ex-inter-
     mediaries to retain their home-farms or "personally cultivated" land; only a handful
     of states placed a limit on the size of such home-farm land retained. The legislation
     loosely defined "personal cultivation" to include cultivation through sharecroppers,
     servants and wage laborers. Most state laws even allowed the intermediary to evict
     tenants from land the intermediary had not been "personally cultivating" but now
     wished to "personally cultivate," and the legislation allowed the ex-intermediaries to
     select the land they wanted to retain. In contrast, the legislation did little to protect
     the actual cultivating tenants. The laws did not confer rights upon tenants-at-will and
     sharecroppers, so the land rights often did not attach to the "tiller" but to an inter-
     mediary one level above the tiller.
15   M.L. Dantwala, one of the foremost authorities on India's land reforms, estimates
     that as a result of the laws to abolish intermediaries, more evictions occurred in the
     first ten years after Indian independence than had occurred in the previous one hun-
     dred years. D. Thakur, POLITICS OF LAND REFORM IN INDIA 58 (New Delhi: Common-
     wealth Publishers 1989), citing THE EASTERN ECONOMIST, Jan. 3, 1958, at 59.
16   Id. at 58-59.
17   B.K. Sinha & Pushpendra, eds., LAND REFORMS IN INDIA: AN UNFINISHED AGENDA 32
     (2000), citing Government of India Planning Commission, Report of the Panel on
     Land Reforms 71-76 (1959). Compare the discussion of (generally much less gener-
     ous) compensation in post-war land-to-the-tiller programs in Chapter 2.

18 Appu, supra note 7, at 79. The uses made of compensation may differ significantly in different cultural settings. RDI research in Taiwan, for example, showed ex-land-lords had been strongly inclined to invest their land compensation in a range of productive activities.

19 Haque & Sirohi, supra note 13, at 40.

20 See discussion in Chapter 2.

21 M.L. Dantwala, *India's Progress in Agrarian Reform*, 19(22) FAR EASTERN SURVEY 240 (1950); see also N.C. Behuria, LAND REFORMS LEGISLATION IN INDIA: A COMPARATIVE STUDY 65-73 (New Delhi: Vikas 1997).

22 Dantwala, supra note 21, at 240-42; see also Appu, supra note 7, at 82-110 (general discussion of tenancy).

23 The national policy on tenancy reform evolved gradually over decades and is embodied in various policy documents issued by the National Planning Commission. The First Five-Year Plan (1951-1956) contained the first authoritative exposition of national tenancy reform policy and included guidelines for state-level legislators on maximum rents, permitting eviction of tenants for landowners resuming land for "personal cultivation" and setting terms for land rights granted to tenants. The Second (1957-1962) and Third (1963-1968) Five-Year Plans essentially reiterated and tried to fine-tune policy guidelines established in the First Plan. By the end of the Third Plan, virtually all states had adopted tenancy reform legislation that broadly followed the policy guidelines.

24 Appu, supra note 7, at 102-103.

25 Ministry of Rural Development Land Reforms Unit, LAND REFORMS IN MAHARASHTRA: AN EMPIRICAL STUDY (1988-1991), at 23-28 (Mussourie: Lal Bahadur Shastri National Academy of Administration 1994).

26 Karnataka Land Reforms Act of 1961, secs. 5, 44, 58, 61, 78.

27 West Bengal Land Reforms Act, 1955, secs. 4, 5, 15-21.

28 Bombay Tenancy and Agricultural Lands Act, 1948, sec. 15; Hyderabad Tenancy and Agricultural Lands Act, 1950; Bombay Tenancy and Agricultural Lands (Vidarbha Region) Act, 1958.

29 Government of India Ministry of Rural Development, Annual Report 2002-2003, annexure XXXVI.

30 The agricultural area figures are taken from *Agricultural Statistics at a Glance, 2006*, available on the website of the Agricultural Census Division, Ministry of Agriculture, Government of India. Population figures used to calculate the number of rural households are reported at *Agricultural Statistics at a Glance, 2005*, at 211. Beneficiary figures are taken from the Government of India, supra note 29, annexures XXXVI, XXXVII & XL.

31 Appu, supra note 7, at 82-124.

32 See results of an RDI 400-household survey reported in T. Hanstad, J. Brown & R. Prosterman, *Larger Homestead Plots as Land Reform? International Experience and Analysis from Karnataka*, ECONOMIC AND POLITICAL WEEKLY (July 20, 2002).

33 The Deccan Development Society ("DDS") in Andhra Pradesh, which has supported groups of poor women in their efforts to access land through tenancy, relies on mutually beneficial tenancy terms that do not comply with legislative restrictions. The DDS program and several other land leasing programs for women are described in RDI's June 2006 report, S*eeking Security and Reducing Risk: Land Leasing by Women in Andhra Pradesh*, on file with the Rural Development Institute.

34 See generally K. Deininger, *Land Policies for Growth and Poverty Reduction* 84-93 (World Bank Policy Research Report 2003); S. Lastarria-Cornhiel & J. Melmed-San-jak, *Land Tenancy in Asia, Africa and Latin America: A Look at the Past and a View to*

the Future, Draft Report for the Food and Agriculture Organization of the United Nations (May 1998).

35 E. Sadoulet, et al., *Access to Land via Rental Markets*, in de Janvry, et al., eds., ACCESS TO LAND , RURAL POVERTY, AND PUBLIC ACTION 196 (Oxford University Press 2001).

36 See, *e.g.*, World Bank, INDIA: LAND POLICIES FOR GROWTH AND POVERTY REDUCTION 70-83 (New Delhi: Oxford University Press 2007).

37 See generally K. Deininger, S. Jin & H.K. Nagarajan, EQUITY AND EFFICIENCY IMPACTS OF RURAL LAND RENTAL RESTRICTIONS: EVIDENCE FROM INDIA (National Council for Applied Economic Research & World Bank Dec. 2005).

38 The study results are reported in World Bank, supra note 36, at 77-78.

39 Hanstad, Brown & Prosterman, supra note 32.

40 Id. This final percentage is surprisingly low given that a great majority of respondents report that the restrictions harm both landowners and the landless and given that 38% of respondents report that such restrictions cause at least one landowner in their village to keep land fallow.

41 Deininger, supra note 34, at 85-86. Land tenancy markets serve an important function in equalizing returns to non-tradable factors of production, such as family labor and bullocks in India. If the distribution of the surplus is not too skewed between landlord and tenant, rental will have an important positive impact on equity. E. Skoufias, *Land Tenancy and Rural Factor Market Imperfections Revisited*, 16(1) JOURNAL OF ECONOMIC DEVELOPMENT 37-55 (1991).

42 Sadoulet, supra note 35, at 217-218.

43 See 17-province survey article at M.R. Carter, Y. Yao & K. Deininger, LAND RENTAL MARKETS UNDER RISK: A CONCEPTUAL MODEL FOR CHINA 784-787 (University of Wisconsin 2002). For example, small landowners with growing non-agricultural work opportunities can lease out, often on a year-to-year basis, to rural families that desire more land, thus allowing the lessor to test the reliability and returns of the job market – including possible testing of the urban job market – without giving up his agricultural land, while the lessee has at least temporary, and often ongoing, access to land his family wants and needs.

44 See T. Hanstad, R. Nielsen & J. Brown, *Land and Livelihoods: Making Land Rights for India's Rural Poor*, FAO Livelihood Support Programme Working Paper No. 12, at 10 (FAO 2004).

45 World Bank, supra note 36, at 74-79 (describing studies indicating that laws prohibiting or placing substantial restrictions on agricultural tenancies constrain productivity and prevent landless and marginal farmers from accessing land).

46 Government of India, *Eleventh Five-Year Plan*, secs 1.109-1.113.

47 In several states, landowners successfully challenged the laws on grounds that they violated the right to property granted in Article 19(1)(7) of the Indian Constitution, and the compensation did not meet constitutional standards of fair market value. In response, parliament amended India's Constitution in 1971 to allow the states to pass laws that provided less than fair market value compensation and to validate all previous land reform laws. *The Twenty-Fifth Amendment Act of 1971* that inserted articles 31-B and 31-C into the Constitution. See A.P. Datar, DATAR ON THE CONSTITUTION OF INDIA 293–310 (Nagpur: Wadheva 2001).

48 The ceilings varied from 9.9 acres (4 hectares) in parts of Gujarat to 336 acres (136 hectares) in parts of Rajasthan. Behuria, supra note 21.

49 Haque and Sirohi list 38 types of exemptions which appeared in varying combinations in the various state laws, including land under plantations, tank fisheries, orchards, land held by religious or charitable institutions, private forests, land where heavy investment has been made, land used for fodder and other activities. Haque & Sirohi, supra note 13, at 81-83.

50 See Behuria, supra note 21, at 131-132.

51 See Appu, supra note 7, at 155-169.

52 Where the concept of "standard" or average acres are used, it means that lower qual-
    ity land qualifies for a higher ceiling and higher quality land qualifies for a lower ceil-
    ing.

53 Behuria, supra note 21, at annexures I-III.

54 See id. at annexures I-III (overview of ceiling law provisions).

55 In addition, some states have provisions for setting some ceiling-surplus land apart
    for public purposes (including Andhra Pradesh, Bihar, Jammu and Kashmir, Karnata-
    ka, Kerala, Maharashtra, Madhya Pradesh and Uttar Pradesh). Other states do not
    provide for reservation for public purposes unless the land is unfit for cultivation or
    was used for grazing before vesting in the state. Id. at 131-138.

56 Government of India, Ministry of Rural Development Annual Report, 2005-2006, Annex-
    ure XXXVII.

57 The results of micro-studies conducted in Assam call into question the large
    amounts of ceiling surplus land reportedly distributed. See generally Ministry of Ru-
    ral Development, LAND REFORMS IN ASSAM: AN EMPIRICAL STUDY (1988-1991) (Mussoorie:
    Land Reforms Unit 1994).

58 See, e.g., T. Hanstad & J. Brown, Land Reform Law and Implementation in West Ben-
    gal: Lessons and Recommendations, Rural Development Institute Report No. 112 (Rural
    Development Institute 2001); A. Chakraborti, Beneficiaries of Land Reforms: The West
    Bengal Scenario, State Institute of Panchayats and Rural Development (Nadia: Gov-
    ernment of West Bengal 2002).

59 See, e.g., Chakraborti, supra note 58.

60 Appu, supra note 7, at 175-179.

61 Government of India, Eleventh Five-Year Plan, sec. 1.99.

62 Government of India, supra note 29, annexure XXXIX.

63 S. Das, A Critical Evaluation of Land Reforms in India (1950-1995), in Sinha & Push-
    pandra, eds., LAND REFORM IN INDIA: AN UNFINISHED AGENDA 32 (New Delhi: Sage
    Publications 2000).

64 Government of India, supra note 29, annexure XXXIX.

65 Ministry of Rural Development (Department of Land Resources) Resolution No.
    21013/4/2007-LRD, sec. 4(iii). The Ministry of Rural Development (Department of
    Land Resources) created the Committee on State Agrarian Relations and the Unfin-
    ished Task in Land Reforms by this resolution.

66 Id.

67 Chambers, et al., offer the following, more comprehensive definition of wastelands:
    "Wastelands mean degraded land which can be brought under vegetative cover, with
    reasonable effort, and which is currently lying underutilized and land which is dete-
    riorating for lack of appropriate water and soil management or on account of natural
    causes. Wasteland can result from inherent/imposed disabilities such as by location,
    environment, chemical and physical properties of the soil or financial or manage-
    ment constraints." R. Chambers, N.C. Saxena & T. Shah, TO THE HANDS OF THE POOR:
    WATER AND TREES 42 (1989).

68 G.K. Kadekodi, COMMON PROPERTY RESOURCE MANAGEMENT 44-45 (New Delhi: Oxford
    University Press 2004).

69 The state-level Revenue Departments still control about 50 million acres of waste-
    land. Id. at 44.

70 Government of India, supra note 29, annexure XL.

71 See, e.g., Ministry of Rural Development, LAND REFORMS IN GUJARAT: AN EMPIRICAL
    STUDY (1988-1991), at 46 (1994), concluding that wasteland distribution in the Kutch
    area of the state provided no benefit because the equality of land was poor.

72 K.V. Akella, *New Life for Land Reform: the Potential in a Decentralized Approach*, un-
    published paper on file with the Rural Development Institute (2005).
73 Das, supra note 63, at 38. West Bengal alone claims to have allocated approximately
    500,000 such house sites.
74 Kerala Land Reforms Act, 1963, sec. 80A.
75 Id.
76 B.A. Prakash, *Evolution of Land Tenure in Kerala: A Review*, in P.P. Pillai, ed., AGRI-
    CULTURAL DEVELOPMENT IN KERALA (Agricole Publications Academy 1982).
77 The formal process for application to purchase *kudikidappu* land followed several
    stages. First, the *kudikidappukar* applied to the Land Tribunal, which then notified
    any person interested in the land and posted notice of the application on the village's
    notice board and at the land itself. The tribunal then made inquiries, including to
    the applicant, and issued a decision and an accompanying order. If the application
    was approved, the order would include the purchase price of the land and the extent
    of land available to be purchased. When this order was final, the Tribunal would is-
    sue a "certificate of purchase," which vested the rights, title and interest of the land
    in the *kudikidappukar* free from encumbrances. See Kerala Land Reforms Act, 1963,
    sec. 80B.
78 Id. Some *kudikidappukaran* did not purchase the land on which their huts were situ-
    ated, but rather enjoyed certain increased securities of tenancy. These increases in
    the security of tenancy rights included making *kudikidappus* heritable, reducing the
    possible amount of arrears of rent to no more than one year's rent, making rent very
    low (in the country, the rent was capped at less than two day's wages), and ensuring
    that customary rights that existed between *kudikidappukars* were not abridged. R.J.
    Herring, LAND TO THE TILLER: THE POLITICAL ECONOMY OF AGRARIAN REFORM IN SOUTH
    ASIA 189 (1983), see also T.J. Nossiter, COMMUNISM IN KERALA: A STUDY IN POLITICAL
    ADAPTATION 293 (1982).
79 K.E. Vergehese, SOCIO-ECONOMIC CHANGE IN KERALA 70-71 n. 25 (1986) ; R.W. Franke
    & B. Chasin, KERALA: RADICAL REFORM AS DEVELOPMENT IN AN INDIAN STATE 57 (1994).
    For an alternate view, see J.P. Mencher, *The Lessons and Non-Lessons of Kerala: Agricul-
    tural Labourers and Poverty* 41(15) ECONOMIC AND POLITICAL WEEKLY 1781 (1980).
80 See T. Hanstad, J. Brown & R. Prosterman, *Allocating Homestead Plots as Land Re-
    form: International Experience and Analysis from Karnataka*, ECONOMIC AND POLITICAL
    WEEKLY (July 20, 2002).
81 Government of India, supra note 29, annexures XXXVI & XXXVII.
82 World Bank, supra note 36, at 58-64.
83 West Bengal issued a circular in 1992 requiring government land to be issued jointly
    in the name of husbands and wives, or to women individually, "to the extent possi-
    ble." West Bengal issued the circular 14 years after the land distribution program be-
    gan, and while the state did issue a second circular restating the joint title require-
    ment, it did not require retroactive application of the policy. As a result, joint titling
    was not a requirement for the majority of land distributed. J. Gupta, *Women Second
    in Land Agenda*, ECONOMIC AND POLITICAL WEEKLY 6 (May 4, 2002). Moreover, local
    officials have not uniformly implemented the policy even with regard to land distrib-
    uted after its adoption. In three rounds of field research, RDI encountered few cases
    of government-granted land allocated in the joint names of husband and wife or in
    the independent name of a woman. RDI found several examples of families that had
    received government-allocated land after the adoption of this policy who stated that
    the land was granted solely to the male head of household. J. Brown & S.D. Chowdh-
    ury, *Women's Land Rights in West Bengal: A Field Study*, RDI Reports on Foreign Aid
    and Development No. 116, at 14 (Rural Development Institute 2002).

84 Karnataka is among a small group of states that have attempted to increase women's land rights through ownership of government-distributed housing benefits. Beginning in 1993, the state ordered officials to put government housing benefits (houses and often house plots) in the names of both husbands and wives. Implementation of the requirement was at best uneven. In 2000, Karnataka addressed the problem of implementation and further enhanced the rights of women by requiring officials to title housing benefits in the name of women individually, with limited exceptions. RDI conducted a review of the implementation of the titling directive, and found as of 2003, almost all housing benefits were titled in the name of women. R. Nielsen, N. Bhatla & S. Chatraborty, *Women's Property Ownership: An Examination of the Process and Impact of Karnataka's Rural Housing Program Titling Directive*, an ICRW-RDI publication, on file with the Rural Development Institute (2006).

85 World Bank, supra note 36, at 63-64.

86 See generally A. Seidman, R. Seidman & N. Abeyesekere, LEGISLATIVE DRAFTING FOR DEMOCRATIC SOCIAL CHANGE: A MANUAL FOR DRAFTERS (London: Kluwer Law International 2001).

87 West Bengal's success is instructive. As noted in section II above, West Bengal redistributed one million acres of ceiling-surplus land to 2.6 million land-poor households. In recent years, the state has been allocating ceiling-surplus lands in very small plots, averaging less than one-third of an acre. In a small field study covering two districts, RDI interviewed 34 erstwhile landless land reform beneficiaries who had received plots averaging 0.16 acres (ranging from 0.07 to 0.38 acres). The majority of the households farmed their plots intensively and reported significant increases in food intake, income and social status – a mix of human, financial and social assets that they attributed to the small field plots. T. Hanstad & S.B. Lokesh, *Findings from Micro-Plot Research in West Bengal*, RDI Report No. 115 (Rural Development Institute 2002). Other more comprehensive studies are consistent with RDI's findings: West Bengal's land reform beneficiaries have realized important benefits from plots of land much smaller than an acre. See Chakraborti, supra note 58.

88 *Constitution of India*, sec. 1.98.

89 Id. sec. 1.99.

90 See detailed discussion in Chapter 4.

91 *Constitution of India*, sec. 1.108.

92 Government of Karnataka, Rural Development of Panchayat Raj Department Programme description, Namma Bhoomi – Namma Thota (2005).

93 The information regarding West Bengal's micro-plot program is drawn from the program documents and RDI's review of the program design and implementation. See Government of West Bengal Department of Land and Land Reforms *Chash-O-Basobaser Bhumi-dan Prakalpa* (Cultivation and Dwelling Plot Allocation Scheme) Guidelines, DLLR Implementation Order (Jan. 30, 2006), and DLLR Supplemental Guidelines (Apr. 24, 2007).

94 State officials are considering whether to expand the Andhra Pradesh program to include purchase of land for micro-plots and land leasing activities.

95 Indira Kranthi Patham ("IKP"), formerly known as Velugu, falls under the state Department of Panchayat Raj and Rural Development and is administered by the quasi-governmental Society for Eradication of Rural Poverty ("SERP").

96 A complete description of the program can be found in the Andhra Pradesh Rural Poverty Reduction Project, *Operational Guidelines: Increasing the Rural Poor's Access and Rights to Rural Land*, Sept. 2005 (on file with the Government of Andhra Pradesh, Society for the Elimination of Rural Poverty).

97 Id. at 8-9.

98 A. Panth & M. Mahamallik, Indian Institute of Dalit Studies, *A Report Submitted the Society for Elimination of Rural Poverty, Government of Andhra Pradesh* 54-81 (on file with the Rural Development Institute).

99 The details and achievements of this project are drawn from the following: B.V. Indira, INDIRA KRANTHI PATHAM: LAND ACCESS FOR THE POOR (SERP Publications Nov. 26, 2007), R. Giovarelli, D. Vhugen & K. Vakatui, *Ensuring Secure Land Rights for the Rural Poor in Andhra Pradesh: A Case Study* (draft report for FAO 2008); R. Mitchell & T. Hanstad, *Innovative Approaches to Reducing Rural Landlessness in Andhra Pradesh: A Report on the Experience of the IKP Land Activities* (on file with the Rural Development Institute 2008).

100 For example, the Government of Orissa's Revenue and Disaster Management Department adopted its Mo Jami, Mo Diha (My Land, My Homestead) campaign to investigate the possession of land in rural areas and ensure that the intended beneficiaries of land reforms and tribal rights legislation were in possession. Order No. 34502/R&DM, LD-60/2007, dated August 28, 2007.

101 The decision to use paralegals to work with the community-based organizations and community surveyors was based on a review of other legal aid programs. As part of the process of developing the Project's legal aid activities, IKP's Legal Coordinator visited the Centre for Social Justice in Ahmadabad, Gujarat. The Center for Social Justice has a long-standing, successful legal aid program that is based on the selection and training of village residents to serve as paralegals. The Centre's paralegals provide training on legal matters, assist in resolving legal matters, and identify emerging legal issues within communities for discussion and action at the state level. Examples of other legal aid programs can be found in M. McClymont & S. Golub, eds., MANY ROADS TO JUSTICE: THE LAW-RELATED WORK OF FORD FOUNDATION GRANTEES AROUND THE WORLD (New York: Ford Foundation 2000). Over the last decade, RDI has designed and implemented legal aid activities in several countries, including Kyrgyzstan, Russia, and Muldova. Descriptions of those projects are available from RDI. After studying models from other states and countries, IKP initiated a pilot paralegal program in one district to train educated rural youth as paralegals to work with the community-based organizations to identify and resolve land rights issues.

102 To date, approximately 80% of the youth participating are male because the position requires independent travel and overnight stays in villages, which presents a cultural barrier for most young women in India.

103 As part of their training, paralegals and community surveyors conduct a physical inventory of a village to identify gaps between land records and possession of land. The inventory team obtains copies of maps indicating areas of government land, visits the land to determine who is in possession, compares the findings with the land records, creates a list of all gaps and discrepancies for further inquiry among residents and officials, and notes a plan for addressing the issues, including surveying needs. The inventory process provides training for the paralegals and community surveyors on land records, maps, land laws, interview techniques, and options for the resolution of issues. The process also educates the village about land issues and options for resolving land problems.

104 Andhra Pradesh includes a substantial amount of land that was not surveyed during British rule because it was under the control of regional or local royalty, vacant "wasteland" or forestland.

105 India's Constitution defines Scheduled Tribes as those deemed to be so. As of 2001, there were 664 Scheduled Tribes. Articles 342 and 366. The issues involved in identifying, distinguishing and counting tribes are well described in D. Thakur, ed., TRIBAL LIFE IN INDIA SERIES (New Delhi: Deep & Deep Publications 1994).

106 The 1991 India Census figure was 67,758,380.

107 H. Mander, TRIBAL LAND ALIENATION IN MADHYA PRADESH in LAND REFORMS IN INDIA, VOL VII, at 275 (2002). The British classified populations as "tribal," as used today in India, based on race, culture and religion, although tribal advocates dispute the distinctions made as artificial and suggest that, in practice, the British system classified individuals who were forest-dwellers as tribals, and those who were not, non-tribals. R.K. Sharma & S.K. Tiwari, TRIBAL HISTORY IN CENTRAL INDIA, VOL. III, at 918 (New Delhi: Aryan Books International 2002).

108 M. Raza & A. Ahmad, AN ATLAS OF TRIBAL INDIA (New Deli: Concept Publishing 1990); R.K. Sharma & S.K. Tiwari, supra note 107.

109 M.L. Patel, CHANGING LAND PROBLEMS OF TRIBAL INDIA 26 (Bhopal: Progress Publishers 1974). Forestland issues, including with relation to tribals, is discussed more specifically above.

110 For a complete discussion of the history of forest legislation in India, see J.M. Lindsay, LAW AND COMMUNITY IN THE MANAGEMENT OF INDIA'S STATE FORESTS 15-19 (Lincoln Institute of Land Policy 1994).

111 R.N. Pati & B. Jena, eds., TRIBAL DEVELOPMENT IN INDIA 65 (New Delhi: Ashish Publishing 1989).

112 N. Singh, *Emerging Problems of Ownership and Exploitation of Communal Land in Tribal Society*, 77 MAN IN INDIA 233 (1997). Some estimate that public projects such as dams have displaced as many as 50 million people, 40% of which have been tribals. See Mander, supra note 107, at 281. Tribal displacement is discussed more fully at paragraph 2.114 ff.

113 Mander, supra note 107, at 278-281; A. Baviskar, *The Fate of the Forest: Conservation and Tribal Rights*, ECONOMIC AND POLITICAL WEEKLY 2493-95 (Sept. 17, 1994).

114 In Gujarat, for example, land reform legislation granted tenants who personally cultivated land ownership rights for any non-resumable area, effective April 1, 1957. Amendments expressly prohibited tribal tenants from surrendering land to their landlords and from landlords resuming land occupied by tribals. Despite these prohibitions, 3,300 tribals in one area comprised of 14 tribal *taluks* "voluntarily" surrendered the land they occupied to non-tribal landlords. Another 1,450 landlords resumed 5,100 acres of land occupied by tribals in the same area. H. Trivedi, TRIBAL LAND SYSTEMS: LAND REFORM MEASURES AND DEVELOPMENT OF TRIBALS 108-119 (New Delhi: Concept Publishing 1993); see also K.B. Saxena, *Tribal Land Alienation and Need for Policy Intervention*, XXXVI(2) THE ADMINISTRATOR 89 (1991).

115 *Scheduled Tribes and Other Traditional Forest Dwellers (Recognition of Forest Rights) Act, 2006*, secs. 3-4.

116 Opposition from the conservation community was nonetheless fierce, with environmentalists and wildlife conservationists claiming that the law would result in the destruction of the forests, forest resources and critical habitat. Those favoring the law note that it provides for creation of wildlife sanctuaries and resettlement of forest dwellers, but with procedures preventing arbitrary action and requiring the state to provide for the secure livelihood of those resettled. *Constitution of India*, sec. 4(2); see A. Kothari, *For Lasting Rights*, 23(26) FRONTLINE (Dec. 30, 2006).

117 *Constitution of India*, secs. 4-7.

118 The *gram sabha* and *panchayat* shall have ownership of minor forest produce, the power to prevent alienation of land in Scheduled Areas, to take action to restore unlawfully alienated land, to manage village markets, and to control money lending. See generally M. Pal, *Panchayats in Fifth Scheduled Area*, ECONOMIC AND POLITICAL WEEKLY (May 6-12, 2000).

119 For example, the PESA gives the *gram sabha* or *gram panchayat* ownership of minor forest products, which are the property of the government. The Ministry of Environments and Forests immediately contested the transfer of ownership to the *gram sab-*

ha, precluding enforcement of rights granted by the PESA. U. Ramanathan, COMMON LAND AND COMMON PROPERTY RESOURCES in LAND REFORMS IN INDIA, VOL. 7, at 216-18 (2002).

120 D. Bandyopadhyay & A. Mukherjee, NEW ISSUES IN PANCHAYAT RAJ 33 (Delhi: Concept Publishing 2004). For example, in Madhya Pradesh, the PESA legislation grants *gram sabhas* in Scheduled Areas the power "to manage natural resources . . . in harmony with the provisions of the Constitution and with due regard to the spirit of other relevant laws . . . ." *Madhya Pradesh Panchayat Avam Gram Swaraj Adhiniyam, 1993*, as amended, ch. XIV-A. To similar effect, in Andhra Pradesh and Maharashtra, a tribe's customary mode of dispute resolution is trumped by any conflicting law. See discussion in Pal, *Panchayats in Fifth Scheduled Area*, ECONOMIC AND POLITICAL WEEKLY (May 6-12, 2000); S. Upadhyay, *Tribal Self-Rule and Common Property Resources in Scheduled Areas of India* (paper presented at the Tenth Biennial Conference of the International Association for the Study of Common Property, Oaxaca, Mexico, Aug. 9-13, 2004); N. Sundar, R. Jeffery & N. Thin, BRANCHING OUT: JFM IN INDIA 175 (New Delhi: Oxford University Press 2001).

121 *Constitution of India*, sec. 1.111.

122 Id. sec. 1.113.

123 Id.

124 In some cases, one state may have more than one tenancy law and some states may have distinctly different circumstances in different regions, requiring separate analysis and potentially different approaches.

125 These steps may in some settings be undertaken simultaneously. However, not in areas where groups are resisting revisions to tenancy laws on the grounds that beneficiaries of the reforms will be disadvantaged.

126 In cases where the landlords still retain some rights to this land, providing ownership rights to the tenant should involve compensation to the landlord.

127 See T. Hanstad & R. Nielsen, *From Sharecroppers to Landowners: Paving the Way for West Bengal's Bargadars*, RDI Reports on Foreign Aid No. 121 (Rural Development Institute 2004).

128 That discussion also includes Egypt, a rare case of successful regulation that was deliberately—and with disastrous impact on previously protected tenants—reversed.

129 The sharecropper's share is 50% if the landlord provides inputs, 75% if not. *West Bengal Land Reforms Act*, secs. 15(2) and 15A.

7 From collective to household tenure: China and elsewhere

Li Ping and Roy L. Prosterman

I.   Introduction

This chapter looks at what is often thought of as a further, separate category of land tenure reforms: those involving movement away from collectivized farming and towards the conferral of new, individualized land rights upon the former collective farm workers. We have already noted, at the beginning of Chapter 3, that there are some potentially useful parallels between these experiences and the program-design-and-benefit issues that arise in the redistribution of land held in large private estates. (One major difference, of course, may be that the collectivized land is almost always considered publicly owned, and hence need not be paid for.)

There are also many more experiences of sweeping "decollectivization" than there are of sweeping redistribution of estate land, and we focus here especially on the case of China, where RDI has now worked on the ground and advised policy makers for more than two decades. The Chinese experience offers an opportunity to explore pro-poor land tenure reform issues from three perspectives:

First, and most directly, how the world's most populous country, still containing roughly one-quarter of all those on the planet who depend on farming for a livelihood, has pursued land tenure reform since its revolution in 1949, and with what results.

Second, China was the first centrally planned economy to see the break-up of its collective farms. The methods and consequences both of individualizing tenure on arable land and of making such individual tenure secure have been and remain central to China's post-revolution experience.

Third, China is presently facing the challenge of how to implement a basically well-conceived set of laws that address the security of rural land tenure. The Chinese implementation experience has potential relevance for pro-poor reforms of land tenure, and more generally for the bringing of the rule of law to the countryside, for a wide range of settings not limited to the formerly centrally planned or "transitional" economies.

One key lesson of the Chinese experience has been a confirmation of the importance of ensuring that the rural population enjoys broad-based (indeed virtually universal) individual access to land. A second key lesson has been that, beyond the benefits of broad individualization, there are vitally important benefits from long-term security of those individual rights. And a third key lesson is that any effort to maintain an absolute per capita equality of individual landholdings by governmental fiat (by "administrative means"), in conflict with the goal of long-term security, carries far higher costs than benefits. Much of this chapter's discussion of legal issues thus concerns how to move from bare individual tenure (very beneficial even though insecure) to more adequate, beneficial and secure tenure.

All of the recent lessons from China, however, may be conditioned by the fact that the land is already held in a form of public ownership and that it need not be acquired from private landowners or involve outlays for land costs. But as we shall see, there may be local cadres or officials whose political response to the allocation of stronger land rights to the cultivating farmers may not be too far different from that of private landlords in other settings.

The land tenure reforms that China has undergone under the Chinese Communist Party's rule, beginning regionally as far back as the 1920s, have produced both dazzling successes and horrific failures. Before the People's Republic of China was founded in 1949, the Communist Party was mostly one of poor peasants who had little or no land. Possibly the most salient and successful measure that the Communist Party championed and implemented was "land to the tiller." Such a measure ensured that poor peasants received land in a highly egalitarian manner and thus whole-heartedly supported the Communist Party. In the first seven years of the new China under communist rule (1949-1956), the central government adopted a landmark law that endowed these peasants with full private ownership of land. As a result, China achieved very large gains in agricultural production, and a rapid recovery from the ruins of the decades-long civil war was facilitated. However, inspired by the Soviet Union's model, ideology-oriented Chairman Mao reversed course and started his collectivization campaign, under which all agricultural land became the property of collective farms, and individual peasants were banned from owning any substantial assets, including land. China's agriculture declined precipitously, and tens of millions of people starved to death.

In the late 1970s and after Chairman Mao's death, China finally came to terms with the painful reality and gradually started a process of decollectivization, called the "Household Responsibility System" (HRS). While collective ownership of farmland was maintained, use rights to such collectively owned land were given to individual farmer households for private farming. These broadly held individual land rights gave rise to a notable achievement in poverty reduction during the 1980s, with China's arable land, merely 7% of the world's total, feeding adequately 22% of the world's population. Learning from this success, China has attempted to extend the 3-year use term initially given to a (at least nominal) 15-year term and now to a 30-year renewable term.

China represents a prime example of what a little individualized land tenure can do to dramatically improve lives. But China has a long way to go before the full benefits of secure, long-term land rights can be realized. Importantly and urgently, the income and wealth brought by China's economic growth for the last two and a half decades has not proportionally benefited the countryside. The urban-rural gap in per capita income continues to widen and has recently reached what the Chinese government considers an alarming ratio of 3.33 to 1.[1] The most promising solution to these issues is to provide farmers with greater land tenure security, permitting the farmers to make mid- to long-term investment on the land, thereby increasing the volume, value and diversity of agricultural production. This requires significant legal and policy reforms and their concrete implementation at the grassroots level.

RDI started its work in China in 1987, a few years after China's decollectivization under HRS.[2] Over the past 20 years, RDI has conducted more than 1,000 direct farmer interviews in over 20 provinces and four large-scale sample surveys in cooperation with Renmin University and Michigan State University in 1999, 2001, 2005 and 2008, each covering between 1,700 and 2,000 farmer households in 17 provinces. The findings from such field research have greatly enhanced and regularly updated RDI's knowledge about farmers' relationship to the land which constitutes the primary means of livelihood for approximately 800 million Chinese. Beginning in 1988, this accumulating body of rural observations has then been used as the basis for briefings and recommendations to policy makers in Beijing.

This chapter begins with an historical overview in Section II, followed by a discussion of tenure security benefits in Section III, and a look at some current major issues surrounding land tenure in Section IV. Section V then explores further tasks and reform needs, and Section VI discusses possibilities of still more extensive tenure reform measures.

Finally, Section VII introduces comparisons with the fate of collective farming, and its legal surround, in the former Soviet Union, where RDI began working in 1990.

II.   China's changes in land tenure: An historical perspective

Land tenure was discussed in Chapter 1, where we noted that individualized land tenures can be measured broadly in terms of three criteria: breadth, duration and assurance. Breadth is a measurement of the quantity and quality of the land rights held and may include the rights to possess land, to grow or harvest crops of one's own choice, to pass the land on to heirs, to sell land or to lease it to others, to pledge land rights as security for credit, to prevent trespass, to protect against state expropriation, and many other rights.

Duration measures the length of time for which these rights are valid. Typically, the same duration applies to all of the rights held, but this is not necessarily so. In general, as the duration lengthens, tenure security improves. However, duration need not be perpetual to create an adequate incentive framework for land investments and improvements.

Assurance, the third criterion, is a measurement of the certainty of the breadth and duration of the rights that are held. If an individual is said to possess land rights of a specific breadth and duration, but cannot exert, enforce or protect those rights, they have no assurance. A land "right" that cannot be exerted or enforced is not a right at all.

In China after the communes were broken up in the early 1980s – thus individualizing agricultural landholdings and giving essentially universal access – the central remaining issue of land tenure has been the insecurity of farmers' rights, stemming primarily from shortcomings in duration and assurance, and secondarily from shortcomings in breadth. At least five interrelated factors have contributed to land tenure insecurity in rural China in recent years: (1) the short term or uncertain duration of the rights; (2) the practice of land readjustments to reflect demographic change; (3) the lack of written documentation and certification of land rights; (4) the inability of farmers to enforce and protect their rights; and (5) the ubiquitous and undercompensated takings of land. All are discussed in this chapter.

Pre-1949 land tenure reforms by the communists

It is worth reviewing the early history of Chinese Communist land tenure reform measures because some of the issues faced and approaches taken remain live and debated reform options in China today.

Ever since its founding, the Chinese Communist Party has been keenly aware of the problem of landlessness that Chinese farmers were facing and had constantly placed land tenure reform as one of its top priorities in its fight with the Nationalists for control over China.[3] Soon after it established its first administrative region in northern Jiangxi

Province in the early 1920s, the Chinese Communist Party promulgated its first land law, setting up the basic framework of communist land tenure reforms: confiscation of land from landlords and distribution of the confiscated land among peasants with little or no land.[4] There are five especially salient features in this law. First, the land confiscated is owned by the Soviet government, and its use rights are allocated to peasant households (Article 1). Second, while the land is mainly allocated to peasants for individual farming, the law allows allocation to peasants for joint farming and to Soviet government farms (Article 1). Third, the term of peasants' right to farm the Soviet owned land is unspecified. Fourth, sale of the confiscated land is prohibited (Article 2). Fifth, land is allocated on an egalitarian basis, and men and women have equal right to allocated land (Article 4).

With the expansion of the communist-controlled area, the Land Law of the Soviet Republic of China was adopted in 1931. Unlike the Jinggangshan Land Law, the new Land Law did not explicitly attest that land is owned by the Soviet government; instead, it emphasized that the confiscated land be "distributed to the poor and middle peasants"[5] and "all temple land and other public land shall be granted to peasants without condition."[6] Second, this Land Law was simply silent on the allocation of confiscated land to peasants for joint farming or the allocation of such land to government farms. Third, it allowed the lease and sale of land among peasants, but landlords were still prohibited from repurchasing land, and rich peasants were prohibited from engaging in land speculation (presumably, purchase with intent to resell).[7]

The most important communist land law before the founding of the People's Republic of China in 1949 was the Platform of Chinese Land Law adopted at the CPC national land conference in September 1947. This document was adopted at the height of civil conflict between the Communists and the Nationalists and when the Communists were seeking to win and consolidate peasant support: one may thus see the Platform as the distillation, in effect, of what the Communists' quarter-century of experience in the Chinese countryside had taught them would win that support. For the first time, the Chinese Communists declared the explicit principle that China would adopt an "agrarian system of 'land to tillers.'"[8] In order to fulfill this principle, the Platform further provided that except for some described categories of non-arable land, all land confiscated from landlords and the land traditionally owned by communities was to be distributed among all rural residents and owned by individuals.[9] All rural residents, regardless of age and gender, were to be entitled to a (locally) equal share of land.[10] It required that land ownership certificates be issued to all landowners.[11] It also provided that landowners "have right to freely manage and sell the land, and lease the land under certain circumstances."[12]

Land tenure reforms in the 1950s

In June 1950, the Chinese communist government promulgated the first land tenure reform law that was applicable to all parts of China (except for Taiwan, which was then governed by the Nationalists, who had fled the mainland after their defeat in the civil war). Except for the important fact of explicit confiscation of landlords' lands for distribution, the program was not much different in design from the successful land-to-the-tiller programs carried out around that same period in Japan, Taiwan and South Korea (see Chapter 2). The Land Reform Law of the PRC embodied the major provisions of the earlier platform on land allocation and land ownership. The law provided that China was adopting a "peasant land ownership system."[13] Land confiscated from landlords, except for that owned by the state in accordance with this law,[14] was to be allocated to poor peasants "fairly, rationally and uniformly for them to own."[15] The law also provided that all landowners were allowed to manage, sell and lease their land freely.[16] To evidence land ownership, the law required that a land ownership certificate be issued by the people's government to landowners.[17]

The Land Reform Law also authorized the regional people's government to promulgate implementing rules, taking into consideration local circumstances.[18] One set of regional implementing measures provided that land could be inherited by the owner's spouse, children and other direct relatives upon the owner's death, and could be mortgaged, sold and leased without restriction for most landowners.[19] The implementing measures also emphasized the need to respect women's land ownership rights, explicitly allowing women to have full rights to the land they own free from others' interference upon marriage, divorce and remarriage.[20]

Although the Land Reform Law required the issuance of land ownership certificates to all landowners, it did not spell out any formalities concerning the certificates. However, under the Mid Southern Region's implementing measures, each landowner was given an option either to have his or her own certificate or to have a single certificate covering all land in the household, and required that all names of individual owners in the household be listed on the certificate if a household certificate was to be issued.[21]

In a separate measure, land in suburban areas previously owned by landlords was confiscated and placed under state ownership with the intention of allocating such land to peasants who had little or no land.[22] To secure peasants' use rights to such land, state-owned land use rights certificates were to be issued to peasant land users.[23] However, the land users could not lease, sell or leave idle such state-owned land.[24]

The land reform program distributed 46.7 million hectares of land to about 300 million peasants, thus covering about one-half of the total arable land and more than 60% of the total rural population.[25] The "land to the tiller" program proved a noteworthy success in increasing agricultural productivity: annual grain production went up from 113.2 million tons in 1949 to 166.8 million tons in 1953, and further to 192.7 million tons in 1956. This 70% increase in grain production was accompanied by an increase of 85% in total farm income during the same period.[26]

Collectivization of Chinese agriculture

Despite the impressive economic gains, private ownership and individual farming on rural land did not remain the policy for long. Soon after the completion of these rural land tenure reforms, the Chinese government introduced the concept of collective farming following the example of the USSR (where all farming had been collectivized in the early 1930s). In 1955, the Central Committee of the Chinese Communist Party issued the Decision on Agricultural Cooperation, formally launching the movement to collectivization.

Collectivization through legislative measures began in 1956 when the National People's Congress' Standing Committee passed the Charter of Agricultural Production Cooperatives.[27] Although the charter did not legally change private ownership, it established the creation of public ownership of rural land as a goal for collectivization.[28] According to the charter, all land owned by members of the cooperative "must be submitted to the cooperative for uniform use."[29] Each member was allowed to keep no more than 5% of the village's average landholdings per capita as private plots.[30] Contributors of land were entitled to some compensation for their land contribution, but such compensation was not to exceed compensation for labor contribution.[31]

The nominal private ownership of farmland under the cooperative system was transformed into formal collective ownership only three months later when the Third Plenary Session of the National People's Congress passed the Charter of Advanced Agricultural Production Cooperatives in June 1956. This charter explicitly stated that collective members "must transform privately owned land, draft animals, and large farm equipment and other major production means into collective ownership."[32] Private plots were absorbed into collective ownership; individual households, however, were allowed to keep ownership of the residential land.[33]

Despite problems with farm management and production incentives, the collectivization campaign proceeded rapidly. By the end of 1958, the agricultural collectives had been abruptly merged into Rural Peoples' Communes. Within half a year, approximately 90% of the rural population became members of vast communes averaging 4,000 families each.

From an ownership aspect, the fundamental characteristic of the commune was the abolition of the last vestiges of private property. The commune took sole ownership of all property, including the private plots (which were absorbed into the commonly worked land), private dwellings, livestock and certain consumer durables. Participating in production activities governed by the collective authorities on the collective's land and with the collective's inputs and equipment was the only means of personal earnings for the commune members. Under this system, none of the farmers had an individual stake in the land; they worked together on the land, receiving pay for time spent in the field. The communes effectively severed farmers from their land.

The collectivization campaign proved to be a disaster for China's agriculture and people. Grain production declined substantially for three years in a row starting in 1959, leading to perhaps the planet's worst famine of the 20th century.[34] After 1962, as an attempted response, the effective unit of collective production was scaled back, generally to the production team level (around 40-50 households in a natural village or hamlet), and use of the private plots, although not their ownership, was restored. But recovery was a slow process and further complicated by the society-wide "Cultural Revolution" that began in the mid-1960s.

Decollectivization under the Household Responsibility System

After ten years of the Cultural Revolution and more than 20 years of collective farming, China's rural economy came to the edge of collapsing prior to the tenure reform beginning in the late 1970s. Indeed, 1977 per capita grain production was lower than that of 1956.[35] The sluggish growth in the farm sector was accompanied by extremely slow growth in peasant incomes. In 1978, the average annual rural income was 133 yuan per capita, and more than 250 million rural people were in semi-starvation status.[36] When the new leadership began to clean up the mess left by collective farming after Mao's death in 1976, the most imperative issue was to decide whether to abandon collective ownership of land and, if not, what rural land system to adopt.

Although private ownership of land was deeply rooted in Chinese history, and the Chinese communists had strenuously pushed forward a "land to the tiller" program before and immediately after they took power, more than 20 years of collective farming promoted and insisted on by Mao between the mid-1950s and mid-1970s had left a political legacy of public ownership. The new leadership was clearly aware that any tenure reform would be derailed if it crossed the threshold (one might say the "third rail") of public ownership.

With the death of Mao, the new reform-minded leadership headed by Deng Xiaoping began to explore the way to bring rural China out of poverty and persistent hunger in the late 1970s. At the same time, a group of poor farmers in Anhui Province, driven by the need for survival, invented a land contracting system in which collectively owned land was contracted to participating farmers for private farming who, in return, were committed to meeting collective demands for quota grain, taxes and fees assessed based on the quantity of the land allocated to each participating farm household.

This new form of private farming aroused a fierce debate among policy makers.[37] The key issue in the debate was whether this new model of farming represented a negation of Mao, designed to replace collective ownership of land with private ownership. The pragmatic faction of the new leadership argued that the new model of farming was merely an experimental way of organizing farm production aimed at motivating farmers, instead of changing rural land ownership. Although this argument for physical decollectivization downplayed its potentially profound implications for the collective ownership of land, individual farming itself had to be based on individual rights to land. Thus, a mechanism was created that separated use rights to land from ownership of land, and provided that the collective entity would continue to hold ownership but that use rights would be allocated to members of the collective for individual farming. This approach of emphasizing decollectivization of farming practice prevailed, apparently because most decision makers realized the damage that had been done to China's agriculture by collective farming. A compromise was reached among the leadership to introduce a new land system throughout the country, later called the household responsibility system, or HRS.

Land contracting under the HRS immediately demonstrated its great advantages over collective farming and received strong support from central leaders. By 1983, virtually all arable land had been allocated to individual households, usually on a per capita (though sometimes on a per worker) basis, and more than 20 years of collective farming had finally come to an end.[38]

The initial results were striking, as grain production increased by 8.6% per year during the first years of HRS, in 1980-1984.[39] These productivity increases had a dramatic impact on farmer incomes and consumption patterns, both in absolute and relative terms. Between 1979 and 1984, average net income for rural residents increased by 11% annually, compared to an average annual increase of 8.7% for urban residents, narrowing the income gap between urban and rural residents from 3.03:1 to 2.49:1.[40] The gap in consumption between urban and rural residents also narrowed during this period, from a ratio of 2.8:1 to 2.3:1.[41] It is estimated that, largely under this regime of broad-based individual access to land, the proportion of people living below the one-dollar-a-day poverty line in China declined during the years 1981-1987 (a period when 70% or more of the total population made its livelihood from agriculture) from 64% to less than 30%.[42] Note the current revisions to earlier global poverty data discussed in Chapter 1, with an extreme-poverty line now calculated at US$1.25 a day, and an estimated 16% of China's population now living below that level.[43]

Further improvements of the HRS

The next land tenure reform China adopted following the initial huge success under HRS was to lengthen the duration of farmers' individual land rights and expand the breadth of such land rights. The land rights that farmers received under HRS were uncertain, usually for a term of one to three years, subject to local decisions.[44] At the end of each term, collective cadres conducted a land readjustment within the village in response to demographic changes occurring during that term to ensure absolutely egalitarian possession of land rights among all members of the village.[45] The breadth of farmers' rights had been restricted in several ways. A compulsory production plan was in force to the extent that farmers were required to produce and sell a certain amount of grain to the state, and to do so at a price much lower than market price. Nor were farmers allowed to transfer their land rights.[46]

To address these tenure insecurity issues after the initial success of HRS, the Chinese central government decided to standardize the allocation of land rights for private farming. The first step took the form of attempts to lengthen the duration of farmers' land rights under HRS. In 1984, the Central Committee addressed this issue in its important annual Rural Work pronouncement (Document No. 1). In order to reverse local practices of contracting land to farmers for very short periods, the Document required that farmers' land rights be prolonged to 15 years nationwide. In addition, the Document formally sanctioned an emerging rural land rights market by allowing transfers of such rights.[47] However, the Document did not make any rules on how to assure implementation of the extended term or facilitate transfer of land rights. Studies done by RDI and other organizations showed that the new 15-year rights were still typically subject to a mechanism of a "small readjustment" sometimes as frequently as every year, and a "big readjustment," sometimes every three to five years, which effectively cut farmers' land rights to a term ending at the next readjustment.[48] The uncertain duration of rights to a specific landholding greatly limited the scope for any rural land rights market, leaving room only for short-term and at-will transfers.

Also, the grain quota remained in place, and farmers were required to set aside at least part of their contracted land for growing grain, which represented a limitation on farming autonomy. (Interestingly, re-adjustment was never introduced in Vietnam, which broke up its collective farms in the north and wherever they had been practiced in the south in the 1980s, around the same time as China. One hypothesis might be that the continuing success and indeed general entrenchment of the system of small family farms in the south helped forestall the political pressure for ultra-egalitarianism that had led to periodic readjustment of landholdings in rural China.[49])

Capitalizing on the pervasive existence of unregulated land readjustment practices, local governments and collective cadres in some rural areas started to introduce mechanisms that presented even more serious threats to farmers' tenure security in the late 1980s and through the 1990s. Typical among them were the so-called "two-field system,"[50] "scale farming"[51] and "recontracting" farmers' land to non-villager bosses.[52] Although these mechanisms took different forms, they shared a similar feature: taking back farmers' contracted land through compulsory administrative land readjustment, but now doing so in ways that had little or no linkage with population change at the village or household level and that often selectively favored small groups of people. Because these schemes facilitated rent seeking by local officials and collective cadres, they rapidly expanded throughout large areas of the country. Central-government responses to these new threats to farmers' land tenure security are discussed below.

The duration of farmers' land use rights was addressed again nearly ten years after the issuance of the 1984 Document No. 1, when the central government decided in November 1993 to extend the term of use rights to collectively owned arable land for another 30 years upon the expiration of the 15-year rights nominally mandated in 1984.[53] Although the 1993 Document No. 11 stated that "[i]n order to avoid frequent changes in contracted land and prevent land from being further fragmented, no readjustment in response to population changes should be promoted within the contract period,"[54] it did not provide any guidelines on how to implement this policy. Nor had the policy been stated in the clearest language: "shall be carried out," for example, would have been a much more definitive statement than "should be promoted." This almost certainly reflected a compromise between central government factions, rather than inadequate drafting skills.

It was not until four years later – when the farmers' 15-year land rights (though still generally both undocumented and nonexistent in practice) were nominally about to "expire" in most villages in China –

that the Chinese government for the first time put forward a series of specific policy measures to restrict the land readjustment practice that had been conducted as a norm in most rural villages since the adoption of HRS. The measures were contained in Document No. 16, issued in mid-1997.[55] These policy measures included explicit prohibition of village-wide big readjustments, serious restrictions on small readjustment, prohibition of introducing the two-field system in villages thus far unaffected by such practices, and banning the practice of taking back farmers' contracted land for "scale farming."

These new policy measures were widely interpreted as mandatory policy guidelines for the implementation of a second round of contracting. As compared with the new land system that was about to emerge under Document No. 16 and successive measures, China's rural land tenure system during the first round of contracting (1983-1998) bore the following characteristics:

First, virtually all rural households had access to some arable land. Rural landlessness was essentially non-existent. This is a major accomplishment. Broad, virtually universal access to land in China has provided important household nutritional and income security throughout rural China[56] and creates a solid foundation for rapid and broad-based rural growth.[57]

Second, landholdings were distributed among households in a substantially egalitarian fashion, usually based on one equal land "share" per household member. While land-per-capita differences among regions resulted in inter-regional discrepancies, differences within villages and localities were remarkably small.

Third, the land system rules and practices were not uniform throughout the country. Collective ownership of land and allocation of specific parcels to individual households had been essentially universal throughout China since 1983. However, the duration of those rights, the specificity with which the use rights were defined, the prevalence and type of administrative land readjustments undertaken, and other important qualitative aspects of the land use rights varied considerably among regions and among localities within regions.

Finally, most villages attempted to balance two competing objectives in establishing and implementing land system practices: continuing equal per capita access to land for welfare or subsistence purposes and stable, secure land use rights for productivity purposes. To this was added the desire of many local cadres to assert influence and find sources of financial return through continued meddling in land allocations. As discussed above, in most Chinese villages the vector resultant of these various pressures was a practice of periodically readjusting household land rights to reflect demographic changes in the village and the individual household. The frequency and extent of those readjustments were, however, not uniform among different provinces nor even among different villages within each province.

More recent major legislation on land rights

The first reform-era law – as distinct from the 1984, 1993 and 1997 policy documents – to contain provisions governing farmers' land rights is the revised Land Management Law (LML) adopted by the Standing Committee of the National People's Congress in August 1998.[58] Article 14 of the law contained important provisions that attempted to address three major shortcomings related to rural land tenure security in China: the short or uncertain duration of the use term, the lack of written land use contracts, and the practice of frequent land readjustments. On the duration of use term, the law states that "collectively owned land shall be contracted to the members of the collective economic entity for . . . 30 years." On documentation of land rights, Article 14 further required that "the contract issuing party and the contracting party execute a contract stipulating the rights and obligations of the two parties," and that "farmers' land contracting rights shall be protected by law." Equally important, Article 14 embodied into law the land readjustment provisions of Document No. 16. It ruled out village-wide big readjustment while allowing small readjustment only to be conducted among "isolated households" upon "consent by two-thirds of villagers or villager representatives and approval by township government and county government agencies in charge of agriculture."

However, the LML has only one article and part of another devoted to rural household contracting[59] and fails to deal with a vast range of issues with respect to farmers' 30-year rights. Thus, after more than three years of further drafting and deliberation, in August 2002 the Standing Committee of China's National People's Congress adopted the Rural Land Contracting Law (RLCL), the first modern Chinese law to deal exclusively with the issue of rural land tenure.[60] This law represented the most important legal breakthrough on almost every tenure issue for securing the land rights of China's estimated 187 million farm households since the adoption of the HRS.

The RLCL sets forth a series of legal rules addressing a very broad range of tenure issues. The legal framework governing land readjustments under the RLCL is composed of three basic rules. First, Article 27 establishes the general principle of prohibiting all kinds of readjustment during the 30-year term, with only a narrow exception for "a natural disaster that seriously damaged the contracted land and other special circumstances" under which a small land readjustment may be conducted. Second, to further restrict these narrowly permitted small readjustments under special circumstances, the RLCL reiterates the important procedural requirements that the consent of two-thirds of the villager assembly or two-thirds of villager representatives as well as approval by the township government and the county agricultural administrative body must be obtained prior to the commencement of such a readjustment. Third, the law validates previously issued contracts (issued under the 1993 and 1997 policy documents or the 1998 LML) that completely prohibit land readjustment. The RLCL also explicitly invalidates any provisions of land contracts that violate the mandatory legal rules with respect to land readjustment (Article 55).

On the breadth of farmers' 30-year rights, the law states that farmers' land rights include "rights to use, profit from, and transfer land contracting and operation rights, and the right of autonomy over production operations and disposition of products" and "the right to receive the corresponding compensation" for any land taken by the state or collective for non-agricultural purposes (Article 16).

On the right to carry out land transactions, the RLCL further states that farmers' land rights "may be transferred [to other village households], leased [to non-village households], exchanged, assigned, or transacted by other means in accordance with law" (Article 32). To safeguard farmers' interests in land from being violated by local officials through various kinds of compulsory land transactions, the RLCL emphasizes the principle of "equal consultation, voluntariness and with compensation" (Article 33), establishes farmers as "the party to any transactions of" rural land use rights (Article 34) and explicitly prohibits local officials to "intercept or reduce" the proceeds from such land transactions (Article 35). It is important to note that prior legislation, although permitting transactions of rural land use rights, had not provided any guidance with respect to the scope of this right and the procedures to exercise this right,[61] and the RLCL has filled this legal vacuum.[62]

To evidence farmers' land rights, the RLCL requires that written contracts be issued to farmer households (Article 21). In addition, the RLCL mirrors legal requirements for documenting urban land use rights by requiring that county government or a higher level to issues land rights certificates to farmers to affirm such rights (Article 23). Such requirements are extremely important to protect farmers' land rights because these written land documents provide powerful evidence in any dispute resolution[63] process and offer deterrence against possible violations.

The RLCL also contains improved provisions on the "assurance" aspect of tenure security. Unlike the dispute resolution provisions in the 1998 LML and 1999 Administrative Review Law, which require exhaustion of administrative reviews before a complaint can be filed with the People's Court,[64] the RLCL explicitly gives farmers a choice between consultation, mediation, arbitration and suing in People's Court (Articles 51 and 52). Because collective cadres and local government officials are themselves often parties to land disputes, requiring administrative review makes little sense, especially when such officials have much greater access to the mechanism than farmers. Enabling aggrieved farmers to seek immediate judicial redress at least opens significant possibilities for substantially improving farmers' ability to resolve such disputes satisfactorily (see further discussion below, as well as Chapter 9 on legal aid).

Notably, the RLCL has a series of well-articulated remedial and penalty provisions with respect to the protection of farmers' land rights. It establishes very clear and strong rules prohibiting violations of farmers' land use rights by local officials, including illegal land readjustments, taking back the farmer-contracted land and re-contracting it to others, and forcing farmers to plant crops against their will. Civil penalties, including monetary damages and restitution, and equitable remedies to forestall or reverse the illegal action, now apply to any such violations (Article 54). Indeed, one would be hard-pressed to find more comprehensive remedial provisions in Chinese law on any subject.

The most recent legislative development may well be the most important of all. The Property Law adopted by the annual plenary session of the National People's Congress – not the smaller standing Committee, as was the case for both the LML and RLCL – in March 2007 reaffirms in the most authoritative manner farmers' individual rights to land in several important aspects. With respect to farmers' land rights for agricultural use, for the first time in China's legislative history, farmers' land rights are defined as usufructuary property rights[65] and thus enjoy a much stronger protection under the law than obligatory (contract) rights. Moreover, the law formally permits farmers to continue using their currently contracted land when the present 30-year term expires,[66] providing a possibility for creation of *de facto* perpetual land rights for farmers, or at least implying a permission for repeated renewals whenever the term expires. The law explicitly reaffirms the principle of prohibition of land readjustments, and refers to the RLCL for applying restrictive rules dealing with the small class of permissible land readjustments.[67]

The Property Law also brings important clarity to the concept of "collective ownership," whose vagueness has helped cover up many actions by local cadres that have undermined farmers' use rights and security. China's Constitution states that rural land, except for that under state ownership, is collectively owned.[68] The 1998 LML reiterates this constitutional principle and authorizes collective economic entities at various levels of the rural collective to "operate and manage" their collectively owned land.[69] However, neither the Constitution nor the LML answers the critical question regarding the relationship between village members (farmers) and administrative bodies of the village (collective entity) on questions of land ownership.

This longstanding uncertainty is seemingly resolved by the Property Law. Article 59 provides that collectively owned real properties "are owned by all members of the collective," namely, by all farmers located within the community on which the collective is formed. With respect to the relationship between member owners and the collective entity that "operates and manages" collectively owned land under the LML, the Property Law further prescribes the role of the collective entity as merely "exercising ownership rights on behalf of the collective."[70] That is to say, such exercise of ownership rights must be carried out on behalf of member owners. In order to prevent the collective entity from circumventing member owners in dealing with collectively owned land, the law further requires that members of the collective decide a series of specified matters of importance including land contracting plans, contracting collective land to non-villagers, readjustments in isolated cases, and distribution of land compensation.[71] However, if the decision made by the collective entity, villager committee or the person in charge of such organizations violates the members' lawful rights, the aggrieved member or members may lodge a lawsuit to void the decision.[72] Other important provisions in the Property Law are discussed below.

III.   Benefits of tenure security for Chinese farmers

Benefits under earlier tenure reforms

There have been two notable periods of high growth in farm productivity and incomes since China's revolution, both linked to land tenure reform. Under the Land Reform Law of 1950 the government introduced a system of peasant land ownership, redistributing secure, non-readjustable rights to nearly half of China's arable land to over 60% of the rural population.[73] Even in those very difficult times, under the private ownership system China experienced a 70% jump in grain production from 1949 to 1956 and an 85% increase in farmers' income.[74] This period immediately preceded the collectivization of Chinese agriculture in the mid-1950s.

The second period of accelerated growth was during and immediately following the decollectivization of agriculture under the HRS in the 1980s, when farmers quickly made many short-term, annual improvements in their cropping practices (better timing, proper weeding, more careful application of fertilizer, etc.) that had often been ignored on the collectives. This represented not a shift from one form of individual tenure to a more secure form, as in the earlier period, but a shift from collective tenure to individualized (though not secure) tenure.

Following the introduction of the HRS, China's gross agricultural output value increased, in real (inflation-adjusted) terms, by 86% from 1980 to 1990.[75] This increase occurred despite a sharp decrease in the level of state investment in agriculture following 1978. One study concludes that the total factor productivity of China's agriculture increased by 41% during the 1978-1984 period, and that 32% (32/41) could be attributed to the incentives of decollectivization and individualization of landholding under HRS, with the remaining 9% resulting from price increases.[76]

Benefits of documented 30-year land rights

Specific evidence now appears to be emerging as to a third Chinese experience with improved tenure: the benefits of the enhanced tenure security provided by China's rules regarding farmers' 30-year land rights, as adopted and implemented since 1997. This evidence relates especially to farmers' possession of the confirmatory documents (contracts and certificates) for their land rights required by the law and comes *inter alia* from a 1,962-household, 17-province survey which RDI conducted in cooperation with Renmin University and Michigan State University during July and August 2005.[77]

Broadly, the findings indicate that there were important positive impacts, including farmer investments in the land, associated with Chinese farmers' possession of documentation for their land rights. We first summarize the chief tenure-related findings of the survey, both positive and negative, and then discuss in more detail some behaviors associated with the possession of documentation.

Positive findings include:

- Where farmers have received documentation of their land rights (contract, certificate or both), they have substantially increased their mid- to long-term investment in their land.
- Increases in investments were even greater where the land documents comply with law and are in proper form and were greater still where farmers hold compliant documents and have received information on their land rights from two or more channels.
- Publicity has successfully conveyed to large majorities of Chinese farmers certain basic facts about their land rights, such as that their arable land should be contracted to them for 30 years without readjustment.

- In villages where farmers possess documents complying with the law, farmers are much more likely to regard the compensation package received in cases of land takings as satisfactory.
- The central government appears to have successfully brought about a substantial degree of implementation of the laws and policies it has promulgated in four land-related areas, as reflected in the decline in prevalence of the two-field system, scale farming and re-contracting, and the effective reduction of taxes and fees paid by farmers. Thus, where the central government focuses and makes its will clear, it appears that *it can succeed in making pro-farmer laws and policies effective*, even on matters where the collective cadres have largely contrary interests.

Negative findings include:
- 17% of villages have not yet begun the second round of contracting in even the most nominal way.
- Only 63% of rural households have received any documentation (contract, certificate or both) for their land rights, and only 38% of households have received both documents, as required by law.
- Only one out of every 10 farmers possesses at least one of these documents in the form most fully compliant with law (and it is for this minority group that the rate of land investment has been greatest).
- 30% of the villages that have purportedly given farmers 30-year land rights have subsequently "readjusted" (almost all of them illegally) farmers' contracted land.
- During the 10 years preceding 2005, the frequency of takings of farmers' land for non-agricultural purposes grew more than 15 times, and in only 22% of takings did the authorities actually consult with farmers regarding the amount of compensation.
- Processes for redress available to farmers for their complaints about compensation for takings have been highly inadequate, and have rarely produced a result favorable to the farmers.

On the issue of investments made, the surveyed farmers were asked whether they had made one or more of six specific mid- to long-term investments on their land: fixed or removable greenhouses, trellises, orchards, fish/eel ponds, or domesticated-animal farms.[78] The survey shows that there were only sporadic investments before 1998. After the transitional year of 1998, when the LML was adopted, there was a very large increase in investments that was sustained for a period of four years (1999-2002). After that, investments appeared to revert back to the pre-1998 level. Overall, the year of 1998 seems to be a defining point when China adopted and seriously started publicizing and imple-

Figure 7.1   *Timing of contract issuance, certificate issuance and investments*

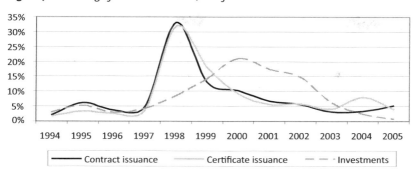

| Contract issuance | Certificate issuance | — — Investments |

Source: K. Zhu, R. Prosterman, J. Ye, P. Li, J. Riedinger & Y. Ouyang, *The Rural Land Question in China: Analysis and Recommendations Based on a Seventeen-Province Survey,* 38 NYU JOURNAL OF INTERNATIONAL LAW & POLITICS 761, 798, fig. 11 (2006).

menting the law. As shown in Figure 7.1, the peak years of investments closely follow, with about a two-year time lag, the peak years of contract/certificate issuance.

The reasons for the drop-off in investments after 2002 may include some satisfaction of "pent-up" investment desires, the growing time-lag since publicity or document issuance, and the increased negative publicity about poorly compensated land takings as well as the growth of illegal land readjustments.

The data analysis further reveals that there is a strong, positive correlation between contract issuance and investments:

Table 7.1.   *Contract issuance and investments, before and after 1998.*

	Investments made before 1998	Investments made in or after 1998
Contract not issued	6.6%	12.3%
Contract issued	8.0%	22.2%

For the no-contract group, investments increased by 1.86 times (86%) during or after 1998, while for the contract-issued group, investments increased by 2.78 times (178%). The correlation between certificate issuance and investments is similar, though less pronounced. Where farmers possess both a contract and a certificate, there is an even stronger correlation with investments, with 24.1% of the households who have received both documents having made one or more of the six investments in or after 1998, versus only 12.5% who received neither.

For those who received both documents, investments increased by 3.44 times (244%) as compared to their pre-1998 investments.[79]

Further, the evidence indicates causation, not just a "correlation" in which both the issuance of documentation and the making of investment might be the twin results of some third factor. This appears to be so for two reasons. First, as in medical tests of the effectiveness of new drugs, we are seeing a desirable response (investment in the land) which is "dose related." Certificates are much more effective than nothing; contracts are somewhat more effective than certificates; both together are more effective than either alone; compliant certificates are much more effective than incompliant ones; and compliant contracts are much more effective than incompliant ones (and somewhat more effective than compliant certificates).

Second, a clear explanation offers itself for the causal mechanism involved. Documented land rights – and the better-documented they are, the better the result is – lead farmers to believe that they will retain possession of their present parcels of land long enough to make a profit from investments that take multiple years to recoup.[80]

This causal relationship is also consistent with what RDI has found in extensive rapid rural appraisal interviewing of Chinese farmers over a period of many years, in which the interviews have repeatedly given insight into why farmers who invest do so, and why those who do not invest refrain from doing so[81] (see Box 7.1).

However, just over one of 10 households in the 17 survey provinces presently possess a land rights document in what appears to be the most efficacious, fully "compliant" form. This invites the question of what would be the likely result in the Chinese context if all or nearly all of the estimated 187 million rural households enjoyed secure, adequately documented land rights.

Box 7.1. Anhui and Jiangxi – A tale of two provinces

In Anhui, RDI interviewed 32 farmers in four counties. The great majority of Anhui farmers, 21 of 25 who expressed an opinion, were highly confident that their land rights would remain free from the process of readjustment for the entire 30-year term. Apparently as a result of this confidence, ten farmers reported that they had made long-term investments on their land to increase productivity or diversify into higher value-added crops. The specific investments included planting fruit trees, shifting from chemical to organic fertilizer, building greenhouses for mushroom or vegetable cultivation, and digging irrigation ponds. On average, farmers who had made such investments reported that their net income per *mu* of land had increased fivefold in the first year following the investment. To make these investments, farmers invested both labor and cash, ranging in amounts from several hundred to as much as 20,000 RMB (at that time, 8.2 RMB = US$1). Farmers paid for the investments using their own savings or loans from friends and family; farmers reported very little formal borrowing from banks or credit cooperatives, and told us that such formal credit was largely unavailable. Access to markets was a particularly important factor in the farmers' decisions to shift from grain to vegetable production. In Fanchang County in Wuhu Municipality, a new highway means that both Shanghai and Nanjing – a combined market of nearly 20 million consumers – are now within a day's drive. However, farmers uniformly stated that without secure land rights, they would not have made investments on their land.

Jiangxi presents a starkly contrasting picture. Only two of 26 farmers expressed high confidence that their land rights would remain secure during the 30-year term. In fact, 16 of the 26 villages had already conducted a land readjustment since purportedly giving farmers 30-year rights under the 1998 Land Management Law. As a result, only four farmers reported making any long-term investment on their land. Among these four, two believed that none of their land would be subject to readjustment, and one had invested only on his dry land because the village announced that dry land would no longer be subject to land readjustments (while readjustments would continue on paddy land). Only one farmer interviewed (the only one reflecting such behavior in either of the two provinces) risked making a long-term investment on land he still considered subject to possible readjustments – and he made sure that the greenhouses he built were movable, just in case.

Source: R. Prosterman & B. Schwarzwalder, *From Death to Life: Giving Value to China's Rural Land,* 8(1) CHINA ECONOMIC QUARTERLY 1 (2004).

Of added interest is the further survey finding that farmers with fully compliant documentation of their land rights were twice as likely – although still a minority – to be satisfied with compensation received for land takings as those who had received no documentation of their rights (39.3% versus 19.1%). Here, however, we may need to be more cautious in attributing causation, since both contract issuance and better compensation in the event of takings might sometimes be the common result of a third factor: local cadres who were better disposed to follow the law and serve farmers' interests.[82]

IV.   Some current major issues surrounding land tenure

Of the issues raised by the "negative findings" in the 17-province survey summarized in the preceding section, two stand out as possibly requiring adoption or clarification of the related legal rules if tenure security is to be further improved: (1) 30% of the villages that have purportedly given farmers 30-year land rights have subsequently "readjusted" farmers' contracted land, and (2) during the 10 years between 1995 and 2005 the frequency of takings of farmers' land for non-agricultural purposes had grown more than 15 times, generally without consultation with or payment of adequate compensation to farmers.

This section discusses possible revisions or clarifications of the legal rules that might forestall these two important tenure-undermining practices. The issue of mortgageability of arable land (presently prohibited) is also briefly explored.

Ending land readjustments

The single most important issue under the RLCL – and its greatest formal achievement – is its general prohibition against readjustments, a prohibition which has now been authoritatively reaffirmed in the Property Law. The RLCL provides:

> ARTICLE 27. During the contract term, the contract issuing party shall not readjust contracted land.
>
> During the contract term, in cases where a natural disaster has seriously damaged contracted land and other special circumstances, and an appropriate readjustment of arable land or grassland between isolated households is necessary, the approval of 2/3 of the members of the Village Assembly or 2/3 of the Village Representatives must be obtained, as well as approval by the township government and the county government administrative unit responsible for agriculture. If there is a land use right contract stipulating that readjustments shall not be conducted, such a contract shall be honored.
>
> ARTICLE 28. The following types of land shall be used in readjustments of contracted land or contracted to newly added population within the village:
> - Flexible land that has been reserved by the village collective in accordance with law;
> - Land that has been added through reclamation and other methods in accordance with legal methods;
> - Land that has been returned by contracting parties voluntarily and in accordance with law.

Viewed against the legislative background and the express language of the law, three points stand out:

First, Article 27 establishes a basic principle of no readjustment within the 30-year contract period and allows limited readjustments only under "special circumstances." Article 28 continues to limit the scope of readjustments by listing types of non-contracted land that could be allocated for readjustments or for newly added population.

Second, by juxtaposing "readjustments" and "newly added population" in Article 28, the legislature presumably has decided that "newly added population" is not covered by Article 27 and cannot be considered one of the "special circumstances."

Third, the law does not allow "big" readjustments. Even under "special circumstances," the readjustments allowed by Article 27 concern only "isolated" households. The same term is used in Article 14 of the 1998 LML. Thus, a village-wide readjustment must be regarded as illegal *per se* after the LML's effective date of January 1, 1999, and emphatically so after March 1, 2003, the effective date of the carefully crafted RLCL.

Nevertheless, the RLCL itself does not directly define what could constitute "special circumstances." This invites abusive interpretations that run afoul of the fundamental non-readjustment principle. And, indeed, the 17-province survey found that population change is the leading reason for post-second-round readjustments, having been cited in 72.8% of those readjustments; natural disaster, the only clearly permitted reason, was cited in only 1.4% of cases.[83]

Provinces and prefectures have adopted implementation rules for the RLCL that offer possible guidance as to what the central government could do to clarify the governing rules, either via national regulations or via amendment to the law.

For example, the Shandong RLCL Implementation Method (article 14) provides the following clarification on "special circumstances":

> During the contract term, where farmer households *lose their land* due to state expropriation or requisition, voluntarily give up the compensation and wish to contract land again, or where households *lose their land* due to special circumstances such as their contracted land being seriously damaged by a natural disaster, the contract issuing party may properly readjust contracted land among isolated households . . . . [Emphasis added.]

Besides reiterating the procedural conditions set forth by the RLCL, the Shandong rule requires that a household must actually "lose land" before a readjustment can be triggered. It logically follows that a household's contracted land remains the same whether or not the household

size grows or shrinks since, in either case, the household has not suffered a "loss of land." This is a significant clarification as it essentially
eliminates population change as a justification for readjustments, and
does so fully consistent with the language of the RLCL.

Certificates drafted by prefecture governments in Hunan Province
are even clearer:

> During the contract term, the collective will not conduct readjustment
> of the contracted land on the ground of population changes. The con-
> tracted land is allowed for like-kind exchange, inheritance, and
> compensated transfers in accordance with applicable laws. The
> collective may take back and redistribute the contracted land if
> the contracting farmer dies without any issue, or if the entire
> household changes their agricultural residence registration to
> non-agricultural registration, or the soil fertility is seriously da-
> maged and contracted land has been idle for an excessive period
> of time. [Emphasis added.]

Inclusion of such an explicit prohibition against readjustments for population reasons in the certificate is an important step forward. Despite
falling short of the RLCL (there is, for example, no power in the collective under that law to take back contracted land due to its being left
idle), the clear restrictions of the village's authority of withdrawing land
are significant in terms of irregular readjustments.[84]

Improving the land takings rules

Farmers' land tenure security is threatened by rampant land takings
from four perspectives: First, although China's Constitution and eminent domain laws permit the state to expropriate farmland for the need
of public interests,[85] such public interests are not defined in any way
under the law, giving the government virtually unlimited power in taking farmland for all non-agricultural purposes. Second, compensation
for taking farmland for either public purposes or commercial purposes
is subject to statutory limits[86] (which are usually well below the fair
market value of the land to be taken),[87] and in most cases are not sufficient to maintain the living standard of the dispossessed farmers.
Third, even this insufficient amount of compensation for the expropriation does not go to the dispossessed farmers in full or in most part,
with other surveys suggesting that farmers get an average of only some
10-15% of the compensation paid.[88] Finally, farmers' right to notice,
participation and appeal in land expropriations is seriously lacking both
in the legal regime and in practice.

RDI's 2005 17-province survey provides the most recent data on the issue of land takings.[89] Farmers reported one or more land takings in 476 of the 1,773 survey villages (or 26.8%) subsequent to when they were granted 30-year land rights (or since 1995 if the village has not implemented the 30-year policy).[90] Of these 476 cases of land takings, almost one-third, 32.7%, were for typical commercial purposes such as factories, urban housing and petrol stations.[91]

With respect to compensation for the farmers' loss of land, the survey found that in only 320 of the 476 cases (67.2%) did farmers receive some actual cash compensation, either in lump sum or installment, or both.[92] Furthermore, in about a third of cases where cash compensation was promised, the promise had not been fulfilled.

Making matters even worse, 26% of villages where takings occurred conducted an apparently illegal land readjustment following the land taking, "spreading the pain" of the taking among all villagers. Such land readjustment essentially reduces the landholding sizes of other village households not directly affected by the land taking, in effect "compensating" land-losing farmers with other farmers' land. Such a scheme also facilitates collective cadres withholding or intercepting cash compensation for their private use.[93]

In only 21.8% of cases were farmers consulted about the amount of compensation. Although 65.5% of farmers were not satisfied with the compensation, only 12.5% demanded a hearing or filed a grievance, and fewer than 1% (only five farmers) went to court.[94]

Largely as a result of such takings processes, disputes and even confrontational protests have in recent years become routine in the countryside.[95] Having realized the potential harm to social stability, the Chinese government has taken some legal and policy measures to improve the regulatory framework, notably the State Council's Document No. 28 of 2004, the Ministry of Land and Resources' Regulations on Public Hearings, and legal measures adopted by some provincial governments in response to the central government's policy guidelines. Most recently, the Property Law has made substantial improvements in the legal regime for ensuring farmers' interests in land when the land is taken. These new developments include:

Compensation for land expropriation. Document No. 28 emphasizes that the amount of compensation be determined based on the principle of preventing the farmer's living standard from being lowered as a result of the land expropriation. It specifically requires that local governments allocate to farmers part of the revenue from granting state-owned land use rights if the maximum sum of land compensation and resettlement subsidies allowed under the Land Management Law (30 times the average annual output value of the land to be expropriated) is still insufficient to restore the affected farmers' livelihoods. It also allows farmers to have an option of "stock-for-land" through which farmers can elect to contribute their land rights directly to a project with stable incomes in exchange for shares of stock in the project.[96] The Property Law, adopted in March 2007, now authoritatively reaffirms the principle that compensation should be adequate to maintain the farmers' living standards.[97] The law also requires that the government make financial arrangements to meet the displaced farmers' social security needs in addition to fully paying the compensation package for the land it takes.[98]

Allocation of compensation. Document No. 28 states that compensation for loss of land must be primarily used for the farmer households who have lost their contracted land through requisition. "Primarily used for" leaves considerable scope for the cadres to exert actual control over the compensation funds. More specific and satisfactory are the Shanxi Provincial government regulations on the allocation of land compensation between collective landowner and affected farmers, promulgated in October 2005. The regulations require 80% of land compensation go directly to affected farmers whose contracted land is expropriated and that 20% go to the collective landowner.[99] The Property Law is closer to – and of course far more authoritative than – the Shanxi regulations, explicitly providing that the holders of rural land contracting and operation rights are entitled to compensation for loss of land, the biggest component of the compensation package under existing Chinese takings law.[100] This provision appears to supercede the prior provisions of law authorizing the collective entity to take exclusive possession of compensation for loss of land.

Procedures for land expropriation. In 2004 the Ministry of Land and Resources promulgated new regulations that require the land expropriating agency to inform affected farmers of their right to a hearing on compensation standards and the resettlement package, and provide that such a hearing must be held if requested within five days after the parties are informed.[101] Document No. 28 takes this further and states that before the expropriation is submitted for approval at the appropriate level of government, its purposes, location, compensation standard, and resettlement and rehabilitation measures should be made known to farmers whose land is to be taken, and the results of the required survey on the existing situation of the land proposed to be taken should be confirmed by the rural collective and farmer households. The Property Law, however, contains nothing on these important procedural issues.

How these new efforts will improve the local practice of land takings – or restrain the frequency and amplitude of such takings – remains to be seen. Widespread publicity for these requirements and putting in place some of the other implementation measures discussed in Section

V below is likely to be helpful. But it would be desirable if the central government adopted an actual "Law on Takings" that would build upon the protections provided in the Property Law, in Document No. 28, and in the best of the local reform measures.

Mortgageability

One further needed reform in the prevailing legal rules in China involves the issue of the mortgageability of farmers' land rights. This is closely linked to the breadth of farmers' land rights and bears on their practical ability both to make improvements on their existing land and to engage in long-term transactions in land rights. The potential importance of measures that would allow farmers to obtain credit for major land improvements is shown in the 17-province survey findings concerning what resources farmers used to make the investments reflected in the survey. Constituting the most prominent resources by far, three-quarters used personal labor, and slightly over three-quarters used personal savings. Much less frequently, one out of six used money borrowed from relatives, and only one out of seven used money borrowed from a bank or credit union.[102]

Chinese law currently prohibits farmers from mortgaging their land rights.[103] This prevents them using land as collateral not only to obtain necessary credit to finance land improvements, but also to finance the acquisition of rights to additional land with a lump-sum payment to the seller (the so-called "purchase money mortgage").

Earlier drafts of the Property Law would have permitted the mortgage of arable land rights under certain conditions. This was omitted, unfortunately, in the final version due to legislative concerns over the farmers' loss of land to foreclosure. Such concerns, while understandable, could be greatly allayed through appropriate provisions in a mortgage law. For example, China could introduce a homestead exemption making part of the household contracted land exempt from foreclosure, and therefore essentially non-mortgageable (enough land to produce sufficient food to meet the household's essential consumption needs). Other options might facilitate credit: crop insurance could help assure repayment; a portion of standing crops could be used as collateral; and micro-credit to farmers, without collateral, could be encouraged and meet important needs.

V.   Further tasks and reform needs: measures for implementation

Much recent land tenure reform experience in China bears on the ever-present issue of implementing the law. Some important tasks related to implementation can be identified, various combinations of which may also bear on implementation in other settings of land tenure reform; indeed one – legal aid, with which RDI has had extensive experience in various country settings – is the subject of Chapter 9.

Publicity, publicity, publicity[104]

The 17-province survey revealed that farmers have heard of the 30-year no-readjustment policy but know few specifics. Virtually none of the farmers knew any provisions of the RLCL, although it had gone into effect more than two years before the survey. Farmers' broadly held knowledge of the 30-year rights policy was traceable to a widespread publicity campaign that coincided with adoption of the LML in mid-1998.[105] Television had been the most widely effective means of communication (the great majority of Chinese farm households have a television). Farmers had retained that broad knowledge, with over 90% still aware of the 30-year rights in mid-2005. But no similar publicity campaign has been conducted for the 2002 RLCL. It remains to be seen if such a publicity campaign will accompany the aspects of the new Property Law that concern farmers' land tenure rights and that reaffirm the RLCL. A repetitive informational and educational campaign using multiple media channels will be necessary for that law and for any additional land tenure protections (such as protections against takings) extended to farmers. The "assurance" aspect of tenure security requires rightholders to be aware of a formally existing right; a right or remedy that is unknown cannot be availed of. And if cadres know that farmers are aware of their rights, this may itself help forestall many rights violations that would otherwise occur.[106]

Issuance of compliant contracts and certificates

The practical importance of formal documentation of land rights, in accordance with Chinese law, is clear from the 2005 survey results. The survey showed that possessing written contracts or certificates – and even better, possessing both contracts and certificates – correlates strongly with decisions to make mid- to long-term investments in the land, and does so in a manner that strongly indicates a causal relationship. This finding alone would amply justify a strong push by the central government to ensure that contracts and certificates are issued to all farmers who have not yet received them. In addition to investment, other important factors such as the farmers' confidence in tenure security and their satisfaction with compensation in cases of land takings are correlated with the presence of documentation – although evidence of causation in the case of takings is less clear than in the case of increased investment.

The survey further showed that issuance of contracts and certificates has slowed in the past four years, leaving nearly two out of five farm households without either document. The first task should be to make sure that 85-90% of all farm households receive at least a contract or a certificate. There seems to be no reason not to set a goal of ensuring that 75-80% of households (versus 38% as found by the survey) receive both documents. The central government should clearly signal now that the achievement of such quantitative goals by an individual locality within a pre-determined timetable will be a key issue on which the adequacy of officials' performance will be judged, and that it will widely publicize success and failure in achieving this goal both within and beyond government circles.

Equally important is that the contracts or certificates to be issued should comply substantially with the controlling laws and regulations. Specifically, a contract or certificate should contain all the essential information that constitutes "compliant" documentation. Existing but inadequate contracts and certificates might be supplemented with a locally appropriate attachment where it is significantly easier to do this than to issue a replacement. Unlike many other implementation needs, this compliant-document goal would require fairly specific regulatory guidelines, preferably from the central government.

Durable "fact sheets"

As part of the apparently successful nationwide campaign to end most taxes and fees assessed against farmers, the government gave each farmer a "fact sheet" in the form of a durable laminated card.[107] The cards contained an accurate but simplified description of the legal rules, likely types of violations, and what to do if rights were violated. RDI researchers found the cards prominently displayed in houses of farmers.[108] The government could cheaply produce and rapidly distribute a similar laminated card containing major legal provisions on farmers' land rights, coordinating the distribution with the needed publicity campaign, reaching farmers before most new contracts or certificates – and supplements to existing ones – were completed, signed and issued.

Legal aid

Besides publicity for laws, RDI experience in Russia, Ukraine and other country settings indicates that one effective method of disseminating legal information to farmers as well as to local cadres is through the establishment of rural land rights legal aid centers. These experiences are discussed in detail in Chapter 9.

Independent rural legal aid services should be established to help farmers and others understand and enforce their land rights. The legal aid offices could be established initially as a pilot project, and later introduced throughout the country if the model proves successful.[109] The offices should be staffed by qualified lawyers and paralegals, be based in places that farmers can visit conveniently – and also from which the legal aid providers can conveniently visit rural villages – and enjoy considerable independence even though they might receive governmental funding. Independence is particularly important in cases where farmers' rights are infringed by government officials.

Experience elsewhere suggests that a large majority of disputes may be resolved in the farmers' interests by negotiation (and education) when the other side perceives that the farmer has competent legal representation. The next recommendation also bears upon the relatively less-common situation where a legal aid lawyer must bring a case to court.

Deploying the Peoples' Court

An entire chapter of the RLCL details farmers' rights to go to court and obtain a wide range of remedies when land rights have been violated. These remedial provisions are reaffirmed in broad terms in the Property Law. However, our impression from extensive rapid rural appraisal interviewing – certainly reinforced by findings from the 17-province survey – is that farmers find it very difficult to bring a land dispute to court, and are often rebuffed in the rare cases where they do so.

China might consider the creation of a specialized court to resolve land disputes, adopting appropriate elements from the models now found in Hong Kong and the state of New South Wales in Australia.[110] But it might be quicker and more effective to establish land panels within the existing Peoples' Courts, to provide farmers with improved access to the legal system, give specialized skills to selected judges and others through training in the resolution of land disputes (and a steadily accumulating experience), and increase the efficiency of land dispute resolution.

A specialized land panel within the Peoples' Court should have exclusive original jurisdiction over cases involving requests to adjudicate disputes such as those over distribution of land by collective units to farm households, deprivation of such land by readjustments or otherwise, land takings compensation and related issues, and disputes between farmers about leases or transfers.

To promote access, these specialized panels might operate in the form of "circuit" courts, with judges traveling to townships (or perhaps even administrative villages, where there had been indications of multiple complaints) throughout each county to hear land disputes according to a pre-announced hearing schedule.

Thus, as farmers learned more about their rights through publicity and other means, they would also have a professionally equipped court to which they could take land disputes. Again, like other measures, this might serve as an important deterrent to would-be violators of farmers' land rights.

Establish an information-collecting and monitoring toll-free hot line

A telephone hotline could be an effective way for the government to link itself to the people and learn from their actual experience. It could take advantage of the now-ubiquitous access to cell phones, including in the countryside. Such a hotline should preferably be operated by a national ministry (e.g., Ministry of Agriculture or Ministry of Land Resources) and be open to the entire country. Certain provinces might be encouraged to establish pilot projects as well. Farmers would call a uniform, publicized and toll-free number to report possible violations of farmers' land rights; hotline operators would receive specialized training on relevant laws and appropriate questions to ask. Anonymous calls should be allowed in order to encourage farmers to expose sensitive problems.

After receiving calls, the operators should record the information on the calls promptly, the call records would then be sorted out and entered into a centralized database. A frequent bulletin could be published to analyze and summarize the calls based on number of calls, geographical origins, nature and content of calls, and so on, with a section describing "hot issues" and "hot areas." The bulletin should be received and reviewed by high levels of the central government and forwarded to provincial-level agricultural and land resources agencies. With respect to areas suffering repeated problems or saturated with farmer complaints, the central government could consider conducting additional independent fieldwork, circulating information about the problems, and requiring the local governments which are responsible to apply specific remedies without delay.

Continue monitoring local implementation progress

To measure implementation in its various dimensions, the central government should conduct continuing assessments through farmer interviews and periodic surveys. Steps must be taken to ensure the objectivity and representativeness of the findings, through random selection of counties, townships, villages and households, and through interviewing farmers directly, outside the presence of local officials (particularly collective cadres). Such assessment tools are essential to provide the government with an accurate and frequently updated picture of the extent of implementation of the RLCL and Property Law, and other land-related issues at both national and local levels. This may also become the basis to evaluate and revise the implementation efforts based on evolving circumstances.

VI.   Possibilities for still more far-reaching tenure reform

The road to more secure and marketable land rights for China's 800 million rural residents will be long and hard, but one must bear in mind how far China has come and how much progress has been made during the last two and a half decades. China actually represents a prime example of what broad and guaranteed individual access to land – even when the rights are readjustable and not assured as to any particular piece of land – can do to bring dramatic improvement to the lives of the rural population.

But the next major advances in farmers' productivity and well being will clearly require greater efforts to ensure their secure tenure on a particular piece of land – a key generator of long-term investment and land value, and a characteristic of all those agricultures that are more productive than China's. As China's urban-rural divide continues to worsen, land takings accelerate, and the competition from foreign agricultural producers intensifies due to China's WTO accession, the rural land question will become ever more important. Powerful evidence supports the view that any solution to these broader issues must also include, as a central element, providing farmers with greater land tenure security. This requires significant legal and policy reforms and their concrete implementation at the grassroots.

Looking beyond the recommendations made in Sections IV and V, including substantially completing implementation of the 30-year rights for all farmers (or, perhaps, if further significant implementation of 30-year rights proved daunting) China should consider one of two next steps: either providing farmers with full private ownership rights to land, or, a less drastic alternative, explicitly giving farmers perpetual use rights to such land. Either approach should remove the main threat to tenure security, that is, those local officials or cadres who typically claim to be acting on behalf of the "collective" as the formal owner of the land (a claim that should be undermined by Article 59 of the new Property Law, as discussed above), but who often act primarily to enrich themselves.[111] The experience of the "land to the tiller" program that made millions of poor Chinese peasants into small but real owners of land in the late 1940s and early 1950s shows that private land ownership not only can trigger enormous economic gain but also accords with the political ideology of a socialist state. As Premier Wen Jiabao put it well in press conferences following annual sessions of the National People's Congress in 2005 and 2006, a reasonable policy would seem to be that farmers' land rights will "not be changed forever."[112]

A first step in that direction – although one going not nearly as far as the two options suggested in the previous paragraph – is the provision in the Property Law that allows the farmer "to continue to contract the land" after the 30-year term expires. Like several important Property Law provisions, however, this would benefit from further clarification in a related regulation: Is the continuation to be for another term of 30 years? Must the farmer affirmatively request renewal of the term, or is it automatic unless he declines to renew? Is the renewal power exhausted by a single exercise, or does it continue – in effect creating the potential for perpetual use rights?

Recently,[113] articles have appeared in the Western media noting that a small but significant movement is afoot – and is facing strong official opposition – to give Chinese farmers full private ownership of the land they till.[114] In one of the same media accounts, a prominent Chinese academic opposed to private ownership was quoted as saying that "if [the Chinese government] want the same problems as India has then they should go ahead and privatize the land," and arguing to maintain "the current system of state [sic] ownership."[115] But, as the detailed discussion in Chapter 6 makes clear, the comparison with India is far off the mark. Except for two or three of its 28 states, India has had little successful land tenure reform in the 60-plus years since independence in 1947. At independence, a high proportion of rural families were comprised of tenant farmers and agricultural laborers, and that proportion has not shrunk appreciably over the past six decades – indeed, as between these two non-landowning groups, there are probably fewer tenant farmers and more agricultural laborers (generally the worse-off of the two groups) today. China, by contrast, would begin any program of full privatization with a farming system in which the great majority of rural families now possess a parcel or (usually) several parcels of land on a highly egalitarian basis, even though most of them remain insecure as to *which* parcel or parcels – and with what relocations, reductions or reconfigurations – they will possess from one year to the next. There are, however, very few tenant farmers, very few agricultural laborers, and virtually no landlords in today's China. Thus, the starting point for any full-ownership-to-the-tiller tenure reform in China would be wholly different than it was, and remains, in India.

However, a persuasive argument can still be made that existing provisions of law, *if effectively implemented*, create land rights for Chinese farmers that are not significantly inferior to full private ownership. Depending on the percentage factor used to discount a future stream of income, the usual formula would assign a 30-year land right, in the first year, roughly 75% to 95% of the value of full private ownership.[116] Moreover, full private ownership does not seem to be a prerequisite for a market economy. Farmers in Hong Kong's New Territories have (and previously had under the British) 50-year rights to their land, while Hong Kong's urban skyscrapers are built on land that is usually held with 75-year rights.[117] Most land in Israel is held under 49- or 98-year rights (the former with a biblical origin).[118] Surely both Hong Kong and Israel would generally be considered market economies. So is Australia, where much privately used land (including extensive grazing land in "stations" held by private parties) is acquired from the government for a single lump sum payment for a "leasehold" period of 99 years.[119] Further examples could be cited.

Moreover, as to the possible psychological significance of "ownership," any market-impeding psychological difficulties arising from "only" having multi-decade rights seem to have been successfully overcome in China's urban sector, where private rights – although never readjustable – now range from 50 to 70 years and are freely bought and sold (and mortgaged).[120] The key psychological need may not be to give farmers formal "ownership," but to help farmers understand and defend the 30-year extendable and non-readjustable property rights that they are supposed to possess under present law. This should also be accompanied by widespread publicity to clarify that the "collective" ownership, as authoritatively defined in Article 59 of the Property Law, is joint ownership by all members of the village community.

The strongest argument in favor of rules giving farmers "private ownership" is likely to be that this would be a more dramatic and more decisive subject of a publicity campaign than the present "30-year rights," would further emphasize the non-existence of any competing collective land rights, and would thus better lend itself to successful implementation of the types of measures described in Section V.

If necessary to placate ideological and political opposition to full private ownership (even though such ownership was successfully put in place by the new communist government in 1949-1956), a series of mutually reinforcing limits and safeguards could be drawn from experience in other countries that would offer reassurance against possible abuses by the well-off or well-connected and would satisfy other policy considerations that might arise as to equity and fairness. It would need to be recognized, however, that by including many of these limits in a new governing law on farmer ownership (such a law would be needed, along with a parallel constitutional amendment) the government would correspondingly limit the marketability of the farmers' ownership rights, and hence the wealth-creating effect of such ownership[121]:

- Do not allow the sale, or even lease, of land rights to anyone other than a self-cultivating farmer. Such a partial moratorium on transfers might be applied for an initial period, such as 15 years, while farmers gained a better sense of land values and the land market (note that the government has not seen any necessity to apply such a restriction on the transfer of the present 30-year rights).[122]
- The foregoing restriction could be reinforced with a requirement that any transferee who purchases the ownership right (even though that transferee is a self-cultivating farmer) could not re-transfer via sale or even lease, for some significant period, such as five or ten years. This would restrain rapid turnover – what some opponents of unrestricted private ownership might call "speculation," or what in the United States housing market has come to be known as "flipping."
- Regardless of the extent of restrictions on sale, or as an alternative to moratorium periods, wherever sales were permitted, there could be a sliding-scale tax on profits the size of which depends on the length of time the land was owned, with a very high percentage tax on sales made after a relatively brief period of ownership. This should not, of course, apply to the present 30-year rightholders who would be the initial beneficiaries of ownership, or their heirs, but only beginning with those who buy from them and then quickly resell.
- Farmers, as owners, should be allowed to capture the value of their land in transfers for non-agricultural purposes, *provided that* they have fully complied with zoning and land-use restrictions. Again, *taxation* of the profits from such non-agricultural transfers (even where permitted and lawful) could be at a high percentage rate – but based on different, and complex, policy considerations. That tax rate, even though it might be high, might well be flat and might apply to the initial beneficiaries as well. Major changes should, in any case, be made in the legal regime for shifting land to non-agricultural uses, as discussed above.

– There could also be restrictions – tailored to specific regions and land types – as to the holding of agricultural land (either as owner or lessee) above specified maximum ceilings. Note that there are no such "ceilings" now, and their absence has sometimes helped pave the way for abuses by the cadres, such as "outside boss contracting" and "scale farming" (note too that large farms are *not* generally more productive or efficient, and certainly not in a setting such as China, which remains short on land and capital but long on labor[123]).

– With a goal similar to that of imposing ceilings, the law might prohibit any purchase or lease of agricultural land by foreign individuals or foreign legal entities, and perhaps also by domestic Chinese legal entities. This, and many of the other restrictions described, could be for a fixed initial period of time, or could later be repealed after policy makers had gained assurance that this could safely be done, in the more developed and less agricultural China of ten or 20 years in the future.

VII.   A brief comparison with land tenure reforms in the former Soviet Union

RDI began working in Russia in 1990, when it was still part of the USSR. After dissolution of the USSR in 1991, RDI worked for extended periods in a number of the republics of the former Soviet Union (FSU), including most prominently Russia, Ukraine, Kyrgyzstan and Moldova.[124]

In comparing the post-collective-farming experience of those countries with that of China (and that of Vietnam), four salient points stand out:

(1) The most fundamental and dramatic difference is that on most of the territory of the FSU, collective farming has ended in name only. Especially in Russia and Ukraine (and also all the Central Asian republics except Kyrgyzstan), the great bulk of farmland is still operated in very large units – typically several thousand hectares with several hundred workers – which generally perform just as poorly as the former collectives. Indeed, those farms are often virtually identical in territory to the old collectives and have simply been reregistered in new corporate forms such as "joint-stock companies" or "production cooperatives." The organizational culture and decision making process appear little changed from those of the previous entities, with the workers (members) still lacking the kind of active input into management that would, for example, characterize the *ejidos* (both collective and individual) in Mexico or the *kibbutzim* or *moshavim* in Israel.

(2) The laws of the various republics have in most cases (including Russia and Ukraine) afforded the workers (members) a formal option to leave the enterprise and start a private farm by claiming their proportionate share of the land formerly used by the enterprise as the private owners of such land. These legal provisions have been in place since the early- to mid-1990s, but only a small fraction of farm families have used them to start private farms in the case of Russia and Ukraine (though used by a somewhat higher proportion of farm families in Moldova and a substantially higher proportion in Kyrgyzstan). The reasons for this sweeping failure to "head for the exits" on the collectives when given the chance in Russia and Ukraine, in stark contract with the experience in China (and in Vietnam), are further explored below.

(3) One expansion of the scope of private farming that has generally taken place, however, is the enlargement of the small plot sector, including the "private plots" on the large farms and the "dacha plots" held by urban residents. These small plots have long been disproportionately productive: in 1990, just prior to the break-up of the USSR, this small plot sector comprised about 2% of the agricultural land in Russia (around 4 million hectares) and already accounted for a disproportionate, roughly 27%, of the gross value of all agricultural output.[125] According to Uzun, "The land in household plots doubled during the 1990s"[126] to 8.6 million hectares, but he believes the figure should be increased to take account of other categories of land allocated to small plot owners for private use, notably land for hay cutting, ultimately leading him to an estimate of 27.2 million hectares, or 14% of agricultural land, from which the small plot owners obtain benefit. The productivity of this sector remains highly disproportionate to the area under utilization, now accounting for an estimated 56% of the gross value of all agricultural output.[127] Small plots, occupying about 5% of the land in the collectives, also existed in China from the end of the giant communes in 1962 until the broad introduction of family farming under the Household Responsibility System after 1978 and were also disproportionately productive in that setting.[128]

(4) As is still the case in China, in three of the four countries where RDI has done most of its FSU work there had been until recently only very limited development of markets for the full assignment or sale of rights to agricultural land.[129] A leasing market in agricultural land rights did develop, however, one which is segmented into three categories: members leasing their land rights to the former collective enterprise; members leasing their land rights to private farmers (here paralleling the farmer-to-farmer lease market in China) when some medium-size private farms were established nearby and wished to expand; and members leasing (perhaps enterprise-wide) their land rights to

large-scale, capital-intensive, sometimes foreign-controlled agribusiness enterprises. Until very recently, the one country exception among the four, where outright sale of agricultural land is increasingly taking place, was Moldova. Now, however, the pattern of acquisitions by large-scale agribusiness enterprises in Russia appears to have shifted decisively from leasing to buying land rights from collective-farm members. There is further discussion of land-market issues below.

Regimes for withdrawal

In the USSR before its break-up, agricultural production had been carried out through a system of 48,856 collective and state farms.[130] These farms averaged 4,136 hectares (41 km^2) in size,[131] employed hundreds of workers engaged in activities across that large area, and were from roughly one to three orders of magnitude bigger than average farm sizes found in the highly productive cropland sectors of the developed market economies.[132] The collective system was very inefficient, required huge subsidies, and did not reward entrepreneurship and hard work. The system treated its workers like "modern-day serfs," as one commentator has put it.[133] Some shortcomings of collective farming are discussed in Chapter 3, and earlier in the present chapter.

These shortcomings were recognized (or not) to widely varying degrees in the 15 republics that emerged from the break-up of the USSR, and the new legal systems addressed the shortcomings with varying degrees of seriousness. The countries of the FSU which took reform relatively seriously all made an effort to give land rights to the workers, retirees and (in some cases) teachers and other "social sphere" workers on the former collective farms, or to return the land to the pre-Soviet owners.[134] The Baltic countries of Estonia, Latvia and Lithuania returned ownership of farm land to the heirs of its pre-Soviet owners, that is, as of around the end of World War II, by way of restitution, a process requiring an administratively fairly complex historical inquiry.[135] In the Caucasus countries of Armenia, Azerbaijan and Georgia, land used by the collective farms was subdivided and transferred directly to ownership of those on the enterprise. And other FSU countries, including the four on which we focus here – Russia, Ukraine, Moldova and Kyrgyzstan – responded to the challenge with a unique and interesting invention: the "land share."[136]

Instead of providing each individual with a specific plot of land, the land share provided the individual a right to claim a physical land parcel of a set size in ownership and leave the collective farm when that person chose to do so. This resembles the right to partition joint property in Anglo-American property law. Until the rightholder sought to exercise the partition-like right, the land share remained an ownership right held in common with the other land share owners on the former collective farm, to a specified quantity of land not yet separately demarcated or identified on the ground. The land share could be leased or sold to a producer.[137] A producer who leased in or purchased anything less than all shares on the farm would have to negotiate with those who had not leased out or sold their shares in order to identify the physical location of the leased or purchased land.

None of the land share systems was well designed. Each has raised serious problems for actual withdrawal in practice, problems it will be useful to bear in mind in case countries with still-collectivized agricultures – such as Cuba, North Vietnam or Belarus – might be tempted to adopt such a system in the future. The key to the full workability of the land share system was whether the holder of the right could actually claim an individually identified land parcel in kind. For the most part, the answer was no. An illustration of the "land-share" system and withdrawal process is given in Box 7.2: clearly much depended on being able to muster a fair decision and a favorable vote at the meeting of all land share owners – something which would vary according to country and local factors. In Russia and Ukraine, the two countries with the largest number of land share owners, no more than 5% claimed land in kind in the first decade of reform. In Moldova, roughly 15-20% of collective farm members left the farms with a corresponding amount of the land. Kyrgyzstan established its land share system in 1992, and by the end of 1996 approximately 50% of this land had moved from collective farms to farms operated by nuclear families or extended families. This move was especially pronounced among the Kyrgyz, Uzbek and Tajik ethnic groups – all the members of an enterprise typically deciding to withdraw their land at once – while the ethnic Russians predominantly resisted withdrawals and remained on large-scale farms.

In 1996-1997 Moldova began to acknowledge the fact that the land share system was not delivering the anticipated results, and in 1999 Ukraine did the same. In response, each country began to execute a vigorous state program to make every land share holder the owner of an individual land parcel. This required platting the parcels, fixing parcel boundaries through boundary surveys, assigning parcels to each land share holder, and registering these parcels in the ownership of their assignees. Moldova's program was implemented during 1998-2000, and Ukraine's during 2000-2006. RDI worked on both programs.

Box 7.2. How the land-share system was supposed to work

A typical Russian collective farm might have employed 250 people and cultivated 3,000 hectares of land. Another 25 people were teachers, medical personnel or other social service providers serving those living on the territory of the collective farm. In addition to these active workers, another 225 pensioners had worked on the farm or as social service providers. All three groups combined totaled 500 people. During the land reform process, 10% of the farm's 3,000 cultivated hectares would have been put into a reserve, with the remaining 2,700 hectares divided equally among those 500 people in the form of land shares. Thus, each land share gave a person the right, at least in theory, to claim 5.4 hectares in-kind out of the 2,700 hectares. Until the land share holder claimed the land, he or she could lease the share to an agricultural producer or transfer the share to relatives or third parties.

To withdraw the corresponding amount of land in kind, one or more individuals (usually a household had two land-share owners, husband and wife) typically needed to apply to the general meeting of enterprise members (technically, the members would be voting as joint owners of the land rather than as enterprise members since the enterprise held no legal interest in the land). In the present example, a husband and wife might be seeking to withdraw a specifically identified 10.8 (2 x 5.4) hectares. The general meeting was then to decide the location of the land the applicants would get, taking a vote on the matter. The allocated land would then be identified on the ground, the parcel boundaries surveyed, and a certificate of rights issued for the parcel.

National programs might also promote and facilitate a general process of enterprise-wide parcel identification and certification. The situation prevailing on that enterprise, and more broadly, might vary from one of widespread support for the process, with mutual accommodation and a general withdrawal by the members, to deep hostility by farm members and farm managers, accompanied by failure to act on an isolated application or by the offer of a remote and ill-suited parcel.

Clearly, these systematic enterprise-wide titling programs obviated the need for approval of individual applications to withdraw land in kind that might otherwise be made by one or a few members at a time. Unfortunately, the country with the largest number of land share holders, Russia, has not taken steps to enable land share owners to widely convert their shares into actual land parcels.

However, in Russia as also in Ukraine and Moldova, it was generally permitted to use a small portion of the land represented by the land share to physically enlarge the "private plots" that nearly all households on the enterprise have. Usually, this was done by choosing a field close to the residential areas where the existing private plots were already located adjoining the house plots, and expanding each private plot by allowing selection of a nearby, but not contiguous, small plot located on the field. There was usually widespread support for such modest extensions of the existing private plots with "field plots." While it is one thing to enlarge the family's private plot, it is quite another to take one's entire proportionate amount of land out of the collective fields and seek to gain the family's livelihood as individual family farmers.

Why the greater resistance to actual break-up in Russia and Ukraine

Compared with China or Vietnam, only a small minority of farmers in Russia or Ukraine have seized the opportunity, once it was given, to leave the former collective and start family farms. In some ways this reluctance to create small farms is even more striking in Ukraine, where nearly every member of a large enterprise now knows exactly where his or her land is, and no longer needs to petition a general meeting to work out and assent to the exact location of the land that is to be withdrawn. Why this striking contrast in behavior between former collective members in Russia and Ukraine, as compared to their counterparts in China and Vietnam?

Several broad contrasts appear to exist between Russia-Ukraine on the one hand, and China-Vietnam on the other that might have explanatory power:

- Collectivized farming had only existed in China and (northern) Vietnam since the mid-1950s, and both decided to permit countrywide family farming roughly 25 years later. Most families, and certainly all villagers in their forties or older, thus had a clear recollection of what it meant to operate a family farm. By contrast, collective farming had existed in Russia and Ukraine since the early 1930s,[138] and the option of leaving the collectives only arose in the early 1990s, a span of some 60 years. Very few were still alive who remembered what it was like to depend on family farming for their whole livelihood.
- A related matter was the need to market the large majority of the farm products produced by agriculture in Russia and Ukraine, each of which was more than four-fifths urban by the 1990s. This was comparatively far more important than the need to market production in China and Vietnam, which remained between three-fifths and two-thirds rural and agrarian. Most farm production in China

and Vietnam was needed and used for home consumption, not to feed the cities, and average distances to urban markets were also far lower in China and Vietnam.

- The agricultural population left behind in the Russian and Ukrainian countrysides was also an ageing one. Indeed, half of all land share holders in those settings were retirees, beyond their peak economically active years, and less likely to welcome a major change in lifestyle.

- Family farms in Russia and Ukraine (comprised of two to four land shares) would typically be 10 to 20 hectares in size, or more. Thus they clearly would require owning, or having assured access to, tractors and other capital equipment, in contrast to the labor-intensive family farms of one hectare (and often less) that families received when exiting the collectives in China and northern Vietnam. But capital equipment or credit to buy it was not readily available in Russia and Ukraine, thus greatly limiting the extent to which families could cultivate their land share.

- Further discouraging the idea of family farming and private land rights was the initial experience of family farming in the USSR after the 1917 Bolshevik revolution. At first, such farming was encouraged, but later Stalin waged a harsh campaign against even modestly successful small farmers (*kulaks*), murdering or deporting to Siberia millions of them in the late 1920s and the 1930s.[139] Many collective farm families retained memories of what had happened to grandparents who had relied on the Bolsheviks' seeming welcome to individual farming in the 1920s. (China had experienced a post-collectivization famine in 1958-1962, but it was the result of disorganization and the destruction of individual motivation, not part of a punishment deliberately visited by the state upon family farmers.)

- Politically, China's and Vietnam's top leadership were clearly calling the economic as well as political signals, and strongly supported the break-up of collectives and a virtually complete reliance on family farming, as well as broadly supporting the development of a market economy. By contrast, Russia especially (despite, or perhaps partly because of, its "big bang" rapid privatization of industry) was experiencing a tug-of-war between supposedly democratic legislative and executive branches, and the pro-privatization, pro-family-farming messages conveyed from Moscow down to the local level were decidedly mixed, with the executive "for" privatization but the legislature "against" throughout most of the period.[140] Neither Yeltsin nor his successor, Vladimir Putin, was apparently willing to expend a great deal of either political or financial capital on actually carrying through reforms in the agricultural sector.

Interestingly, in Moldova, where some of the above factors do not hold (and others hold to a lesser degree), by 2000 an estimated 27% of agricultural land was in individual production (small plots or family farms), versus only 13% in Russia and 18% in Ukraine.[141]

Land market activity

The problems initially associated with creating a market for private land rights in Russia – where, at the time the USSR dissolved in 1991, such rights and such a market had not existed for almost 75 years (since 1917) – are illustrated by the anecdote recounted in Box 7.3. This anecdote underscores the problems of starting up a rural land market "from scratch" where no legal framework or even customary practice for such a market has existed for an extended period of time.

Some of those problems have persisted to the present day. Except for the small plots – household plots on the successors to collectives, and dacha plots around urban areas, usually including a house – it appears that virtually no sales of rural land plots or of land shares had been occurring in Russia as recently as 2005,[142] and in Ukraine such sales have languished due to a legislative moratorium. Considerable leasing of rights to agricultural lands, however, has been occurring. The following specific developments with respect to rural land markets in this group of countries are worth noting:

Land sales in Moldova. Extending back at least to 2002 there has been a developing market in sales of smallholder land plots, with family farmers well represented among the buyers. Field research in 2008 found a price range of roughly US$500 to US$1600 per hectare.[143]

Reverse tenancy in Ukraine, with and without titling. As a prominent form of "reverse tenancy" – with small owners leasing to large lessees – land rights have for a number of years been leased out by the rightholders chiefly to the successor organizations of the former collectives. But there have been at least four positive changes with the introduction of individually demarcated and titled land plots in Ukraine, changes reflected in an 800-household survey: (1) the same amount of land that was formerly represented by an undivided and undemarcated land share now commands a payment from the lessee that averages 32% more per hectare; (2) the lessee of the demarcated parcel is substantially more likely (85% versus 66%) to make the full rental payments agreed to in the lease contract; (3) the lessee of the demarcated parcel is also substantially more likely (84% versus 61%) to make the rental payments on time; and (4) a much higher proportion of land thus individually demarcated and titled (18% versus 2%) is self-cultivated by the owner – usually by adding some of it to the owner's private plot – than holds true for the land still formally held in common.[144]

Box 7.3. An anecdote from the early days of reform

Very early in the reform process, in 1991, two RDI lawyers met with a group of generally progressive Russian officials and academics convened by the All Union Academy of Agricultural Sciences with the request that we discuss the experience of private ownership of agricultural land in the United States, including the question of purchase and sale. After an extensive presentation by RDI lawyers, a round of questions began. One prominent Russian participant raised his hand vigorously near the back of the room and was recognized by the moderator. His question: "But who decides the price?"

Nearly three-quarters of a century of communism and central planning had clearly taken its toll. To those from a developed market economy, the question may seem absurd, but it is not as absurd as it might seem: the parties to a land sale in a country such as the United States are drawing upon a long history of past transactions and prices paid. What could parties participating in such a transaction in the FSU countries draw upon if a land market were to be introduced (as would be the case for Russia and most others) for the first time since 1917?

Reverse tenancy in Ukraine and Russia – the appearance of large agri-business. Beginning around 2000, in both Ukraine and Russia, a new kind of large tenant has appeared, in the form of large private agri-business concerns, sometimes funded with foreign capital. One recent account projected large future investments in Ukraine's agriculture, especially if the existing moratorium on sale of agricultural land is allowed to expire in 2009; but even now, the same account reports that investors have been leasing land in the hope that they can later buy and resell the land, and that lease prices doubled in 2007 and were predicted to double again in 2008.[145]

Growing land sales in Russia. In Russia, where sales of agricultural land have been permitted since 2002, but especially developing since 2006, it appears that large agri-business investors had driven the average price of farmland up from US$570 per hectare in 2006 to US $1000 as of mid-2008, often consolidating former collective farms into very large "factory farms." By one account, as much as 14% of Russia's agricultural land has now gone through such an acquisition-and-consolidation process.[146] But whether the individuals who hold land rights – and whose land shares have not been individually demarcated and

titled in Russia, as most such rights have been in Ukraine and Moldova – have a sufficient perception of the reality and value of their private
ownership rights, or whether much or most of the land price is being
directed to the entity that had succeeded the collective or its individual
managers (compare the discussion of "takings" for non-agricultural
purposes in China, above) is a crucial question. So far as we are aware,
no field research has yet been done on this question – and, troublingly,
the same account noted above reports that each member (land share
owner) of an enterprise whose land was acquired three years ago was
offered about US$100 per hectare for land now worth US$1100 per
hectare.[147]

As the land markets described above grow – both for longer-term
leases and sales – there will be an urgent need to "level the playing
field" between the small transferor and the large transferee. Various aspects of how to overcome land-market inadequacies or "imperfections"
have been discussed earlier in this chapter and are discussed in the
two following chapters. They include publicity for farmers' land rights
as they stand under the law, legal aid (certainly agri-business land
buyers or land lessees who are increasingly on the other side of the
transaction have legal representation), further formalization of rights
(perhaps by applying the Ukraine and Moldova demarcation and titling
approaches in Russia – but this will have to be done before the land is
transferred, not after), reduced transaction costs (thus enlarging the
pool of potential transferees), and monitoring of what is actually happening on the ground including publicity for transaction prices and
terms.

Notes

1   Calculated based on rural net income per person (4,140 RMB) and urban net income
    (13,786 RMB) per capita. See State Statistics Bureau, 2007 *Statistic Bulletin of National
    Economy and Social Development*.
2   For an account of RDI's early China fieldwork up to the mid-1990s, see R. Proster-
    man, T. Hanstad & L. Ping, *Can China Feed Itself?*, SCIENTIFIC AMERICAN 90 (Nov.
    1996).
3   A substantial majority of those Chinese agricultural families who owned little or no
    land were tenant farmers rather than landless laborers. See E. Moise, LAND REFORM
    IN CHINA AND NORTH VIETNAM 29-33 (University of North Carolina Press 1983); W.
    Hinton, FANSHEN: A DOCUMENTARY OF REVOLUTION IN A CHINESE VILLAGE 26-27 (Uni-
    versity of California Press 1997).
4   Mao Tse-Tung, *Jinggangshan Land Law (adopted in December 1928 on the Jinggang-
    shan)*, in S.R. Schram & N.J. Hodes, eds., MAO'S ROAD TO POWER: REVOLUTIONARY
    WRITINGS 1912-1949, VOL. 3, at 128 (M.E. Sharpe 1995).
5   Land Law of the Chinese Soviet Republic, art. 1 (1931).

6   Id. art. 6. The lawmakers' intention to grant to peasants full ownership is more visible when comparing the language of land allocation in Article 6 and the language in Article 8 concerning allocation of the confiscated farming tools and draft animals. Article 8 specified that the confiscated tools and draft animals should be "allocated to poor and middle peasants for use in cultivating land," and the users should pay a user fee.
7   Id. art. 12.
8   Platform of Chinese Land Law, art. 1 (1947).
9   Id. art. 6. The exceptions were large forests, irrigation projects, large mining sites, large and contiguous tracts of grassland and wasteland, and lakes. Id. art. 9, sec. B.
10 Id. art. 6
11 Id. art. 11.
12 Id. Local communist governments promulgated specific rules for implementing the Platform. For example, the Northeast Administrative Commission adopted an implementing rule for the Northeast Liberated Region requiring that a region-wide uniform land ownership certificate be designed by the Commission and issued to all landowners by governments at county level. Supplemental Measures for Implementing the Land Law Platform in the Northeast Liberated Region, art. 11. In its implementing rule, the Shanxi-Hebei-Shandong-Henan Border Region Government made distinction between arable land and the land used for fish farming, fruit production, and bamboo growing and let peasants decide whether to distribute these categories of non-arable land for private ownership. Shanxi-Hebei-Shandong-Henan Border Government Supplemental Rules on Implementing the Land Law Platform, art 7.
13 Land Reform Law of the People's Republic of China (1950), sec. 1, art. 1.
14 Several categories of land are listed as state owned under the Land Reform Law, which are: large tracts of forestland, the land on which large irrigation facilities are erected, large tracts of wasteland, large tracts of salt-producing land, mines, rivers, lakes and harbors. The large and contiguous tracts of land for growing bamboo, fruits, tea and mulberries which were previously owned by landlords were also converted to state-owned land. See id. sec. 4, arts. 18 & 19.
15 Id. sec. 3, art. 10.
16 Id. sec. 5, art. 30. Unlike the Platform, which allows land lease only under "certain circumstances," the Land Reform Law does not contain such a restriction.
17 Id.
18 Land Reform Law of the People's Republic of China (1950), sec. 6, art. 39. A region was composed of several provinces. Regional people's government was abolished in the mid-1960s when the Cultural Revolution began.
19 Measures of the Mid Southern Military and Administrative Committee on Implementing the Land Reform Law, art. 9(vii) and 9(ix). The landowners who were previously landlords but currently did not engage in agricultural production were prohibited from possessing such rights to transfer for "a certain period" after the land allocation. Id. art. 9(ix).
20 Id. art. 9(viii).
21 Id. art. 9(xi).
22 Regulation of Suburban Land Reform (1950), art. 9.
23 Id. art. 17.
24 Land Reform Law of the People's Republic of China (1950), sec. 4, art. 27.
25 China Institute of Reform & Development, HISTORY OF CHANGES AND INNOVATIONS OF CHINA'S RURAL LAND SYSTEM 31-32 (Nanhai Publishing 1999). See J. Bruce & P. Harrell, *Land Reform in the People's Republic of China 1978-1988*, LTC Research Paper No. 100, at 3 (Land Tenure Center 1989); Y. Wu & H. Yang, *Productivity and Growth*

in China: A Review, in K. Kalirijan & Y. Wu, eds., PRODUCTIVITY AND GROWTH IN CHI-
NESE AGRICULTURE 30 (MacMillan 1999).

26 China Institute of Reform & Development, supra note 25, at 32; Z. Gensheng, RURAL
REFORM IN CHINA 3-4 (Shenzen: Haitian Publishing House 2001)

27 Standing Committee of the National People's Congress, *Decision on the Charter of Rural Production Cooperatives*, PEOPLE'S DAILY (Mar. 18, 1956).

28 Article 1 of the Charter of Rural Production Cooperatives states in part, "Collectives
shall uniformly use its members' land, draft animals and agricultural production
tools, and gradually realize the goal of public ownership of these production means."
See also Decision of the Sixth Plenary Session (expanded) of the Seventh Central
Committee of CPC on Agricultural Cooperation, PEOPLE'S DAILY (Oct. 11, 1955). The
decision defined agricultural cooperatives as a form of semi-socialist organization in
the transition to full public ownership of rural land.

29 Id. art. 17.

30 Id.

31 Id. art. 18.

32 Charter of Advanced Agricultural Production Cooperatives (1956), art. 13.

33 Id. art. 16.

34 Fifteen to thirty million incremental deaths occurred, as agricultural production
plummeted. See S. Weigelin-Schwiedrizik, *Trauma and Memory: The Case of the Great
Famine in the People's Republic of China (1959-1961)*, 1(1) Historiography East & West
41-43, 61 (2003); X. Peng, *Demographic Consequences of the Great Leap Forward in China's Provinces*, 13(4) POPULATION & DEVELOPMENT REVIEW 658 (1987).

35 C.A. Carter & F. Zhong, CHINA'S GRAIN PRODUCTION AND TRADES: AN ECONOMIC
STUDY 5 & table 1.2 (Westview 1988); see also N. Lardy, *Agricultural Reforms in China*,
39(2) JOURNAL OF INTERNATIONAL AFFAIRS 91 (1986).

36 China State Statistics Bureau, Analytical Report on 50 Years of New China: Part Sixteen, available at http://www.stats.gov.cn/tjfx/ztfx/xzgwsnx1fxbg/t20020605_21433.
htm.

37 Wu Xiang, RECORDS OF CHINA'S RURAL REFORMS [ZHONGGUO NONGCUN GAIGE SHILU]
139-206 (Hangzhou 2001).

38 Id. at 172; see also H. Qinghe, REVIEW AND CURRENT ISSUES ON THE RURAL LAND POL-
ICY IN CHINA in *Transition of China's Rural Land System: Papers from International
Symposium on Rural Land Issues in China* 7-8 (University of Wisconsin Land tenure
Center 1995).

39 State Bureau of Statistics, National Economic & Social Development Bulletin (1980)
and (1984).

40 State Bureau of Statistics, Compilation of 50-Year Statistical Information of New China (1999).

41 Xinhua News Agency, Economic Statistical Data: Citizen Consumption Level and Index, available at http://news.xinhuanet.com/ziliao/2003-01/25/content_707561.htm.

42 See J. Sachs, THE END OF POVERTY 154-155 (Penguin Press 2005); S. Chen & M. Ravallion, *How Have the World's Poorest Fared Since the Early 1980s?*, World Bank Policy
Research Working Paper No. 3341, at 17, 30 (June 2004).

43 See generally note 1 in Chapter 1. The current 16% estimate is found in S. Chen &
M. Ravallion, *The Developing World is Poorer than We Thought But No Less Successful
in the Fight Against Poverty*, World Bank Policy Research Working Paper No. 4703, at
31, table 6(a) (Aug. 2008) (15.9% living below $1.25 a day).

44 D. Runsheng, Z. NONG CUN ZHI DU BIAN QIAN [TRANSFORMATION OF CHINA'S RURAL
SYSTEM] 38 (Sichuan People's Publishing 2003).

45 Land readjustment as household and village population numbers change is designed
to ensure absolute equality of per capita (or sometimes per worker) landholdings in a

given community. Not all land readjustments are of the same magnitude. "Big" or comprehensive readjustments involve an overall change in the landholdings of all farm households in the village. In a big readjustment, all farmland in the village is given back to the collective entity and reallocated among village households so that each household receives entirely new land. A "small" or partial readjustment consists of adding to or taking from a household's existing landholdings when that household's size changes. Under small readjustments, households that neither add nor lose members will continue to farm the same landholding. Such readjustment for population change is not found in any of the world's highly developed agricultures, but can be found in a few customary tenure regimes in Africa. See J. Ensminger, *Changing Property Rights: Reconciling Formal and Informal Rights to Land*, in J. Drobak & J. Nye, eds., FRONTIERS OF THE NEW INSTITUTIONAL ECONOMICS 165-196 (Academic Press 1997). There are also historical examples in a few other societies, including pre-communist Russia, where communal tenure took two forms, hereditary (passing by inheritance) and repartitional, where land was subject to periodic reallocation. S. Williams, LIBERAL REFORM IN AN ILLIBERAL REGIME: THE CREATION OF PRIVATE PROPERTY IN RUSSIA, 1906-1915, at 39-49 (Hoover Institute 2006); *Formal and Informal Rights to Land*, in Drobak & Nye, supra, at 165-196. There are also historical examples in a few other societies; it appears to be contemplated, though with a far longer duration of 49 years and "readjustment" in the fiftieth, in the Old Testament reference to reallocation in the "year of the Jubilee" (Leviticus 25:23) (it is unclear, however, whether this reallocation was ever actually practiced).

46 As to assurance of farmers' land rights (see the discussion of "duration, breadth, and assurance" in Chapter 1), the impact was qualified in the sense that farmers were not assured possession of *this* piece of land for the future, but of *some* piece of land, though it might be a different and lesser piece (or pieces), dependent on population changes at the village and household level. That is, unlike a tenant farmer evicted by a landlord, an HRS farmer "readjusted" by the local cadres was intended to end up with *some* land, which would generally represent the proportion of village arable land that his household's population bore to the total population of the village.

47 Central Committee of CPC, *Circular of the Central Committee of CPC on rural work in 1984*, Sec. 3 (the third No. 1 document) (Jan. 1, 1984), in Gensheng, supra note 26, at 469-470.

48 J. Kung, *Equal Entitlement versus Tenure Security under a Regime of Collective Property Rights: Peasants' Preferences for Institutions in Post-reform Chinese Agriculture*, (21)1 JOURNAL OF COMPARATIVE ECONOMICS 88-96 (1995). See also R. Prosterman & T. Hanstad, *Land Reform in China: A Fieldwork-Based Appraisal*, Rural Development Institute Monographs on Foreign Aid and Development No. 12, at 36-41 (Rural Development Institute 1993).

49 See the discussion of the land-to-the-tiller program in South Vietnam and its sequels in Chapter 2. See generally R. Prosterman & T. Hanstad, *Agrarian Reform in Vietnam and the 1993 Land Law*, RDI Monographs on Foreign Aid and Development No. 14 (Rural Development Institute 1994).

50 The two-field system breaks with the typical pattern of distributing all farmland on a per capita basis. Instead, cultivated land is divided into two categories: "consumption land" and "responsibility land." Consumption land is divided in each village on a per capita basis to meet each household's basic needs. The remaining land is contracted to farm households as responsibility land through a variety of methods which in many cases results in a non-egalitarian land distribution. Unlike consumption land, on which farmers are only responsible for collective contributions, an additional contracting fee is typically charged for responsibility land. For an analysis of the two-field system and its implementation in China, see R. Prosterman, T. Hanstad & L. Ping,

Land Reform in China: The Two-Field System in Pingdu, Rural Development Institute Reports on Foreign Aid and Development No. 86, at 1-23 (Rural Development Institute 1994).

51 Scale Farming involves the consolidation of small, labor-intensive farms into larger, mechanized farms. Scale Farming can be accomplished through a variety of approaches, but typically involves the contracting of large areas of arable land to a few farmers or the operation of large-scale farms by the collective landowner. Recollectivization of farmland was the ultimate goal of at least some experiments with Scale Farming in the early 1990s. R. Prosterman, et al., *Large-Scale Farming in China: An Appropriate Policy?,* 28(1) JOURNAL OF CONTEMPORARY ASIA 74 (1998).

52 Compulsory re-contracting means that collective cadres, usually in cooperation with township officials, take farmers' land back and re-contract it out to non-villagers or corporations, including foreign corporations, without consulting farmers and with no or little compensation to the farmers whose land is affected. The motivation behind re-contracting is rent seeking by collective cadres, who cannot legally impose contracting fees on the land allocated among village households, but can impose such fees on the third party contractor through the process of re-contracting.

53 Central Committee of CPC and the State Council's Policy Measures on the Current Agricultural and Rural Development, Nov. 5, 1993 (Document No. 11 of 1993). See also the more general *Decision of the CCP Central Committee on Some Issues Concerning the Establishment of a Socialist Market Economic Structure,* adopted by the 14th Central Committee of the CCP at its third plenary session on 14th November 1993, sec. VI, art. 31 available at LEXIS [database on-line], News Library, BBCSWB File (Nov. 18, 1993).

54 Document No. 11, sec. 1.

55 Notice Concerning Further Stabilizing and Protecting the Rural Land Contracting Relationship (1997) No. 16, issued by the Central Committee on August 27, 1997 [hereinafter Document No. 16].

56 See R. Burgess, *Land and Welfare: Theory and Evidence from China,* London School of Economics Working Paper 1-2, 7 (2001).

57 Empirical studies show that – at the country level – broad-based access to land is associated with higher rates of economic growth. See K. Deininger & P. Olinto, *Asset Distribution, Inequality, and Growth* 3-4, 9 (World Bank 2000).

58 Law of Land Management (promulgated at the 4th Meeting of the Standing Committee of the Ninth National People's Congress on August 29, 1998, effective Jan. 1, 1999), *translated in* LEXIS (last visited Oct. 6, 2006) (P.R.C.).

59 In addition to Article 14, Article 2 relates, in part, to transfer of farmers' land use rights.

60 Law of the People's Republic of China on the Contracting of Rural Land (promulgated by the Standing Committee of the Ninth National People's Congress; Aug. 29, 2002, effective Mar. 1, 2003), *translated in* LEXIS (P.R.C.).

61 Article 2 of the 1998 Law of Land Management of the People's Republic of China had simply repeated the general principle that "land use rights may be transferred in accordance with the law."

62 For example, the RLCL Article 21 requires that transactions of rural land rights, except leases for one year or less, be evidenced with a "signed contract" and that such transaction contracts should contain such elements as "the name and address of each of the parties; name, location, area and quality class of the land to be transferred; the transfer period and the starting and ending dates of the transfer contract, . . . transfer fees and the payment methods."

63 RDI was informed in recent discussions with Chinese officials that the People's Court will refuse to consider any farmer's complaint regarding the non-payment of

compensation in takings of land for non-agricultural purposes if the farmer cannot produce one of these documents showing that the farmer holds rights to the land in question.

64 See Land Management Law of the People's Republic of China, Chapter 2, art. 16 (1998); Administrative Review Law of the People's Republic of China (1999), art. 30.

65 People's Republic of China, Property [Real Rights] Law of the People's Republic of China (2007), ch. III.

66 Id. ch. XI, art. 126.

67 Id. ch. XI, art. 130.

68 Constitution of the People's Republic of China, art. 10.

69 1998 Land Management Law, art. 10.

70 Property Law, art. 60(i).

71 Property Law, art. 59.

72 Property Law, art. 63.

73 See supra note 13 and accompanying text.

74 See supra note 14 and accompanying text.

75 W. Colby, F. Crook & Shwu-Eng H. Webb, AGRICULTURAL STATISTICS OF THE PEOPLE'S REPUBLIC OF CHINA, 1949-1990, at 14, 40 (1992).

76 Wu & Yang, supra note 25, at 37, citing J. McMillan, J. Whalley & L. Zhu, *The Impact of China's Economic Reforms on Agricultural Productivity Growth*, 97(4) JOURNAL OF POLITICAL ECONOMY 781-782 (1989).

77 See K. Zhu, R. Prosterman, J. Ye, P. Li, J. Riedinger & Y. Ouyang, *The Rural Land Question in China: Analysis and Recommendations Based on a Seventeen-Province Survey*, 38(4) NEW YORK UNIVERSITY JOURNAL OF INTERNATIONAL LAW & POLITICS 761, 807-822 (2006). The sample – 1,962 households in 1,776 villages – is sufficient to give results that should be descriptive of the situation in the 17 provinces as a whole to an accuracy of +/- 2.2% for household-level questions and +/- 2.3% for village-level questions (e.g., "how many persons are in your household" versus "has your village carried out a post-second-round-of-contracting readjustment"). Id. at 768. Approximately 83% of China's agricultural households are present in the 17 provinces surveyed. Id. at 767.

78 Id. at 797-798. The six named types of investments which were selected to be the subject of survey questions are ones virtually never made except by individual farm households.

79 Id. at 811-814. Moreover, when either a contract or certificate has been received in a form that closely conforms with the law (including formalities, start and end dates, and land description via map or sketch), the investment rate is still higher than for recipients of documents that do not comply, reaching 28.8% in the case of compliant contracts. Id. at 815. The additional factor of exposure to publicity for land rights from multiple sources is correlated with further increases in investments. For example, for those with a certificate issued and having heard of the RLCL through multiple channels, 29.5% of them invested in or after 1998, a 4.21 times (321%) increase over their pre-1998 investments. Id. at 819.

80 Id. at 817, n.89. Note too that contracts are supposed to be signed by both the farmer and by local cadres. The cadres represent the chief potential threat to tenure security via illegal land readjustments or interception of already-low compensation paid by the state for land takings. Such contracts may thus provide somewhat more reassurance than certificates signed or sealed at higher levels, even where both contracts and certificates contain the same information. This also seems consistent with the findings as to the likelihood of engaging in a two-year or longer compensated transfer, versus documentation possessed, discussed below.

81 Id. at 817-818; R. Prosterman & B. Schwarzwalder, *From Death to Life: Giving Value to China's Rural Land*, 8 CHINA ECONOMIC QUARTERLY 19 (2004); T. Hanstad & P. Li,

Land Reform in the People's Republic of China: Auctioning Rights to Wasteland, 19 LOYO-LA OF L.A. INTERNATIONAL & COMPARATIVE LAW JOURNAL 545 (1997) (including discussion of farmers' investment behavior on non-readjustable "wasteland" covered by written long-term contracts, versus their investment behavior on arable land, the latter at that time readjustable and not documented).

82 Zhu, et al., supra note 77 at 822-823.

83 Id. at 794.

84 As to readjustments carried out in the wake of land takings for non-agricultural purposes, it is clear from the existing standards of the Land Management Law (see discussion the subsection on land takings below), however inadequate they may be, that readjustment of landholdings is not contemplated as a potential mode of compensation in the case of takings. Again, however, it would be desirable to state this explicitly in normative measures of national application.

85 Constitution of the People's Republic of China, ch. 1, art. 10 (adopted Dec. 1982); People's Republic of China, 1998 Land Management Law, ch. 1, art. 2.

86 Under Chinese takings law, compensation for arable land expropriations includes: (1) compensation for the loss of land, which is limited to 6-10 times the average annual yield of the land over the three years prior to the expropriation; (2) compensation for young crops (usually the value of the land's agricultural output for one year) and fixtures; and (3) a resettlement subsidy which is valued at 4-6 times such average annual output. See 1998 Land Management Law, art. 47. However, compensation for the loss of land, the biggest component of this seemingly unfair compensation package, has been designated, at least until recently, to go to the collective landowner for "development of collective economy" under Chinese takings law. See Implementing Regulations of the 1998 Land Management Law, art. 26.

87 For example, in Fuyang Municipality of Anhui Province, the published market price in 2003 was 160,000 yuan to 300,000 yuan per mu, but RDI's findings in the same area indicated that the highest compensation paid to farmers in the same area was 23,000 yuan per mu. See *Introduction of Granting Use Rights to State Owned Land in Anhui Province*, ZHONGGUO GUOTU ZIYUAN BAO [CHINA LAND & RESOURCES NEWS] (Aug. 12, 2003). See also R. Prosterman, et al., *Reform on the Land Takings System: Fieldwork Findings and Recommendations for Further Reform*, China Rural Survey, No. 6 (2004)

88 Prosterman, et al., supra note 87.

89 Zhu, et al., supra note 77.

90 Id. at 779.

91 Id. at 781.

92 Id. at 782.

93 Prosterman, et al., supra note 87.

94 Of the farmers who went to People's Court, three left with compensation unchanged, and two left with a satisfactory increase in compensation.

95 See, e.g., J. Yardley, *Farmers Being Moved Aside by China's Real Estate Boom*, NEW YORK TIMES (Dec. 8, 2004); J. Kahn, *China Crushes Peasant Protest, Turning 3 Friends into Enemies*, NEW YORK TIMES (Oct. 13, 2004); H. French, *Protesters Say Police in China Killed Up to 20*, NEW YORK TIMES (Dec. 1, 2005).

96 However, for a discussion of defects that have appeared in other Chinese "stock-for-land" programs, see R. Prosterman & D. Bledsoe, *The Joint Stock Share System in China's Nanhai County*, Rural Development Institute Reports on Foreign Aid and Development No. 103, at 17-22 (RDI 2000). The Beijing municipal government recently reversed the usual maximum standard approach by adopting a "minimum protection standard" and requiring the expropriating agency to negotiate with the collective on the basis of "no less than the minimum protection standard." Beijing Municipality

Regulations on Compensation and Resettlement for Land Expropriations (2004), art. 9 and art. 10. In Guangdong Province, the new rules on compensation for land expropriation for commercial purposes go one step further. The rules are completely silent on the agricultural yield method and multiplier standard as provided under the 1998 Land Management Law; instead, the rules require that conversion for non-agricultural and non-public purposes be conducted in the open market at a price reached through negotiation between the collective and the end user or through auction, bidding and public listing. The Guangdong Provincial Measures on Management of Transactions of Use Rights to Collectively Owned Construction Land (2005), art. 15. It appears at least in Guangdong, the standard of fair market value begins to emerge. However, the Guangdong rules apply to commercial non-agricultural use of farmland only; government expropriation of land for authentic public interests is expected to be governed by the 1998 Land Management Law.

97 People's Republic of China, Property [Real Rights] Law of the People's Republic of China (2007), art. 42.

98 Id.

99 Shanxi provincial Measures on Allocation of Land Compensation for Expropriation of Collectively Owned Land (2005), art. 13. While the requirement that such compensation go directly to the farmers is a clear improvement over the vague "primarily used for" language of Document No. 28, the exact mechanism of such payment remains of vital importance: payment into an escrow account held by a third party such as a bank would, for example, be far better than payment to local officials with instructions to pay over a set proportion to the land-losing farmers.

100 Property Law, supra note 65, art. 132.

101 Ministry of Land and Resources, Regulations on Land Resources Hearings (2004).

102 Zhu, et al., supra note 77, at 799.

103 Guarantee Law of the People's Republic of China, art. 37 (1995). There is an exception for wasteland, which, when contracted to farmers, falls under a regime separate from that for arable land.

104 The repetition refers to the answer supposedly given by a celebrated real-estate investor when an aspiring young entrepreneur asked him what were the three most important things to look for when buying urban real estate. The answer: "Location, location, location."

105 As had been found in two previous rounds of the 17-province survey in mid-1999 and mid-2001. See R. Prosterman, B. Schwarzwalder & Y. Jianping, *Implementation of 30-Year Land Use Rights for Farmers Under China's 1998 Land Management Law: An Analysis and Recommendation Based on a 17-Province Survey*, 9(3) PACIFIC RIM LAW & POLICY JOURNAL 512 (2000); B. Schwarzwalder, R. Prosterman, Y. Jianping, J. Riedinger & L. Ping, *An Update on China's Rural Land tenure Reforms: Analysis and Recommendation Based on a Seventeen Province Survey*, 16(1) COLUMBIA JOURNAL OF ASIAN LAW 223 (2002).

106 A.W. Seidman, R.B. Seidman & J. Payne, LEGISLATIVE DRAFTING FOR MARKET REFORM: SOME LESSONS FROM CHINA (St. Martin's Press 1997).

107 Development Research Center and the Rural Development Institute, *The Rural Land Contracting Law: Strengthening Implementation and Supporting Institutions*, Project Final Report (2006); see also Zhu, et al., supra note 77, at 824-825.

108 The villages and households where the interviews were held had been randomly selected by RDI. Id.

109 The establishment of rural legal aid centers falls within existing Chinese policies. For example, in June 1997, a notice issued jointly by the Ministry of Agriculture and the Ministry of Justice called for judicial departments at various levels to provide legal

aid to farmers. *Notice on Legal Aid to the Poor in China's Rural Areas*, PEOPLE'S DAILY (June 23, 1997)

110 See Zhu, et al., supra note 77, at 118, citing I. Ng, *Compulsory Purchase and Compensation in Hong Kong: A Study of the Role of the Land Development Corporation in Urban Renewal*, 20(2) PROPERTY MANAGEMENT 167-181 (2002); J. Crawford & B. Opeskin, AUSTRALIAN COURTS OF LAW 254-257 (Oxford University Press 1982).

111 A cautionary tale on lodging formal "ownership" in – or where it is exercisable by – individuals other than the farmer, even where the farmer has supposedly been given all or nearly all the beneficial enjoyment of the land, can be found in the reversal of Egypt's radical and longstanding regime of landlord-tenant regulation, described in Chapter 2. The two alternatives proposed in the text – full private ownership for the farmers, or nationalization coupled with perpetual use rights – would definitively end the cadres' ability to act, purportedly, on behalf of the collective as "owner" of the land.

112 Press conference transcripts (Mar. 14, 2005 and Mar. 14, 2006), available at http://news.sina.com., cn/c/2005-03-14/10106077756.shtml and http://news.sohu.com/20060314/n242284498_3.shtml.

113 Portions of the following have been adapted from R. Prosterman, *If Chinese Farmers Were to be Given Full Private Ownership of their Land, What Measures Might Contribute to this Being Most Confidently and Successfully Done?*, paper for discussion at Meeting of China Task Force on Institutional Design for China's Evolving Market Economy, University of Manchester, England, June 25-26, 2008.

114 See, e.g., J. Bajoria, CHINA'S LAND REFORM CHALLENGE (Council on Foreign Relations, March 10, 2008); J. Anderlini, *Losing the Countryside, A restive peasantry calls on Beijing for land rights*, FINANCIAL TIMES, Feb. 20, 2008, at 7; *This land is my land*, THE ECONOMIST, Feb. 14, 2008.

115 FINANCIAL TIMES, supra note 114. Ownership of rural arable land in China is collective, as discussed above.

116 Based on the common formula for net present value (where C*t* is net cashflow during time *t*, r is the discount rate, and *t* is the time of cashflow), the present value of 30-year rights, after discounting future streams of income at any likely range of discount rates, should equal somewhere between 75% and 95% of the value of full private ownership.

117 See Government of Hong Kong, *Sino-British Joint Declaration: Exploratory Notes on Annex-II-III* (Nov. 7, 1996), available at http://www.hkbu.edu.hk/~pchksar?JK?jd-full8htm; Lands Department, Government of Hong Kong SAR (28 Nov. 2005), available at http://www.lansd.gov.hk/en/service/landpolicy.htm.

118 See Israel Land Administration, *General Information* (March 11, 2007), available at http://www.mmi.gov.il/Envelope/indexeng.asp?page=/static/eng/f_gen.

119 See ACT Planning & Land Authority, *Leasehold–Lease availability, length and selling*, available at http://www.actpla.act.gov.au/topics/property_purchases/leases_licenses.

120 The urban rights are now renewable at the end of their term. Property Law, art. 149.

121 For a broad comparative discussion that encompasses these issues with special reference to approaches taken by the transitional systems in the former Soviet Union and Eastern Europe, see R. Prosterman & T. Hanstad, eds., *Legal Impediments to Rural Land Relations in Eastern Europe and Central Asia: A Comparative Perspective*, World Bank Technical Paper No. 436, at chs. 2 & 7 (World Bank 1999).

122 Under the RLCL, "assignment" of the full 30-year term does require approval by the collective; but this requirement is largely meaningless since a "lease" for 29 years and 364 days (including one with a lump-sum payment up front for the entire term) does not require any approval.

123 See generally the discussion of this issue in Chapter 3.

124 Also, more briefly in Kazakhstan, Georgia and Tajikistan. See generally R. Prosterman & T. Hanstad, eds., supra note 121; Z. Lerman, C. Csaki & G. Feder, AGRICUL-
TURE IN TRANSITION: LAND POLICIES AND EVOLVING FARM STRUCTURES IN POST-SOVIET
COUNTRIES (Lexington Books 2004).
125 See V. Uzun, *Large and Small Business in Russian Agriculture: Adaptation to Market* 47
(1) COMPARATIVE ECONOMIC STUDIES 92, fig. 2 (2005) (note that the only individual
farming in 1990 was on the small plots).
126 Id. at 89.
127 Id. at 89 & 98, table 1. In 2001, household plots accounted for 581 billion of the
1029 billion rubles of gross agricultural output, or 56.5%. The table also shows gross
value of agricultural output per hectare on the household plots as 7.7 times as great
as on the large "corporate" farms – that is, the successors to the collectives. The small
plots are, however, labor intensive: they account for 75% of all agricultural employment, while the corporate farms with their mechanization produce 2.3 times as
much gross value of agricultural output per worker.
128 See T.G. Rawski, ECONOMIC GROWTH AND EMPLOYMENT IN CHINA 78 (Oxford University Press 1979); J.S. Prybla, THE CHINESE ECONOMY: PROBLEMS AND POLICIES 57-58
(University of South Carolina Press 1978).
129 None in the case of Ukraine, where a moratorium on all sales of agricultural land –
whether to domestic buyers or foreigners – is set to expire in January 2009 after several extensions. See Land Code of Ukraine, Transitional Provisions sec. 15 (as
amended); USDA *Foreign Agriculture Service, Commodity Intelligence Report: Ukraine
Grain Production Prospects for 2008/09*, at 5 (May 15, 2008).
130 Lerman, et al., supra note 124, at 58.
131 Id. Looking at the focus countries, farms in Moldova averaged 1,718 hectares of arable
land, Russian farms averaged 4,756 hectares, Ukrainian farms averaged 3,199 hectares, and Kyrgyz farms averaged 2,613 hectares.
132 Ranches with grazing land for cattle and sheep, as in Australia or the Western United
States, are, of course, a very different and typically large-scale form of agricultural enterprise. These are not common in most of the FSU.
133 Uzun, supra note 125.
134 Belarus, Kazakhstan, Tajikistan, Turkmenistan and Uzbekistan have not addressed
the problems of the collective farm system in any serious manner.
135 Lithuania, for example, had only completed the process of identifying and formally titling the owners of 37% of its agricultural land by 1997-1998. See Lerman, et al.,
supra note 124, at 90, table 3.13.
136 Lerman, et al., supra note 124, at 70, 93-95.
137 If it was a transaction involving the collective or a successor enterprise, separate demarcation was not likely to be a necessity; but if it was a transfer to, say, a nearby private farmer (where these existed), a physical withdrawal and demarcation of that
quantity of land would be needed.
138 It is true that nearly all collective farm families in Russia and Ukraine had a separate
private plot, but these did not supply the family's whole livelihood.
139 See generally R. Conquest, THE HARVEST OF SORROWS: SOVIET COLLECTIVIZATION AND
THE TERROR-FAMINE (Oxford 1986).
140 It will be recalled that at one point President Yeltsin ousted the Duma, the elected
legislature – elements of which were attempting a coup – with a tank bombardment
of their legislative building. There were entire political parties within the Duma (notably the Agrarian Party) whose chief *raison d'etre* was the preservation of collective
farming. But even within the executive entourage, there were those who opposed
adoption of a Land Code that would permit the purchase and sale of farmland, as
well as opposing easy exit with one's individual land share. See C. Freeland, *New de-*

cree threatens Russian farm reform, Financial Times, Feb. 21, 1995; R. Prosterman, *Looming Land Code*, THE MOSCOW TIMES, Aug. 12, 1998). In the absence of action by the Duma, several favorable presidential decrees were issued by Yeltsin in the mid-1990s, notably Presidential Decree No. 1767, *On the Regulation of Land Relations and the Development of Agrarian Reform in Russia* (Oct. 27, 1993) (allowing the full range of land transactions for agricultural land plots and land shares), but without either implementing regulations or a corresponding enactment by the Duma, these decrees had little influence. Not until the adoption of a generally favorable Land Code by the Duma under President Putin in 2002, followed by a specific law on Agricultural Land Turnover later that same year (amended in 2003 and 2005), was the full legal framework for transactions in agricultural land shares in place.

141 See Lerman, et al., supra note 124, at 113, table 4.2. As compared to Russia and Ukraine, Moldova spent less time collectivized, markets are generally closer to farms, the ratio of people to land is larger, and Moldova was not part of the USSR during Stalin's campaign against family farming.

142 Id.

143 Communication to the authors from Leonard Rolfes, Sept. 18, 2008 (chart), on file with the Rural Development Institute (reporting on his field research in seven *raions* (counties)).

144 See L. Rolfes, Jr., *The Impact of Land Titling in Ukraine: The Results from an 800 Person Random-Sample Survey*, RDI Reports on Foreign Aid and Development No. 119, at 1-11, 8-14 (Rural Development Institute 2003)

145 R. Olearchyk & S. Wagstyle, *Business eyes Ukraine's fertile land*, FINANCIAL TIMES, June 19, 2008. See also USDA Foreign Agricultural Service, supra note 129, at 3-5.

146 A. Kramer, *Russia's Lazy Collective Farms Are a Hot Capitalist Property*, NEW YORK TIMES, Aug. 31, 2008.

147 There is also some question as to the process by which foreign investors can make such land investments, since the Land Code prohibits ownership of agricultural land by foreigners or companies more than 50% owned by foreigners. It appears that the actual owners are Russian subsidiaries of foreign investors. See id.; Vedomosti, *Russian and non-Russian companies buying up farm land in Russia*, in RIA Novost – Opinion & Analysis – What the Russian Papers Say, July 21, 2008, available at http://en. rian.ru/analysis/20080721/114561999.html. It is still unclear how, or whether, the "more than 50% owned by" proviso is being dealt with. Rolfes, supra note 144, indicates reports to the effect "that these mega-farms actually weren't making much money because of high management costs. I.e., just like collective farms. They're being subsidized by their parent organizations. . . ."

8   Formalization of rights to land

Robert Mitchell

I.   Introduction

This chapter discusses general considerations bearing upon the registration of rights to land in the developing world. Given the great variety
of rights regimes applicable to land in the developing world, it is important to acknowledge that our analysis only touches on some of the
many issues that are likely to arise in any particular setting. In fact, different land regimes often exist side by side within the same country.
And across much of the world, most notably in Africa, customary
groups govern themselves according to customary law that also regulates the land rights of members within the group. Where such groups
exist, complicated questions arise regarding each group's relation to
the state, other customary groups, and its own members.

Developing and transitional country governments formalize rights to
land to pursue at least two distinct (but overlapping) goals: economic
development and poverty alleviation.[1] Development banks and bilateral
donors are the usual sponsors of such projects. RDI has participated in
the design and implementation of a number of national programs to
formalize land rights, including multi-year programs in Moldova and
Ukraine, and has worked with policy makers on these issues in a number of other countries, including Albania, Russia, Indonesia, Rwanda,
China and the Kyrgyz Republic.

Two topics frame our discussion: First, under what circumstances
does the formalization of rights to land – defining, certifying and registering such rights in a public registry – benefit the poor and promote
broader economic development in less developed countries? Second,
how do legal, social and bureaucratic systems influence the creation
and effective operation of rights registration systems?

The first set of questions concerns whether the state should formalize land rights, and what types of rights should be formalized. These
questions include: What types of rights do people claim? Do customary
groups claim rights to territory according to customary law? Do non-
traditional communities claim the right to use village commons? Are
local elites in a position to displace the poor during the implementation of state formalization programs? Is formalization likely to benefit

the poor directly – through increased tenure security, increased property values, access to credit, etc.? Is formalization likely to benefit the
poor indirectly by promoting broader economic growth? Apart from
the potential benefits accruing to the poor through formalization, what
are the inherent risks for the poor? Is formalization likely to result in
elite capture and the poor losing control over land they currently possess or use?

The second set of questions relates to the nature of the system used
to formalize rights to land if policy makers have concluded that those
rights should be formalized. This discussion focuses primarily on the
registration of transactable rights to land, which are more likely to be
held by individuals or families than groups. The questions include:
When rights are first registered, how can the state ensure that the interests of the poor – including interest in access to commons – are not
harmed? How can the interests of women be recognized and protected
during registration? How can citizens be encouraged to participate in
the system (and bureaucrats encouraged to make the system accessible)? How can the system be made trustworthy, sustainable and affordable?

Section II presents several examples that typify the broad range of
projects that attempt to formalize rights to land. Section III reviews the
theoretical benefits that formalization may bring to the poor, and Section IV examines the evidence from various settings as to whether and
to what extent formalization has benefited the poor in practice. Section
V reviews elements and principles that underlie functioning land rights
registration systems, and Section VI reviews the types of rights that
might be registered in such systems. Section VII takes a closer look at
issues that arise when rights to a parcel of land are formalized for the
first time. And Section VIII presents conclusions.

II.   Projects to formalize land rights

In this discussion we distinguish between titling (certification) of land
rights and registration of rights in a public registry. The land titling
process formalizes the landowner's legal right in the land and results
in the creation and issuance of a land title or some similar document.
The land title may take the form of a stand-alone document, often in
the nature of a certificate, that defines and memorializes the legal land
right. Land rights registration is the process whereby land titles are entered into a catalogue or compilation of legal land rights and related descriptions of the land parcels upon which they are based. The resulting
land registry serves as a database of land parcel descriptions and of the
rights associated with each parcel.[2] It is possible to title land rights

without registering them, but the typical goal in most settings is to title and register the land rights as part of the same process. In this chapter, unless the context indicates otherwise, the terms "titling and registration" are generally treated as being integral parts of a connected process.

Land titling and registration efforts take different forms in different settings. Understanding how best to approach land titling and registration, or the potential impacts (positive and negative) of titling and registration presupposes a basic understanding of the differing settings, contexts and objectives. For example, a titling and registration effort aiming to title occupied but as yet undocumented land in the remote regions of a particular country is certain to involve different objectives, approaches and impacts than a titling effort focused on individual land rights belonging to the members of a recently reorganized collective farm. The following descriptions of several recent and notable titling and registration efforts around the world illustrate the range of settings.

Projects that seek to formalize land rights often end up defining (and changing) the nature and scope of rights that people exercised previously. It is usually not the case that each neighbor in a community has exactly the same understanding regarding the location of parcel boundaries or even the nature of each person's rights to specific plots of land.

Following the break-up of the USSR, governments of some of the new states which emerged decided to move land formerly owned by the state into private hands. Some projects to individualize state land have involved land parcelization and titling on a massive scale. In Moldova, for example, a national program created about 2.4 million land parcels by sub-dividing land previously used by 901 collective and state farms. The government issued a land title for each parcel, establishing land rights for some 783,000 individual owners over six years. In this case the process of formalizing rights occurred simultaneous with assigning parcels to individuals who previously had no claim to any particular parcel. In this way, each landowner's rights were both created and defined in the same process.[3] Each owner's rights were initially registered in the village land registry, and the great majority of titles were thereafter registered in district offices of the national land registry. The USAID-financed project also included extensive legal and regulatory, public education and legal aid programs. An RDI attorney served as chief legal advisor and later as project manager.[4]

The Latin American experience with land tenure reform and the titling and registration of land rights has a long history, reflecting unequal land distribution, large agricultural laborer populations, insecure smallholder land rights, and interjections of conflicting indigenous rights. Seen as abundant in land but carrying large populations of land-less poor, most Latin American countries have initiated land titling and registration programs.[5] In Honduras, for example, several land admin-istration and titling and registration projects have been implemented in recent years. From 1997 through 2003, a land management project financed with World Bank loans registered 72,000 urban and 77,000 rural properties. The project included components addressing natural resources management, assistance to uplands producers, and biodiver-sity conservation.[6]

At the risk of gross oversimplification, African titling and registra-tion efforts have generated paradoxical results that make for a difficult puzzle. Different efforts have sought to advance individualization and common use, informal tenure regimes and formalization of tenure, commercial land uses and community land uses, as well as support for traditional cattle grazers and traditional small-plot farmers.[7] Some ex-perts have condemned the formalization of individually controlled rural parcels as inconsistent with and destructive of an otherwise functional common property tradition,[8] while other experts consider the formali-zation of community-held, commonly used land to be an attractive op-tion.[9] Still others emphasize the need for the formalization of rights to millions of residential parcels in informally settled urban areas.[10]

The results of formalization projects in Africa vary considerably. Ken-ya probably stands as the most extensive and "Westernized" example of land plot individualization, titling and registration in Africa. Beginning in the 1960s, the Kenyan government individualized and formalized ownership of large portions of several Kenyan districts.[11] The results were widely criticized as being inconsistent with local land tenure re-gimes and thus, in part, resulting in a land grab by local elites.[12] In Uganda, since passage of the 1998 Land Act, the government has con-sidered land demarcation and titling pilot projects as a means of stimu-lating land markets, anticipating that local demand will drive any sub-sequent titling of rights.[13] The authors of a recent land assessment in Rwanda recommended a two-tier land titling and registration system consisting of a more informal system at the local level and a more for-malized system at the national level that would title commercial con-cessions.[14]

III.   Formalization of land rights and the poor

There is growing interest in formalizing the land rights of impover-ished individuals and families in a manner that helps the poor increase the value of their capital, amass additional capital, mitigate economic shocks, and broaden their civic and economic participation.[15] This concept of formalization usually involves documenting, certifying and registering ownership and other land rights claimed by individuals or families. This undertaking is motivated in part by the notion that citizens, including the poor, are more likely to invest in improving their land if they hold secure rights to it. It is also motivated by the notion that if land rights are made transactable, and if a larger potential market for such rights develops, this will naturally lead to increases in property values and ensure that properties move towards a higher and better use. According to the theory, if the poor have secure land rights and they can transfer their rights in the market, their assets will become more valuable, and they will be able to take important steps to escape poverty and otherwise improve their economic well-being.

However, the concept of formalization should not be limited to the process of certifying, documenting and registering land rights held solely by individual families. Where the poor claim land rights on a group basis – whether according to customary law or in the form of community commons exercised historically – it may be appropriate to extend state protections to such rights as they are characterized by the poor and their customary groups. This can be done without converting the customary rights into an individualized land rights regime. In this way, formalization is a much broader concept and includes state protection for many different types of land rights.

Documentation and registration of individual land rights are not a panacea. In fact, if not handled correctly, it may not help the poor and may actually hurt them. Thus, in any attempt to certify and register land rights on an individual basis, it is important to identify the contexts in which an approach advances or hinders the interests of the poor, as well as the inherent risks, both to the poor generally and to women and minority groups specifically.

How might formalization of land rights benefit the poor?

Land rights typically play many important roles in the lives of the poor. This point bears emphasis since observers who focus on only one benefit often miss other very important benefits. Such oversights may result in reforms that promote one benefit, while undermining others. Therefore, it is important to apply a critical lens to the potential benefits of formalized land rights since they are often assumed, rather than demonstrated or really understood. The relative importance of these benefits is likely to vary from context to context. Moreover, some benefits carry with them corresponding risks, which policy makers must understand how to evaluate and mitigate.

One potential benefit – security against eviction – deserves special consideration since it has the potential to help not only individuals subject to state law, but also communities that claim group rights.
- *Security against eviction.* Many poor families who lack secure rights to the land and housing where they reside face the threat of eviction by the state or at the hands of more powerful individuals.[16] This threat not only creates psychological stress, it introduces constant economic stress in the lives of the poor. Eviction looms especially in many settings where there are significant market pressures to make different, higher-value uses of land, which often characterizes urban and transitional peri-urban areas, and rural areas endowed with natural resources coveted by state and private corporations.

Customary groups are subject to the same types of predations. In fact, some groups are especially vulnerable because some state officials may regard the claims of customary groups as unfounded and their use of the land as inefficient, rendering the claims unworthy of protection.

A number of other potential benefits of formalization arise in the case of transactable rights, which are more likely to be held by individuals or families than groups:
- *New opportunities for investment and savings.* Families who have secure rights to land and housing can better invest on and improve their property (see Box 8.1 and the discussion in Chapter 7). When their rights are secure and long-term, holders can be more confident that they will realize the benefits of such improvements. If the rights are transferable, the family has the option of selling the property rights to cash out their investment and pursue other opportunities. In this way, land rights become a vehicle for storing and accumulating capital. Such investments can take the form of agricultural improvements (e.g., terracing, draining land, tree planting, greenhouses, improved crop storage), construction of shelter for animals, and construction or improvement of housing.
- *Higher productivity and higher incomes.* Increased investments in farming can help farmers to intensify and diversify their production, which should translate over time to increased production and higher incomes.[17] In addition, if formalization of rights allows the family to reduce the amount of time it must spend on defending its land rights, this can allow them to participate more fully in productive work not tied to the land.[18]
- *Capturing increases in property value.* If land is transactable, increased tenure security should increase the market value of the property by giving buyers confidence that their purchase is secure.[19] Where demand for land is high (e.g., on the periphery of cities), the

value of securely held land is likely to increase whether or not the owner improves the land.[20]

- *Access to services.* Secure land rights that encompass a homestead allow families to have a stable address, which can be essential in establishing the personal identity necessary to access a range of public and private services. Formalized land rights are often a requirement in order to benefit from government agricultural or other land-related programs. In addition, lenders and other businesses may feel more comfortable doing business with a family which has an address and may be more willing to offer unsecured credit or to offer it at a lower interest rate.[21]

- *Access to credit.* Land is a preferred form of collateral for lenders because it is immovable. Lenders typically will not accept land as collateral to secure loans unless rights to that land have been formalized. Given the importance of access to credit for economic development, this potential benefit flowing from the formalization of land rights is frequently highlighted by development planners.

- *Enhanced social status and stability.* In addition to economic benefits, a family that obtains secure land rights is likely to experience a heightened sense of social status within the community. Families in rural India report that after receiving formal title to land they had purchased years earlier, they received their first invitation to attend the village meeting. These families had attended the meetings in the past, but had never been invited and were not expected to participate.[22] When families have a greater stake in the stability of their community through secure land rights, they are less inclined to support violent political action.[23] Such families may also be less likely to move precipitously to already crowded cities.[24] These hard-to-quantify social and political benefits may sometimes be even more important to the poor than the economic ones.

- *Peace of mind.* Improved tenure security is also associated with reduced stress, improved peace of mind, and a greater hope for the future for individuals, families or groups who receive it.[25]

- *Reduced incidence of disputes.* Although the process of defining rights to land, including the location of boundaries, can expose latent conflict among neighbors, once the rights are defined and documented, the scope for further conflict is likely to be diminished. Short-term costs associated with the definition of rights should produce long-term benefits.

- *Improved stewardship of the land.* Individuals who are assured of retaining a long-term relationship to a plot of land may feel more inclined to preserve the land by reducing soil erosion and other forms of onsite environmental degradation. At the same time, more inten-

sive cultivation of land can negatively impact the environment, including offsite impacts not borne directly by the farmer.[26]
- *Improved economic atmosphere*. The case is sometimes made that registration of land rights for the general population – that is, not targeted specifically on the poor – also benefits the poor by increasing
general economic activity, which leads to more jobs and opportunities for all members of society, including the poor. According to
this concept, trade in land is presumed to benefit the larger society
by placing property in the hands of those who are most willing and
able to invest in improving the land. Trade in land naturally leads
to higher values for property, and ownership of property becomes a
secure place for families to invest savings and build capital that is
reinvested in the economy.

Of the foregoing benefits, proponents of formalization often single out
benefits associated with investments that owners are likely to make following formalization of their rights.[27] According to the theory, as an
active market for land transactions develops, banks are able to determine the market value of land. They also become more willing to accept land as collateral for loans. In this way, the value of land is un-
locked and owners can mortgage their property to purchase materials
that will improve the property, thereby further increasing its value, or
to invest in other wealth-generating activities, such as the expansion of
a business. As market values become clearer and transactions more frequent, a further big boost to transactability occurs if banks begin offering "purchase-money mortgages" to finance the sales transactions
themselves, thus offering new market entrée to buyers who do not
have cash or savings in hand. Repeated thousands of times throughout
a community, over a period of years, mortgage lending can lead to a
general improvement of local living standards. This is less likely in the
absence of an active and secure land market, and such markets depend
upon a reliable and affordable system for registering rights in land.[28]

Settings in which formalization may not benefit the poor

Formalization of individual rights is unlikely to benefit the poor in settings where the state, or strong private actors, have stripped the poor of
land rights in the recent past (paving the way for certification and registration of rights claimed by the dispossessors), or where they can
subvert the registration process itself to accomplish such dispossession,
or in settings where large segments of the poor do not possess land.

Formalization of individual land rights may be inadvisable in settings where families base their claim of right upon customary law
administered by customary law institutions, especially where poor fa-

milies exercise multiple subordinate rights to use land possessed by another. State registration of individual rights in such a context might have the effect of undermining customary institutions.[29]

However, formalization of rights is likely to benefit the poor in settings where their land rights are under threat from the powerful, or where the property could gain substantial value by becoming more transactable. Even in such settings special care must be taken to ensure that this process does not privatize community lands – "commons" – from which the very poorest families gather products for their daily needs.

In urban settings, the state's fear that certifying and registering the land rights of squatters on public land will encourage additional squatting can be a serious obstacle to reform efforts.[30] The high value of land (and consequent high opportunity costs of allocating land to the poor) may also dissuade states from working to certify and register land rights for the urban poor. The state may also fear that the poor will transfer formalized rights prematurely to non-poor transferees at an inadequate price, and that the benefits of formalization will largely bypass the poor.

In addition to the state, local elites may object to certification and registration efforts that benefit the poor. State and corporate interests may have their own claims to natural resources used and claimed by the poor, especially forests and unimproved rangelands. If there is a serious likelihood that the state formalization program will result in unleashing the energy of local elites and corporations to claim lands used by vulnerable groups, formalization of such lands should generally not be attempted. These examples underscore the need to ensure that local conditions will permit the formalization of land rights that will benefit the poor.

Special considerations regarding rights of customary groups

Different cultural settings often involve different land regimes, and many cultures and sub-cultures place a high value on group property claims administered through customary law institutions. Often, a compelling case can be made for the need to formalize such rights through a process of formally recognizing the legitimacy of customary law institutions and territorial claims by the customary group. In settings where groups claim group rights to land and natural resources, policy makers should consider how state action can protect and advance the interests of the poor by registering the land rights of customary groups. Identification and registration of customary group land rights is one way in which the state can insulate the group against encroachment by either the state or private corporate interests.

ROBERT MITCHELL

The state may protect group rights by mapping the territory claimed by the group and adjudicating any conflicting claims with neighboring groups. In this process, the state must define the membership of each group, identify the structure that the group will use to administer land use within its territory, and identify the process the group will use to deal with outsiders. This process should be described in special legislation that ensures that group members are informed regarding the process by which the group rights are being protected. (It cannot, for example, be automatically assumed that chiefs, elders or other group leaders will not act in self-seeking ways in cases such as approving, for cash payments, the opening of parts of the group territory for private corporate logging or mining, with corresponding displacement of group members presently enjoying use of that area.)

States may be reticent to cede too much authority to customary law institutions for fear of strengthening groups that may challenge the state politically with respect to broader issues of local governance. States may also fear that any recognition of customary land rights will lead to demands that the state relinquish all claims over extraction of minerals and timber resources on that territory.

In addition, recognition of customary group tenure can require the state to adjudicate competing claims among rival groups, including claims between neighboring forest communities and claims between sedentary farming communities and migrating pastoralists. Such adjudication can exacerbate latent tensions if not handled carefully and in a way that citizens accept as fair and transparent.[31]

If policy makers are not willing to protect customary group rights and commons, and if it appears that titling and registration of individual rights may encroach upon common property resources used by the poor, it may be inadvisable to proceed with such titling and registration.

It is also important to note that the formalization of group rights is very different from formalizing whatever individual rights to land are held by members of the group. Group members often hold individual or family rights to land ultimately controlled by the group. States should work very closely with customary groups to determine whether and under what circumstances the group would like to see registration of the individual rights of group members. This type of registration may or may not undermine the authority of the group to manage its territory.

Women's rights to land

The importance of formalizing women's rights to land is only beginning to receive serious attention from international development pro-

fessionals.[32] Development planners should not assume that programs
that are framed to stabilize the rights of whomever program administrators accept as the head of the household – who is almost always the
husband – benefit all members of the household adequately or equally.
There is often an imbalance of rights within the household that limits
the ability of women and children (especially girls) to benefit from the
formalization of rights extended to (or expressly naming only) the husband individually. The implications of this imbalance are explored in
Chapter 5.

Formalizing women's rights to land that is controlled by the household should lead to improvements in child welfare, including improved
nutrition and greater household spending on child education.[33] In addition, women who have received formalized rights to land are better
able to withstand disruptions to the family caused by divorce, or the
husband's death or abandonment. In the absence of formalized rights,
women and their children may be left with little or no access to land if
the family structure breaks down.

The issue of women's rights to land should be addressed in every
discussion of rights formalization. This issue is complicated by local
customs and is likely to be a sensitive issue for state officials. It is important to involve state planners in research to shed light on the effects
that women's lack of land rights has on families within the society.

Figure 8.1 summarizes a number of issues, arising out of the above
discussion, that planners should examine when analyzing individual
and group rights to land in a given setting.

Other state goals in formalizing rights to land

Historically, states have created inventories of land parcels and owners
to assess and collect land taxes.[34] Such parcel inventories are often
called "cadastres." The earliest cadastres were created to calculate land
taxes and to assign tax bills to the correct owner or user. The land cadastre included measurements of the surface area of land and the productive value of land as compared with other similar lands. When land
registries were later created to ensure the legal protection of landowner
rights, the registries were often built using data contained in the land
cadastre. Land cadastres exist in some developing countries, but these
tend to cover only part of the territory and are often out of date.

If the primary purpose of the land register is to protect private rights
to land and facilitate transactions, it is probably inadvisable for the register to contain all information required by the land tax authority.[35] In
fact, by allowing the land register to contain data that are not necessary
to protect private rights, there is a risk that such data will become mandatory and that the (perceived) need to correct such data will interfere

with land transactions. On the other hand, there are very good reasons for designing the land register in a way that allows the tax authority to use the land rights database as a foundation to create the tax database. If the databases are linked early on, this will make it much easier for lending institutions to make underwriting decisions involving land collateral.

Cadastral offices may also aspire to provide data for use in regional planning, such as roads and other public infrastructure, or, for example, to provide the government with a basis for estimating crop yields. Therefore, in addition to containing data on parcel boundaries, a "multi-purpose cadastre" might contain data on land tax rates and payments, land use restrictions, soil quality, environmental conditions, crop performance, etc. A full-fledged, multi-purpose cadastre may not be affordable even in many developed economies and is unlikely to be affordable in less developed countries in the near term. Although it may make sense to create a system framework that allows the registry to develop into a multi-purpose cadastre,[36] it is prudent to build in safeguards to prevent the registry from being populated with data not essential for registering rights to land.

Administrative capacity and commitment

Those living in poverty are not likely to obtain land rights if national and local governments lack either the will or institutional capacity to design and implement measures that identify and protect such rights. At the national level – and at the state or province level where land is a "state subject" as in India – capacity is important for designing laws and regulations that take into account the interests of the poor.

Perhaps most important of all on the administrative point, state institutions at the national and local levels require clear direction regarding institutional roles in establishing and protecting the land rights of the poor. Successful implementation will require the state to prioritize the land rights of the poor and to earmark sufficient funds for programs. It is important to consider the types of incentives that will motivate public institutions to treat the poor as clients whose rights and interests are worth protecting. Information is key: judicial and land administration institutions cannot work effectively with the poor unless they have clear information regarding both land rights law and the needs and interests of the poor. If a state lacks the will or institutional capacity to carry out reforms, any half-hearted attempt to formalize land rights risks injuring the poor.

A good place for the state to begin is by conducting research on the challenges facing poor families who might, at least in theory, benefit from certification, documentation and registration of their rights to

Figure 8.1. *Threats to tenure security, interventions and risks*

Land rights claimant	Threats to possession (if any)	Possible intervention	Risk to vulnerable population	Transactability an issue?	Women's land rights an issue?
Customary law group	State, natural resource extractors, developers, individuals outside of group, neighboring groups	Register rights in name of incorporated group	Expose latent conflict between neighboring groups	No	Yes
Community claiming commons	State, natural resource extractors, developers, local elites	Register rights in name of community	Displace informal use by some individuals	No	Yes
Family or individual claiming ownership or lease rights	State, natural resource extractors, developers, other individuals [Neighbors may encroach gradually]	Register rights in name of husband and wife (or unmarried individual)	Elites claim rights in place of current holder, cancellation of subordinate rights, omission of wife from ownership, encroachment upon commons, encroachment upon land claimed by customary law group	Yes	Yes
Individual claiming personal subordinate rights to land owned by another (e.g., passage easement, pasture of animals, gathering wood)	Owner of land	Preserve unregistered subordinate rights	Preservation of unregistered rights does not pose risk to vulnerable population, but may cloud title	No	Yes

Source: Adapted from R. Mitchell, *Registration of Rights to Real Property in the Developing World* 8, fig. 1 (2007) (paper commissioned by First American Corporation, on file with the Rural Development Institute).

land. Some questions to consider include: Are the barriers to registration – both formal and informal – so high in the current system that the poor simply have no real opportunity to register their rights? How can the system be designed so that these barriers are removed? Are citizens interested in registering their land rights, and what changes in the system would motivate citizens to participate in the system? This research can help to demonstrate the state's commitment to addressing the needs of vulnerable populations in the design and implementation of a new rights registration regime.

Planners should also consider carefully whether the state has the capacity and will to maintain the registry once it is created. If the system is to sustain development of the land market, the capacity and will to register transactions and other transfers must exist on the day that officials first begin registering rights to land.

IV.   Evidence regarding benefits to the poor

The economic benefits of titling and registration can, but do not necessarily, help alleviate poverty. For the poor to benefit, the economic benefits of titling and registration must reach them, and some experts assert that there is very little evidence that titling and registering rights to land provide significant benefits to rightholders in the developing world.[37] Lack of capital to fuel local land markets and general malaise of the local economy may do more to dampen the development of the land market than lack of titles and registration. And even if land markets are developing in some regions of the country, is it likely that titling and registration of rights held by the poor will attract investment in their neighborhoods and increase their property values? How can one predict that conditions are such that lack of titles and registration is a significant drag on development of the market? Surely governments and citizens should not invest heavily in titling and registering rights to land if there is no social or economic demand for these systems.

The benefits to the poor are likely to depend upon the specific context in which titling and registration are conducted. And benefits in one setting may not justify an assumption that these benefits will translate to other settings.

The Thai titling and registration effort is one of the few to include data collection and an econometric multivariate analysis. The analysis generally indicates that capital-to-land ratios, land improvements, land values, and outputs and inputs per unit of land were higher for the titled land than the untitled land.[38] Another study, using data from land registration in Thailand during the period 1960-1996, projected the effect of Thai land registration on broader financial and economic growth patterns. The study concluded that registration has had a significant effect on the longer-term economic growth, which occurred after an initial negative impact over two years and after an extended period of recovery from this initial impact.[39]

A 2005 survey conducted by RDI showed that where Chinese farmers possess documentation (land rights contracts or certificates) issued by the government according to the 2002 Rural Land Contracting Law, they, such farmers invested in substantial improvements to their arable land much more frequently than did farmers who lacked such documentation; for example, a farmer with a land contract which complies with the law is 2.4 times as likely to make such an investment as a farmer who has not received any land contracts. Yet according to the law both farmers have the same land rights regardless of documentation.[40] Other significant findings regarding the documentation of land rights in China are shown in Box 8.1 and are discussed in Chapter 7.

Box 8.1. Formalization of agricultural land rights in China

A 17-province survey that RDI conducted in mid-2005 in cooperation with Renmin University and Michigan State University found several important positive impacts associated with Chinese farmers' possession of documentation for their land rights, including the following:

– Farmers who received documentation of their land rights via contracts or land certificates were much more likely to increase mid- to long-term investment in their land.
– In villages where farmers have contracts or certificates that comply with the law, farmers are much more likely to receive satisfactory compensation in cases of land takings.

These findings are discussed in greater detail in Chapter 7.

Few Latin American programs have been systematically evaluated to confirm the existence of linkages between tenure security and economic development. However, recent studies of titling in Honduras and Paraguay showed links between tenure security and increased investment as well as links between land titling and increased productivity However, the studies also indicated that a small minority of farmers, who were not the poorest or those with the least land, obtained most of the benefits.[41] Another recent study of tenure insecurity and investment and productivity in Nicaragua showed some positive connection between tenure insecurity and lower production levels, although there was no indication that insecurity reduced investment.[42]

In Buenos Aires, Argentina, however, a "natural experiment" in the formalization of the land rights of urban squatters has found that formalization resulted in significant increases in investment. The squatting began in the 1980s with about 1,800 families moving onto what they thought was government-owned wasteland on the edge of Buenos Aires. The land was in fact privately owned. After several attempts at eviction, the government sought to expropriate the land from the private owners and award titles to the squatters. A number of owners accepted the offered expropriation compensation, while others rejected the offers and began legal challenges to demand higher compensation. In 1989-1991, those occupying the land of owners who accepted the government's offer of compensation received formal land titles, while those on land still subject to litigation did not. These events, by exogenously creating an "untitled" control group and a "titled" group – with no other difference between them – presented an opportunity to examine the effects of titling.

The study showed that those holding formal title invested substantially more in housing construction features (total house footprint, walls, roofs and sidewalks) as compared to the group lacking titles. Overall housing quality was 37% higher (in terms of the quality of housing features and components) for the titled homeowners.[43] And although the titled households had larger houses, the researchers found that families without titles had an average of six household members, while families with titles had an average of five members.[44] In addition, the school-age children of the titled households attended school for an average of 0.4 years more than the children of untitled households and were less likely to be absent from school.[45] There was no difference between the two groups with respect to access to either formal or informal credit.[46]

A 2003 study by RDI in Ukraine compared the experience of owners who had received titles to specific parcels with that of individuals who held only a "land share" document representing a right in large, undivided fields. On average, the titled owners were able to rent out their land for 32% more, were substantially more likely to receive the rent payment in full and on time, and were much more likely to cultivate some of the land themselves rather than rent it out.[47] However, this style of formalization really amounts to a special case since titling did not involve land already possessed, but instead occurred simultaneously with the conversion of the undifferentiated land share right into a right to a specific parcel.

In African settings, there is little or no evidence that land titling and registration of individual parcels has spurred investment or consequently led to increased agricultural production.[48] In Kenya and Burkina Faso, there is evidence that titling has not increased investment.[49]

In Uganda some argue that specific forms of tenure insecurity actually spur investment, in the sense that improvements made or added to the land can increase the possessor's tenure security by denoting permanency and owner-like status. Parcel occupiers may increase investment in perennial crops and other improvements so as to make eviction more costly by virtue of higher mandated compensation amounts (where compensation requirements are enforced).[50] One study of 36 Ugandan villages concluded that, through tree planting, land possessors increased their security of land rights over inherited land.[51] In any event, the notion that investment might increase security must be accounted for in any analysis of African titling and registration. Research suggests that not accounting for this notion will yield results showing that increased security has prompted the investment.[52]

Other findings tend to establish that some customary tenure systems in Africa, and even those that provide for less than full transfer rights, provide sufficient rights and security to prompt investments in the land. Land tenure security under customary systems may be stronger than it first appears to outsiders, and what seem at first inspection to be precarious rights may in fact be stronger than suspected. Methods of measuring land tenure security do not always make distinctions between levels of security as they actually exist.[53] Assumptions of insecurity are among the matters that should be explored and confirmed before future titling and registration are undertaken in African settings where customary land rights prevail.

Despite these African examples, it is probably useful to remember that land titling and land rights registration – particularly in Africa – is contextual. Most African examples described above illustrate the individualization and formalization of small parcels of agricultural land. But what might not be useful in one situation might be useful in another. For example, because of the intense urban and peri-urban informal settlements that make up and surround so many African cities, titling and registration of rights to urban residential plots may be a sensible way to formalize the related investment, create assets for the urban poor, and prevent displacement and landlessness. Moreover, none of the examples have addressed the potential impact of documenting customary group or community rights to protect them against outside incursions.

Perhaps the lesson to be drawn is that although titling and registration may benefit the poor, the benefits cannot be assumed. Planners should investigate the effects of titling and registration projects on the poor in each context. With respect to each component of the project, planners and implementers should ask whether the design is consistent with the protection of the interests of the poor, and whether the system, as implemented, protects such interests.

V.   Registration of individual rights to land

The system used to register rights to land, broadly speaking, defines how rights to land are acquired, proven and protected, as well as what recourse citizens have if state officials do not register the rights correctly. In addition to certification of rights during first registration, the contents of a functioning registration system for transactable rights is an important element to consider. Transactability is generally not an issue for customary group rights, commons and certain types of customary subordinate rights, but is usually an important reason for registering rights held by individuals, families and legal entities.

A principal justification for formalizing and registering individual rights to land is to support the development of an efficient land market. Registration of rights should promote two closely related objectives: (1) continued protection of private rights to land such as rights of ownership, mortgage and lease; and (2) facilitation of land rights transfer by sale, lease and inheritance, as well as the creation of mortgage rights.

Private land rights face tenure insecurity threats from both public and private sources. In many countries a common threat to private rights is that the state may expropriate the rights for some public purpose without adequately compensating the private owner. Once the state has registered the owner's private rights, it is much more difficult for the state to expropriate the land without compensating the rightful owner.[54] Private rights may also be under threat from more powerful individuals within the community.[55] States may take steps other than titling and registration to enhance the security of those who physically possess land.[56]

Another common threat to the holder's rights to land relates to the stability of parcel boundaries. Over time, neighboring parcel owners may encroach upon the parcel, occupying and using small amounts of land along the common boundary of the parcel. If parcel boundaries are defined as part of the process of registering rights to each parcel, each owner will have a basis for resolving disputes that may arise regarding the location of the common boundary.[57]

The second objective of the rights registration system – facilitating transactions in land – is accomplished through instituting procedures that make the transfer of rights to land simple and affordable. But it is worth noting that the first objective – protection of private rights – also serves to promote trade in land. Protection of rights to land encourages a prospective buyer to have confidence that if he purchases the property, he will receive legal and enforceable rights to it. That is, to the extent a prospective buyer has confidence that the seller owns the land, the buyer will be more willing to buy. Buyers are naturally willing to pay more for more secure rights than for less secure rights.

In the same way, protection of ownership rights to land encourages a lender to have confidence that when the lender accepts the mortgage of an object of land as security for the loan, it will be able to enforce the mortgage and dispose of the land to satisfy the loan in the event that the owner defaults on repayment.

Prospective buyers will also be interested to know about all significant rights that encumber the ownership right, such as multi-year lease rights and mortgage rights. Thus, registration of such lease rights and mortgage rights not only protects the lessee and the lender who holds the mortgage right, but also protects the buyer, who might suffer losses if she buys the property without knowing about the encumbering rights. And whereas a prospective buyer's visit to the land might reveal rights claimed by an earlier, unregistered buyer, the prospective buyer cannot easily learn about non-possessory rights such as mortgage rights if they are not registered.[58]

Elements of the registration system

The registration system should contain information on the owner (or equivalent rightholder), the owner's rights and the land itself including: (1) textual data on the owner's name, address and other identifying characteristics; (2) textual data regarding the owner's specific rights to the land parcel (as well as the rights of other persons created by lease agreement, mortgage agreement, etc.); and (3) spatial data regarding the parcel boundaries and its location relative to other parcels.[59]

Identification of the owner. Legal identity requirements must take into account the ability of citizens, and especially the poor, to obtain whatever proof of identity is necessary to hold and use land rights. Registration programs should allow for practical means for enabling the poor to establish their legal identity for purposes of registration (e.g., public acknowledgment by neighbors or a community leader, if they lack documentation).

Identification of rights to be registered. Conceptually, it may be helpful to understand that an owner's rights to a parcel do not describe the owner's relationship to the parcel so much as they describe the owner's *relationship with others* as regards the possession and use of the parcel. The owner's rights typically include, for example, the right to exclude others from the land, the right to sell the land to others, the right to use the land without being disturbed, etc. The most common types of rights registered include ownership (or long-term use rights in societies that do not allow private ownership) and subordinate rights, such as lease and mortgage rights, which are registered as encumbrances

upon the ownership rights.[60] All rights should be organized and records indexed according to the unique parcel number assigned to the
parcel.[61]

Identification of the parcel. The parcel must be differentiated from the
larger territory in some way. The process of determining boundaries
has both a legal and a technical aspect. Boundaries are essentially legal
constructions although they are described with reference to natural or
artificial monuments or with respect to GPS coordinates. Based on the
identification of boundaries, it is useful to construct an index map describing all parcels in a defined area, and then assign a unique number
to each parcel. The parcel number becomes an essential element for
registering rights to the parcel. Aerial photographs and satellite images
may be a cost-effective way of preparing base maps that can be used to
create parcel index maps, particularly where the scale allows identification of parcel boundary features such as irrigation canals and hedges.
The basic process is illustrated in Figure 8.2.

In addition, the system for registering rights must be "dynamic" in
the sense that it allows for changes in owners, changes in rights and
changes in parcels. For example, owners and rights may be changed
either through court order, sale or inheritance. Such changes are likely
to begin occurring immediately after the first registration of rights begins. Parcels may be changed (and created) through division or
through consolidation with other parcels.

Figure 8.2.   *Relation of rights registration and parcel cadastre functions*

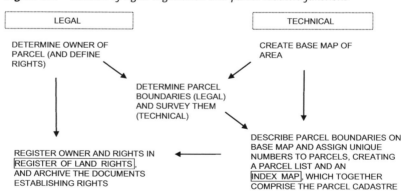

Source: R. Mitchell, *Registration of Rights to Real Property in the Developing World* 8, fig. 3
(2007) (paper commissioned by First American Corporation, on file with the Rural Development Institute).

Transfer of rights

When considering the benefits of formalization, it is useful at the outset to acknowledge that some citizens will transfer rights to land whether or not the state recognizes the legality of the transfer. The parties to such transactions may be willing to accept the risk that the transfer might be challenged, especially if the cost of legalizing the transfer is high. The challenge for planners is to design a system that can be operated in such a way that citizens prefer to formalize their transfers.

Procedures established for registering rights in land should be designed in a way that makes the process for transferring rights (or creating new land objects through subdivision or merger of objects) relatively simple and affordable, rather than cumbersome and expensive. A sound registration system should have the following characteristics:[62]

Simplicity. The system should be simple to operate and simple to explain to the public. It should not contain extraneous data. The public must be able to understand precisely why the system exists and what benefits it provides.

Accuracy. It is essential that the system contain accurate information and that the information is protected against unauthorized manipulation or loss. The system must be updated whenever transfers occur. An inaccurate register is likely to create more problems than it solves.

Promptness. The system must be capable of processing transactions without delay. If the system allows registration officials to delay processing transactions, this will tend to undermine its usefulness to the public. Moreover, a system that allows delay for the great mass of transactions, but which allows officials to expedite only some transactions, provides opportunities for corrupt practices.

Affordability. The system must be affordable, based upon the local population's standard of living costs and the market value of the rights being registered. If registration processes are unreasonably costly, the public may find ways to avoid formally registering transfers of interests, opting for informal methods of dealing. Such informality exposes the public to significant risks that they may not appreciate, and results in a registry of rights that does not reflect the actual possession of land.

Suitability to circumstances. The registration system must be suitable to the national conditions. It is inappropriate to introduce an elaborate, multi-functional database of land objects in settings where the national budget and users of the system cannot pay for its creation or maintenance. This is related to the question of simplicity, but also relates to other questions, such as the degree of precision required in boundary measurement (with more precise measurement generally costing more).

One important issue to consider is whether the system will be a "conclusive" system (in which registration conclusively establishes the legitimacy of rights) or a "declaratory" system (in which registration provides only evidence of what rights are claimed), or perhaps something in between.

Conclusive systems are based upon a positive assertion from the state that the registered owner is the legal owner of the land. State officials undertake to verify that submitted documents are legally sufficient to transfer rights from the seller to the buyer, and registration is often necessary to create and terminate rights to land. Some conclusive systems also provide compensation to innocent parties who suffer losses as a result of reliance on the system. The law deems the register to be legally conclusive, and third parties can rely upon it and need not inspect transfer deeds or other right-establishing documents. Such systems are often referred to as "title registration" systems.

A declaratory registration system provides only a public register of documents that purport to effectuate the legal transfer of rights to land. In a declaratory system, state officials do not attempt to verify the sufficiency or accuracy of documents submitted for registration, and instead place the burden upon private parties to determine whether the registered documents are legally effective. Such systems are often referred to as "deed registration" systems.

Registration systems are most likely to fall somewhere along the continuum between a purely conclusive system and a purely declaratory system. And it is possible to begin with a declaratory system and over time introduce features of conclusive systems. In a developed market economy the uncertainty associated with the declaratory system can be greatly reduced through private "title insurance," which is a contract by which the insurer guarantees to compensate the registered owner for losses suffered in case the owner's property right is declared invalid.

Incentive for bureaucrats to process applications to register rights

State bureaucrats who operate the registry stand to benefit from any government mandate requiring registration of rights since they will have enhanced job security and may also have perverse opportunities for demanding illicit payments from registry users. It is quite common to see government ministries clashing over which one will be entrusted with the creation and operation of the land rights registration system.

Opportunities for corrupt practices will be greater if the registration process is non-transparent or inefficient. Backlogs create an especially fertile ground for economic rent seeking (i.e., demands for payment of bribes to officials) since owners may be willing to pay to move to the front of the queue. Well-enforced time limits for processing applications to register rights may reduce opportunities for corruption.

By the same token, to the extent that registration rules limit the discretion of state registry officials and require them to document their decisions, opportunities for rent seeking diminish. In a conclusive registration system, for example, the law should require the clerk to receive into the system all applications, even if the clerk believes the application is incorrect or the documents submitted do not comply with the law. If registration is to be denied, a senior official should issue a written decision explaining the basis for the refusal. Designed correctly, it should be possible to limit or eliminate cases in which an official can demand an illicit payment for accepting an application to register rights.[63]

Finally, registration officials must receive an adequate salary to make the job worth keeping. It may be useful to base compensation, job security and career advancement on meeting registration targets for timeliness and accuracy.

Promoting use of the system

Citizens are unlikely to register rights to land unless they perceive that the benefits outweigh the costs. Apart from cases in which the individual is about to sell the property, benefits are more likely to outweigh costs if two conditions are satisfied: (1) that citizens face threats to tenure security; and (2) registration costs are predictable and relatively affordable, given the value of land and citizen income. If either condition is not met, citizens may rationally conclude that registration is not worth the cost. Some may also be inclined to register only if they anticipate that registration will enhance the market value of the property; however, this is mainly a consideration for properties that are likely to be developed in the foreseeable future, such as properties in and around cities. Even in that case, the anticipated increase in the value of the property may not offset the cost of registration and the time needed to register. If the government can create trust among citizens that the benefits of using the registration system outweigh the costs, more citizens are likely to use the system, which, in turn, will likely help the system to perform in a way that produces benefits. Public trust is an essential element to a well performing registration system.

Public education relating to registration and its benefits will be important for creating understanding and trust of the system. In Moldova, public education was an integral part of a four-year project to privatize land formerly used by collective farms, issue titles to individual parcels to former collective members, and register the ownership in a new registry. The project created a monthly newspaper – "Farmers'

Hour" – to help beneficiaries understand the privatization process and their new land rights.[64] A similar privatization and titling project in Ukraine made extensive use of national radio and television programming to reach the rural population.[65]

Financing operation and setting fees

Unless registration fees are affordable to citizens, they will not use the system and it will become increasingly out of date and less trustworthy over time. If the users cannot afford to pay the entire cost of operating the system, then the state must subsidize its operation, whether through taxes on land or from the general budget. Prior to launching the system, planners should make a careful assessment of what fees citizens are able (and willing) to pay, and then determine what level of state subsidy, if any, will be needed. If the business plan does not make sense, it will not be prudent to launch the system.

There are important business reasons for eliminating opportunities for officials to collect bribes during registration. Bribes dissuade citizens from using the system and are not recorded as revenue for the registry. This is doubly damaging to the registry since it reduces the demand for services without producing an increase in system revenue. It is much better to set a higher registration fee, which will support adequate salaries, and eliminate corruption than allow low fees and tolerate corruption. Ultimately, corruption is a management issue that must be resolved by leaders.

VI.   Rights subject to registration

Individual rights

The legislation should define clearly what types of individual rights to land are recognized by law, and which of these rights are subject to registration. With respect to individual rights, it is desirable to limit the number of registered rights to only the most important, such as private ownership, long-term lease and mortgage of privately owned land. In addition, any valuable private right to publicly owned land, such as permanent use rights (and temporary rights, provided the term is sufficiently long), should also be registered.

Protecting women's rights to land

The laws of many developing countries do not require, or even provide for, the registration of rights of married women and women living in consensual unions. Even where the law does require such registration, it is almost always ignored in practice, either because the system is not designed to facilitate the registration of the rights of both spouses, or because registry officials are ignorant of the law. Failure to register a wife's rights to property can limit her control over resources within the household, reducing the proportion of resources spent on the family's basic needs, particularly the needs of the children. Failure to register spousal rights also exposes women to the risk of great hardship following abandonment, divorce or the husband's death.

To address this need, one approach is for the law to require the registration of spousal rights to land, but for the law also to presume that when a married individual registers his or her rights to land, an unregistered spouse is entitled to assert the same rights. In other words, it is useful for the law to require all persons dealing with land to inquire into the marital status of the registered owner, as well as whether the owner's spouse, or former spouse, has rights to the land.

This requirement could be enforced in various ways. The law might provide, for example, that any person seeking to acquire a right to land must obtain one of the following: (1) proof that the seller has never been married; (2) proof that the owner's spouse has no legal claim to the property (i.e., proof that the property was inherited separately by the husband or is not otherwise subject to the legislation governing marital property); or (3) a notarized statement signed by the spouse consenting to the transaction.

Of course, admitting the continued legal force of unregistered spousal rights would tend to cloud the title and make it harder for people who seek to deal with the property to determine whether the property right is burdened with unregistered rights. In developing countries, it may well be that such clouds on a title are appropriate since they serve to protect the legitimate interests of women who are otherwise less able to protect their interests. By recognizing the continued legal force of unregistered spousal rights, the cost of resolving whether such rights exist would be shifted to persons who seek to deal with the property. Provided that the rule is well known, this approach is not inconsistent with the operation of a conclusive registration system. To ensure that the public receives adequate notice of this exception to the conclusive effect of registration, rules could require that the registration records (including certificates or registry excerpts issued to those dealing with the land) explicitly state that unregistered spousal rights continue in force.

Protecting subordinate rights to land

In many developing countries, it is common to find traditional personal subordinate rights, such as the personal right to gather fruits on land owned by another. Such rights often play a substantial role in the subsistence strategies of the most vulnerable members of rural societies. As with the spousal rights, it seems fair to require the law to protect unregistered personal subordinate rights. In creating a presumption that these unregistered rights remain valid, the law should also establish a process by which people who seek to deal with the property right can determine whether such rights exist in fact. Again, all persons dealing with land should be required to inquire whether any person asserts unregistered personal subordinate rights of this type. Furthermore, it is probably appropriate for the law to make it difficult to extinguish such rights and to require, for example, that any extinguishment of the right must require the owner to buy out the unregistered subordinate rights according to the same legally prescribed process required for transfer of other land rights.[66]

Group rights and rights to commons

In countries where traditional groups claim group territory managed by customary law institutions, the law should provide some process by which the state works with the group to define the territory and register the group's rights. In order to protect the group against loss of the rights, the law should provide for registration of caveats (specific restrictions) prohibiting the sale, mortgage, license or other transfer of the land rights, perhaps subject to some process whereby the group as a whole can decide to transfer rights to a delimited portion of their land. The territory should be mapped and should appear in the index mapping system to prevent encroachment by other owners.

It is also very useful to register the commons (taken to mean lands held within the formal property system, but reserved for common use), though it will require legal research to determine the nature of the right and the holder of the right. For example, it is necessary to determine whether the law allows villages to incorporate, or whether the village can hold, for example, a permanent use right to state land. If the law allows the village to dispose of commons, the law should provide a transparent public process for making such decisions based on public meetings and documented public testimony by members of groups using the commons, including the poor.

VII.   First registration

Process of adjudication, demarcation, land survey, posting, certification

"First registration" of rights is the series of initial steps concerning a given area or parcel to determine for the first time who holds rights to that land, document those rights, and enter them into the public record. First registration is more typically associated with the initial establishment of a land title registry to support a conclusive registration system; however, it could also be undertaken to support the creation of a declaratory system, especially if the existing record of rights is generally out of date or otherwise untrustworthy, or if the society is creating the registry for the first time.

At least in a system that is intended to be, if not strictly conclusive, at least tending significantly in that direction, first registration consists of five main steps: (1) adjudication to determine who has the legitimate claim to own which parcels of land; (2) demarcation, in which land claimants physically mark the limits of each parcel on the ground (not needed for boundaries already marked with a fence, soil berm or other installation); (3) land survey, which involves the measurement and mapping of the physically marked parcel boundaries; (4) public posting of the parcel maps and ownership claims to allow others to challenge the claims asserted; and (5) preparation of land certificates and entry of relevant information on land rights and land parcels into the land rights register.[67] Of the foregoing, steps (1) and (4) are less likely to apply, at least in full-fledged form, the more the system tends toward the declaratory model.

In the adjudication process, officials and citizens jointly determine existing rights in particular land parcels. The main questions to be answered concern who holds what rights to which land parcels and structures. Simultaneously, claimants of parcels that adjoin each other must visit the parcels to agree on the location of mutual boundaries, which are then demarcated (if not already demarcated) on the ground. Once neighbors agree, it is usual to set temporary pegs in the ground to mark the location of boundaries, except in areas where fences or berms or equivalent clear delineations already exist. The land survey official may also prepare a rough sketch of the parcels and may ask the neighbors to sign the sketch. This process can be greatly facilitated with the use of aerial photographs and satellite images, especially where many boundaries are physically marked with fences, berms, etc. that are visible from the air.

After the neighbors have agreed on the location of parcel boundaries, the land surveyor measures the location of the boundary markers with respect to local fixed monuments, or perhaps by using global positioning system technology (GPS). The main purpose of land surveying is to record the location of parcel boundaries so they can be re-established in the future in case of dispute. The surveys also provide a basis for producing parcel index maps that assist in land administration.

Survey methods range from simple and inexpensive to complex, detailed and costly. In many settings, especially in agricultural areas where land values are lower and there is minimal risk of constructing buildings across parcel boundaries, owners require much less precise definition of boundary location. In urban areas, relatively higher land values and the need to avoid construction across boundaries help justify the higher cost of more precise measurement of boundaries. The choice of surveying and mapping methods should balance cost with accuracy, taking into account local needs, local land values and the local availability of various survey technologies. Planners should never base their decisions upon the mere fact that certain standards are used by more developed economies or based upon a desire for technical perfection. And donor agencies seeking to fund registration systems should be conscious of such potential biases in making recommendations, especially when they may coincide with the donor's own interest in making a larger loan or grant (or a preference to purchase equipment rather than fund salaries). Planners must be careful to pay special attention to per-parcel costs, with the overarching goal of identifying a usable system of least cost (in China, for example, a nationwide registration system for farmers' land rights, when it is established, will need to encompass over one billion separate parcels).

As an example of suitable practices, in the Moldova land titling project, land survey costs averaged US$2.25 per parcel, including the measurement of existing parcel boundaries and the creation of new parcel boundaries through a subdivision process.[68] Although simplified, the land survey techniques produced a very small number of errors.[69] In addition, land survey costs were controlled through strict pricing procedures that established fixed price ceilings for bids by survey contractors. In Indonesia, the per-parcel costs of using satellite images was estimated in 2003 to be about US$3 per hectare, including correction with GPS technology, as compared to approximately US$12 per hectare for corrected aerial photography. The cost for ground surveys was much greater.[70]

After the parcel index map is prepared, registration officials may ask land claimants to sign a copy of the map to signify their concurrence with the parcel descriptions. At the very least, registration officials should post the registration map publicly for some specified minimum period to allow local residents an opportunity to raise questions and challenge ownership claims or claims regarding the location of boundaries. After challenges are resolved, the index map and associated information on land claimants should become the legal basis for preparing the land ownership registry and the preparation of title certificates for distribution to the owners.

Proving rights to land during first registration

In many developing countries, large segments of the population claim rights to land based upon occupation or upon the fact that they have purchased the right to occupy the property from someone whose claim was based on occupation. These transactions may or may not be documented, and there may not be documentary evidence of occupation. In some countries, occupants may have tax receipts showing that they have paid land taxes over a period of years, even though they do not have a formal title to the property.

The law should specify the grounds upon which ownership can be proven, either according to customary law or according to legislation that provides for rights to arise through prescriptive possession, including with respect to rights acquired on land designated as state land. In most developing country settings, the law should probably provide that the adjudication process shall allow claimants to present oral testimony to prove their ownership or other long-term rights, and should not presume that documentary proof is superior to oral testimony that contradicts the documents. Neighbors usually know very well who has occupied each piece of property and for what term. Immediate neighbors are likely to have very clear ideas about the location of parcel boundaries that have been respected in practice. If the law is not clear regarding the basis for proving undocumented ownership, planners must ensure that the law is changed to clarify this process.

It is also important that the adjudication process be public. Preliminary results of each local adjudication should be posted publicly in the neighborhood to allow community members to raise objections before the rights are registered. Again, the law should set forth this process.

Costs and benefits of systematic vs. sporadic first registration

Adjudication, certification and registration of rights can be performed either sporadically or systematically. In a sporadic process, officials perform the necessary tasks at the request of the rightholder, parcel by parcel according to demand, often facilitated by a legal requirement that land parcels must go through the process before they can be transferred or subdivided. In the systematic process, officials set out to perform the necessary tasks with respect to all parcels (or at least all privately claimed parcels) within a given area.

The sporadic approach is piecemeal and haphazard, but low-income countries with significant resource and personnel constraints are often forced to proceed in this way. The sporadic approach allows the government to defer costs and makes it easier to pass costs on to beneficiaries.[71] Using a sporadic approach typically means, however, that the land register will remain incomplete for many years or decades and will be less beneficial both to the state and to landowners as long as unregistered titles also exist in the same locality.[72]

Sporadic approaches can exclude poor rights holders because the poor often lack the resources (time, money, information and education) needed to take advantage of opportunities to register their own land or purchase and register the land of others. For example, expensive land surveys can deter poor rightholders from formalizing their rights and, because owners usually fund sporadic titling and registration services (at least in part), high costs can become onerous and create accessibility problems.[73]

The exclusionary nature of sporadic approaches is manifested by the great length of time needed to conduct sporadic registration of most properties. One estimate, made in 1998, of the time to complete sporadic titling in Indonesia and to bring all eligible properties within the system at the then-current rate was set at 90 years.[74] Until well into that 90-year period, most land rights holders – the overwhelming majority of them poor – would be excluded from the intended benefits of titling and registration.[75]

In the long term, a systematic approach is preferable to a sporadic approach for several reasons. First, economies of scale make it less expensive.[76] Second, it is less likely to lead to encroachment upon the rights of the poor because it gives maximum publicity to the determination of land rights within a given area, enhancing transparency and grassroots participation. Third, women may also be more likely to have their rights registered through a systematic process since this allows greater scope for public education and may allow local women to focus community attention on the importance of registering women's rights. Finally, it is more certain because adjoining land parcels are investigated simultaneously, helping to ensure that boundaries of adjacent parcels are mapped without gaps or overlaps.[77] However, if a systematic approach is used, it is likely that the state will need to subsidize the cost, or at least a substantial portion of the cost, since many landowners, especially in rural areas, cannot afford registration fees and land survey costs outside the context of an individual market transaction.

USAID has demonstrated a preference for systematic titling of land ownership in some settings despite the absence of a fully functioning state system for registering rights to land. The large-scale privatization and titling efforts in Moldova and Ukraine are prime examples of this approach. The argument in favor of these approaches is very much centered on providing immediate and tangible benefits to the poor. The primary benefit conferred in these projects was a valuable land right in place of a less valuable and much more tenuous land share right.[78] An important emphasis in such projects is to keep the price per beneficiary as low as reasonably possible, allowing the project to benefit a large universe of owners and provide a model that would allow the government to finance titling without foreign assistance.[79]

However, systematic titling and registration can also exclude certain rights holders. During systematic efforts, holders of uncertain or irregular rights – including parcels subject to dispute, for which the owner lacks documentary evidence, or on which the owner has erected constructions without the necessary permissions – can be excluded from obtaining title.[80] Because of the costs related to resolving the status of these "problem parcels," they are often left unregistered and their titles left subject to later resolution, or officials simply register the problem parcels in the name of the state. In the Republic of Georgia, at one point systematic registration had failed to register up to 50% of residential plots in some places because of encroachments and irregularities.[81] In Albania, as many as 30% of parcels were registered in the name of the state in some places because of unresolved issues.[82] In such cases, the very people who have a clouded title, and whose rights are consequently most in need of resolution and formalization, are excluded from the process. Inevitably, it is the poorest rightholders who lack sufficient resources to clear those rights.

Provisional titles

Provisional titles are one legal tool that can be used to prevent exclusion of the poor. The English title registration system, set forth in large part by the Land Registration Act (1925), allows for the registration of possessory titles.[83] Possessory title is provisional in the sense that the rights are registered "as is" and the act of registration does not cure any existing defect, although the act of registration combined with the passage of a period of time without any challenges could turn the provisional title into an absolute title. Registration of possessory titles could reduce the costs of cleaning up title for registration and still preserve latent rights, allowing a rightful claimant to appear and reassert rights to the land. According to the English legislation, a registered possessory title remains subject to all latent rights existing at the time of registration, but the possessory title automatically converts to absolute title after the "as is" registered rights have existed for 15 years without challenge. The Singapore land title registration system also recognizes provisional titles, similar to the English system, but provides for conversion of title from provisional to absolute in only five years.[84]

This type of legal tool might be particularly suitable in an environment where it is suspected that there are many conflicting (and difficult to resolve) claims to the same land parcels. Where poor populations do not have the resources to make and support a claim, these tools can provide a legal safety net that preserves the rights until such time as the claimant is able to pursue the claim. Of course, a disadvantage of possessory titles is that – until they become absolute – they provide more limited protections and less certainty for the titleholders, and may impair marketability.[85] Legislators must strike the proper balance between facilitating efficient registration of rights and protecting the rights of those who are not able to participate fully in the process. The use of provisional titles is most likely to protect the interests of the poor when used in conjunction with a systematic registration process that maximizes participation of the poor.

Financing first registration

If the state cannot afford to finance the costs of first registration it is reasonable to ask whether the population is in a position to finance these costs. Even if citizens might be able to scrape together the money necessary to pay registration fees and survey costs, it is often unlikely that they would prioritize such purchases over other purchases, except in the specific instance of sporadic registration in the context of a transaction. Where a system is in place to collect land taxes, including for agricultural land, one solution might be to add the fees for first registration to the annual land tax, and allow them to be paid over a short period of time (say, five years), which would reduce the immediate impact upon property owners. A variant on this approach would be to collect the fees for a systematic first registration at the time of the first sale or mortgage of the property (but not upon inheritance), following first registration. This would require the state to finance most of the costs of first registration up front and collect reimbursement gradually as the land market develops.

If the state does not finance first registration, it may also be unable to finance the day-to-day operation of the system. Although the state may design a registration system with the intention of making it self-financing, paid for through registration fees charged to applicants and fees charged for providing information to market participants, the state should be prepared to subsidize the system in the event that fees do not generate enough income to sustain the system.

VIII. Conclusion

Systems that formalize land rights offer opportunities to improve the lives of the poor in many developing countries. Potential benefits include security against eviction, opportunities for investment and savings, capture of increased property values, access to credit, and enhanced social status and stability. However, the needs and opportunities are likely to differ from setting to setting, and planners must clearly understand both their goals in formalizing rights, as well as the particular features of the specific setting in which they will work. Importantly, planners should test – through field research – hypotheses about the benefits and risks of formalizing rights before embarking on an expensive program to do so.

Evidence as to the benefits of formalization appears to be highly situation specific, and it appears, moreover, that there will be settings in which the general principle of "do no harm" is likely to be significantly violated. The challenge is to determine whether in a given situation formalization is likely to benefit the poor, or at least likely to benefit the general population without harming the poor.

The following are settings in which formalization may be more likely to benefit the poor:

– Settings in which the poor have received land rights under government programs, including under redistributive land tenure reform programs.
– Settings in which squatters have occupied public lands (and private lands) for long periods of time.
– Settings in which rightholders do not have formalized rights, but face a serious external threat such as, for example, owners (or equivalent rightholders) of peri-urban lands that might be a target for takings via eminent domain for commercial or "development" purposes. (Reasonable care would need to be taken, however, that the legal rules and administrative arrangements for such titling did not open the way for a reverse phenomenon: government or private interests successfully claiming to already be the priority rightholders.)
– Settings in which customary group rights are not yet formally protected against the threat of outside incursions. Formalization should consist of documenting and registering the external boundaries of the group's lands within which they will carry on their chosen customary arrangements.
– In almost all settings it is desirable to give greater weight to women's land rights via formalization. This may take several forms, ranging from adding the wife's name to existing titling documents and registry entries, to adding the wife's name in supplements or

reissues for existing documents, to creating a presumptive rule of law that deems wives to have rights in common to all land documented in a husband's name, unless the contrary is shown.

Formalization is unlikely to benefit the poor – and may positively harm the poor – in other settings, some of which may overlap (and thus may negate) settings described above. These include:

- Settings in which the legal and administrative arrangements cannot offer adequate protection against the interception of benefits by local officials or local elites, as via their successful assertion of false claims, or their simply using the occasion to undertake an illegal "squatter clearing" operation, especially for valuable lands.
- Situations of premature insistence upon "Westernization" and individualization of land rights, as in customary rights within the boundaries of traditional communities. To similar effect, lands such as unimproved pasturelands or rangelands used by traditional herders (although documenting the *external* boundaries of such lands is likely to be beneficial).
- Situations – often also found on lands of customary or indigenous groups – where there are likely to be many subordinate rights, often held by women or by other weaker members of the community, which it would be difficult to memorialize and preserve in the formalization process, and which are therefore likely to be lost (although it may be possible to formulate rules that preserve such subordinate rights, at the cost of some derogation from any desired "conclusive" aspect of the registration system).
- Situations where there are lobbies or groups, such as surveyors or notaries, who insist upon a titling and registration process that would involve financial or other transaction costs far higher than is reasonably necessary. This might take the form, for example, of ground-survey costs per parcel far higher than what international best practice shows is possible.

In determining when and whether and to what extent to move ahead with titling and registration, planners should bear in mind at least four general observations.

First, there should be no general presumption that individualized titling and registration are always to be done. This chapter has attempted to lay out some of the considerations that should be the subject of empirical investigation before decisions are made. Yet failure to act is also a decision, and one must take care that an extended research agenda does not simply become an excuse for inaction: the potential benefits, for the poor, from this most important of productive assets, land, are too significant to put off decision making for an extended period. Thus, conduct research, but also decide.

Second, where research does not point a clearer way or where there are major variables still to be determined as to a possible titling and registration system, planners should consider implementing pilot projects to test whether formalization is likely to provide benefits, if the nation's legal system permits such a legal regime to be adopted for application in only one or a few areas. As with all pilot projects, it will be necessary to keep replicability in mind, not lavishing financial or administrative resources that are too generous to be extended on a national scale.

Third, wherever possible, use the comparative international experience as a guide to lower the per-parcel costs of titling and registration. Consider, for example, whether newer technologies such as satellite surveying and GPS can be used to reduce the costs of surveying and mapping drastically, used in conjunction with practically minded legal rules about the accuracy of boundaries, especially for rural lands. Or, if traditional ground surveying is to be used, keep in mind that there have been large differences in costs-per-parcel in different country settings, depending on such factors as whether competition among private surveyors is demanded and bidding processes are used.

Finally, planners would do well to keep in mind that fundamental aspects of system design may make a system more or less affordable and, especially when corruption is a basic concern, more or less open to rent seeking by officials involved in the registration process. Certainly, a declaratory system is likely to be much less expensive for the state to operate than a conclusive system and involves much less official discretion and hence less room for rent seeking (where that is perceived to be a major threat). On the other hand, what the register provides in a declaratory system is essentially notice of claims and no strong assurance of rights. Other important legal variables in design that may put less pressure on perfection of the information in the registry are the recognition of rights by prescription (including prescription effective against the state, at least for smallholders), and clear rules as to inquiry notice, holding prospective transferees liable to have the knowledge they should gain as a consequence of inspecting the property. A highly promising intermediate approach, without going to a declaratory system, but offering potentially large cost savings, is the use of provisional titles that will be perfected if they are not challenged within a prescribed period.

Land rights registration systems are fundamentally human systems that operate within a complex environment of existing power relations, including relations between citizens and public officials, and among citizens who may possess differing amounts of power. Successful introduction and operation of a system will depend in part upon creating a workable legal framework, and creating appropriate knowledge and technical capacity among registry officials. But the greater challenges may arise with regard to matching the capacity of the system to the needs of the public, ensuring that the system provides services that are useful and affordable to citizens. Mere legislative fiat – making registration of land rights mandatory – is unlikely, by itself, to ensure that the system is used in practice. An unused registration system is unlikely to serve the needs of either the state or citizens, and may create many more problems than it solves.

Notes

1   Australian Agency For International Development (AusAID), *Improving Access to Land and Enhancing the Security of Land Rights: A Review of Land Titling and Land Administration Projects*, Quality Assurance Series No. 20, at xiii, 11–12 (AusAID 2000); L. Strachan, *Assets-Based Development: The Role for Pro-Poor Land Tenure Reform* 4 (Discussion Paper, Canadian International Development Agency 2001); World Bank, WORLD DEVELOPMENT REPORT 2002: BUILDING INSTITUTIONS FOR MARKETS 31–38 (World Bank 2002); A. Galal & O. Razzaz, *Reforming Land and Real Estate Markets*, World Bank Policy Research Working Paper No. 2616, at 5–9 (World Bank 2001).

2   T. Hanstad, *Designing Land Registration Systems for Developing Countries*, 13(3) AMERICAN UNIVERSITY INTERNATIONAL LAW REVIEW 647, 649-652 (1998); H. Dekker, THE INVISIBLE LINE: LAND REFORM, LAND TENURE SECURITY AND LAND REGISTRATION 121-125 (Ashgate 2003); G. Larsson, LAND REGISTRATION AND CADASTRAL SYSTEMS: TOOLS FOR LAND INFORMATION AND MANAGEMENT 9-10, 41-42, 112-114 (Longman Scientific & Technical 1991).

3   The process of converting "land shares" into ownership rights to particular parcels is discussed in Section VII of Chapter 7.

4   S. Dobrilovic & R. Mitchell, *Project to Develop Land and Real Estate Markets in Moldova: End of Contract Report* 3-6, 9-15 (USAID 2000). RDI attorneys also served as legal advisors to the USAID-funded Ukraine Land Titling Initiative, a six-year nationwide land privatization and titling program with many parallels to the Moldova titling program. By its close in 2006, the project had issued just over 1.5 million titles for agricultural land to approximately 1.25 million citizens. The titles were registered at the district level because no national land rights registry yet exists. This project also included significant legal and regulatory, public education, and legal aid components. United States Agency for International Development, *Ukraine Land Titling Initiative 2001-2006: Final Report* 18-9 (USAID Sept. 2006), available at http://pdf.usaid.gov/pdf_docs/PDACI600.pdf [hereinafter *ULTI Final Report*].

5   See generally R. Lopez & A. Valdez, *Fighting Rural Poverty in Latin America: New Evidence and Policy*, in R. Lopez & A. Valdes, eds., RURAL POVERTY IN LATIN AMERICA 19-24 (MacMillan 2000); C.D. Deere & M. León, EMPOWERING WOMEN: LAND AND PROPERTY RIGHTS IN LATIN AMERICA 292 (University of Pittsburgh Press 2001).

6   The World Bank, *Implementation Completion Report on Credits in the Amount of US $42.3 million to Honduras for a Rural Land Management Project* 3-9 (World Bank 2004). A follow-on project, also financed through World Bank loans, is expected to run for 12 years in three four-year phases. During the first phase (2004-2008), project plans call for the survey and registration of 745,000 land parcels. This phase will

also include policy and regulatory and institutional capacity building components. The World Bank, *Project Appraisal Document on a Proposed Credit in the Amount of SDR 16.9 Million (USD 25.0 Million Equivalent) to Republic of Honduras for a Land Administration Project in Support of the First Phase of a Land Administration Program* 32-39 (World Bank 2004).

7   See generally J.W. Bruce, *Country Profiles of Land Tenure: Africa 1996*, Land Tenure Center Research Paper No. 130 (Land Tenure Center 1998); M. Rwabahungu, *Tenurial Reforms in West and Central Africa: Legislation, Conflicts, and Social Movements*, in K. Ghimire, ed., WHOSE LAND? CIVIL SOCIETY PERSPECTIVES ON LAND REFORM AND RURAL POVERTY REDUCTION 165-191 (International Fund for Agricultural Development 2001); E. Koch, J.M. Massyn & A. van Niekerk, *The Fate of Land Reform in Southern Africa: The Role of the State, the Market, and Civil Society*, in Ghimire, supra, at 129-161; J.W. Bruce & S.E. Migot-Adholla, eds., SEARCHING FOR LAND TENURE SECURITY IN AFRICA (Kendall/Hunt 1994); F. Muhereza & D. Bledsoe, *Final Report – Land Sector Analysis: Common Property Resources Component* (Government of Uganda 2002).

8   J.W. Bruce, LAND TENURE ISSUES IN PROJECT DESIGN AND STRATEGIES FOR AGRICULTURAL DEVELOPMENT IN SUB-SAHARAN AFRICA 81-84 (Land Tenure Center 1986); J. Quan, *Land Tenure, Economic Growth and Poverty in Sub-Saharan Africa*, in C. Toulmin & J. Quan, eds., EVOLVING LAND RIGHTS, POLICY AND TENURE IN AFRICA 35-38 (IIED & Natural Resources Institute 2000); J. Platteau, *Does Africa Need Land Reform?*, in Toulmin & Quan, supra, at 66-67.

9   United Nations Office for the Coordination of Humanitarian Affairs (UNOCHA), *Angola: Land Reform Needed*, IRIN News, Apr. 26, 2002, at 1; Republic of Uganda, Land Act sec. 5 (1998).

10 Development Workshop, *Terra Firme: Oportunidades e Constrangimentos para uma Gestão Apropriada da Terra Urbana em Angola* (Development Workshop 2003).

11 See Bruce & Migot-Adholla, supra note 7, at 145-46.

12 A threshold problem, however, may have been that a major part of the Kenya program was politically geared to ignore the group with traditional land claims, in favor of a more distant favored group, as well as favoring local elites. See the discussion in Chapter 3.

13 Republic of Uganda, *Land Sector Strategic Plan: 2001–2011*, at 36-38 (Republic of Uganda 2002).

14 P. Brinn, et al., *Assessment of Rwanda's Land Registration, Land Information Management, Land Use Planning and Land Management Systems* 5 (Natural Resources Institute, University of Greenwich 2004).

15 Hernando de Soto's *The Mystery of Capital* presents perhaps the most popular recent argument that formalization of land rights will bring needed assets into the formal economy and allow millions of the poor to become economic actors and to prosper. Among other things, de Soto suggests that the formal law has done a poor job of mirroring and responding to the many existing extra-legal but firmly established rules that govern the social and economic relations of the poor and their "dead capital" assets. See generally H. de Soto, THE MYSTERY OF CAPITAL: WHY CAPITALISM TRIUMPHS IN THE WEST AND FAILS EVERYWHERE ELSE (Basic Books 2000).

16 Often, the state poses the greatest threat of dispossession, especially to the poor and especially to customary group rights in areas where customary law institutions are not robust. As compared to local elites and corporations, the state often has greater power to displace poor individuals and weak groups. Titling and registration, which is a recognition by the state of the validity of individual or group rights, make it more difficult for the state to lay claim to physical possession of the land without paying adequate compensation. See R. Mitchell, *Property Rights and Environmentally Sound*

Management, in J. Bruce, et al., eds, LAND LAW REFORM: ACHIEVING DEVELOPMENT POL-
ICY OBJECTIVES 197 (World Bank 2006).

17 See J. Hayes, M. Roth & L. Zepeda, *Tenure Security, Investment and Productivity in
Gambian Agriculture: A Generalized Profit Analysis*, 79(2) AMERICAN JOURNAL OF AGRI-
CULTURAL ECONOMICS 369, 377 (1997); T. Besley, *Property Rights and Investments In-
centives: Theory and Evidence from Ghana*, 103 JOURNAL OF POLITICAL ECONOMICS 903
(1995); Q.T. Do & L. Iyer, *Land Rights and Economic Development, Evidence from Viet
Nam*, World Bank Policy Research Working Paper No. 3120 (World Bank 2002); Guo
Li, et al., *Tenure, Land Rights, and Farmer Investment Incentives in China*, 19 AGRICUL-
TURAL ECONOMICS 63 (1998).

18 J. Strasma, *Unfinished Business: Consolidating Land Reform in El Salvador*, in W. Thie-
senhusen, ed., SEARCHING FOR AGRARIAN REFORM IN LATIN AMERICA 427 n.5 (Unwin
Hyman 1989); E. Field, *Property Rights, Community Public Goods, and Household Time
Allocation in Urban Squatter Communities: Evidence from Peru*, 45(3) WILLIAM AND
MARY LAW REVIEW 837, 867-868 (2004).

19 G. Feder, *The Intricacies of Land Markets: Why the World Bank Succeeds in Economic
Reform through Land Registration and Tenure Security* (paper presented at the Confer-
ence of the International Federation of Surveyors, April 19-26, 2002, Washington D.
C.).

20 It is unclear whether more secure land rights are also likely to lead to increases in
land speculation (in the sense of purchasing only to resell, not to use or develop), or
whether such speculation, in net effect, injures the poor.

21 See E. Field & M. Torero, *Do Property Titles Increase Credit Access Among the Urban
Poor? Evidence From a Nationwide Titling Program*, Mimeo (2006).

22 R. Mitchell, *A Productive Convergence: Report on the Pilot Program of the Revenue Department and Rural Development Department to Regularize Ownership Based on Sada
Bai Nama Transactions* 9 (on file with the Rural Development Institute, Apr. 2008).

23 See generally R. Prosterman & J. Riedinger, LAND REFORM AND DEMOCRATIC DEVELOP-
MENT chs. 1, 5 & 6 (Johns Hopkins 1987).

24 M. Fay & C. Opal, *Urbanizations without Growth, A Not-So-Uncommon Phenomenon*,
World Bank Policy Research Working Paper No. 2412, at 6 (World Bank 2000); D.F.
Bryceson & V. Jamal, FAREWELL TO FARMS: DE-AGRARIANISATION AND EMPLOYMENT IN
AFRICA (Ashgate 1997).

25 R. DiTella, S. Galiani & E. Schargrodsky, *The Formation of Beliefs: Evidence From the
Allocation of Land Titles to Squatters*, 122(1) QUARTERLY JOURNAL OF ECONOMICS 209-
241 (Feb. 2007).

26 Mitchell, supra note 16, at 191.

27 See generally de Soto, supra note 15.

28 Of course, an efficient system for registering rights to land, by itself, is not likely to
create a land sale market or mortgage market. The general level of the economy, the
preferences of citizens and lenders, and the opportunities for other investment,
among other factors, will influence the extent to which citizens engage in land transactions and lenders finance such transactions. But an efficient system for registering
rights to land is surely a major facilitator for the development of robust property markets.

29 In settings where customary law regimes discriminate against the most vulnerable,
including women, there may be pressure to register individual and family rights of
group members and protect such rights against claims by the larger group. This ob-
viously weakens the group's control over the group territory and raises complicated
issues regarding administration of rights.

30 Compare the discussion of invasions of agricultural land in Chapter 3, recognizing too that many cases of urban squatting occur on publicly owned land, often a consideration weighing in favor of regularization.

31 But in the absence of some form of adjudication of group rights, the state itself may introduce conflict by resettling or transmigrating land-poor populations from elsewhere to what the state erroneously regards as unused "public" lands. See the discussion of resettlement in Indonesia in Chapter 3.

32 Women's land rights is the subject of Chapter 5. Also, see generally R. Giovarelli, *Overcoming Gender Biases in Property Rights Systems*, in J.W. Bruce, et al., eds., LAND LAW REFORM: ACHIEVING DEVELOPMENT POLICY OBJECTIVES 79-84 (World Bank 2006).

33 B. Agarwal, A FIELD OF ONE'S OWN: GENDER AND LAND RIGHTS IN SOUTH ASIA 31-32 (Cambridge University Press 1994).

34 See generally Larsson, supra note 2, at 15-17.

35 The taxing authority may require additional information such as the quality of the soil, the estimated value of constructions, or the identity of temporary land users.

36 For example, the system framework could include some number of open (i.e., unused) fields for data that will give operators flexibility to modify the system in the future as new needs arise.

37 D. Bledsoe, *Can Land Titling and Registration Reduce Poverty?*, in J.W. Bruce, et al., eds., LAND LAW REFORM: ACHIEVING DEVELOPMENT POLICY OBJECTIVES 143 (World Bank 2006). For a somewhat harsh assessment of the value of state-guaranteed titles, see D. W. Bromley, *The Empty Promises of Formal Titles: Creating Potempkin* [sic] *Villages in the Tropics* (undated), available at http://otto.idium.no/desotowatch.net/?module=Articles; action=Article.publicOpen;ID=2935.

38 See G. Feder, T. Onchan, Y. Chalamwong & C. Hongladarom, LAND POLICIES AND FARM PRODUCTIVITY IN THAILAND 101-114 (Johns Hopkins University Press 1988).

39 F. Byamugisha, *How Land Registration Affects Financial Development and Economic Growth in Thailand*, Policy Research Working Paper Series No. 2241, at 19, 22 (World Bank 1999). Given that the longer-term positive impact reflects the theoretical expectations, the effects of early speculation and related land price increases, and some initial caution on the part of financial agents, were suggested as the causes of the initial negative impact. Id. at 22.

40 Survey results showed that although the frequency of investments by all farmers increased after 1998, farmers who had both contracts and certificates had increased the frequency of their investment by 244% while farmers who had neither contracts nor certificates increased the frequency of their investments by only 64%. Z. Keliang, R. Prosterman, Y. Jianping, L. Ping, J. Riedinger & O. Yiwen, *The Rural Land Question in China: Analysis and Recommendations Based on a Seventeen-Province Survey*, 38(4) NYU JOURNAL OF INTERNATIONAL LAW & POLITICS 761, 811-818 (2006).

41 M.R. Carter & E. Zegarra, *Land Markets and the Persistence of Rural Poverty: Post-Liberalization Policy Options*, in R. Lopez & A. Valdes, eds., RURAL POVERTY IN LATIN AMERICA 81-82 (MacMillan 2000); see also R. López & T.S. Thomas, *Rural Poverty in Paraguay: The Determinants of Farm Household Income*, in R. Lopez & A. Valdes, eds., RURAL POVERTY IN LATIN AMERICA 252-257 (MacMillan 2000).

42 J. Foltz, B. Larson & R. López, *Land Tenure, Investment, and Agricultural Production in Nicaragua*, Development Discussion Papers: Central American Project Series 17-18 (Harvard Institute for International Development 2000).

43 S. Galiani & E. Schargrodsky, *Property Rights for the Poor: Effects of Land Titling* 1-6, 16-21 (Universidad Torcuato Di Tella 2005).

44 This might be explained by the fact that the heads of household for titled families were less likely to have non-nuclear family members (such as brothers or sisters of

the head) living in the house, and were less likely to have had offspring born after the titling. Id. at 25-26.

45   Id. at 27.

46   Id. at 28-29.

47   See L. Rolfes, Jr., *The Impact of Land Titling in Ukraine: the Results from an 800 Person Random-Sample Survey*, RDI Reports on Foreign Aid and Development No. 119, at 1-11, 8-14 (Rural Development Institute 2003). The Ukraine experience is discussed in Section VII of Chapter 7.

48   See, e.g., R. Barrows & M. Roth, *Land Tenure and Investment in African Agriculture: Theory and Evidence*, 28(2) JOURNAL OF MODERN AFRICAN STUDIES 265 (June 1990).

49   See Quan, supra note 8, at 35–36; A. Brasselle, F. Gaspart & J. Platteau, *Land Tenure Security and Investment Incentives: Puzzling Evidence From Burkina Faso*, 67 DEVELOPMENT ECONOMICS 373, 395-396 (2002); Barrows & Roth, supra note 48, at 265, 275.

50   J. Mackinnon & R. Reinikka, LESSONS FROM UGANDA ON STRATEGIES TO FIGHT POVERTY 38 (Centre for Study of African Economies & World Bank 2000).

51   J. Baland, F. Gaspart, F. Place & J. Platteau, POVERTY, TENURE SECURITY, AND ACCESS TO LAND IN CENTRAL UGANDA: THE ROLE OF MARKET AND NON-MARKET PROCESSES 27-28, 30 (World Bank 1999).

52   See Brasselle et al., supra note 49, at 375, 391.

53   Id. at 379-381.

54   In cases where the owner of a land parcel does not regularly inspect the land, other persons might occupy the land and claim it as their own. If the owner's rights are registered, the owner should have less difficulty in obtaining the assistance of courts and police to remove the occupier. The owner's right may be limited by rules on prescription (that is, rules as to whether, and after how many years, unauthorized occupation of the land or of part of the land by another person will terminate the owner's right to reclaim it, and transfer ownership of the land, by operation of law, to the unauthorized occupant).

55   In Ukraine, for example, former members of collective agricultural enterprises who hold land shares that have not yet been allocated in kind may be vulnerable to losing their land rights to more powerful individuals and enterprises before they are able to convert the land shares into identifiable parcels and receive a certificate documenting their ownership of land.

56   For example, Mozambique's 1997 land law provides for "automatic" recognition of exclusive rights to land of individual citizens who have worked on the land "in good faith" for ten or more years; there is no need for the state to issue a title certificate or perform registration. Admittedly, the unregistered rights do reduce tradability of land, at least for those transactions involving persons from outside the village; however, the cost of proving ownership (in the case of Mozambique, of proving exclusive use rights) is only borne by the parties at the time of a transaction. See Mitchell, supra note 16, at 194-196.

57   Legal tools other than strict enforcement of registered boundaries may provide owners with more effective and more reasonable means for resolving boundary disputes. In particular, judicial recognition of prescriptive rights (also known as adverse possession) to land that a neighbor occupies for a long period in an obvious way can provide a clear and rational basis for awarding property rights to the possessor. See generally D. Irving, *Should the Law Recognize the Acquisition of Title by Adverse Possession?*, 2 AUSTRALIAN PROPERTY LAW JOURNAL 1, 6-9 (1994).

58   Just as a prospective buyer of the land object will be interested to know about encumbrances to the owner's rights, the prospective lender will also be interested to know about all existing encumbrances of the owner's right (including existing mortgages)

since the lender's mortgage rights may have a lower priority than the rights of the holders of the encumbrances.

59 See S.R. Simpson, LAND LAW AND REGISTRATION 16-17 (Cambridge University Press 1976). Although the data on owners and rights may be contained in a separate database from the spatial data on parcel boundaries, the databases should be maintained by one institution that includes some officials with expertise in rights registration and other officials with expertise in cadastral mapping.

60 Usually only lease agreements exceeding some specified length, such as three years, should be registered; otherwise, the frequency of lease registrations becomes a burden on citizens and the registry system. Some systems may also register servitudes, and in particular servitudes of passage across privately owned land.

61 Although parcel-based indexes are usually associated with conclusive registration systems, they are used in declaratory registration systems. See J. Zevenbergen, SYSTEMS OF LAND REGISTRATION: ASPECTS AND EFFECTS 57-58 (Delft: Netherlands Geodetic Commission 2002).

62 This list is adapted, with modification, from Simpson, supra note 59, at 17-18.

63 This type of rule also provides other protections to the applicant since, if the registrar makes no record of the refusal, the applicant will have much more difficulty in appealing the refusal because there would be no conclusive evidence that the applicant ever submitted the application. There is also a risk that a second applicant may register rights regarding the land while the first applicant is appealing the registrar's refusal. The second applicant would have no notice of the first applicant's application since the registrar had refused to accept the first applicant's application.

64 Dobrilovic & Mitchell, supra note 4, at 13-14, 26. The newspaper, which was delivered monthly to subscribers in every village of the country, also contained articles on other issues of interest to farmers, including farming techniques, animal husbandry, farm finance and prices for farm products in various markets.

65 *ULTI Final Report*, supra note 4, at 15-21. The most popular program was a national radio program – Agronovyny – that the project developed to answer letters from citizens who had questions about how to obtain and use their land rights, and how to resolve disputes over land. The project's legal staff provided general information about the applicable law and placed citizens in contact with the project's regional legal aid staff for further follow-up.

66 As with the exception for spousal rights, a rule that establishes the legitimacy of unregistered subordinate rights (of a defined character) is not necessarily inconsistent with operation of a conclusive registration system, again provided that the public is generally aware that such exceptions exist. To ensure that the public receives adequate notice of this exception to the conclusive effect of registration, rules could require that the registration records (including certificates or registry excerpts issued to those dealing with the land) explicitly state that unregistered subordinate rights of a defined character continue in force.

67 See P. Dale & J. McLaughlin, LAND ADMINISTRATION 28 (Oxford University Press 1999).

68 Dobrilovic & Mitchell, supra note 4, at 52.

69 Land Privatization Support Project in Moldova, *Report on Project Activity* 24 (2004) (an estimated 2.75 of parcel surveys contain some type of survey error).

70 Author conversations with land survey experts of the Indonesian National Land Agency, June 2003. At 10 parcels per hectare, the cost of ground surveys was approximately eight times as expensive as the corrected surveys based on aerial photography, and more than 30 times as expensive as the corrected surveys based on satellite imagery.

71 See Dale & McLaughlin, supra note 67, at 30 (noting some positive traits of the sporadic approach).

72 Simpson, supra note 59, at 268.

73 Also, registration procedures and requirements can be opaque, further deterring access by the poor. L. Holstein, *Towards Best Practices from World Bank Experience in Land Titling and Registration* 16-17 (paper presented at the International Conference on Land Tenure Administration, University of Florida Geomatics Program, Nov. 12-14, 1996). In addition, rent seeking by registration officials can keep poor rightholders away.

74 C. Grant, *When Titling Meets Tradition* 2 (paper presented at 39th Australian Surveyors Congress, Launceston, Australia, Nov. 8-13, 1998).

75 Cambodia provides some examples of the shortfalls of sporadic registration. There the approach initially focused on registering rights to residential and commercial land, and tended to exclude agricultural parcels because the registration infrastructure is most lacking in rural areas. Cambodia also had problems with a lack of trained staff at the local level, a failure by staff to follow procedures consistently, insufficient equipment and archiving capacity at the local level, inaccurate land survey plans, the entry of inaccurate or fraudulent information (to avoid transfer taxes) and corruption. The Cambodian government later decided to move resources to systematic mass registration to take advantage of mapping economies, opportunities for widespread dispute resolution, and appropriate land survey detail. The approach will promote accessibility by displaying graphic and textual documentation in the villages for 30 days, soliciting input and appeals, and resolving disputes through bodies composed of local community leaders and titling program representatives. M. Törhönen, *Systematic Registration for Cambodia: Why and How?* 1-6 (paper presented at the International Conference on Spatial Information for Sustainable Development, Nairobi, Kenya, Oct. 2-5, 2001). The Cambodian government is simultaneously exploring ways to improve the sporadic titling system, focusing on simplicity, transparency and accuracy. H.E.S. Setha, *Discussion Paper* 4-5 (paper presented at the Regional Workshop on Land Issues in Asia, Phnom Penh, Cambodia, June 4-5, 2002)

76 One reason a systematic program will produce a reduced unit cost is that land survey professionals will measure and map each common boundary only once. If rights to land parcels are registered sporadically, then the majority of common boundaries will be measured at least twice since there is no general registration map upon which the parcel boundaries can be identified.

77 Simpson, supra note 59, at 194-207; E. Dowson & V.L.O. Sheppard, LAND REGISTRATION 94 (Her Majesty's Stationary Office 1952). In addition, a systematic approach is likely to reduce greatly the number of cases in which a common boundary measured earlier by one land surveyor does not correspond to the location of the same boundary measured later by a different land surveyor.

78 Because the rights created during this process often relate to parcels that are located in the middle of a large field, the prospects for leasing or trading such land are necessarily limited. However, the land right can be leased or sold to any citizen. By contrast, a lessee who leases in one or more land shares must negotiate, through a general meeting or the equivalent, with other land share owners (and, potentially, also with other lessees of shares) regarding the location of land to be leased from the large massif owned in common by all holders of land shares. This cumbersome process usually results in all land shares being leased in by a single large lessee, often a successor to the former collective, and often on terms rather unfavorable to the land share owners.

79 A further expectation is that once land surveyors and the public find that appropriate land survey services need not be exorbitantly expensive, market fees for land survey

services are likely to be much more affordable for any subsequent land market activity requiring land survey.

80 See Holstein, supra note 73, at 17.

81 J. Salukvadze, *Comparative Analyses of Land Administration Systems: With Special Reference to Armenia, Moldova, Latvia and Kyrgyzstan* 37 (2002) (on file with the Rural Development Institute).

82 R. Gaynor & D. Bledsoe, EVALUATION OF THE ALBANIA LAND MARKET PROJECT 5 (USAID/ARD 2000).

83 T. Fiflis, *English Registered Conveyancing: A Study in Effective Land Transfer* 59 NORTHWESTERN UNIVERSITY LAW REVIEW 470, 482-483 (1964).

84 Simpson, supra note 59, at 214-216.

85 See id. at 216-218.

9   Land rights legal aid

Robert Mitchell

I.   Introduction

Of all possible pro-poor interventions relating to reform of land tenure, legal aid for poor families who use, own or seek access to land may be the most generally applicable and least risky. It is less risky because it is more flexible than other interventions: client demands can daily help shape the nature and focus of the intervention. Legal aid is important for implementing other land tenure interventions discussed in this book, and it can help project implementers maintain their focus squarely on the poor. Land rights legal aid to the poor also provides a feedback loop for project implementers, which can provide an early warning of project missteps. And legal aid provides ample "real life" material to support advocacy and public information campaigns directed at the public and government officials. Finally, legal aid tests the government's commitment to assisting the poor; a government that cannot accept and support a program of legal aid for the poor may be a weak candidate as a partner for other pro-poor land-related interventions.

Legal aid seeks to assist the poor to take control over their own lives. Designed and delivered properly, provision of legal aid services to the poor represents a "bottom-up" strategy that focuses on the needs of the poor and approaches the legal system from the standpoint of the poor. This is very different from the much more common approach that international development agencies take, of reforming judicial systems in the hope of benefiting the poor.

> [T]he basic needs of the rural poor are more than merely physical. The rural poor hunger besides for justice, for respect for their dignity, and for control over their lives. . . . To the extent legal aid can help the rural poor gain justice and greater control over their lives, it does meet a basic need.[1]

This point is illustrated by the comment of a Chinese farmer who told RDI that he was not primarily concerned with winning his case over a land dispute; rather, he was most concerned that his position should be heard and considered.[2] Thus, there is reason to believe that the poor derive important benefits from participating in the process of understanding and pressing their rights, even if they do not immediately succeed.[3] At the same time, to be truly successful, a legal aid program should materially improve the lives of clients.

Designed and delivered with appropriate sensitivity and focus, legal aid can help to protect the poor's access to land and use of land. This chapter discusses lessons learned regarding how to provide legal aid services in a manner that promotes and protects the access to and use of land by the poor. Section II presents an overview of two broad styles of legal aid: traditional and structural. Section III discusses the relationship between traditional legal aid and rural land rights. Section IV explores further the representation of clients. Section V looks at land rights education and use of mass media, and Section VI discusses financing, organization and staffing.

Lessons described here are based primarily on RDI's experience in organizing and supervising legal aid services in Russia, Moldova and Ukraine, and are informed by our involvement with legal aid in the Kyrgyz Republic and India. In 1996 RDI established the first land rights legal center in the former Soviet Union, the Center for Land Reform Support of Vladimir Oblast, which celebrated its tenth anniversary in August 2006. In 1998 RDI established a second center in Samara, Russia, which operated until 2005. As part of a USAID land privatization program in Moldova, RDI helped create a national system of rural legal aid centers that operated until the project ended in December 2000. RDI also helped design a national system of legal aid centers in Ukraine. The first centers opened in February 2003 and the twenty-fifth center opened in 2005; these operated until March 2007.[4] Since 2002 RDI has provided technical assistance to a statewide paralegal program working with the rural poor in the Indian state of Andhra Pradesh (See Chapter 6).

II.   Styles of legal aid

Legal aid services may be divided into two broad types: traditional and structural. In general terms, "traditional" legal aid undertakes to provide clients with legal protections on the basis of existing legislation. Traditional legal aid does not seek to change the letter of the law, but to enforce the law as written. In the process of enforcing the written law, a well-designed traditional legal aid program should also seek to generate public discussion of government policies, laws and legal processes in terms of the real experience of legal aid clients.

The traditional approach may be contrasted with structural legal aid, also called "developmental" legal aid, which uses a political approach to challenge legal and political structures that generate and perpetuate injustice to the poor.[5] Proponents of structural legal aid advocate this approach in settings where the legal system is believed to be fundamentally biased against the poor. Structural legal aid seeks to assist the poor as a class rather than specific individuals.[6]

Advocates of structural legal aid charge that traditional legal aid, at best, is a way of giving alms to the poor, providing temporary relief without addressing the structural problems that generate poverty.[7] Another charge is that traditional legal aid may even provide cover to those in a position of power who maintain unfair policies. In making the case for structural legal aid, Nasution argues that the legal aid must have a political motivation in addition to a humanitarian motivation, and must both inform people of their rights and encourage them to develop the moral courage to demand such rights.[8]

Diokno argues that structural legal aid lawyers must confront the government with the detrimental human effects of government policies and programs, demonstrating the inconsistencies between the values that the government professes (and values that accord with international standards) on the one hand, and the government's actual policies, as implemented, on the other. This strategy is premised on the belief that appeals to conscience are not doomed to fail, and on the belief that governments seek respect from other governments.[9] Diokno further argues that legal aid should help the poor understand the causes of their situation and help them to organize and mobilize themselves to overcome the causes.[10]

Structural legal aid can surely serve a very valuable role in challenging government policies and the fundamental structure of legal protections available to the poor. Such aid may be the only type of assistance relevant to the poor in settings where the law, as written, excludes protection for the poor, and where the justice system, either through design or practice, routinely deprives the poor of access.

But traditional legal aid may also perform a valuable role in many settings. If designed and implemented correctly, traditional legal aid can inform people of their rights as embodied in existing law and motivate them to find the moral courage to demand their rights, and can expose inconsistencies between the values the government professes in the law as written and the values evident in the government's policies. Providers of traditional legal aid may also advocate changes in law, though this is unlikely to be a primary focus. Perhaps the only structural legal aid activity that is outside the purview of traditional legal aid is protest (and advocacy of public protest) against the government.

Box 9.1. Classifying legal aid tactics

By way of example, one might consider the possibility of various alternative approaches by which lawyers might help landless rural people to gain ownership of an unused large estate or portion of a large estate.

(1) Identify a group of such people as client and ask the country's land administration authorities to take over control of that land under existing legal rules applicable to unused or abandoned land, and to allocate the land to the clients as defined beneficiaries under the law; or

(2) Perhaps after a rebuff under (1), file suit in court to force the land administration authority to act; or

(3) Urge the legislature or the land administration authority to adopt rules under which the clients can acquire control of such land; or

(4) Represent a group of clients who already occupy the land, under circumstances in which the law may recognize in principle their entitlement to control that land (e.g., they were previous owners or had customary rights and were wrongfully displaced); or

(5) Represent the occupying clients in arguing to the government for the need to change the law to accommodate the needs of these clients, or the need for conferral of control rights to the clients on an ad hoc basis.

Options (1), (2) and (4) might appropriately be categorized as examples of traditional legal aid, while options (3) and (5) might appropriately be categorized as structural legal aid.

Even in fundamentally unjust societies, there may be space to enforce the existing law for the benefit of the poor, to expose deficiencies in the law, to sensitize the courts and the press regarding injustices, and to compel the law actually to deliver to the poor that which it promises on the books. Traditional legal aid programs address this gap: to expose the hypocrisy in law by helping the powerless to enforce the law as written.[11] The defense of the interests of those who lack access to secure land may contribute to erosion of the sense that powerlessness is an immutable condition. Box 9.1 offers some specific examples of tactics that might be classified as traditional and others that might be classified as structural legal aid.

Some governments may not allow structural legal aid tactics that question the government's legitimacy. In settings where structural legal aid is not an option, traditional legal aid may be an appropriate means for assisting the poor. For example, Chinese legal aid providers "are able to challenge local authorities, or persons with powerful connections, precisely because the goals they are pursuing are consistent with those of the State."[12]

An argument can also be made that traditional legal aid may sometimes better serve the interests of the poor, even in settings where the government tolerates structural legal aid. Sometimes, structural legal aid providers may have strong ideological viewpoints, occasionally even to the point of superseding the needs or best interests of their clients. Moreover, the poor may prefer to use existing law to make incremental and immediate improvements in their lives rather than expend energy on improvements that are more fundamental, but more distant and perhaps less certain.[13] Finally, the rational motivations of poor individuals may well differ from the rational motivations of groups of the poor.[14] If this is correct, poor families may be more willing to participate in legal tactics that improve their life now rather than participate in legal (or political) tactics that provide no immediate benefit to the family, but which may benefit the larger group in the future.

Nothing just said, of course, precludes the possibility that in some circumstances both traditional and structural legal aid activities may be proceeding in parallel towards a common goal. Nor should it be inferred that traditional legal aid operates in settings and in a manner free of controversy: to the contrary, local landlords or officials on the other side of a legal dispute may be quite unhappy to see the poor receiving legal assistance.

III.   Legal aid and rural land rights

Although legal aid programs typically address all types of problems for a given population, legal aid programs can also be effective when they develop individual specialization or model approaches to common issues.[15] This specialized approach acknowledges that the poor are a heterogeneous body, and that while the poor have a number of features in common, such as a lack of control over goods and services, the dissimilarities among groups of the poor require different approaches for addressing and reducing poverty.[16]

We focus here on the provision of traditional legal aid relating to a narrow set of issues – land rights and access to land – affecting the rural poor.[17] This focus implies both a means test and an issue test. This narrow focus is justified to the extent that secure control of land is fundamental to the livelihoods of the poor, the case for which is made elsewhere in this book.

Land rights legal aid may be initiated as a stand-alone program or in support of larger land tenure interventions. Where land rights legal aid complements other land tenure interventions (such as redistributive land tenure reform, or systematic land titling, to name but two), the legal aid services allow project implementers to ensure that the principal intervention remains focused on delivering benefits to the poor. It is possible to implement land rights legal aid on any scale, from one attorney to many hundreds, depending upon resources and circumstances.

International experience with land rights legal aid is limited. In the Philippines, local NGOs do occasionally help resolve land disputes, but local NGOs are reluctant to provide such aid since this type of dispute tends to create direct conflicts with powerful local landowners.[18] National NGOs may be more willing to provide assistance in land disputes, but they are not based in rural areas where the needs arise most often. In Bangladesh, legal aid providers focus only a small percentage of their time on land disputes.[19] What legal aid exists in China is mostly limited to major cities; few functional legal aid programs operate in rural areas, where lawyers are few, and it is difficult for lawyers to earn a living.[20]

Several African legal aid initiatives focus a portion of their activities on land rights issues, including the Land Reform Project operated by the Legal Resources Centre in South Africa. The project focuses on litigating in order to establish precedent, to secure settlements for clients outside of court, and to facilitate access to land for clients through the government's Department of Land Affairs.[21] It is also actively involved in state deliberations on land reform legislation and has advocated specific law and policy reform, such as the passage of the Communal Land Rights Act of 2004. Another example is the Legal Assistance Centre (LAC) in Namibia, which in 1997 launched the Land, Environment and Development (LEAD) project to provide legal advice on land rights to rural communities. The four main activities of the project are: (1) lobbying for legal reform; 2) legal training on land laws for farmers, small-scale enterprises and NGOs; (3) providing educational materials on land rights; and (4) providing advice, mediation and litigation services on land and environmental issues to rural communities.[22] The center has often met resistance from regional officials; it was forced to request a court order from the High Court to meet with the community leaders without harassment from local police and government officials.[23]

Legal aid is especially needed in less developed areas of any country since people there lack the money to pay for lawyers, have a lower level of legal consciousness, have less access to lawyers generally, and have much less access to lawyers who can afford to provide pro bono services.[24] The same can surely be said for rural populations throughout the developing world.

It is important for legal aid providers and those designing and funding legal aid to conduct research regarding the legal needs of the poor. In order to understand whether and how one can devise programs to provide legal assistance to have-nots, it is also crucially important to examine the structures of power in the society. Study must not be a substitute for action, however, and the needs of the poor will be understood more clearly once legal aid services begin to be provided. It is necessary to monitor service provision intensively at the beginning of the program to ensure that clients both desire and benefit from the services provided.

Legal aid services may include a wide range of activities. The time and resources of service providers are not unlimited, so it is important to decide what time and other resources the providers will devote to each activity. Here we examine four activities: land rights education; advice to clients regarding specific matters; representation of clients engaged in a dispute; and changing the climate of expectations.

Land rights education

In many (though not all) settings where RDI has worked to provide information to the poor regarding land rights, rural citizens do not have frequent access to newspapers, television or even radio. Print and broadcast media rarely devote much coverage to land rights issues, and whatever coverage exists is often incomplete or inaccurate. Literacy varies widely in countries where legal aid for land rights is needed, and this influences the mode of delivering information. It is self-evident that if a person is unaware of her land rights, she is not in a position to know whether – or to what extent – her rights are being violated. The question of considering remedies is never reached. Rural elites may rely upon such ignorance to their advantage in dealings with the rural poor.

Of course, it is dangerous to generalize regarding the extent to which the rural poor understand their rights. In their study of the legal needs of the poor in an Indian village, Gordon and Lindsay found that the poor did in fact know something about the law. They dismiss outright the assertion that the poor are mystified by the law and courts and found, to the contrary, that however deficient the understanding of outsiders might be regarding the legal needs of the poor, the rural poor they met with clearly understood their needs and aspirations.[25]

In settings where the law is undergoing rapid change, as in countries that emerged in the 1990s from the former Soviet Union, it is especially difficult for rural citizens to obtain sound information on land rights. In the half-dozen countries of the region in which RDI has worked with rural populations in the last decade, it is still quite common to find extremely low levels of legal fluency regarding land rights. Although people are not completely ignorant of the law, there is often no reliable institution from which they can receive accurate information. In many rural areas, citizens do not have regular access even to local newspapers. Even where newspapers and other mass media are available, these rarely present a thorough discussion of land rights. The present limitations of knowledge of the changing (improving) formal land rights in rural China are discussed in Chapter 7.

Nor can people regularly rely upon local officials to provide accurate information. Officials may not know the law themselves or may be unaware of more recent changes in law. Even where local officials have information regarding land rights, they are often more likely to view land questions from the perspective of the non-poor, either because the officials come from non-poor families or because they perceive their political futures to be aligned with the interests of the non-poor.

Even among the poor, some constituencies may require additional, special outreach in land rights education. These may include socially disadvantaged populations and also, in many settings, women (see Box 9.2).

Box 9.2. Legal aid and the protection of rural women's land rights in Guangxi, China

Women are often at a distinct disadvantage in obtaining information regarding land rights. It is important to ensure that public education campaigns targeted to reach the poor are designed in ways that address the needs and interests of women, which feature women in roles of understanding and enjoying their land rights, and which are delivered at times and places where women are likely to feel comfortable receiving the information.

In cooperation with Guangxi University Law School, in January 2007 RDI prepared a training manual and provided training to legal aid lawyers and staff of Guangxi Province (China) on the protection of rural women's land rights. A majority of attendees had encountered inquiries or cases concerning rural women's land rights, but knew little about specific laws and regulations controlling rural women's land rights, especially recent regulations and notices from the Ministry of Land and Resources and the Supreme Court.

The training focused on several questions that are common in the countryside regarding securing women's land rights, including, for example, protecting a daughter's land rights when she marries and moves to a different village, ensuring a woman's land rights are preserved after divorce or abandonment, ensuring that women receive compensation equal to that provided to men in the case of land takings by government, and procedures for initiating a formal lawsuit related to rural land.

Advice in specific matters

While important, public education does not usually provide sufficient protection to the poor. There are at least two reasons. First, a poor citizen may reasonably conclude that land rights that appear to be granted in laws are not truly available since he or she cannot afford to challenge the interests of officials or the non-poor who benefit from lack of enforcement of such rights. Second, a poor citizen may not even be interested in learning about land rights in the absence of some demonstration that the society – through such institutions as the courts and legal aid – is prepared to ensure that the rights are enforced.

People may use knowledge of rights in a number of ways short of going to court. They may, for example, negotiate with a neighbor about repairing a fence based on knowledge of the relevant law. Although citizens have not taken the matter to court, this does not mean that they have not mobilized the law.[26] Legal aid providers in some settings have long provided services to help the poor resolve legal issues without entering the formal legal system. In the Ukraine and Vladimir, Russia, legal aid centers, non-litigation assistance complements litigation services. Legal aid attorneys receive letters from clients and meet with clients who request advice in specific matters. The attorneys are often able to advise clients regarding how the client can resolve the issue personally by, for example, preparing a particular application, or presenting the claim to a particular government office.

Representation of clients engaged in a dispute

The provision of advice to clients – that is, explaining the client's options, but not offering to assist the client in pursuing any option – may fail to protect the client's interests adequately. Advice alone may be insufficient in cases where the client's rights are obstructed by a citizen or official who has much more power than the client. In such cases the legal aid service provider can best serve the client by actively representing the client in the dispute. This principle is stated explicitly in the guidelines of the land rights legal aid network that operated for several years throughout rural Ukraine:

> The legal aid centers will focus upon identifying and solving disputes and other problems related to land rights of land parcel owners. The centers will not merely provide information to land parcel owners, but will accompany the land parcel owner to meetings with other parties to the dispute or problem, and then advocate a solution on behalf of the land owner.[27]

Other observers have noted that filing court cases should not be measured only in terms of winning or enforcing a court victory, and that the poor often use the legal system as a way to increase their leverage in settling disputes outside of court.[28]

Even if one believes the courts to be corrupt, or at least biased against the interests of the poor, filing cases in court may place pressure on judges and increase the costs to those who obstruct the rights of the poor. Elites often find that illegal manipulation of the court system carries certain costs, and that if one is "clearly wrong and expects to lose a case, bribing judges or the police becomes an expensive proposition."[29]

Although it is sometimes necessary for the legal aid service provider to represent the client's interests in court, it is often the *threat of filing the claim in court*, rather than the actual prosecution of the claim in court, that is most important in advancing the client's interests. The lawyers of the Ukraine Land Titling Initiative (ULTI) legal aid network took only about 2% of client disputes to court, while solving the vast majority of disputes outside of court.[30] But the lawyers were able to settle so many cases outside court precisely because they had the wherewithal and the confidence to take cases to court if the violation of rights was clear.[31]

Changing the climate of expectations

One fundamental objective of legal aid should be to make the delivery of justice and respect for the rights of the poor "routine" in the sense that these outcomes and practices are expected in the normal course. Legal aid should seek to change expectations which regard injustice as the norm.[32] Such a change in expectations should be regarded as an integral part of the establishment of the rule of law in a society.

Perhaps the best place to begin reversing low expectations is with routine cases that involve clear, but nevertheless frequently occurring, violations of rights. It is true that the routine cases may be easier to prosecute in the sense that they have a lower profile and are therefore less likely to attract strong resistance from groups that have no interest in seeing the poor succeed in defending their rights. But an important reason for preferring routine cases is that the resolution of such cases, whether they are resolved in court or outside court, can more effectively serve to establish the basic principle that the rights of the poor – rights provided in national law – must be respected. Resolution of routine matters may thus have a more dramatic impact on the lives of the poor than victories in so-called "impact" litigation that is undertaken for its dramatic appeal, and "small victories . . . not only make the crucial difference for the immediate clients, but also make it possible for wider change."[33]

If legal aid services provide concrete victories in routine cases over time, and as news of the victories travels throughout the community – and, where possible, is broadly publicized though the media – these successes should gradually increase the confidence of the poor as a class and motivate more individuals to demand that their rights be respected. Researchers who studied the impact of legal aid services provided to poor women in Ecuador concluded that the program may have a positive influence even on those not directly involved in the program. The researchers surmised that recipients of legal aid may serve as disseminators of information, and the successful prosecution of claims should create precedents that induce non-litigants to change their behavior. They conclude that the indirect benefit on non-litigants may be the major potential impact of effective legal and judicial reform.[34] The ultimate objective is to promote a respect for equal application of the law to the poor:

> The sum total [of the work of legal advocacy NGOs] is far greater than the number of evictions they stop or the amount of maintenance payments they obtain for poor women. They help to create a culture of rights in which community standards are raised, so that it is no longer acceptable for a man to unilaterally declare an oral divorce and leave his wife and children with nothing, where a municipal government cannot bulldoze a shanty town with impunity, where factory owners cannot assume government safety officials will simply ignore hazardous workplace conditions, and where poor people begin to believe that rights are not just something that exist for others.[35]

Some routine problems may not be easy to solve and may require much of the legal aid service provider's time to resolve. But if the problem recurs with frequency, it may be worth spending a large amount of time to pursue several "test cases." The pursuit of such cases may help to expose problems in how courts and local government handle them, and even expose problems in the law.

IV.   Representation of clients in practice

Representation of clients vs. mediation

Although there may be a place for mediation in cases involving disputants who are of more or less equal status, mediation is less likely to be

effective in cases where one party has much greater power than the
other party. Mediation and other "neutral" processes are often decidedly
not neutral in cases involving disputes between the poor and the non-
poor (or between the poor and government officials) since such processes inevitably reinforce unequal relations that precede the dispute.
When a dispute is passed from the formal system of justice to the informal system, there is evidence that pre-existing inequalities between
the parties will carry over into the informal system. If a landlord or
large company is the party against which the poor tenant is proceeding,
the powerless person remains at a substantial disadvantage in the new
context.[36]

Legal aid services that provide representation to poor clients constitute a very different approach to dispute resolution, an approach that
acknowledges the importance of the power imbalance between the
poor and the non-poor. This imbalance of power usually contributes to
the dispute in the first place and makes it difficult to resolve. In RDI's
experience working with legal aid providers in Russia, Ukraine and
Moldova, disputes between the poor and local elites (or local officials)
rarely come down to a question over confusion of the legal norm;
rather, the dispute almost always amounts to a case of the more powerful party taking advantage of the less powerful.

Resolution of cases prior to court

Almost all disputes presented to the ULTI legal aid centers in Ukraine
relate either to the denial of client land rights by village or district officials, or the refusal of agricultural enterprises to honor the terms of
lease contracts signed with client landowners. After the legal aid attorney gathers sufficient background information, the attorney meets with
the local official or land lessee to learn his or her side of the dispute
and to attempt to find a solution that protects the interests of the client. The ULTI legal aid attorneys report that they resolve 98% of cases
prior to filing a claim in court. In the usual case, once the attorney
meets with the official or leasing-in enterprise on the other side of the
dispute to explain the law and offer a solution, the official or enterprise
accepts the solution proposed. This occurs not only because the law
usually supports the client's claim, but because the party who is confronted with an explanation of the law is better able to save face by
feigning ignorance of the law and accepting the attorney's explanation
as an assistance rather than as an affront. If the official or leasing enterprise decides to resist the solution offered by the attorney, the official
or enterprise risks losing face in the event the attorney successfully
uses administrative and court process to compel a solution.[37] And in
the great majority of cases taken to court by the ULTI legal aid centers

or the Vladimir legal aid center in Vladimir, Russia, the legal aid attorneys prevailed.

It is usually much preferable for legal aid service providers to help their clients to resolve disputes without resorting to court. Resolution of disputes outside of court takes much less time and is therefore a much more efficient use of the legal aid staff's time. Resolution outside of court is also likely to provide much quicker relief to clients. Where court administration is not efficient – a condition in no way limited to, but especially prevalent in, developing countries – resort to court may doom the client to protracted and time-consuming litigation. In Andhra Pradesh state in India, for example, long backlogs of land cases in the Revenue Court serve to preserve the status quo, delaying justice for poor litigants who cannot afford to pay attorneys to press their cases.

Resolution of disputes outside of court is also likely to create much less friction between the client and the opposing party, with whom the client will continue to live and work in the same community. Minimization of social discord is often in the best interests of the poor, and this concern may reduce their interest in pursuing claims in court. Legal aid service providers in Vladimir, Russia, report that the overwhelming majority of rural citizens are still reluctant to file claims in court and attribute this unwillingness to their distrust of the judicial system and their opposition to conflict with the agricultural organizations and state management bodies on which they depend.[38] In other cultural settings, resort to litigation in the courts may carry with it social stigma, resulting in a "reluctance, particularly among the poor, to become entangled with the courts."[39] Of course, there is likely to be a natural limit to people's propensity to endure injustice: for example, a family that faces losing their land rights as the result of official action may have very little to lose in challenging the officials as publicly and strongly as possible. Two examples from Ukraine, one resolved in court and the other prior to court action, are given in Box 9.3.

Resolution outside court saves the client court fees, which are often a considerable barrier to the poor. And resolution outside court may give clients a greater sense of control over the situation and lay the groundwork for informal resolution of disputes that arise in the future between the same parties, reducing the need for the legal aid provider to become involved.

Finally, resolution outside court may allow all parties to save face. The importance of this factor should not be underestimated. A local elite whose actions are challenged often has a strong interest in resolving the dispute in a way that allows the elite to excuse the dispute as a misunderstanding of the law or difference of opinion regarding the facts. This is much easier to do during an informal negotiation between the legal aid service provider and the opposing party.

Box 9.3. Two cases in Ukraine

The following are examples of typical cases reported by ULTI rural legal aid centers during November 2005.

The right to receive land. Ukraine law provides that members and pensioners of collective and state farms are entitled to receive an equal share of land previously used by the farm. A pensioner of the Shevchenko state farm was passed over when the farm distributed land shares in 1995. Early in 2005 the pensioner, then 93 years old, and her daughter heard about the Mykolaiv oblast legal aid center while listening to the Agronovyny radio program and applied to the legal aid center for help. After confirming the pensioner's right to receive a land share, the center prepared a court claim for the daughter to present. The claim was uncontested, and in August 2005 the court ordered the village to provide the pensioner with a land share for 5.3 hectares.

Collecting past rents. In March 2005 a poor pensioner wrote to the enterprise leasing his land and requested payment for rents due for 2003-2005, to which he received no reply. He heard about the Zaporizhzha oblast legal aid center from the provincial radio program "Land, hopes and expectations," and applied to the center in September. The center wrote to the enterprise in October asking for documentation related to the overdue rents in preparation for filing a court claim. The center received a letter from the enterprise later the same month stating that the rent had been paid in full in sunflower seed, grain and cash, for a total value of UAH 3,143 (then approximately US$628), which the pensioner confirmed.

Source: Ukraine Land Titling Initiative (July 2006).

Moral suasion

In cases in which it is obvious that the rights of the poor have been violated, moral suasion becomes a valuable tool for resolving the case short of litigation in court. Moral suasion – the act of convincing the rights violator that it is manifestly unjust to proceed with the violation – can be an effective and efficient method of resolving disputes.

Although this is not universally true, in many cultures it is important for the non-poor and poor alike to save face and not to be per-

ceived as flaunting the law. To the extent that elites depend on the stability of social institutions, including laws, to protect their interests,
they may be reluctant to challenge laws and social norms directly. For
example, in India, "perhaps one of the more important allies of the
lower *jatis* [that is, the lower caste groups] is the legitimacy, albeit
strained, of the legal system in the minds of the upper *jatis*."[40] Legal
aid providers in Ukraine have found that once a legal aid attorney explains the law to the adversary in the presence of the poor clients, the
adversary often concedes in order to save face, explaining that he or
she had misunderstood the law.

Explanation of the law by an outsider – especially an outsider who
has the credential of being law-trained – can carry great moral force,
making threat of court litigation unnecessary in many types of cases.
Thus, in a range of cases, merely making known to an adversary that
the poor claimant or defendant has legal representation can greatly improve the bargaining position of the poor.

Representation in court

Where an official or local elite has a significant personal financial stake
in maintaining a particular position, embarrassment or moral condem-
nation by the community may not be enough to compel compromise.
In such cases, the willingness of the client and the legal aid service
provider to take the case to court is the only method left for forcing
resolution of the claim.

After a legal aid service provider has pressed several cases in court,
the advocate's reputation for being willing and able to prosecute cases
in court will also give the advocate greater credibility in the region the
advocate serves.

Legal aid service providers must carefully choose which cases to take
to court. One important consideration should be the chances of winning the case and obtaining some practical relief for the client. This
may seem obvious, but there may be situations in which both the client and the legal aid staff undertake to prosecute cases in which the
likelihood of success is small. One reason for prosecuting such a case
may be to call attention to an unjust situation. It is extremely important for the legal aid service provider to discuss with the client the prospects for success in court so that the client can make an informed decision about whether to participate. Some clients may very reasonably
decline to undergo the stress and other costs of litigation (even where
there will be no direct financial cost) where the litigation is not likely
to improve the client's situation in the near term.

The legal aid service provider must decide whether to accept all types
of cases, or to accept only those cases in which the rights of the poor

are violated by an adversary who is wealthy or otherwise powerful enough to influence the outcome of the dispute through formal and informal means. Participation in cases between unequally situated parties can help to even the playing field, providing relief in cases that would otherwise be unwinnable or whose pursuit would otherwise be unthinkable.

Although there is no shortage of cases in which one poor citizen disputes with another poor citizen over access to land or other land issues, the legal aid service providers may reasonably decline to become involved, concluding that the disputants have relatively the same access (and the same limits to access) to courts and other decision makers. If the service provider does wish to become involved in disputes among the poor, the service provider may be most effective acting as a mediator of the dispute, provided that all parties agree that the service provider may play this role.

These observations are not intended to minimize the needs of the poor for resolution of disputes among themselves, but only to suggest that the use of the limited time and resources of the legal aid service provider must be prioritized, and that those poor who have a dispute with more powerful interests may have fewer avenues of relief to pursue, and may therefore legitimately claim a higher priority for legal aid services.

Legal aid service providers must also take pains not to prosecute cases in which the client does not advance a meritorious claim. Although ordinarily an attorney hired by a private client might have an ethical obligation to prosecute the client's claims without regard to whether the client "deserves" to win, the legal aid attorney who serves the poor owes an obligation to other prospective clients not to squander time on less than meritorious claims since this reduces the amount of time that the attorney has to devote to meritorious claims. Thus, the attorney will often be justified in refusing to prosecute a case that, even while having a basis in law, does not rise to the status of a meritorious claim or an efficient use of resources.

V.   Land rights education and use of mass media

Village seminars

The ULTI legal aid centers in rural Ukraine found village seminars to be an efficient and effective way of transmitting basic legal information to villagers regarding rights to receive ownership of land and the exercise of ownership rights through cultivating land, leasing land to others, exchanging land, bequeathing land to heirs, etc. Legal aid center staff typically travelled to a number of villages in a day to meet with mayors and other citizens to make arrangements to hold a village-wide seminar during a subsequent visit. On seminar days, villagers gathered at the village hall to hear a presentation on land rights by the legal aid staff, who then invited villagers to pose questions and present concerns related to land relations in the village. Although the focus was on agricultural land, the attorneys were able to respond to general questions regarding other types of land, as well as questions related to pensions, labor contracts, and other matters of concern to the villagers.[41]

As part of their seminar presentations, ULTI legal aid staff stated their availability to represent villagers in matters related to the exercise and protection of land rights. In this way, seminars were an essential source of clients during the first months of center operations. The Vladimir legal aid center in Russia has long used village seminars to inform villagers of their land rights and to publicize the center's availability for consultation.

Educating officials

Provision of legal information to local officials, judges and administrators can be as important as providing it to rightholders, especially where the law is changing or judicial training has not adequately focused on the rights of the poor. Regional officials can be an important ally in resolving local disputes. Judges and public prosecutors are often not well versed in land law, particularly where the law has recently changed. Even land administration officials may not fully understand the law, especially as it regards the land rights of the poor.[42]

It can be effective for legal aid attorneys to meet with such officials to present training on land rights, including review of cases handled by legal aid attorneys in other districts. In addition to representing clients, the Qianxi legal aid center in China holds seminars with judges and other court officials to raise awareness of laws relating to the protection of women's rights.[43]

Seminars with officials can also help to establish the legal aid attorney as an expert on land law in the eyes of local officials. In Ukraine, upon establishing a new provincial legal aid center, one of the first acts of attorneys of the ULTI legal aid network was to meet with provincial justice officials and land administration officials to explain the purposes and working guidelines of the center, and to offer the center's services to officials who receive appeals for help from rural landowners.

Box 9.4. The importance of rural presence

Land rights legal aid attorneys cannot provide appropriate service to poor rural landowners and the landless unless they travel frequently to rural areas. This is important so that attorneys may see firsthand evidence related to specific disputes, and to understand the context of land tenure issues. And travel to villages is important to facilitate meetings with groups of clients who cannot easily travel to the legal aid office. But another, often overlooked benefit of frequent travel to rural areas is that this allows the legal aid attorney to gain a sense of the daily life of the rural poor and to appreciate the importance of land tenure issues in their lives. The presence of legal aid attorneys in the village also helps to establish the reputation of the legal aid attorneys in the eyes of clients and to serve notice to third parties that the attorney takes the work seriously. For these reasons, effective legal aid programs must ensure that legal aid staff have adequate transportation to rural areas to accomplish their work.

Mass media

The mass media – including print, radio and television – can help to advance the aims of legal aid in several important ways, including public education on legal rights (including publicizing the results of litigation), raising expectations with regard to enforcement of rights, and even influencing the outcome of particular disputes.

Public education is perhaps the most obvious way in which the mass media can support legal aid work. Journalists who develop a specialized focus on laws and legal disputes can translate these issues "into everyday language in order to implant the feel for justice in society."[44] It is important in such cases for the reporter to explain not only the legal outcome of cases, but the legal basis and important considerations that produced the outcome.

One effective and low-cost means of promoting public education is for the legal aid service provider to submit articles for publication in local and regional newspapers, which rural citizens are more likely to read. For example, during the final quarter of 2006, the Center for Land Reform Support of Vladimir Oblast published three articles in some twenty district newspapers in Vladimir oblast (province) and four neighboring oblasts. The articles explained the rights of citizens to engage with administrative agencies as established under a new law, explained recent changes to a federal law that establishes local commissions to decide, in the event of a dispute, which land parcel a person who wishes to leave the former collective farm will receive in individual ownership, and explained recent changes reducing land tax rates for agricultural land.[45]

One very popular device is the question and answer column in which a legal aid service provider (or other qualified attorney) responds to readers' questions regarding various matters. In Ukraine the ULTI legal aid attorneys participated in a weekly national radio program in which they answered general questions mailed in by program listeners.[46] In Moldova, a question and answer column was used with great success in "Ora fermierului" ("Farmer's Hour"), a national monthly magazine published during 1998-2000 to support private farming and the privatization and subdivision of formerly collectivized agricultural land.

Many Chinese public interest lawyers pursue their goals through appeals to the press, which has been increasingly active in reporting legal injustices.[47] Although it is important to publish news of legal disputes in which the outcome appears to be less than just, it is also helpful to find and report news of cases in which the poor succeed.

The objective of legal advocacy for the poor should be not only to protect the interests of individual clients of the legal aid service, but to use the victories as lessons to other similarly situated individuals who might otherwise be unaware of their rights or too intimidated to demand that their rights be respected. "The most important method of disseminating information about legal strategies is through their successful pursuit. Nothing spreads like a success story. The active promoting of such uses of courts will, by itself, result in others following similar strategies."[48]

Publication of victories serves several purposes. First, it may encourage similarly situated poor disputants to press their case. Second, it serves to educate public officials, including court officials, as to the existence of the law and the fact that the rights of the poor are being enforced, at least in some quarters. Third, publication of victories by the poor may influence the degree to which local elites and others feel they have a free hand in violating the rights of the poor, in effect influencing the climate of expectations generally. Finally, where the legal aid service provider has been instrumental in obtaining the victory, publication of the victory helps raise the profile of the provider, perhaps enhancing the provider's effectiveness in other cases and attracting new clients to the legal aid service. The Wuhan University Center for the Protection of the Rights of Disadvantaged Citizens states that its support from the municipal government is due in part to the center's favorable treatment in the national press.[49]

VI.   Financing, organization and staffing

Financing

Financing is the single most important factor in the ability of legal aid organizations to plan and meet program objectives. A source of multi-year, stable funding gives the legal aid program a much better chance of retaining trained staff and allows service providers to focus on delivering services without being overly concerned about job security.

The primary sources of financing for legal aid organizations in the developing world are international and national foundations, religious organizations, foreign government donors, contributions from lawyers and other individuals, member dues and court-ordered fees, and most receive financing from multiple sources.[50] Funding often includes "soft money" grants that support a particular program aim and which expire after a given period. These can be very useful, but can complicate the work of the legal aid organization by requiring the organization to track specific types of clients and cases separately.

Personnel costs should be the largest budget category. For legal aid organizations that focus on solving specific disputes, investigation costs are likely to be a substantial portion of operating expenses. The Center for Land Reform Support of Vladimir Oblast in Russia currently operates on a budget of roughly US$2,000 per month, with which it maintains a staff of three full-time attorneys. In Moldova, each legal aid center operated on a budget of approximately US$1,800 per month, which paid the salaries of three specialists (either three attorneys or two attorneys and an agronomist), a clerical staff person, office rent, fuel for local travel, an internet connection and other office expenses.[51]

The higher costs for the ULTI legal aid centers was attributable to higher salaries and the fact that each center was responsible for making visits to villages across a territory whose average size was approximately 24,000 square kilometers (just over 9,000 square miles), an area larger than either El Salvador or Israel. Attorneys traveled to villages to provide land rights legal education through village seminars, to gather information related to client claims, and to negotiate with opposing parties on behalf of clients. See Box 9.4 on the importance of travel outreach.

Travel to rural areas is important to African legal aid programs as well. Despite the fact that the majority of the South African LRC's clients are from rural communities, its seven offices are all in predominantly urban areas. The LRC services its rural clients through regular travel and by maintaining relationships with over 50 "advice offices" in rural towns across the country.[52] Lawyers and paralegals frequently travel to some of the most remote regions in the country, including

Northern Cape Province and the interior of KwaZulu Natal.[53] In Namibia, LAC attorneys are often forced to limit expensive and lengthy travel to remote areas when the organization is experiencing financial instability. The center compensates by working with locally based NGOs and community organizations to provide legal assistance to rural clients and has also helped establish advice offices in rural regions, which are managed by volunteer paralegals.[54]

The national government is a potentially stable source of financing for legal aid. And government provision of legal aid to protect the rights of particular groups – such as women, the elderly and children – helps send a message that the government places particular value on these protections[55] and serves to legitimize the work of legal aid providers. Although potentially a stable source of financing for legal aid, government financing may bring with it unwanted influence on legal aid activities. Such influence is likely to be particularly unwelcome with respect to structural legal aid, more so than with respect to traditional legal aid.[56] In the case of the latter, while government officials might intercede in the work of legal aid providers to protect particular important persons, they are less likely to intervene in a general class of cases since the legal aid providers are, presumably, working to uphold current law. Nevertheless, public financing of legal aid can create an inappropriate dynamic of state-supported attorneys litigating against state interests and the interests of elites, and this dynamic can lead to restrictions on activities or the threat of loss of financing.[57]

Where the focus of traditional legal aid is the enforcement of land rights of the poor, national government financing may be especially problematic because a fair number of land disputes are likely to involve state action. One common source of dispute involving the poor, for example, is the taking of land for public (or ostensibly public) purposes. Other common types of disputes involve state regulation of the landowner's use of land, and complications arising from the registration of rights to land. In China, for example, the Ministry of Justice and other Chinese government institutions such as the National Labor Union, consumer organizations and local governments have begun providing legal aid, including legal aid services for disabled persons.[58] However, some local governments in China object to financing legal aid because they believe lawyers have become exceedingly wealthy, while other local governments object to the idea of paying lawyers to litigate against the local government.[59]

Just as national government funding of legal aid for the poor sends a message that the government supports the protection of the poor, international financial support for land rights legal aid sends a similar message with respect to the values of the outside world. International recognition can give the legal aid program some political insulation from government interference.[60] And legal aid programs financed by sources other than the national government may be more likely to take on cases that government-supported programs might feel obliged to avoid.[61]

The land rights legal aid programs in Moldova and Ukraine are examples of legal aid programs funded by a foreign government, in this case USAID, and established independent of existing NGOs. These programs, which were part of larger programs primarily devoted to privatizing and titling agricultural land, greatly benefited from secure funding. In the case of the ULTI centers in Ukraine, funding continued from 2003 until the spring of 2007. Both programs had the support of the respective national government, and because the land privatization was very popular in rural areas, the legal aid programs enjoyed strong support in the villages.

It can be difficult for legal aid programs to survive in the absence of outside funding. The legal aid program in Moldova ended almost immediately after the close of the USAID-financed program of which it was a part. In Ukraine, the ULTI legal aid network survived the close of the USAID-financed project in September 2006 and registered as an independent legal entity. The centers continued operating with USAID support but closed in the summer of 2007 when USAID support ceased.

Another potential source of funding is client fees. The question of charging fees for services relates not only to sustainability, but also to the value clients place on services. Are clients likely to value services received free of charge? Should legal aid centers charge nominal fees for services, both as a way of dissuading prospective clients from presenting less serious claims, or as a way of encouraging clients to participate in the prosecution of the claim? Although the ULTI legal aid centers in Ukraine and the Vladimir center in Russia have not charged fees, this did not lead to the presentation of frivolous claims and did not cause clients to behave passively. The legal aid center in Guangzhou, China, uses a unique approach. The center charges clients a small fee when they apply for legal assistance from the center. If the center accepts the case, it returns the fee to the client at the conclusion of the case. If the center does not accept the case, it keeps the fee. This practice is intended to discourage people from presenting non-meritorious applications for assistance.[62]

It is not appropriate to require that legal aid programs have the potential to become wholly self-supporting in order to justify funding them over the medium term. As Golub observes, "NGOs engaged in challenging the status quo may always depend on foreign sources of funding in many parts of the developing world, just as equivalent groups depend on foundations and other outside sources in many far more affluent industrialized societies."[63] If legal aid services in developed nations are not wholly self-supporting, it is unrealistic to suppose that legal aid services in developing nations can support themselves. If a legal aid program is eventually forced to close due to lack of funding, this is no reason to regard the resources invested in the program as having been wasted. In particular, legal aid services that are targeted at resolving actual disputes are worth providing even if only for a limited time since such services make an immediate difference to the lives of clients receiving assistance, and because resolution in favor of one poor client is bound to raise expectations among others similarly situated.[64]

Organization

Some suggest that legal aid services are best provided by grassroots social action organizations, in part because such organizations may have the local political clout necessary to help successful litigants withstand pressures (in some other area of village life) brought by local elites who have lost a case in court.[65] This is a fair point, and highlights the need for the legal aid service provider to be sensitive to local power relations and to make sure that it is the client who ultimately determines whether and how to proceed in prosecuting the case. The goal of legal aid is not to "win cases," but to improve the client's situation. It is for the client to decide whether a particular victory is worth achieving, taking into account the types of pressures local elites may bring to bear.

University programs provide another means of delivering legal aid to rural populations. In China, for example, legal aid services have in large part been developed by local justice bureaus and university law departments.[66] Non-government legal aid programs established by Chinese universities receive no government support, though some are supported by foreign foundations, such as the Ford Foundation.[67] University programs may be preferable in certain settings. The fact that the Beijing University Center for Women's Law Studies and Legal Services is part of the university's law department reportedly provides the center with more credibility than it would have if it were completely independent of an established institution. The Wuhan University Center for the Protection of the Rights of Disadvantaged Citizens reports that because it is affiliated with a university rather than the government, its status is attractive to clients who have grievances against government departments or entities and who are therefore reluctant to seek assistance from a government legal aid program. In addition, the position of legal aid programs within Chinese universities may help insulate them from scrutiny by the state.[68]

University-based legal aid clinics have recently developed throughout much of Africa, including in Kenya (Moi University), Zimbabwe (University of Zimbabwe), and Lesotho (University of Lesotho). In no African country, however, have university-based law clinics become as widespread as in South Africa. Since 1972 each of South Africa's 21 law schools has created its own legal aid clinic. These clinics have been lauded as both practical academic tools for law students and beneficial resources for poor and marginalized communities in the school's surrounding area.

While many of these clinics differ in size and resources, most are staffed by a small number of practicing attorneys, current law students and administrators. Often, working at the clinic is voluntary for students, but in some cases can be required in the final year of law school. A number of these university-based clinics have teamed up with the Legal Aid Board (LAB) and been subsumed into the local "justice centre." Others remain mostly independent, funded partly by the LAB and partly by the university. Most clinics rarely ask clients to pay fees. Many South African university law clinics specialize in a particular legal issue, such as children's rights, refugees or domestic violence. The clinics tend to be located near the university, forcing rural dwellers to travel to the city to seek legal aid.

Another potential method for providing legal services to the poor is "judicare," which is a general term given to programs that enlist private attorneys to take on individual cases, usually on a reduced fee basis, with fees paid by the state. This approach is an alternative to providing legal aid through full-time attorneys whose only work is with legal aid clients.

One criticism of judicare services is that private attorneys do not understand the needs of the poor and have no experience in working on issues important to the poor. A 1989 study contains the following assessment:

> Few solicitors' offices are located in deprived areas where the poor have most need of them, and solicitors receive little training in social welfare law. The problem is circular – the poor do not think of using a lawyer for advice with their problems, hence lawyers do not develop skill and expertise in these areas, and the service is not available to those who wish to use it.[69]

In the UK, dissatisfaction with the ability of judicare to address the legal needs of the poor led to a movement to create legal aid centers.[70]

Another important issue is the possible conflict of interest of the private attorney, who may very reasonably conclude that it is risky to represent poor clients who have disputes with either local elites (who may be prospective clients) or local officials (upon whom the attorney may need to rely in other matters). In other words, "private lawyers will be constrained in their legal work for the poor by established interests in the local community whom they rely on for resources."[71] This is likely to be especially true in rural areas where there are few attorneys and fewer paying clients.

For thirty years the LAB in South Africa operated a judicare system, but reorganized its activities in 1998 to move towards a "justice centre" system that employs salaried legal practitioners solely to provide services to the poor. The 1998 National Legal Aid Forum cited the following as its main reasons for the transition away from judicare services: (1) a new constitutional requirement for legal representation; (2) widescale fraud by legal practitioners; (3) cost concerns; and (4) the success of public defender pilot programs.[72] Since the transition to justice centers, the LAB has created better access to legal aid in South Africa but disproportionately in favor of criminal cases in urban areas.[73] The LAB currently has 44 justice centers throughout the country in chiefly urban areas, but a major goal of the organization is to establish centers gradually in rural areas.[74]

On the other hand, the establishment of legal aid centers may sometimes be perceived as a threat to private attorneys. Private attorneys in the UK objected to the "political and quasi-political" law reform activities of publicly financed legal aid centers and also objected that the centers competed unfairly with private attorneys by providing services free of charge. A compromise was reached whereby the centers agreed not to compete with private attorneys with respect to issues such as personal injury litigation, marital disputes and probate. It soon became apparent that referrals of these matters from legal aid centers actually generated clients for private attorneys.[75] In Ontario, Canada, lawyers and social activists concluded that poor people often have very different legal needs than fee-paying clients, leading them to call for the introduction of community legal aid clinics to complement judicare services being providing by private attorneys.[76]

Use of attorneys

If a primary function of the legal aid service is to represent clients in resolving disputes (as opposed to advising clients how they can solve their problems themselves), attorneys are likely to be far more qualified to provide this service than paralegals. In most countries, only attorneys are authorized to prosecute claims in court. Even if the goal of the legal aid service is to avoid taking the clients' claims to court, the legal aid service provider may find that the threat of going to court can provide highly useful leverage in negotiating the resolution of disputes.

Attorneys are also likely to command more respect in negotiations with adversaries. The attorney's explanation of the law applying to the merits of the client's case may be more readily received by adversaries. And a powerful adversary may be more willing to negotiate with a licensed professional, perceiving that this helps the adversary to preserve his dignity.

Of course, attorneys are likely to command a much higher salary than paralegals, which reduces the number of legal aid service providers who can be hired within a given budget. But if the legal aid service aims to negotiate favorable outcomes for clients involved in disputes with more powerful adversaries, attorneys may be necessary.[77]

Ideally, legal aid service providers will be committed to social reform. Lev notes that the founders of the LBH in Indonesia determined that because the work "extended beyond legal representation to legal and social reform, law graduates were screened for commitment and social awareness as well as social skills."[78] On the other hand, attorneys and other legal aid providers must be paid a living wage. Workers who are not fairly compensated for their time will not perform at the highest standard.[79] Salaries for professional staff are likely to be the most significant expense of the legal aid operation, greatly exceeding rent, transportation and other expenses.

Land rights legal aid service providers should be carefully and competitively interviewed and selected for energy, commitment and capability rather than supposed existing knowledge of land law; the latter can be learned but not the former. If a significant part of the legal aid service will involve negotiating settlements on behalf of clients, it is helpful if the attorneys have some experience in court, either as prosecutors or private litigators. This type of experience gives the attorney the confidence to press cases in court, which greatly strengthens the attorney's hand in negotiating the resolution of disputes.

For legal aid service providers to be effective, they must respect and listen to clients. "There is often a social, economic, educational or identity gap between lawyers and their clientele that must be bridged."[80] In India, poor families may be reluctant to seek lawyers from a higher ranking *jati* (caste), thus limiting their access to legal aid.[81]

It may not always be possible for organizers of legal aid services to hire attorneys from the same social background as the program's clients. But where possible, legal aid service providers should be drawn from the local region rather than transplanted from the national capital. Regional attorneys are more likely to understand the local conditions. In the Moldova and Ukraine legal aid programs, care was taken to hire regional attorneys, agronomists and economists.[82]

Some social scientists postulate that individuals who provide needed services establish power over the person receiving the services, and that unilateral dependence occurs when the receiver is unable to reciprocate by bestowing benefits upon the provider.[83] One way to counter this supposed tendency might be for the provider of legal aid services to emphasize that the legal aid program has an interest in ensuring that the law is respected and that the resolution of personal problems also benefits the larger society, including others who may be situated similarly, but who do not have immediate access to assistance. In this way, the client's acceptance of aid actually redounds to the benefit of others, especially if the legal aid provider is able to publicize any good outcome the provider helps the client achieve.

Use of paralegals

Paralegals play an important role in many legal aid programs. In places where the ratio of lawyers to the rural population is very low, it may be very difficult to staff legal aid centers only with lawyers. The Legal Resources Center in South Africa trains paralegals and others to monitor law violations, take statements, provide information and give legal advice to communities in times of emergency.[84]

The primary argument against using paralegals is that they lack the necessary training and are not qualified to provide legal services. However, with proper training and guidance, paralegals can significantly enhance the delivery of legal aid services, especially where a significant part of the services consists of advising clients on how to solve their problems themselves. An interesting example is provided by the client advice bureaus established throughout the UK in 1939 to help citizens cope with the disruptions of war; by 1940 the bureaus had dealt with 4 million applications for advice. Although the legal profession was not involved in setting these up, much of the advice the bureaus gave related to legal matters.[85]

Staff of the UK client advice bureaus relied upon a 150-page set of "Citizens Advice Notes" prepared by the central organization. These notes gave the bureaus a clear advantage over attorneys who had earlier undertaken to assist the poor through "Poor Man's Lawyer" schemes active in the 1920s and 1930s. Whereas attorneys of the earlier program had little knowledge of the areas of law important to the poor, the lay volunteers staffing the advice bureaus had access to quality information that addressed the right issues.

In the case of land rights legal aid, it is useful for paralegals to be knowledgeable regarding rural society and agronomy. The staff of a legal aid project providing advice and assistance to rural landowners in Moldova contained a number of agronomists and agricultural economists working alongside the attorneys. Legal aid clients consisted of poor rural citizens who had recently received agricultural land in ownership and were either farming it themselves or leasing it to large agricultural enterprises. Attorneys supervising the work provided these specialists with basic instruction in the national laws applicable to agricultural land relations. For their part, the agronomists and agricultural economists were highly motivated to work with rural landowners and had particular insight into problems relating to agricultural production. Since many land disputes related to the lease of agricultural land under production, the agronomists and economists were often able to fashion solutions that made economic sense to both the landowners and the agricultural enterprises which leased in their land.[86]

In any event, legal aid services should be overseen by attorneys, assisted where appropriate by paralegals trained in the appropriate area of law. The supervision by attorneys is necessary to ensure that paralegals have a sound understanding of the relevant law and that advice to clients keeps up with changes in the law. The attorneys will also be able to take over particularly difficult cases and represent clients in court or other official proceedings if necessary.

Since 2003 the Society for Eradication of Rural Poverty SERP has operated an innovative paralegal program in the Indian state of Andhra Pradesh as part of the Indira Kranthi Patham (IKP) program established by the state Department of Rural Development (DRD). The program trains village youths to serve as paralegals and community land surveyors dedicated to identifying and resolving land issues on behalf of impoverished rural families.[87] In each sub-district, a federation of village-level women's self-help groups (established earlier by the DRD) hires the paralegals. The fact that the paralegals report to the women's groups is significant since it helps to ensure that they will focus on the priorities of the women they serve.

Each paralegal concentrates on three villages per year, focusing primarily on land claims related to: (1) land the government previously allocated to landless families (though often not completing the allocation process), (2) government lands occupied by the poor, and (3) private lands that poor families have purchased but for which they have not formalized their rights in the state registration system. The paralegal identifies land issues confronting particular poor families, gathers facts and documents, prepares reports for land administration officials and files petitions in the administrative courts, assists the claimants and the court officials to address the issues, and tracks the cases until they are resolved. With the assistance of the paralegals and other project staff, the land administration officials hold village courts, resolving as many claims as possible on the spot.

In response to the chronic shortage of trained surveyors in rural areas, the program has also hired village youths in each district to train as apprentices with government surveyors to help settle the survey-related issues of the poor. The community surveyors are trained at the state survey training academy and then apprentice for one year before being eligible to receive a license as a surveyor.

In each district the government has established a Land Rights and Legal Assistance Center to support the paralegals and community surveyors. The district-wide federation of women's self-help groups hires a retired government land administrator to manage the community surveyors and support the work of the paralegals. Each district federation also hires a legal coordinator to provide functional support to the paralegals. The centers also provide training to land administration officials to expose them to the methods and pro-poor approach of the program's activities.

These activities have helped to place the issue of land rights and claims of the poor back onto the agenda of state land administrators and have helped ensure that the issues are viewed within a development perspective. Importantly, the paralegals, who are typically from the most exploited and vulnerable families, are able to identify the issues affecting the poor and bring them onto the agenda of government administrators. In what is a two-way bridge, the paralegals can also help the poor to understand the requirements of the state land administration system. As of October 2007, paralegals and community surveyors had resolved land disputes and other land issues on behalf of 21,716 poor people, which represents 27.5% of the issues presented to the program to date.

Ultimately, legal aid staffing in any given setting will largely depend upon the program budget and the decisions of the organizers regarding the nature of the aid to be provided. RDI's experience in Russia, Moldova and Ukraine leads us to value the work of committed attorneys who place a high priority on resolving land disputes on behalf of poor rural clients, including the very small percentage of disputes that the attorney and client decide to pursue in court. At the same time, our experience with the paralegal program in Andhra Pradesh, India, persuades us that well designed and well managed paralegal programs can be an efficient means of reaching large segments of the rural poor, particularly where paralegals are drawn from the rural sector.

VII.   Conclusions

Of all possible interventions designed to improve the ability of the poor to obtain and exercise rights to land, traditional legal aid may be the most generally applicable and least risky. Legal aid is more flexible in that it can be adjusted to fit particular circumstances to respond to the specific demands of a given segment of the poor. It can be an impor-

tant tool for implementing other land tenure interventions, helping implementers maintain a focus on the poor and correct flaws in project
design. And legal aid may be implemented on any scale, from one attorney to many hundreds, depending upon resources and circumstances. Although some successful models rely exclusively on attorneys
to provide services, well trained and well supervised paralegals can also
provide specific legal services to the rural poor and can do so at a lower
cost per client.

Designed and delivered with appropriate sensitivity and focus, traditional legal aid – the form of aid that seeks, in principal part, to implement current law – can inform people of their rights, motivate them to
demand that their rights be respected, and expose inconsistencies between the values expressed in the law as written and values evident in
the way public policies actually affect the poor. This exercise may serve
to sensitize the courts and the press regarding the plight of the poor
and compel the legal system to deliver the rights promised in the law.

One key component of land rights legal aid is education of the public. This can be especially important in countries where the land rights
regime is changing rapidly. Legal aid can sometimes represent the only
reliable source of information on land rights that is available to the
poor. But information is often not enough; in many settings the poor
are likely to require some form of direct assistance in enforcing their
rights. The legal aid service provider can best serve by actively representing the poor client seeking to enforce land rights and helping the
client deal with officials and private parties whose actions interfere
with the client's exercise of rights. A fundamental objective of legal aid
should be to make respect for the rights of the poor "routine" in the
sense that the poor begin to expect that their rights will be respected.

To be most effective, legal aid providers should actively take the side
of the poor in disputes between the poor and the non-poor, rather than
act as neutral mediators or arbitrators. This approach acknowledges
the importance of the power imbalance between the poor and the non-
poor. At the same time, legal aid providers should seek to resolve disputes efficiently and minimize confrontation. The goal is not to avoid
confrontation, but to avoid *unnecessary* confrontation and escalation of
disputes to the point that they risk damaging the long-term interests of
the client. Where disputes can be resolved prior to court, this is often
not only more efficient, but also minimizes damage to social relations.
Where it is obvious that the rights of the poor have been violated, moral suasion can be a valuable tool for resolving the case short of litigation in court, especially in settings where elites depend on the stability
of laws and other social institutions to protect their interests.

Land rights legal aid should strive not only to protect the interests of
individual clients of the legal aid service, but to use the victories as les-

sons to other similarly situated individuals who might otherwise be
unaware of their rights, or too intimidated to demand that their rights
be respected.

Notes

1   J.W. Diokno, DEVELOPMENTAL LEGAL AID IN RURAL ASEAN: PROBLEMS AND PROSPECTS in
    INTERNATIONAL COMMISSION OF JURISTS AND CONSUMERS' ASSOCIATION OF PENANG, RU-
    RAL DEVELOPMENT AND HUMAN RIGHTS IN SOUTH EAST ASIA 175, 176 (Penang, Malaysia:
    Sun Printers Sendirian Berhad 1982).
2   Authors of a study of legal services provided to poor women in Ecuador were struck
    by the extent to which women clients valued access to justice for non-financial rea-
    sons. M. Dakolias & B. Owen, IMPACT OF LEGAL AID: ECUADOR 51 (World Bank 2003).
3   "Legal empowerment is both a process and a goal. As a *process*, it involves activities
    aimed at increasing disadvantaged populations' control over their lives. As a *goal*, le-
    gal empowerment refers to their actual achievement of that control. Thus, the pro-
    cess can take place even if the goal has yet to be achieved." S. Golub, *Beyond Rule of
    Law Orthodoxy: The Legal Empowerment Alternative*, Rule of Law Series Working Paper
    No. 41, at 26-27 (Carnegie Endowment for International Peace, Washington, D.C.
    Oct. 2003), available at http://www.carnegieendowment.org/files/wp41.pdf.
4   See generally United States Agency for International Development, *Ukraine Land Ti-
    tling Initiative 2001-2006: Final Report* 18-9 (USAID Sept. 2006), available at http://
    pdf.usaid.gov/pdf_docs/PDACI600.pdf [hereinafter *ULTI Final Report*].
5   R.J. Wilson & J. Rasmusen, PROMOTING JUSTICE: A PRACTICAL GUIDE TO STRATEGIC
    HUMAN RIGHTS LAWYERING 10 (International Human Rights Law Group 2001). See
    generally M. McClymont & S. Golub, eds., MANY ROADS TO JUSTICE: THE LAW-RELATED
    WORK OF FORD FOUNDATION GRANTEES AROUND THE WORLD (New York: Ford Founda-
    tion 2000).
6   "In principle, legal aid should be interpreted as a war against poverty." T.M. Lubis, *Le-
    gal Aid: Its History and Its Role*, in LEGAL AID IN INDONESIA (FIVE YEARS OF THE LEMBA-
    GA BANTUAN HUKUM) 25, 29 (Lembaga 1976).
7   Diokno, supra note 1, at 178.
8   A.B. Nasution, BANTUAN HUKUM DI INDONESIA (LEGAL AID IN INDONESIA) 107 -108
    (Jakarta: LP3ES 1981), quoted in D.S. Lev, *Legal Aid in Indonesia*, Centre of Southeast
    Asian Studies Working Paper No. 44, at 21-22 (1987). Others hold that government
    funding of legal aid for the poor creates "an illusion of justice and an image that the
    state does not truly wish to rectify inequality through more substantive means," en-
    courages the poor and social activists to neglect more meaningful political activity,
    and "may legitimate existing inequalities inherent in society." R. Gordon & J. Lind-
    say, *Law and the Poor in Rural India: The Prospects for Legal Aid*, 5 AMERICAN UNIVER-
    SITY JOURNAL OF INTERNATIONAL LAW & POLICY 655, 659 (1990) (generally citing D.
    Kairys, ed., THE POLITICS OF LAW: A PROGRESSIVE CRITIQUE (1982)).
9   Diokno, supra note 1, at 181. We could also add, with occasional noteworthy excep-
    tions, that governments also seek respect from their own citizens.
10 Id. at 182. Mobilization may involve protest against the government with the objec-
    tive not only of changing the law, but of eroding support for the government. The ob-
    jectives of confronting the government over its policies is, first, to make the govern-
    ment "begin to doubt its own legitimacy and thus blunt the cutting edge that unchal-
    lenged belief in its righteousness could give it" and, second, to erode public support
    for the government, both at home and abroad. Development legal aid lawyers use

several tactics in confronting the government over its policies. They may urge an interpretation of existing law that favors the rights of the poor. Or they may expose inconsistencies between the law and constitutional norms, the statements of public officials or international human rights norms. The point is to shock the conscience of government officials and the public. Id.

11 "Providing attorneys to assist the poor with their routine legal problems is an important step in ensuring some measure of equality in the civil justice system. . . . [I]n simply forcing local legal systems and decisionmakers to apply established laws, legal services attorneys provide important benefits to the poor." M. Kessler, LEGAL SERVICES FOR THE POOR: A COMPARATIVE AND CONTEMPORARY ANALYSIS OF INTERORGANIZATIONAL POLITICS, Studies in Social Welfare Policies and Programs No. 6, at 144 (Greenwood Press 1987). Approaches that enable the poor to access legal resources advance the rule of law in the sense that where the poor have more power they are better able to compel government officials to implement the law and make influential private parties comply. Golub, supra note 3, at 7.

12 B.L. Liebman, *Legal Aid and Public Interest Law in China*, 34 TEXAS INTERNATIONAL LAW JOURNAL 211, 279 (1999).

13 See S. Popkin, THE RATIONAL PEASANT 8, 18-19 (University of California Press 1979). The political economy approach, in which individuals calculate how likely they are to benefit from some action, may be contrasted with a moral economy approach, in which individuals act from a need to correct injustice. Of course, these sets of motivations are not mutually exclusive, and some litigants may want to have their day in court even if the odds of winning are perceived to be low, and quite apart from any desire to change the rules governing the issue at stake.

14 Id. at 245 -246, 251.

15 During a series of workshops in 1999 and 2000 involving representatives of 125 organizations providing legal aid in developing countries, relatively few defined their clients as suffering from a particular rights violation. Wilson & Rasmusen, supra note 5, at 20.

16 C. Dias, OBSTACLES TO USING LAW AS A RESOURCE FOR THE POOR: THE RECAPTURING OF LAW BY THE POOR in REPORT OF THE SEMINARS ON LEGAL SERVICES FOR THE RURAL POOR AND OTHER DISADVANTAGED GROUPS, SOUTH-EAST ASIA AND SOUTH ASIA 154 (International Commission of Jurists Geneva 1987). In Australia, legal aid is characterized by generalist centers that provide services within a geographic area, and specialist centers that provide services to individuals confronting particular problems (such as tenants, young people, refugees, etc.). The generalist centers tend to focus on providing referrals, information, advice and education, while the specialist centers focus on test cases and law reform. F. Zemans & A. Thomas, *Can Community Clinics Survive? A Comparative Study of Law Centres in Australia, Ontario and England*, in F. Regan, et al., eds., THE TRANSFORMATION OF LEGAL AID: COMPARATIVE AND HISTORICAL STUDIES 67 (Oxford University Press 1999). The Peking University Center for Women's Law Studies and Legal Services provides legal aid to women in three topic areas: family or marriage disputes, labor disputes and personal injury claims. Liebman, supra note 12, at 235.

17 In Northern Europe, legal aid is generally available to all citizens, while in English-speaking societies it is usually targeted at the poor. F. Regan, *Why Do Legal Aid Services Vary Between Countries? Re-examining the Impact of Welfare States and Legal Families*, in F. Regan, et al., supra note 16, at 179.

18 K.B. Ghimire, *Peasants' Pursuit of Outside Alliances in the Process of Land Reform: A Discussion of Legal Assistance Programmes in Bangladesh and the Philippines*, UNRISD Discussion Paper No. 102, at 15 (Mar. 1999).

19 Id. at 11 (in 1996, only 25 of 1,037 cases involved land disputes).

20 Liebman, supra note 12, at 251-252.
21 Legal Resources Centre, *Land Reform Project*, available at www.lrc.co.za/focus_areas/landform.asp.
22 Legal Assistance Center, *Land, Environment and Development Project Overview* (Sept. 15, 2006), available at www.lac.org.na/lead/default.htm.
23 A. Corbett, A *Case Study on the Proposed Epupa Hydro Power Dam in Namibia* 15 (contributing paper to the World Commission on Dams, Dec. 1999).
24 Liebman, supra note 12, at 252. In China, as of 1999, provincial and local justice bureaus had established 180 legal aid centers or offices; however, at that time programs were concentrated in economically developed urban areas, and lawyers remained out of reach for the majority of the country's rural poor. Id. at 212, 214.
25 Gordon & Lindsay, supra note 8, at 750.
26 Regan, supra note 17, at 182.
27 Ukraine Land Titling Initiative, *Legal Aid: Strategic Goals and Beneficiary Focus* (ULTI Legal Aid Training Program document) (Kyiv, Ukraine, Jan. 2003, on file with the Rural Development Institute).
28 Gordon & Lindsay, supra note 8, at 754.
29 Id. at 755.
30 The level of activity of the legal aid teams in Moldova, Ukraine, and Vladimir, Russia, were roughly comparable, with an average of 19-23 new cases per month involving an average of 14-23 clients per case. S. Dobrilovic & R. Mitchell, *End of Contract Report: Project to Develop Land and Real Estate Markets in Moldova* 36 (report submitted to United States Agency for International Development, on file with the Rural Development Institute 2000) (Moldova); *ULTI Final Report*, supra note 4, at 36 (Ukraine); A. Pulin, *Quarterly Report for Center for Support of Land Reform in Vladimir Oblast* 6 (Dec. 2006) (on file with the Rural Development Institute)
31 Similarly, a report on legal services to poor women in Ecuador found that some clients used the threat of legal action to achieve out-of-court settlements with the absent father. Dakolias & Owen, supra note 2, at 46.
32 A.B. Nasution, *Legal Service in Developing Countries: An Indonesian Case*, in LBH, LEGAL AID IN INDONESIA (FIVE YEARS OF THE LEMBAGA BANTUAN HUKUM) 33, 41 (1976).
33 D. Manning, *The Role of Legal Services Organizations in Attacking Poverty* 17 (paper presented at World Bank Conference, St. Petersburg, Russia, July 8-12, 2001). Groups of the poor are emboldened to take action if they are confident that legal representation is available to protect group members from retaliation. Id.
34 Dakolias & Owen, supra note 2, at 49. The Qianxi legal aid center in China believes that its work has a similar "deterrent and proactive effect" in protecting the rights of women. A. McCutcheon, *Contributing to Legal Reform in China*, in McClymont & Golub, supra note 5, at 182.
35 Manning, supra note 33, at 32.
36 Wilson & Rasmusen, supra note 5, at 38. Commentators familiar with mediation in rural India report that while the Indian court system is not immune from the influence of local elites, it is relatively more immune than village mediators, and that local non-coercive settlement institutions are unlikely to help the poor in disputes with local elites. Gordon & Lindsay, supra note 8, at 677. In India, villagers within the same *jati* (caste) may look to a respected member of the *jati* to mediate the land dispute; however, the mediation is non-binding, and the loser frequently takes the dispute to court. Id.
37 Author interviews of ULTI legal aid staff, February 2004 and November 2005. Similarly, LBH of Indonesia will take a case to court only after exhausting other remedies, including informal negotiations and presentation of the case to the media. Nasution, supra note 32, at 38. To leave a final opportunity to save face is a reflection of the ba-

sic principle that is sometimes expressed as "you catch more flies with honey than with vinegar," a principle that RDI has found useful in many aspects of the work. Sometimes, of course, vinegar may be needed.

38 Center for Land Reform Support of Vladimir Oblast [Russia], Annual Report 2004, at 10, available at www.zrv.ru/english.

39 M. Anderson, *Access to Justice and Legal Process: Making Legal Institutions Responsive to Poor People in LDCs*, IDS Working Paper 178, at 16-17 (Institute of Development Studies 2003). This reluctance is sometimes attributed to the "strong social stigma attached to any encounter with the law, no matter how innocent" and "litigation may be seen as making trouble." Id. at 17.

40 Gordon & Lindsay, supra note 8, at 755.

41 Author interviews with ULTI legal aid staff, February 2004. The centers estimated that they spent about 35-40% of their time conducting seminars, including preparation and travel time.

42 District officials in Vladimir, Russia, cite the availability of legal aid attorneys to answer legal questions to be the center's greatest attribute. L. Rolfes & B. Rorem, *Legal Assistance in Rural Russia: A Report on the Activities of the Center for Land Reform Support of Vladimir Oblast*, RDI Reports on Foreign Aid and Development No. 93, at 10 (Rural Development Institute 1997).

43 Liebman, supra note 12, at 231; McCutcheon, supra note 34, at 182.

44 A.R. Saleh, *The Press and the Lembaga Bantuan Hukum*, in LBH, LEGAL AID IN INDONE-SIA (FIVE YEARS OF THE LEMBAGA BANTUAN HUKUM) 45, 46 (1976).

45 The center earlier experimented with publishing articles in the provincial (oblast) newspaper, but found that it did not reach rural citizens. Rolfes & Rorem, supra note 42, at 4-5.

46 *ULTI Final Report*, supra note 4, at 18-19.

47 Liebman, supra note 12, at 278. The Peking University Center for Women's Law Studies and Legal Services, for example, maintains close ties to the press. Id. at 236.

48 Gordon & Lindsay, supra note 8, at 771.

49 Liebman, supra note 12, at 234. Influential Indonesian newspapers and magazines have exhibited an interest in legal and political reform. Lev, supra note 8, at 31. LBH reports, "Very often also, a person under arrest has been freed by the Legal Aid Institute with the help of one release in the press, when numerous letters of protest of the Institute have been unsuccessful." Saleh, supra note 44, at 47.

50 Wilson & Rasmusen, supra note 5, at 27.

51 R. Mitchell, budget materials from USAID Project to Develop Land and Real Estate Markets in Moldova (on file with the Rural Development Institute).

52 Personal correspondence with Annette Reed, Donor Liaison of Land Resources Centre, Oct. 17, 2006.

53 Id.

54 Personal correspondence with Norman Tjombe, Project Coordinator for the LAC's Land, Environment and Development Project, Oct. 18, 2006.

55 See Liebman, supra note 12, at 246 (discussing legal aid in China).

56 With respect to structural legal aid, several factors make it difficult for government-financed legal aid providers to engage in effective law reform, including the fact that political change generally requires a broad political strategy, of which legal work and litigation are only one component, as well as the fact that law reform may draw unwelcome criticism from the government, exposing the legal aid provider to suspension of public financing for all legal activities. Zemans & Thomas, supra note 16, at 78-79. In Ontario, law reform activities have increased protections to the poor, but have also made the publicly financed legal aid clinics politically vulnerable, exposing

them to critics who contend that it is inappropriate to expend public money on "political" activity. Id. at 77-78.

57   Gordon & Lindsay, supra note 8, at 658.

58   Liebman, supra note 12, at 232.

59   Id. at 266.

60   Lev, supra note 8, at 31 (discussing international reputation of LBH of Indonesia).

61   Liebman, supra note 12, at 271 (discussing non-governmental NGOs in China); Wilson & Rasmusen, supra note 5, at 24.

62   Liebman, supra note 12, at 244.

63   Golub, supra note 3, at 21.

64   Id.

65   Gordon & Lindsay, supra note 8, at 766.

66   Liebman, supra note 12, at 224.

67   Id. at 233.

68   Id. at 236 (discussing Beijing University), 234 (discussing Wuhan University) and 279 (discussing state insulation).

69   NCC, Ordinary Justice 99–100 (HMSO, London 1989), quoted in T. Goriely, The English Approach to Access to Justice 3 (paper presented to a World Bank Workshop, Washington, D.C., Dec. 11, 2002), available at http://www1.worldbank.org/ publicsector/ legal/EnglandWhales/pdf.

70   Zemans & Thomas, supra note 16, at 79.

71   Kessler, supra note 11, at 148.

72   H. van As, Legal Aid in South Africa: Making Justice Reality, 49(1) JOURNAL OF AFRICAN LAW 59 (2005).

73   Id. at 60.

74   Legal Aid Board, Justice Centres, available at www.legal-aid.co.za/staff/justicecentres. php. In the meantime, the LAB has entered into agreements with advice offices run by Lawyers for Human Rights in rural areas on an experimental basis. D. McQuoid-Mason, Legal Aid Services and Human Rights in South Africa, available at www.pili. org/2005r/content/view/155/26/. These offices are staffed by trained paralegals and refer clients who qualify for legal aid to attorneys. Through these advice offices, Lawyers for Human Rights offer litigation assistance, training workshops and a legal advice telephone hotline for some of the most rural parts of South Africa. Lawyers for Human Rights, Security of Farm Workers Project, available at www.lhr.org.za/sfwork/ pageo.php. Due to their reliance on paralegals, rather than attorneys, advice offices in rural areas are often utilized as legal education centers and referral offices, not specific legal assistance to address grievances. J. Sarkin, Legal Aid: Promoting Access to Justice, 19(3) UNIVERSITY OF NATAL INDICATOR 4 (2002).

75   Zemans & Thomas, supra note 16, at 82-83.

76   Id. at 71.

77   Attorneys may sometimes have other motives for entering into legal aid work. In Indonesia in the 1970s legal aid was attractive to lawyers committed to social change, in part because the political parties were meaningless. Lev, supra note 8, at 27.

78   Id. at 29.

79   Studies in the UK have found that paid specialist staff usually provide much better service than unpaid volunteers. Goriely, supra note 69, at 15

80   Wilson & Rasmusen, supra note 5, at 50.

81   Gordon & Lindsay, supra note 8, at 769.

82   Another good reason for hiring regional attorneys is that they are more likely to remain in the regions throughout the program's existence and after the program ends.

83   Dias, supra note 16, at 156.

84   Wilson & Rasmusen, supra note 5, at 35.

85 Discussion of the UK experience is based on Goriely, supra note 69, at 11-14.

86 Dobrilovic & Mitchell, supra note 30, at 36.

87 R. Mitchell & T. Hanstad, *Innovative Approaches to Reducing Rural Landlessness in An-
    dhra Pradesh: A Report on the Experience of the IKP Land Activities*, report prepared for
    the Andhra Pradesh Department of Rural Development and the Society for Eradica-
    tion of Rural Poverty (Jan. 2008), available at http://www.rd.ap.gov.in/IKPLand/
    RDI_analysis_IKP_Land_activities.pdf. See also R. Nielsen & T. Hanstad, *APRPRP
    Land Component Land Purchase Subcomponent: Assessment of Purchases* (unpublished
    mimeograph on file with the Rural Development Institute, Sept. 2005); Society for
    Elimination of Rural Poverty, *Operational Manual: Increasing the Rural Poor's Access
    and Rights to Rural Land* (Andhra Pradesh Department of Rural Development, Dec.
    12, 2002). RDI has served as a technical consultant to the IKP paralegal program
    since its inception.

10 Concluding reflections

Roy L. Prosterman

As this book was being completed, we learned of the new research (see Chapter 1) that has greatly increased the estimate of the numbers presently living in extreme poverty – now calculated as less than US$1.25 a day in purchasing power parity terms – from just under 1.0 billion to 1.4 billion people. This new estimate does not yet take into account the sharp increase in food and energy prices since 2005. Roughly three-quarters of these very poor are rural, and a majority of them lack secure rights – several hundred million of them lack any access – to a piece of land.

Providing secure land property rights, especially to the poor and marginalized, is a challenge that remains at the root of many development problems today. Feasible tools and solutions do exist. These tools – which fall under our definition of "pro-poor land tenure reforms" reflected in Box 1.2 in Chapter 1 – vary widely in their specific objectives and design. Globally, while there have been some significant reductions in the prospects and occasions for carrying out pro-poor land tenure reforms over the past four decades, there have been, on balance, even more important expansions in the possibilities for such programs and the recognition of their importance. The global and comparative experience over the past 40 years has much to teach about what works and what does not work.

The present volume is an effort to capture and distill many of those lessons, based largely on the work and learning of the Rural Development Institute (RDI). RDI's work, and its precursor labors under the umbrella of the University of Washington School of Law in Seattle, began in 1966. Those efforts have now covered more than 40 countries, and they provide the core perspectives for the present volume.

When RDI's work on behalf of land access and secure land rights for the rural poor began, Lyndon Johnson was the U.S. President, the Cold War was near its nadir, and the first moon landing was still three years in the future. In the intervening four decades, much has changed, even our preferred terminology: this book has avoided the term "land reform" but refers throughout to "land tenure reform." This has been done in part because the land reform sobriquet has been identified, in some parts of the world – notably in much of Latin America –

with narrow, confiscatory and punitive approaches, and in some other settings has been used as a political leader's Orwellian terminology – as in the case of President Mugabe in Zimbabwe – for measures that have harmed the poor while enriching well-connected cronies.

Terminology aside, there has been major evolution over those 40 years in what the cumulative experience suggests should be done to improve the land access and security of the hundreds of millions of people in poor rural families who still lack such property rights. Drawing upon what the previous chapters have reflected of RDI's experience and that of governments, civil society, practitioners and scholars, the following broad changes in the perception, prospects and practice of land tenure reform seem the most fundamental:

– Little scope remains for traditional land-to-the-tiller programs that use expropriatory methods to obtain private land for the allocation of full-sized farms to tenant farmers.
– Somewhat more, albeit only modest, scope remains for programs that distribute estate lands to agricultural laborers.
– The greatest scope for land redistribution to the completely landless poor in developing countries now appears to reside with the distribution of micro-plots – fractions of an acre on which they can build houses, plant gardens or crops, grow trees, keep livestock and maintain micro-enterprises.
– In many settings where agricultural tenancy has been the subject of intrusive regulation or has been prohibited, much could probably be gained on behalf of the poor by legalizing and encouraging such tenancy.
– The "household" should not be treated as a mysterious black box whose interior workings are unknown or irrelevant, and the intra-household allocation of land rights to women – at least equally with men, and even preferentially where possible – must be viewed as a critical goal of land tenure reform.
– Hundreds of millions of families of non-tenant possessors would benefit from having their insecure land rights made more secure. While programs to formalize individual land rights through titling and registration may provide one possible solution, formalization is not a uniform solution and also involves numerous risks that can undermine the land rights of the poor. Where it is not yet appropriate to define or document individualized rights, a repertoire of good practices has evolved that can give recognition to group or community rights. The devil is in the details.
– Where it is otherwise appropriate to recognize and document individualized land rights, the law should generally provide that they are held in ownership or some other long-term tenure, that a system is instituted for protecting the rightholder's interests against the state

as well as other private actors, and that the rights are, or are at least on track to become, transferable and mortgageable.

- That collective farms were nearly always a bad idea already appeared evident when we began this work four decades ago. More recent experience confirms this and provides a basis for distinguishing the cases where collective farm members will quickly exit with their pro rata portion of enterprise land if given the opportunity, and those where they will not, and identifying how to preserve practicable opportunities for the latter to exit later or otherwise translate their land rights into economic benefit.

- Land tenure reform involving the redistribution of private lands should, wherever possible, be done at market prices through voluntary market transactions and not through involuntary takings. In the exceptional cases of involuntary takings, the land losers should receive a fair and adequate price and not be targeted for punitive measures any more than the owner of land being taken for a highway.

- Land tenure reform policies and legislation must be developed against the background of a thorough comprehension of the grassroots realities and the social, historical, economic and political surround. It is now much better understood that this requires input from a broad range of stakeholders. At the same time, one must be cognizant of the possible existence of windows of opportunity and the consequences of lengthy delay in the lives of the desperately poor.

- More universally recognized during the course of the four decades – though still a struggle to put into practice – is that developing and adopting appropriate policies, laws and programs forms only the first part of the challenge. Implementation is key and is fully as important and typically more challenging than the adoption of laws and policies. Concomitantly, increasing attention is now paid to the need to track implementation through systematic and independent monitoring and evaluation.

- Legal aid for poor families who use, own or seek access to land can be an important tool for implementing land tenure programs that target the poor. It is a flexible tool in that the demands of legal aid clients – the poor – can help implementers of the principal program ensure that the program remains focused squarely on the poor. Land rights legal aid also provides a very useful feedback loop for project implementers, providing an early warning of project missteps.

This final chapter adds a brief gloss to these leading developments in perception, prospects and practice that have emerged during the past four decades and that seem likely to be largely determinative of whether we may indeed see "one billion rising" out of rural poverty through the land tenure reform of coming decades.

ROY L. PROSTERMAN

I.   Leading changes in prospects and practice

Declining relevance of "old" land-to-the-tiller approaches in combating landlessness

The cumulative experience, discussed in Chapter 2, teaches much about what legal and administrative parameters must be met to support a mandatory land-to-the-tiller program giving ownership to tenant farmers. Even where those design lessons can be absorbed and applied, a combination of political and financial constraints now make the prospects for such reforms in the future rare. Countries where substantial tenancy exists today generally have governments that are less authoritarian than they were decades ago, are much less likely to face threatening rural rebellions centered on the land issue, and are likely to have much higher land prices than in the past (after adjusting for inflation). Thus, thinking in terms of the landlords whose lands would need to be mandatorily acquired under such a program, there would today usually be no government that could credibly impel them, no insurgency whose existence might persuade them of the need to cooperate, and little likelihood of adequate compensation for their land.

Limited relevance of estate-land distribution

The prospects for acquiring agricultural estates to provide laborers ownership rights – either individually or as a pro rata share – to land equivalent to a full-sized or close to full-sized farm are discussed in Chapter 3. Such prospects may be modestly greater than the prospects for providing tenants with ownership of their present holdings. Even where the government is now non-authoritarian and no impelling land-related insurgency exists, some significant part of a country's estate lands may still have a low enough value to be affordable in a mandatory taking at a market or near-market price. This will not be true of plantation land producing high-value crops but may well be true of unused or underused estate lands, including private unimproved pasture that could be used for growing food crops. Even in such cases, important design parameters would need to be observed – for example, acquiring and allocating modest enough landholdings per beneficiary family to allow replication over most or all of the needy beneficiary universe.

Prospects for using micro-plots to address landlessness

Although micro-plots have existed in many settings from time immemorial, their connection to the needs of the landless in traditional developing countries is only now being recognized and applied in practice, as discussed in Chapter 4. Even where some developing countries have had small-plot allocation programs, they have often failed to recognize the full potential benefits, either considering such plots solely in terms of housing benefits and thus failing to provide the small additional area beyond the footprint of the house itself that would permit significant agronomic and other non-housing benefits, or actually providing some area beyond the house footprint (largely by accident, rather than as a deliberate policy) and then failing to discover how such households are using the unbuilt portion of the land to improve their livelihoods. Unlike hypothetically projected land-to-the-tiller programs and many hypothetically projected estate-lands programs, programs distributing micro-plots are much more likely to be affordable to developing country governments, with or without donor assistance. Indeed, with appropriate design safeguards to prevent inflating land prices, the needed land can often be acquired on the market from willing sellers. Thus, governments now have a generally affordable micro-plot option that is hard to ignore in settings where distribution of full-sized farms to the landless is impracticable. India appears now to be moving towards replication of such programs countrywide, as discussed in Chapter 6.

Deregulation of tenancy

Once policy makers in a particular country setting determine that it is not feasible in today's circumstances to provide multi-acre or "full-sized" farms in ownership to wage laborers working in the small-and-medium-holding sector, legalization and deregulation of tenancy may become another attractive option. Especially for landless agricultural laborers, becoming a tenant farmer may represent the first rung up on the ladder out of poverty. Laborers who become tenants are likely to achieve increased income, increased absorption of underused family labor power, increased scope for decision making, and increased agronomic knowledge.

Legalization and deregulation may also produce benefits where tenants already hold land, but under formally illegal arrangements. Public acknowledgement of lease terms that have been concluded in secret may afford tenants a measure of protection against serious violations of such terms by the landlord, and tenants may gain useful bargaining power from more freely circulating information on rental rates and other lease terms. And if landlords are free to rent out land without fear that tenants may claim ownership (or may assert other not-bargained-for rights, such as a cap on rent), this may greatly enlarge the pool of people to whom landlords are willing to rent. Thus, an energetic and motivated young laborer family may replace an indifferent (but previously "safe") relative of the landlord as a tenant when a true market for rentals begins to operate. Ending a purported right to be-

come owner for tenants who are allowed to stay on the land more than
a short time may also permit longer-term leasing, with prospects for
better stewardship and multi-year improvements by tenants such as
use of organic fertilizer.

The land rights of women

Until very recently – an omission only beginning to be recognized and
remedied even now – the land rights of impoverished women have received little attention. Chapter 5 examines in depth the challenges associated with the land rights of women.

Land rights, including those conferred in reform programs, have almost always been considered as though they are solely those of or solely under the control of the "head of household," who is almost always
a man.

"Family law," moreover, often embodies customs that are extremely
difficult to influence by means of changes in formal law. In rural cultures in developing country settings, customs related to land typically
give wives far less voice and control over the family's land and its at-
tachments than is given to husbands. In decisions regarding land
transactions, inheritance of land, and rights to land in cases of divorce,
separation or abandonment, wives often have far lesser or even no acknowledged rights to household land.

These customary arrangements are extremely difficult to change
with respect to land for which rights are already held. But where the
government is conferring rights to additional parcels of land or formalizing rights already held (especially where existing rights are perceived
to be uncertain), it is often possible to confer and document those new
rights either in the joint names of wife and husband or even exclusively in the name of the wife. The recognition that women's rights
must be treated explicitly and at least equally, in programs that allocate
new land (or stronger rights) to beneficiaries represents a further
extremely important evolution in the concept of land tenure reform.

But wherever the wife's rights are to be documented, it is not
enough just to make the proper notations or entries. It will also be important – and the more widespread and deeply rooted the contrary customs are, the more necessary this will be – to carry out a campaign of
education that underscores the land rights that women now have. In
some circumstances, special legal aid programs or initiatives under
broader legal aid programs may be needed to offer protection and education focused on women's enhanced land rights and all that they
entail.

Whether and how to document land rights

Forty years ago, when confronted with the question of whether to formalize and document land rights, the general answer would have been, "If the land is being used in fact on an individual household basis, and there are no other private actors claiming a better right, then yes." Today, as discussed in Chapter 8, the answer is more nuanced.

Among other considerations, it is important to recognize that complex mosaics or layers of customary land rights are very difficult to capture and represent in the types of land titles commonly found in more developed market economies. Women and others on the margins may hold secondary or subsidiary rights – perhaps unperceived or seemingly "minor" to outsiders, but of great moment to such customary rightholders – that may be overlooked, weakened or entirely lost during a formal individualization and documentation process. Even if the formalization process succeeds in securing the rights of women (or children, as in the case of orphans) who hold primary rights, the cost may be the diminishment of important secondary rights previously exercised by other women (or others in weaker positions). It is clearly difficult to assess the degree to which the potential gains of some may justify the potential losses of others in such cases. Some types of subsidiary rights (gathering fallen branches for firewood, grazing animals in the off-season, foraging mushrooms, etc.) may also be difficult or administratively impossible to capture in a formalization process. However, to the extent that it is natural to suppose that the existing holders of undocumented secondary or subsidiary rights are generally likely to be less powerful than existing holders of undocumented primary rights, then the burden of any process that favors the latter is likely to fall on those least equipped to bear it.

Still another risk is that the well connected will make exaggerated or even entirely false assertions of land rights in the course of a rights formalization process. And where the process of formalizing rights must be financed by the rights claimants, the poor may not be able to afford to participate, and thus may find that their rights are less protected (relatively speaking) than they were before the formalization occurred. This is a sound argument in favor of public financing of land formalization programs. Design issues, including standards applied to land description requirements, should be resolved in favor of modern, effective, lowest-cost technologies.

Many cultures place a high value on group property claims administered by customary law institutions. In certain cases, these group rights can be protected through formal recognition of the customary law institutions and the territorial claims by the group. Formalization of group rights is very different from formalizing whatever individual rights are held by members of the group. The state must work closely with the customary group to determine whether and under what circumstances the group would like to see registration of the individual rights of its members.

If these fundamental issues can be addressed successfully in program design, the formalization of land rights may benefit the poor. But the design challenges are complex, and the decision of whether to embark upon formalization should be taken only after a thoughtful consideration of the risks, costs and benefits of the program, in particular with relation to the poorest and most marginalized segments of society. There is much greater scope for conducting an analysis that is aware and nuanced on those issues than would have been the case 40 years ago. The devil is in the details.

The sticks in the property rights bundle

In cases where formal individualization of land rights is deemed desirable, it now appears much more clearly than it did four decades ago that the "bundle" of rights confirmed should generally include all of the characteristics usually associated with full private ownership and marketability. Much like the issue of women's land rights, issues relating to transferability and the importance of wealth creation through land ownership or its equivalent were largely ignored and relegated to the background three and four decades ago.

Ideally, the bundle of rights confirmed during formalization should consist of a set of documented and perpetual (or at least very long-term) rights that include the powers to sell, lease, mortgage and pass such rights by inheritance. Under special circumstances it may be appropriate, at least initially, for the government to impose some restrictions. For example, the government may decide to impose a brief moratorium on sales where land markets are newly developing and unfamiliar, or a moratorium on sales to foreigners (who may come from wealthier countries). Even if such measures do not respond to any real threat, the government may find that such measures respond to popular fears and reduce public resistance to the individualization of rights. Similarly, mortgage rules might include a limited homestead exemption, and debtor protections like crop insurance could be simultaneously introduced.

But the longer the duration and greater the scope of the restrictions on sale and lease, the more likely it is that owners will be motivated to transfer their rights through extra-legal means, driving the land market underground. And if such transactions cannot be acknowledged, they cannot be placed upon the public records, nor can they receive bank financing via a mortgage. The resulting uncertainty and lack of finance

are likely to reduce the market value of the land rights and simultaneously act as a drag on land market development. Moreover, restrictions on sale and lease that do achieve compliance will, so long as they
remain in place, correspondingly restrict the land market and its generally desirable "wealth creating" effect.

Once land rights are individually formalized, all rights that extend
beyond the lifetimes of the present holders will pass by law or by will,
at least to the extent the holders have not previously transferred such
rights in lawful transactions. Here, a further important application of
the women's land rights principles suggested above should be to ensure that the wife inherits upon the death of the husband. Preferably,
such inheritance should not be merely a severable one-half interest,
but ownership of the entirety of the property such as would follow
from adopting "community property" type rules. (Of course, *pari passu*,
the husband would then inherit the whole if the wife died first.) To
protect the interests of the wife more fully, the law should stipulate
that one spouse's attempted testamentary disposition through will
could not alter the other spouse's entitlement, and should specify strict
procedural requirements for the wife's formal consent to any transfer
attempted by the husband during his lifetime.

Successfully winding up decollectivization

After China and Vietnam allowed near-universal exit from their collective farms in the 1980s, and farm members departed rapidly to establish small family farms, it was assumed by many in the development
community that the same permission, if given in what was then the
USSR, would have the same results. In the years since communism
and central planning began to lose their grip in 1989 – and the former
Soviet republics went their separate ways in 1991 – the experience in
this region has been much more variable.

Excluding those settings where there has been no real permission given by the government to break up the collectives, such as in Belarus,
it is now possible to look at more than a decade-and-a-half of post-com-
munist experience in prominent settings such as Russia and Ukraine,
and identify key factors that seem to have kept their collective farms
from following the radical break-up path seen in China and Vietnam.

Important variables, discussed in Chapter 7, seem to include the
length of time the farmers were collectivized, the likely need for and
scarcity of capital equipment for a resulting family farm (such farms
being much larger in settings like Russia than in settings like China),
the difficulty of accessing markets distant from the farm, and the farmers' lack of confidence that the reforms will not be reversed. The possi-

ble role of such differences was not even the subject of serious speculation prior to 1990.

But even where the collectives have not been broken up by a general
exodus of members, it is clear that some degree of land reallocation
and some benefits of privatization can be conferred upon such members. For example, rules can allow and encourage the expansion of existing "private plots" held by the farm members – compare the discussion of micro-plots above – which have historically been used for higher-value crops and more intensive animal husbandry. Also, the law
might at least be changed to remove barriers that make it difficult for
individuals to own or lease in enough land to create small and mid-size
farms. Governments or NGOs could also provide rural legal aid to enhance the likelihood that small landowners or land share owners – including those who lease or sell land rights to the former collectives and
to new private enterprises in "reverse tenancy" or "corporate factory
farm" arrangements – receive basic protections. The law could thus
play a useful role in leveling the playing field between small transferors
and large transferees.

Analysis of the decollectivization experience (as explored in Chapter
7) remains highly relevant, of course, to facilitating future transitions
in the two most prominent holdouts still mandating a collectivist organization of agriculture – North Korea and Cuba – as well as for others
like Belarus and Kazakhstan. And some combination of further enlargement of the private plots and policies to address constraints in starting full-sized private farms may yet have an impact on the future shape
of farming in Russia and Ukraine.

Paying an adequate price for land to be acquired

The issue of how the government should obtain private land for public
purposes – including for reallocation to the poor – has been the subject
of dramatic new thinking over the past four decades. Indeed, this issue
was the entry point in 1966 for the first land tenure work that preceded RDI's formation. For reasons discussed in Chapter 2, it is generally best to pay the market price for any private land that is to be used
in a land tenure reform program.

This, in turn, means that the needed land should usually be acquir-
able – wherever a rural land market has developed – on the basis of
market transactions involving a willing buyer and willing seller. Exceptions may arise in the case of acquisition of estate land where the existing market price is excessive relative to the land's present income flow,
whether due to its role as a source of political power or for other reasons that are not directly economic. In such cases, the government
might reasonably invoke its eminent domain power to acquire the land

at a price reflecting a reasonable capitalization of its projected net income flow.

But even this non-confiscatory and non-punitive "eminent domain" model should be rarely involved. Wherever possible, the program should be entirely without compulsion and based on the payment of market prices. And to the extent that micro-plot allocation programs come to "occupy the field" in lieu of older approaches focused on full-sized farms, the amounts of land needed will be correspondingly much smaller, and the prospects for land acquisition through market purchase correspondingly much better. Such market-based approaches, of course, as discussed in Chapter 3, do not preclude the use of measures to ensure that the program of government or government-financed purchases does not inflate the price of land, such as the protective measure of a Dutch auction in which would-be sellers compete to offer a buyer the best deal.

Creating new norms

The development of land tenure reform policies and legislation is a labor-intensive and demanding task. A full comprehension of the on-the-ground realities and the social, historical, economic and political context is needed. Those designing such policies and legislation must seek input from a broad range of interested parties: the rural poor and landless themselves, landowners, government officials, knowledgeable NGOs and other civil society participants, academics, and others with relevant knowledge and perspectives. Focused desk research must be followed by extensive field interviewing (sometimes called "rapid rural appraisal") and, often, by full-scale sample surveys.

There are no cookie-cutter solutions that obviate the need for this demanding labor. And while the comparative experience can be instructive, cautionary, even enlightening, good policies and laws cannot be simply imported across national boundaries.

At the same time, "windows of opportunity" do in fact open and close. Bad advice may also rush in to fill a vacuum, especially where a new government or leader – perhaps urban in experience and outlook, but well-disposed toward the rural poor and their needs – has come to power. And there must be a constant awareness that long delays in formulating programs, if they are allowed to occur in an otherwise receptive environment, will come in a setting in which the rural poor and landless continue each day to suffer and have needs – with chronic malnutrition, for example, the most important contributing factor in child deaths globally.

Ultimately, one reason why we write this book is the hope that it may help to make such delays in program formulation shorter, in so

far as the accumulated experience may bear on the introduction of
practicable solutions in a specific setting.

From norm creation to norm fulfillment

A recurring theme in this book has been that it is essential not just to
adopt or already possess "good laws" on the books, but to have those
laws widely and effectively implemented in the countryside. As compared to 40 years ago, there is a much greater awareness today both of
key litmus tests that an adequate implementation process must meet,
and of the need to assess actual accomplishments systematically.

Key elements for the adequate implementation of laws must always
involve reiterated publicity, delivered by means that are highly accessible to the intended beneficiaries of the tenure reform. In some settings
(such as rural China), television may be a highly suitable medium, but
will be of little use in rural settings that lack electrification. Planners
must clearly consider literacy levels when crafting and using printed
materials, including the literacy rates of women who should be included as at least equal beneficiaries. In-person education about new
land rights programs is also often critical, and typically must be delivered to groups of beneficiaries by effectively trained local officials and
civil-society actors desiring to help support the program. Legal aid programs are an especially promising method of providing local educational outreach both to local officials and program beneficiaries, and
RDI's experience with them has been discussed in detail in Chapter 9.

The need for systematic monitoring and evaluation of actual accomplishment through well-designed sample surveys is much more widely
recognized today. Such surveys can also be supplemented by more frequent and less formal "rapid rural appraisal" interviews. This monitoring can yield crucial information for refinements and "mid-course corrections" as land tenure reform programs are being implemented. New
and supplemental approaches for gathering information from beneficiaries, such as via telephone hotline or text messaging to a central in-
spectorate, could now be in prospect in many countries with the rapid
spread of cell phone technologies. And information gathered by NGOs
and reports by local media should be carefully monitored as affording
early warnings of possible problems.

Disputes over land rights will arise, of course, and some local officials or the well-connected may seek to intercept benefits or deprive
the poor of what is rightfully theirs. Intended beneficiaries together
with administrators and implementing agencies must, wherever possible, be backed up by adequate judicial or quasi-judicial institutions that
administer some form of dispute resolution.

And just as it is important to budget adequately for such central elements of a land tenure reform as, for example, the purchase of private land for allocation to the poor, policy makers must also identify and make available the human and financial resources necessary to sustain the various measures of implementation.

Legal aid

Legal aid programs may help land tenure reform beneficiaries access judicial or quasi-judicial institutions that can offer protection in case of disputes with local officials or the well-connected. But the past decade or so has yielded experience showing that land rights legal aid can have impacts on program implementation that go well beyond litigation. Legal aid providers – pro-actively traveling to the places where both beneficiaries and local implementers are – can serve a vital educational function, educating beneficiaries as to what their rights are, and informing those charged with front-line implementation as to the specifics of relevant laws and regulations. Information gathered by the legal aid providers about what is happening in the countryside and what kinds of disputes may be arising or on the horizon can, in turn, be carried back to the makers of policy and the crafters of implementation strategies in national or provincial capitals to give early warning of problems and also mid-course corrections in implementation approaches (also, in effect, another source of program monitoring).

And, when disputes arise, litigation – though it may be highly successful when pursued, even in seemingly unpromising institutional environments – is usually a measure of last resort that is, in practice, rarely necessary. A motivated, energetic and informed legal professional on the side of a disputant poor family is able in a wide range of settings to gain a satisfactory outcome in the great majority of disputes, even against the powerful, with a trip to court comprising a tacit threat that rarely needs to be invoked.

II. The continuing relevance of land tenure reform today

On balance, the needs for land tenure reform around the globe are almost certainly greater than they were four decades ago, when the precursor work that led to the creation of RDI began.

In some respects, of course, those needs have diminished. Most notably, the UN Food and Agriculture Organization estimates that the proportion of the world's population dependent on agriculture, excluding the long-time developed economies, has fallen from about 66% in 1970 to around 51% currently. However, the number of people counted in the agricultural sector in those countries has actually increased, by some three-fifths, as a result of the large overall increases in population and is today more than 3 billion people.

Certainly there are some countries, such as Brazil, where the proportion of those engaged in agriculture has fallen so far over the past four decades that one might argue the land issue has now greatly declined in relative importance and that formulation of responses to urban poverty must now receive much higher priority. Shortly after RDI first did fieldwork in Brazil in 1968, looking at the land tenure issue and conceivable solutions (theoretically feasible, but not then politically possible), the FAO estimated 45% of the population was economically active in agriculture. Today it is 16%, and even the absolute number of those counted in the agricultural sector has declined, from 37 million to 31 million. Is addressing the rural land tenure issue in contemporary Brazil, or in other countries with seemingly similar demographics of urbanization just "locking the barn door after the horse is stolen"? The question will be considered further below.

Another seeming source of decline for the importance of the land tenure reform issue is the end of the Cold War. Even well before the Cold War ended around 1989-1990, there had been a sputtering decline in major civil conflicts in which largely rural-based Marxist movements used the land issue to organize threats to existing regimes. With the exception of Nepal (where a political settlement had seemingly been reached shortly before this was written), the last national insurgencies that embodied serious threats of that kind were the interimly successful one in Nicaragua, the failed one in El Salvador, and the non-Marxist one still in power after nearly three decades in Zimbabwe, each of which had led to major and highly disparate programs to address the land issue. Other current violent movements that seem to threaten governments with some degree of seriousness – among them, Afghanistan, Iraq, Somalia, Algeria and Kashmir – have much less or nothing to do with the land tenure issue. But to say that violent Marxist movements that seek to mobilize the rural poor around land-based grievances are no longer as widespread as they were in the 1960s, or even as salient as they were in the 1980s, may not necessarily be to say that dangerous instability is not a threat traceable to the poverty of the rural landless, in at least some critical settings. Again, this will be considered further below.

Both urbanization and Marxism's decline may thus have diminished the relevance of rural land tenure reform, at least upon first glance. On the other side of the ledger, the possibility and need for pro-poor land tenure reform initiatives have clearly increased over the past four decades in four important ways.

First, rural land tenure reform has become a live topic and ongoing process in most of the former centrally planned economies. Coinciding with the diminution of serious Marxist insurgencies in non-communist developing countries that grew out of the end of the global confrontation between communism and capitalism, there has also been a broad resurgence of the importance of the rural land issue within the former centrally planned economies themselves. Many have now embraced "capitalist" and market-based approaches that have led to the significant reorganization of their agricultural sectors including their rural land systems. The transformations in these countries would not have been predicted, or even imagined, four decades ago. However, the transformation of the rural land tenure systems is not yet complete in these transition economies. Whereas land tenure reform was not a live topic in these former centrally planned economies 40 years ago, it remains an important topic of unfinished business today. Of these, China alone contains about one-fourth of the agricultural population of the planet. Other countries, notably North Korea and Cuba, have yet to transition away from unsuccessful collective farming but presumably will at some future time; and in the former Soviet republics there is a wide spectrum of experience, from persisting collectivization (Belarus, Kazakhstan) to "land shares" and formal privatization side-by-side with variations on continuing collective or other large-scale operation (Russia, Ukraine) to near-complete exit into family farms (Baltic states, Georgia, Kyrgyzstan).

Second, new approaches to land tenure reform, through the distribution of micro-plots and through liberalizing tenancy, mean that land tenure reforms could now reach additional tens of millions of households of the rural landless – especially agricultural laborer households – and could provide major benefits in settings in which governments had given up on the land tenure issue over previous decades. The need for new measures to aid rural laborer households that must presently use a cash wage to acquire their entire daily sustenance is especially critical in light of the startling, and likely to persist, crisis in the price of basic foodstuffs. Furthermore, the new focus on intra-family allocation of benefits offers promise of bringing land rights to a large new segment of the neediest and most marginalized: women and, through them, young children. The additional number of poor rural persons in traditional developing countries for whom the land issue can thus once again be revitalized – by intelligently re-imagining the forms that tenure reform can take – is probably at least as great as the numbers for whom the possibility of tenure reform has been newly created by the withering of central planning.

Third, giving the poorest a stake in the rural economy can slow the process of excessively rapid urbanization. This matter takes on ever-greater urgency as governments see the anomie, suffering and violence that can arise out of "desperation urbanization" in which large numbers of the landless poor are impelled to the cities by the push of poverty, with no real prospect for steady employment or for educating their children, and with no assets other than the clothes on their back. Such desperation urbanization may create new potentials for instability. For example, some of the teenage sons of the migrating families – instead of becoming rural Marxist guerrillas – may now join or support radical political groups (e.g., Pakistan, Egypt) or secular criminal gangs (e.g., Brazil, South Africa) in the new urban setting. Here, the wealth-creating aspect of the conferral of rural land rights in forestalling premature and unprepared urban migration may be especially relevant, and involves the increasing recognition of the importance of the marketability of such rights. There may also be settings in which recent premature urbanization might be partially reversed if, for example, ownership of micro-plots is made available in peri-urban areas.

Fourth, some of the most vexing and difficult land tenure reform issues now arise in post-conflict or post-disaster settings, in which some great trauma has set the stage for widespread local contentions as to which household or group has the more legitimate claim to possess and use particular lands. Many such conflicts over land arise in African settings, of which the post-apartheid land restitution program in South Africa is perhaps the most widely known example. It is hard to judge whether the need for post-conflict resolution of land disputes is greater today than it was 40 years ago; certainly the international awareness of the problem is greater. And one huge and continuing disaster that has multiplied the number of such land disputes greatly is the global HIV/AIDS pandemic, with its death toll now at 25 million, much of this concentrated in sub-Saharan Africa, the hardest hit region. The effects of the pandemic raise many issues related to women's access to land, in particular: what are a wife's land rights when her husband has died of HIV/AIDS? What are the land rights of an aunt or other female care-giver when parents of the children she cares for are dead? What are the land rights of orphans, female or male? By what affordable and replicable processes are humane and acceptable resolutions of these issues to be reached?

In sum, there will be no dearth of land tenure reform issues to demand the attention of specialists, governments, funders, NGOs, academics, members of the media, concerned citizens and vast numbers of direct stakeholders for many years to come. As long as poverty, hunger, distress and instability prevail among large numbers of the world's rural population, and many of them still lack a secure relationship, often even access, to the chief source of rural livelihoods, hope and status, these land issues will have to be addressed.

Select bibliography

Anderson, D. & E. Lochery, *Violence and Exodus in Kenya's Rift Valley, 2008: Predictable and Preventable?*, 2(2) JOURNAL OF EASTERN AFRICAN STUDIES 328 (July 2008).

Appu, P.S., LAND REFORMS IN INDIA (New Delhi: Vikas Publishing 1996).

Behuria, N.C., LAND REFORMS LEGISLATION IN INDIA: A COMPARATIVE STUDY (New Delhi: Vikas 1997).

Berry, R.A. & W.R. Cline, AGRARIAN STRUCTURE AND PRODUCTIVITY IN DEVELOPING COUNTRIES (John Hopkins University Press 1979).

Besley, T., *Property Rights and Investments Incentives: Theory and Evidence from Ghana*, 103 JOURNAL OF POLITICAL ECONOMICS 903 (1995).

Binswanger, H., K. Deininger & G. Feder, *Agricultural Land Relations in the Developing World*, 75(5) AMERICAN JOURNAL OF AGRICULTURAL ECONOMICS 1242 (1993).

Black, R., S. Morris & J. Bryce, *Where and Why are 10 Million Children Dying Every Year?*, 361 THE LANCET 2226 (Elsevier 2003).

Bromley, D.W., ed., MAKING THE COMMONS WORK – THEORY, PRACTICE, AND POLICY (ICS Press 1992).

Brownrigg, L., HOME GARDENING IN INTERNATIONAL DEVELOPMENT: WHAT THE LITERATURE SHOWS (League for International Food Education 1985).

Bruce, J.W., et al., eds., LAND LAW REFORM: ACHIEVING DEVELOPMENT POLICY OBJECTIVES (World Bank 2006).

Burgess, R., *Land and Welfare: Theory and Evidence from China*, London School of Economics Working Paper (2001).

Burgess, R., LAND, WELFARE, AND EFFICIENCY IN RURAL CHINA (London School of Economics 1997).

Burns, T., C. Grant, A.M. Brits & K. Nettle, COMPARATIVE STUDY OF LAND ADMINISTRATION SYSTEMS: CRITICAL ISSUES AND FUTURE CHALLENGES (World Bank 2003).

Bush, R., *An Agricultural Strategy Without Farmers: Egypt's Countryside in the New Millennium*, 27(84) REVIEW OF AFRICAN POLITICAL ECONOMY 235 (2000).

Bush, R., ed., COUNTER-REVOLUTION IN EGYPT'S COUNTRYSIDE (Zed Books 2002).

Calvo, G.A. & S. Wellisz, *Supervision, Loss of Control, and the Optimum Size of the Firm*, 86(5) JOURNAL OF POLITICAL ECONOMY 943 (1978).

Carter, C.A. & F. Zhong, CHINA'S GRAIN PRODUCTION AND TRADES: AN ECONOMIC STUDY (Westview 1988).

Center on Housing Rights and Evictions, *Bringing Equality Home: Promoting and Protecting the Inheritance Rights of Women: A Survey of Law and Practice in Sub-Saharan Africa* (Geneva 2004).

Chambers, R., RURAL DEVELOPMENT: PUTTING THE LAST FIRST (Longman 1983).

Chen, C., LAND REFORM IN TAIWAN (China Publishing 1961).

Chen, S. & M. Ravallion, *The Developing World is Poorer than We Thought But No Less Successful in the Fight Against Poverty*, World Bank Policy Research Working Paper No. 4703 (Aug. 2008).

China Institute of Reform & Development, HISTORY OF CHANGES AND INNOVATIONS OF CHINA'S RURAL LAND SYSTEM (Nanhai Publishing 1999).

Clark, S., THE SOCIAL ORIGINS OF THE IRISH LAND WAR (Princeton University Press 1979).

Conquest, R., THE HARVEST OF SORROWS: SOVIET COLLECTIVIZATION AND THE TERROR-FAMINE (Oxford 1986).

Dale, P. & J. McLaughlin, LAND ADMINISTRATION (Oxford University Press 1999).

Dakolias, M. & B. Owen, IMPACT OF LEGAL AID: ECUADOR (World Bank 2003).

Das, S., A Critical Evaluation of Land Reforms in India (1950-1995), in Sinha & Pushpandra, eds., LAND REFORM IN INDIA: AN UNFINISHED AGENDA (New Delhi: Sage Publications 2000).

De Janvry, A., et al., eds., ACCESS TO LAND, RURAL POVERTY, AND PUBLIC ACTION (Oxford University Press 2001).

de Soto, Hernando, THE MYSTERY OF CAPITAL: WHY CAPITALISM TRIUMPHS IN THE WEST FAILS EVERYWHERE ELSE (Basic Books 2000).

Deere, C.D. & M. León, EMPOWERING WOMEN, LAND AND PROPERTY RIGHTS IN LATIN AMERICA (University of Pittsburgh Press 2001).

Deininger, K., LAND POLICIES FOR GROWTH AND POVERTY REDUCTION (World Bank 2003).

Deininger, K. & P. Olinto, Asset Distribution, Inequality, and Growth (World Bank 2000).

Demsetz, H., Toward a Theory of Property Rights, 57(2) AMERICAN ECONOMIC REVIEW 347 (1967).

Dias, C., OBSTACLES TO USING LAW AS A RESOURCE FOR THE POOR: THE RECAPTURING OF LAW BY THE POOR IN REPORT OF THE SEMINARS ON LEGAL SERVICES FOR THE RURAL POOR AND OTHER DISADVANTAGED GROUPS, SOUTH-EAST ASIA AND SOUTH ASIA (International Commission of Jurists Geneva 1987).

DiTella, R., S. Galiani & E. Schargrodsky, The Formation of Beliefs: Evidence From the Allocation of Land Titles to Squatters, 122 (1) QUARTERLY JOURNAL OF ECONOMICS 209 (Feb. 2007).

Diokno, J.W., Developmental Legal Aid in Rural Asean: Problems and Prospects, in International Commission of Jurists and Consumers' Association of Penang, RURAL DEVELOPMENT AND HUMAN RIGHTS IN SOUTH EAST ASIA (Penang, Malaysia: Sun Printers Sendirian Berhad 1982).

Dobrilovic, S. & R. Mitchell, Project to Develop Land and Real Estate Markets in Moldova: End of Contract Report (USAID 2000).

Dore, R.P., LAND REFORM IN JAPAN (Oxford University Press 1959).

Dowson, E., & V.L.O. Sheppard, LAND REGISTRATION (Her Majesty's Stationary Office 1952).

Drobak, J., & J. Nye, eds., FRONTIERS OF THE NEW INSTITUTIONAL ECONOMICS (Academic Press 1997).

Duncan, J., K. Rasmussen & A. Tabyshalieva, Women's Rights to Land in the Kyrgyz Republic (World Bank 2001).

Eckstein, S., G. Donald, D. Horton & T. Carroll, Land Reform in Latin America: Bolivia, Chile, Mexico, Peru, and Venezuela, World Bank Staff Working Paper No. 275 (World Bank 1978).

Ellickson, R., Property in Land 102(6) YALE LAW JOURNAL 1315 (1993).

Feder, G., T. Onchan, Y. Chalamwong & C. Hongladarom, LAND POLICIES AND FARM PRODUCTIVITY IN THAILAND (Johns Hopkins 1988).

Field, E., Property Rights, Community Public Goods, and Household Time Allocation in Urban Squatter Communities: Evidence from Peru, 45(3) WILLIAM AND MARY LAW REVIEW 837 (2004).

Fitzpatrick, D., Best Practice for the Legal Recognition of Customary Tenure, 36(3) DEVELOPMENT & CHANGE 449 (2005).

Gajaseni, J., & N. Gajaseni, Ecological rationalities of the traditional homegarden system in the Chao Phraya Basin, Thailand, 46(1) AGROFORESTRY SYSTEMS 3 (1999).

Galiani, S., & E. Schargrodsky, *Property Rights for the Poor: Effects of Land Titling* (Universidad Torcuato Di Tella 2005).

Ghimire, K., ed., WHOSE LAND? CIVIL SOCIETY PERSPECTIVES ON LAND REFORM AND RURAL POVERTY REDUCTION (International Fund for Agricultural Development 2001).

Giovarelli, R., & E. Eilor, *Land Sector Analysis, Gender/Family Issues and Land Rights Study* (Government of Uganda 2002).

Giovarelli, R., & S. Lastarria-Cornhiel, *Shared Tenure Options for Women: A Global Overview*, UN-HABITAT AS/785/05E (UN-HABITAT July 2005).

Golub, S., *Beyond Rule of Law Orthodoxy: The Legal Empowerment Alternative*, Rule of Law Series Working Paper No. 41 (Carnegie Endowment for International Peace, Washington, D.C. Oct. 2003).

Gopal, G., *Gender-Related Legal Reform and Access to Economic Resources in Eastern Africa*, World Bank Discussion Paper No. 405 (World Bank 1999).

Gordon, R., & J. Lindsay, *Law and the Poor in Rural India: The Prospects for Legal Aid*, 5 AMERICAN UNIVERSITY JOURNAL OF INTERNATIONAL LAW & POLICY (1990).

Hammond, J.L., & B. Hammond, THE VILLAGE LABOURER (Longman 1966, originally published in 1911).

Hanstad,. T., *Philippine Land Reform: The Just Compensation Issue*, 63 WASHINGTON LAW REVIEW 417 (1988).

Hanstad, T., & J. Brown, *Land Reform Law and Implementation in West Bengal: Lessons and Recommendations*, Rural Development Institute Report No. 112 (Rural Development Institute 2001).

Hanstad, T., J. Brown & R. Prosterman, *Larger Homestead Plots as Land Reform?: International Experience and Analysis from Karnataka*, 37(29) ECONOMIC & POLITICAL WEEKLY 3058 (2002).

Hanstad, T., R. Nielsen & J. Brown, *Land and Livelihoods: Making Land Rights for India's Rural Poor*, FAO Livelihood Support Programme Working Paper No. 12 (FAO 2004).

Haque, T., & A.S. Sirohi, AGRARIAN REFORM AND INSTITUTIONAL CHANGES IN INDIA (New Delhi: Concept Publishing 1986).

Heath, D.B., C.J. Erasmus & H.C. Buechler, LAND REFORM AND SOCIAL REVOLUTION IN BOLIVIA (Praeger 1969).

Heller, M., *The Tragedy of the Anticommons: Property in the Transition from Marx to Markets*, 111(3) HARVARD LAW REVIEW 621 (1998).

Henderson, G., Korea: THE POLITICS OF THE VORTEX (Harvard University Press 1968).

Herring, R.J., LAND TO THE TILLER: THE POLITICAL ECONOMY OF AGRARIAN REFORM IN SOUTH ASIA (1983).

Hinton, W., Fanshen: A DOCUMENTARY OF REVOLUTION IN A CHINESE VILLAGE (University of California Press 1997).

Hoogerbrugge, I., & L.O. Fresco, *Homegarden Systems: Agricultural Characteristics and Challenges*, International Institute for Environment and Development, Gatekeeper Series No. 39 (1993).

International Crisis Group, *Blood and Soil: Land, Politics, and Conflict Prevention in Zimbabwe and South Africa*, ICG Africa Report No. 85 (International Crisis Group Press 2004).

Izumi, K., *Liberalisation, Gender, and the Land Question in Sub-Saharan Africa*, in C. Sweetman, ed., WOMEN, LAND, AND AGRICULTURE VOL. 9 (Oxfam Publishing 1999).

Jannuzi, F., & J. Peach, THE AGRARIAN STRUCTURE OF BANGLADESH: AN IMPEDIMENT TO DEVELOPMENT (Westview 1980).

Johnson, N.L., & V.W. Ruttan, *Why are Farms so Small?*, 22(5) WORLD DEVELOPMENT 691 (1994).

Kalirijan, K., & Y. Wu, eds., PRODUCTIVITY AND GROWTH IN CHINESE AGRICULTURE (MacMillan 1999).

Katz, E., & J.S. Chamorro, *Gender, Land Rights and the Household Economy in Rural Nicaragua and Honduras*, paper prepared for the Regional Workshop on Land Issues in Latin America and the Caribean (USAID 2002).

Khan, M., UNDERDEVELOPMENT AND AGRARIAN STRUCTURE IN PAKISTAN (Westview 1981).

Kluck, P., *Small Farmers and Agricultural Development Policy: A Look at Brazil's Land Reform Statute*, 38(1) HUMAN ORGANIZATION 44 (Spring 1979).

Koo, S.W.Y., G. Ranis & J.C.H. Fei, THE TAIWAN SUCCESS STORY: RAPID GROWTH WITH IMPROVED DISTRIBUTION IN THE REPUBLIC OF CHINA (Westview 1981).

Kumar, S.K., *Role of the Household Economy in Child Nutrition at Low Incomes: A Case Study in Kerala*, Occasional Paper No. 95 (Department of Agricultural Economics, Cornell University 1978).

Landauer, K., & M. Brazil, eds., TROPICAL HOME GARDENS: Selected papers from an international workshop held at the Institute of Ecology, Padjadjaran University, Bandung, Indonesia, 2-9 December 1985 (United Nations University Press 1990).

Larsson, G., LAND REGISTRATION AND CADASTRAL SYSTEMS: TOOLS FOR LAND INFORMATION AND MANAGEMENT (Longman Scientific & Technical 1991).

Lastarria-Cornhiel, S., *Impact of Privatization on Gender and Property Rights in Africa*, 25(8) WORLD DEVELOPMENT 1317 (1997).

Lerman, Z., C. Csaki & G. Feder, AGRICULTURE IN TRANSITION: LAND POLICIES AND EVOLVING FARM STRUCTURES IN POST-SOVIET COUNTRIES (Lexington Books 2004).

Lev, D.S., *Legal Aid in Indonesia*, Centre of Southeast Asian Studies Working Paper No. 44 (1987).

Liebman, B.L., *Legal Aid and Public Interest Law in China*, 34 TEXAS INTERNATIONAL LAW JOURNAL 211 (1999).

Lindsay, J.M., LAW AND COMMUNITY IN THE MANAGEMENT OF INDIA'S STATE FORESTS (Lincoln Institute of Land Policy 1994).

Lipton, M., LAND REFORM IN DEVELOPING COUNTRIES: PROPERTY RIGHTS AND PROPERTY WRONGS (Taylor and Francis, in press).

Marsh, R., *Building on Traditional Gardening to Improve Household Food Security*, Food, Nutrition and Agriculture No. 22 (Food and Agriculture Organization 1998).

McAuslan, P., BRINGING THE LAW BACK IN: ESSAYS IN LAND, LAW AND DEVELOPMENT (Ashgate 2003).

Meinzen-Dick, R.S., L.R. Brown, H.S. Feldstein & A.S. Quisumbing, *Gender, Property Rights, and Natural Resources*, 25(8) WORLD DEVELOPMENT 1303 (1997).

Mitchell, K., *Market-Assisted Land Reform in Brazil: A New Approach to Address an Old Problem*, 22(3) NEW YORK LAW SCHOOL JOURNAL OF INTERNATIONAL AND COMPARATIVE LAW 576 (2003).

Mitchell, R., *Property Rights and Environmentally Sound Management of Farmland and Forests*, in J.W. Bruce, et al., eds., LAND LAW REFORM: ACHIEVING DEVELOPMENT POLICY OBJECTIVES 175 (World Bank 2006).

Mitchell, R., & T. Hanstad, *Small Homegarden Plots and Sustainable Livelihoods for the Poor* (FAO 2004).

Mitchell, R., R. Prosterman & A. Safik, *Productivity of Intensively Used Homestead Plots in a Central Javan Village*, RDI Reports on Foreign Aid and Development No. 122 (Rural Development Institute 2006).

Miura, S., O. Kunii & S. Wakai, *Home Gardening in Urban Poor Communities of the Philippines*, 54(1) INTERNATIONAL JOURNAL OF FOOD SCIENCES & NUTRITION 77 (2003).

Moise, E., LAND REFORM IN CHINA AND NORTH VIETNAM (University of North Carolina Press 1983).

Myrdal, G., ASIAN DRAMA: AN INQUIRY INTO THE POVERTY OF NATIONS (Twentieth Century Fund 1968).

Nair, P.K.R., AN INTRODUCTION TO AGROFORESTRY (Kluwer Academic Publishers 1993).

Nasution, A.B., *Legal Service in Developing Countries: An Indonesian Case*, in LBH, LEGAL AID IN INDONESIA (FIVE YEARS OF THE LEMBAGA BANTUAN HUKUM) (1976).

Netting, R.M., SMALLHOLDERS, HOUSEHOLDERS: FARM FAMILIES AND THE ECOLOGY OF INTENSIVE, SUSTAINABLE AGRICULTURE (Stanford University Press 1993).

Nielsen, R., T. Hanstad & L. Rolfes, *Implementing homestead plot programmes: Experience from India*, LSP Working Paper No. 23 (FAO 2006).

Ninez, V., *Working at half-potential: Constructive analysis of home garden programmes in the Lima slums with suggestions for an alternative approach*, 7(3) FOOD AND NUTRITION BULLETIN (2005).

O'Grada, C., IRELAND BEFORE AND AFTER THE FAMINE: EXPLORATIONS IN ECONOMIC HISTORY 1800-1925 (2d ed. Manchester University Press 1993).

Panda, P., & B. Agarwal, *Marital Violence, Human Development and Women's Property Status in India*, 33(5) WORLD DEVELOPMENT 836 (2005).

Prosterman, R., *Land Reform as Foreign Aid*, 6 FOREIGN POLICY 130 (1972).

Prosterman, R., & J. Riedinger, LAND REFORM AND DEMOCRATIC DEVELOPMENT (Johns Hopkins 1987).

Prosterman, R., & T. Hanstad, eds., *Legal Impediments to Effective Rural Land Relations in Eastern Europe and Central Asia: A Comparative Perspective*, World Bank Technical Paper No. 436 (World Bank 1999).

Prosterman, R., T. Hanstad & P. Li, *Can China Feed Itself?*, SCIENTIFIC AMERICAN 90 (Nov. 1996).

Prosterman, R., M. Temple & T. Hanstad, eds., AGRARIAN REFORM AND GRASSROOTS DEVELOPMENT: TEN CASE STUDIES (L. Rienner 1990).

Randell, L., ed., REFORMING MEXICO'S AGRARIAN REFORM (M.E. Sharpe 1996).

Riedinger, J., AGRARIAN REFORM IN THE PHILIPPINES: DEMOCRATIC TRANSITIONS AND REDISTRIBUTIVE REFORMS (Stanford University Press 1995).

Robertson, A.F., THE DYNAMICS OF PRODUCTIVE RELATIONSHIPS: AFRICAN SHARE CONTRACTS IN COMPARATIVE PERSPECTIVE (Cambridge University Press 1987).

Rolfes, Jr., L., *The Impact of Land Titling in Ukraine: the Results from an 800 Person Random-Sample Survey*, RDI Reports on Foreign Aid and Development No. 119 (Rural Development Institute 2003).

Runsheng, D., Z. NONG CUN ZHI DU BIAN QIAN [TRANSFORMATION OF CHINA'S RURAL SYSTEM] (Sichuan People's Publishing 2003).

Sachs, J., THE END OF POVERTY (Penguin Press 2005).

Seidman, A., R. Seidman & N. Abeyesekere, LEGISLATIVE DRAFTING FOR DEMOCRATIC SOCIAL CHANGE: A MANUAL FOR DRAFTERS (Kluwer Law International 2001).

Seidman, A., R. Seidman & J. Payne, LEGISLATIVE DRAFTING FOR MARKET REFORM: SOME LESSONS FROM CHINA (St. Martin's Press 1997).

Simpson, R., LAND LAW AND REGISTRATION (Cambridge University Press 1976).

Springborg, R., *State-Society Relations in Egypt: The Debate Over Owner-Tenant Relations*, 45(2) MIDDLE EAST JOURNAL 232 (1991).

Strickland, R., *To Have and to Hold: Women's Property and Inheritance Rights in the Context of HIV/AIDS in Sub-Saharan Africa*, ICRW Working Paper (ICRW June 2004).

Thiesenhusen, W., ed., SEARCHING FOR AGRARIAN REFORM IN LATIN AMERICA (Unwin Hyman 1989).

Thiesenhusen, W., BROKEN PROMISES: AGRARIAN REFORM AND THE LATIN AMERICAN CAMPESINO (Westview 1995).

Thomas, H., THE SPANISH CIVIL WAR (Harper & Row 1977).

Toulmin, C., & J. Quan, eds., EVOLVING LAND RIGHTS, POLICY AND TENURE IN AFRICA (IIED & Natural Resources Institute 2000).

UNFAO, *Good Practice Guidelines for Agricultural Leasing Arrangements*, FAO Land Tenure Studies No. 2 (UNFAO May 2001).

United States Agency for International Development, *Ukraine Land Titling Initiative 2001-2006: Final Report* (USAID Sept. 2006).

Uzun, V. *GE and Small Business in Russian Agriculture: Adaptation to Market* 47 (1) COMPARATIVE ECONOMIC STUDIES (2005).

van Zyl, J., J. Kirsten & H.P. Binswanger, eds., AGRICULTURAL LAND REFORM IN SOUTH AFRICA: POLICIES, MARKETS AND MECHANISMS (Oxford University Press 1996).

Wilson R.J., & J. Rasmusen, PROMOTING JUSTICE: A PRACTICAL GUIDE TO STRATEGIC HUMAN RIGHTS LAWYERING (International Human Rights Law Group 2001).

Wolf, E.R., PEASANT WARS OF THE TWENTIETH CENTURY (Harper & Row 1969).

World Bank Agriculture & Rural Development Department, *Gender Issues and Best Practices in Land Administration Projects: A Synthesis Report,* Report No. 32571-GLB (World Bank 2005).

World Bank, INDIA: ACHIEVEMENTS AND CHALLENGES IN REDUCING POVERTY, WORLD BANK COUNTRY STUDY (World Bank 1997).

World Bank, INDIA: LAND POLICIES FOR GROWTH AND POVERTY REDUCTION (New Delhi: Oxford University Press 2007).

Wu Xiang, RECORDS OF CHINA'S RURAL REFORMS [ZHONGGUO NONGCUN GAIGE SHILU] (Hangzhou 2001).

Wylie, J.E.W., IRISH LAND LAW (2d ed. Butterworths 1986).

Yelling, J.A., COMMON FIELD AND ENCLOSURES IN ENGLAND (MacMillan Press 1977).

Yoong-Deok, J., & Y. Kim, *Land Reform, Income Redistribution, and Agricultural Production in Korea,* 48(2) ECONOMIC DEVELOPMENT AND CULTURAL CHANGE 253 (2000).

Zakaria, F., THE FUTURE OF FREEDOM: ILLIBERAL DEMOCRACY AT HOME AND ABROAD (Norton & Company 2007).

Zemans, F., & A. Thomas, *Can Community Clinics Survive? A Comparative Study of Law Centres in Australia, Ontario and England,* in F. Regan, *et al.,* eds., THE TRANSFORMATION OF LEGAL AID: COMPARATIVE AND HISTORICAL STUDIES (Oxford University Press 1999).

Zevenbergen, J., SYSTEMS OF LAND REGISTRATION: ASPECTS AND EFFECTS (Delft: Netherlands Geodetic Commission 2002).

Zhu, K., R. Prosterman, J. Ye, P. Li, J. Riedinger & Y. Ouyang, *The Rural Land Question in China: Analysis and Recommendations Based on a Seventeen-Province Survey,* 38(4) NEW YORK UNIVERSITY JOURNAL OF INTERNATIONAL LAW & POLITICS 761 (2006).

Zusman, P., INDIVIDUAL BEHAVIOR AND SOCIAL CHOICE IN A COOPERATIVE SETTLEMENT – THE THEORY AND PRACTICE OF THE ISRAELI MOSHAV (Magnes Press, Hebrew University 1988).

List of Contributors

The Editors:

Roy L. Prosterman is Founder and Chairman Emeritus of the Rural Development Institute (RDI) in Seattle, Washington, and Professor Emeritus at the University of Washington School of Law.

Tim Hanstad is Chief Executive Officer and President of RDI, and Affiliate Associate Professor of Law at the University of Washington School of Law.

Robert Mitchell is Program Chair and Senior Land Tenure Expert at RDI, where he currently directs RDI's India Program, and Affiliate Assistant Professor of Law at the University of Washington School of Law.

Additional Authors:

Jennifer Brown is a Staff Attorney at RDI.

Renée Giovarelli is Senior Fellow at RDI, where she directs RDI's Women and Land Program, and Adjunct Professor at Seattle University School of Law.

Li Ping is a Staff Attorney at RDI.

Robin Nielsen is a Staff Attorney at RDI.

Index